AMERICAN JEWRY

AMERICAN JEWRY

TRANSCENDING THE EUROPEAN EXPERIENCE?

Edited by Christian Wiese and Cornelia Wilhelm

Bloomsbury Academic
An imprint of Bloomsbury Publishing Plc

B L O O M S B U R Y
LONDON · OXFORD · NEW YORK · NEW DELHI · SYDNEY

Bloomsbury Academic

An imprint of Bloomsbury Publishing Plc

50 Bedford Square	1385 Broadway
London	New York
WC1B 3DP	NY 10018
UK	USA

www.bloomsbury.com

BLOOMSBURY and the Diana logo are trademarks of Bloomsbury Publishing Plc

First published 2017

© Christian Wiese, Cornelia Wilhelm and Contributors, 2017

British Library Cataloguing-in-Publication Data
A catalogue record for this book is available from the British Library.

ISBN:	HB:	978-1-4411-8809-0
	PB:	978-1-4411-2622-1
	ePDF:	978-1-4411-6343-1
	ePub:	978-1-4411-8021-6

Library of Congress Cataloging-in-Publication Data
A catalog record for this book is available from the Library of Congress.

Cover design: Eleanor Rose
Cover image: Food will win the war by Charles Edward Chambers / Library of Congress

Typeset by RefineCatch Limited, Bungay, Suffolk
Printed and bound in India

CONTENTS

Contents

LIST OF ILLUSTRATIONS

NOTES ON CONTRIBUTORS

Yaakov Ariel is Professor of American Religion in the Department of Religious Studies at the University of North Carolina, Chapel Hill. He is also Director of the Minor of Christianity and Culture and Co-director of the Center for Jewish Studies. His areas of scholarly interest include Judaism and Evangelical Christianity in America, and the relationship between the two religious communities. Among his publications are the books *On Behalf of Israel: American Fundamentalist Attitudes Towards the Jewish People and Zionism* (1991); *Evangelizing the Chosen People: Missions to the Jews in America 1880–2000* (2000); and *An Unusual Relationship: Evangelical Christians and Jews* (2013).

Judah M. Cohen is the Lou and Sybil Mervis Professor of Jewish Culture and Associate Professor of Jewish Studies and Folklore and Ethnomusicology at Indiana University (Bloomington). His work focuses on the history of Jewish music scholarship in the United States, musical theatre works that address Holocaust memory, contemporary forms of Jewish musical expression, and musical representations of such cultural figures as Anne Frank and Shylock. His writings include *Through the Sands of Time: A History of the Jewish Community of St. Thomas, U.S. Virgin Islands* (2004); and *The Making of a Reform Jewish Cantor: Musical Authority, Cultural Investment* (2009); *Sounding Jewish Tradition: The Music of Central Synagogue* (2011).

Kathleen Neils Conzen is Thomas E. Donnelley Professor Emerita of American History at the University of Chicago. Her research and teaching focus on the social and political history of the United States in the nineteenth century, with a special interest in issues of immigration, ethnicity, religion, western settlement, and urban development. Her publications include *Making Their Own America: Assimilation Theory and the German Peasant Pioneer* (1990); *German-Americans and Ethic Political Culture: Steams County, Minnesota, 1855–1915* (1989); and *Germans in Minnesota* (2003).

Hasia R. Diner is the Paul S. and Sylvia Steinberg Professor of American Jewish History and Director of the Goldstein-Goren Center for American Jewish History at New York University. Her works include *In the Almost Promised Land: American Jews and Blacks, 1915–1935* (1995); *The Lower East Side Memories: The Jewish Place in America* (2000); *Hungering for America: Italian, Irish and Jewish Foodways in the Age of Migration* (2002); *The Jews of the United States, 1645 to 2000* (2004); and *We Remember With Reverence and Love: American Jews and the Myth of Silence after the Holocaust, 1945–1962* (2009). She is also the editor of *Remembering the Lower East Side: American Jewish Reflections* (with Jeffrey Shandler and Beth S. Wenger, 2000); *Her Works Praise Her: A History of Jewish Women in America from Colonial Times to the Present* (with Beryl Lieff Benderly, 2002); and *From Arrival to Incorporation: Migrants to the U.S. in a Global Age* (with Elliott

Barkan and Alan Kraut, 2007); *Roads Taken: The Great Jewish Migrations to the New World and the Peddlers Who Forged the Way* (2016).

Eli Faber is Professor of History at John Jay College in New York. He is the author of *A Time for Planting: The First Migration, 1654–1820* (1992) and *Jews, Slaves and the Slave Trade: Setting the Record Straight* (1998). For six years he was the editor of *American Jewish History*, the quarterly scholarly journal of the American Jewish Historical Society.

Henry Feingold is Director of the Jewish Resource Center at Baruch College and Professor Emeritus of History at Baruch College and The Graduate Center, CUNY. His most important works are *The Politics of Rescue: The Roosevelt Administration and the Holocaust, 1938–1945* (1971) and, more recently, *Bearing Witness, How America and Its Jews Responded to the Holocaust* (1995). Further works on American Jewry include *Zion in America: The Jewish Experience from Colonial Times to the Present* (1974); *A Midrash on the History of American Jewry* (1982); *A Time for Searching: Entering the Mainstream, 1920–1945* (1992); *Lest Memory Cease, Finding Meaning in the American Jewish Past* (1996); *Jewish Power in America: Myth and Reality* (2002); and *Silent No More: Saving the Jews of Russia, the American Jewish Effort, 1967–1989* (2006). He is also the General Editor of the five-volume series published by Johns Hopkins University, *The Jewish People in America* (1992); *American Jewish Political Culture and the Liberal Persuasion* (2014).

Karla Goldman is the Sol Drachler Professor of Social Work and Jewish Studies at the University of Michigan, where she directs the Jewish Communal Leadership Program. She previously taught American Jewish history at Hebrew Union College-Jewish Institute of Religion in Cincinnati and served as historian in residence at the Jewish Women's Archive in Brookline, Massachusetts. She is the author of *Beyond the Synagogue Gallery: Finding a Place for Women in American Judaism* (2000).

Arthur A. Goren is Russell and Bettina Knapp Professor Emeritus of American Jewish History at Columbia University. His books include *New York Jews and the Quest for Community: The Kehilla Experiment, 1908–1922* (1970); *Dissent in Zion: From the Writings of Judah L. Magnes* (1982); *The American Jews* (1982); and *The Politics and Public Culture of American Jews* (1999).

Jeffrey S. Gurock is Libby M. Klaperman Professor of Jewish History at Yeshiva University. His numerous publications include *When Harlem was Jewish: 1870–1930* (1979); *American Jewish Orthodoxy in Historical Perspective* (1996); *A Modern Heretic and a Traditional Community: Mordecai M. Kaplan, Orthodoxy and American Judaism* (1997); *Judaism's Encounter with American Sports* (2005); *Orthodox Jews in America* (2009) and *Jews in Gotham: New York Jews in a Changing City, 1920–2010* (2012).

Susannah Heschel is the Eli Black Professor of Jewish Studies at Dartmouth College. Her scholarship focuses on Jewish-Christian relations in Germany during the nineteenth and twentieth centuries, the history of biblical scholarship, the history of anti-Semitism, and the history of European Jewish scholarship on Islam from the 1830s to the 1930s. Her numerous publications include *Abraham Geiger and the Jewish Jesus* (1998), which won a National Jewish Book Award, and *The Aryan Jesus: Christian Theologians and the Bible in Nazi Germany* (2008). She has also edited several books, including *Insider/ Outsider: American Jews and Multiculturalism* (with David Biale and Michael Galchinsky, 1998); *Betrayal: German Churches and the Holocaust* (with Robert P. Ericksen, 1999); and *Moral Grandeur and Spiritual Audacity: Essays of Abraham Joshua Heschel* (2001).

David E. Kaufman is Associate Professor and the Florence and Robert Kaufman Endowed Chair in Jewish Studies at Hofstra University. Previously he was Associate Professor of Contemporary American Jewish Studies at Hebrew Union College, Los Angeles. He has been a consultant for the restoration of synagogues in Boston, Hartford, Baltimore, and Los Angeles, and is currently the head of a research project for Synagogue 3000 on the subject of sacred space, i.e., synagogue design and renovation. His publications include *Shul with a Pool: The "Synagogue-Center" in American Jewish History* (1999); and *Jewhooing the Sixties: American Celebrity and Jewish Identity—Sandy Koufax, Lenny Bruce, Bob Dylan, and Barbra Streisand* (2012).

Laura Arnold Leibman is Professor of English and Humanities at Reed College. She is the author of *A Cultural Edition of Experience Mayhew's Indian Converts or, Some account of the lives and dying speeches of a considerable number of the Christianized Indians of Martha's Vineyard, in New-England (1727)* (2008); and *Messianism, Secrecy and Mysticism: A New Interpretation of Early American Jewish Life* (2012). She is currently working on a book on a black Jewish family in early New York.

Tony Michels is George L. Mosse Professor of American Jewish History at the University of Wisconsin-Madison. His specialization includes American Jewish history, Yiddish culture, Russian Jewish history, socialism, working-class history, and nationalism. His book *A Fire in Their Hearts: Yiddish Socialists in New York* (2005) won the Salo W. Baron Prize from the American Academy for Jewish Research in 2006. He is the editor of *Jewish Radicals: A Documentary History* (2012).

Gil Ribak is an Assistant Professor of Judaic Studies at the University of Arizona. He served as the Director of the Institute on American Jewish-Israeli Relations at the American Jewish University in Los Angeles (2012–14), and as a Fulbright Scholar. His publications include the book *Gentile New York: The Images of Non-Jews among Jewish Immigrants* (2012), as well as numerous articles in various journals such as *American Jewish History, Israel Studies Forum, Journal of American Ethnic History,* and *Polin: A Journal of Polish-Jewish Studies.*

Jonathan D. Sarna is the Joseph H. and Belle R. Braun Professor of American Jewish History in the Department of Near Eastern and Judaic Studies at Brandeis University, Director of the Hornstein Program in Jewish Professional Leadership, and Chief Historian of the National Museum of American Jewish History in Philadelphia. His most important works include *JPS: The Americanization of Jewish Culture, 1888–1988* (1989); *Religion and State in the American Jewish Experience* (1997); *Minority Faiths and the American Protestant Mainstream* (1998); and *American Judaism: A History* (2005). He is also the editor of *Jews and the Civil War: A Reader* (2010), *Jewish Renaissance and Revival in America* (with Eitan P Fishbane, 2011), *When General Grant Expelled the Jews* (2012), and *Lincoln and the Jews: A History* (2015).

Michael E. Staub is Professor of English at Baruch College, New York. He is the author of *Voices of Persuasion: Politics of Representation in 1930s America* (1994); *Torn at the Roots: The Crisis of Jewish Liberalism in Postwar America* (2002); *Madness Is Civilization: When the Diagnosis was Social, 1948–1980* (2011). He is also the editor of *The Jewish 1960s: An American Sourcebook* (2004); *Love My Rifle More Than You: Young and Female in the U.S. Army* (2005); and *Madness Is Civilization: When the Diagnosis was Social, 1948–1980* (2011).

Stephen J. Whitfield holds the Max Richter Chair in American Civilization at Brandeis University, where he specializes in twentieth-century politics and culture. He has also published widely on the American Jewish experience. His most recent books include *Into the Dark: Hannah Arendt and Totalitarianism* (1980); *The Culture of the Cold War* (1991, rev. ed. 1996); *American Space, Jewish Time: Essays in Modern Culture and Politics* (1996); and *In Search of American Jewish Culture* (1999). He is editor of the *Blackwell Companion to Twentieth-Century America* (2004).

Christian Wiese holds the Martin Buber Chair in Jewish Thought and Philosophy at the Goethe University in Frankfurt. His publications include *Challenging Colonial Discourse: Jewish Studies and Protestant Theology in Wilhelmine Germany* (2005); and *The Life and Thought of Hans Jonas: Jewish Dimensions* (2007). He has edited numerous volumes, including *Janusfiguren: "Jüdische Heimstätte," Exil und Nation im deutschen Zionismus* (with Andrea Schatz, 2006); *Redefining Judaism in an Age of Emancipation: Comparative Perspectives on Samuel Holdheim (1806–1860)* (2007); *Modern Judaism and Historical Consciousness: Identities—Encounters—Perspectives* (with Andreas Gotzmann, 2007); *Judaism and the Phenomenon of Life: The Legacy of Hans Jonas: Historical and Philosophical Studies* (with Hava Tirosh-Samuelson, 2008); *Years of Persecution, Years of Extermination: Saul Friedländer and the Future of Holocaust Studies* (with Paul Betts, 2010); *German-Jewish Thought Between Religion and Politics: Festschrift in Honor of Paul Mendes-Flohr on the Occasion of his Seventieth Birthday* (with Martina Urban, 2012); *Jüdische Existenz in der Moderne: Abraham Geiger und die Wissenschaft des Judentums* (with Walter Homolka and Thomas Brechenmacher, 2013); and *Reappraisals and New Studies of the Modern Jewish Experience: Essays in Honor of Robert M. Seltzer* (with Brian Smollett, 2014).

Cornelia Wilhelm is currently DAAD Visiting Professor at the Department of History and the Tam Institute for Jewish Studies, Emory University, Atlanta. She is also Professor of Modern History at the Department of History at the University of Munich. Her publications include *Bewegung oder Verein? Nationalsozialistische Volkstumspolitik in den USA* (1998); *German Jews in the United States: A Guide to Archival Collections* (2008); *Deutsche Juden in Amerika: Bürgerliches Selbstbewusstein und jüdische Identität in den Orden B'nai B'rith und Treue Schwestern* (2007); and *The Independent Orders of B'nai B'rith and True Sisters: Pioneers of a New Jewish Identity, 1843–1914* (2011). She is currently working on a history of German refugee rabbis in the United States, 1933–90.

CHAPTER 1
EUROPE IN THE EXPERIENCE AND IMAGINATION OF AMERICAN JEWRY: AN INTRODUCTION[1]

Christian Wiese

1

In her programmatic essay that opens the present volume, Susannah Heschel sets the tone by introducing the notion of "The Myth of Europe in America's Judaism," in fact, by introducing varying and competing myths embraced by American Jewry at different times, including the present. Analyzing the changing perceptions of Europe and European Judaism during the nineteenth and early twentieth centuries, and addressing such phenomena as Reform-Jewish references to Christian-Jewish relations in Europe, reflections on Europe during the Holocaust, or constructions of the memory of Eastern European Jewry by Jewish intellectuals after the Nazi genocide, she convincingly argues that Europe always loomed large in the American Jewish imagination, with America being conceived of as a sort of counter-world, a promised land allowing for a constant creative reconfiguration of Judaism in an exceptional environment. Contradictory at times, the myth included various facets, depending on the changing circumstances both in Europe and America. A dominant perception, particularly among liberal Jewish intellectuals in the nineteenth century, was that of Europe as a place of Christian hegemony, intolerance, anti-Semitic discrimination and violence, from which only American democracy could offer redemption. European Judaism, according to this view, was characterized by the persistence of an Orthodox mindset that defied the challenges of modernity, whereas the liberation of Jewish thought and morality from such confinement would allow Judaism's true essence to prevail and its spiritual mission to unfold in a society marked by unprecedented freedom and diversity. The influx of millions of Eastern European Jews since the 1880s fostered convictions regarding the backwardness of European Jewry as well as concepts of Americanization aiming both at facilitating integration and overcoming the European model. After the "Old World" had turned into a place of catastrophic political failure and utter destruction, turning away from Europe appeared to be the only possibility.

However, Heschel's chapter points to other, much more differentiated, ambivalent references to the European legacy since the mid-twentieth century which were linked to a marked disillusionment with America in an age of materialism and rapid assimilation. Particularly among religious circles who sought inspiration for a Jewish spiritual renewal, the departure from such Western European assimilationist traditions went hand in hand with a fascination with alternative voices from the vanished "inner worlds of the Jew in Eastern Europe," in Abraham J. Heschel's words, which were deemed to provide religious and cultural orientation for American Jewry. In the end, however, as the opening essay argues, the general impression to be gained from the history of the transnational relationship between the two diasporic communities is that of a profound reversal: it is now American Judaism with its internal diversity and its firm place within a multicultural society that offers European Jews a model for a re-definition of its religious and political self-understanding.

With her reflections, Heschel turns our attention to the complexities any historiography devoted to American Jewry's transnational history and particularly to the role Europe played in the memory and imagination of American Jews at different times in their history in the "New World" is confronted with. It serves as a reminder that an unqualified notion of America's "exceptionalism," which tends to pervade the historiography on American and American Jewish history, may be counterproductive when addressing the main question explored in this collection of essays: namely whether, to which extent and in which ways the multi-faceted history of American Judaism involves a process of "transcending the European experience."[2]

The very concept of "exceptionalism," i.e., the idea that the history of the United States constitutes a unique case in world history, unaffected for instance by the historical forces that have determined the path of the European nations and thus superior to them, has, of course, been and continues to be the object of substantial historiographical controversy. In contrast to approaches that tend to make the case for the uniqueness of American political culture, delineating its commitment to civil liberty, egalitarianism, and individualism (since the American Revolution at the latest) radically from the political realities and elsewhere,[3] scholars involved in the "transnational turn" in American historiography have strongly challenged such notions, examining instead the intensive interactions and mutual influences that connected the United States with political and cultural processes unfolding in other national contexts, particularly in Europe.[4] Emerging in the early stages of American history as a narrative that "provided a way to explain the connection of the United States to Europe within a story about its geographic and political disconnection," i.e., as an instrument to express a distinctive national identity, the exceptionalist view, according to Joyce Appleby, turns out to be inadequate as a historiographical perspective because it raises "formidable obstacles to appreciating America's original and authentic diversity."[5] However, the many-voiced and often contradictory versions of the transnational approach, whose common denominator has been mainly the anti-exceptionalist attitude, have themselves been exposed to serious criticism as well as to self-critical revisions and differentiations.[6] The spectrum of these more recent perspectives ranges from renewed emphasis on America's exceptional character[7] to most interesting attempts to historicize the rhetoric of exceptionalism and thus to interpret it as a phenomenon that is in itself inherently transnational in that it originated in the European discourse about the uniqueness of the "New World": even though the self-image of the immigrants to America and the emerging American nation was dependent on its contrast with an imagined Europe, its self-attributed exceptionality was also strongly influenced by the European discourse on nationality[8] and the dreams harbored among Europeans of a "world-transforming future" on American soil.[9]

Irrespective of the complex debates regarding the plausibility of the concept of "American exceptionalism," the notion of American Jewry's unique political and social situation in the modern period as well as its distinctive religious and cultural character in comparison to the European Jewish experience is a recurring theme in much of the historiography devoted to American Judaism, albeit with varying nuances. One dominating element of that perception is that the United States, as an inherently pluralistic new nation, has, indeed, a unique history that has, until today, necessarily determined both the opportunities American Jews enjoyed in contrast to their European contemporaries and the way American Judaism developed. Benny Kraut, in his introduction to Marc Lee Raphael's collected volume of essays, *What is American about the American Jewish Experience?* (1993), emphasizes the creative religious and cultural syntheses that, over the centuries, resulted from the confrontation with American values such as freedom, pluralism, and voluntarism. As nuanced as they are, he suggests, they all are expressions of a confluence of Jewish and American ideals, and "they all articulate an existentialist tie of fate binding America and its Jews, in which American Jews are perceived to be irrevocably linked to this country by historical destiny and, for the more religious, by Providence itself."[10] American Jewish history is exceptional, according to Kraut, in terms of the singular Jewish presence in an American culture that, more than any other host society in world history, offered Jews an environment in which they "could even dream of becoming cultural insiders while daring to devise an existential American-Jewish symbiosis of soul," and which allowed them to actively contribute to the project of American pluralism.[11] In this regard, he argues, a strong case can be made for "American Jewish historical exceptionalism," even though historians should avoid embracing the almost mythical elements of some of the narratives involved, and instead, be mindful of the significant anti-Jewish sentiments that persisted throughout the history of American Jews.[12]

Similar limits to the notion of an American Jewish symbiosis, untroubled by anti-Semitism, are identified in a volume entitled *Why is America Different?* (2010), which includes a wealth of essays devoted to the Jewish experience in the United States, among them comparative reflections on European and American anti-Semitism. While emphasizing the consensus according to which American Jews were "largely exempted from demonization, ghettoization, exclusion, submission, and other persecutions that tormented them in the "Old World," Fredric Cople Jaher, for instance, warns about an all too "triumphalist assessment of American liberalism" that would underestimate the transfer of anti-Jewish prejudice from Europe to America, even though it was, most of the time, counterbalanced by the prevailing democratic culture.[13] Other historians, such as Leonard Dinnerstein, when speaking about the phenomenon of heightened anti-Semitism in America during the interwar years and the Nazi period, tend to insist on its fundamental difference in comparison to the "savagery of the prejudice that existed at that time in Poland, Rumania, and Germany," concluding that, for "myriads of reasons, America has always been different for Jews."[14] Europe and America, according to this view, are absolutely incomparable:

For Jews, there have always been less intense feelings against them in the United States than existed in Europe. The history of the Jews in Europe, despite the periodic good times, has been one of slander, stoning, expulsions, hanging, and drowning. Jews have been charged with causing riots, poisoning wells, kidnapping and mutilating Christian children for religious purposes, and fomenting wars and revolutions. In their economic dealings they have been suspected of shady and ruthless practices which they foisted on Christians. While several of these charges have also been attributed to Jews in the United States they have not been as many, as severe, or as quickly supported by church and governmental institutions. In fact, even when churches and members of the government have quietly supported and/ or encouraged blatant anti-Semitism, the official rhetoric has always been circumspect and more often critical of public bigotry. In Europe, however, it would be difficult to find centuries where Christian voices were officially accepting of Jews as simply people of a different faith.[15]

In the majority of the publications that appeared on the occasion of the 350th anniversary of American Jewry in 2005, this very question—why (and how) America is, indeed, different—necessarily played an important role, not only regarding anti-Semitism, but with respect to almost all aspects of American Jewish history. In his programmatic essay, "Some Thoughts on American Jewish Exceptionalism," Steven T. Katz has addressed the continuing concern of scholars of American Jewish history, which also occupies center stage in this present volume, namely "whether the American Jewish experience represents a singular communal circumstance or whether it repeats, with obvious and unavoidable variation, the older European pattern of Jewish existence."[16] His own answer is very clear: Jewish history in America, since the very beginning, has been "a significant deviation from prior historical Jewish experience,"[17] for all the reasons that have come to define American society—its character as a socio-political order with no unified ethnicity and religion, its success in implementing the ideals of European Enlightenment, its inherent myth of America as the "New Israel" that would offer refuge to all human beings, the absence of the sort of debate on a "Jewish question" that undermined the process of Jewish emancipation in Europe, and, most importantly, its essentially pluralistic culture which shaped the equally diverse and pluralistic nature of American Judaism.

Within the context of the 350th anniversary, the manifold facets of the historical, sociological, and cultural developments underlying the distinctiveness of American Jewish history have been explored in numerous books and collections of essays. Based on the substantial achievements of American Jewish studies during the last quarter of the twentieth century,[18] new questions have been posed and fresh avenues of research developed from a variety of interdisciplinary perspectives. Anthologies such as *The Cambridge Companion to American Judaism* (2005), and *The Columbia History of Jews and Judaism in America* (2008) cover almost every aspect of historical and contemporary American Jewry, providing an ever more detailed image of the transformations it underwent during the different periods that can be identified in American Jewish history, and analyzing a wealth of specific aspects that define the latter's distinctive character.

Topics addressed in these anthologies include the development of the different Jewish denominations, religious culture and institutional practice, Jewish religious life and practice, the tension between ethnicity and religion, Jewish responses to Nazism and the Holocaust, feminism's confrontation with Judaism, Jewish politics within the context of American democracy, or the role of Judaism in a multicultural society, to name just a few.[19]

A monographic synthesis of recent trends in American Jewish historiography published on the occasion of the celebration of 350 years of American Jewry, Hasia R. Diner's comprehensive and nuanced book, *The Jews of the United States* (2004),[20] which offers an equally rich portrayal of the path Jews and Judaism took and the dramatic transformations that occurred between the colonial period and the year 2000. Her overview of the multifaceted story of American Jewry, starting with Jewish communities which were initially just "American outposts of the Jewish communities of Amsterdam, London, and several others scattered around the Caribbean,"[21] and focusing strongly on the "great era of European Jewish immigration to America" from 1820 to 1920,[22] a century also characterized by her as a century of the establishment of Jewish life and of Jewish politics in America, strongly emphasizes the need to give weight to both the Jewish *and* the American context that determined the American Jewish experience. The narrative provided is that of a "constant process of negotiation" between American and Jewish identities, between their will to be Jews rooted in their historical traditions and to fully participate in American society and culture—a process in which the successive generations of immigrants, first from Germany and Central Europe, and later from Eastern Europe, self-consciously redefined Judaism according to both American and Jewish sensibilities, thus creating a community whose character was "distinctive from that of other Jewries."[23] At times setting American Jewry apart from other parts of the Jewish Diaspora, "while at other times putting them at odds with the behaviors and attitudes of other Americans," Diner argues, this process of negotiation entailed varieties of possibilities for Jewish individuals and groups throughout that period, from embracing American values as part of their Jewish identities to leaving Jewishness behind as a burden or to the attempt to immunize their own spiritual and social world against American culture. One important aspect of Diner's interpretation, however, that makes it extremely relevant for the questions explored in the present volume, is the strong emphasis it puts on the crucial role Europe and the "transnational Jewish path" of religious, intellectual and political currents that shaped the Jewish experience in the modern period plays in American Jewish history, at least until the Holocaust. This history can, therefore, not be adequately understood without considering that, for centuries, American Jews not only "articulated, albeit in American forms, similar ideas, sensibilities, fears, hopes, and beliefs" as did Jews in Europe, but were profoundly shaped by the forces of European (and European Jewish) culture:

> For much of its history American Jewry functioned as a kind of outpost of Europe. It was in the great population centers in Poland, Russia, and Germany that Jewish high culture was created. Warsaw, Berlin, Vienna, Odessa, Vilna, and other cities of

Europe were the cradles of Jewish political and artistic inspiration, while America was a kind of sideshow. Although these ideas and movements also flourished in New York, Chicago, Los Angeles, and Philadelphia, the basic flow went from east to west.[24]

While almost all expressions of American Jewish culture, including the Reform movement, modern Orthodoxy, Jewish nationalism, socialism, the emergence of Yiddish and Hebrew literature, and new trends in literature, theatre and film before the First World War were nurtured by European influences, even though they were often thoroughly Americanized, the decades between 1920 and the end of the Second World War were a crucial turning point, according to Diner, in two regards: firstly, "a population of Jewish immigrants transformed itself into a population of native-born American Jews" during that period, with the result that, by the 1960s, there were no strong immediate links to Europe; secondly, the destruction of the Jewish world in Europe made American Jewry the dominant center of Diaspora Jewish life (with Israel as a new reality and reference point) and, in a radical reversal of historical circumstances, started turning it into a "model for the older communities."[25] The years between 1948 and 1967 which Diner characterizes as a "golden age" of American Jewry, even though it was overshadowed by the confrontation with the memory of the Nazi genocide, saw an abundance of developments, unprecedented in Europe, that turned Judaism into "a mainstream American faith, becoming a third jewel in the crown of American civic religion."[26] During the decades since the Israeli Six-Day War in 1967, Europe seems largely absent as a formative element of the American Jewish identity debates which were, instead, revolving around the significance of the relationship to the State of Israel as well as the question regarding American Jewry's distinctiveness within a multicultural society.

A second masterful history of the American Jewish experience published amidst the 350-year-celebrations is Jonathan D. Sarna's book, *American Judaism: A History* (2004) that is, at the same time, a historian's response to the "haunting fear" among observers of American Judaism's situation at the beginning of the twenty-first century "that Judaism in the New World will wither away" as a result of various developments leading to a potentially alarming demographic decline.[27] In the face of such challenges, Sarna points to the contemporary relevance inherent in a comprehensive, differentiated study of its history, particularly if it succeeds in reminding American Jews of the creative responses found in the history of American Judaism's transformations and reinventions in the past and in bringing to mind the "dynamic story of people who lose their faith and a story of people who regain their faith, a story of assimilation, to be sure, but also a story of revitalization."[28] With his emphasis on social, economic and cultural history, his broad definition of religion that includes also secular phenomena, and his insight into American Judaism's diversity, and by situating American Jewish history in its manifold contexts (Jewish history, American history as well as the history of American religion), Sarna identifies a number of past revivals and awakenings that give hope for the future: the revitalization engendered by the immigration of Eastern European Jews since the late nineteenth century, or the revival of American Jewish life that took place after the severe crises in the wake of the First World War and the unfolding European Jewish catastrophe, eventually preparing American Jewry for its new responsibilities: "Whereas before, the Jews of Europe represented the demographic and cultural center of world Jewry, now that designation fell to America."[29] The postwar revival, according to Sarna, must be seen as a history of enormous religious and cultural transformation, followed by yet another awakening in the 1970s, a "veritable explosion of self-consciously Jewish culture of every sort,"[30] and characterized even in the present by signs of religious and cultural vitality that seem to defy the predictions of a gloomy future.

Even though Sarna sharply emphasizes the contrast between the European Jewish experience and American Jewry's unique opportunities in an environment shaped by freedom and diversity, characterizing American Jewish history as a history "without expulsions, concentration camps, and extermination,"[31] he shares Hasia R. Diner's views regarding the significance of Europe for the shape Judaism took during the different periods of American history. His book, therefore, includes extensive reflections on the development of European Jewry even before the colonial period, starting in Spain before 1492 and the ensuing history of crypto-Jews as well as their open return to Judaism in seventeenth-century Amsterdam, or on the political and cultural situation of Russian Jewry in the late nineteenth century. In his programmatic afterword to the *Cambridge Companion to American Judaism*, transnational studies are attributed crucial importance among the five new directions of the study of American Judaism which he identifies as the most significant desiderata for future research (the other four being: detailed studies of religious practice among American Jews; studies of the Jewish book in America; local and regional studies that would challenge the image of a homogenized "American Judaism"; and studies devoted to the different variants of secular Judaism in American history).[32] In contrast to overly "internalist" interpretations that tend to accentuate the uniqueness and self-sufficiency of American Jewish history at the expense of its transnational elements, ignoring Judaism's character as "the paradigmatic 'transnational faith,'" Sarna suggests a systematic examination of American Judaism's cultural and political ties to and interaction with the rest of the Jewish world in different historical periods as well as the present:

> A transnational understanding of American Judaism would explore more closely the involvement of European and, more recently, Israeli Jewish leaders in Jewish religious life in America—and vice versa. It would examine the ties linking American Jewry with the other major communities within the English-language Jewish diaspora: Canada, the Caribbean, England, South Africa, Australia, and New Zealand. It would reinterpret the role of rabbis and scholars who repeatedly crossed borders in search of learning, collegiality, and employment, and whose correspondence and publications likewise spanned the globe, shaping different Jewish communities' images of one another. In short, a transnational approach would remind us that American Judaism was never "an island entire of itself," and would help to restore American Judaism to its rightful place within a global universe.[33]

The few reflections presented above about current historiographical perspectives on the history of American Jewry and American Judaism, particularly on the partially controversial discussions regarding the distinctive character of its development under the circumstances offered by the "new promised land" in comparison to the situation in Europe, raise important questions that have not yet been fully answered. Building on Hasia R. Diner's emphasis on the crucial role Europe, European ideas as well as religious and cultural developments within European Jewry played in the course of American Jewish history at least until the mid-twentieth century, and on Jonathan D. Sarna's insistence on a decidedly transnational approach, the present volume focuses mainly on the way American Jews perceived the history, challenges, and legacy of their European experience, while negotiating their self-understanding as Americans *and* Jews as part of the complex ethnic and religious texture of American society and culture since the colonial period. One of the main question examined in these collected essays with their various disciplinary approaches is in which regard and for which reasons American Jews did, indeed, deviate from the patterns of their European past, which aspects of the "Old World" they retained and continued to cherish, and what facilitated the unmistakable re-invention of Jewish identity in America over the last centuries. To what extent did the construction of the "European experience" serve the process of Judaism's "Americanization" that unfolded from the initial arrival of a few Sephardic Jews in New Amsterdam in 1654 to the establishment of a large and diverse Jewish community in the twentieth century? Indeed, did Jewish life in America facilitate a national and religious experience that made American Jews find a "New Zion" and overcome the sense of *galut* that continued, to varying degrees, to shape and overshadow European Jewry? Or did they also encounter boundaries limiting their integration into surrounding society, in this case the limits of "American Exceptionalism?" Did the hopes of establishing an independent American Judaism in a free, pluralistic country held by the Jewish immigrants from Western and Eastern Europe come true or did they fail at times, because patterns of prejudice and exclusion also persisted in the "New World?" In which ways did the American Jewish experience specifically differ from the European model during the centuries since the colonial period, with Jews being influenced by the changing political, social, and cultural circumstances in America as well as by the complex developments in various parts of Europe? How did American Jews define their relationship to the "Old World," before and after the vicissitudes of the late nineteenth and early twentieth centuries, which culminated in the explosion of mass violence during the Second World War and the Holocaust? How did the memory of these earth-shattering events impact American Jewish self-understanding during the last seventy years? And what does it mean that, since then, the State of Israel seems to have replaced the European Diaspora as the main object of American Jews' imagination, concern, and criticism?

This book does neither intend to provide a comprehensive survey of all the facets of American Jewish history nor can it cover all potential dimensions of the transnational approach it is devoted to. Like other anthologies exploring the manifold elements of what has, with regard to the American Jewish experience, been defined as an emerging new paradigm addressing the "cultural, religious, social, institutional, and economic linkages that spanned political borders and boundaries,"[34] it is a modest attempt to develop new perspectives regarding the extremely rich and complex history of the transnational relationship between European Jewish history and American Jewish history from the early modern period to the present. A fine group of acknowledged scholars of American Studies, Jewish Studies, and History join forces to present lesser known facets of the history and the present situation of what, during the twentieth century, became the largest Jewish Diaspora and—alongside the State of Israel—the most important Jewish community worldwide. Based on a transnational and comparative approach, the contributions in this volume explore the gradual emergence of the leading role American Jews have played and continue to play with regard to religious trends, secular Jewish culture, and Jewish politics. By providing a thorough analysis of the way Jews in America interpreted their own European past and the events affecting their European Jewish contemporaries, the authors shed new light on the question why and how American Jewry was able to develop such a distinctly "American" identity and capitalize on the religious, legal and political framework the English colonies and later the United States offered them as the first modern nation. By doing so, the essays collected here also critically expose the limits of the dream of American freedom and equality, and analyze where this dream was shaped by European models, individuals and thought, or where it differed or deliberately dissociated itself from the "Old World." The key elements of the comparison of the American and European diasporic communities' history and identity include, among others, the modernization of religious currents within Judaism in their respective non-Jewish religious worlds, the phenomenon of newly emerging secular or political identities (such as Jewish socialism or Zionism) as well as questions regarding social, cultural and economic lifestyles. Finally, the volume will address the question whether the specifically American context, including the reigning legal and social situation as well as the religious and cultural environment weakened or strengthened Jewish distinctiveness, and how the relationship between the American and European Jewish communities reversed in the wake of the Holocaust and the Cold War.

Part I: Colonial identities: the early modern period

As seen above, one of the central elements of the historical self-understanding of the United States of America has been the nation's self-awareness as the "New Zion," a refuge for the persecuted peoples of the world and a unique opportunity to depart from European patterns. By virtue of its deeply rooted ideal of religious and social freedom, "America" became symbolic of a modern and pioneering counter-model to Europe's political, social and cultural parameters, and concepts of the relationship between Church and State.

This model of the United States as the embodiment of a promised land of freedom, tolerance, and equality versus an "Old World" characterized by discrimination, persecution, and religious violence, formed the core of an American civil religion, which had its roots in the hopes and visions of the persecuted Pilgrim Fathers. Since the latter had arrived in the "New World," this notion of a civil religion has been of central significance for the various religious and ethnic minorities who immigrated between the seventeenth and the twentieth century and who underwent a deliberate and voluntary, albeit complex process of "Americanization." The Puritan-inspired Biblicism, including the concomitant myth according to which America was the "New Jerusalem" and Americans were the "new chosen people," had no detrimental impact on the integration of Jews and Judaism into American culture, on the contrary: it has become a crucial element of what has been termed "the Judaic quality of the American cultural ambience," and thus a factor that strengthened the latter's inclusive character also with regard to Jews and Judaism.[35]

Based on the British policies in the establishment of settler colonies, the thirteen British colonies in North America soon became a safe haven for the religious dissenters who were fleeing from ecclesiastical and state authority in Europe, and later for those immigrants who, in more general terms, hoped for better political and socio-economic circumstances across the Atlantic. The British colonial experiment and the endeavor to establish prospering settlements on the American continent resulted, at least in some of the colonies, in the practice of religious tolerance and in early forms of self-government. Both were unheard of in Europe, where feudal society and confessionalization had left a strong mark on society.

The eventual emergence of the American nation codified this development and provided the model for a "modern nation" that allowed its citizens to create and sustain a new civic identity. The concept of a separation of Church and State rooted in the Constitution of the United States of America, the warranty of religious freedom as well as the non-establishment clause, and a legal system enabling the citizens to claim their rights, shaped the contours of a society that continued to attract numerous European immigrants after the American Revolution. The emergence and flourishing of a free market, the absence of the traditional corporative privileges as well as the far-reaching political and social liberties that accompanied the American model created a new society that retained its great appeal to European minorities during the nineteenth and twentieth centuries as well.

There has probably been no other group of immigrants for whom the hopes in the new "promised land" have turned out to be as captivating as for the American Jews. For them, America represented and continues to be a unique place that allowed them to leave the European historical experience behind and to re-invent themselves as well as their religious and cultural identities. The disillusionment brought about by long-standing traditions of anti-Jewish hatred, discrimination, and persecution prevalent in early modern Europe on the one hand, and the emergence of attractive economic opportunities in the colonies on the other, prompted a small minority of Sephardic Jews to settle on American soil during the seventeenth and eighteenth centuries. The period between 1654 and 1820, from the colonial beginnings through the American Revolution and to the beginning of the mass migration of Jews from Central Europe, saw increasing liberties for the Jewish communities, allowing them to blend in into American society, interact with the Christian majority, and create their institutions as they wished, without necessarily looking to Europe "for guidance in how to be Jewish."[36]

While the history of American Judaism, according to the common narrative, tends to symbolically commence with the arrival of the famous twenty-three Sephardic Jews in New Amsterdam, the story presented by *Judah M. Cohen* in his essay, "Trading Freedoms? Exploring Colonial Jewish Merchanthood between Europe and the Caribbean," broadens the historiographical perspective by turning to the pre-history of Jewish migration to colonial America from the South American coast whose Jewish communities were shaped by the experience of Spanish and Portuguese Jews in Western Europe. In explicit contrast to the somewhat mythical image of a direct transatlantic migration of European Jews in search of a sanctuary in the "New World," the story told in this essay challenges dominant narratives about the origins of American Judaism by incorporating the history of the role played and the experiences made by Jews in the mercantile trade between Europe, the Caribbean, and colonial America before 1654. The counter-narrative suggested is that of a Jewish community of merchants who were part of the European project of westward colonial expansion in the age of mercantilism, enjoying new opportunities of religious freedom and economic participation, moving back and forth between Europe and the Caribbean depending on the political circumstances, and occupying a place in the "other America" that tends to be neglected in American Jewish historiography. A meeting place between Europe and America in the early modern period and a space in between the Americas well into the twentieth century, the Caribbean remained important for both European and American Jewish history much beyond the episode of the first group of pioneering Jewish immigrants. Cohen's essay thus advocates accentuating the relevance of Caribbean Jewish history within a transnational historiographical framework that would reconfigure more conventional interpretations to include elements that have been unjustly eclipsed by the dominant focus on North America.

An excellent example of the significance of this perspective is provided by *Laura Arnold Leibman*'s chapter, "Early American *Mikva'ot*: Ritual Baths as the Hope of Israel," which explores the religious meaning and cultural practice of ritual purity as expressed by the tradition of ritual baths in the early Americas, particularly in Caribbean Jewish communities with their strong link to the world of Sephardic and Ashkenazi Jewry in Amsterdam. Against the background of religious developments related to the Early Enlightenment in seventeenth- and eighteenth-century Amsterdam—and subsequently in its colonies in the Caribbean—the essay interprets the significance attributed at that time to the concept of purification and the institution of the *mikveh* as an expression of a yearning for messianic redemption, combined with an enlightened medicinal discourse on the benefits of "water cures" for women. The detailed comparison of the idea as well as the construction and use of ritual baths in Amsterdam to the early Jewish communities of the Americas aims at a clearer understanding of the specific religious implications of the colonial *mikva'ot*. The strong messianic symbolism inherent in the new tradition of making use of underground springs rather than rainwater, as in Amsterdam, reflects, as

Leibman suggests, the two main distinctive aspects of the colonial model: first, the influence exerted by messianic revivalist trends in the Protestant American colonies, and second, a sense of messianic hopes connected to the experience of *conversos* who, far from the shores of Europe, felt free to return to Judaism, but remained in need of redemption; both elements led to an understanding of Jewish settlements in the Americas as the sign of the impending "ingathering of Israel." The "New World," in contrast to Europe, thus became the embodiment of the hope for the fulfillment of Israel's and humankind's messianic future.

Eli Faber's comparative chapter, "Early American Jewry and the Quest for Civil Equality," explores the political aspects of the early modern Jewish communities in British North America. Starting with the first small settlements during the mid-seventeenth century, but with a focus on the eighteenth century, he addresses the conspicuous difference between European and American Jewry in the modern period with regard to the process of emancipation and social participation. While initially Jews in Europe and in America were equally caught in a state of permanent exclusion, separated from the Christian population by insurmountable boundaries, the eighteenth century already saw a marked difference between Europe and America, as anti-Semitism in America tended to be less violent, Jews were less exposed to economic and social restrictions, and social interaction with non-Jews was much more intense than in the "Old World." Even though the circumstances gradually changed in Western and Central Europe after the French Revolution, the process of emancipation there was generally much more protracted and encumbered by obstacles than in America, where the only realm that remained barred to Jews before the American Revolution was that of political participation. As the crucial turning point in American Jewish history toward full inclusion in a civic society, the analysis of Jewish political activities during and in the wake of the Revolution reveals, according to Faber, a significant difference to Europe: in contrast to the passivity of European Jews, who tended to be much more cautious in challenging the political status, American Jewry took political initiative, asserting their vision of civic equality and religious pluralism in a manner that led to a new and hitherto unknown political order for the Jews of America that separated their experience radically from that of their European contemporaries.

Part II: Finding a "new Zion" in America's civic culture?

The second wave of migration between the 1820s and the 1880s that brought, along with almost seven million non-Jews, about 280,000—mainly German-speaking—Ashkenazi Jews from Central Europe to America, revolutionized American Jewry in many respects—demographically as well as in cultural and political terms. Followed by another, even larger group of millions of Eastern European Jewish immigrants between the 1880s and 1924, they stood at the beginning of what would eventually become the "two worlds of American Judaism," in Jonathan D. Sarna's words, which created the dynamic process of competing and converging cultural phenomena that were to change the course of American Jewish history forever.[37] According to Hasia R. Diner, this makes the entire period between the 1820s and 1924 (which marks the year of the implementation of strict immigration restrictions) the "pivotal century" of American Jewry, shaped by the experience of migration, the process of religious and ideological diversification, the establishment of increasing numbers of Jewish institutions, and Jewish politics within a rapidly changing American environment.[38] This century was marked, at the same time, by a history of both Europeanization and De-Europeanization, with a constant new influx of European immigrants, ideas, traditions, and memories on the one hand, and intense negotiations with the challenges, offers and needs of American culture on the other.

This section of the book is devoted to the first of the "two worlds of American Judaism" and explores the complex process by which the Jewish immigrants since the 1820s, mainly from a German-speaking background, contributed to and found their place in the civic culture emerging in America during the nineteenth and early twentieth centuries. This culture offered Jews unique opportunities and allowed them to prosper economically, enjoy religious freedom, and participate culturally and politically in a society to a degree that seemed unattainable even in the most liberal European contexts. While the social structure of the different immigrant groups who came to the United States in the 1820s, 1840s, and 1860s, their experience during the Civil War, the religious and cultural character of the American Jewish Reform movement and the delayed "Americanization" of these "German" immigrants have been researched extensively,[39] a more nuanced comparative and transnational examination of the way they related to the European component of their emerging cultural self-understanding is still a desideratum.

Kathleen Neils Conzen's essay, "German Jews and the German-speaking Civic Culture of Nineteenth-century America," addresses, at the same time, the rarely told story of how the German Jewish immigrants negotiated their relationship to their cultural roots by intervening in contemporary debates among the vast non-Jewish German immigrant community regarding the legitimacy of continuing German ethnic and linguistic distinctiveness within American society. Based on a thorough reading of German Jewish periodicals and journals in America over several decades, the chapter is devoted to the fundamental question: whether or not there was a significant Jewish voice within those debates and how it related to the shared cultural heritage and concept of *Bildung*. Having experienced the controversies about the terms and conditions of a religious minority's integration in Germany, and being confronted with a challenge to which the non-Jewish German immigrants were now equally compelled to respond—namely, that even the liberal cosmopolitan voices within American society tended to define American cultural identity as necessarily evangelical Protestant—Jewish intellectuals were among those who fiercely rejected such views and contributed to a discourse on an appropriate balance between assimilation, pluralism, and democracy. Without intending to present an exclusively Jewish perspective, many of them, by emphasizing the value of cultural difference within American democracy, did, in fact, advocate a model of identity that included several elements: Jewish religious convictions, German ethnicity, and belonging to the American nation. The essay further examines the complex and often contradicting ways in which, toward the end of the nineteenth century, German Jewish immigrants, in the face of rising anti-Semitism in Germany and increasing immigration from Eastern

Europe, asserted their own religious-cultural identity, while negotiating their relationship to the German language and German culture and combating anti-Jewish sentiments among non-Jewish Americans. The controversies about the need for an accelerated Americanization process and linguistic unity of the Jews, as embodied in Isaac M. Wise's polemics against those who sought to maintain their German roots, was, as Conzen argues, an intervention in a more general German debate in America and, at the same time, the expression of a central concern of American Jewry vis-a-vis its European past—namely the role of cultural diversity and difference within American civic society.

Cornelia Wilhelm turns to a different aspect of civic society's promises for American Jewry. In her comparative essay, "Unequal Opportunities: The Independent Order B'nai B'rith in Nineteenth-century Germany and in the United States," accentuates the striking contrast between the political and cultural conditions of German-speaking Jewry and the American Jews during the nineteenth century. The German Jewish immigrants who came to America since the 1830s had left behind a society that, despite the impact the Enlightenment had on early concepts of civic emancipation and the integration of religious or ethnic minorities, caused a high degree of disillusionment among the Jews. The Haskalah and hopes for civic equality had inspired Reform-oriented Jewish intellectuals in Europe to modernize Judaism by reinterpreting crucial concepts such as the "chosenness" of the Jewish people and replacing it by the notion of a universal "Jewish mission to humankind." Their goal of constructing a—secular—civic identity that would include the right to maintain a distinctively Jewish identity failed, however, due to the non-Jewish authorities' strategy of offering equality only in a frustratingly protracted process, a strategy that revealed German society's deeply rooted will to uphold its politics of exclusion and to deny equal participation to the Jewish minority and particularly Judaism as a cultural tradition. In contrast to the situation in Germany, soon to be aggravated by nationalist, racist, and anti-Semitic discourses, the Jewish immigrants encountered, according to Wilhelm, a uniquely favorable context: American society embraced the enlightened concepts of diversity and pluralism to a hence unknown extent that allowed American Jews to occupy their legitimate space within the pluralistic realm of American civil religion without giving up their distinctive identity as a religious and ethnic group. Focusing on the example of the Independent Order of B'nai B'rith, founded in 1843 in New York, with its characteristic blend of German Jewish Reform principles, Masonic-style organization, and identification with American values, the essay explores the opportunity for American Jewry to combine the message of Judaism's universal mission with an unprecedented involvement in the public political sphere. With this creative and successful strategy, American Jews could have become a role model for the Jewish minorities in the European context, had not the political circumstances in Germany, particularly the reigning "integral nationalism," with its polarizing confrontation of "Germanness" and "Jewishness," posed an insurmountable obstacle for the endeavor of institutions such as the German B'nai B'rith to convince German society of the benefits inherent in America's cultural pluralism.

A defining moment in the history of the American Reform movement as well as with regard to its transnational links to reformers and reform ideas in Germany was the

Philadelphia Conference in 1869 which formulated the theological assumptions and practical guidelines that shaped the agenda of a specific generation of reform-oriented immigrants for the Jewish communities in post-Civil War America. *Christian Wiese*'s chapter, "The Philadelphia Conference (1869) and German Reform: A Historical Moment in a Transnational Story of Proximity and Alienation," explores the dynamics between the German and American Reform movements as reflected in the sharp public ideological controversy between the historian Abraham Geiger, one of the pioneering protagonists of *Wissenschaft des Judentums* in Germany, and the reform philosopher David Einhorn, who became a dominating voice within the American rabbinate in the 1860s and 1870s. This conflict that erupted between them in 1870 and the decades-long ambivalent relationship between the two thinkers, characterized as it was by a mixture of friendship, intellectual affinity, and ideological difference, is interpreted as the symbolical expression of a gradually emerging tension between those Reform rabbis who immigrated to America and those who remained in Germany. By analyzing the mutual perceptions within the context of this debate, this essay captures a particular historical moment that sheds light on the increasingly discernible inclination of American Jewish reformers to both cherish and transcend the European experience by contesting the dominating role of the German Jewish matrix, without dissociating themselves from the continuing inspiration originating from it. The image portrayed is that of a gradual emancipation of the American rabbis from the conspicuous paternalistic attitude of German reformers like Geiger, and of a distinctive path of the American Reform movement that responded to the different political and cultural contexts it was confronted with in the "New World."

As *Karla Goldman*'s chapter, "Beyond the Synagogue Gallery? Women's Changing Roles in Nineteenth-century American and German Judaism," demonstrates, the distinctiveness of the American Reform Movement in contrast to its German model crystallized not merely in the theological realm, but also in regard to crucial elements of religious practice. One of these elements was the endeavor to redefine the nature of female religiosity and women's role in the synagogue as part of the project of adapting Judaism to the expectations of modern society. Through an in-depth comparative approach, the chapter sheds light on the profound impact the differing bourgeois cultures in nineteenth-century Germany and America had on the gap that opened up between the realities Jewish women were confronted with in both contexts. While the attempts of the German Reform movement to transform traditional gender roles were limited by much stronger restraints when it came to revolutionizing given practices in the synagogue as well as by a cultural environment that often tended to confine female religiosity to the domestic realm, the circumstances in America were much more favorable for the visible inclusion of women in the public sphere. The crucial significance of public worship in American Protestantism, very much in contrast to increasingly secularizing German society, and the deviating codes of bourgeois respectability which expected women's participation in the public display of religiosity and morality, forced the American Reform rabbinate to rethink the place assigned to women in the synagogue service and thus to depart from the more traditional European model. The image emerging from Goldman's comparison is that of a process in which the American Reform movement was strongly influenced by the—sometimes quite radical—modernizing theories of its German model, but was also prompted by the differing political and social context to a much more progressive redefinition of gender roles in Judaism. This combination, in conjunction with the voluntary, pluralistic character of religious communities in America, led to a unique American Jewish ritual and synagogue practice that was to become the starting point for more recent developments in the twentieth century.

Yaakov Ariel's chapter, "Something Old, Something New ... Something Blue: Negotiating for a New Relationship between Judaism and Christianity, 1865–1917," shifts the attention to the specific religious and cultural encounter between Judaism and Christianity in the post-Civil War period which was brought about by changing perceptions of Judaism among Christian intellectuals as well as by Jewish efforts to programmatically assert the role of the Jewish religious tradition within contemporary society. Analyzing the way Christians and Jews re-negotiated their relationship in a period of increased immigration, amidst the emergence in America of both a liberal Christian theology, whose triumphalism was at least alleviated by the most recent trends in historical, philological and literary studies, and given an elite of Reform-oriented Jewish intellectuals, who strongly challenged traditional Christian constructions of Judaism, this essay also includes important comparative reflections upon the European roots of this process. While American Christianity was influenced by traditions such as English Reform or Pietism which were less permeated with anti-Jewish sentiments than other currents within the European context, the protagonists of Jewish apologetics in America, often belonging to the German Jewish leadership, were profoundly indebted in particular to the German discipline of *Wissenschaft des Judentums* and appropriated the latter's project of using academic scholarship to undermine Christian prejudice and to assert Judaism's providential messianic role in modern society. What gradually came to distinguish these Jewish scholars from their German predecessors was that, despite their characteristic historical critique of early Christianity, they were more inclined to envision a reconciliation of both religious traditions, because they encountered, among at least parts of the Christian leadership, a willingness to pay respect to Judaism—an experience that Jewish scholars in Europe never enjoyed before the Holocaust. Even though many of the scholarly arguments used by American Jewish scholars echoed the Jewish discourse in Western and Central Europe, the uniqueness of American Christianity, with its more inclusive outlook and its openness toward interreligious dialogue (even if it was under the guise of conservative Evangelical interest in Jews as the heirs of the historical children of Israel), facilitated the emergence of a comparatively dialogical relationship which anticipated and influenced more recent developments in the European context since the mid-twentieth century, as well.

Christian Wiese's essay, "Translating *Wissenschaft*: The Emergence and Self-emancipation of American-Jewish Scholarship, 1860–1920," explores a similar tension between the obvious indebtedness of American Jewish scholars to the European Jewish scholarly tradition of the nineteenth century and the equally unmistakable distinctiveness of the emerging Jewish scholarship in America. It is devoted to the process of transformation that took place when Jewish migration from Europe to America since the

1840s led to the transplantation of the scholarly tradition of *Wissenschaft des Judentums* into a different social, cultural and linguistic context. The—anything but straightforward— emergence of English as a new, independent language of Jewish scholarship and the establishment of a distinctly American tradition of scholarly approaches to Jewish history and literature reflect the history of the Jewish experience in Europe and America during this period, including the complexities inherent in the way American Jewish intellectuals, immigrants as well as members of the subsequent generation, negotiated the relationship between their European origins and cultural heritage and what they considered to be the "new Zion," the land of Judaism's future. The development toward more independence and a certain sense of superiority among American Jewish scholars, demonstrated by the emergence of an abundance of new scholarly institutions at the beginning of the twentieth century, was accelerated by the tragic fate of Jewish scholars and Jewish scholarship under Nazi persecution. By interpreting the protracted process of the transfer of Jewish Studies from Europe to America, including the changes it underwent in the new cultural context, the chapter thus points to the significance of the much more profound transition that occurred in Jewish history during this period in which the center of the Diaspora shifted from Europe to the "new promised land," whereas particularly Germany, once regarded as the origin of its most important values, eventually came to embody the experience of discrimination, persecution and genocide suffered by the Jewish people in Europe.

Part III: New roles and identities in an age of mass migration

The demographic, cultural, and political impact of the massive wave of Jewish immigration from Russia, Romania, and Austria-Hungary between 1880 and 1924, triggered by discrimination, poverty, and pogroms, marks an entirely new phase of American Jewish history that brought about a thorough reconfiguration of the social realities, religious affiliations as well as political concerns of the rapidly growing Jewish minority in America.[40] It also engendered a gradual reversal of the power relations between established German Jews and the around 2.5 million new immigrants from Eastern Europe, who brought a variety of diverse alternative religious, cultural, and ideological attitudes or lifestyles from a region in Europe in which the Jewish experience had strongly differed from the one in the societies of Western and Central Europe. The diversification of American Judaism that went along with these immigrants who embodied a plurality of Jewish responses to the challenges of modernity, including different variants of religious traditionalism, secular self-definitions of socialist or nationalist provenance, and linguistic preferences, and the accelerating transformation of the American economy and society, challenged the predominance of the bourgeois urban Reform Jewish elite and led to new priorities and identities. As far as the religious landscape was concerned, the first decades of the twentieth century saw a number of crucial developments that were to fundamentally alter the religious face of American Judaism during the first half of the century: a reorientation of the Reform movement, the ascent of Conservative Judaism, the confrontation of Orthodox Jews with the forces of

Americanization,[41] and the emergence of Reconstructionism as an attractive, alternative interpretation of Judaism's significance to the American context.

The tectonic shifts in the life of European Jews brought about by the First World War, the mass violence in parts of Eastern Europe, the revolutions and crises in Central Europe during the interwar years, the unprecedented escalation of anti-Semitism, the rise of Fascism and Nazism and the destruction that followed "demonstrated, emphatically," as Hasia R. Diner argued, "how differently American Jews experienced history from their sisters and brothers" in Europe,[42] witnessing the events in the "Old World" from afar, often in horror, and undertaking rescue attempts when they became aware of the unfolding genocide.[43] At the same time they were confronted with political, economic, and cultural challenges of their own, including the defense against the spreading American variant of anti-Semitism, the crisis of the Great Depression, and the consequences of the accelerating middle-class Americanization. Forming an "anxious subculture," as Jonathan D. Sarna called it,[44] American Jews actively faced these challenges, engaging in intensive debates on the various religious and national identities and transforming the self-understanding of the different currents within American Jewry, including Reform Judaism, Orthodoxy, and Zionism in the face of the events in Europe and Palestine. What unfolded during these two decades can only be described as a dramatic process whose true nature would only become apparent in the wake of the Second World War: "As the Nazis reduced European Jewry to ashes, Judaism in America was gathering strength."[45]

This section of the volume opens with two essays that engage in a self-critical re-reading of the respective authors' earlier research on American Jewry's religious and cultural self-understanding. *David E. Kaufman*, in his chapter, "'Shul with a Pool' Reconsidered," revisits crucial elements of his own interpretation of the institution of "synagogue-center" in the post-First World War period as a signifier of the uniqueness of the American Jewish experience. Was this institution—a dialectical combination of Jewish identity constructions based on religiosity or ethnicity—rooted in Jewish tradition, in an analogous version of social Christianity's forms of religious and social interaction, or in a truly unique expression of a "New American Judaism" characterized by the attempt to transform the synagogue into a center of Jewish peoplehood? And why did it emerge in America rather than in Europe? In his attempt to identify the origins of what he continues to perceive as a unique American Jewish phenomenon, Kaufman identifies a number of heterogeneous influences, including from the Reform movement, cultural Zionism, and modern Orthodoxy, which lent themselves to a creative response to the need to overcome traditional hierarchical relations between rabbinical or lay leaders and the constituency of the synagogue center with its diverse religious and social needs. The contrast to the European *kehillah* in the nineteenth and early twentieth centuries, the chapter assumes, may be attributed to the latter's lack of democratic communal structures and diversity which the Jewish immigrants overcame when confronted with the need to adapt to the American context.

"Americanization" is also a main theme of *Jeffrey S. Gurock*'s "'Resisters and Accommodators' Revisited: Reflections on the Study of Orthodoxy in America"—a critical revision of distinctions made earlier in his analysis of the development of two camps within American Orthodoxy since the 1880s, both with different biographical roots in Europe: on the one hand, there were the "resisters," as he calls them, who usually received their training at Eastern European *yeshivot* and were aiming at transplanting their religious convictions and lifestyle to America, refusing to accept the forces of acculturation; on the other hand, the "accommodators," who had been shaped by their studies at American Jewish theological seminaries, were inclined to a much larger extent to adapt to more liberal American cultural and esthetic categories as well as to the social needs of their congregants in order to reach out to those who had already undergone a process of Americanization. Gurock's reinterpretation dissolves the notion of a fundamentally polarized opposition between these two trends, allowing for a more nuanced image of the flexibility between and within respective camps. By closely examining the attitudes of individual rabbis and Orthodox organizations, the chapter points to a number of more ambivalent features to be found among the "resisters," including the willingness of Jews with a European-style Religious Zionist background to join forces with less Orthodox or secular Jews, or to adapt to the modern American educational system. But not only did the Eastern European Jewish legacy, to which the "resisters" felt committed, undergo significant changes during the encounter with America, the more accommodationist attitudes were also more diverse and ambivalent than previously thought. With these differentiations regarding the dynamics of the encounter of the different generations and factions of Orthodox immigrants in their new environment, the chapter provides an excellent example of the complexities involved in the inner-Jewish discourse on religion within twentieth-century American society.

Apart from the transformation of the character of American Jewish religious life after the end of the "German phase" of American Jewish history, one of its most crucial new dimensions was the emergence of a secular, often Yiddish-speaking Jewish socialist movement triggered by the working conditions in the urban contexts of New York, Chicago, Philadelphia, and other larger cities. This phenomenon, which thoroughly changed the character and self-understanding of American Jewry, both in terms of its social structure and the accelerating discourse on the "Americanization" of the new group of immigrants, can be read, as it has often been done, as another chapter of European influence absorbed and transformed by American Jewry. However, *Tony Michels'* chapter, "Exporting Yiddish Socialism: New York's Role in the Russian Jewish Workers' Movement," with its accent on mutual transnational links between socialism in the "New World" and in Eastern Europe, gives this narrative a surprising new twist. Contrary to traditional views, according to which Yiddish socialism was imported from the Russian Empire, this essay emphasizes the marginal character of the pre-existing socialist tradition and labor movement in Russia before the mid-1890s, whereas New York's first Jewish socialist organization was created a decade earlier. While the large proportion of Jewish revolutionaries, members of the *Bund* and other Jewish political parties, who did eventually immigrate to America after the abortive 1905 revolution and who transplanted their ideologies onto American soil, tends to obscure the fact that the Jewish labor movement in New York had developed for almost twenty years without a strong Russian influence, there seems to be much evidence for an alternative story: the cultural and ideological influence Jewish socialists from New York exerted on socialist and revolutionary circles back in Russia. As with the Yiddish press, which flourished in New York years before it did anywhere in Europe, Yiddish socialism emerged primarily as a response to New York's volatile social conditions and the growth of a massive Jewish proletariat, eventually playing a pivotal role in the development of the movement in Russia. By pointing to the intensity of the export of Yiddish literature—newspapers, fiction, plays, socialist propaganda—and by analyzing the secret routes it took from New York via Austria-Hungary, Germany or Switzerland to Vilna, Bialystok, Minsk, Odessa, and other places that were home to socialist networks and organizations, Michels challenges the notion of a unilateral linguistic and ideological transfer from Eastern Europe to America, contrasting it with the image of a much more complex, transnational, and reciprocal relationship. Even after the establishment of the *Bund* in Eastern Europe in 1897 and the growth of the revolutionary movement that rendered Jewish socialists in Europe in many respects more independent, the transatlantic relations continued to be characterized by reciprocity well into the Soviet period.

Apart from revolutionary socialism, another European-born movement coming from Europe, taking roots in America, and challenging American Jewish culture by the turn of the nineteenth century, was Jewish nationalism with its different ideological variants. In his essay, "Zionism in the Promised Land," *Arthur A. Goren* focuses on two defining moments in the history of American Zionism's endeavor to find a balance between its fascination with the quest for a Jewish homeland in Palestine, and its conviction, profoundly rooted in the narrative of America as the "new Zion," that American Jews were not in exile and thus had a different role to play in the movement than the European Zionists, particularly in Eastern Europe. The early phase of Zionism's emergence as a major factor within American Judaism, between 1898 and 1920, was dominated by the awareness of the increasing plight of the Eastern European Jews in light of the poverty and anti-Jewish violence at the beginning of the century, and by the developments during the First World War, including the Balfour Declaration in 1917. Much beyond the philanthropic efforts triggered by the news from Europe, the Louis Brandeis-style pragmatic advocacy of Jewish settlement in Palestine during that period strongly transformed the political discourse and created a pervasive new element of American Jewish identity: the affirmation of Jewish ethnicity as a legitimate part of "Americanism." The Holocaust and the establishment of the State of Israel made this attempt to reconcile the existence of two promised lands, the one in America and the one in Palestine, even more urgent, as the new Jewish state rebelled against the politics of American Zionism. The first Zionist Congress that took place in Israel in 1951 became, according to Goren's interpretation, symbolic in that it revealed the political tensions between the two centers of world Jewry after the destruction of European Jewry, with two clearly conflicting views of the relationship between a sovereign Jewish state and American Diaspora Zionism. For American Jews these tensions made clear that the main reference point of their identity had irrevocably shifted away from their European past to the State of Israel, fascinating and disconcerting as it was, and that this new constellation meant, at least for those who did not embrace leftist anti-Zionist attitudes, a new form of dual identity involving both firm loyalty to their American home and a strong relationship to and responsibility for the other promised land.

As the example of Zionism demonstrates, the First World War turned out to be a watershed moment for American Jewish perceptions of Europe in many respects, one of them being the challenge of anti-Semitism and anti-Jewish violence. As *Gil Ribak* emphasizes in his chapter, "'You Can't Recognize America': American Jewish Perceptions of Anti-Semitism as a Transnational Phenomenon after the First World War," the period after the Great War and the ensuing mass violence against Jews in Eastern Europe in the early 1920s triggered fears and debates among American Jews that did not only concern the events beyond the Atlantic but also the domestic situation, including the relations with non-Jewish Eastern European—particularly Polish—immigrants in America who were perceived as instigating anti-Jewish hatred. While the Jewish public closely monitored the fate of the Jewish population in Europe during and after the war, turning away from their initial pro-German attitudes after the Bolshevik Revolution and in view of increasing anti-Semitism in Germany, the traditional certainty that America was immune to anti-Semitism was seriously undermined by ominous signs of increasing vulnerability: the anti-Jewish implications of American anti-Bolshevik fears, the experience of social exclusion and discrimination, and the immigration restrictions of the 1920s. Such signs were interpreted as an alarming tendency, in fact a "Europeanization" of American society that threatened to put an end to the golden age of American Judaism. Adopting European anti-Semitism and, at the same time, exporting its own variants back to Europe, America seemed, as Ribak describes the contemporary Jewish perception, to become an indistinguishable part of a truly transnational anti-Jewish enmity in the entire Gentile world.

Part IV: Challenges for American Jewry after the Holocaust

The catastrophe of the Second World War for European Jewry, which changed the course of Jewish history in a most dramatic way, had a tremendous impact also on American Jewry, its internal development and political perceptions, and the challenges it faced after the mid-twentieth century.[46] Much has been written about the postwar renewal of American Judaism in the aftermath of the First World War, a golden age shaped by the almost unrestricted access to American life.[47] The same is true for the political involvement in the Civil Rights Movement, for the suburbanization of American Jews and its consequences for the American Jewish religious landscape, for the significance of Jewish feminism,[48] for the impact the establishment and development of the State of Israel had on the self-understanding and politics of America Jewry, and finally for the emergence of a broad and self-conscious American Jewish culture.[49] Among the grand themes that dominated the Jewish discourse especially after 1967, the remembrance of the Holocaust and the relationship to Israel were particularly important, to the extent that Jonathan D. Sarna has described them as the new "civil religion of the American Jews."[50]

With regard to the impact of the European experience on American Jewish history, it is certainly the confrontation with the unprecedented trauma of the destruction of European Jewry that came to occupy center stage in the historical, political, and theological debates among American Jews from the very beginning of the postwar period and even stronger since the 1960s.[51] While Israeli society since the establishment of the Jewish State and the surviving Jewish communities in the European Diaspora after 1945 have been and continue to be haunted and overshadowed by the awareness of living in a post-Holocaust world, the significance of Holocaust remembrance for American society in general and American Jews in particular seems to be characterized by a number of distinctive elements which require detailed scrutiny. Works by Jeffrey Shandler and other historians have provided a profound insight into the various dimensions of what can be seen as a distinguishing feature of American Jewish identity as it developed over the last seven decades. Apparently linked to the awareness among American Jews of their new leading role in representing the Jewish Diaspora, the comparatively stronger and more public confrontation with the remembrance of the Holocaust among American Jews, multifaceted as it was depending on religious affiliation or secular self-understanding, biographical background, or political proclivity, tended to transcend such differences to the extent that critics have defined its function as that of a unifying surrogate identity in the face of increasing assimilation. The culture of remembrance, starting from less visible and more internal forms of memorializing the Nazi genocide, had, as Shandler has argued, an evolving history of its own that eventually resulted in the full-fledged phenomenon we recognize today: since American Jews witnessed the atrocities in Europe from afar, were confronted with the enormity of the Nazi crimes within the context of war trials, were involved in debates about the immigration of survivors, and saw the Eichmann trial in 1961 and the Six-Day War in 1967 as decisive turning points, a specifically American variant of Holocaust remembrance emerged in which the role of mediation—through literature, cinematic representation, documentaries, art, historical scholarship, collection of testimonies, and museums—played an eminent role, absent in Europe and Israel to the same measure.[52] This trend is equally relevant for the pervasive influence the memory of the Holocaust—as a unique historical experience of the Jewish people and a paradigmatic event for humankind at the same time—exerted on the political and moral discourse in broad areas of the American public sphere, making the Jews an embodiment of the obligation to remember past suffering and to be aware of its moral implications for the present.[53]

Europe, particularly Germany and Eastern Europe, remained a constant, albeit changing reference point of this culture of remembrance: a continent of unprecedented horror, where anti-Semitism and persecution tended to persist, and—after the end of the Cold War and with the increasing opportunities to travel back to places once inaccessible behind the Iron Curtain—a destination of Jewish tourism to Europe that has transformed sites of Jewish persecution into sites of "mass Jewish Holocaust pilgrimage."[54] The essays collected in this part provide important insights into crucial aspects of American Jewry's development during the twentieth and early twenty-first centuries, without, however, being able to cover the full story of its perceptions of Europe and European Judaism: a more systematic interpretation would have to include a variety of other facets, among them the involvement of American Jewish institutions in the project of revitalizing Judaism in Eastern Europe after the Cold War, the history of the immigration of Jews from the former Soviet Union to the United States,[55] and the emergence of what Larissa Remenick has described as a transnational diaspora of immigrants in the United States with strong ties to Russia,[56] as well as the currently growing concerns about the viability of Jewish life in Europe in view of the rising tide of anti-Semitism that appears to be threatening the Jewish minorities in Western and Central Europe.

Jonathan D. Sarna's chapter, "From Periphery to Center: American Jewry, Zion, and Jewish History after the Holocaust," is devoted to the question how the fundamental reversal of European and American Jewry's roles after 1945 transformed the community, particularly in its self-understanding and its relationships to the European Diaspora and the newly established State of Israel. Even though the process leading to American Jewry's demographic, cultural, and political centrality had already begun half a century earlier with the East European Jewish immigration and its consequences, the 1950s saw the emergence of a new, self-confident American Jewish self-understanding that defied other, more problematic experiences, such as the persistence of anti-Semitic sentiments and the inclination of American society in the McCarthy era to identify all Jews with the threat of communism. Apart from describing how the majority of American Jews responded to the latter suspicion by embracing a liberal, anti-Communist stance, which shaped their attitudes toward American policy in Europe and the Middle East as well as toward questions of civil liberty within the USA, the essay focuses on what it characterizes as two "seismic shifts" that had to do with Europe and the growing role of the recently established State of Israel. First, it addresses the profound influence of the hundreds of thousands of Jewish refugees and survivors from Europe between 1933 and the 1950s, including those intellectuals, mostly from Eastern Europe, who became crucial figures within the revival and reinterpretation of all segments of American Jewish religious culture, thus making America into a dominating spiritual and intellectual center of world Jewry. Secondly, a more long-term development was the increasing importance of Israel that soon started to challenge the centrality of American Jewry, to claim the role of the Jewish state, to seek to attract American immigrants or at least Zionist sympathies in America. The essay concludes with reflections on the imminence of a new era defined by a reconfiguration of the relationship between the two centers—Europe, however, seems to play only a rather marginal role in this process.

The overwhelming and lasting impact of the Holocaust on American Jewish self-awareness can be seen in the underlying motives of the movement that responded—between the 1960s and 1980s—to the precarious situation of the Jews and the marginalization of Judaism in the Soviet Union. *Henry Feingold's* chapter, "Can Less be More? The American Jewish Effort to 'Rescue' German and Soviet Jewry," interprets this episode of profound American Jewish concern for the largest surviving Jewish community in post-Holocaust Europe as an expression of a search for redemption from the feelings of guilt that haunted the younger generation with the failure of America (and American Jewry) to come to the rescue of European Jews during the Nazi persecution and the Holocaust. From a historical perspective, a comparison between Nazi politics and the politics of the Soviet Union as well as between the situation of German Jewry in the 1930s and 1940s and Soviet Jewry after the Second World War reveals fundamental differences, particularly with regard to the political intentions of both regimes and the nature of the respective anti-Semitic ideologies. And, while two emigrant groups also differed in almost any respect, the dominant perception was nonetheless that of an analogous situation and a Jewish community under equally dramatic threat. This time, however, after an unprecedented genocide that neither the United States, nor American Jewry, nor the *Yishuv* in Palestine had been able to prevent, American Jews felt the urgent responsibility to help as efficiently as possible. The fact that American Jewish leaders acted with much more self-confidence and determination than in the past, even though American Jewry was probably smaller in numbers and less cohesive than a few decades earlier, stemmed, according to this essay, from a combination of aspects: the relatively stronger Jewish political influence in the United States after the Six-Day War in Israel in 1967, the link of the rescue efforts to American interests during the Cold War, and the widely acknowledged Jewish role as historical victim of genocidal politics that allowed American Jews to invoke the solidarity of the American public. The "Holocaust obsession," as Feingold would call it, with its painful memories of Europe as a place of loss and utter destruction, had defined the perception of contemporary developments behind the Iron Curtain to the extent that they were conflated with the horrors of the past, challenging American Jews to confront what they imagined as the failed responsibility of the previous generation by undertaking any effort to avert the renewed threat to the remnant of European Jewry.

After 1948—and increasingly with every new crisis or war in the Middle East—it is Israel even more than Europe that occupies the attention of and defines the diverse self-understanding and intense ideological controversies among the American Jewish public. In his chapter, "American Jews and the Middle East Crisis," *Michael E. Staub* explores the transformation of the political landscape since the terror attacks on American soil in 2001 and the second Gulf War in 2003, with its twists and turns defining the attitude toward Israel on the part of Jewish intellectuals on the left and on the right side of the political spectrum. His reflections revolve around two historical moments: First, the years after the re-election of the Bush-administration in 2004 saw controversial debates among influential Jewish opinion-makers regarding the legitimacy of the war in Iraq, Israeli settlement policies, and the prospects of American-style democratization in the Middle East. While more conservative observers attacked leftist criticism of the implications of the occupation for Israeli democracy, characterizing it as a dangerous de-legitimization of the Jewish state, the attitude of the general American Jewish public was more progressive, tending toward advocacy of a Palestinian state and Israeli territorial concessions. The more than problematic coalitions of conservative American Jewish organizations with the Christian Zionism of evangelical Christian groups in the United States, who supported the politics of the Israeli right were but one of the factors of decline of public pro-Israel sentiment among American Jews. Second, the chapter describes the dramatic shift of the political atmosphere in 2011 following the increasingly obvious failure of the hopes invested in the "Arab Spring": anxieties surrounding the increasing political isolation of the State of Israel, even from its European partners, skepticism regarding the concept of a two-state solution, debates about the threat emerging from the Iranian nuclear program, and a sense of disconcertment in view of growing tensions between secular and ultra-orthodox voices in Israeli society. These factors created the impression of a crisis whose repercussions, also for Jews in the Diaspora, were difficult to assess.

The analysis of the challenges linked to the Middle East are followed by reflections characterized by a somewhat surprising note: a thoughtful contemplation that sets an interesting counterpoint to the sentiment that, despite all differentiations regarding the theme of the impact of "American exceptionalism" on American Jewry, tends to run, most of the time quite rightly so, through the latter's historical representation. In his essay, "The Meaning of the Jewish Experience for American Culture," *Stephen J. Whitfield* reflects on a specific trait of American national culture that was an integral part of what attracted European Jewish immigrants to the "promised land" and occupied their imagination of America: the promise of happiness as the ultimate goal of life and the almost legal guarantee for every citizen to enjoy it. Citing literary and cinematic expressions of this quasi-messianic hope for a place in which the suffering, persecution, cruelty, and poverty that Jews had been exposed to throughout the centuries of exilic existence in Europe were absent, the chapter depicts the tensions inherent in the fact that, despite the unprecedented sense of security, the cultural and social participation, and the astonishing upward mobility Jews experienced in twentieth-century America, they were not exempt from the realities of discrimination and marginality. However, while in Eastern Europe there was no escape from the bitterness of exile, American Jews immersed themselves in the optimism of mass culture in the United States, where cultural pessimism, loss, tragedy, and despair seemed to have no legitimate place, to the extent that even the representation of the Holocaust had to accommodate the audiences' wish for some happy endings. The memory of a much more somber European experience, with the tragic aspects of Exile, Whitfield concludes, points to a dimension of Jewish tradition that would do more justice to the reality of human suffering, moral challenge, and the need for resilience, and that could be an important contribution to an otherwise less rich and varied culture. Transcending the European experience by embracing the "pursuit of happiness," he implies, would, as desirable as pure felicity may be, mean to deny American culture a religious and historical insight Judaism brought with it to the shores of the "New World."

Reflecting on symbolic anniversaries and landmarks in the history of an ethnic or religious group such as American Jewry permits both evaluating its past, including the latter's historiographical representation, and looking into its present self-understanding, including its hopes for the future. In her concluding essay, "Looking Back on American Jewish History," *Hasia R. Diner* analyzes how the history of American Jewry was constructed in 2004 and 2005, during the celebrations of the 350th anniversary of Jewish settlement in North America in 1654. Reflecting on essential elements of the historiographical discussion on American Jewry voiced within the context of the abundance of academic and public events in the USA on that occasion, she explores the manifold ways in which American Jews interpreted their history at the beginning of the new millennium. The shared narrative emerging from the publications, lectures, and exhibitions resulting from the celebrations of the anniversary is that of a distinctive historical path taken by a community of immigrants that achieved an extraordinary degree of religious, social and economic equality and left behind the European experience of discrimination, oppression, and poverty. It is the story of a religious and ethnic group that did not merely benefit from the opportunities offered by the unprecedented circumstances but played an active and significant role in shaping America as a pluralistic society which transcended the obstacles and boundaries that Jews—and other immigrant groups—had been confronted with in the "Old World." America, in contrast to this, empowered Jews to assert their claim for a legitimate space as a distinctive minority. Even though Diner agrees that there was indeed a strong connection between America's exceptionalism and the valuable contributions of its Jewish population since the seventeenth century, she is critical of the overly celebratory tone she identifies in the rhetoric of 2004/5 and offers an alternative, more nuanced interpretation of the long history of Jewish existence on American soil. Europe as the symbol of the life the Jewish immigrants of different backgrounds (Sephardi, German, or Eastern European) had left behind marks a significant element of the five overarching realities of the American context explored in the essay: the affinity of the Jewish immigrants with the experience of other European immigrant communities focused on the cultural diversity that spared them from being branded as the "Other" of American society; the fact that the concepts of otherness differed from those reigning in Europe, with Jews benefiting from their whiteness, due to the American preoccupation with color; the ascent of those Jewish immigrants who had often fled from economic hardship rather than from anti-Jewish violence; the absence of religious demonization, so characteristic for many European societies, and the inclusive character of the American religious landscape; and, finally, the degree of political participation offered to individual Jews and Jewish institutions. The specific nature of the American Jewish experience, this essay suggests, needs therefore to be understood against the background of the synergy of these favorable circumstances, which history denied to the majority of European Jews.

Notes

1. I would like to thank my co-editor, Cornelia Wilhelm, for her important input to this introduction and for generously allowing me to make use of an unpublished German article devoted to aspects of American Jewish history relevant for the crucial questions examined in this volume. I also thank her for her thorough reading of the introduction and her valuable bibliographical advice. Furthermore, I am very grateful to my colleague Matthew Handelman (Michigan State University) for his comments and for improving the English style.

2. The title of this volume has partly been inspired by Stuart E. Rosenberg's idiosyncratic book, *America is Different: The Search for Jewish Identity* (London, New York, and Toronto: Thomas Nelson & Sons, 1964), in which the author, who served as rabbi at the conservative Beth

Tzedek Synagogue in Toronto from 1956 to 1976, embraced the narrative of America's uniqueness, emphasizing how strongly it is rooted in the American and American Jewish experience since the colonial period, when all immigrating religious groups tried to forget their deprivations in the "Old World": they all were convinced that "the European experience had to be exceeded and transcended," if they truly wanted to affirm their new identities as Americans and revolutionize reality (4); however, as Rosenberg argues, there was also a profound ambivalence that prevented the immigrants, generation after generation, from erasing the cultural heritage they had brought with them: America remained, for many, Jews as non-Jews, "a new world that could never altogether forget the old" (16).

3. See, e.g., Seymour Martin Lipset, *American Exceptionalism: A Double Edged Sword* (New York: W.W. Norton & Co., Inc. 1996).

4. See, e.g., David Thelen, "The Nation and Beyond: Transnational Perspectives on United States History," *Journal of American History* 86 / 3 (1999): 965–75; Daniel Thelen, "Of Audiences, Borderlands, and Comparisons: Toward the Internationalization of American History," *Journal of American History* 79 / 2 (1992): 432–62; Ian Tyrell, "American Exceptionalism in an Age of International History," *American Historical Review* 96 / 4 (1991): 1031–55; Daniel T. Rogers, "Exceptionalism," in *Imagined Histories: American Historians Interpret the Past*, ed. Anthony Molho and Gordon S. Wood (Princeton, NJ: Princeton University Press, 1998), 21–40.

5. Joyce Appleby, "Recovering America's Historic Diversity: Beyond Exceptionalism," *The Journal of American History* 79 / 2 (1992): 419–37, here 420.

6. For a representation of that process, see Donald E. Pease, "Introduction: Re-Mapping the Transnational Turn," in *Re-Framing the Transnational Turn in American Studies*, ed. Winfried Fluck, Donald E. Pease, and John Carlos Rowe (Hanover, NH: Dartmouth College Press by University Press of New England, 2011), 1–48; see also the interdisciplinary contributions in Winfried Fluck, ed., *Towards a Post-Exceptionalist American Studies* (Tübingen: Narr, 2014).

7. See, e.g., Eric Rauchway, *Blessed Among the Nations: How the World Made America* (New York: Hill & Wang, 2006).

8. See Thomas Bender, *A Nation among Nations: America's Place in World History* (New York: Hill & Wang, 2006), esp. 116–81.

9. Appleby, "Recovering America's Historic Diversity," 423. For the discourse in Europe about America's uniqueness, see Jack Greene, *The Intellectual Construction of America: Exceptionalism and Identity from 1492 to 1800* (Chapel Hill, NC: The University of North Carolina Press, 1993). As an example for this kind of approach, see the analysis of the ongoing transatlantic interaction and dialogue between American and European intellectuals during the late nineteenth century in Daniel T. Rogers, *Atlantic Crossings: Social Politics in a Progressive Age* (Cambridge, MA: Harvard University Press, 1998).

10. Benny Kraut, "What is American About American Jewish History and American Judaism? A Historiographic Inquiry," in *What is American about the American Jewish Experience*, ed. Marc Lee Raphael (Williamsburg, VA: The College of William and Mary, 1993), 1–23, here 7.

11. Ibid., 12.

12. Ibid., 13.

13. Frederic Cople Jaher, "American Exceptionalism: The Case of the Jews, 1750–1850," in *Why is America Different? American Jewry on Its 350th Anniversary*, ed. Steven T. Katz (Lanham, MD: University Press of America, 2010), 28–53; with regard to later periods of American Jewish history, see Michael N. Doblowski, "American Antisemitism: The Myth and Reality of American Exceptionalism," in ibid., 154–68; Donald Weber, "To Make 'a Jew': Projecting Antisemitism in Post-War America," in ibid., 169–97.

14. Leonard Dinnerstein, "Jews in the United States: How Good has it Been," in ibid., 198–212.

15. Ibid., 204; see also Leonard Dinnerstein, *Antisemitism in America* (New York and Oxford: Oxford University Press, 1992).

16. Steven T. Katz, "In Place of an Introduction: Some Thoughts on American Jewish Exceptionalism," in Katz, ed., *Why is America Different?*, 1–17, here 1.

17. Ibid.

18. Major monographs that precede those of more recent years include Arthur Hertzberg, *The Jews in America: Four Centuries of an Uneasy Encounter* (New York: Simon and Schuster, 1989); Howard M. Sachar, *A History of the Jews in America* (New York: Knopf, 1992); Jacob Rader Marcus, *The American Jew, 1585–1990: A History* (Brooklyn, NY: Carlson Publishing, 1995); Gerald Sorin, *Tradition Transformed: The Jewish Experience in America* (Baltimore: Johns Hopkins University Press, 1997).

19. See, among others, the contributions in Dana Evan Kaplan, ed., *The Cambridge Companion to American Judaism* (Cambridge and New York: Cambridge University Press, 2005), and in Marc Lee Raphael, ed., *The Columbia History of Jews and Judaism* (New York: Columbia University Press, 2008).

20. Hasia R. Diner, *The Jews of the United States, 1654 to 2000* (Berkeley, CA: University of California Press, 2004); see also Hasia R. Diner, *A New Promised Land: A History of Jews in America* (Oxford and New York: Oxford University Press, 2000).

21. Diner, *The Jews of the United States*, 3.

22. Ibid., 4.

23. Ibid., 2.

24. Ibid., 6.

25. Ibid., 7.

26. Ibid., 260.

27. Jonathan D. Sarna, *American Judaism: A History* (New Haven, CT and London: Yale University Press, 2004), xiv. Among the many other—optimistic or pessimistic—voices regarding the "future of Judaism in America," see the conclusion of Dana Evan Kaplan, *Contemporary American Judaism: Transformation and Renewal* (New York: Columbia University Press, 2009), 379–85. Kaplan stresses the irony inherent in the fact that "Judaism has established itself as an important component of American culture, while Jews themselves are losing much of the distinctiveness that made them a historical people" (380); however, despite the corrosion of the ethnic component of Jewish religion, he also discovers "signs of vitality in Jewish religious life in America" (382). For the question regarding Jewish identity in multicultural America, see David Biale, "The Melting Pot and Beyond: Jews and the Politics of American Identity," in *Insider/Outsider: American Jews and Multiculturalism*, ed. David Biale, Michael Galchinsky, and Susannah Heschel (Berkeley, CA: University of California Press, 1998), 17–33.

28. Sarna, *American Judaism*, xiv.

29. Ibid., 274.

30. Ibid., 331.

31. Ibid., xvi.

32. Jonathan D. Sarna, "Afterword: The Study of American Judaism: A Look Ahead," in Kaplan, ed., *The Cambridge Companion*, 417–21.

33. Ibid., 420. For broader reflections on the relevance of transnational approaches to the history of Jewish migration, see Tobias Brinkmann, *Migration und Transnationalität* (Paderborn: Ferdinand Schöningh, 2012).

34. See the editors' introduction in *Transnational Traditions: News Perspectives on American Jewish History*, ed. Ava F. Kahn and Adam D. Mendelsohn (Detroit, MI: Wayne State University Press, 2014), 1–8, here 5.

35. Kraut, "What is American About American Jewish History and Judaism," 11. For the concept of civil religion, see Robert N. Bellah, "Civil Religion in America," *Daedalus* 96 (1967): 1–21; Will Herberg, "America's Civil Religion: What It Is and Whence It Comes," in *American Civil Religion*, ed. Russell E. Richey and Donald G. Jones (New York: Harper & Row, 1974), 76–88; see also S. Daniel Breslauer, *Judaism and Civil Religion* (Atlanta, GA: Scholars Press, 1993), esp. ch. 2 (29–52).

36. Diner, *A New Promised Land*, 19; for a detailed history of that period, see Henry Feingold, ed., *The Jewish People in America*, vol. 1: *A Time for Planting: The First Migration, 1645–1820*, ed. Eli Faber (Baltimore: Johns Hopkins University Press, 1992); Diner, *The Jews of the United States*, 13–67; Sarna, *American Judaism*, 1–61; Eli Faber, "America's Earliest Jewish Settlers," in Raphael, ed., *The Columbia History of Jews and Judaism*, 21–46.

37. See Sarna, *American Judaism*, 135–207; see, however, Hasia R. Diner's reflections on the need to differentiate the strong historiographical divide of those two waves of migration in Diner, *The Jews in the United States*, 77–99.

38. Ibid., 71–202; Dianne Ashton, "Expanding Jewish Life in America, 1826–1901," in Raphael, ed., *The Columbia History of Jews and Judaism*, 47–69.

39. See Avraham Barkai, *Branching Out: German-Jewish Immigration to the United States, 1820–1914* (New York and London: Holmes & Meier, 1994); Michael A. Meyer, *Response to Modernity: A History of the Reform Movement in Germany* (New York and Oxford: Oxford University Press, 1988), 225–334; Henry L. Feingold, ed., *The Jewish People of America*, vol. : *A Time for Gathering: The Second Migration, 1820–1800*, ed. Hasia R. Diner (Baltimore: Johns Hopkins University Press, 1992); Sarna, *American Judaism*, 63–134.

40. See Henry L. Feingold, ed., *The Jewish People of America*, vol. 2: *A Time for Building: The Third Migration, 1880–1920*, ed. Gerald Sorin (Baltimore: Johns Hopkins University Press, 1990); Sarna, *American Judaism*, 135–207; Eric L. Goldstein, "The Great Wave: Eastern European Jewish Immigration to the United States, 1880–1924," in Raphael, ed., *The Columbia History of Jews and Judaism*, 70–92.

41. For the history of American Orthodoxy, see Jeffrey S. Gurock, *Orthodox Jews in America* (Bloomington and Indianapolis: Indiana University Press, 2009).

42. Diner, *The Jews of the United States*, 206.

43. For the discussion about Jewish rescue efforts, see ibid., 215–25; Henry L. Feingold, *Bearing Witness: How America and its Jews Responded to the Holocaust* (Syracuse, NY: Syracuse University Press, 1995); Sarna, *American Judaism*, 258–71; Rafael Medoff, "American Jewish Responses to Nazism and the Holocaust," in Raphael, ed., *The Columbia History of Jews and Judaism*, 291–312.

44. Sarna, *American Judaism*, 208–271; for the development of American Judaism during this period, see Henry L. Feingold, ed., *The Jewish People of America*, vol. 4: *Entering the Mainstream, 1920–1945* (Baltimore: Johns Hopkins University Press, 1992); Diner, *The Jews of the United States*, 205–58; Lloyd P. Gartner, "American Judaism, 1880–1945," in Kaplan, ed., *The Cambridge Companion to American Judaism*, 43–60; Jeffrey S. Gurock, "American Judaism between the Two World Wars," in Raphael, ed., *The Columbia History of Jews and Judaism*, 93–113.

45. Sarna, *American Judaism*, 271.

46. For the history of American Jewry since 1945, see Henry L. Feingold, ed., *The Jewish People of America*, vol. 5: *A Time for Healing: American Jewry since World War II*, ed. Edward S. Shapiro

(Baltimore: Johns Hopkins University Press, 1992); Dana Evan Kaplan, "Trends in American Judaism from 1945 to the Present," in Kaplan, ed., *The Cambridge Companion to American Judaism*, 61–87; Riv-Ellen Prell, "Triumph, Accommodation, and Resistance: American Jewish Life from the End of World War II to the Six-Day-War," in Raphael, ed., *The Columbia History of Jews and Judaism*, 114–41; Stephen J. Whitfield, "Influence and Affluence, 1967–2000," in ibid., 142–66; Sarna, *American Judaism*, 272–355.

47. Diner, *The Jews of the United States*, 259–304.

48. See Paula Hyman, "Jewish Feminism Faces the American Women's Movement: Convergence and Divergence," in *American Jewish Identity Politics*, ed. Deborah Dash Moore (Ann Arbor, MI: The University of Michigan Press, 2008), 221–40; Annelis Orleck, *Rethinking American Women's Activism* (London: Routledge, 2014).

49. See Stephen J. Whitfield, *In Search of American Jewish Culture* (Hanover, NH and London: Brandeis University Press by University Press of New England, 1999); Stephen J. Whitfield, "Declarations of Independence: American Jewish Culture in the Twentieth Century," in *Cultures of the Jews: A New History*, ed. David Biale (New York: Schocken, 2002), 1099–1146; Jeffrey Shandler, "What is American Jewish Culture?," in Raphael, ed., *The Columbia History of Jews and Judaism*, 337–65.

50. Sarna, *American Judaism*, 337.

51. See Hasia R. Diner, *We Remember with Reverence and Love: American Jews and the Myth of Silence after the Holocaust, 1945–1962* (New York: New York University Press, 2009); Lynn Rapoport, "The Holocaust in American Jewish Life," in Kaplan, ed., *The Cambridge Companion to American Judaism*, 187–208; see also the chapter on "Rethinking the Holocaust after Post-Holocaust Theology: Uniqueness, Exceptionalism, and the Renewal of American Judaism," in Magid, *American Post-Judaism*, 186–239.

52. See Jeffrey Shandler, *While America Watches: Televising the Holocaust* (New York and Oxford: Oxford University Press, 1999); Jeffrey Shandler, "Jewish Culture," in *The Oxford Handbook of Holocaust Studies*, ed. Peter Hayes and John K. Roth (New York and Oxford: Oxford University Press, 2010), 465–85; see also Hilene Flanzbaum, ed., *The Americanization of the Holocaust* (Baltimore: Johns Hopkins University Press, 1999).

53. For the discussion about the role of the Holocaust for American politics and identity, see Peter Novick, *The Holocaust and Collective Memory: The American Experience* (London: Bloomsbury, 2000); Michael A. Staub, "Holocaust Consciousness and American Jewish Politics," in Raphael, ed., *The Columbia History of Jews and Judaism*, 313–36.

54. See the chapter on "Mass Jewish Holocaust Pilgrimage" in Erica T. Lehrer, *Jewish Poland Revisited: Heritage Tourism in Unquiet Places* (Bloomington and Indianapolis, IN: Indiana University Press, 2013), 54–99.

55. See, e.g., Steven J. Gold, "Soviet Jews in the United States," *American Jewish Yearbook* 94 (1994): 3–54; Annelis Orleck, *The Soviet Jewish Americans* (Westport, CT: Greenwood Press, 1999).

56. Larissa L. Remenick, "The Russian-Jewish Transnational Space: An Overview," *Journal of Jewish Identities* 4 / 1 (2011): 1–11.

CHAPTER 2
THE MYTH OF EUROPE IN AMERICA'S JUDAISM[1]
Susannah Heschel

Since the early nineteenth century, American Jews, optimistic about the United States as a promised land whose political values are exemplified in Jewish thought, have creatively reimagined Judaism, both religious and secular. As the place of Jews in American culture changed, they re-created American Judaism with another place and culture in mind: Europe, which loomed as a mythic presence, sometimes a place of persecution, intolerance, and narrow-minded orthodoxy, at others a center of intellectual vibrancy and Jewish religious inspiration. The varying myths of Europe have shaped and inspired American Judaism to this day.

The Jewish experience in the United States is often regarded by rabbis and historians as one of growing assimilation and abandonment of Jewish identity. Lacking institutions of higher Jewish education, and without strong rabbinic leadership, the small American Jewish community in the first half of the nineteenth century did not participate in the explosion of scholarship and theological creativity that took place in Europe during the same period. Later in the century, the mass immigration of Eastern European Jews to the United States was perceived, in its day and subsequently, as an assimilatory process: the immigrants and their children shed their religious observances, their distinctive dress, and their language. The rising rate of intermarriage between Jews and Gentiles in the late twentieth century seemed to give further proof that American Jews were abandoning their Jewish identity.

Yet assimilation, even conversion, its peak of expression, can create its own kind of psychosocial heritage. The initial group of Jews who arrived in Peter Stuyvesant's New Amsterdam in 1654 were Marranos, Jews who had converted to Catholicism under pressure from Spanish authorities and who often continued to practice Judaism in secret, or at least to maintain a surreptitious sense of Jewish identity. Their experience as Marranos, which was far from assimilationist, gave them a sense of social and political entitlement. In an essay celebrating the three hundredth anniversary of the arrival of the original twenty-three Jews in New Amsterdam, Salo W. Baron drew three important conclusions from this group's Marrano backgrounds that contradicted the assimilationist paradigm found in most of Europe.[2]

First, their practice of holding religious services in private during their early years in New Amsterdam—the first synagogue was not built on the American continent until the 1730s—is not surprising because that was what they had done as Marranos. Second, as Marranos in Europe they had adjusted to Christian conversion, holding significant roles as Christians in the government, the army, and in the church, a practice that had accustomed them to positions of honor and authority, not subservience. Third, because they did not come from ghettos but were assimilated into Christian society, they were not about to take discrimination lying down. They fought against the anti-Jewish actions of the Dutch colonial director-general Peter Stuyvesant and they won. Even though subsequent generations of Jews in America did not come from Marrano backgrounds, the initial experience, Baron suggested, set a pattern of political and cultural self-assertion in America that was far more prominent than in Europe.

While the Marrano backgrounds of these early Jewish settlers spurred them to establish an American Jewish cultural and political community assertively different from what they had known in Europe, the past experiences of Jews in Europe nonetheless retained a forceful mythic presence in the minds of American Jews. Liberal rabbis and Jewish thinkers of the nineteenth and early twentieth centuries spoke of America not as posing an anti-Semitic or assimilationist danger but as offering the great hope for the Jewish future because American democratic principles embodied the true moral essence of Judaism. Only in America could Judaism come to its full fruition as a religion, they argued, because the absence of democracy in Europe encouraged discrimination against Jews and hindered their cultural self-realization. Indeed, America as a center of Jewish liberation became one of the guiding myths of the modern Jewish imagination. America in the eyes of modern Jews meant redemption from Europe, which symbolized both Judaism's subservience to Christianity and the confinement of Jews within the strictures of an unbending Orthodox Judaism. In the nineteenth and early twentieth centuries, American Jews thought of their Judaism as the authentic Judaism, a manly Judaism, while that of Europe was distorted by centuries of persecution and economic discrimination.

1 The nineteenth century

In the nineteenth century, American Jews skillfully created an image of a Europe beset by intolerance and anti-Semitism, in contrast to America, the Jewish promised land. In dedicating a new synagogue in Charleston, South Carolina in 1841, Gustav Poznanski proclaimed, "This country is our Palestine, this city our Jerusalem, this house of God our temple." The Other was not only Europe, but European Judaism, which American Jews like Poznanski represented as oppressive, backward, and authoritarian. In fleeing Europe, the Jews who came to America could also flee European Judaism. Reform Rabbi Samuel Adler, just after arriving in New York in 1857, declared, "Behind us lies Egypt, the Middle Ages, before us the sea of Talmudic legalism . . . The spirit indwelling here in the West, the spirit of freedom, is the newly-born Messiah." The goal, wrote David Einhorn in his inaugural sermon in Baltimore in 1855, was "the liberation of Judaism for ourselves and for our children, so as to prevent their estrangement from Judaism."[3]

For Jewish thinkers, Protestantism could not stand alone in claiming a privileged place in America; Judaism, the original Israel, had to stand beside it as the religion informing the American democratic enterprise and bearing its own manifest destiny in the world. In an 1898 resolution, leaders of Reform Judaism in America declared that "America is our Zion.... The mission of Judaism is spiritual, not political ... to spread the truths of religion and humanity throughout the world."[4] This was a Jewish echo of what Protestant thinkers, during and after the colonial period, had been doing: identifying the New Land with the Bible, and themselves with Israel; as Herman Melville declared in *White Jacket* (1850), "We Americans are the peculiar, chosen people—the Israel of our time; we bear the ark of the liberties of the world."

The sense of liberation that Jews experienced in America would also bring about a new kind of Jew. For the Reform rabbi Kaufmann Kohler, America would restore the Jewish "manliness" that life in Europe had undermined: America was "a country that rolled off the shame and the taunt[s] of the centuries from the shoulders of the wandering Jew, to place him, the former Pariah of the nations, alongside of the highest and the best, according to his worth and merit as a man."[5]

As much as Jews viewed America as an embodiment of Jewish values, they transformed Judaism in accordance with American principles into a religion of democracy. If European Judaism signified a backward-looking, Orthodox religiosity, Judaism in America meant freedom to develop a liberal religious expression by means of a democratic process. This entailed, for example, eliminating the role of chief rabbi, which dominated Jewish communities in Europe. It also meant strengthening the control of the laity over decisions regarding liturgy and ritual that in Europe had been under rabbinic authority. Mordecai M. Kaplan, the founder of Reconstructionist Judaism, expressed it: "The ancient authorities are entitled to a vote—but not to a veto," a radical repudiation of classical Judaism's authoritarian structure.[6] Even Zionism, when it attained support from liberal Jews, was viewed as an essentially American phenomenon. For Louis Brandeis, Zionism was not only compatible with American Judaism but expressed the ideals of the Pilgrims, the American Revolution, and American democracy.[7]

The writings of nineteenth-century Reform rabbis energized Jewish thought in America. They failed to develop into a formal theology, however, owing in part to the absence of institutions of Jewish higher learning and of an educated audience of laity, as existed in Europe. In addition, the rabbis' arrival coincided with an era of Christian revivalism that militated against theology. American evangelicals were, by the nature of their undertaking, uninterested in formal theology or intellectual debate and as a result, created no intellectual structure for their movement precisely at a time when German Protestants, by contrast, were reaching a pinnacle of sophisticated theological speculation. As Henry Steele Commager has commented, "During the nineteenth century and well into the twentieth, religion prospered while theology went slowly bankrupt."[8]

The absence of an intellectual Christian theological tradition in the United States during the nineteenth century affected Jewish thought. There was no sophisticated academic community with which Jewish thinkers could engage and hone the intellectual level of a formal Jewish theology. As a result, the publications of Jewish thinkers in the United States were not received by a critically attuned academic audience, in contrast to Germany, where Jewish thinkers found a lively (if critical or even hostile) audience among their Christian counterparts.

This void also meant that no formally articulated Christian theological anti-Judaism was being developed (apart from whatever was transmitted from abroad, or from earlier theological writings), whereas in Germany, Christian theological denigrations of Judaism grew sharply in the nineteenth century and contributed significantly to negative perceptions of Jews. Such theological denigrations stemmed not only from rabble-rousing ministers like Adolf Stöcker, court preacher in Berlin, but also from scholars who claimed training in rabbinic literature, such as Emil Schürer. By contrast, the role of Christian theological seminaries in the United States was marginal to academic life, and while Stöcker was ranting against emancipation of the Jews, American preachers were debating the abolition of slavery. Whatever negative attitudes toward the Pharisees or the Old Testament were held in common by German and American Christian ministers, they resonated considerably differently in the two political and cultural contexts. For example, in listing the various factors that shaped negative views of Jews in America, the historian Jonathan Sarna presents American Christianity as inhospitable to anti-Semitism, a conclusion inconceivable to a student of European Jewry.[9]

Various explanations have been offered for American Protestants' tolerance of Judaism: Calvinists' appreciation of the Old Testament (in contrast to Lutheran denigrations), the focus of Protestant hostility on Catholicism, the overriding preoccupation with slavery, and the problems of integrating numerous national immigrant groups in addition to Jews. Unlike Europe, with its public and often violent anti-Semitism, America seemed a golden land of tolerance and opportunity for Jews. Yet that tolerance may not have been intentional or even deeply rooted in American culture but simply the result of an unusually low population density. Sidney Mead has observed that "there really was not much time in America for the traditionally antagonistic religious groups to learn to live together in peace. But there was space." Or, as Perry Miller writes, more cynically, Protestants "did not [willingly] contribute to religious liberty, they stumbled into it, they were compelled into it, they accepted it at last because they had to, or because they saw its strategic value."[10] If Jews had not been present in America, issues of religious tolerance would have revolved around Protestant acceptance of Catholics; the presence of Judaism stimulated a broader consideration of religious pluralism.

As Protestantism in America grew more nationalistic it did not turn to anti-Semitic racism as German Protestantism did. Religion, writes James Turner, "waxed fat and prosperous in the Gilded Age."[11] The theological universalism of the era implied both a striving for Christian hegemony over the entire world, not just America, and also a belief in the "moral proprietorship over the nation."[12] This was in striking contrast to the Christian theological justifications for imperialism developed in Germany, where the German *Volk* was elevated above all others, a Volk from which Jews were excluded. Indeed, the winds of *völkisch* theology began to blow stronger in Germany during the first decades of the twentieth century, until a *Volksnomostheologie* (people's theology) ultimately emerged as a dominant religious force within the Protestant church during the 1930s, according to which the German Volk was the measure of all things religious.[13] Religious teachings, such as the role of the Old Testament and the nature of Jesus, came to be measured according to these Protestant theologians by their accord with the political and cultural interests of the racist nationalism that became National Socialism.

Christian claims inspired Jewish thinkers to assert competitively that not Christianity but Judaism held the rightful claim to a universal religious message. One of the most important figures in American Jewish thought, Kaufmann Kohler (1842–1926), became the spokesperson for liberal Judaism during that era after he arrived from Germany in 1869. In defining Judaism as essentially an "eternal moral idea" rooted in subjective experience, Kohler declared, "The Bible is holy not because it is inspired, but because and insofar as it does still, inspire. It is not true because God has spoken the word, but because in the truth, the comfort, the hope, the final victory of justice which it holds out, you hear God speak to you in soul stirring strains."[14] The goal of the Reform movement's Pittsburgh Platform, formulated by Kohler, was "to solve, on the basis of justice and righteousness, the problems presented by the contrasts and evils of the present organization of society," a formulation that encompassed the goals of the Protestant Social Gospel movement as well.[15]

Reform Jews identified the ills of modernity, but they did not reject modernization, technology, and rationalism. Instead they embraced modernity, as did Protestants, as a means to improve the world, to create God's kingdom on earth. Kohler used a lofty bourgeois voice, like the voices of the liberal Protestants of his day, to direct contempt at Jewish displays of ethnicity, piety, and poverty. Kohler's Judaism was exclusive, disdainful of the massive influx of impoverished Eastern European Jewish immigrants who represented the medieval religious Judaism from which American Jews thought themselves liberated. The immigrants' arrival introduced a wedge into the previous arrivals' comfortable identification of Judaism with America.

In "trumpeting a symbolic definition of self which Jews and Americans shared," as Arnold M. Eisen describes the effort,[16] what was left of Jewish uniqueness, of the singularity of Judaism's religious message? Why be Jewish if simply being American represented the same thing? Since Judaism could not be identified by exclusive truths, Reform Jewish thinkers turned instead to the status of Jews. They defined Jewish chosenness not as indicating a supernatural quality inherent in Jews, but as signaling an obligatory Jewish mission to spread biblical monotheism to the world. Even while touting the significance of the Jewish mission, however, Reform thinkers rejected Jewish nationalism, removing any hints of present-day or eschatological peoplehood from their liturgy and theology. The Reconstructionist Mordecai M. Kaplan, on the other hand, "intended to take the Jewish response to Emancipation represented by Kohler and carefully turn it on its head ... While the Reform accepted chosenness in the form of mission and denied Jewish peoplehood, Kaplan did precisely the opposite. He accepted peoplehood and denied chosenness."[17]

The first major Jewish thinker in America who came from Eastern Europe, rather than Germany, Kaplan represents a new stage in American Jewish thought: the introduction in American theological terms of the sense of cultural identity that was fundamental to European Jewish life. Like those in earlier generations, Kaplan sought to shape a Judaism distinctive to America by making Jewish values accord with American ones, but his emphasis was on Jewish culture, ethnicity, and nationhood, and he helped set the American foundations for Zionism. The story of the Exodus from Egypt, for example, functioned for Jews, Kaplan argued, the way the Declaration of Independence did for Americans.[18] America was not a melting pot, but an opportunity to live in a Jewish subcommunity, a "cultural nationhood" that embodied the values of American democracy, to the extent that Americanism took precedence over Judaism. Indeed, one of the motivations for his rejection of Jewish chosenness was democracy, which Kaplan, following John Dewey, viewed as a religion that helped people achieve self-realization, which for him meant salvation.

For Kaplan, understanding Jewish peoplehood as the central pivot of Jewish life made Judaism the creation of Jewish civilization, its "language and culture." He viewed Judaism's various religious manifestations as the *sancta* through which the Jews expressed their identity, which functioned, in turn, to preserve their identity through centuries of Diaspora. God, too, is such a *sancta*, and not the supernatural deity of traditional Judaism. Viewing Judaism as the product of Jewish civilization gave a historical impetus to Kaplan's cultural Zionism without suggesting a negation of diasporic life, and the dynamic view of Jewish society contributed to Kaplan's endorsement of religious life as active, not passive. Kaplan and a growing number of Jews in the 1920s did not believe that Zionism would conflict with American Jewish loyalties, but would instead revitalize them.

The problem for American Zionists, like those of pre-1933 Germany, was the sense that they were already at home, not in the Diaspora. Yet the democracy that fostered their sense of home in America was precisely what endangered the Zionist dream, as did the possibility of a multi-ethnic democracy in Palestine that would include Arabs as well as Jews.

Following the Second World War, a broad disdain by intellectuals for all forms of nationalism arose in response to the course of National Socialism in Germany and undermined, in their eyes, the nationalist aspirations of the Zionists. At the same time, Jewish optimism regarding America, and American Jews' desire to be liberated from the confines of European Judaism, ended, and in the second half of the twentieth century, reversed itself. American Jews no longer believed that the United States was a place where Judaism could be nurtured or experience a renaissance. Instead, life in the United States became a source of worry, as it enticed Jews to assimilate and intermarry at rates that would soon lead to a sharp diminution in the size of the community. In addition, many secular Jewish intellectuals argued, post-Second World War America itself seemed to have lost its ideals and values and needed Judaism to save it from moral disintegration. In a reversal, American Jews no longer viewed Europe as a place of confinement but instead saw it as a source of inspiration that would help them rescue American Judaism from its moribund state. Moreover, many argued, America needed Judaism to rescue it from sinking into moral and political lethargy. Thus began the great reconception of the Marrano-American accord established in 1654. Instead of being Christian on the outside and Jewish on the inside like the Marranos, American Jews affirmed their identity in public as an expression of their internal commitments.

Jewish involvement in the Civil Rights Movement was a watershed for their Jewish identity, both religiously and politically. No longer did Jews enter the political scene disguised as Christians—now they marched as Jews alongside African Americans. The photograph of Abraham Joshua Heschel marching in Selma has become iconic because it marks a watershed shift in American Jewish identity. Heschel noted at the time: "I am here because I am involved in the fate and dignity of my fellow man."[19] Judaism was no longer a religion practiced in secret, as it had been with the Marranos, but the very text of the movement in its identification with the Exodus and the Hebrew prophets. Jews were now fighting not for their own rights, but for the rights of others and for the good of American society, a remarkable turning point in Jewish political history.

A significant number of rabbis who took part in the Civil Rights Movement were themselves refugees from Germany: Joachim Prinz, Ernst Lorge, Max Nussbaum, and Heschel, among others. These were people who had been repudiated by their own country, Germany, and wanted to express their dignity and their values in public political activism. Through the Civil Rights Movement, they enacted a rebuke of the Germans, showing how one ought to behave in a racist society and defining their Judaism through principles of justice, truth, and compassion. German Jews and Eastern European Jews joined together in the movement, overcoming a long history of antagonism. Their alliance also made it clear that to be Jewish was to publicly express one's Jewish identity, rather than persist in the assimilationist traditions of Western Europe. The iconic impact of Heschel, with his beard and head covering, marching at Selma with Martin Luther King, Jr., was derived from the visual impression Heschel made as a Jew.

For Heschel the inspiration for joining the Civil Rights Movement came from the prophets, while for others the turn to social justice came through politics. Eugene Goodheart, in his memoir *Confessions of a Secular Jew* (2001), describes the socialist movement he had been involved with before the war as a false progressivism that nonetheless imbued him with a sensitivity to social injustice that survived the movement's contamination with Stalinism.[20] For Heschel, however, there was no distinction between the religious and the political; he told me that in Selma he felt as though his legs were praying.

Religious inspiration, both for Heschel and for the younger generation of American Jews whom he inspired, was drawn not from the liberal movements of Central and Western Europe but from the pietistic movements of Eastern Europe, especially from Hasidism and its mystical traditions. The revival of neo-Hasidism in America in the 1960s led to major changes in the religious services of Reform, Reconstructionist and Conservative synagogues, and to the creation of the Jewish Renewal movement, led by Arthur Waskow, Zalman Schachter, and Michael Lerner. Yet after the Second World War, Europe could no longer serve as a source of Jewish leaders, especially rabbis, even as it could no longer be held up as a paragon of culture and intellectual life for secular Jews. Younger, American-born Jews saw themselves as the saving remnant of European Jewry; but for the immigration of their parents and grandparents, they too might have perished. Others came here directly from the Displaced Persons camps of post-Nazi Europe. The Judaism they created tried to preserve the European legacy both in an ethnic, particularist way, yet also with a universal message of political commitment to all peoples. Born after the war, mine is the generation that would not let the Jewish people disintegrate after the Holocaust. The revival of Judaism demanded reinterpretation; simply to preserve the old ways was "spiritual plagiarism," in Heschel's phrase.[21]

The assertiveness of the American Jewish legacy that Salo Baron noted in connection with the arrival of the first Jews in New Amsterdam led to dramatic innovations in Jewish religious life, particularly the role of women in the synagogue and as ordained rabbis. Jewish feminism was a product of America, exported to Israel, Europe, and other diasporic communities, although it was not well-received, even among liberal Jews. Yet the fight against discrimination, initiated by the first American Jews in protest of Peter Stuyvesant, inspired feminists in their struggle against Judaism's relegation of women to a secondary status.

2 Intellectuals

While Jewish religious thinkers regarded Europe as medieval, and America as a place where Jews could be liberated not only from European anti-Semitism but from European Judaism, secular Jewish intellectuals turned to Europe as a suckling to its mother, seeking intellectual and political nourishment For them America was crude and garish, the home of the "booboisie," in Henry L. Mencken's phrase. In the1920s Jews were not particularly well-represented at American universities or other sites of intellectual exchange, and they looked instead to Europe as the seat of culture, politics, and intellectual refinement. European liberalism and Marxism were two of the strong currents that pulled the attention of Jewish intellectuals away from America. While modernity for Americans implied technological and economic progress, for Europeans it carried the taste of capitalism and commodification. Europe preserved the higher dimensions of human autonomy and fulfillment, the idea of freedom and culture, the utopia of a better life or at least a better education.

The admiration American Jewish intellectuals had for Europe came to an end with the Second World War. As a result, they had to drastically reconceive America. Europe, the source of intellectual life and the forefront of political advancement, was now the home of unbridled anti-Semitism, fascism, Stalinism, and the utter failure of liberalism, a failure that the philosopher Leo Strauss argued was no accident, but intrinsic to liberalism.[22] After all, it was liberalism that, despite having been the great supporter of Jewish Emancipation in Europe, had allowed the rise of the communism and fascism that had destroyed European Jewish life.

In a symposium held in the pages of *Partisan Review* in 1952, about a dozen American intellectuals, among them Leslie Fiedler, Philip Rahv, David Riesman, and Lionel Trilling, were asked to comment on their new regard for America and its institutions. "We have obviously come a long way from the earlier rejection of America as spiritually barren." "The end of the American artist's pilgrimage to Europe is the discovery of America," Leslie Fiedler wrote. Socialism ceased to figure in intellectual discussion, and American democracy, Rahv wrote, looked like the real thing: "At least [it] exists, not a mere theory or deduction from some textbook of world salvation."[23]

What is striking about the *Partisan Review* symposium is not just that the participants were all men but that Jews played a prominent role, even though they never articulated the word *Jew* or talked about Jewish interests. Religion played no role in the symposium. Personal affiliations were not disclosed. Nor did anyone discuss the implications of Nazism's defeat for Jews. The group praised the United States for its political freedoms, its economic strength, its traditions of nonconformity, its political security, and its avenues of social mobility. Yet they had concerns. David Riesman and Philip Rahv worried that the job of intellectuals—remaining in tension with their audience and milieu—would be difficult, given the comforts of American life and the embourgeoisement of the country's intellectuals. Trilling asked, "Where in American life can the artists and intellectuals find the basis of strength, renewal, and recognition, now that they can't depend on Europe as a cultural example?" There were the old Jamesian concerns about the barrenness of the native scene—"the flower of art blooms only where the soil is deep."[24]

They stood, in 1952, in the early years of a right-wing course away from socialism and communism and toward liberalism and neo-conservatism. Irving Howe characterized the New York Jewish intellectuals in a 1969 essay as "the first group of Jewish writers to come out of the immigrant milieu who did not define themselves through a relationship, nostalgic or hostile, to memories of Jewishness."[25] Yet it is that very denial of relationship to Jewish memory that came to be in itself a form of Jewish identity, much like the woman writer who says she is a writer, not a woman writer. Indeed, the New Criticism of the era sought to eliminate the biography of the author and focus on the ideal reader— the Protestant white male as generic human.[26] Part of the reason was that in the postwar years the United States was uninterested in identity, universities were not particularly philo-Semitic, and modernism was elitist and anti-Semitic—think of the orthodox modernism created by the expatriates T. S. Eliot and Ezra Pound. The commitment to communism had had a religious intensity and its unmasking was a brutal experience,[27] similar to what a later generation of Jewish feminists experienced in the unmasking of Judaism's patriarchy.[28] In both cases, the response had a strong measure of conservative politics.

3 Conclusion

Even while secular American Jewish intellectuals turned away from Europe in the 1950s, many of them moving from socialism to neo-conservatism, religious Jews turned increasingly toward the memory of Eastern European religious Judaism as a source of inspiration—yet they identified that Judaism with left-wing politics. What they were experiencing, however, was not their own memory of that vanished world, but a postmemory, to use Marianne Hirsch's term, a memory appropriated from their parents and grandparents.[29] That memory inspired a renaissance of Jewish creativity. Today it is no longer Europe that provides the inspiration for American Jews; Israel does that to some extent, but it is, primarily, America and American Judaism that offer political and religious inspiration to European Jews and, to some extent, to Israeli Jews. The major questions facing Jews have to do with multiculturalism, within both the community and the larger society; women's rights, which have brought the most radical changes in the synagogue since it was established; and the question of who is a Jew. On each of these questions, both European and Israeli Jews have remained negative, unable to respond to the challenges because their paradigms cannot cope.

Klaus Milich, a German scholar of American culture, has offered a useful distinction between the paradigm of modernity that has dominated postwar German and European thought—and Israeli thinking as well—and the paradigm of postmodernism that dominates American culture.[30] Whereas Europeans worry about the clash between culture and civilization, Americans attempt to expose the epistemological and ontological foundations of those antagonisms. In a similar fashion, we might observe that today's European Jewish communities think they can return to the structures of modernity: recognizing only Reform and Orthodox Judaism, retaining rabbis as the gatekeepers of their communities, and appealing to the state for protection against the anti-Semitism of the society. Within the American Jewish community, however, the concerns are with postmodernity: issues of cultural diversity are raised by feminism, critiques of Zionism, and multiculturalism.

In the United States, the diffusion of Jewishness throughout popular culture and as a result of intermarriage has brought it to ever-increasing swaths of the non-Jewish population. Consequently, traditional Jewish definitions of boundaries and rabbinic determinations of Jewish identity have become unwieldy and meaningless. Postmodern America has invented a uniquely multiform Judaism, and the openness of America's multicultural society has encouraged a mixture of identities. American Jews are creating new forms of Judaism—Reconstructionist, Renewal, Feminist—stemming from their interrogation and rejection of religious regimes of chosenness, patriarchy, authority, imitation of the Christian, and the old-fashioned modern; and they are participating in the restructuring of America as an immigrant, multicultural society that controls the state.

The older sense that Europe was in the forefront of modernization while the United States lagged behind has been altered. European intellectuals find themselves pallbearers of the Enlightenment while Americans theorize cultural diversity through poststructuralism, creating a useful model for Europe. Indeed, the flow of young Jewish intellectuals to Berlin since the mid-1990s has brought with it the introduction of postmodern paradigms that may help Germany come to grips with its increasingly multicultural society.

The American Jewish vision of Europe is no longer defined by confrontation with the Christian world but with the Muslim and Arab world on European soil, and with a resurgent anti-Semitism that reveals, yet again, the inability of European culture to cope effectively with it. Europe's only hope lies in following the American model of multiculturalism and radical democracy if it is to survive with its moral and political integrity intact. Similarly, the Zionism that originally developed as the repudiation of European anti-Semitism, as Arthur Hertzberg has argued, cannot now be blamed for European anti-Semitism.[31] Yet Zionism, too, like Europe, needs to be modified by the American political model and transformed from a repudiation of modern European culture into an embodiment of the principles of American democracy and multiculturalism.

The problematic side of postmodernism is its dissolution of boundaries and fixed identities, in which the cultural boundaries in America become so porous that Jewishness develops into a free-floating identity open to appropriation by anyone, including Jews. That is, Jewishness becomes staged, blurring the distinction between Jews and Gentiles, and obfuscating the nature of Jewish identity. Such staging is not unprecedented; at the Passover Seder, for example, the liturgy demands that all Jews view themselves as if they had come out of Egyptian slavery and recreate the experience for a week.

While Jewishness is not an empty identifier—references to Israel, the Holocaust, holy days, and the Torah abound in American Jewish life, along with plenty of heroic political events—the act of being Jewish, whether Orthodox or secular, can become a performance. Just as the Marranos became outwardly Christian while remaining inwardly Jewish, American Jews also had to prove that they fit into the larger society, which, in the United States, was categorized by color. "White" and "black" were not only skin colors but social constructs and identifiers of social status. In yet another kind of performance, when Jewish vaudeville acts appropriated "blackface" in the early part of the twentieth century they signified their entry into white American society. Michael Rogin has shown how blackface functioned to identify Jews within white America—only if you were white was it necessary to adopt blackface.[32] In a similar way, postmodernity leads American Jews to appropriate a "Jewface," a kind of *imitatio Iudei*, imitation of the Jewish.

The Marranos who came to these shores in the seventeenth century were strengthened by their experiences in Europe as Christians on the outside, Jews on the inside. They were able to establish themselves here successfully, while also teaching America how to become a pluralistic and tolerant society. Now it is Americans, having been inspired by their Jewish community, who can demonstrate to the rest of the world how a democratic, multicultural society can foster a flourishing Judaism.

Notes

1. This essay was first published in Barbara Kirshenblatt-Gimblett, ed., *Writing a Modern Jewish History: Essays in Honor of Salo. W. Baron* (New Haven, CT and London: Yale University Press, 2006), 91–104, 115–16. I would like to thank the publisher for permission to reprint it in this volume.

2. Salo Wittmayer Baron, "Some of the Tercentenary's Historic Lessons," in *Steeled by Adversity: Essays and Addresses on American Jewish Life*, ed. Jeanette Meisel Baron (Philadelphia: Jewish Publication Society, 1971), 473–84.

3. Poznanski, Adler, and Einhorn, quoted in David Philipson, *The Reform Movement in Judaism* (New York: Macmillan, 1907), 467, 483, 481.

4. Jonathan Sarna, "Converts to Zionism in the American Reform Movement," in *Zionism and Religion*, ed. Shmuel Almog, Jehuda Reinharz, and Anita Shapira (Hanover, NH and London: Brandeis University Press by University Press of New England, 1998), 188–203, here 189.

5. Kaufmann Kohler, "American Judaism," in *Hebrew Union College and Other Addresses* (Cincinnati: Ark Publishing Co., 1916), 195–213, here 198.

6. Mordecai M. Kaplan, *Not so Random Thoughts* (New York: Reconstructionist Press, 1966), 263.

7. Sarna, "Converts to Zionism," 198.

8. Commager, quoted in Sidney Mead, *The Lively Experiment: The Shaping of Christianity in America* (New York: Harper and Row, 1963), 55.

9. Jonathan Sarna, "American Anti-Semitism," in *History and Hate: The Dimensions of Anti-Semitism*, ed. David Berger (Philadelphia: Jewish Publication Society, 1986), 115–28.

10. Mead, *The Lively Experiment*, 19; Miller, quoted ibid., 13.

11. James Turner, *Without God, Without Creed: The Origins of Unbelief in America* (Baltimore, MD: Johns Hopkins University Press, 1985), 226.

12. James H. Moorhead, *World Without End: Mainstream Protestant Visions of the Last Things* (Bloomington and Indianapolis, IN: Indiana University Press, 1999), xvii.

13. The most prominent figure associated with *Volksnomostheologie* is Wilhelm Stapel, but for a broader study of its influence, see Wolfgang Tilgner, *Volksnomostheologie und Schèopfungsglaube: Ein Beitrag zur Geschichte des Kirchenkampfes* (Göttingen: Vandenhoeck & Ruprecht, 1966). See also Cornelia Weber, *Altes Testament und völkische Frage: Der biblische Volksbegriff in der alttestamentlichen Wissenschaft der nationalsozialistischen Zeit, dargestellt am Beispiel von Johannes Hempel* (Tübingen: Mohr-Siebeck, 2000).

14. Kohler, quoted in Michael A. Meyer, *Response to Modernity: A History of the Reform Movement in Judaism* (New York and Oxford: Oxford University Press, 1988), 273, fn 25.

15. For the text of the Pittsburgh Platform, see *Encyclopedia Judaica* (Jerusalem: Keter, 1971), vol. 13, 571.

16. Arnold M. Eisen, *The Chosen People in America: A Study in Jewish Religious Ideology* (Bloomington and Indianapolis, IN: Indiana University Press, 1983), 6.

17. Ibid., 2.

18. Mel Scult, *Judaism Faces the Twentieth Century: A Biography of Mordecai M. Kaplan* (Detroit: Wayne State University Press, 1993), 252.

19. Abraham Joshua Heschel, personal communication to the author.

20. Eugene Goodheart, *Confessions of a Secular Jew: A Memoir* (New York: Overlook Press, 2001); Eugene Goodheart, personal communication to the author.

21. Abraham Joshua Heschel, *Man Is Not Alone* (New York: Farrar, Straus & Young, 1951), 164.

22. Leo Strauss, *Liberalism, Ancient and Modern* (New York: Basic, 1968); see also Shadia B. Drury, *Leo Strauss and the American Right* (New York: St. Martin's, 1997).

23. Newton Arvin et al., "Our Country and Our Culture: A Symposium," *Partisan Review* 19 (1952): 282–326, here 283, 294, 304.

24. Ibid., 306, 314, 322–23; Henry James, quoted ibid., 305.

25. Ethan Goffman, "The New York Intellectuals and Beyond: Editor's Introduction," *Shofar* 21 (2003): 1–6, here 1; Howe, quoted ibid., 2.

26. Daniel R. Schwarz, "Eating Kosher Ivy: Jews as Literary Intellectuals," *Shofar* 21 (2003): 16–28, here 19.

27. Ibid.

28. Goffman, "The New York Intellectuals," 2.

29. Marianne Hirsch, *Family Frames: Photography, Narrative, and Postmemory* (Cambridge, MA: Harvard University Press, 1997).

30. Klaus Milich, *Die frühe Postmoderne: Geschichte eines europäisch-amerikanischen Kulturkonflikts* (Frankfurt am Main and New York: Campus, 1998).

31. Arthur Hertzberg, "Introduction," in *The Zionist Idea: A Historical Analysis and Reader*, ed. Arthur Hertzberg (Westport, CT: Greenwood Press, 1970), 15–100.

32. Michael Rogin, *Blackface, White Nose: Jewish Immigrants in the Hollywood Melting Pot* (Berkeley, CA: University of California Press, 1996).

PART I
COLONIAL IDENTITIES: THE EARLY MODERN PERIOD

CHAPTER 3

TRADING FREEDOMS? EXPLORING COLONIAL JEWISH MERCHANTHOOD BETWEEN EUROPE AND THE CARIBBEAN

Judah M. Cohen

As an arbitrary yet meaningful moment in American Jewish history, the 2003–5 celebration commemorating the 350th Anniversary of Jewish life in America has been a boon for affirming and reclaiming American Jewish identity. Communities across the United States (and Europe) employed the milestone date to open spaces for reflection, action, and discussion about the roles Jews played within American life: both as actors within a historic American chronicle, and as propagators of Judaism who sometimes had to act in counterpoint with that chronicle. "350th" events provided a platform for connecting with the scholarly community as well, providing the general public with an opportunity to learn about (or, often, celebrate) particularly salient issues of "American" Jewish life, and giving scholars the opportunity to focus their efforts on determining overarching narratives or paradigms the American Jewish experience has fostered.

While many within United States borders have justifiably found such reenactments of collective memory appropriate for framing their own identities as "American Jews," however, their efforts also prove highly problematic in representing the scope of "American Jewish" history: particularly with the way scholars have centered the American experience in the United States even before the country actually came into being. Viewed from *outside* the north American colonies, as I will show, American Jewish history takes a significantly different shape: one that challenges some of the field's foundational assumptions, and points the way to a reassessment of what it meant to be Jewish at a time when the centers of Jewish life and culture occurred elsewhere in the hemisphere.

For the purpose of this essay, I will approach American Jewish history from the perspective of the Caribbean region: primarily the islands and sections of the South American coast where communities of Spanish and Portuguese Jews first travelled into the Western hemisphere *as Jews*. From this seemingly oblique vantage point, the 350th anniversary commemorating a continuous presence of Jews in "America" came late, and would actually have taken place sometime in the 1980s, if not earlier. With a bit of a head start on what we now call the United States, in other words, the *other* part of America has historical relevance in the North American saga, not to mention a direct connection. In a sense, Jewish life in the Caribbean laid the groundwork for North American Judaism to emerge: particularly upon recognition that the trip starting the chronicle of 350 years did not cross the Atlantic from east to west, but rather took place roughly from south to north. *From* America, *to* America.

Recast within a broader context, the now fabled landing of twenty-three Jews in New Amsterdam in 1654 had both nothing and everything to do with Europe. These Jews, chased from a failing Dutch-occupied region of northeastern Brazil due to a local rebellion, represented a tiny minority of a fleeing Jewish community.[1] Many among this evicted population returned to Amsterdam, or headed to other European and Caribbean locations. The twenty-three Jews credited with starting the North American saga, however, sailed up to another Dutch possession in North America; and upon their arrival, they had to dismantle the protests of Peter Stuyvesant, a former governor of the Dutch Caribbean island of Curaçao (which had the hemisphere's largest Jewish population at the time), before the age of American Jewry as celebrated today could begin.

Thus, bringing the Caribbean and its surrounding territories into the trajectory of American Jewish settlement adds significant coloration to both interpretations and implications of the broader story. The clean, direct migration sometimes envisioned between Europe and America during this time proves far more complicated and multi-faceted than American Jewish origin accounts tend to portray, and suddenly must reckon with issues associated with the nerve center of transatlantic trade. Likewise, the motives for such migrations, often tied by implication to a mythic Puritan-like quest for sanctuary, also face significant challenges based as much on what occurred *outside* the continental borders as inside. To arrive in North America in the sixteenth, seventeenth, and eighteenth centuries, then, sojourners invariably had to negotiate the aggressively mercantile culture pervading the region. Within this schema of trade routes, the Caribbean's status as an important point of transfer—the destination of trans-Atlantic currents—allowed the volatile archipelago to become an important gateway to the Americas, and a prime site for intercontinental exchange through the promise of mercantilism.

What did it mean for Jews to make those transitions between Europe and the Caribbean, often again and again, through their dealings and their travels? The common oscillations of people and goods during this time suggest alternate approaches to viewing American Jewry of the era: rather than physically bounded and geographically based, the North American settlements depended upon such movement for their livelihood, and valued the shipping industry as a way to exchange information (news and intelligence), expand business and matrimonial opportunities, maintain ties to the religious hierarchy (complete with publications and rabbinic rulings), and hold onto the cosmopolitanism of the lands left behind. Such a reading proves invaluable, moreover, for incorporating the *rest* of the Americas into this narrative of Jewish history. The year 1654, after all, marks the beginning of a beloved story, but one that should acknowledge its emergence from a larger, pre-existing fabric of settlement, politics, and negotiation already well-established in the "new world."

Many layers of this history have been researched and described independently, but attempts to fashion them into a narrative have thus far been difficult and piecemeal due precisely to the overbearing weight of the American (i.e., United States) narrative. Several possible signposts exist for establishing such a history. Looking beyond 1654, the presence of Jews in America could start in 1651, when Jewish merchants and their families established what would become a permanent congregation on the island of

Curaçao.[2] Current research suggests that organized, openly Jewish religious life in the hemisphere dates to the late 1630s, when Jews founded Congregation *Zur Yisrael* in Dutch-occupied Recife, Brazil.[3] Questions of how to incorporate "secret" Jewish identities into the American narrative gain relevance through the case of Mexican Judaizer Luis de Carvajal, whom Inquisitors burned at the stake in a 1596 *auto da fé*.[4] And, with additional research, it is possible to go back still further into places and situations that hardly register on the American Jewish history map.

In order to open up a space for exploring this discourse, I intend to present a fleeting glimpse into that world from three perspectives: First, I will explore the issues involved in studying Caribbean Jewish life in existing academic frameworks. Following that, I will provide a Caribbean mercantile case study from my own work illustrating the difficulty in framing the region as a place for politicized Jewish self-realization (often described in terms of "freedom"). I will then conclude by briefly following the Caribbean Jewish historical narrative into the nineteenth and twentieth centuries, in order to assert its relevance as a history in its own right, and a counternarrative that both complements and challenges often dominant North American Jewish historical discourses.

1 Situating Caribbean Jewish studies

Paralleling its geographical location, the study of Caribbean Jewry tends to find itself stuck between disciplinary fault lines, often evincing minority counternarratives in the face of dominating (perhaps even colonizing) literatures in larger fields.

From one perspective, the Caribbean has strong ties with European history: European colonization of the islands, after all, still serves as the Western hegemonic narrative that even postmodernists and new historians use as a point of reference. Throughout the colonial period, the region provided important bases of trade and territorial expansion for the Dutch, British, French, Spanish, Danes, and others, administered by both nationalized West India companies and colonial governments serving as proxies for their mother countries. Western Europe treated the Caribbean islands as a remote battle theater for its wars, due in part to their relative wealth and strategic locations for accessing the mainland; frequent, brief (and usually benign) takeovers of poorly defended islands took place well into the nineteenth century, often representing a microcosm of conflicts taking place on the European continent. Despite the Caribbean islands' miniscule size, they thus held important symbolic, strategic, and financial capital, and served as a gateway for European ambitions to flush themselves into America, and a funnel for transporting the best of America back to Europe.

Accounts of European Jewish activities during this age of mercantilism provided by Jonathan Israel, Renate G. Fuks-Mansfeld, and Miriam Bodian provide important perspectives on the conditions that led to Jewish forays across the Atlantic, though they often view the islands themselves through a rather fuzzy lens as a distant destination *for* merchants.[5] Historians of European Jewish history such as Yosef Yerushalmi and Yosef Kaplan, meanwhile, took pains to include the Caribbean (mainly Curaçao) into their conceptions of European westward expansion, even as they framed that conception mainly in Continental terms (yet notably, such works exist mainly because the Curaçao congregation commissioned them, presumably with the intent of asserting its story within the European narrative).[6] Perhaps the most important contribution to this area, however, has been the recent collection *Jews and the Expansion of Europe to the West 1450–1800*, edited by Paolo Bernardini and Norman Fiering. Bringing together both young and veteran scholars, largely of European and colonial history, this collection makes significant inroads in traversing conventional disciplinary borders to translating the center of Jewish mercantilism out from the Continent into the Atlantic, exploring how Jews negotiated the Caribbean and the Americas in the context of European expansion. Among the thorniest issues the book handles with increasing finesse are how scholarship can be sensitive to the ambiguous differentiations between Judaism and Marranism, Sephardic and Ashkenazic background, self-identification and imposed identification; how Jews operated within a broader society that itself had variable concepts of Judaism; and how Jewish life in these small communities carried on in a cultural, as opposed to numeric or anecdotal, sense. It is, hopefully the first of many works that aim to traverse disciplinary, geographical and conceptual borders through the qualitative and creative use of primary sources.[7]

Just as the Caribbean could be claimed as emerging from European Jewish history, however, so American (i.e., United States-based) Jewish historians look to the area to bolster their own narrative, though in a way that more or less continues to distance the European component. Many works of American Jewish history cite the Caribbean in passing, often highlighting the origins of one or another American Jewish personality— such as Florida senator David Levy Yulee or American confederate higher-up Judah Benjamin[8]—or mentioning it as an interesting "elsewhere" described in correspondence and family histories. Recent histories of Judaism in the United States by Jonathan Sarna and Hasia Diner acknowledge the Caribbean as having a part in early American Jewish history, but also struggle with the significance of its role in North American Jewish affairs (in large part, admittedly, because few studies have really considered the Caribbean in this kind of framework).[9] Publications and archives, meanwhile, clearly saw their mission as extending south of the United States almost from the start: prominent American Jewish historian Jacob Rader Marcus led an American Jewish Archives expedition down to the Caribbean in the early 1950s to collect material for the archive's collections; and since then, the Archives' journal has actively sought articles and printed special issues on Jews in the Caribbean and Latin America.[10] The American Jewish Historical Society also holds materials from the Caribbean, including a significant collection from Jamaica; and *its* journal, *American Jewish History*, has professed an interest in publishing primary materials from the Jewish Caribbean, particularly in the lead-up to the 350th year celebration. Such actions clearly ascribe value to these Caribbean communities, especially for their great age and their role as predecessors to presumably greater Jewish communities in the United States; yet most historians have not looked deeply at these communities, perhaps due in part to a skewed perception of the communities' lack of necessary documentation.[11] After the colonial era, moreover, the Caribbean's frame of reference in American Jewish history virtually disappears. Books such as Malcolm Stern's *First American Jewish Families*, as well as numerous articles on specific families or the contents of Caribbean cemeteries have laid out the continued Caribbean connection to American Jewish history rather impressively from a genealogical perspective.[12] Aside from these approaches, however, Jewish Caribbean communities of the late nineteenth and twentieth centuries essentially vanish from the American Jewish history landscape.

The experiences of Caribbean Jewry might seem a natural fit in Latin American studies, a well-developed field with numerous departments and programs at both American and Israeli universities (and a field that in some places already claims Caribbean studies in its purview). Yet here, too, investigations pose vexing problems. Latin American studies indeed occupies itself heavily with the dynamic interplay of Europe and the Americas; yet in doing so, it places a strong (albeit proportional) emphasis on the Iberian American colonies—Central America, South America, Cuba, the Dominican Republic, and Puerto Rico—which tend to serve as ambiguous vanishing points for colonial era narratives of Judaism. Although the Caribbean did house early seventeenth-century communities of unambiguously Jewish residents, moreover, their existence in territories not owned by the Spanish and Portuguese, and their relatively late appearance in the context of Spanish colonization, relegates them to the margins of discourse. Numerous liaisons between the Caribbean and Latin America would take place in the nineteenth century, as Latin American countries achieved their independence, liberalized, and began to disengage from the anti-Jewish attitudes installed by the Inquisition: what is often described as the first post-emancipation Jewish community in a former Spanish colony, for example, consisted largely of Dutch Jews who moved from Curaçao to Coro, Venezuela in the early nineteenth century.[13] Latin American studies scholars, however, tend to treat such Caribbean associations as peripheral to broader questions of Latin American history; and the fast-growing, energetic research currently taking place in Latin American Jewish Studies similarly centers on Spanish-speaking and Lusophone studies, and leaves references to the non-Spanish-speaking Caribbean primarily to biographical, family history, and locally produced historical accounts.

The much smaller, more fragmented field of Caribbean studies frequently bases its narratives on relationships with more powerful influencing nations as well, but focuses predominantly on the journey of its majority populations from slavery to self-rule.[14] Jews manifest themselves as a visible if minor element in this narrative, often gaining exposure through their own minority status as non-Christians. Inevitably, however, their racially variable (and often marginally white) status clashes with the more powerful and populated discourses associated with the Black Atlantic.[15] As a result, and due especially to the Nation of Islam's potent 1991 polemic *The Secret Relationship Between Blacks and Jews*, recent scholarly accounts of Caribbean Jewish history have spent significant efforts reassessing Jews' status in local, transnational, social, and racial hierarchies, while paying particular attention to the perceptions associated with slave holding and trading.[16] Important works such as Eli Faber's systematic *Jews, Slaves and the Slave Trade* and Jonathan Schorsch's encyclopedic *Jews and Blacks in the Early Modern World* have provided self-described correctives to arguments claiming Jews' disproportionate "role" in the slave trade, and added increasing degrees of nuance and complexity to the understanding of race (both historical and retrospective) within Jewish colonial life.[17] Although these works still occupy a peripheral space within the broader Caribbean studies literature (perhaps because the writers' own orientations lie more toward American and European Jewish history respectively), such deep investigations into how Jews functioned during colonial times successfully present Europe and the Caribbean as a continuous cultural arena, complete with its requisite philosophies, theories of race, and ties with mercantile activity. Conversely, perhaps these works even argue—admittedly under duress—for serious reconsideration of the Africa's role in shaping Jewish colonial discourse as it moved between Europe and the Americas. Framed within the context of Caribbean history, as communities ever interacting within intimate public and private spaces, these works, in rising to a challenge, both shy away from a sense of Jewish "exclusiveness" often assumed in other studies, and hold the potential for employing inter-community interactions to explore further the meaning of living in a trans- and multi-national environment—complete with its biases, its contradictions, and its social hierarchies.[18]

Last, and perhaps most influential, is popular Euro-American sentiment toward the Caribbean. Although not a discipline *per se*, these attitudes, which tend to portray the Caribbean (and much of Latin America) as a place of exoticism existing outside modern history, weigh heavily on the region's treatment within European and North American academic discourses. The recent promotion of such locations as St. Thomas, Recife, and Curaçao as Jewish "destinations," complemented by the appearance of travel guides to the Jewish Caribbean for well over thirty years, has led amateur historians and journalists to publish short accounts continually repackaging available materials in terms of novelty, surprise, and discovery.[19] (That the sites themselves often play up this very image to increase tourist revenue, moreover, complicates studies of the region still further.) Treating the area as a curiosity from the 1940s while American and European Jewish historians occupied themselves with more mainstream (and mainland) populations, such publications often saw light at the hands of journalists, usually after consultation with local congregational representatives; they focused at best around limited primary materials, and slanted toward appealing and notable occurrences that inflated the local area's status.[20] In some cases, notably, academically oriented outsiders with personal ties to an island would create more in-depth, systematic works as labors of love, or as side projects associated with the researcher's other scholarly work. Such was the case with Isaac and Suzanne Emmanuel for the Dutch West Indies, Julius Hartog with St. Eustatius, Eustace M. Shilstone with Barbados, Mordecai Arbell for Jamaica and the Dominican Republic (and the Caribbean in general), and to a certain extent myself with St. Thomas (I lived there between 1974 and 1976, while my parents were pursuing their own adventure).[21] Until recently, many of these histories provided the dominant narratives for understanding Jewry on the various islands. The work of trained historians such as Stephen Fortune, Robert Cohen and Thomas August, and, more recently Aviva Ben-Ur and Wim Klooster, has begun to change this insular historical image and broaden interest, to the point where it is now just beginning to congeal into its own academically engaged literature.[22]

The Caribbean thus both reinforces and defies the very borders American and European historians so often require in order to hold up their narratives. Comprising numerous nation states with frequently shifting allegiances, a highly mobile population, a highly stratified society, active questions of race (discussed as *a part of* Jewish identity), populations small enough to challenge religious, national, colonial and hegemonic identity, and a variety of concurrent timelines that do not fit easily into the narratives of either American or European life, the Caribbean region thus forces the discourses of European and American history to face each other in difficult but necessary ways, even as it demands its own set of historical paradigms.

2 Challenging the freedom motive

One of the Caribbean issues that seems to go without questioning, however, is that Jews came to the new world in part to avail themselves of expanded freedoms negotiated through the colonizing nation. To some extent, there is justification for this view: Yosef Hayim Yerushalmi, Thomas August, and a host of others (including myself) describe the progressive enfranchisement of Jews in island life throughout the seventeenth and eighteenth centuries along a relatively standardized modernity/enlightenment narrative, albeit one that often preceded similar occurrences on the European continent. Yet did this enfranchisement truly represent religious freedom? Perhaps, as James Homer Williams has noted, such freedoms may have been merely a front for furthering more important aims. "At an official level," Williams notes, "religious difference mattered, but at the practical level, economic, military, or political utility counted for more."[23] When religious difference gained greater currency—as occurred, in part due to economic competition, in Martinique in 1685—the Jews again became subject to restrictions and expulsion.[24]

How various Caribbean Jewish populations negotiated these restrictions (or lack thereof) thus could become as maddeningly complicated as the Caribbean itself, fluctuating according to the island/nation, the ruling power, the economic situation, and events in the European political theater. Going *outside* the progressivist narrative of Jewish "emancipation," in other words, may provide a more nuanced and interesting understanding of Caribbean mercantile life, and one that takes into account a multivalent view of the world in which Judaism was one issue subject to many other nationalist, economic and competitive factors. Rules concerning Jews, after all, could only be enforced within bounded polities, and often required well delineated areas of land to be effective. For merchants who supervised the exchange of goods across the Atlantic, the very idea of location was itself highly contingent, and the concept of restrictions far more difficult to enforce. Caribbean Jewish merchants had expansion offices, possessions, homes or families in several sites, on either side (and sometimes both sides) of the ocean. Those who travelled for business spent months at a time away from their primary residence, sometimes several times per year. "Freedoms" within this context thus represented a multi-layered set of variables that changed based on the flag under which a merchant sailed, the merchant's reputation and business status, and the merchant's various sites of trade. As part of such a culture frequently in motion, Jewish mercantile activities thus could fluctuate as much due to the home country's desire to increase their colony's revenue as to any "genuine" desire to address Jewish needs.

The islands themselves, meanwhile, provided their own disadvantages: their consistently hot and humid climates, often minimal rainfall (particularly on the smallest islands), ever-encroaching vegetation, and mostly poor natural resources constantly challenged the residents' abilities to focus on business. The isolated nature of the islands, combined with the density of their settlements, led to frequent outbreaks of cholera, yellow fever, smallpox, and other microbe-borne diseases (typically introduced by ships coming from abroad); and before the mid-nineteenth century, the dense, mostly wooden buildings in the shipping villages suffered particular devastation from fires. Their location at the western end of the trade winds and currents, so crucial to their mercantile success, also placed the islands right in the path of oncoming hurricanes; and the tectonic plates that induced the volcanic activity creating the islands in the first place also made them susceptible to frequent earthquakes and occasional tidal waves. Though several of these sites (particularly Curaçao and St. Eustatius) had become relatively cosmopolitanized by the late eighteenth century, and served as important intercultural meeting points between east and west, they were still rather undesirable, expensive, and risky places to live, cut off from the best education, devoid of extended community, and (particularly for the Jews) lacking a dynamic system of hierarchically regulated religious leadership.

What did it mean, then, for a Jewish merchant to experience a life bracketing the Atlantic? There are many answers, some of which have been considered by Stephen Fortune from an economic, plantation-based perspective. Here, however, I will provide one contrasting story for illustration: that of Emanuel Alvarez Correa, of both Altona (at the time a part of Denmark) and St. Thomas, in what was then the Danish West Indies.[25] Correa lived during the first half of the nineteenth century, and therefore may have led a life somewhat different from earlier merchants in locations such as Jamaica, Curaçao and Barbados.[26] Yet the struggles he faced in trying to come to terms with his religious beliefs and his international occupation nonetheless provide a uniquely telling window upon which to view the issues facing Jewish merchanthood between Europe and the Caribbean.

St. Thomas, located just east of Puerto Rico in the northwest Caribbean, came relatively late to the mercantile scene: benefitting from a combination of Denmark's decision to make the island a free-trade zone in 1767, and economic and social crises taking place in other port cities in the area, the island's population and mercantile industry began to flourish mainly in the late eighteenth century.[27] Although a handful of Jewish settlers spent time on the island throughout the 1700s, the majority came over in the mid-1790s, due in part to economic crises in the Dutch islands of St. Eustatius and Curaçao, and what would later be known as the Haitian Revolution in St. Domingue. Fragmentary records suggest the community first organized as a burial society (likely called *Gemilut Hasadim* or "Acts of Lovingkindness"); but in 1796, a core group received clearance from the government to establish a Jewish congregation named "Bracha

VeShalom" ("Blessing and Peace") and build a sanctuary. Within a few years, the congregation and burial society had unified under a single entity, combining their names to serve as the island's sole Jewish institution.[28]

Like the rest of the island's white residents (with which they associated by the early nineteenth century), most of the Jews on St. Thomas lived a cosmopolitan lifestyle.[29] As full members of a free trading society, they spread out across town, affiliating more by socio-economic bracket than by religious affiliation. With the exception of an occasional ceremonial winecup or Sabbath candelabrum, their possessions were little different from those of anyone else. Businesswise, schedules of ships and sales centered around Saturdays. While some Jews refused to open shop on their Sabbath, many others had little choice, or simply did not care. The auction houses, owned by Jewish merchants, ran their swiftest business on Saturdays, and many Jewish stores stayed open for the same reason. Lacking governmental impediments since the congregation's founding, and with options for full citizenship from 1814, many Jews lived the lifestyles of their neighbors, identifying with Judaism primarily on an institutional level. They supported the synagogue, but also served important roles in the island's welfare, as Brand Corps volunteers, board members for the local bank, and honored members of the Knights of the Dannebrog.

Within this environment lived Emanuel Alvarez Correa. Born in Curaçao in 1794, Correa moved in the late 1810s to St. Thomas, where he set up business.[30] Two years later, he married Judith Julien, and over the next thirteen years fathered five children with her.[31] Shortly after the last of these births, however, Judith died, leaving Correa to raise his children alone. It appears that, following a custom of many St. Thomas merchants to send their children to Europe for a proper education and upbringing, Correa placed his daughter and four sons in the hands of a trustworthy friend in Altona, and remained in St. Thomas to cultivate his firm.

Correa maintained his status as a member in good standing at the island's synagogue and likely retained some practices of Judaism in both home and communal settings. His personal library (compiled after his death) contained a Holy Bible, a Hebrew Bible, at least one printed copy of the Torah, six copies of the High Holiday liturgy, the works of Josephus, American rabbinic figure Isaac Leeser's *Discourses . . . on the Jewish Religion*, and Leeser's translation of Joseph Johlson's *Instruction in the Mosaic Religion*.[32] Although Correa apparently accepted his duty toward his religious institution, he never became particularly active in synagogue life. With the exception of a contribution to the rebuilding of the synagogue in 1832 (after a town-wide fire decimated it), not a single reference in the local paper—the trade journal *Sanct Thomae Tidende*, which ran several of his advertisements—linked him to the Jewish community in any way between his arrival on the island and his death. Correa's attitude toward his children's religious upbringing held similar connotations: with his consent, he allowed their guardian in Altona to raise them as Christians, while asserting the children's freedom to choose a religion for themselves once they reached a mature age.

In May 1837, Correa left St. Thomas for Europe, where presumably he spent some time with his children in addition to pursuing business ventures. Soon after his return to the island on December 31, he fell mortally ill. Facing his end, Correa suddenly added a codicil to his will, desiring, "That my children shall be made acquainted with the religion in which they were born and a Hebrew Master employed to teach them the custom and usage of the Jewish congregation." He appointed two acquaintances in Altona "to supervise the education of my Children, and to act as guardians for the same in case any thing should prevent the executors named in my will from acting."[33]

Correa died on January 5, 1838. Noting the codicil, the executors of the will (Correa's business partners S. Bahnsen, John Marshall, and J. H. Osorio) sent a letter to Altona appraising the guardians of Correa's final wish. Yet the response they received proved far from conciliatory. Sixteen-year-old Rachel, the eldest child, protested the provision, proclaiming:

> Some years ago we have had a Jewish teacher for some time, but the lessons were very tedious to us and so our dear father just being here, allowed us to leave them off, and I think it would be perfectly superfluous to begin it once more, as it would expose us to great inconveniences. As we have been brought up in the Christian religion, according to the wish of our dear father, we have a predilection for it, which I think is very natural. [Our guardian] . . . told me that whenever [he] spoke on this subject to our good father, he always said, that we could do whatever we should like, when we were old enough to reflect upon such things. Now I have attained the age and have really very often thought about it, and have always found that the Christian agrees the most with me. As I shall be seventeen next month, and as almost all the young girls are confirmed with sixteen or seventeen years, I have no time to loose. I hope therefore you will have nothing against it if we get baptized.[34]

Rachel's younger brother Maurice (birth name Moses), even more distraught with the news, threatened to go through a baptism against the executors' wills should they not consent, arguing that without such action, his future business career could be greatly challenged.[35]

The guardian, Mr. O. G. C. Degetau, accompanied these exhortations with a rather badly composed letter in English, urging the executors to drop their request. While respectful of Correa's dying wish, Degetau nonetheless saw little merit to it, since "any delay [in the conversion to Christianity] may prove injurious to the future welfare of the children."[36]

Although such arguments appeared puzzling in the context of the Caribbean Jewish trade, they reflected a longstanding cultural bias within Europe. Officially, by this point, Jews had the same rights in both Danish-controlled Altona and St. Thomas; there is even some evidence Altona's Jews received a favored stature during this time.[37] Correa—and by extension his Jewish and non-Jewish executors, all of whom had significant transatlantic trade experience—seemed to see this status as a means for Jews to retain their religious identities while participating in a society dominated by Christians. In contrast, Degetau saw such rights as an opportunity for the Jews to join the Christian world, eliminating their differences. Such attitudes reflected the separation between Europe and St. Thomas, and revealed the conflicts that complicated matters for "respectable" Jews of the Caribbean.

The fate of these children is unknown, but, after several months of further exchanges involving the executors' polite but firm persistence and Degetau's demurring resistance, chances are they nominally fulfilled their father's dying wish and subsequently converted to Christianity. This situation was not unique in Europe, but appeared to be exceedingly rare in the Caribbean based on available studies; at the same time, it showed the religious tensions that existed between the Caribbean Jewish merchants and the society in which they operated. St. Thomas's small free population, with a significant Jewish component, gave little advantage to Christians (save a seemingly required nominal donation to the Lutheran [i.e., state] church in wills of the era); thus, Jews there could wander as they wished philosophically, with little pressure to disavow their affiliation unless they wished to do so. Twenty-five years after the Correa affair, a Jew who no longer wished to have an association with the St. Thomas Hebrew congregation simply declared himself a free Unitarian, while in 1871 a group of reformers within the Jewish community finally gained governmental recognition as a separate congregation by declaring their practices to constitute a religion different from the Judaism practiced by the main congregation.[38] Europe, in contrast, represented a series of institutionalized Christian states, a situation that often gave Jews the choice of either facing the prejudices associated with their religion, or leaving Judaism altogether. Caribbean Jews, traveling frequently from one region to another, thus faced two different standards: in the Caribbean, merchants could be nominally Jewish and remain a significant part of society, even as uncertain resources and a precarious island existence limited their options. In Europe, which sported stronger economic and social infrastructures as well as more consistent resources, the task proved far more difficult. Negotiating between these different standards, and the freedoms and expectations each implied, proved a constant challenge that may well have seemed ever out of balance.

3 Caribbean Jewry beyond the colonial period

It is easy to think of the Jewish merchant communities of the Caribbean fading away once their mercantile usefulness had run its course in the nineteenth century. Yet these communities in fact continued to exist, adapt, and play important if understated roles in American and European Jewish history. Synagogues in St. Thomas, Curaçao and Jamaica maintained a continuous presence on their respective islands from the colonial period to the present day, with each staying viable through difficult periods due to different combinations of consolidation, intermarriage, in-migration, amateur leadership, support from larger Jewish communities, and sheer serendipity. The oldest organized Jewish communities in Panama, Costa Rica, and Venezuela, meanwhile, have their roots in Caribbean Jewish ancestors. Other islands, epitomized by Barbados, house Jewish communities that have recently expanded or been reconstituted by new generations of recently arrived island residents, who see themselves and their activities as continuing a Jewish tradition abandoned decades or centuries ago.[39] Important ethnographic studies by Frances P. Karner, Carol Holzberg, and Alan Benjamin, meanwhile, have made inroads into understanding how the complicated histories of the region's Jewish communities impact upon island life in the present—for both Jews and non-Jews, and everyone in between.[40] Most of the congregations, meanwhile, have affiliated with international Jewish religious movements and organizations, allowing them access to a range of resources (including rabbis) and a network of coreligionists: St. Thomas's synagogue joined the Union of American Hebrew Congregations (today the Union for Reform Judaism) in 1967; Barbados's congregation belongs to the American Conservative movement; and Curaçao's United Netherlands Portuguese Congregation Mikvé Israel-Emanuel affiliates with the Jewish Reconstructionist Federation. Compared with other communities in the United States at the turn of the twenty-first century, these congregations are tiny. Yet their continuous fluctuations in size, their struggles for survival, and their constant searches for current and chronologically cumulative identity—notably within the shadow of the United States—provide unique case studies that continue to challenge a border-based concept of American Jewish religious life.

The Caribbean also plays an important part in American history as a region constantly under scrutiny by American interests. A victim of the steamship industry and the delays presented by the Panama Canal, the region became increasingly oriented around United States policies as its constituent islands changed hands or headed toward independence. From the accession of Cuba and Puerto Rico during the Spanish American War, to the purchase of the Danish West Indies in 1917 and their subsequent transformation into a US naval base (after failed attempts dating back to 1867), to the succession of presidential doctrines asserting *de facto* control over or politically quarantining selected islands, to the colony-like development of specific island sites as both American and European vacation lands, the Caribbean has remained a significant part of the American purview. Such is the case with Jewish life as well: in the months leading up to the Second World War, several island governments opened their arms to German-Jewish refugees, only to have their plans derailed by an overcautious and imposing American government.[41] The rise of the commercial airline industry, combined with increased vacation time in the United States, has been an important influence to the establishment of Jewish life in Puerto Rico. B'nai B'rith (District XXIII) and other international organizations founded in the United States have also extended into the region, just as they have done with much of Latin America. These are part of the American Jewish legacy as well, and need to be acknowledged as such: not as early blips on the radar, but as a continuous and significant narrative of small but theoretically relevant communities who can bring new perspectives to the ever-transcendent borders of American Jewish life.

Although the Caribbean has been the focus of my essay, it is worth adding that Central and South American Jewry, despite their considerable scholarly literature, remains a black hole in the discussion of American Jewish history as well—even as they house equally fascinating questions on numerous levels about transcending the European Jewish experience in the Western hemisphere. How do we deal with the vexing (and these days political) issue of new world "crypto-Judaism," especially in its constructed manifestation in the American southwest? How did countries such as Argentina, Mexico, Cuba and Brazil offer alternate visions of the American golden land in the late nineteenth and early twentieth centuries, especially when Jews who *wanted* to enter the United States could not? How can American Jewish historians deal with figures such as Marshall Meyer, the American rabbi who established Latin America's first Liberal Jewish Seminary, and subsequently cultivated a model synagogue in New York's Congregation B'nai Jeshurun with the help of two of that seminary's graduates? More so than Caribbean Jewry, Latin American Jewry has developed a well-established scholarly organization and several research centers, and much of their literature has been published in English. This work is a rich resource that once again challenges the border-based focus of North American Jewish history, and provides those who wish to access it important perspectives on the meaning of being Jewish in America—including the United States.

The crucial issue for both regions thus becomes less their relevance for American Jewish historical studies, and more a matter of framing meeting places between the Americas, wherever their physical geography, as an important if not illuminating part of American Jewish studies. Paolo Bernardini, in his guidelines for contributors to what would become the 2001 collection *Jews and the Expansion of Europe to the West*, suggested that "European and American history should not be separated," and "one should also not separate between North American history and South American history."[42] I would underline these suggestions in the hope that by lifting borders we can discover a still richer landscape of culture and continuum awaiting us in the American Jewish experience.

And so I end where I began. Between 2003 and 2005, Jewish communities in the United States and beyond celebrated the 350th anniversary of the arrival of Jews in an abstract land named "America"—a land that European countries were trying to reshape in their own images and exploit for their own profits; a land that, in the north, would only gain its identity as the United States over a hundred and twenty years *after* that fateful 1654 landing. Yet just as important to recognize in the North American narrative is that the pioneering Jews who arrived to New Amsterdam *came* from America as well: an America to the south that Europe subjected to its same hopes of profit and influence. Why one America became the site of record while the other America drifted into exoticism was the result of events, attitudes, politics, migration, and scholarship that developed much later.

Now that United States Jewry has had the opportunity to honor itself, perhaps it can begin to let in the lives of those who remain buried under its dominant narrative. There is much more to tell in the story of American Jewry: it is not just a history of laying down roots in a new land. It is also a story of constant movement back *and* forth across geographic, spiritual and legal borders—borders that served as both convenient realities and necessary fictions. Did the Jews come to the future United States for the freedom of observing their own Jewishness? Maybe that is something we can now read backward into history, particularly if we like to frame history as a form of progress. Yet we must also understand the desire of Jewish merchants who ventured forth into this world to be a part of a broader sense of exploration, and recognize the sacrifices in resources and religious and social continuity such exploration entailed. The Caribbean at the time was a site more than a destination to these and many other merchants: a veritable European diaspora in which Jews could participate. Consequently, the Jews found themselves trading not just in goods, but also in freedoms.

Notes

1. James H. Williams, "An Atlantic Perspective on the Jewish Struggle for Rights and Opportunities in Brazil, New Netherland, and New York," in *The Jews and the Expansion of Europe to the West 1450–1800*, ed. Paolo Bernardini and Norman Fiering (New York and Oxford: Berghahn Books, 2001), 369–93, here 377. Williams estimates the Jewish community of Recife, Brazil to number c. 600, thus causing the 23 New Amsterdam-bound Jews to comprise less than 4 percent of the total.

2. Isaac S. Emmanuel and Suzanne A. Emmanuel, *History of the Jews of the Netherlands Antilles* (Cincinnati, OH: American Jewish Archives Press, 1970).

3. Beit Hatefutsot, "The Kahal Zur Israel Synagogue, Recife, Brazil." http://www.bh.org.il/Communities/Synagogue/Recife.asp.

4. See Martin A. Cohen, *The Martyr Luis de Carvjal: A Secret Jew in Sixteenth-Century Mexico* (Albuquerque: University of New Mexico Press, 2001), *inter alia*.

5. Jonathan I. Israel, *European Jewry in the Age of Mercantililsm, 1550–1750*, 2nd ed. (New York and Oxford: Oxford University Press, 1989); Renate G. Fuks-Mansfield, *De Sefardim in Amsterdam tot 1795: Aspecten van een joodse minderheid in een Hollandse stad* (Hilversum: Uitgeverij Verloren, 1989); Miriam Bodian, *Hebrews of the Portuguese Nation: Conversos and Community in Early Modern Amsterdam* (Bloomington and Indianapolis, IN: Indiana University Press, 1997).

6. Yosef Haim Yerushalmi, "Between Amsterdam and New Amsterdam: the Place of Curaçao and the Caribbean in Early Modern Jewish History," *American Jewish History* 72 (1982): 172–92; Yosef Kaplan, "The Curaçao and Amsterdam Jewish Communities in the 17th and 18th Centuries," *American Jewish History* 72 (1982): 193–211.

7. Also worth mentioning here is Stephen A. Fortune's book, *Merchants and Jews: The Struggle for British West Indian Commerce, 1650–1750* (Gainesville, FL: University of Florida Press, 1984). Although Fortune tends to identify Jewish merchants themselves rather uncritically, he does succeed in providing a nuanced context in which to describe their operation.

8. On Yulee, see Bernard Postal, "David Levy-Yulee, the First Jewish Senator," *Judaica Post* 7 (1979): 929–31 *inter alia*. Judah P. Benjamin has been the subject of two books, neither of which expounds particularly effectively on his Caribbean birthplace. See Robert Douthat Meade, *Judah P. Benjamin: Confederate Statesman* (Baton Rouge: Louisiana State University Press, 2001 [1943]) and Eli N. Evans, *Judah P. Benjamin: The Jewish Confederate* (New York: Free Press, 1988).

9. Hasia R. Diner, *The Jews of the United States* (Berkeley, CA: University of California Press, 2004); Jonathan D. Sarna, *American Judaism: A History* (New Haven and London: Yale University Press, 2004). Sarna's essay "The Jews in British America," in Bernardini and Fiering, eds., *The Jews and the Expansion of Europe*, 519–531, both attempts to outline such a schema, and illustrates the extent of research needed to bring the two regions together more fully.

10. Jacob R. Marcus, "The West India and South America Expedition of the American Jewish Archives," *American Jewish Archives* 5 (1953): 5–21. See also *American Jewish Archives* 44

(Spring/Summer 1992), a special issue edited by Martin A. Cohen entitled *Sephardim in the Americas*.

11. Franklin B. Krohn, "The Search for the Elusive Caribbean Jews," *American Jewish Archives* 45 (1993): 146–56. Krohn's assertions hold some merit in that materials on Jewish Caribbean communities may not be as focused or as centrally located as those in the United States; yet as my own work and that of others suggests, it is still possible to piece together in-depth, significant research on these communities by seeking out and relying on other forms of historical information in addition to pulling together perhaps far-flung but often extant and relatively extensive archival materials.

12. Malcolm H. Stern, comp. *First American Jewish Families: 600 Genealogies, 1654–1988*, 3rd ed. (Baltimore: Ottenheimer Publishers, 1991); Emma Fidanque Levy, "The Fidanques: Symbols of the Continuity of the Sephardic Tradition in America," *American Jewish Archives* 44 (1992): 179–207; Rochelle Weinstein, "Stones of Memory: Revelations From a Cemetery in Curaçao," *American Jewish Archives* 44 (1992): 81–140, *inter alia*.

13. Isidoro Aizenberg, *La Comunidad Judia de Coro 1824–1900: Una Historia* [Biblioteca Popular Sefardi, No. 11] (Caracas, Venezuela: Centro de Estudios Sefardís de Caracas, 1995).

14. One of the most popular books on Caribbean history in the 1970s and 1980s, for example, was Eric Williams's provocatively titled volume *From Columbus to Castro: The History of the Caribbean, 1492–1969* (New York: Vintage Books, 1984 [originally published in London by A. Deutsch, 1970]).

15. See, for example, Paul Gilroy, *The Black Atlantic: Modernity and Double Consciousness* (Cambridge, MA: Harvard University Press, 1993).

16. Historical Research Department of the Nation of Islam, *The Secret Relationship Between Blacks and Jews* (Chicago, IL: Nation of Islam, 1991). For a critique of the ways American Jewish historians treated slavery before and after the publication of *The Secret Relationship*, see Jonathan Schorsch, "American Jewish Historians, Colonial Jews and Blacks, and the Limits of *Wissenschaft*: A Critical Review," *Jewish Social Studies* 6 (2000): 102–31.

17. Eli Faber, *Jews, Slaves, and the Slave Trade: Setting the Record Straight* (New York: New York University Press, 1998); Jonathan Schorsch, *Jews and Blacks in the Early Modern World* (Cambridge and New York: Cambridge University Press, 2004).

18. The developing field of Sephardic studies, which tends to overlap American, European and Latin American studies, also has a place for the Caribbean as a site for Sephardic Jewish merchants. See, for example, Eugene Cooperman, "Portuguese *Conversos* and Jews and their Trade Relations Between the New and Old Worlds," in *Studies on the History of Portuguese Jews*, ed. Israel J. Katz and M. Mitchell Serels (New York: Sepher-Hermon Press, 2000), 125–63. What studies there are, however, tend to fit the Caribbean into a geographical migration pattern rather than consider it as its own area.

19. Bernard Postal and Malcolm H. Stern, *Tourist's Guide to Jewish History in the Caribbean* (New York: American Airlines, 1975); Ben G. Frank, *A Travel Guide to the Jewish Caribbean and Latin America* (New York: Pelican, 2004); Boris Fishman, "Discovering Jewish Roots on Caribbean Soil," *New York Times*, March 27, 2005: 5, col. 3, *inter alia*.

20. For St. Thomas alone, this includes Alexander Alland, "The Jews of the Virgin Islands: A History of the Islands and Candid Biographies of Outstanding Jews Born There," *The American Hebrew*, March 29, 1940: 5, 12, 13, 16; April 5, 1940: 6–7; April 26, 1940: 5, 12, 13; May 17, 1940: 5, 12; Janet Steinberg, "The U. S. Virgin Islands: A Sun-Sational Vacation Destination," *Metrowest Jewish News* (Whippany, NJ) 54, No. 10: 48; Ronnie Greenberg, "Exhilarating Flair and Excitement of the Caribbean's Barbados," *Metrowest Jewish News* 51, No. 39: 64, *inter alia*.

21. Isaac and Suzanne Emmanuel, *History of the Jews of the Netherlands Antilles*, passim; Isaac Emmanuel, *Precious Stones of the Jews of Curaçao* (New York: Bloch, 1957); Julius Hartog, *The Jews and St. Eustatius* (Aruba: J. Hartog, 1976); Eustace M. Shilstone, *Monumental Inscriptions in the Jewish Synagogue at Bridgetown, Barbados with Historical Notes from 1630* (New York: Macmillan, 1988); Mordecai Arbell, *The Portuguese Jews of Jamaica* (Mona, Jamaica: Canoe Press, 2000); Mordecai Arbell, *The Jewish Nation of the Caribbean: The Spanish-Portuguese Settlements of the Caribbean and the Guianas* (Hewlitt, NY: Gefen Books, 2002); Judah M. Cohen, *Through the Sands of Time: A History of the Jewish Community of St. Thomas, U. S. Virgin Islands* (Hanover, NH and London: Brandeis University Press by the University Press of New England, 2004).

22. Fortune, *Merchants and Jews*, passim; Robert Cohen, *Jews in Another Environment: Surinam in the Second Half of the Eighteenth Century* (Leiden: Brill, 1991); Thomas August, "Family Structure and Jewish Continuity in Jamaica Since 1655," *American Jewish Archives* 41 (1989): 27–42; Aviva Ben-Ur, "Still Life: Sephardi, Ashkenazi and West African Art and Form in Suriname's Jewish Cemeteries," *American Jewish History* 92 (2004): 31–9; Wim Klooster, "The Jews of Suriname and Curaçao," in Bernardini and Fiering, eds., *The Jews and the Expansion of Europe*, 350–68.

23. Williams, "An Atlantic Perspective on the Jewish Struggle for Rights and Opportunities," 377.

24. Abraham Cahen, "Les Juifs de la Martinique au XVIIme Siècle," *Revue des Etudes Juives* 31 (1895): 93–121; Mordechai Arbell, "Jewish Settlements in the French Colonies in the Caribbean (Martinique, Guadeloupe, Haiti, Cayenne) and the 'Black Code'," in Bernardini and Fiering, eds., *The Jews and the Expansion of Europe*, 288–95.

25. Fortune, *Merchants and Jews*, passim; Altona, notably, was a part of the Danish kingdom from c. 1640–1864.

26. For more on these communities, see Fortune, *Merchants and Jews*, passim; Wilfred S. Samuels, "A Review of the Jewish Colonists of Barbados in the Year 1680" (London: Purnell & Sons, 1936); Isaac and Suzanne Emmanuel, *History of the Jews of the Netherlands Antilles*, passim.

27. Isaac Dookhan, *A History of the Virgin Islands of the United States* (Mona, Jamaica: Canoe Press, 1994 [1974]), 89–91; Cohen, *Through the Sands of Time*, Chapter 1.

28. See Cohen, *Through the Sands of Time*, Chapters 1 and 2.

29. The rest of this section is an adaptation of material found in Cohen, *Through the Sands of Time*, 60–3.

30. Obituary of E. A. Correa, *Sanct Thomae Tidende*, January 10, 1938: 2.

31. Wedding announcement of E. A. Correa and Judith Julien, *St. Thomae Tidende*, September 4, 1818: 4.

32. Isaac Leeser, *Discourses, Argumentative and Devotional, on the Subject of the Jewish Religion: Delivered at the Synagogue Mikveh Israel, in Philadelphia, in the Years 5590–5597*, (Philadelphia: Haswell and Fleu, 5597 [1837]); Joseph Johlson, *Instruction in the Mosaic Religion*, tr. Isaac Leeser (Philadelphia: Adam Waldie, 5590 [1829–30]). Knowledge of the books in Correa's possession comes from an accounting of his estate, held in the Copenhagen *Rigsarkiv* (*Danske Vestindiske Lokalarkiv*, St. Thomas Byføgedarkiv, Eksekutor og Konkurboer, 1778–1868, V. Cor-Dec. [herein "Correa Papers"]) along with Correa's will and all the correspondence discussed in this section.

33. Will of E. A. Correa, Correa Papers. The codicil is dated January 4, 1838.

34. Letter from Rachel Correa to Bahnsen, Marshall and Osorio, July 27, 1838. Correa Papers.

35. Maurice's letter appears to be lost, but is described in a letter from Bahnsen, Marshall and Osorio to Degetau dated November 4, 1838. Correa Papers.

36. Letter from Degetau to Bahnsen, Marshall and Osorio, July 28, 1838. Correa Papers.

37. St. Thomas's Jewish community petitioned for the same rights as those given Jews in Copenhagen since at least 1803, when they placed the request explicitly in the community's by-laws (Cohen, *Through the Sands of Time*, 22, 24). King Frederick VI's 1814 proclamation that Jews in Danish lands "should be permitted to enjoy equality with the rest of the citizens" would provide those blanket rights, although the Jewish community of St. Thomas had to wait until 1815, when the British returned the island to Denmark after eight years of occupation (Ib Nathan Bamberger, "The Royal Decree of 1814," in *The Viking Jews: A History of the Jews of Denmark* [New York: Shengold, 1983], 50–64). Evidence of the Jews as a privileged minority in Altona is provided in Arthur Arnheim, "Don Gratuit—En gave fra jøderne i Altona" ["Don Gratuit—A Gift from the Jews of Altona"], *Rambam* 6 (1997). (English summary at http://www.rambam.dk/rambam_6_1997_sum.htm.)

38. See Cohen, *Through the Sands of Time*, 106, 130–1.

39. Donald H. Harrison, "Who are the Bearded Ones?: Reclaiming the Jewish Past in Barbados," *San Diego Jewish Press-Heritage*, April 6, 2001.

40. Frances P. Karner, *The Sephardics of Curaçao: A Study of Socio-Cultural Patterns in Flux* (Assen: Van Gorcum, 1969); Carol Holzberg, *Minorities and Power in a Black Society: The Jewish Community of Jamaica* (Lanham, MD: The North-South Publishing Company, 1987); Alan F. Benjamin, *Jews of the Dutch Caribbean: Exploring Ethnic Identity on Curaçao* (London and New York: Routledge, 2001).

41. See, for example, Tony Martin, "Jews to Trinidad," *The Journal of Caribbean History*, 28 (1994): 244–57; William R. Perl, "The Holocaust and the Lost Caribbean Paradise," *The Freeman* 42 (1992): 7–10; William R. Perl, "Paradise Denied: The State Department, the Caribbean, and the Jews of Europe," *The National Interest* 42 (1995–96): 78–84, *inter alia.*

42. Paolo Bernardini, "A Milder Colonization: Jewish Expansion to the New World, and the New World in Jewish Consciousness of the Early Modern Era," in Bernardini and Fiering, eds., *The Jews and the Expansion of Europe*, xiii.

CHAPTER 4

EARLY AMERICAN *MIKVA'OT*:
RITUAL BATHS AS THE HOPE OF ISRAEL[1]

Laura Arnold Leibman

1 Introduction

On July 27, 1656, at the age of twenty-three, Baruch Spinoza was cast out of the Jewish community of Amsterdam. In a proclamation read publicly in the Portuguese Synagogue, the "Lords of the *ma'amad*" (Synagogue Board) declared that

> having long known of the evil opinions and the acts of Baruch de Spinoza ... [and] having failed to make him mend his wicked ways, and, on the contrary, daily receiving more and more serious information about the abominable heresies which he practiced and taught and about his monstrous deeds ... [we] have decided ... that the said Espinoza should be excommunicated and expelled from the people of Israel.

By placing Spinoza in *ḥerem*—a ban or excommunication—the elders declared him not only forbidden, but a source of pollution or corruption; he was *menuddeh*—"defiled." To escape further contagion, not only other congregants, but also all the "people of Israel," were forbidden to communicate with him either in person or in writing. As if Spinoza carried a contagious disease, community members were told to remain at least four cubits distance from the rebel at all times.[2]

For many scholars and intellectuals, Spinoza's rejection of Jewish law and the supernatural epitomizes and foreshadows later Jewish involvement in the Enlightenment. For example, Jonathan Israel characterizes Spinoza as the "supreme philosophical bogeyman of Early Enlightenment" and the "chief challenger of the fundamentals of revealed religion, received ideas, tradition, morality, and ... divinely constituted political authority." As philosopher Rebecca Goldstein puts it, Spinoza is the "renegade Jew who gave us modernity"; hence, his expulsion from the Amsterdam community seems to signal the impasse between religion and Enlightenment thought. As Jonathan Israel and David Sorkin have argued, however, one should think of Spinoza's philosophy as part of a "family" or "plurality" of Enlightenments that range from the radical, antireligious Enlightenment of Spinoza, to a "genuinely religious" and providential Enlightenment.[3] This chapter is about that other Enlightenment: the Enlightenment of the men who cast out Spinoza. Moreover, it is about that seemingly most "unmodern" of practices: the laws of pollution and ritual purity.

Israel."[19] Through their use of the *mikva'ot*, Jewish women played a crucial role in the redemption of the Jewish people.

For Sephardic Jews in Amsterdam and the American colonies, the pun of "gathering" and "hope" embedded in *mikveh* took on specific messianic associations during the seventeenth and eighteenth centuries. Just as the Enlightenment brought a wave of messianic revivals throughout the Protestant American colonies, so, too, early American Jews dreamed of the messiah's imminent approach.[20] The messianic subtext of *mikveh* is one of two key ways that seventeenth- and eighteenth-century Jews in Amsterdam and the colonies changed and adjusted the symbol of the *mikveh* to meet their current religious needs. *Mikveh Israel* is a popular name for colonial Jewish synagogues: the most famous examples are the original congregation in Curaçao (founded 1651) and in Philadelphia (founded 1740). One impetus for this name came from an influential seventeenth-century work by Dutch Rabbi Menasseh ben Israel (1604–57): his book *Mikveh Israel* [*Esperanza de Israel/The Hope of Israel* 1650/52] supported his plea to readmit the Jews to England.[21] In *Mikveh Israel*, Menasseh ben Israel argued that the establishment of synagogues in England and the Americas fulfilled the prophecy that before the messianic ingathering of the Jews could occur, the scattered of Israel would establish synagogues in the four corners of the earth.[22] Most of the other early Jewish congregations in the Americas played upon this messianic idea of America as a site of "ingathering"; thus, early congregations used names such as Nephuse [*nefuẕe*] Israel (the Scattered of Israel), Yeshuat Israel (Salvation of Israel), Shearith Israel (the Remnant of Israel), and Nidhe Israel (Scattered/Exiles of Israel).

The idea of *mikveh* was an important part of the early American congregations' perception of their role in the arrival of the messiah: these congregations were to be both a "hope" and "source" for the reconnection to God that the messiah would bring. Indeed the congregation in Curaçao—itself an offshoot of the Portuguese congregation in Amsterdam—became a wellspring for the other New World Jewish congregations: for example, Curaçao's *Mikvé Israel* helped fund other early synagogues built throughout the American colonies. The vision of the Americas as a wellspring for a messianic future may help to explain the preference in early American *mikva'ot* for the use of underground water source. Underground springs reinforced the symbol of *mikveh* as a "source" (rather than pit) and recalled the spring of water that Ezekiel claimed would run from beneath the third messianic Temple.

The reconnection and hope provided by the *mikveh* had important ramifications for early American Jews. If the early Jews of the Caribbean and American colonies were obsessed both with their estrangement from God and their imminent redemption, these dual concerns were most likely tied to the communities' strong *converso* presence. Many early American Jews were descendants of Spanish-Portuguese Jews forced to convert (*convertir*) to Catholicism during the Inquisition. Although many *conversos* had practiced a form of crypto-Judaism in private while on the Iberian Peninsula, before they could rejoin Jewish communities elsewhere, men were required to be circumcised and female *conversos* needed to immerse in the *mikveh*. For women, then, the physical ceremony marking their personal reconnection to the divine paralleled the larger movement of the scattered "remnant" of Iberian Jews back to God and was inherently tied to the ritual bath.

The second readjustment of the symbol of *mikveh* during this era was the association of immersion with secular water cures; thus we see a change in the decoration of *mikva'ot* to reflect the rise of spa culture during the seventeenth and eighteenth centuries. Although bathing for pleasure decreased in the sixteenth century, during the late seventeenth and early eighteenth centuries there was a rise of bathhouses or "spas" devoted to water cures throughout Europe and England. Spas were believed to cure a number of physiological ailments, ranging from rheumatism, paralysis, skin disease, lameness, hip cases, jaundice, vertebral deformities, gout, and infertility.[23] Although by the end of the eighteenth century, doctors were using "chemistry" to validate the healing properties of mineral springs, in the seventeenth and early eighteenth centuries, physical and spiritual health were seen as deeply interconnected. Thus, when colonist Cotton Mather published his medical treatise in 1722 he titled it *The Angel of Bethesda* and used as his inspiration the passage from John 5:1–15 that recounts the miraculous healing of the sick through a pool of water blessed by an Angel of the Lord. In general, spas were associated with spiritual as well as physical health, and often with elites. Drawings of spas from this era often feature tiling and water heaters like those that began to be used in *mikva'ot* in this epoch. The use of tiling as well as the preference for spring-fed *mikva'ot* in early American *mikva'ot* may be related in some part to the rise of a spa culture more generally during this era.

The alignment of *mikva'ot* with spas highlights an important difference between the perception of women in Judaism in this era and their Protestant counterparts. As Kathleen Brown notes, in the "fervently Protestant [conception of the] early modern body ... proscribed sexual acts were loathsome not simply because they sullied the purity of the soul, but because of their location in the 'lower regions' of the body, strongly associated with organic filth."[24] Women were particularly susceptible to this contagion: Protestant ministers, for example, sometimes argued that "the 'unclean' state of the woman's body functioned as a clear, knowable sign of an unregenerate spirit."[25] In Judaism, sexual acts committed within the framework of ritual immersion and the laws regarding intimacy between husbands and wives did not "sully" the soul, but rather elevated sex to a spiritual act: the couple sanctify themselves ("*se santifika*") through following the law and hence merited pious children who would not fall prey to the evil inclination ("*tener ijos buenos judyos ke no tendrá el* yēṣer hā-rá").[26] Thus while grace saved only select Protestant women, *mikveh* offered a means to spiritually cleanse all married Jewish women on a regular and ongoing basis. Moreover while men and women used spas equally, the practice of *mikveh* directly connected women's immersions with the salvation of all of Israel.

The spiritual cleanliness offered to Jewish women by the *mikveh* was accompanied by an enhanced social value associated with cleanliness during the early Enlightenment that was unlikely to be available to gentile women of the same social rank. Scholars such as Richard and Claudia Bushman, Kathleen Brown, and Georges Vigarello have noted that during the seventeenth century and particularly the eighteenth century a change occurred in the understanding of water among gentiles. During the seventeenth century, most Europeans and American colonists "embraced what we might call a 'linen-centered' standard for personal cleanliness: that is, changes in clothes and linen along with the washing of hands, face and hair—rather than bathing—made one "clean." Immersion such as in spas was primarily therapeutic and reserved for people with money. Cleanliness was increasingly associated with manners, propriety, elegance, and social distinction: that is, cleanliness was connected to the people who could afford to change their shirts frequently and keep their hands and faces clean. During the second half of the eighteenth century, bathing for cleanliness became increasingly common in Europe and the colonies: getting "wett all over at once" spread from being something done only by elites to something merchants and the middling sort might do. As Bushman and Bushman note, prior to the inclusion of shower boxes and the like in late eighteenth-century American homes, bathing was gendered, as gentile men had more avenues for cleanliness than gentile women: "men bathed in streams and oceans, a privilege usually denied to women." Likewise early public baths in America were primarily for men, until the advent of women's sections.[27] Thus Jewish women of this era were both spiritually and physically cleaner than their gentile counterparts, not only because of their regular immersion in ritual baths, but also because of the thorough bathing required prior to immersion in *mikva'ot*. This cleanliness brought with it new associations of nobility, decorum, and elegance. This social distinction must have been pleasing to the Sephardic women in particular, who in spite of being the wives of merchants often called attention to their nobility and "pure" bloodlines.[28] When it came to bathing and cleanliness, Jewish women were ahead of the curve.

With these two symbolic readjustments in mind, I would like to turn now to some of the physical hallmarks of seventeenth- and eighteenth-century *mikva'ot* and connect them to the specific spiritual and social symbolism of the *mikveh* for early American Jews.

3 A model for understanding New World *mikva'ot*: Amsterdam *mikva'ot*

If the rise of spas and the messianic associations of the word *mikveh* help us understand the symbolism ritual baths held for Jewish colonists, the *mikva'ot* in Amsterdam are perhaps the best physical model we have for understanding ritual baths in the New World. Amsterdam was not only a major port of refuge for *conversos* fleeing the Inquisition, but also a wellspring for most of the openly Jewish settlements in the colonies. Early American Jews often appealed to Amsterdam's Rabbis to settle questions of Jewish law, and many New World Jews went back and forth between the New World and Amsterdam, either because of trade, marriage, or the pursuit of education. Thus Amsterdam's *mikva'ot* provide an important model for understanding the construction and use of ritual baths in the colonies.

Architectural historian Thomas Hubka has argued that eighteenth-century Ashkenazi (Eastern European) synagogues tended to be built near a water source and the community's *mikveh*. This pattern is duplicated in Amsterdam's Portuguese synagogue (the Esnoga, 1675), which served as the parent congregation for all of the early Sephardic synagogues in the New World. One of the innovations found in Amsterdam, however, is that the *mikveh* was built as part of the synagogue complex itself, rather than merely nearby. This "innovation" harkened back to antiquity, much in the way that the Amsterdam Esnoga deliberately invoked the lost Temple in Jerusalem.[29]

The pattern of including the *mikveh* within the synagogue complex holds among early Jewish congregations in Holland, and, as I will argue, in the New World.[30] Thus across the street from the Amsterdam Esnoga, we find that the Ashkenazi Jews built two *mikva'ot* in 1671 and 1752 in buildings attached to the *Grote Synagoge* (Great Synagogue) and *Nieuwe Synagoge* (New Synagogue) respectively. There is no *halakhic* (legal) basis for having discrete Sephardic and Ashkenazi *mikva'ot*, nor are there any known standard design differences between Ashkenazi and Sephardic *mikva'ot* during this era.[31] However, in general Amsterdam's Sephardic community tended to separate themselves for reasons of status from their poorer Ashkenazi brethren. This social separation was not usually an option for the small Jewish communities in the colonies; congregations tended to be mixed, but followed the Sephardic rite.

Today the Great and New Synagogue *mikva'ot* are our best resource for understanding expectations for *mikva'ot* for Jewish colonists who settled in the Americas during this era.[32] Although there is a general paucity of information about seventeenth- and eighteenth-century European *mikva'ot*, a wealth of information remains about the Great

Figure 1: Excavated and restored Great Synagogue *mikveh* (1671), Amsterdam. Photo by Peter Langer, 2006. Courtesy of the Collection of the Jewish Historical Museum, Amsterdam.

Figure 2: Excavated New Synagogue *mikveh* (1752), Amsterdam. Courtesy of Bureau Monumenten & Archeologie, Amsterdam.

and New Synagogue *mikva'ot* (Figures 1, 2, and 3). The Esnoga *mikveh* was rediscovered in 1955–59; yet, this *mikveh* was never excavated because it was situated in the weakest spot in the building. In contrast, images of the New Synagogue *mikveh* were printed during the eighteenth century, and both the Great and New Synagogue *mikva'ot* have been excavated.[33] Because of the large influx of both Sephardic and Ashkenazi Jews from Amsterdam to the colonies, these *mikva'ot* provide an important model for understanding what the colonial American *mikva'ot* might have looked like. Although the Ashkenazi congregation was considered to be less wealthy than the Sephardic congregation, the Great and New Synagogue *mikva'ot* are quite luxurious. Given the competition between Sephardim and Ashkenazim in Amsterdam for social status, it is logical to assume that the Portuguese *mikveh* had many of the same luxury elements. Moreover several of these "luxurious" aspects are found in colonial American *mikva'ot*.

When compared to ancient and medieval *mikva'ot*,[34] several features of the Great and New Synagogue *mikva'ot* stand out (Figures 1, 2, and 3). These elements help us understand the standard to which early American *mikva'ot* should be compared. First, the *mikva'ot* could be heated: indeed a brick oven was located adjacent to the New Synagogue *mikveh*, presumably for this purpose. The technology for heating *mikva'ot* was known in Palestine as early as the Roman era, but was re-popularized by Hasidim during the eighteenth century. We know that at least some early *mikva'ot* in the Americas were heated in colder climates, because in 1760 Congregation Shearith Israel in New York approved an allowance of fifty shillings a year for cleaning the *mikveh* and heating the water.[35] Second, like most New World *mikva'ot*, the Amsterdam *mikva'ot* provide ample room for immersion: for example, the New Synagogue baths are 1.65 meters deep, and each side of the bath is fitted with a drain and has a water supply.[36] Third, whereas many *mikva'ot* have built in steps to make descending into the bath easier, no steps were found in the New Synagogue bath; rather a wooden ladder was probably used. A fourth important feature that is shared by most of the colonial *mikva'ot* is the use of tile. Whereas in earlier centuries, *mikva'ot* were often lined only with plaster to make them watertight (as required by Jewish law), the Great and New Synagogue *mikva'ot* are further lined with decorative white ceramic tiles. This tiling is similar to that of health spas of this era and may reflect the association of spiritual and physical health during this era. Moreover since spas were associated with social distinction, the tiling may have been seen as providing a greater sense of elegance and decorum.[37]

One final physical element of the Amsterdam *mikva'ot* requires analysis. The Great and New Synagogue *mikva'ot* (like the Esnoga *mikveh*) are located indoors, although outdoor water sources were plentiful in Amsterdam. Recent religious books about *mikva'ot* have emphasized the lengths to which women have gone to immerse after menstruation: these include immersing in the ocean, or women who broke "the frozen surface of a lake" in order to "immerse in the ice-water beneath." While it is technically permissible to immerse in the ocean or certain rivers and lakes, because of the strict rules regulating immersion, the chance of an immersion being done improperly increases dramatically when done outdoors, a point emphasized by Sephardic commentators during this era.[38]

Indeed, indoor immersion was the norm in the seventeenth through nineteenth centuries for reasons of modesty, comfort, and Jewish law. Routine outdoor immersion would clearly be uncomfortable (in fact life threatening) in harsh winters such as those found in New York, Philadelphia, and Newport: as we will see, even in warm Caribbean climates, Jewish communities chose to build indoor *mikva'ot*. Moreover, according to Jewish law, a woman's immersion must take place in an area "where there is sufficient privacy," since a woman who immerses in the presence of other people is cursed and like an animal.[39] As Stefanie Hoss points out, for both men and women

> Nakedness was a cause for shame in Judaism … [it] was a sign of poverty and vulnerability and even purposefully used to shame persons. Somebody who is naked is at least ridiculous in Judaism; at worst he or she loses his or her "honour."[40]

Like most *mikva'ot* of this era, the Great and New Synagoge *mikva'ot* had a separate, private entrance. Because a woman's immersion signals her availability to her husband, other men should not be aware she has immersed, as it might lead them to have impure thoughts. The indoor location was not a luxury but standard for the day.

Our understanding of the physical features of the New Synagogue *mikveh* is complemented by insights into its ritual use provided by the Jacobsz/Wagenaar print from 1783 (Figure 3).[41] The high degree of accuracy in Wagenaar's depiction of the *mikveh*'s architecture suggests that he had access to the building when it wasn't in use.

Figure 3: Engraving of Amsterdam *mikveh*. Drawn by P. Wagenaar and engraved by C. Philips Jacobsz, 1783. Author's collection.

Presumably Wagenaar also interviewed members of the community to learn about how the *mikveh* might have been used, since it would have been *halakhically* impermissible (as well as immodest) for him to witness the immersion he depicts.[42] The ritual details depicted by Wagenaar correspond to the description of immersion provided by Rabbi Culi in the first volume of *Me'am Loez* (1730). Wagenaar's engraving depicts a woman on the left undergoing a *tevilah* (immersion). In contrast to early American Protestants of this era who tended to take only sponge baths without soap, before immersing the Jewish woman would have bathed completely in clean, hot water ("*labarse bien kon agua todo su kuerpo . . . sea agua pura . . . sola mente debe labarse kon agua kaliente*"), and eliminated any *ḥaẓiẓah* (barriers), such as dirt, food particles, scabs, jewelry, or tangled hair.[43] Indeed in Wagenaar's image, the woman immersing has her hair combed straight forward to ensure proper immersion. She would probably have immersed three times (or perhaps seven if she were Sephardic or Hasidic), and have recited a blessing either before or after her immersion.

As is required, the immersion depicted by Wagenaar is supervised by a *balanit* (or *shomeret*), the woman directly to her right. This woman must be "religious and godfearing": neither a non-Jewish woman ("*de resto de nasyones*") nor a girl under twelve ("*no puede ser ĉika, ke si no tiene doze anyos i un día*") were considered reliable witnesses.[44] The *balanit* signals an important difference between the status of women in Jewish and Protestant households: whereas Protestant husbands were the "'heads' of the household's body," Jewish women had authority over their bodies when it came to impurity and purification.

Women self-regulated (and proclaimed) their status as either in *niddah* (forbidden/separated) or not, and turned to male authorities only if they had questions about their status. Likewise the *balanit* had authority over immersions: no males were in attendance.[45]

The *mikveh* attendant has at least four important functions: (1) she must inspect the woman before she immerses to ensure that there is no loose hair, scabs, hangnails, etc. that might interfere with the immersion. (2) She must ensure that the woman immerses completely below the water and that her hair does not float up and her body and feet do not touch the sides (or bottom) of the *mikveh*. In this engraving, the *balanit* has a candle for this purpose and she peers over the edge to make sure that the woman immerses properly. (3) She may provide the woman immersing with a cloth with which to cover herself while reciting the blessing; thus, notice that Wagenaar's *balanit* holds a cloth in her hand.[46] (4) She guards the woman's life in case of an accident in the water. If a *mikveh* meets *halakhic* (legal) standards it will still purify even if it contains algae and the like; hence, before the advent of chlorine *mikva'ot* were sometimes slippery. One horror story will suffice to explain the significance of this role of guarding the immersee: in 1741 and in 1771 two women in Frankfurt drowned in the *mikveh*. Presumably they immersed without an attendant, as one of them "remained undiscovered for nine months, because the body had slipped under a wooden cover that covered the larger part of the *miqveh*."[47]

There are also a few unusual elements of the image that may point to errors on the part of the engraver or unusual practices within Amsterdam. First, the water is quite low, particularly if one compares the engraving to the excavated *mikveh*. As Culi notes, the water in the *mikveh* should reach at least up to the woman's waist (47–49 inches) when she is standing.[48] The water level may have been an error on the part of the engraver: for example, perhaps he saw the water at this level when the *mikveh* wasn't in use, but didn't realize that hot water would have been added before immersion. Second, the *balanit* stands in the second half of the *mikveh*. If this is accurate, this is an interesting innovation; more likely it is an error. Third, there appears to be a servant attending the immersee. This woman stands at the far right of the engraving and holds the woman's clothes. The servant's presence is odd: in Judaism, "Seeing the nakedness of social superiors … is a humiliation for the superior and a forbidden, punishable act for the inferior."[49] Indeed as Culi himself notes:

> *I debe la mujer de ser muy onrada de ir a la ṭᵉbîlāʰ en sekreta mente, ke ninguno se lo sepa; i toda mujer ke se da a sentir delantre de la jente kuando se ba a ṭᵉbîlāʰ es pekadora, i sobre esto dize la Ley: <<Maldito sea yazién kon bestya>> (Dt 27²¹; supra).* [And a woman should receive much honour who immerses in secret without anyone knowing; and a woman who lets people know when she immerses is a sinner, and about this the Torah says, "Cursed be he who lies with a beast."][50]

Since women had to immerse at night, it is possible that for reasons of safety, a female servant accompanied women to the *mikveh*.

Having outlined the norm for *mikva'ot* in both Jewish law and in practice in seventeenth- and eighteenth-century Amsterdam, I want to turn to the evidence we have for *mikva'ot* in the colonies and use this context to analyze these baths.

4 *Mikva'ot* in the New World in context

To date, remains of six seventeenth- and eighteenth-century American mikva'ot are known to exist: (1) the *mikveh* in Recife (1636–54), (2) the *mikveh* in Barbados (c. 1650s), (3 and 4) the *mikva'ot* in Paramaribo (c. 1719[?], 1735), (5) the *mikveh* in Curaçao (1728), and (6) the *mikveh* in St. Eustatius (c. 1739)[51]. These *mikva'ot* follow several of the trends outlined in my analysis of the Amsterdam *mikva'ot*: they are part of the synagogue complex and they generally reflect the rise of spa culture. Moreover, they tend to reflect colonists' messianic dreams: while the Amsterdam *mikva'ot* appear to have been fed by rainwater, the New World *mikva'ot* display a preference for being fed by underground springs.

(1) Recife

The oldest remains of an early American *mikveh* are from the Dutch colony of Recife in Brazil. Like the Amsterdam *mikveh*, the Recife *mikveh* was built as part of the synagogue complex. Like the other early American *mikva'ot* I will discuss, this congregation had messianic leanings. There has been almost no scholarly analysis of the Recife *mikveh*, but I will argue that based on the comparison to the Amsterdam *mikveh* and other new World *mikva'ot*, this bath should be understood as a *kelim mikveh*;[52] that is, a *mikveh* for immersing vessels made of metal and glass to be used for food and that were bought from (or made by) a non-Jew, rather than a *mikveh* used for people. According to compendiums of Jewish law such as the *Shulkhan Arukh*, the immersion of these vessels is a necessary part of *kashrut* (kosher laws). As with the immersion of people, vessels are immersed in order to "complete" them so that they can fulfill their ritual purpose. For vessels this purpose would be making and serving kosher food. As with humans, the vessel must be completely cleaned physically prior to immersion.[53]

The Recife *mikveh* was built as part of the first synagogue in the New World: Kahal Zur Israel (Congregation Rock of Israel). The synagogue and *mikveh* were used for less than twenty years before the Portuguese recaptured the colony in 1654, and the Jewish population fled to Curaçao, Barbados and other ports of refuge. Archeologists discovered the *mikveh* in 2000 beneath several layers of flooring. As Dr. Alberquerque (Federal University of Pernambuco) notes, the structure is clearly a *mikveh* and not a well, since in Brazil wells were always outside the house, and never inside; indeed, inspection of the *mikveh* by orthodox Rabbis revealed that it was a kosher *mikveh*—that is it was built according to Jewish law. The building above the *mikveh* dates to around 1640, and hence is the original structure. Above the level with the *mikveh* was a two-story building: the first floor contained shops, while the second floor had the synagogue. Like other early synagogues, the congregation's name is a messianic reference: *zur Israel* is a phrase from 2 Samuel 23:2 that is generally seen to be a prediction of the messiah through the Davidic line. The *mikveh* was fed by "*uma agua limpida e fluente*" (clear, flowing water); that is, by an underground stream.[54]

Having seen the 1671 Great Synagogue *mikveh* in Amsterdam built only a few decades later, we should be surprised by the shape of the Recife *mikveh* (Figure 4). Although at its

Figure 4: Kahal Ẓur Israel *mikveh* (1636–54), in Recife, Brazil. Photo by and courtesy of Joan Glanz Rimmon, Los Angeles, 2006

peak, Recife's Jewish population contained around 1,450 Jews (nearly half of the white population and close to the number of Jews in Amsterdam),[55] the Recife *mikveh* itself is simpler, rougher, and much smaller than either the seventeenth- or eighteenth-century *mikva'ot* from Amsterdam. The size and shape presents two (or three) problems: (1) the *mikveh* would have to be quite deep, as one would have to plunge straight down (rather than bend forward) to immerse. This is not impossible, but it would make it more difficult to use. (2) It would be difficult to immerse without touching the sides of the *mikveh*, thereby invalidating the immersion. Likewise if one scratched or cut oneself on the sharp edges, the immersion would be invalidated, and indeed a rabbinical authority would need to be consulted before one could immerse again. (3) If a woman were large, it would be impossible to immerse in the *mikveh* without running into these problems (or not fitting at all).

All of these problems disappear if we understand that this *mikveh* is a *kelim mikveh*—that is, a *mikveh* specifically designed for immersing vessels that were made of metal and glass, bought from (or made by) a non-Jew, and intended to be used for food.[56] Although these vessels could have been immersed in the nearby ocean, such a practice is often not realistic, as items can be easily broken or lost in the waves. In larger and prosperous communities such as Recife, a *kelim mikveh* would have been a desirable and not overly expensive option and would prevent the community from having to drain the regular *mikveh* if and when glass was broken in it. In sum, a *kelim mikveh* is not a substitute for a regular *mikveh*; rather it is a luxury that would only be built after a *mikveh* for people was already available. If the Recife *mikveh* is indeed for *kelim*, a larger "human" *mikveh* still probably lies below ground somewhere else in the city—perhaps in the basement of the Rabbi's house, or that of another god-fearing individual.

(2) Barbados

In spring of 2008, the second oldest Caribbean *mikveh* was discovered and excavated in Barbados. Jews settled in Barbados perhaps as early as 1628; however, the community grew after the fall of Recife.[57] The island's main congregation, Nidhe Israel, built their first synagogue around 1654. The *mikveh* was part of the synagogue complex and located in the basement of the Rabbi's house; the rubble stone construction suggests that it also dates to the 1650s.[58] If this turns out to be the case, it would be the oldest discovered non-*kelim mikveh* in the Americas.

Whether it is the oldest, the Barbados *mikveh* (Figure 5) is the most luxurious of the early American *mikva'ot* so far discovered. Like *mikva'ot* in Amsterdam, the *mikveh* reflects the influence of spas; like the Recife *mikveh*, it demonstrates the early American preference for spring-fed baths. The *mikveh* is quite large: it is just slightly over 12 feet deep, 4 feet wide, and 8 feet long. Karl Watson notes that the *mikveh* is fed by "underground flowing water" that is fresh to the taste and fills the *mikveh* with about four feet of water. However, the *mikveh* also responds to tidal changes of the nearby sea. According to Watson, the "Inside is plastered with three alcoves presumably for lamps since it is deep and would have been dark. It is not internally tiled but plastered ... however the three flights of steps leading down to it are a mix of marble and slate tiles" and several more steps leading the immersee into the water itself. The floor is covered in red-grey granite tiles. With its use of marble, slate, and granite, this *mikveh* is the most luxurious of all of the early American *mikva'ot*, and the tiles underscore the status accorded to *mikveh* use. The *mikveh* also has an intriguing design element: wall alcoves that could be used for placing candles for lighting. There are a large number of alcoves in the *mikveh*; hence, they may have also been used for the purposes of placing one's clothes, cloths for drying off, cloths for covering oneself while saying the *berakha* (blessing), or even for a text of the blessing itself.[59] These thoughtful design elements reveal a community that was concerned with making *mikveh* use a pleasurable, safe, and enriching experience.

(3 and 4) Suriname

The *mikva'ot* of the former Dutch colony Suriname similarly reveal the value early American communities placed upon ritual baths: the *mikva'ot* are conveniently located, well planned, and richly built both in terms of architecture and tiling. As in Recife and Barbados, the

Figure 5: Nidhe Israel *mikveh* (c. 1650s), in Bridgetown, Barbados. Photo by and courtesy of Stevan Arnold, 2010

Figure 6: Neveh Shalom *mikveh* building (c. 1719[?], renovated 1830) in Paramaribo, Suriname. Photo by Laura Leibman, 2008.

trend of having a *mikveh* in the synagogue complex and in a dedicated building is found in Suriname. Sephardic Jews began to settle in Suriname in the 1660s. Although the earliest synagogue complex (1685) was downriver in the plantation town of Jodensavanne, in 1716 the joint Sephardic-Ashkenazi community in the port town of Paramaribo acquired a property on Keizerstraat and in 1719 they began construction on Neveh Shalom synagogue. According to the community's historian and *balanit* Lily Duym, the two-story *mikveh* building (Figure 6) is from the original 1719 construction, although an inscribed tile indicates that the immersion pool was at least renovated or retiled in 1830. In 1735 the community split: Neveh Shalom became the Ashkenazi synagogue and the Sephardim built the ẓedek ve-Shalom synagogue complex a couple of blocks away on Herenstraat. A second *mikveh* (c. 1735) was built on this property (Figure 7).

Perhaps the most intriguing feature of the Neveh Shalom *mikveh* is its ingenious design: the *mikveh* is on the first floor (rather than sunk into the ground), and the bather descended into it by climbing up a set of stairs and entering the *mikveh* from the second floor. This *mikveh* has had an extremely long history: it was in continual use from its inception until the end of the twentieth century.[60] Although the *mikveh* was altered in the late-twentieth century, originally the unusual two-story design was a stunning example of the only known early American *bor al gabei bor mikveh* ("one pit on top of another pit" *mikveh*). Originally rainwater was collected into two brick cisterns adjacent to the *mikveh* building that connected to an underground reservoir (*ozar*) below the immersion pool.[61] This underground reservoir fed the aboveground *mikveh*.[62] Although medieval Rabbis mention the *bor al gabei bor* design, it was (and is) not considered normative practice, except by followers of Rabbi Shneur Zalman of Liadi (1745–1821), first Rabbi of the Chabad Lubavitch Hasidim.[63] Since the Suriname *mikveh* predates Rabbi Zalman's ruling, it is unlikely that the design reflects a Hasidic presence in the colonies. One possible explanation for the design is the high water table in Paramaribo: by placing the immersion pool above (rather than next to) the *ozar*, sediment could fall to the bottom of the *ozar* and leave a clean bottom to the immersion pool as well as clearer water for immersion. Hence the design element would have been useful for cities such as Paramaribo with brackish water, as eighteenth-century commentators warned that if

Figure 7: Ẓedek ve-Shalom *mikveh* (c. 1735), in Paramaribo, Suriname. Arrow indicates the location of the *mikveh*, which is shown in the inset. Photos by Laura Leibman, 2008

there were mud on the tiled floor of the immersion pool, it might adhere to the woman's feet and invalidate the immersion.[64]

In contrast to the Neveh Shalom *mikveh*, the immersion pool of the Ẓedek ve-Shalom *mikveh* is below ground and today is covered by a trapdoor. The *mikveh* is found in the synagogue complex in a small building adjacent to the synagogue (Figure 7). The *mikveh* is no longer in use, but was used by the community until the 1970s. This *mikveh* is of a more standard design and is fed by underground water. The water table is high in this area, and the street (Gravenstraat) behind the synagogue and adjacent to the *mikveh* building serves as a dyke to prevent flooding from the nearby waterway called Van Sommelduck Kreek. The crushed seashells used to build the dyke would provide a nice filter for the rain and ground water, and hence may have made the two-story design of the Neveh Shalom *mikveh* unnecessary for this location. The *mikveh* is brick lined with the same elegant slate tiles that were originally used in the Neveh Shalom *mikveh* and on the roofs of the synagogues. Unlike the Neveh Shalom *mikveh*, which had a ladder to descend into the pool, the Ẓedek ve-Shalom *mikveh* has slate covered stone steps (inset Figure 7). The Surinamese *mikva'ot* reflect the Amsterdam practice of having separate Sephardi and Ashkenazi *mikva'ot*, even when the synagogues are in close proximity to one another. Although Suriname was known in the colonial era for its decadence, usually the examples cited of the colony's opulence emphasize how it was at once "crassly materialistic and spiritually empty": planters bathed their children in imported wine and had large numbers of slaves to perform the most mundane of domestic tasks.[65] The attention early Jewish Suriamese settlers paid to the *mikva'ot* suggests they accorded grandeur to their spiritual lives as well, even to elements associated primarily with women's ritual lives.

(5) Curaçao

Curaçao, like Suriname, was known for its important economic and social role in the American colonies. The Curaçao *mikveh* was placed at the heart of this vibrant community. The Curaçao *mikveh* is the fourth oldest in the Americas, but was the first to be recovered: it was uncovered during the restoration of the synagogue complex in the 1970s. The *mikveh* was housed in a small building adjacent to the Rabbi's house, both of which were built in 1728. Four years later, the island's fifth (and oldest remaining) synagogue was built next door.[66] As with the Recife synagogue, Curaçao's congregation had messianic leanings. Like the Recife *mikveh*, there has been almost no scholarly attention to the structure; the style, however, is reminiscent of the Amsterdam *mikveh* and reflects the rise of spa culture during this era.

As with the Recife *mikveh*, this *mikveh* served a large and prosperous community. Indeed, up through the first quarter of the nineteenth century, Curaçao was the "New York" of the colonial world. The congregation was aptly named Mikvé Israel: it had the largest and best educated Jewish community in the entire Western Hemisphere, and it provided funds to build most of the New World Synagogues. By 1750, the Jewish population reached roughly 2,000 individuals.[67] When the *mikveh* was built in 1728, Curaçao's community was at its peak, and the *mikveh* reflects the community's status.

Figure 8: Mikvé Israel *mikveh* (1728), in Willemstad, Curaçao. Photo by Laura Leibman, 2008.

Like the *mikvaot* in Barbados and Suriname, this *mikveh* is in keeping with the standard set by the Amsterdam *mikveh*: it is large, smooth, and well decorated. The *mikveh* is of a size appropriate for people: "It measures four by seven feet and two and a half feet deep. It was probably used until the mid-nineteenth century." Whereas the Recife *mikveh* used rough stones, the top of the Curaçao *mikveh* was decorated with "a line of red bricks." Like most of the other known early American *mikvaot*, it was fed by an underground water source, and was indoors, in spite of the near proximity of a warm and safe body of water.[68] As in Amsterdam, Barbados, and Suriname, the entrance to the *mikveh* was separate from the synagogue, insuring the modesty of the users.

(6) St. Eustatius ("Statia")

Although the St. Eustatius ("Statia") Jewish community was smaller and poorer than that of Curaçao, Suriname, or Barbados, their *mikveh* is spacious and well decorated (Figure 9). As with the previous examples, the *mikveh* was built as part of the synagogue complex. St. Eustatius Center for Archaeological Research (SECAR) has excavated this *mikveh* and the adjacent synagogue. This *mikveh* is a fine example of how even in less

Figure 9: Honen Dalim *mikveh* (c. 1739), in Oranjestad, St. Eustatius. Photo by and courtesy of R. Grant Gilmore III, SECAR

prosperous communities, financial resources were dedicated to making the *mikveh* a pleasurable and elegant experience.

If Curaçao was the center of the Jewish colonial world, Statia was a relatively poor outpost. In 1722, there were 524 free inhabitants on the island: of these only twenty-one were Jews. By 1781 when the British took the island, there were 101 Jewish heads of households, or roughly a population of 400 Jews. Thus, at its peak, the island's Jewish population was at most 20 percent of that of Curaçao. This population was not known for its wealth: many of the Jewish inhabitants had had their way paid to the colony by the community in Amsterdam in order to alleviate the burden of caring for the poor in Holland.[69] Indeed this may explain the congregation's unusual name, *Honen Dalim* ("Gracious to the Needy"). The Jewish cemetery reflects this relative poverty: of the twenty-two gravestones that are identifiable today, few have any decoration and none match the beauty and elegance of the carvings found in Curaçao and other islands. In spite of the paucity of Jews and resources, the community built both a synagogue in 1738 and a *mikveh* in an adjacent building. This presence of the *mikveh* in Statia reinforces the primacy of the *mikveh* for eighteenth-century Jews in the colonies.

Despite the community's limited resources, the *mikveh* is well adorned and reflects both attention to Jewish law and the influence of spa culture. Archeologist Stefanie Hoss found that all of the *mikva'ot* in Palestine from the Hasmonean Era through the Muslim

Conquest "were plastered at least up to the water level with several layers of water-resistant plaster, in order to prevent the water from leaking and thus to meet the religious requirements of an impermeable pool."[70] The inside of the Statia *mikveh* was covered in fine white plaster; however, SECAR's analysis of architectural remains at the site indicates that, like the Suriname and Barbados *mikva'ot*, the *mikveh* originally had a tiled floor. In addition it was decorated along the upper edge with a yellow brick border. The tiles helped congregants view their *mikveh* experience as akin to a spa. Another important feature of the St. Eustatius *mikveh* is the built-in cut stone steps that helped ease the bathers into the roughly two meter deep water. Unlike most of the other known early American *mikva'ot*, this *mikveh* was fed by rain, which was collected in a cistern.[71] Like other early American *mikva'ot*, the Statia *mikveh* was built not only to ensure the user's modesty and spiritual well-being, but also to provide the user with a sense of elegance, propriety, and social distinction.

5 Conclusions

By surveying these six known early American *mikva'ot* and placing them in the context of *mikveh* practice in Amsterdam during this era, I hope to both challenge some common misconceptions about early American Jewish life and to show how Enlightenment ideologies about redemption and spa culture shaped religious practice. The foremost misconception this survey challenges is the idea that it would have been common practice for early American Jews to immerse ritually in the ocean, rivers, or streams. Even in small and relatively poor communities in warm climates with water sources nearby, early American Jews built *mikva'ot*. Second, many early American *mikva'ot* were built as part of synagogue complexes and were fed by underground water sources. This can help us understand the location of other early synagogues: for example, the first synagogue in New York (the Mill Street Synagogue of Shearith Israel) was built alongside a stream, Yeshuat Israel congregation of Newport (RI) was built along an underground stream, and the Jodensavanne Synagogue (Suriname) was also built alongside a water source. This consistency in placement suggests that in at least some cases, the needs of the *mikveh* (a water source) must have been driving the location of the synagogue (which has no need for water), rather than vice versa. Thinking of the *mikveh* as the determining factor in Jewish urban planning inverts the usual hierarchy art historians use to analyze the "synagogue complex."

Third, the strong predilection for underground water sources in New World *mikva'ot* may reflect messianic symbolism. The prophet Ezekiel had predicted that a large stream of fresh water would run beneath the Third Temple (Ezekiel 47:2–5), and early Americans saw their synagogues as predictors of this messianic structure. *Mikva'ot* were an important part of early American Jewish life, and they represented the "hope" American Jews had for their future. Through their monthly use of ritual baths, Jewish women helped bring about this redemption. In this way, *mikveh* use accorded early American Jewish women a higher status than we might otherwise imagine. Moreover, by incorporating elements of spa culture, *mikva'ot* allowed bathers to envision themselves as socially as well as spiritually elevated. Changes in *mikveh* structure are an important reminder of how religions assimilate and respond to the challenges people face. *Mikva'ot* represented one way that early American Jews reinvented Jewish symbols to face a new world.

Notes

1. This chapter originally appeared as an article in the journal *Religion in the Age of Enlightenment* 1 (2009): 109–45, and I am grateful to the editors for allowing it to be reprinted here. The article would not have been possible without the help and/or suggestions of the following people: Eric Leibman, Karl Watson, Jonathan Sarna, Gail Sherman, Lily Duym, Myrna C. Moreno, Rabbi Kenneth Brodkin, R. Grant Gillmore III, Rebbetzin Devora Wilhelm, Abraham W. Rosenberg, Philip Dikland, Bert Lippincott III, Kent Coupé, Barbara Siegel, Jodi Schorb, Margot Mindari, Aviva Ben-Ur, and Rachel Frankel. I am also indebted to resources or people at the following museums and archives: Jewish Cultural Historical Museum (Curaçao), Ets Haim Library (Amsterdam), Joods Historisch Museum (Amsterdam), Centro Cultural Judaico Pernambuco (Brazil), AJHS Archives (New York), Newport Historical Society, SECAR, and Mikveh Shoshana (Oregon). Funding for research done for this article and my book, *Messianism, Secrecy and Mysticism: A New Interpretation of Early American Jewish Life* (London and Portland, OR: Vallentine Mitchell, 2012) more broadly was provided by the National Endowment for the Humanities, the Mellon Foundation, Stillman Drake and Ruby Lankford Grants, and Reed College. Any mistakes are of course my own.

2. Steven Nadler, *Spinoza: A Life* (Cambridge and New York: Cambridge University Press, 1999), 87, 120–1.

3. Rebecca Goldstein, *Betraying Spinoza: The Renegade Jew who Gave Us Modernity* (New York: Schocken Books, 2006). Jonathan Israel, *Radical Enlightenment: Philosophy and the Making of Modernity 1650–1750* (New York and Oxford: Oxford University Press, 2001), 159, 445–562. David Sorkin. *The Religious Enlightenment: Protestants, Jews and Catholics from London to Vienna* (Princeton, NJ: Princeton University Press, 2008), 1–5.

4. Death impurity is the pollution caused by contact with a corpse or items touched by a corpse. Some scholars, such as Jacob Milgrom, argue that the "common denominator" of all ritual defilement is death, which stands in opposition to God as the source of life and holiness. See Jonathan Klawans, *Purity, Sacrifice, and the Temple: Symbolism and Supersessionism in the Study of Ancient Judaism* (New York and Oxford: Oxford University Press, 2006), 56–7; Jacob Milgrom, *Leviticus 1–16* [The Anchor Yale Biblical Commentaries, 3] (New York: Doubleday, 1992), 766–8, 1000–04.

5. Nadler, *Spinoza*, 87, 94–5; Mary Douglas, *Purity and Danger: An Analysis of the Concept of Pollution and Taboo* (New York: Praeger, 1966), 51.

6. This practice was popular both among men in the *Hasidic* movement and among Sephardic Kabbalists. As Hyam Maccoby notes, after the destruction of the Temple there was no technical need for men to immerse; hence, male immersion in *mikva'ot* following 70 CE is voluntary and a purely pietistic exercise. See Hyam Maccoby, *Ritual and Morality: The Ritual Purity System and its Place in Judaism* (Cambridge and New York: Cambridge University Press, 1999), 43.

7. Historical analyses of early American *mikveh* use (but not the baths themselves) include Joshua Hoffman, "The Institution of *Mikvah* in America," in *Total Immersion: A Mikvah*

Anthology, ed. Rivkah Slonim (Northvale, NJ: Jason Aronson, Inc., 1995), 76–92; Karla Goldman, *Beyond the Synagogue Gallery: Finding a Place for Women in American Judaism* (Cambridge: Harvard University Press, 2001), 68–75; and Hyman Bogomolny Grinstein, *The Rise of the Jewish Community of New York, 1654–1860* (Philadelphia: Jewish Publication Society, 1945), 297–8.

8. Jerzy Gawronski and Ranjith Jayasena, "A mid-18th-century *mikveh* unearthed in the Jewish Historical Museum in Amsterdam," *Post-Medieval Archaeology* 41 / 2 (2007): 213–21. R. Grant Gilmore, III, "Recovering Jewish Heritage on St. Eustatius," *ARCHEObrief* 10 / 1 (2006): 7–10; Coenraad L. Temminck Groll, *De architektuur van Suriname: 1667–1930* (Zutphen: Walburg Press, 1973), 98–100; Jean Louis Volders, *Bouwkunst in Suriname; driehonderd jaren nationale architectuur* (Paramaribo: Kersten & Co. 1966), 81.

9. Rahel Wasserfall, ed., *Women and Water: Menstruation in Jewish Life and Law* (Hanover, NH and London: Brandeis University Press by University Press of New England, 1999), 2. Jacob Rader Marcus, *The Colonial American Jew, 1492–1776* (Detroit, MI: Wayne State University Press, 1970), 134–5.

10. Jacob Kullí, *Me'am Loez: El Gran Comentario*, ed. David Gonzalo Maeso and Pascual Pascual Recuero (Madrid: Editorial Gredos, 1969), Vol. 1, 171. This text was originally published in 1730 in Ladino, the *lingua franca* of Sephardic Jews. Non-italicized words are Hebrew.

11. Kullí, *Me'am Loez*, Vol. 1, 172

12. Janet Liebman Jacobs, "The Return to the Sacred: Ritual Purification Among Crypto-Jews in the Diaspora" in Wasserfall, ed., *Women and Water*, 217–31; David M. Gitlitz, *Secrecy and Deceit: The Religion of the Crypto-Jews* (Philadelphia: Jewish Publication Society, 1996), 209, 272–3.

13. Jonathan Sarna, "Port Jews in the Atlantic: Further Thoughts," *Jewish History* 20 (2006): 213–19, here 215; Aviva Ben-Ur, "Still Life: Sephardi, Ashkenazi, and West African Art and Form in Suriname's Jewish Cemeteries," *American Jewish History* 92 / 1 (2004): 31–79, here 40, 44–5.

14. Many of Luzzatto's works follow this theme, but see in particular Moshe Chaim Luzzatto, *The Knowing Heart—Da'ath Tevunoth*, tr. Shraga Silverstein (Jerusalem: Feldheim, 1982).

15. Jill McMillan, "Institutional Plausibility Alignment as Rhetorical Exercise: A Mainline Denominationé as Struggle with the Exigence of Sexism," *Journal for the Scientific Study of Religion* 27 (1988): 326–44.

16. Michael A. Meyer and W. Gunther Plaut, eds., *The Reform Judaism Reader: North American Documents* (New York: Union of American Hebrew Congregations Press, 2001), 7.

17. As Hyam Maccoby notes, today the purity gained by corpse-avoidance and immersion following handling the dead is "only nominal, since the absence of the ashes of the Red Cow means that all priests [and indeed all Jews] are in a state of corpse-impurity anyway"; see Maccoby, *Ritual and Morality*, 2.

18. Rabbi Kenneth Brodkin, "Fountain of Truth" (Congregation Kesser Israel, Portland, January 16, 2008); Tamar Frankiel, "To Number our Days," in Slonim, ed., *Total Immersion*, 13–22, here 18–19; Midrash Toras Cohanim; Schneur Zalman Lesches, *Understanding Mikvah: An Overview of Mikvah Construction* (Montreal: Rabbi S.Z. Lesches, 2001), 37; *The Holy Scriptures* (Jerusalem: Koren Publishers, 1992), 128.

19. Brodkin, "Fountain of Truth"; Rivka Slonim, ed., *Total Immersion*, xxx–xxxi; Mishnah Yoma 8.9 85b.

20. Sarna, "Port Jews in the Atlantic," 215; Ben-Ur, "Still Life," 40, 44–5.

21. Notably the pun embedded in *mikveh* for ritual bath/hope is lost when it is translated into Spanish as a choice must be made: the ritual bath is referred to as "*baño*" (*banho* in

Portuguese), whereas the *mikveh* in the title of Menasseh ben Israel's book is translated as "*esperanza.*"

22. Daniel 12:7; Menasseh ben Israel, *The Hope of Israel Translation by Moses Wall, 1652*, ed. Henry Méchoulan and Gérard Nahon (London, Oxford, and New York: Littman Library of Jewish Civilization and Oxford University Press, 1987), 58–60, 142–4, 148, 158. Rivka Schatz-Uffenheimer, "Messianism in the Jewish-Christian Context," in *Menasseh ben Israel and his World*, ed. Yosef Kaplan, Henry Méchoulan, and Richard H. Popkin (Leiden: E.J. Brill, 1989), 244–61, here 253.

23. Françoise de Bonneville, *The Book of the Bath* (New York: Rizzoli, 1998), 40–2; L.W.B. Brockliss, "The Development of the Spa in Seventeenth-century France," in *The Medical History of Waters and Spas*, ed. Roy Porter (London: Wellcome Institute for the History of Medicine, 1990), 23–47; Christopher Hamlin, "Chemistry, Medicine, and the Legitimization of English Spas, 1740–1840," in ibid., 67–81; Audrey Heywood, "A Trial of the Bath Waters: the Treatment of Lead Poisoning," in ibid., 82–101, here 96.

24. Kathleen Brown, "Murderous Uncleanness: The Body of the Female Infanticide in Puritan New England," in *A Centre of Wonders: The Body in Early America*, ed. Janet Moore Lindman and Michele Lise Tarter (Ithaca, NY: Cornell University Press, 2001), 77–94, here 81. Cited in Jodi Schorb, "Buried Child: Infanticide's Affects in *Warnings from the Dead*" (ASA, Philadelphia, October 10–13, 2008), 4.

25. Jodi Schorb, "Uncleanliness is Next to Godliness: Sexuality, Salvation, and the Early American Woman's Execution Narrative," in *Puritan Origins of American Sex: Religion, Sexuality, and National Identity in American Culture*, ed. Nicholas Radel, Tracy Fessenden, and Magdalena Zaborowsky (London and New York: Routledge, 2000), 72–92, here 73.

26. Kullí, *Me'am Loez*, Vol. 1, 172.

27. Brown, "Murderous Uncleanness," 86–7; Georges Vigarello, *Concepts of Cleanliness: Changing Attitudes in France Since the Middle Ages*, tr. Jean Birrell (Cambridge and New York: Cambridge University Press, 1988), 58–9, 64, 78–9; Richard L. Bushman and Claudia L. Bushman, "The Early History of Cleanliness in America," *The Journal of American History* 74 (1988): 1213–38, here 1214–15.

28. Sephardic scholars of this era often signed their names with the phrase "*Sephardi tahor*" (pure Sephardi) and heraldic symbols are popular on early Sephardic gravestones and documents in the colonies.

29. Thomas Hubka, "A Spatial/Cultural Analysis of Jewish Communities in 17th–19th Century Poland" (The 13th Annual Conference of the Western Jewish Studies Association. Portland State University, Portland, March 18, 2007). Thomas Hubka, *Resplendent Synagogue: Architecture and Worship in an Eighteenth-century Polish Community* (Hanover, NH and London: Brandeis University Press by University Press of New England, 2003); Laura Leibman, "Sephardic Sacred Space in Colonial America," *Jewish History* 25 (2011): 13–41; Lee I. Levine, *The Ancient Synagogue: The First Thousand Years* (New Haven, CT and London: Yale University Press, 2005), 70.

30. For example when the 1782 Philadelphia synagogue was built, space was set aside for a *mikveh*; see Karen J. Spiegel, "A *Mikveh* in early 19th Century Philadelphia" (American Jewish Archives, 1978), 2. Edwin Wolf and Maxwell Whiteman, *The History of the Jews of Philadelphia* (Philadelphia: Jewish Publication Society, 1975), 140.

31. The only group that has distinct legal requirements for *mikva'ot* are Lubavitcher Hasidim. See my discussion of this issue in the section on the Suriname *mikva'ot*.

32. Another possible resource would be German *mikva'ot*; however, there were many fewer immigrants from Germany to the colonies during this era and they did not tend to control

the synagogues (or synagogue finances). For more on German *mikva'ot* see Georg Heuberger, ed., *Mikwe: Geschichte und Architektur jüdischer Ritualbäder in Deutschland* (Frankfurt am Main: Jüdisches Museum, 1992).

33. Abraham W. Rosenberg [Librarian, Ets Haim Library, Amsterdam], e-mail to author, March 18, 2008; Gawronski and Jayasena, "A mid-18th-century *mikveh*," 213–21.

34. For example, the medieval *mikva'ot* found in London and Speyer, Germany.

35. "From the 2nd Volume of the Minute Books of the Congn: Shearith Isreal in New York." *Publications of the American Jewish Historical Society* 21 (1913): 83. Indeed although it is usually forbidden to immerse by day, Rabbi Culi allows women to do so if the woman "*tiene miedo de entrar de noĉe en agua yelada, ke aze munĉo frío*" [is afraid to immerse at night in freezing cold water, that makes one very chilled]; see Kullí, *Me'am Loez*, Vol. 1, 168.

36. There are several possible explanations for this dual system. One is that the second pit is an *oẓar* (reservoir); however there is no connecting pipe between the two pits, as would be necessary. A second more likely explanation is that it may reflect the increased use of baths by men during this era due to the influence of *Kabbalah*. Although this dual system has not been found in the colonies, it was also found in the Great Synagogue *mikveh* in Amsterdam and the Amersfoort *mikveh* (the latter of which did have a connecting pipe, and hence may be an *oẓar* and a *mikveh* rather than two *mikveh* pools); Jerzy Gawronski, e-mail message to author, December 19, 2008.

37. Stefanie Hoss, *Baths and Bathing: The Culture of Bathing and the Baths and Thermae in Palestine from the Hasmoneans to the Moslem Conquest, with an Appendix on Jewish Ritual Baths (Miqva'ot)* (Oxford: Archaeopress, 2005), 33–6, 111–17; Lesches, *Understanding Mikvah*, 64; Gawronski and Jayasena, "A mid-18th-century *mikveh*," 213–21.

38. Slonim, ed., *Total Immersion*, 144, 203, 206–7. Some of the problems one is likely to encounter when immersing outdoors are as follows: (1) one is liable to get mud or pebbles between one's toes and thereby invalidate the immersion; (2) if one were to cut oneself on an object in the river (such as a stone) the immersion would be invalid; (3) changes in the level of a river due to rain or drought may invalidate the river for use as a *mikveh*; (4) it may be more difficult to insure that the person is completely submerged; (5) many Jews hold that if one sees an unclean animal when leaving the immersion site, one would have to immerse again. Rabbi Yaakov Culi, *Me'am Loez: The Torah Anthology*, tr. Aryeh Kaplan (New York: Moznaim, 1988), vol. 1, 150–2; Lesches, *Understanding Mikvah*, 38–9.

39. Culi, *Me'am Loez*, vol. 1, 150, 152.

40. Hoss, *Baths and Bathing*, 12.

41. This print was used in the 1783 Dutch edition of William Hurd's *A New Universal History of the Religious Rites, Ceremonies, and Customs of the Whole World*, in which Hurd used a comparative approach to world religions to show both that "religion is of the rational faculties" and differences between Christianity and the "absurd and inconsistent" ceremonies of other religions; see William Hurd, *A New Universal History of the Religious Rites, Ceremonies, and Customs of the Whole World: or, a Complete and Impartial View of all the Religions in the Various Nations of the Universe.* (London: n.p., [1780?]), iii.

42. Even the woman's husband would not be allowed to witness it.

43. Bushman and Bushman, "The Early History of Cleanliness in America," 1214–15; Culi, *Me'am Loez*, vol. 1, 149; Kullí, *Me'am Loez*, Vol 1, 166, 169.

44. Culi, *Me'am Loez*, vol. 1, 151; Kullí, *Me'am Loez*, Vol 1, 170.

45. Robert Blair St. George, "Witchcraft, Bodily Affliction, and Domestic Space in Seventeenth-Century New England," in *A Centre of Wonders: The Body in Early America*, ed. Janet Moore

Lindman and Michele Lise Tarter (Ithaca; NY: Cornell University Press, 2001), 13–27, here 19; Culi, *Me'am Loez*, vol. 1, 130–1.

46. It is forbidden to say the name of God while one is naked; see Hoss, *Baths and Bathing*, 74. However, God's name forms part of the blessing that must be said upon immersions. There are several ways that women get around this prohibition: some say the blessing just prior to immersion while wearing a robe, while others cross their arms under their chest and/or cover their head. Culi suggests that Sephardic women in the eighteenth century placed the cloth over their breasts (*"se kobizará el peco kon algún dimalo"*) while in the *mikveh* before reciting the blessing; see Culi, *Me'am Loez*, vol. 1, 151; Kullí, *Me'am Loez*, Vol. 1, 170.

47. Hoss, *Baths and Bathing*, 109, 110 fn. 84. Another extreme example of the disparity between spiritual and physical cleanliness was the early *mikveh* in Philadelphia: congregant Jonas Phillips, for example, threatened to remove his children from the Jewish school next door if the stench from the *mikveh* couldn't be controlled; see Spiegel, "A *Mikveh* in early 19th Century Philadelphia," 3; Wolf and Whiteman, *The History of the Jews of Philadelphia*, 258.

48. Culi, *Me'am Loez*, vol. 1, 150; Lesches, *Understanding Mikvah*, 43

49. Hoss, *Baths and Bathing*, 12. Although today some Sephardic women hold "*mikveh* parties" for brides, it would be unusual for an unnecessary woman to know about the time of immersion for another woman during her a regular menstrual cycle. It is possible that since a servant would have been required to draw the bathwater at home, she would have known about the immersion anyway.

50. Kullí, *Me'am Loez*, Vol. 1, 171.

51. In addition since the time of the original publication of this article a *mikveh* was found in Coro Venezuela. Although archeologists originally estimated the date to be the mid-1770s, historical evidence suggests the 1820s is more likely the earliest date. In addition, remains of a structure that appears to be a *mikveh* were found in Jodensavanne, Suriname.

52. I am grateful to Eric Leibman for first making this point.

53. *Shulkhan Arukh*, 120:14.

54. Larry Rohter, "Recife Journal; A Brazilian City Resurrects Its Buried Jewish Past," *New York Times*, May 19, 2000, A4. "Jewish Community of Recife, Brazil." *Beth Hatefutsoth*. http://www.bh.org.il/. Arquivo Historica Judaico Brasileiro, Nachman Falbel, and Francisco Moreno-Cavalho. *A Fenix, Ou, O Eterno Retorno: 460 Anos Da Presenca Judaica Em Pernambuco* (Brasília: Publicações Monumenta—Ministerío da Cultura, 2001), 227.

55. Jonathan Israel and Stuart B Schwartz, *The Expansion of Tolerance: Religion in Dutch Brazil (1624-1654)* (Amsterdam: Amsterdam University Press, 2007), 27.

56. Rabbi Avraham HaCohen Soae, *The Kosher Kitchen*, tr. M. Steinberger (Benei Berak, Israel: Bene Aharon, 1996), Vol 2., 183–5.

57. "In 1680, the Jews were about 2.5 percent of the white population; they reached about 3 percent in 1750, the year the Jewish population was between 400 and 500 souls"; see Mordechai Arbell, *The Jewish Nation of the Caribbean: The Spanish-Portuguese Jewish Settlements in the Carribean and the Guianas* (New York: Gefen, 2002), 192–6, 199.

58. Karl Watson, e-mail message to author, March 18, 2008.

59. Karl Watson, e-mail messages to author, March 18, 20, and 22, 2008.

60. Volders, *Bouwkunst in Suriname*, 81. The *mikveh* in Amersfoort (Holland) was similarly used from 1737 to 1943; "Amersfoort," Jewish Historical Museum, http://www.jhm.nl/. Although it may seem surprising that a ritual bath would be used for so many years, the *mikveh* in

Friedberg, Germany was in use from around 1260 until the early nineteenth century, and then was reactivated from 1875 to 1939; "Mikwe in Friedberg (Hessen)," http://wapedia.mobi/de/Judenbad_(Friedberg).

61. Since the publication of this article, Yonatan Adler has argued that previous archeologists have misidentified ancient structures previously thought to be examples of *oʒar*. He dates the earliest *oʒar* to nineteenth-century Europe. If he is correct, this suggests the Surinamese *oʒar* is a later addition. Yonatan Adler, "The Myth of the Osar in Second Temple-period Ritual Baths: An Anachronistic Interpretation of a Modern-era Innovation." *Journal of Jewish Studies* 65/2 (2014): 263–83

62. Toward the end of the twentieth century the aboveground immersion pool was split into a pool and *oʒar*, and the connection to the belowground *oʒar* was eliminated.

63. Rabbi Berel Wein notes that "*Bor al gabei bor* is mentioned in early *Rishonim*, especially the Raavad in Baalei Hanefesh." E-mail to author, June 2, 2008.

64. I would like to thank Morris Engelson for first pointing out to me the advantage of the pit on top of a pit design for eliminating sediment in areas with brackish water; Culi, *Me'am Loez*, vol. 1, 150; Kullí, *Me'am Loez*, Vol. 1, 169.

65. John Gabriel Stedman, *Narrative of the Five Years Expedition against the Revolted Negroes of Surinam*, ed. Richard and Sally Price (Baltimore: Johns Hopkins University Press, 1988), xiv. Gordon K. Lewis, *Main Currents in Caribbean Thought: The Historical Evolution of Carribean Society in Its Ideological Aspects, 1492–1900* (Baltimore: Johns Hopkins University Press, 1983), 109.

66. Jane Gomes Casseres, *Generation to Generation: The Continuing Story of Congregation Mikvé Israel-Emanuel 1963–2000* (Amsterdam: Drukkerij Arno van Orsouw, 2003), 118; Arbell, *The Jewish Nation of the Caribbean*, 134.

67. Arbell, *The Jewish Nation of the Caribbean*, 165.

68. Gomes Casseres, *Generation to Generation*, 118. While rainfall is common throughout the year in Amsterdam, in some locations such as Curaçao the average yearly rainfall is only 570 mm (22 inches). Twenty-odd inches would not have been sufficient for a rainwater *mikveh*. The predilection for using the underground water source is undoubtedly due to necessity in locations such as Curaçao; however, the community also interpreted the water symbolically. When the synagogue's construction crew struck water in 1730, the community recorded the event and held a ceremony; see *Our "Snoa": 5492–5742* (Curaçao: Congregation Mikvé Israel-Emanuel, 1982), 22. Even if completely filled, the *mikveh* would have been 17–20 inches shallower than Rabbi Culi recommends: the length would have allowed women to immerse length-wise, however, eliminating this problem.

69. Most of the Jewish poor shipped to St. Eustatius were Ashkenazim (Eastern European Jews). In fact the island had a large proportion of Ashkenazim, but they did not control the Synagogue rites; see Arbell, *The Jewish Nation of the Caribbean*, 174, 176. Robert Cohen, *Jews in Another Environment: Surinam in the Second Half of the Eighteenth Century* (Leiden: E.J. Brill, 1991), 19–21, 24–5, 28–9; Johan Hartog, *The Jews and St. Eustatius* (Philipsburg: Privately Printed, 1976).

70. Hoss, *Baths and Bathing*, 115.

71. Gilmore, "Recovering Jewish Heritage on St. Eustatius," 8–9; R. Grant Gilmore, III, Gay Soetekouw, and Carol MacHendrie, "St. Eustatius Synagogue Project Restoring Honen Dalim" (unpublished report, 2008).

CHAPTER 5
EARLY AMERICAN JEWRY AND THE QUEST FOR CIVIL EQUALITY
Eli Faber

The year: 1761. The place: Newport, Rhode Island. The event: Two Jewish merchants, one of them, Aaron Lopez, well on his way to becoming Newport's wealthiest man, and colonial America's most successful Jewish businessman, apply for naturalization. They do so on the basis of a law enacted by the British Parliament in 1740, a statute that authorized the naturalization of foreigners, Jews included, who resided in the colonies for seven years. Let us be precise about one thing: Britain's 1740 naturalization act did not confer citizenship on Jews. That is, the form of naturalization that it bestowed did not include the right to vote or to serve in office; but it was nonetheless worth obtaining because it lifted trade restrictions that applied to resident aliens. And so, the two foreign-born Rhode Island Jews, one of them a prominent refugee from Portugal, applied for naturalization, only to be rebuffed, first by the colony's legislature and then by its high court. The reason the two bodies gave for highhandedly flouting an act of Parliament—the colony certainly had no authority to supersede Parliamentary legislation—was that Rhode Island, both legislature and court averred, had been established for "the free and quiet enjoyment of the Christian religion and a desire of propagating the same." Thwarted by such reasoning in their own colony, the two merchants briefly took up residence in other colonies, one in New York, the other in Massachusetts, where they applied for and promptly received naturalization. If any colony in British North America had originated for the purpose of advancing the cause of Christianity, it was Massachusetts, while Rhode Island had originated as a haven for religious dissenters, and had institutionalized religious toleration, even for Jews, in the mid-seventeenth century.[1]

Musing later on this incident, the Reverend Ezra Stiles, a prominent Newport clergyman, a future president of Yale, and an intimate friend of one of the rebuffed merchants, reflected in his diary on what had occurred, and penned the following statement, one that is highly relevant to the theme of the present volume:

> Providence seems to make everything to work for mortification of the Jews, and to prevent their incorporating into any nation; that thus they may continue a distinct people ... The opposition it has met with in Rhode Island, forebodes that the Jews will never become incorporated with the people of America any more than in Europe, Asia, and Africa.[2]

Insofar as the Reverend Stiles was concerned, there was no difference between America and Europe with regard to what he called "the incorporation of the Jews." In contemporary

European societies, of course, Jews were defined as permanent outsiders, members of another nation, one that would always be separate from the nations in whose midst they resided. There was no crossing the boundary, and hence Jews could not become citizens by meeting residency requirements, by paying fees, or by taking an oath of allegiance; consequently, they could never obtain the right to vote or to serve in public office. Others in European society who belonged to this category of permanent outsiders included Gypsies, while in what eventually would become the United States of America, Native Americans would likewise be defined as members of separate nations. Indians did not become citizens of the United States until 1924; they were referred to as the Navaho Nation, the Iroquois Nation, and so forth, and because they belonged to foreign nations, the US government concluded treaties with them, as it did with nations that lay abroad. And as far as the Reverend Ezra Stiles could foretell, the status of Jews as outsiders would never change, not even in America.

The fact is, of course, it did change, almost everywhere by 1820, or within two generations of Stiles's prediction. It would begin to change, too, in Europe, in 1791, with the advent of the French Revolution, although the "incorporation" of the Jews—defining them as members of the nation rather than as permanent outsiders, bestowing citizenship, and incorporating them within the body politic in practical terms by conferring the rights to vote and serve in public office—in short, emancipation—would take much longer in Europe than it did in America, stretching across much of the nineteenth century. Moreover, in America, the Jewish population would itself press for incorporation. And this leads me to pose a question to historians of European Jewry, to wit: to what extent did Jews in Europe make the case for emancipation, for inclusion in the political body? To what extent did they feel secure and comfortable enough to press openly for the right to become citizens? Did emancipation in Europe come primarily, if not exclusively, because it was conferred, because it was granted from on high, as it were? Or as in the American case, did the Jews in effect demand, however politely they may have put their case, equality in the civic realm? I do not mean to imply that the Jewish population of early America achieved incorporation entirely on their own. In the highly influential case of Virginia in 1785, and in Connecticut and Massachusetts, in 1818 and 1821, respectively, Jews were not significantly present, and they did not figure in the discussions and debates that led to the elimination of religion as a requirement for civic equality.[3] In other settings, however, they did speak out—and this may be one of the most interesting of the contrasts between European and American societies during the era of emancipation on the two continents.

Throughout the early and mid-eighteenth century, the condition of the Jewish population in the British colonies already differed profoundly in one key respect. Anti-Semitism, while it certainly existed through the perpetuation of traditional stereotypes, did not take the violent forms it sometimes did in Europe, nor did it encompass the kinds of economic restrictions and legal disabilities that prevailed in many European jurisdictions. Jews could reside anywhere; they owned land; they engaged in retail trade; and they could (and did) become artisans and craftsmen. Because the general environment was a benevolent one, one in which toleration prevailed, Jews and Christians established business partnerships, formed personal friendships, summered together, belonged to the same Masonic lodges, and even on occasion fell in love and married one another.[4] Furthermore, in contrast to certain restrictions on economic enterprise in the mother country—although England, itself, stood out as quite benevolent, according to contemporary Jewish observers who contrasted it favorably with the Continent[5]— colonial legislatures bestowed commercial privileges upon Jews. In 1754 in Rhode Island, for example, the legislature conferred a ten-year monopoly upon a Jewish merchant who had petitioned for the right to produce potash using a secret process. In South Carolina, a Jewish inhabitant held the vitally important position of inspector-general of indigo for a decade, sorting and certifying the quality of that crop harvested for export. Indigo, at the time, was an important element in the colony's economy.[6]

There was, however, one area to which toleration and acceptance did not extend: the political—with one exception described below. Jews in the British colonies had no civic existence; they could not vote or serve in public office. In America, too, therefore, they were in effect regarded as members of a separate nation; they were not included within the body politic. There is no evidence to suggest they served as advisors to members of the raucous political factions that salted life during the American colonial era, or marched in the riotous crowds that sometimes formed for political action, or participated in public debates regarding policy. Not yet citizens, they sat on the sidelines; to our knowledge, they did not express political preferences or take public stands. Public policy, office in government, and political activity was the one sector in which colonial-era Jews did not mix with other colonial Americans.

But there did exist one exception: the colony of New York, especially New York City— but apparently the Reverend Ezra Stiles did not know about the latter. For reasons unknown, New York took steps to "incorporate" its Jewish population well in advance of any other jurisdiction in the Western world. Remarkably, as early as 1715, the colony approved legislation that offered naturalization to any foreigner in the colony who owned real estate. Thirteen Jews were naturalized under this law before Parliament enacted its own naturalization law in 1740. Then too, New York City admitted Jews to the status of "freeman," eliminating religious qualifications for it, retaining only the gender requirement (men only) and a small property test. Freemanship permitted one to vote in municipal elections. Between 1688 and 1770, fifty-seven Jewish New Yorkers became freemen; and we know for certain that they voted. They did so even in elections for seats in the colony legislature, until barred on grounds of religion by a statute enacted in 1737 as a result of a disputed election that year. Thereafter, however, they continued to vote in municipal elections. Finally, and most astonishingly of all for the period in which this occurred, they served as constables in New York City. This actually placed them in positions of authority over Christian New Yorkers, for constables, pre-modern policemen, albeit highly amateurish as law-enforcement officers, served warrants, made arrests, kept the peace, walked the night watch in the city, and were responsible for monitoring vice, Sabbath violations, and excessive drinking in taverns.[7]

But New York City, as mentioned, was the exception to the rule. Everywhere else in England's mainland colonies, the prevailing European concept that Jews did not belong to and could not become part of the community's public life prevailed. Nor did America's Jews challenge the status quo. No doubt they knew that any attempt to do so would be decisively rebuffed. This is what occurred in 1750 in Jamaica, England's most important colony in the Caribbean, which had a larger Jewish population than in any of the mainland colonies, when one Abraham Sanches petitioned the island's legislature for the right to vote on the grounds that he owned a large tract of land and had been naturalized. The reaction was swift and it was uncompromising. Kingston's Christian inhabitants counter-petitioned that the Jews had "renounced their right of government to the governor, Pontius Pilate, in favour of the Roman emperors, in order to destroy, and put to the most cruel and ignominious death, Jesus Christ, the lord and saviour of mankind." In another petition, the Christian residents of the parish of St. Catherine, the location of the island's capital, cited another well-established truism: that Jews were not loyal to the societies in which they resided. As the protesters wrote: "The Jews are a foreign nation . . . and pay no voluntary obedience to our laws; but on the contrary, abhor both them and our religion . . . To admit a nation, under such circumstances, to exercise a share in the legislature . . . might be destructive to our religion and constitution." Needless to say, Abraham Sanches's petition quickly died. In view of the fact that the Jews of North America were in constant contact with the Jews of Jamaica, it is entirely reasonable to suppose that they knew about this abortive attempt to enter the political order.[8]

With the advent of the American Revolution, however, Jews in America began to behave in a strikingly different manner. They began to comport themselves as if they actually had a role to play in public life; for them, in other words, the Revolution precipitated a revolution. One senses in them an interest in political expression that for years had been of necessity self-repressed but that emerged finally when circumstances permitted. And this occurred everywhere—not just in New York City, where the Jewish population had already enjoyed political inclusion, even if only on the municipal level, for several decades. In Philadelphia, the new assertiveness was manifest as early as 1765, when several Jewish merchants signed the non-importation agreement, with its pledge to boycott all English merchandise. In Savannah, Georgia, the city's committee for revolutionary activities included two Jews who played highly visible roles; one served as its chairman, no less. In nearby Charleston, South Carolina, Francis Salvador was elected to the colony's first and second provincial congresses between 1773 and 1776, despite the fact that Jews had not yet been "incorporated" there. Salvador played a highly visible role by serving on several of the congresses' committees, helping to draft South Carolina's first state constitution (which, by the way, required a Christian oath in order to vote and serve in office), and by sitting in the new state legislature after independence had been declared.[9]

Nor were these declarations of political choice limited to just a few. Throughout the new nation, most Jews took sides in the struggle, declaring themselves in most cases for the American side, but in some cases for the British. Many who supported the American side in the struggle abandoned their homes and businesses when their towns fell under British control, and crossed over behind American lines. Many of Newport's Jews left for Massachusetts, most of New York's for Connecticut and Philadelphia, Savannah's for

Charleston, and when the latter fell to the British, most of the Jewish population there, Savannah's as well as Charleston's, also made for Philadelphia, which thus became a national gathering place for the country's Jews, a great proportion of whom ended up there during the course of the hostilities. In turn, when Philadelphia fell into British hands, they retreated from it into the interior, toward western Pennsylvania. Leaving their places of origin was not a sign of cowardice, for had they remained they would not have been molested by the British. Rather, it amounted to a declaration of political affiliation, as it did for the smaller number of Jews who backed the British and remained in Newport and New York.[10] Furthermore, Jews who supported the American side demonstrated their commitment even more vividly by volunteering for military service. Approximately one hundred fought in the Continental army or the state militias.[11] Openly taking a political stand could take no more vivid form.

The American Revolution, therefore, was a decisive turning point, with the Jewish inhabitants of the colonies publicly taking political stands for the first time anywhere in the Western world by declaring either for England or America. They need not have done so. According to the well-known formulation attributed correctly or incorrectly to John Adams, one-third of the population supported the American side during the struggle with Great Britain, one third-remained loyal to the Crown, and the remaining third elected to sit on the fence—and the latter were not made to suffer for their neutrality.[12] Without penalty, recriminations, or untoward consequences, America's Jews could easily have chosen to stand aloof from the conflict between the colonies and the mother country, to maintain their civic non-existence. The Revolution, therefore, represents a watershed in the history of the Jewish people in America, as it consequently does for Western Jewry everywhere; it proved to be a milestone in the shift from outsider status to membership in the civic order, doing so, as we shall see, by providing ammunition for making the claim to equal citizenship.

Why, then, did they choose to involve themselves, if neutrality would have served them well? They were probably permitted to do so because each side in the contest could use as much support as it could get. But did they recognize in the Revolution an opportunity to set the stage for a demand for civic inclusion, for the neutralization of religion as a requirement for membership in the political order? The records and sources that have come down to us do not provide anything that illuminates their motives; it would be too much to argue, therefore, that they planned it that way. But the sources demonstrate that, following the Revolution, the Jewish population did press for inclusion, citing their loyalty and service to America during the conflict. The Revolutionary experience, in other words, became the justification for the "incorporation," whose seeming impossibility the Reverend Ezra Stiles had lamented. Significantly, the rhetoric they employed did not center around natural rights, but rather their record during the Revolution.

Despite the heady talk about the natural rights of man before and during the Revolution, and the equality of all men, as well as the definition of the struggle as one to secure the civil rights and liberties of Englishmen, twelve of the thirteen state constitutions adopted during the course of the conflict prescribed religious tests for voting and serving in office. Again there was only one exception: New York State's constitution, adopted in 1777, prohibited any religious test for voting and serving in office, and this not just in New York City but throughout the state.[13] In all other twelve states, however, the old order was still the rule, as new state constitutions included Christianity among the qualifications for political participation. The country's Jewish population reacted by speaking out assertively, even confrontationally. When the officers of the Jewish congregation of Philadelphia protested in 1783 against the clause in the Pennsylvania state constitution that required members of the legislature to swear that the Old and the New Testament were divinely inspired, a requirement that obviously disbarred Jews, they pointed to their affiliation with the American cause during the recent struggle. As they wrote to the relevant state officials,

> The conduct and behavior of the Jews in this and the neighboring states has always tallied with the great design of the revolution; that the Jews of Charleston, New-York, New-Port and other posts, occupied by the British troops, have distinguishedly suffered for their attachment to the revolution principles ... The Jews of Pennsylvania in proportion to the number of their members, can count with any religious society whatsoever, the whigs among either of them; they have served some of them, in the continental army; some went out in the militia to fight the common enemy.[14]

Pennsylvania's officials did not respond positively to this representation on behalf of equal citizenship. But a major breakthrough did occur a little more than a year later, in Virginia, where, in 1785, with the way charted by Thomas Jefferson, the Virginia legislature proclaimed religious freedom, disestablished the Episcopalian (formerly the Anglican) church, and abolished all religious tests for participation in public life. Virginia thereby joined New York in extending citizenship to all its inhabitants. Jews did not play a part in this vitally important development—only a handful were present in the state—underscoring that emancipation in early America hardly occurred solely because of Jewish initiative; the ideology and the principles that emanated from the Revolution did count, too, after all. And in the light of this dramatic development, the nation's Jews continued to make the case for inclusion based upon their contributions to the Revolution. Thus, a year after the Virginia statute for religious freedom went into effect, one of Philadelphia's Jewish leaders undertook to contact the men who were meeting behind closed doors in Philadelphia during the summer of 1787 to create the Constitution of the United States, in order to make the case for ending their status as permanent aliens. As he wrote to them,

> It is well known among all the Citizens of the 13 united states that the Jews have been true and faithful whigs, & during the late Contest with England ... [were] foremost in aiding and assisting the states with their lifes and fortunes, they have supported the cause, have bravely fought and bled for liberty, which now they can not enjoy.[15]

In time, the Constitution would emerge with its clause prohibiting religious tests for office under the federal government. But what about the remaining eleven states in which Jews were yet barred from having a political existence? Here, too, in many cases the Jewish population made a stand.

An unparalleled opportunity to do so occurred when George Washington visited Newport, Rhode Island, in the summer of 1790. The small Jewish congregation that remained there after the Revolution wrote to him as he neared the town, thereby initiating what is undoubtedly the most important exchange of letters in American Jewish history between a president and the Jewish population. The incident is more than sufficiently well-known because of Washington's assertion that the government of the United States "to bigotry gives no sanction, to persecution no assistance," a line in the congregation's letter that Washington's secretary lifted and worked into the president's reply.[16]

Few, however, realize how important this episode was in furthering the cause of Jewish inclusion in the body politic, thanks to other wording cleverly, but appropriately, included by Newport's Jewish inhabitants. In their letter to the president, they wrote that, throughout the course of history, Jews had been denied, in their words, "the invaluable rights of free citizens," but, in a reference to the new federal government, there now fortunately existed "a Government . . . deeming every one, of whatever nation, tongue or language equal parts of the great governmental machine." Here, indeed, was an assertion of that to which they aspired: "every one, of whatever nation . . . equal parts of the great governmental machine," rather than relegation permanently to the sidelines. It was a government under which "all [have] liberty of conscience and immunities of citizenship." And in his reply, as his secretary shaped it, Washington closely repeated that phrase, writing that "all possess alike liberty of conscience and immunities of citizenship," thereby, in that short phrase, gathering the Jews of America under the mantle of equal citizenship. By implication, the hero of the Revolution, the father of the nation, could be said to have supported the case for Jewish emancipation, thereby becoming the first head of state in the emerging modern world to do so, employing the word "citizenship" in connection with Jews. But what is most significant in the background to this critical breakthrough is the initiative taken by the Jews of Newport that created the opportunity for Washington to respond as he did. Did this happen fortuitously—or did Newport's handful of Jews with forethought shape the opportunity? There is no way to know; but the context—the fact that America's Jews had already for some time been openly making the case for political inclusion—suggests that their letter to the president was part of an ongoing program to revolutionize the position of the new nation's Jews in the larger community.

Whatever the circumstances behind the exchange of letters in Newport may have been, opinion in several others states was swinging in any case to the side of civic equality. In the same year, 1790, that Washington visited Newport, South Carolina and Pennsylvania extended the right to vote and to serve in office to their Jewish inhabitants. Delaware did so in 1792, and Georgia followed suit in 1798. Inasmuch as this still left seven of the original thirteen states with religious qualifications for citizenship in their constitutions, Jewish spokesmen continued openly to press their case. In Maryland, for example, where Jews were beginning to settle in Baltimore, merchant Reuben Etting repeatedly submitted petitions to the legislature in the late 1790s and early 1800s, although emancipation would not come until 1826, and only after a lengthy, bitter struggle that began in 1818, a battle initiated and fought by non-Jews who subscribed to liberal principles. (Maryland, incidentally, was the only jurisdiction in which the "incorporation" of the Jews was fought out in the presence of overt anti-Semitism.)[17] In North Carolina, again a Jewish spokesman took a bold stand. In 1809, Jacob Henry, elected to the legislature, was challenged when he sought to take his seat, on the grounds that the state's constitution required an oath affirming the New Testament's divinity. Henry argued, successfully as it turned out, that he supported the principle that officeholders did have to subscribe to religious beliefs; but which beliefs could not be required.[18] Even more eloquently, in Charleston in 1816, Isaac Harby argued against barring anyone on the basis of religion from appointment to a position in government, in the process articulating a vision of America as a society in which equal inclusion and pluralism were bedrock principles: in which the equal incorporation of all under the umbrella of citizenship was the norm (though at the time, "all" meant only white males). Harby formulated his challenge to any religious test for government service, when Secretary of State James Monroe recalled the country's Jewish consul to Tunis, explaining that the Tunisians' religion (Islam) made a Jewish diplomat unacceptable there. In his reaction, Harby wrote to Monroe that Jews were

> by no means to be considered as a Religious sect, tolerated by the government; they constitute a portion of the People. They are, in every respect, woven in and compacted with the citizens of the Republic. Quakers and Catholics, Episcopalians and Presbyterians, Baptists and Jews, all constitute one great political family.[19]

Harby's was arguably the most eloquent formulation of all offered by a Jewish spokesman on behalf of the creed that all belong equally to the nation, that none could be excluded on the basis of religion, that all were incorporated, as Harby put it, in "one great political family." While it did not sway the Secretary of State, its significance lies in the mere fact that it could be uttered—that a Jewish individual in America could speak in this way to power and advocate the notion of political inclusion.

Jewish assertiveness about belonging to the political order began during the American Revolution and continued right through to Harby, with voting and service in office as the hallmarks of emancipation. A new world order had indeed emerged in the New World for the Jews of America. It is their assertiveness that, in retrospect, is so striking.

Notes

1. The other individual who sought naturalization was Isaac Elizer. The incident may be followed in its entirety in Stanley F. Chyet, *Lopez of Newport: Colonial American Merchant Prince* (Detroit: Wayne State University Press, 1970), 34–40. For the text of the naturalization act of 1740, see Morris U. Schappes, ed., *A Documentary History of the Jews in the United States, 1654–1875*, 3rd edition (New York: Schocken, 1971), 30.

2. Chyet, *Lopez of Newport*, 37–8. Stiles was a close friend of Lopez's; their association can be followed in ibid., *passim*.

3. On the elimination of religious requirements for political participation, see Stanley F. Chyet, "The Political Rights of the Jews in the United States: 1776–1840," in *Critical Studies in American Jewish History: Selected Articles from American Jewish Archives*, Vol. 2 (Cincinnati, OH and New York: American Jewish Archives and KTAV, 1971), 27–88.

4. For a discussion of the ease with which Jews in colonial America related to the non-Jewish majority, see Eli Faber, *A Time for Planting: The First Migration, 1654–1820* (Baltimore, MD and London: The Johns Hopkins University Press, 1992), 84–93.

5. Thus, for example, the observations of Moses Cassuto, a traveler from Florence who visited England in 1735: see Richard Barnett, "The Travels of Moses Cassuto," in *Remember the Days: Essays on Anglo-Jewish History Presented to Cecil Roth*, ed. John M. Shaftesley (London: Jewish Historical Society of England, 1966), 103–5.

6. Charles Reznikoff and Uriah Z. Engelman, *The Jews of Charleston: A History of an American Jewish Community* (Philadelphia: Jewish Publication Society of America, 1950), 23–33; Abram Vossen Goodman, *American Overture: Jewish Rights in Colonial Times* (Philadelphia: Jewish Publication Society of America, 1947), 51.

7. Leo Hershkowitz, "Some Aspects of the New York Jewish Merchant and Community, 1654–1820," *American Jewish Historical Quarterly* 66 (1976–77): 13, 16–18; Beverly McAnear, "The Place of the Freeman in Old New York," *New York History* 21 (1940): 418–30, here 419, 425; Goodman, *American Overture*, 111–12, 114. For the office of constable in colonial America, one may still consult profitably Carl Bridenbaugh, *Cities in the Wilderness: The First Century of Urban Life in America, 1625–1742* (New York: Capricorn, 1964), 63–4, 215–16, 374–5, and for examples of Jews who served as constables (or refused to do so after election to the position), see Leo Hershkowitz, ed., *Wills of Early New York Jews (1704–1799)* (New York: American Jewish Historical Society, 1967), 36, 56, 65, 75, 99, 118, 140.

8. Assembly of Jamaica, *Journals of the Assembly of Jamaica*, 14 vols. (Jamaica: Alexander Aikman, 1811–29), Vol. 4, 238, 246–7, 249; Samuel J. Hurwitz and Edith Hurwitz, "The New World Sets an Example for the Old: The Jews of Jamaica and Political Rights, 1661–1831," *American Jewish Historical Quarterly* 55 (1965–66): 37–56, here 42–5.

9. William V. Byars, *B. and M. Gratz, Merchants in Philadelphia, 1754–1798* (Jefferson City, MO: Hugh Stephens Printing, 1916), 14; Jacob R. Marcus, "Jews and the American Revolution: A Bicentennial Documentary," *American Jewish Archives* 27 (1975): 116–19, 124–5, 128–9; Samuel Rezneck, *Unrecognized Patriots: The Jews in the American Revolution* (Westport, CT: Greenwood, 1975), 23–4.

10. "Items Relating to Congregation Shearith Israel, New York," *Publications of the American Jewish Historical Society* 27 (1920): 31; Chyet, *Lopez of Newport*, 156–62; Byars, *B. and M. Gratz*, 20, 158; David De Sola Pool, *The Mill Street Synagogue (1730–1817) of the Congregation Shearith Israel* (New York: n.p., 1930), 56; Reznikoff and Engelman, *Jews of Charleston*, 50; Edwin Wolf and Maxwell Whiteman, *The History of the Jews of Philadelphia from Colonial Times to the Age of Jackson* (Philadelphia: Jewish Publication Society, 1957), 84; Morris A. Gutstein, *The Story of the Jews of Newport: Two and a Half Centuries of Judaism, 1658–1908* (New York: Bloch, 1936), 182; Ezra Stiles, *Literary Diary*, ed. F. B. Dexter, 3 vols. (New York: Scribner's 1901), Vol. 2, 29, 151.

11. Rezneck, *Unrecognized Patriots*, 21–66.

12. I am indebted to Professor Stephen J. Whitfield of Brandeis University for pointing out to me that there is no clear evidence that Adams ever made this statement. Despite this, its basic thrust, that the American population was deeply divided during the conflict, is accurate.

13. The relevant provision is the thirty-eighth article of *The Constitution of the State of New York* (Fishkill, NY: n.p., 1777).

14. Schappes, *Documentary History*, 65.

15. Ibid., 69.

16. The text of the correspondence is in ibid., 79–81.

17. For the entire history of the progressive emancipation of the Jews in the original thirteen states, see Stanley F. Chyet, "The Political Rights of the Jews in the United States: 1776–1840," cited above at note 3, and for the references here, especially 35–62. To follow the struggle in Maryland: Edward Eitches, "Maryland's 'Jew Bill,'" *American Jewish Historical Quarterly* 60 (1970–71): 258–79; and Joseph L. Blau and Salo W. Baron, eds., *The Jews of the United States, 1790–1840: A Documentary History* (New York: Columbia University Press, 1963), Vol. 1, 33–55, including Etting's petitions.

18. For the text of Henry's address to the North Carolina legislature, see Schappes, *Documentary History*, 122–5.

19. For the full text of Harby's correspondence, see Blau and Baron, *Jews of the United States, 1790–1840*, vol. 2, 318–23; for Harby see Gary P. Zola, *Isaac Harby of Charleston: Jewish Reformer and Intellectual* (Tuscaloosa, AL and London: The University of Alabama Press, 1994).

PART II
FINDING A "NEW ZION" IN AMERICA'S CIVIC CULTURE?

CHAPTER 6
GERMAN JEWS AND THE GERMAN-SPEAKING CIVIC CULTURE OF NINETEENTH-CENTURY AMERICA
Kathleen Neils Conzen

"It is too early," lamented Isidor Busch in 1849 as he announced the suspension of *Israels Herold*, his pioneer venture in Jewish-American German-language journalism, after only twelve issues. The newly arrived immigrant's effort to combine support for Jewish communal activities in America with commentary on European Jewish developments, literary offerings, and a neutral forum for discussions of reform had failed, he argued, because the American Jewish community was too divided and its literary talents still too undeveloped. But just before he was forced to suspend *Israels Herold*, Busch laid out a program for converting it into a very different kind of American Jewish journal. Committed to the twin principles of religion as self-cultivation (*Bildung*) and politics and public life as reflections of divine providence (*die göttliche Waltung*), his revamped journal would place expanded coverage of American Jewish affairs within the context of reporting on more general American conditions. A central goal was to speak from a Jewish viewpoint to non-Jews as well as Jews. He planned extensive coverage of European freedom movements, essays on Jewish history, editorials that would go beyond purely confessional concerns to address all the important issues of the day, and, of course, poetry and novels to entertain female readers. He proposed, in sum, a journal that would project a specifically Jewish voice into America's rapidly expanding German-language public arena.[1]

Busch soon turned his attention elsewhere and never succeeded in publishing this ambitious German-language Jewish journal of public commentary.[2] Nor did others ever fully take up his project. The Jewish press that emerged in mid-nineteenth-century America would be primarily neither German nor political. As historians of this press have noted, it would be mainly an English-language one for almost over-determined reasons. Jews in America came from a variety of linguistic traditions, including significant numbers of English speakers both long present in America and newly immigrated; Jews' economic niches encouraged rapid Americanization, and they had little reason to indulge in sentimental preservation of old world languages often themselves only recently acquired. It would also be primarily a religious press, reflecting the religious basis of collective Jewish identity, the pressing religious issues that confronted and divided Jews in America, and the constitutional grounds of freedom of religion and separation of church and state on the basis of which they claimed equality of rights in their new American homeland. Initially, at least, only when those constitutional rights were threatened, whether by Sunday closing laws, tax-supported Christian schools, or discriminatory treaties would an antebellum Jewish journal like Isaac Mayer Wise's widely circulated *Israelite* move aggressively into the public arena of national debate— and then primarily in English. For much of the century, in any case, Jewish numbers were too small to support a more broadly focused ethnic press that could compete with the English- or German-language weeklies and dailies to which American Jews could turn for news.[3] There would be, by one count, as many as forty-three German-language Jewish serials published in the nineteenth-century United States.[4] Some thirty-eight are identifiable in a book-length bibliography of all German-language American serials— most of them short-lived, many either mixed English and German or German supplements to English-language papers, most local and/or religious in focus. Only Wise's *Die Deborah*, initially a supplement to the *Israelite*, developed both longevity and a broader focus.[5]

Was there, then, no significant Jewish voice within mid-nineteenth-century America's rapidly expanding German-language arena of civic debate? And if there was, how can that voice be characterized, and what was its significance? The campaign to reconcile cultural difference with American democracy that was conducted within the country's nineteenth-century German-language public arena, this essay argues, lends particular significance to such questions regarding the Jewish role in its shaping. Jews, a brief look at several examples of editorial participation suggests, had an important presence even as they denied seeking an explicitly Jewish non-religious voice. Speaking within America's German-language public sphere—sometimes simply as Germans, sometimes identifiably as Jews—Jews helped shape a nineteenth-century discourse on assimilation, pluralism, and democracy that was as contentious and consequential as its better known twentieth-century counterpart.[6]

1

Questions concerning the Jewish role in America's mid-nineteenth-century German language print debates arise both from the distinctive character of the German immigrant press as it emerged at this time, and from the sustained debate conducted within it on the ability of a democracy to survive and thrive in the face of significant cultural differences among its citizens. The more than five million immigrants from German-speaking Europe who arrived in the United States between 1820 and 1900 made up nineteenth-century America's largest linguistic minority. By 1870, first-generation Germans comprised almost 9 percent of the nation's population, heavily concentrated in the rural states of the Midwest and the industrializing cities of the east; their proportion of the electorate was even higher, since their children inflated the numbers of the native-born.[7] The *Deutsch-Amerikanisches Journal für Buchdruckerkunst* estimated in 1873 that there were about six million German speakers and readers in the United States—about 16 percent of the total population.[8]

America's German-language press could trace its origins back to a monthly printed in Germantown, Pennsylvania in 1739. At the time of the constitutional debates in 1789 there were about a dozen German papers of widely varying quality. By 1837, a German-American commentator could identify, among a host of undistinguished publications, fifteen reasonably well-edited German-language weeklies serving descendants of the colonial Pennsylvania immigration, as well as eight major papers catering to the rapidly increasing new immigration from German-speaking Europe.[9] By the early 1840s, such weeklies were joined by the first monthly journals of opinion and literature, whose numbers, influence, and frequency of publication would increase in the following decade. By the mid-1840s, the largest of the German papers were moving to thrice weekly and soon to daily editions, and developing more systematic coverage of local, national and international news, drawing on well-informed correspondents in Europe, in Washington and New York, and in state capitals, as well as on exchange papers and bulletins from the new telegraph. In 1860 there were over 200 German-language newspapers and magazines in the USA—a number that would peak at about 800 near the end of the century. By 1880, eighty German dailies had a combined circulation of 448,000, and 466 weeklies counted over 1.3 million readers.[10] A 1973 effort to tabulate all German-language periodicals ever published in the USA came up with approximately 5,000 separate titles.[11]

This was by far the largest ethnic press in nineteenth- and early twentieth-century America, but it was distinctive in two other ways as well. First, as James Bergquist (and Carl Wittke before him) has observed, it was less an immigrant press than an American press published in the German language. Theorizing about the functions of the immigrant press, going back to Robert Park, has stressed that it provided needed information about the new homeland and events in the old, expressed group values and changing sense of identity, helped socialize readers to American life, and promoted group pride and power.[12] But America's German-language press was born and raised in the context of colonial-era political debates, and along with fulfilling the classic adaptive functions of an immigrant press, it aspired to the same kinds of broad-based coverage and public influence as its English-language counterparts; like them it quickly became a political press dependent on party subsidies, and responded to similar technological and journalistic innovations.[13] By the middle decades of the nineteenth century in many parts of the American north, a good quarter of the American electorate was probably reading, discussing, and forming its political opinions in this German-language public arena.

The development of this national arena for public debate and opinion formation is, then, the other distinctive characteristic of the German press that should be stressed. Particularly after the failure of the 1848 revolutions in Europe, a large cadre of educated, opinionated Germans took over many of the old, and established many new, journals. Their arrival coincided with the intensification of the slavery debate in the USA, the collapse of one party system and the emergence of another, and the ensuing crises of Civil War, emancipation, and national reconstruction. Many of these editors had already known one another in revolutionary Europe, and moved frequently from one newspaper to another in America; they constituted a well-integrated community of debate in which discussion ricocheted rapidly from one paper to the next across the country and back. Well-edited and widely circulated journals in cities like New York, Philadelphia, Cincinnati, and St. Louis were manufacturers and wholesalers of opinion, more local newspapers served as retailers, while consumers absorbed and discussed the product at their kitchen tables, in saloons and clubs, in debating societies and public mass meetings. In effect, German editors functioned for this immigrant community in a fashion similar to the editors of early national party papers who, Jeffrey Pasley has argued, in the course of their battles for circulation, found themselves crafting not only party positions but also a national identity for the new American republic.[14] What these immigrant German editors crafted in analogous fashion was not only German ethnic identity, but also a legitimation of ethnicity itself.

Educated German newcomers by the 1830s had been formed in a German environment where culture had been heavily politicized—where language, music, gymnastics, and simple sociability carried national and liberal connotations suppressed in the formal political realm. They arrived in an America which, despite its liberal cosmopolitan ideology, was in the midst of an aggressive campaign to define American identity and public culture in evangelical Protestant terms, drawing on both perfectionist millennial religious aspirations and a conviction that only the internal constraints of shared religious belief could restrain the excesses of democracy in a rapidly developing economy. Evangelicals quickly turned to government to achieve ends like temperance, Sunday observance, appropriately Protestant public schools, and—when immigrant voters helped oppose such efforts—a nativist project to restrict immigrant access to naturalization. Catholics were particular targets of nativist concern, but all immigrants were potentially affected by suffrage limitations, while restrictions on Sunday socializing and alcohol-enhanced conviviality directly attacked defining forms of German-American cultural expression. In reaction, a national German-language effort began to take shape by the later 1830s to formulate, for an external audience, a theoretically defensible and practically effective argument for the legitimacy and harmlessness of cultural difference within American democracy; to define for an internal German audience what the acceptable and indeed necessary contours of ethnic difference were and how best to maintain them; and then to work out which political party could make the best ally in the fight. By the mid-1850s, these efforts were coalescing into a coherent theory of cultural difference as an intrinsic component of personal liberty and equality of rights within a democracy, only to fragment again in subsequent decades under changing national pressures, increasing differentiation and assimilation within the German-speaking community, and new theories of racial distinctiveness.[15]

Where then were German-speaking Jews in these debates? Jews admittedly constituted only a small fraction of the immigration from German-speaking Europe, and the extent and significance of their involvement in America's German community remains a subject of scholarly debate.[16] Stanley Nadel, for example, cites the well-documented and prominent presence of Jews in German-American associational, cultural, and political life to argue for the "organic unity" of Jewish and non-Jewish German-speaking groups.[17] But Hasia Diner stresses that such involvement was often limited only to marginal cultural activities unavailable within the Jewish community, declined over time, and was in any case most attractive to the disaffiliated.[18]

The point at issue here, however, is neither how many nor how deeply Jews participated, but the nature and strength of the voice provided by those who did. A variety of factors could bring Jews who spoke German into this broader German-language civic space, even those whose primary commitments were to their Jewish co-religionists. Some were practical. There were large numbers of Germans who were potential customers for businessmen, voters for aspiring politicians, readers and pupils for journalists and teachers. The sheer appeal of language itself should also not be dismissed. The peculiar power of one's cradle language for the full integrity of self was a frequent subject of nineteenth-century German-American theorizing, and those Jews who grew up speaking German, and particularly those educated at German universities, were not immune to that appeal, no matter how competent in English they became. But above all, many modernizing Jews shared with other Germans a concept of *Bildung* embodied in bourgeois aspirations toward culture and sociability that only the broader German-speaking community was large enough to support.[19] Yet those same leisure-time social and cultural activities that drew Jews into close association with other German-speakers—music and drama, gymnastics, target-shooting, public festivity—brought them also into the cultural core of what came to define German ethnicity, and to fuel German efforts to develop and defend their theories of cultural pluralism.[20] Thus someone like Simon Wolf, a long-time leading figure of Washington, DC and indeed, through the B'nai B'rith, national Jewry, was also the city's acknowledged German-American leader for decades, and as prominent a figure in national German-American organizations as he was in Jewish ones.[21]

Jews in nineteenth-century America cultivated their public identity as a religious group, and as such a comparison with other religious groups among America's German speakers may provide a useful way to think about this Jewish role within America's German civic culture. For German speakers in America never constituted a homogeneous or cohesive community. Divided by region of origin, dialect, class, degrees of cultivation, and above all by often mutually antagonistic religious orientations, any unity they constructed was pragmatic, opportunistic, and cultural.[22] German-speaking Lutherans, like Jews, found English-speaking co-religionists already present in America, and shared their religion with other non-German-speaking immigrants. But for strongly confessional Lutherans, fellowship with those not in complete agreement on theological issues was impossible, and political activism undesirable among a people who felt themselves counseled by their Bible to obey constituted authority. Their choice, then, was one of continuing German usage but separation from the broader German-speaking public arena; only in the 1870s, with a rising second generation and increased American efforts to ban foreign-language parochial schools would they finally seek to project a specifically Lutheran voice within the broader German arena.[23] On the other hand, German Catholics, 30–40 percent of the whole in the mid-nineteenth century, already felt the need for a public voice in the face of nativist attacks, and differed sufficiently from their Irish co-religionists in culture that an English voice was not an option. Yet contemporary state efforts to marginalize the power of Catholicism in European civic life found their echo in German America, and by the 1850s German Catholics in America as in Europe were retreating into their own defensive milieus, with organizations and a press that paralleled—and quarreled with—those of other German Americans.[24] In effect, while secular Germans had both a presence and a voice in the German arena, and confessional Lutherans sought neither, Catholics in their parallel world withdrew their presence but spoke in a loud, distinctive voice. By contrast, it might be suggested, Jews may well have had a significant presence in that German arena—as members of German organizations, leaders of German-speaking constituencies, editors of German-language newspapers— even if they seldom sought to project within it an explicitly Jewish voice.

But was that voice necessarily uninflected by distinctive Jewish experience? Even Jews who chose to remain at least partially within the broader German-speaking community in America certainly understood the logic of those who rejected the discriminatory associations of their European countries of birth and insisted on complete Americanization. They brought to America their own intimate familiarity with German debates about the terms on which a minority could be incorporated into the body of the nation. For many, moreover, the move into the broader German-speaking world had been a relatively recent one, and unlike most other Germans they understood from personal experience or familial memory what cultural assimilation could involve—and the consequences of exclusion. Some might take heart that the process of cultural change could readily be repeated again in America, but others might desire all the more to retain the German cultural identity so hardly won. One important place to look for such Jewish-inflected German-American voices is among the Jewish journalists who wrote for America's German-language press, and Max Cohnheim can serve as a case study. But, as several briefer examples will also suggest, even the nation's explicitly Jewish press chose to engage in debates within the broader German-American arena more directly and frequently than is generally assumed.

2

It is, to be sure, difficult to estimate how many Jews wrote for, edited, or owned secular German-language newspapers in nineteenth-century America. Pioneers included Joseph Cohn, founder of two successful German newspapers in New Orleans between 1842 and 1853, and Moritz Loeb, for almost half a century a prominent spokesman for Bucks County's Pennsylvania Dutch as owner and editor of Doylestown's *Der Morgenstern*.[25] The ranks of Jewish German-language newspapermen ranged from well-known antebellum radicals like New York's Sigismund Kaufmann, editor of *Die Turnzeitung* (the official organ of the Turners) and contributor to the *New Yorker Staats-Zeitung*, Lewis N. Dembitz of Louisville's *Beobachter am Ohio*, and Moritz Pinner of Kansas City's *Missouri Post*, to lesser lights like Nehemiah Miller, proprietor of a post-Civil War Washington, DC German newspaper, and Conrad Jacoby, who established the *Süd-California Post* in Los Angeles in 1869.[26] Some of these editors may have had little or no affiliation with formal Jewish community life, but to the extent that they were raised within the Jewish tradition, they could well bring a distinctive Jewish perspective to issues facing this ethnic press.[27]

Max Cohnheim provides a case in point. With much of his career spent editing German-language journals of humor and political satire, he was admittedly atypical of

German-American journalists. Yet his witticisms were frequently quoted by others, and for a few critical years in the mid-1860s he was in a position of real influence as owner-editor of the only German-language newspaper in the nation's capital. Historians have encountered Cohnheim at various moments of his life in Europe and America, but his editorial voice gains coherence when his full biographical trajectory is traced. By 1848, no longer part of the traditional world of eastern European Jewry into which he was born, it was the revolutionary events of that year that would shape his life.

He came into the world as Marcus Raphael Cohnheim in 1826 in Fraustadt in Prussia's Grand Duchy of Posen, the youngest of seven children of a Jewish merchant and community leader whose German assimilation was affirmed by Prussian naturalization in 1833, shortly after the privilege was extended to qualified Posen Jews. The outbreak of revolution in March 1848 found young Max, as he was now known, a shop assistant by profession, reportedly doing his required year's military service with the Gardeartillerie in Berlin.[28] Already enjoying a certain reputation in the raucous, caustic world of Berlin popular humor, he quickly emerged as a popular revolutionary speaker, author of radical democratic broadsides, and co-editor of *Der Satyr: Blatt für offene Meinung und freies Wort*, whose first and only issue appeared on May 1.[29] A week later *Kladderadatsch*, another satirical political journal destined for far greater longevity and fame, made its first appearance, and although Cohnheim later claimed a role in its early authorial collective, by early July he was in flight to Switzerland to avoid prosecution for his revolutionary activities.[30]

From his Zürich exile, Cohnheim initiated a correspondence with Marx and Engels' *Neue Rheinische Zeitung*, but soon joined the revolutionary forces in neighboring Baden, and by November found himself detained with fellow revolutionaries in Bruchsal's formidable new prison and debating whether to accept American exile. Mob action forced open his prison in mid-May 1849 as revolution again crested in Baden, and Cohnheim saw renewed service as a military and deputy civil commissar. With the final collapse of the Baden revolution in July, he found refuge once again in Switzerland, this time in Geneva, where he and other comrades—the *Schwefelbande* ("little devils") they called themselves—soaked up cheap wine and lovely scenery, and even published a couple of issues of a satirical paper, *Rummeltipuff: Organ der Lausbubokratie*, complete with its editors' portraits on the masthead. Expelled from Switzerland in late spring 1850, Cohnheim and a Baden comrade arrived in Schleswig-Holstein in time to participate as volunteers in the bloody losing battle against the Danes at Idstedt in late July, and soon joined the large German refugee community in London. Here they gravitated to the anti-Marx circle of Baden revolutionary leader Gustave Struve, and from here, in late April 1851, they departed for New York.[31]

Much about Max Cohnheim's life in New York remains obscure, but it is clear that he saw in New York's large and vibrant *Klein Deutschland* a chance to recapture some of the excitement and opportunity of the Berlin that he had been forced to abandon. He soon attracted notice as a publicist for one of two not very scrupulous German firms competing for the lucrative business of forwarding German immigrants and their baggage westward from New York, and clerical and accounting jobs, including, by 1858, his own shipping agency, continued to provide a basic income.[32] But he kept equally busy honing his comedic skills on the makeshift stages of the Bowery, and on December 10, 1853, his three-act Berlin-style farce, *Fürsten zum Lande hinaus, oder die Schul' ist aus* opened at the St. Charles Theatre.[33] Cohnheim soon became the most successful of the dramatists writing Berlin- and Vienna-style farces and melodramas for antebellum New York's German stage. His farce *New York und Berlin, oder wo macht man am besten aus* reportedly earned about $4,000 in eleven New York performances in the spring of 1857, and more than $500 in one evening alone the following year; his plays were performed by German companies as far afield as New Orleans and San Francisco.[34] Equally popular were the operetta lyrics that he composed for the carnival masked balls of the Arion, one of New York's two leading singing societies.[35] He became an American citizen as soon as possible, threw himself into New York radical and reform politics and the new Republican Party, and found time to marry and father two daughters; his parents joined him in New York in 1855.[36]

But political satire seems to have remained his central ambition, and after a couple of abortive efforts to inaugurate a New York counterpart to Berlin's now successful *Kladderadatsch*, Cohnheim launched the *New Yorker Humorist: Illustrirte Wochenschrift für Humor, Satyre, Kunst und Belletristik* in late spring 1858 in partnership with Otto Brethauer, a political refugee from Franconia.[37] The four-page weekly combined light stories, sketches, and poetry with an opinionated summary of local, national, and European political developments; an overview of cultural news; reviews of concerts, plays, and operas; political and other cartoons; and bitingly humorous commentary on current events and social foibles. Cohnheim himself soon began touring as far west as St. Louis and as far south as New Orleans to present humor "soirees" to German audiences and collect *Humorist* subscriptions along the way. But the journal's finances remained insecure, and in late June 1859 Jacob Pecare, a New York Jewish pawnbroker and real estate speculator, took over its ownership while retaining Cohnheim and Brethauer as editors. Under the new regime, the outspoken news summary disappeared, while cultural coverage and fiction increased and satirical commentary continued unabated.[38]

At some point during the crisis leading up to the Civil War the *Humorist* ceased publication, and on June 6, 1861, the 35-year-old Cohnheim mustered in as a first lieutenant in Company F of the Forty-first New York Volunteer Infantry, the DeKalb Regiment, an elite all-German unit raised with support from prominent New York Germans. His Civil War participation was quite literally a continuation of his German fight for freedom: some 700 of the regiment's men, including its colonel, Leopold von Gilsa, were reportedly, like Cohnheim, veterans of the Schleswig-Holstein war, and twenty-three of its thirty-three field officers had, like him, seen European military service.[39] Initially detailed to construct fortifications around Washington, the regiment was assigned in early 1862 to the new all-German division commanded by Brigadier General Louis Blenker, an old comrade from Baden, and Cohnheim, now a captain, probably received his baptism of fire during the ill-conceived "mud march" into the Shenandoah Valley and the losing battle of Cross Keys that ended Blenker's military career. In the resulting reorganization, the Forty-first became part of a new Corps commanded by the popular German-American hero, Major General Franz Sigel, yet another Baden veteran. In late July, Cohnheim became one of Sigel's aides-de-camp, and seems to have remained with him through the season's disastrous Northern Virginia campaigns until the following spring when Sigel, upset at perceived anti-German discrimination, was maneuvered out of his command. Just days before Sigel's former Corps departed for what would become a deadly disaster for the German-American troops at Chancellorsville, Cohnheim resigned his commission and soon was ensconced in a Washington patronage position as a Treasury Department clerk. On October 17, 1863, the first issue of his new German weekly, *Columbia*, appeared, financed by two local German businessmen and printed on the press of a failed predecessor.[40]

Columbia began life as a literary and satirical journal very much in the *Humorist* mold, addressed particularly to wartime Washington's swelling numbers of German-speaking soldiers, civil servants, and military suppliers. But as the 1864 presidential campaign heated up, Cohnheim expanded his weekly news commentary into full newspaper coverage and aggressive support for Lincoln's reelection, while also taking an increasingly prominent role in the city's German and political life. He chaired the planning committees for German participation in the ceremonies after Lincoln's assassination, and for Washington's great Peace Festival for the benefit of sick and wounded German soldiers that followed; he was elected an honorary member of the *Turnverein*, and helped found the *Schützenverein*, Washington's leading German association for decades. With the end of the war, Cohnheim cut back *Columbia*'s political coverage, but retained the scathing satire of its humor page, directed increasingly now at President Andrew Johnson for betraying Lincoln's legacy. In March 1866 a German rival denounced him to the administration, and he was forced to resign his Treasury position. Without the benefit of a regular salary, he could not long sustain *Columbia* in the depressed postwar economy, and published his last issue on January 12, 1867. A month and a half later, buoyed by the proceeds of a special benefit performance of one of his plays in New York, he departed on a Panama steamboat for San Francisco.[41]

His San Francisco career can be quickly summarized. His wife and daughters had apparently been in California for several years by this time, and Cohnheim was soon able to again combine a patronage position (as an abstract clerk in the Court House) with editing and co-publishing a newspaper, the *San Francisco Abend Post*.[42] He threw himself into Republican and radical labor politics in this city with its significant German and Jewish population, but again encountered financial and legal problems. He left the *Abend-Post* in June 1870 to co-found the *Sonntags-Gast*, a belletristic and humorous weekly more like his previous ventures, and a year later established the long-lived San Francisco *Humorist*. Though he soon lost control of the journal, he remained associated with it for the remainder of his career while also pursuing his comedy interests.[43] Stalked by personal tragedy, he lost a daughter in 1870, his wife in 1876, and his left leg to a fall on a snow-covered San Francisco street in 1887; nine years later he died at the age of 70.[44]

Throughout his career, Max Cohnheim's public voice was primarily German rather than Jewish.[45] His humor, heavily dependent on wordplay and cultural conventions, would have translated poorly into English, while his political engagement, editorial livelihood, and comedic vocation all necessarily depended on the broader community of German-speaking voters, readers, and playgoers. His publications, in their humor as much as in their editorial commentary, participated fully in the broader Forty-Eighter project to rally German-Americans against American political corruption, Puritanism, and cultural crassness. The political convictions molded in his revolutionary youth continued to inform his editorial voice. But that voice may also have been inflected by his own outward movement from Posen's Jewish community into the boisterous popular culture of *Vormärz* Berlin in at least three respects: his light-handed inclusion of Jews and Jewish themes in the German-American community constituted by his journals, his stance toward American assimilation, and his skepticism toward *Deutschthümelei*— those overblown pufferies of the glories of German culture and the need for German recognition in America that were so much a part of German-American journalism, including that of his Washington predecessors and successors.

Fiercely anticlerical like so many Forty-Eighters, Cohnheim probably avoided Jewish congregational affiliation. Congregational doings of any religion found no coverage in *Columbia's* pages, in sharp contrast to the German newspapers that preceded and followed it in Washington (only one of them edited by a Jew), all of which gave as careful attention to Jewish as to Christian affairs, printing sermons and covering both religious and social events. Washington's Jewish literary society was well-reported in *Columbia* but never identified as Jewish. Yet Cohnheim found many of his own associates within the Jewish community, and was active, for example, in Washington's Jewish cultural and charitable endeavors. Simon Wolf, who worked closely with him in Washington, later included him in his catalog of Jewish Civil War officers. Cohnheim agreed to publicize and accept subscriptions for Isaac Mayer Wise's Jewish journals, and Wise returned the favor by praising his "humoristic lectures ... full of excellent humor, and not unfrequently of biting sarcasm, the spice of wit."[46] Jewish themes were as casually present as non-Jewish ones in the humorous and literary pieces he published.[47] More serious concern occasionally broke through, as when a report about a Patterson, New Jersey congregation's difficulty finding someone familiar with Jewish burial rites concluded, "Commentare sind überflüssig." Prussian rejection of a monument for the Jewish composer, Giacomo Meyerbeer, offered occasion for scornful reference to the controversy surrounding the election of a Jewish officer in a Baltimore singing society, while efforts of newly rich Jews to buy culture could provoke humorous but heartfelt poetic notice.[48]

If Jews were matter-of-factly present, without specific identification as such, in the German-American world shaped by Cohnheim's journals, the problem of assimilation received more sustained consideration. Cohnheim's three-year stint as a Treasury clerk suggests his own ability to function in an English-speaking setting. He reserved special and frequent comic scorn for the half-assimilated, for those who mixed English into their German and German into their English, who translated German idioms too literally, mis-heard English expressions, and misinterpreted American social conventions; he complained when English was spoken at German ethnic events.[49] His implicit message was that German immigrants had a duty to integrate fully into American life but also to respect and preserve the integrity of the German culture that had nurtured them. He was both a vigorous advocate for cultivating German literature, drama, and sociability within American cultural life (and an early defender of Wagner's new music), and an insistent proponent of active German participation in the American public sphere.[50] Assimilation in this model did not mean abandoning the best of the older culture, but it definitely meant mastering the new.

For Jews like Cohnheim, German experience may have provided a model for the feasibility of cultural assimilation, but it also bequeathed mistrust of German ethnic chauvinism. Cohnheim, who had fought for a free Germany, did not seem to share Isaac Mayer Wise's bitter judgment that the land of his birth "rejected me, I have no old fatherland."[51] The construction and maintenance of German community in America was a central task of Cohnheim's journals, with their coverage of German-American cultural and social events and their advertising from German-American businesses and associations. *Humorist* gave strong support to events like the 1859 Schiller festival that sought to raise the cultural standing of Germans in American eyes, and printed without comment John Bernhard Stallo's Humboldt festival speech emphasizing immigrants' duty to sow the seeds of German culture in American furrows. But at the same time it deplored the focus of so many German associations on wine, lager beer, and dance, and mocked the "genuine German persiflage" of celebrations that equated Gambrinus with the giants of German culture.[52] It was not only American realism gained on the Virginia battlefields that kept Cohnheim from joining other Forty-Eighters—*Radikalissimi*, he called them—in their quixotic 1864 effort to dump Lincoln from the Republican ticket as soft on slavery; he also used his stock Berlin alter ego, the master tailor Willem Schulze, to ridicule their pretensions to German cultural superiority.[53] *Sonntags-Gast* found a "peculiar charm" in a diverse San Francisco where immigrant communities, unlike in eastern cities, neither melted into American society nor kept themselves completely separate; even Chinese immigrant culture merited the journal's moderate defense.[54]

3

The muted Jewish sensibility in Max Cohnheim's German public voice seems to exemplify the segmented character of the Jewish presence within the German-American public arena, reflecting the sharp distinction between the religious role as Jew and the public role as citizen that Isaac Mayer Wise espoused for his co-religionists in America. But Jews—including Wise himself—could also choose to speak in that German ethnic arena with an explicitly Jewish voice. Most of the Jewish serials that opted to publish fully or partially in German did so for reasons internal to the Jewish community itself: in order to participate in a trans-Atlantic Reform dialogue, as in the case of David Einhorn's *Sinai* (Baltimore, 1856–63) and Moritz Ellinger's bilingual *The Jewish Times* (New York, 1869–77), or to speak to Jewish community members (women in particular) who were not yet fluent in English, as in the case of *Die Deborah* (Cincinnati, 1855–1902), the German-language supplement to Wise's *Israelite*. Some bilingual journals, like Philo Jacoby's *The Hebrew* (San Francisco, 1863–1921) clearly reflected their editors' personal involvement with German associational life, while Milwaukee's Reform journal edited by Adolph Moses and Isaac S. Moses, *Der Zeitgeist: Ein israelitisches Familienblatt* (1880–82), also expressed the assertive German ethnicity characteristic of that period and particularly of that city.[55] But whatever their differences, none of these journals, or others that might similarly serve as examples, aspired to the broader voice within the German-American community earlier proposed by Busch and achieved by publications of other German-speaking groups. They remained essentially journals of internal communication and religious discussion, or local community bulletin boards with infusions of Jewish history, literature, and instruction.

Nevertheless, it seems that few editors with German capability in place could resist launching Jewish viewpoints into the greater German-American sea of opinion when the occasion arose. From *Sinai*'s 1857 campaign against the discriminatory Swiss treaty to *Der Zeitgeist*'s 1881 protests against anti-Semitism in the German-American press, defense of Jewish interests was a central motive for editorial engagement with the broader German-speaking community.[56] Thus Moritz Ellinger, who usually reserved the German section of *The Jewish Times* for serious religious discussion, literary contributions, and occasional B'nai B'rith news, publishing most other news and commentary in English, moved quickly to German when it was a matter of defending Sigismund Kaufmann, recently nominated as Republican candidate for lieutenant governor of New York, against the "religious hate" of some German-American journals.[57]

But editors of Jewish journals could also use their German pages to contribute to broader ethnic discussions as members of the German-American community, and to bring those discussions back into the Jewish arena. While Philo Jacoby, San Francisco's famous Jewish champion sharpshooter, wrestler, and weightlifter, published most of his religious material as well as city news, political commentary, and local and national Jewish news in English, he used his German pages not only for material lifted liberally from European papers but also for extensive coverage of the local German sporting and theatrical scene in which he and numerous other San Francisco Jews participated. When he wanted to comment approvingly on a California court ruling that exempted household items needed to practice "the Mosaic dispensation" from executions for debt, he chose the English appropriate for Jewish discussion and for reprinting in both California English-language newspapers and other Jewish journals. But when he wanted to speak out forcefully against the Puritanism, nativism, temperance fanaticism, and Sabbatarianism that he saw infecting the Republican Party, he used a German that could be picked up readily by German-American exchange papers and influence fellow German voters.[58] In New York, Ellinger, a long-time B'nai B'rith leader, was equally involved in German social and political life, holding a series of public offices in the German interest. During the period of heightened German awareness surrounding the Franco-Prussian War, he used the English pages of *The Jewish Times* to laud German sociability, intellectuality, and civilization, urge the teaching of German in the public schools, and promote political reform as a German-American mission; at the same time, he printed occasional German speeches, usually by Jews, exploring the role of Germans in America. In effect he advocated an identity that was Jewish in religion, German in ethnicity, and American in nationality and politics.[59] A decade later, at a time of renewed German anti-Semitism, growing Jewish immigration from Slavic Europe, and reviving American nativism, the *Zeitgeist*'s repeated consideration of the relationship among racial, national, ethnic, and religious identities fed into an increasingly urgent German-American conversation about the probabilities of maintaining ethnicity itself in America.[60]

But no editor interjected specifically Jewish perspectives into the German-American public arena more repeatedly and skillfully than Isaac Mayer Wise himself. For all his insistence that *Die Deborah* was simply an accommodation to (particularly female) linguistic weakness and a means to inform European Jews about American Jewry, Wise took clear linguistic delight in his German organ, and quickly abandoned his vow to avoid polemics; indeed by 1868, he was willing to admit publicly not only that *Die Deborah* provided an outlet for men who expressed their thoughts best in German, but that it also allowed him to say things that should not be said to an English-speaking public.[61] He established an extensive set of exchanges with other German-American papers, and monitored them carefully for inaccuracy or insult toward Jews. He engaged in frequent controversy with German-American radicals about their extremism, contempt of religion, and scorn for non-abolitionist Jews. But he also joined their campaigns against German Catholic editors and Yankee nativists, Sabbatarians, and temperance fanatics, and recruited their support on Jewish issues like the Swiss treaty or the proposed Christian amendment to the Constitution. He was shy neither about requesting that other German-American papers reprint his articles, nor about recommending and reprinting theirs.[62] His advocacy of German schools and encouragement for German theater and music forged further links to other German speakers.[63] But most importantly, *Die Deborah*'s repeated inquiries into the religious basis of Jewish identity, its relationship to ethnicity and citizenship, and its links to language and culture, became part of analogous explorations of the boundaries of ethnic allegiance within the broader German-American public arena, carried into that arena not only on the printed page, but through the ideas and words of *Die Deborah*'s Jewish readers who also identified as German-Americans. When Wise probed the emotional resonance of speaking one's mother tongue, when he insisted on linguistic unity as a necessity for American nationhood, when he pointed to the rapid Americanization of the second generation, or when he assessed the consequences of group separation from the national mainstream, he was intervening willy-nilly in a German as well as a Jewish debate.[64]

4

A central concern within America's nineteenth-century German-language public arena, this essay has suggested, was the role of cultural difference within democracy. To the extent that Jews defined and defended themselves in purely religious terms, this was a debate that they could avoid. German immigrants, whose quarrel with America was based on cultural difference, could not. Jews who chose, even if only for some of their leisure activities, to enter that German sphere in segmented fashion, also entered that debate. They would make it their own in the early twentieth century, when an educated Jewish second generation sought to develop the cultural basis for a secular Jewish life and to defend it with a theory of cultural pluralism against the intense Americanization pressures of the period.[65] We can't know how Isidor Busch would have entered the nineteenth-century debate, had he been able to publish his proposed German-language journal with a Jewish voice. But other Jews participated one way or another, and even when speaking as Germans they brought their own Jewish background and perspective with them. Their distinctive voice within America's German-speaking civic culture and its defense of ethnic pluralism is one that should be heard.

Notes

1. *Israels Herold: Versuch einer Zeitschrift für Israeliten in den Vereinigten Staaten* was published by Isidor Busch in New York between March 30 and June 15, 1849. For the reasons behind its suspension, see the editor's "Schlusswort" bound with its first (and only) quarter's issues; for his proposal for revamping the journal, see "Unser neues Programm," *Israels Herold*, June 15, 1849. (For the sake of economy, all nineteenth-century journal articles will be cited by date only; all translations are my own.) Busch (1822–98) was the son of a prominent Jewish printer and scholar in Vienna; he himself edited a pioneering Jewish literary and scientific annual in Vienna between 1842 and 1847, founded an important Jewish weekly advocating religious and political freedom during Vienna's 1848 revolution, and promoted an *Auf nach Amerika!* movement for Central European Jews before he himself emigrated, arriving in New York on January 8, 1849; see Guido Kisch, "*Israels Herold*: The First Jewish Weekly in New York," *Historia Judaica* 2 (1940): 65–84 (Kisch does not comment on Busch's projected revamping of his journal); James A. Wax, "Isidor Busch, America Patriot and Abolitionist," *Historia Judaica* 5 (1943): 183–203.

2. Busch (or Bush) soon moved to St. Louis, where he made a career as a businessman, winegrower, abolitionist and Republican Party activist, and prominent member of the city's German and Jewish communities; see Wax, "Isidor Busch."

3. Arthur A. Goren, "The Jewish Press," in *The Ethnic Press in the United States*, ed. Sally M. Miller (New York: Greenwood Press, 1987), 201–28; Robert Singerman, "The American Jewish Press, 1823–1983: A Bibliographic Survey of Research and Studies," *American Jewish History* 73 (1984): 422–43; Barbara Straus Reed, "Pioneer Jewish Journalism," in *Outsiders in 19th-Century Press History: Multicultural Perspectives*, ed. Frankie Hutton and Barbara Straus Reed (Bowling Green, OH: Bowling Green State University Popular Press, 1995), 21–54.

4. Cited in Avraham Barkai, *Branching Out: German-Jewish Immigration to the United States, 1820–1914* (New York: Holmes & Meier, 1994), 170.

5. Tabulated from Karl J. R. Arndt and May E. Olson, *The German Language Press of the Americas*, Vol. I (Munich: Verlag Dokumentation, 1973).

6. See Gary Gerstle, "Liberty, Coercion, and the Making of Americans," *Journal of American History* 84 (1997): 524–58.

7. Kathleen Neils Conzen, "Germans," in *Harvard Encyclopedia of American Ethnic Groups*, ed. Stephan Thernstrom, Ann Orlov, and Oscar Handlin (Cambridge, MA: Harvard University Press, 1980), 405–25.

8. Cited in Arndt and Olson, *German Language Press*, Vol. I, 10.

9. Willi Paul Adams, "The Colonial German-language Press and the American Revolution," in *The Press and the American Revolution*, ed. Bernard Bailyn and John B. Hench (Worcester, MA: American Antiquarian Society, 1980), 162–200; Wilhelm Weber, "Die Zeitungen in den Vereinigten Staaten; mit besonderer Berücksichtigung der in deutscher Sprache erscheinenden Blätter," in *Das Westland: Nordamerikanische Zeitschrift für Deutschland* (Heidelberg: J. Engelmann, 1837), reprinted in *The German Language Press of the Americas*, Vol. III (Munich: K. G. Saur, 1980), 473–513.

10. James M. Bergquist, "The German-American Press," in *The Ethnic Press in the United States*, ed. Sally M. Miller (New York: Greenwood Press, 1987), 130–59; Carl Wittke, *The German-Language Press in America* (Lexington: University of Kentucky Press, 1957).

11. Arndt and Olson, *German Language Press*, Vol. I.

12. Sally M. Miller, "Introduction," in Miller, ed., *Ethnic Press*, xi–xxii; Robert E. Park, *The Immigrant Press and Its Control* (New York: Harper and Brothers Publishers, 1922).

13. See Adams, "Colonial German-language Press"; Bergquist, "German-American Press"; Wittke, *German-Language Press*.

14. Jeffrey L. Pasley, *"The Tyranny of Printers": Newspaper Politics in the Early Republic* (Charlottesville, VA: University of Virginia Press, 2001).

15. See Kathleen Neils Conzen, "Phantom Landscapes of Colonization: Germans in the Making of a Pluralist America," in *The German-American Encounter: Conflict and Cooperation between Two Cultures, 1800–2000*, ed. Frank Trommler and Elliott Shore (New York and Oxford: Berghahn Books, 2001), 7–21.

16. Granting the lack of reliable data on the size of the German Jewish immigration, Barkai's estimate that they constituted approximately 4 percent of the total 1830–1914 emigration from the region that came to make up the German Reich seems a reasonable one; see Barkai, *Branching Out*, 9.

17. Stanley Nadel, "Jewish Race and German Soul in Nineteenth-Century America," *American Jewish History* 77 (1987): 6–26; see also Rudolf Glanz, *Jews in Relation to the Cultural Milieu of Germans in America Up to the Eighteen Eighties* (New York: By the Author, 1947).

18. Hasia R. Diner, *A Time for Gathering: The Second Migration 1820–1880* (Baltimore, MD: Johns Hopkins University Press, 1992), 163–5; see also Barkai, *Branching Out*, 175–90, who acknowledges extensive engagement with German-American cultural activities, but stresses both the temporal and geographical limits of other forms of interaction, and the barriers of prejudice; Naomi W. Cohen, *Encounter With Emancipation: The German Jews in the United States 1830–1914* (Philadelphia: The Jewish Publication Society of America, 1984), 58–63, suggests that German Jews developed a dual ethnicity in the middle decades of the nineteenth century, but that it dissipated rapidly after 1871.

19. See the careful discussion of the role of such cultural Germanness for Jewish immigrants aspiring to middle class status in Maria T. Baader, "From 'the Priestess of the Home' to 'the Rabbi's Brilliant Daughter': Concepts of Jewish Womanhood and Progressive Germanness in *Die Deborah* and the *American Israelite*, 1854–1900," *Yearbook of the Leo Baeck Institute* 43 (1998): 47–72.

20. Kathleen Neils Conzen, "Ethnicity as Festive Culture: German-America on Parade," in *The Invention of Ethnicity*, ed. Werner Sollors (New York and Oxford: Oxford University Press, 1989), 44–76; Kathleen Neils Conzen, "German-Americans and the Invention of Ethnicity," in *America and the Germans: An Assessment of a Three-Hundred Year History*, Vol. I, ed. Frank Trommler and Joseph McVeigh (Philadelphia: University of Pennsylvania Press, 1985), 131–47.

21. Esther L. Panitz, *Simon Wolf: Private Conscience and Public Image* (Rutherford, NJ: Fairleigh Dickinson University Press, 1987); Kathleen Neils Conzen, "*Die Residenzler*: German Americans in the Making of the Nation's Capital," in *Adolf Cluss Architect: From Germany to America*, ed. Alan Lessof and Christof Mauch (New York and Oxford: Berghahn Books, 2005), 55–67.

22. Frederick C. Luebke, "Three Centuries of Germans in America," in Luebke, *Germans in the New World: Essays in the History of Immigration* (Urbana and Chicago: University of Illinois Press, 1990), 157–89.

23. This characterization applies particularly to members of conservative synods like Missouri and Wisconsin that were created by the nineteenth-century immigration; despite sporadic efforts to found a newspaper reflecting a conservative Lutheran perspective, more narrowly church-focused organs dominated their German-language press until a group of Milwaukee laymen succeeded in establishing the *Germania* to reflect a Christian viewpoint on the news of the day. See Angelika Dörfler-Dierken, *Luthertum und Demokratie: Deutsche und amerikanische Theologen des 19. Jahrhunderts zu Staat, Gesellschaft und Kirche* (Göttingen: Vandenhoeck & Ruprecht, 2001); Frederick C. Luebke, "Politics and Missouri Synod Lutherans: A Historiographical Review," *Concordia Historical Institute Quarterly* 45 (May 1972): 141–8; August Suelflow, "St. Louiser Volksblatt," *Concordia Historical Institute Quarterly* 18 (1946): 108–10; Wittke, *German-Language Press*, 176–81.

24. The first German Catholic newspaper was founded in Cincinnati in 1837; over the course of the nineteenth century, 60 others followed, along with a host of purely religious and more specialist periodicals; see Kathleen Neils Conzen, "The German Catholic Milieu in America," in *German-American Immigration and Ethnicity in Comparative Perspective*, ed. Wolfgang Helbich and Walter Kamphoefner (Madison, WI: Max Kade Institute for German-American Studies, University of Wisconsin-Madison, 2004), 69–114.

25. Reinhart Kondert, "The German Press of New Orleans, 1839–1909," in *The German-American Press*, ed. Henry Geitz (Madison, WI: Max Kade Institute for German-American Studies, University of Wisconsin-Madison, 1992), 144–6; Hans G. Reissner, "The German-American Jews (1800–1850)," *Yearbook of the Leo Baeck Institute* 10 (1965): 57–116, here 95–6; Henry Samuel Morais, *The Jews of Philadelphia: Their History from the Earliest Settlements to the Present Time* (Philadelphia: The Levytype Company, 1894), 336–7; Joseph Gutmann and Stanley F. Chyet, "Introduction" to Moritz Loeb, "Abraham Urjella or the Struggle Over Principle," *American Jewish History* 83 (1995): 471–2; Arndt and Olson, *German Language Press*, 515.

26. Wittke, *German-Language Press*, 110; Isaac Markens, *Abraham Lincoln and the Jews* (New York: by the author, 1909), 32, 36; *Doron Zeilberger–Moritz Pinner (1828–1911)* (online), http://www.math.rutgers.edu/~zeilberg/family/moritz.html (April 3, 2006); *Washington Post*, November 28, 1889; Lamberta Margarette Voget, "Germans in Los Angeles County California 1850–1900," ms. 1933, (online), http://ftp.rootsweb.com/pub/usgenweb/ca/losangeles/germans/chapter4.txt (July 10, 2003).

27. Heinrich Boernstein and Charles L. Bernays of the influential antebellum St. Louis *Anzeiger des Westens* exemplify the difficulties of ascribing Jewish identity; though both, at the time and since, have been identified as Jews, Boernstein was the son of a Galitzian Catholic father and a North German Protestant mother who was educated as a Catholic, while Bernays' obituaries likewise stressed his Catholic education; Steven Rowan, "The Return of Henry Boernstein," in Henry Boernstein, *The Mysteries of St. Louis*, ed. Steven Rowan and Elizabeth Sims (Chicago: Charles H. Kerr Publishing Company, 1990), vii; H. A. Ratterman, "Karl Ludwig Bernays," *Der Deutsche Pionier* 11 (1880): 458–68.

28. His parents were Raphael Pincas Cohnheim and Fagel (Philippine) Rosenthal; see Max Cohnheim, Civil War Military Service and Pension Records, U.S. National Archives and

Record Service, Washington, D.C., R.G. 94 (for approximate birth date and father's name); "Geburten 1802–1833," "Namen des Kindes," and "Vorsteher der Gemeinde," ms. lists in Jüdische Gemeinde Fraustadt, *Matrikel, 1763–1936* (5 microfilm reels; Koblenz: Bundesarchiv, 1958), LDS Microfilm Nos. 1184412 (for the first two lists) and 1184413; Edward David Luft, comp., *The Naturalized Jews of the Grand Duchy of Posen in 1834 and 1835* (Atlanta: Scholars Press, 1987), 18; Heinrich Raab, *Revolutionäre in Baden 1848/49: Biographisches Inventar für die Quellen im Generallandesarchiv Karlsruhe und im Staatsarchiv Freiburg* (Stuttgart: W. Kohlhammer, 1998), 139; Sigismund Borkheim to Karl Marx, London, February 12, 1860, in Karl Marx and Friedrich Engels, *Gesamtausgabe* (Berlin: Dietz, 1975), vol. 10, 245. Max Cohnheim was known officially to authorities in Berlin and Baden as "Markus Cohnheim." For helpful background, see Sophia Kemlein, *Die Posener Juden 1815–1848: Entwicklungsprozesse einer polnischen Judenheit unter preußischer Herrschaft* (Hamburg: Dölling und Galitz Verlag, 1997).

29. "Der Kaufmann: Humoristische Vorlesung von Max Cohnheim, Gehalten zur Stiftungs-Feier der Gesellschaft junger Kaufleute" (Berlin: Bloch, n.d.); Siegfried Weigel, *Flugschriftenliteratur 1848 in Berlin: Geschichte und Öffentlichkeit einer volkstümlichen Gattung* (Stuttgart: J. B. Metzlersche Verlagsbuchhandlung, 1979), 52–7; Max Cohnheim and Adolph Reich, "Die konstitutionellen Zehn Gebote: Den Männern aus dem Volke gewidmet: Frage: Wie lauten die konstitutionellen zehn Gebote?" (Berlin: Bartz, March 20, 1848) (online). http://edocs.ub. uni-frankfurt.de/volltexte/2006/6404 (September 22, 2007). For *Vormärz* popular humor in Berlin, see Mary Lee Townsend, *Forbidden Laughter: Popular Humor and the Limits of Repression in Nineteenth-Century Prussia* (Ann Arbor: University of Michigan Press, 1992).

30. Klaus Schulz, *"Kladderadatsch": Ein bürgerliches Witzblatt von der Märzrevolution bis zum Nationalsozialismus 1848–1944* (Bochum: Studienverlag Dr. N. Brockmeyer, 1975), 19; Raab, *Revolutionäre in Baden*, 139; Rüdiger Hachtmann, *Berlin 1848: Eine Politik- und Gesellschaftsgeschichte der Revolution* (Bonn: Verlag J. H. W. Dietz Nachfolger, 1997), 318–19; Weigel, *Flugschriftenliteratur*, 169. This was part of a mid-summer wave of Berlin prosecutions for press law violations; public pressure forced the court to free his associates in early October, but on appeal Cohnheim (in absentia) and a colleague were sentenced to 10-years' imprisonment for high treason in June 1849. The founding trio of *Kladderadatsch* editors grew up within the Jewish community of Breslau, not far from Cohnheim's hometown of Fraustadt.

31. Max Cohnheim to Redaktion der *Neue Rheinische Zeitung*, Zürich, September 20, 1848, in *Karl Marx, Friedrich Engels, Briefwechsel, Mai 1846 bis December 1848*, vol. 000, 474; Borkheim to Marx, February 12, 1860; Raab, *Revolutionäre in Baden*, 139, 254, 764. Eckhart Pilick, ed., *"Mein Kopf ist voll Hass und Rache!" Unbekannte Briefe aus dem Jahr 1848 von Adelbert von Bornstedt aus dem Zuchthaus Bruchsal* (Rohrbach/Pfalz: Verlag Peter Guhl, 2004); Borkheim to Marx, February 12, 1860; Karl Marx and Friedrich Engels, *Werke*, Vol. 14 (4th ed.; Berlin: Dietz Verlag, 1972), 389–97; Rolf Dlubek, "Ein Fund aus den journalistischen Anfängen von Sigismund Ludwig Borkheim: Der 'Rummeltipuff!' (Genf 1849/1850)," in *Vom mühseligen Suchen und glückhaften Finden: Rückblicke und Erlebnisse von Marx-Engels-Forschern und Historikern der Arbeiterbewegung* (Berlin: Helle Panke, 2003), 35–44; Ship Passenger Lists, http://ancestry.com. Cohnheim sailed on the appropriately named *Independence*. His companion, Eduard Rosenblum, a German doctor's son from Odessa, soon returned to Britain and then reportedly emigrated to Australia.

32. Correspondence from New York dated August 7, 1854, *Atlantis* (Dessau), 2:17 (1854): 478; *Trow's New York City Directory* 1855–56, 169; 1856–57, 162; 1857–58, 164; 1858–59 160; 1859–60, 168; *New Yorker Humorist und Illustrirte Novellenzeitung*, February 5, March 26, 1859.

33. *Amerika, wie es ist: Ein Buch für Kunde der neuen Welt* (Hamburg: Serie III der Volksschriften des Deutsch-amerikanischen Vereins, 1854); Fritz A. Leuchs, *The Early German Theatre in New York: 1840–1872* (New York: Columbia University Press, 1928), 63–5, 68–74. "Fürsten zum Lande hinaus," dating back to the *Hambachfest* in 1832, with its catchy tune and angry lyrics demanding the departure of prince after prince by name, was a popular song of the 1848 revolution, and Cohnheim's play took place in various New York radical settings (including the Gasthof zum Königsmörder—inn at the sign of the regicide) at "the next harvest time of the republicans"; http://www.volksliederarchiv.de/tet1493.html (September 29, 2007); *New Yorker Staats-Zeitung*, December 10, 1853, cited in Leuchs, 65.

34. Leuchs, *Early German Theatre*, 96–7, 241, 258, 260, 267, 271; Geo. C. Odell, *Annals of the New York Stage*, 15 vols. (New York: Columbia University Press, 1927–49), vol. 6, 321–2, 402–3; vol. 7, 169, 341, 421, 508, 593, 670; vol. 8, 197; New *Yorker Humorist*, September 17, 1859; *New York Herald*, April 2, 1860; Heinrich Kadelburg, *Fünfzehn Jahre des Deutschen Theaters in San Francisco* (San Francisco: Rosenthal & Roesch, 1883), 17, 19, 25. Other titles include *Herz und Dollar*, *Der Sohn des Jongleurs*, *Der Mord an West Broadway*, and *Reise durch San Francisco in 80 Stunden*; his last documented play, *Der Pownbroker von Harlem*, opened in New York in 1882; Odell, *Annals*, vol. 12, 70. I have found no indication that scripts of any of these plays survive.

35. *Arion New York, von 1854 bis 1904: Ein Rückblick auf fünfzig Jahre deutschen Strebens in Amerika anlässlich des goldenen Jubiläums des Vereins* (New York: privately printed, 1904), 6; the Arion's 1856 operetta, *Ephraim Levy, oder Der Gang nach dem Eisenhammer*, was regarded as particularly successful.

36. His citizenship sponsor was Jewish immigrant and Berlin revolutionary Julius Brill, a photographer prominent in German Republican politics in New York; Max Cohnheim, Petition for Naturalization, Superior Court, New York City, October 6, 1856, http://www.ancestry.com; Stanley Nadel, *Little Germany: Ethnicity, Religion, and Class in New York City, 1845–80* (Urbana and Chicago: University of Illinois Press, 1990), 20 (1857 Kommunisten Klub membership), 135 (among notables at 1856 Republican rally). His wife was Holstein-born Elise Lorenzen; Elise Cohnheim passport application March 9, 1858, http://www.ancestry.com (December 20, 2007); 1870 U.S. Census of Population, San Francisco, http://www.ancestry.com. Cohnheim's parents arrived in New York from Bremen on August 2, 1855; his mother died in New York in the spring of 1865, while as late as 1880 the widowed Raphael Cohnheim, aged eighty-four, was a resident of New York's Home for Aged and Infirm Hebrews; *Columbia* (Washington, D.C.), May 13, 1865; New York Passenger Lists, and 1880 U.S. Census of Population, New York City, http://www.ancestry.com (April 23, 2006).

37. *Amerika, wie es ist; Humorist*, February 5, 1859, when it appeared in enlarged format as *New Yorker Humorist und Illustrirte Novellenzeitung*. The title, *Der Humorist*, echoed that of older comic papers published in Breslau (1833) and Vienna (1837–58); see Andreas Graf, *Die Ursprünge der modernen Medienindustrie: Familien- und Unterhaltungszeitschriften der Kaiserzeit (1870–1918)*, originally in *Geschichte des deutschen Buchhandels im 19. und 20. Jahrhundert*, Vol. I, Part 2, ed. Georg Jäger (Frankfurt am Main: MVB Marketing- und Verlagsgeschellschaft des Buchhandels GmbH, 2003), 409–522, http://www.zeitschriften.ablit.de/graf/gz054htm. The *New Yorker Humorist* seems to have emerged from the Sunday humor page that Brethauer edited for the radical *New Yorker Abend-Zeitung*; Brethauer (1830–1882) remained in the New York area and subsequently published books of humor and his own humor journal; Eitel Wolf Dobbert, *Deutsche Demokraten in Amerika: Die Achtundvierziger und ihre Schriften* (Göttingen: Vandenhoeck & Ruprecht, 1958), 40–1.

38. *Humorist*, February 5, April 16, May 28, July 9, August 13, September 10, 1859 (on Cohnheim's travels); June 25, August 13, 1859 (on Pecare's takeover); Pecare may have had personal connections to the Jewish community in Fraustadt; on Pecare, see *New-York Spectator*,

June 11, 1835; *New York Herald*, June 3, 1848, April 8, 1854, May 21, August 31, 1856, November 7, 1858.

39. Max Cohnheim, Military Service Record, National Archives; Harry W. Pfanz, *Gettysburg—Culp's Hill and Cemetery Hill* (Chapel Hill, NC: University of North Carolina Press, 1993), 245–6; David G. Martin, *Carl Bornemann's Regiment: The Forty-First New York Infantry (DeKalb Regt.) in the Civil War* (Hightstown, NJ: Longstreet House, 1987), 5–8, 17–30; Tim Engelhart, *Zu den Waffen! Deutsche Emigranten in New Yorker Unionsregimentern während des Amerikanischen Bürgerkrieges 1861–65* (Zella-Mehlis/Thüringen: Heinrich-Jung-Verlagsgesellschaft, 2000), 33–9; New *York Herald*, October 17, 1861.

40. Cohnheim, Military Service Record; Stephen D. Engle, *Yankee Dutchman: The Life of Franz Sigel* (Fayetteville: University of Arkansas Press, 1993); *Register of Officers and Agents, Civil, Military, and Naval, in the Service of the United States, on the Thirtieth of September 1863* (Washington, DC: Government Printing Office, 1864); Klaus G. Wust, "German Immigrants and their Newspapers in the District of Columbia," Society for the History of the Germans in Maryland, *Thirtieth Report* (Baltimore, 1959), 49.

41. Kathleen Neils Conzen, "*Die Residenzler*: German Americans in the Making of the Nation's Capital," passim; *Columbia* (Washington, D.C.), April 29, June 17, 1865, February 17, March 3, March 10, March 31, 1866, January 12, 1867; Wust, "German Immigrants"; *New York Times*, March 2, 1867.

42. *San Francisco Daily Evening Bulletin*, May 23 and 26, June 15, 1864; *Columbia*, June 18, 1864; A. C. Freeman, comp., *The American Decisions: Containing the Cases of General Value and Authority Decided in the Courts of the Several States from the Earliest Issue of the State Reports to the Year 1869*, XCIX (San Francisco: Bancroft-Whitney Company, 1888), 363–4; *San Francisco City Directory 1868–69* (Research Publications microfilm, *United States City Directories 1861–81*), 146; Arndt and Olson, *German Language Press*, 25–6.

43. *San Francisco Daily Evening Bulletin*, October 15, 1868, August 31, September 9, 1869, April 28, August 7, 9, and 29, 1871; Jacques Freymond and Henry Burgelin, eds., *La Première Internationale* (Geneva: E. Droz, 1962), Vol. I, 587; San Francisco *Sonntags-Gast*, June 25, 1871; San Francisco City Directories, 1870 through 1881; Armin Tenner, *Amerika: Der Heutige Standpunkt der Kultur in den Vereinigten Staaten* (Berlin: Stuhr'sche Buchhandlung, 1886), 172, Appendix 61–2; Odell, *Annals*, Vol. 12, 70.

44. Index, "San Francisco Deaths August 1870–1873," California Genealogical Society (online): http://www.calgensoc.org/web/cgs/cgshp.nsf?Open; *San Francisco Daily Evening Bulletin* October 24, 1876; Max Cohnheim Pension File, in Case Files of Pension Applications, Record Group 15: Records of the Department of Veterans Affairs, National Archives, Washington, D.C.

45. The following observations draw on my survey of surviving issues of Cohnheim's papers: *New Yorker Humorist*; February 5 to December 17 1859; *Columbia*, October 17, 1863 to June 2, 1866; San Francisco *Sonntags-Gast*, June 4 to December 12, 1871 (I have not been able to consult the one or two extant issues of the San Francisco *Humorist*). Since two of these journals were co-edited, and most articles in all three were unsigned, it is impossible to attribute specific contributions to Cohnheim, but it seems fair to assume that he was in general agreement with the positions reflected in these journals.

46. *Washington Post*, December 10, 1891; *New Yorker Humorist*, June 8, 1859; *The Israelite* (Cincinnati), December 8, 1859. Wise's Washington lectures on Jews in art, science, and literature received approving coverage in *Columbia*, December 19, 1863, while Wise, who defended Cohnheim when he was attacked as a Jew by German radicals for his support for the Lincoln administration, in turn lauded *Columbia* as "witty, humorous, full of seriousness and jest, beautifully nuanced and pleasant-featured"; see *Die Deborah*, October 3, 1863, January 8, 1864.

47. E.g., *Humorist*, February 5, 12, May 7, 1859; *Columbia*, January 9, 1864, October 21, 1865, March 10, June 2, 1866; *Sonntags-Gast*, July 9, 23, November 19, 1871.

48. *Humorist*, June 11, 1859; *Columbia*, November 11, 1865, June 2, 1866; *Sonntags-Gast*, November 19, 1871.

49. E.g., *Humorist*, March 19, 26, May 21, July 18, November 5, 1859; *Columbia*, November 21, 1863, April 16, 1864, March 10, 1866; *Sonntags-Gast*, June 4, November 19 and 26, 1871.

50. On Wagner, see *Humorist*, March 5, April 4, 1859; *Columbia*, April 2, 1864.

51. *Die Deborah*, December 18, 1857.

52. *Humorist*, November 5, July 16, February 26, March 5, June 4, October 15, 1859; *Columbia*, May 14, 1864, July 15, December 16, 1865.

53. *Columbia*, June 18, August 13, 1864, October 24, 1863; Schulze's later "advice" to "fellow tailor" President Andrew Johnson was among the offenses for which Cohnheim was forced to resign his Treasury position.

54. *Sonntags-Gast*, November 9, June 4, October 29, 1871.

55. Michael A. Meyer, *Response to Modernity: A History of the Reform Movement in Judaism* (New York and Oxford: Oxford University Press, 1988), 252–5; Baader, "Priestess of the Home;" William M. Kramer and Reva Clar, "Philo Jacoby: California's First International Sportsman," *Western States Jewish History* 22 (1989): 3–17, 243–57; *Der Zeitgeist*, January 1, 1880.

56. *Sinai* 2 (September–December 1857): 8–11 surveyed February 1856 to December 1857; *Zeitgeist*, April 14, 1881, surveyed 1880–1882.

57. *Jewish Times*, September 30, 1870, surveyed March 5, 1869 to November 8, 1872.

58. *Hebrew*, November 6, 1868, October 16, 1868; surveyed from July 5, 1867 through August 27, 1869. Wise had nothing but scorn for the inclusion of sporting news in Jacoby's "Jewish-religious organ"; see *Die Deborah*, May 4, 1866.

59. *Jewish Times*, August 13, 1869; February 25, July 22, September 16, 1870; April 14, June 2, 1871; April 29, 1870; April 14, 1871; August 19, 1870.

60. *Zeitgeist*, January 1 and 15, September 30, December 9 and 23, 1880; December 8, 1881; June 8 and 22, July 6, 1882.

61. *Die Deborah*, August 22, 1856; July 10, 1868; surveyed August 22, 1856 to July 1, 1859, April 10, 1863 to November 19, 1869. See Baader, "Priestess of the Home"; Sefton D. Temkin, *Isaac Mayer Wise: Shaping American Judaism* (New York and Oxford: Oxford University Press, 1992), 124.

62. E.g., *Die Deborah*, December 12 and 19, 1856, October 30, November 20, 1857, January 1, September 24, 1858, October 3, 1863, April 24, 1868 (radicals); November 28, 1856, July 3, 1857, November 2, 1859, April 17, 1868 (Catholics); August 7, 1857, January 22, June 14, December 10, 1858, February 17, 1864, March 3, 1865, April 17, 1868 (cooperation); November 21, 1856, January 2, August 7, 1857, March 19, 1858, November 11, 1864, March 3, 1865 (requests, reprints).

63. E.g., *Die Deborah*, November 21, December 12, 1856, June 19, 1857, February 12, March 9, 1858, September 3, 1869; theater and concert reviews were a regular feature of the paper.

64. *Die Deborah*, December 18, 1857, January 29, July 9, 1858, June 16, 1865, November 30, 1866, February 22, 1867, October 9, 1868.

65. Daniel A. Greene, *The Jewish Origins of Cultural Pluralism: The Menorah Association and American Diversity* (Bloomington and Indianapolis, IN: Indiana University Press, 2011); William Toll, "Horace M. Kallen: Pluralism and American Jewish Identity," *American Jewish History* 85 (1997): 57–74.

CHAPTER 7
UNEQUAL OPPORTUNITIES: THE INDEPENDENT ORDER B'NAI B'RITH IN NINETEENTH-CENTURY GERMANY AND IN THE UNITED STATES

Cornelia Wilhelm

It was the Enlightenment and the rise of the modern nation state in German-speaking Central Europe which opened new venues for religious and ethnic minorities to become citizens and thus depart from their prior status as mere subjects, or even "outsiders"— often entangled in complicated and insecure legal definitions as well as social, economic and political restrictions. The modern era introduced the ideal of a civil society, shaped by the civil involvement of its individual members, a society in which everyone who qualified by skill, civic activity, and virtue was entitled to participate. Such a society was not supposed to be based on heritage, kinship or religious ties and traditional boundaries, rather it was a *civil society* by definition, based on rational thinking, free choice, self-improvement and tolerance.[1] *Bildung*, character formation and virtue, economic enterprise, civic involvement, political activity, and the ideal of humanity were now deemed to be the preconditions for societal participation, determining an individual's access to bourgeois civil society and one's place therein: a society as represented by the United States of America, the first modern nation uniquely shaped by Enlightenment thinking and an emerging market society.

While, from its very inception, the United States presented an ideal of modern bourgeois civil society and nation, Europe's rulers had also started to re-structure their territories into modern states. This proved, however, to be a much more difficult process, as historic societal and religious structure as well as responsibilities resulting from a medieval lien system and fellowship within that system based on landownership and Christian religious affiliation had to be overcome in order to open venues for the construction of civil equalities within a society that was based on traditional inequalities. Accordingly, the process of civil emancipation started opening new opportunities for one of the oldest minorities in Central Europe, namely its Jews, to define their place within the emerging modern states and within a newly civil arena. The *Haskalah*, the Jewish Enlightenment, created a class of modern Jewish thinkers and intellectuals who started to question the traditional particularism of Jewish life as well as certain forms of Judaism. Modern German Reformers introduced a reinterpretation of Israel's covenantal relationship with God, which used to legitimize pre-modern Jewish distinctiveness as an incorporated community apart from Christian society at large. The old motif of Jewish "chosen-ness" as a people that needed to preserve their separate identity was re-interpreted and used as a basis to follow the opposite pattern: due to their *chosen-ness* modern Jews were now obliged to serve as a "priestly people" within society at large, and were consequently challenged to engage with the larger society to provide a model of ethical behavior.[2]

As several historians have shown, it became a challenge for modern Jewish life and thought to construct a new "secular" civil identity in practice, and still give it a particular *Jewish*, albeit *civil,* meaning and vision; one that would allow Jews to conquer a space in civil society to blend with the society while maintaining a sense of Jewishness. This was important as otherwise the idea of their "mission to humankind" would lose its meaning and potential.[3] This proved to be very difficult and depended on how civil society responded to the desire as to whether its own identity and structures allowed modern Jews to blend with the nation while retaining a modern ethnic and/or religious identity as Jews. As can be seen particularly in the German case, the process of Jewish emancipation and political liberalism was tied to the question regarding the modern nation state.

In Central Europe the Napoleonic era triggered a series of major legislative initiatives for the emancipation of the Jewish minority in the German territories. Political restoration, ongoing German territorialism, and the lack of a consistently pursued modernization of German society left German Jews as an incompletely emancipated and economically, socially, and politically suffering minority until the establishment of a German nation state in 1871, when the first German constitution finally permitted emancipation for all German Jews. The long delay of nationhood went hand in hand with old elites holding on to their liberties and supported the emergence of a romantic chauvinism whose supporters claimed to represent a uniquely *German* development toward the formation of a nation and modern statehood. In the late nineteenth century, this movement culminated in an ideology which put the category of race (folk) at the core of modern German identity and defined itself through common kinship and fate.[4] Such an ideology seriously torpedoed the effort to establish a civil society open to all former subjects based on their merits, and it limited access to society based on religion and ethnic background.[5]

Since the 1830s the ongoing delay of emancipation contributed to the continuing dispersion of German Jews through emigration. By 1914, an estimated 280,000 German-speaking Jews had chosen immigration to the United States alone, which was their preferred destination.[6] Their main discontent was based on bitter disappointment with the protracted emancipation process, which was perhaps most inconsistent in Bavaria and Posen from where most immigrants originated from the early 1830s onwards. The situation was particularly difficult and confusing for a young generation of Jews who had attended public schools and learned "non-Jewish" professions, or some of the intellectuals and the rabbinate, who had received modern training at state universities but were too radical and too modern for their congregations, Jewish authorities, or for state authorities. In Bavaria young people were virtually forced to leave due to the restrictive Matrikel law, which continued to restrict the number of Jews permitted to settle in its communities and earn a living.[7]

In this context the transition toward a *civil* albeit *Jewish* identity created communal problems and ruptures—or left individual Jews simply alone. This was frequently the first step toward conversion, which appeared to be the goal of Christian authorities. In practice, it continued to be extremely difficult finding ways to maintain religious community and venture into civil society. Both political repression during the restoration era as well as the lasting territorial split did not permit the establishment of large-scale German and Jewish representations or organizations capable of reaching out to the public sphere, carve out a space for the integration of an ethnic identity or teach their members democratic practice, civil virtues and participation, merging these concepts with a "national" German vision or communicating "Jewish" concerns. None of the existing communal societies met the mobility of this young generation or managed to accommodate such secular needs. None of the existing institutions offered a role model to facilitate this. Early in the nineteenth century, there had been attempts to create an association outside the Jewish sphere that would serve as a mediator between Jews and non-Jews in the civil bourgeois sphere. This secular society, the Verein der Freunde,[8] had religious and humanitarian undertones and elevated "brotherhood" to its members' core value, but based its forms on Masonic rituals. This was no surprise, since masonry, as a philosophical system and organizational form, was in many regards attractive for modern Jews: not only was it based on the same motto as the emerging modern Judaism—"the fatherhood of God and the brotherhood of men"; it also permitted its members to socialize beyond confessional boundaries and to embrace key values of bourgeois society as well as Enlightenment thinking. Above all, it offered a protected space within society—among brothers—to practice what qualified them for the participation in civil society.[9] However, within Central European Masonic orders, Jews continued to be excluded and thus this model did not really contribute to enhancing a civil, albeit explicitly Jewish identity.

This was different in the United States where German-Jewish mass migration found a unique environment in which to develop their ideal of social and civil integration into a modern civil society. In America, Jews encountered a modern nation that represented a common value system rather than a kinship-based understanding of nationhood. The narrative of the nation was constructed around the history of the first settlers of the original thirteen colonies and harked back to the early Puritan experience, describing the nation as emerging from a covenant of its first settlers with God, a haven, or "New Zion" for the persecuted and oppressed peoples of the world—a conscious departure from European societies. Although the United States strictly separated church and state, thus preventing the establishment of a state religion and securing the free profession thereof, the nation expressed itself in a Civil Religion based on the biblical narrative of the Jews, who defined themselves through a covenant and as a chosen people, destined to bring humanity to the world.[10]

While church and state were also increasingly separated during the formative period of modern statehood in Europe, the process of secularization in the German lands never led to a complete separation of church and state, or the privatization of religion; rather, the nation continued to maintain a certain role in shaping the framework of religious life in the nation.

Unlike Germany, the United States provided self-definition and a society which embraced diversity and was open to the integration of Jews as an ethnic and religious group, while integrating them into the nation. Its motto "e pluribus unum" came true for its Jewish immigrants, whereas other ethnic groups, such as Native Americans or African Americans were left behind.[11] The opposite was the case for many immigrants with European backgrounds. It was the visibility of their very identity as ethnic or religious groups, while adhering to the common value system of the Protestant nation, which *made them* true Americans and became the foundation for an "American exceptionalism," an American self-understanding as a nation departing from European traditions.[12] Their group identity was important in the explanation of nation and society and created an unprecedented ethnic and religious pluralism. Although historians of American ethnic history might argue that, from the inception of American nationhood, certain ethnic groups, such as Native Americans and African Americans were excluded from such pluralism, at least in the eyes of the European settlers the American experiment was extremely successful. This new definition of the American nation shaped a distinctly American civil religion that permitted religious groups to spell their own religious meaning and mission within the nation's religious definition and inscribed their narrative into that of the nation. Like modern Jews, Americans defined their identity and historic role in terms of a mission on behalf of humanity and were quite comfortable with America stressing its conscious departure from the Old World. This was even more so the case with American Jews, who defined themselves as an ethnic as well as a religious group and could blend the idea of the Jewish covenant and mission almost ideally in the Old Testament imagery of the American nation. Perhaps more than other ethnic groups in America during the mid-nineteenth century, Jews sought to become citizens, after having pursued this goal for a while in the German lands and having acquired not only motivation, but also a large amount of social capital in the process of political and societal change in central Europe.[13]

The new American environment helped the German Jews in particular, who had strongly internalized a "mission" motif that commanded them to engage in society in order to solve the question of how to enable the modern Jews to do so both as Jews and citizens. Partly pressured by the concepts of "citizenship" and "civil society," partly deeply aware that the United States at mid-century had already internalized such concepts and offered them at a special moment in time, thus providing unique opportunities to put their ideals into practice, the new immigrants actively ventured to form communities and the shaping of a new Jewish mentality. Although deeply embedded in the German-Jewish ideal, their solution to this problem was modelled to meet the *American* challenges of modernity and found expression in a new type of Jewish organization; this organization was uniquely modelled toward reaching out into the public sphere, national in scope, serving the needs of the local community beyond religious lines, and at the same time representing the idea of moral mission and respectability within society. Jews in America quickly noticed that only such a new form of organization would serve the purpose to find a balance between their Jewish and American identities, between group and society, thus communicating both American and Jewish role models.[14]

It was only a secular Jewish organization outside the *kehillah*, which, unprecedented as it was, provided a new model to fill the new civil spaces. The Independent Order of B'nai B'rith represented the first such "secular" Jewish organization and was founded as a voluntary association in 1843 in New York City. Here a unique blend of German-Jewish principle and thought started to play a vital role in the design and wide dissemination of modern Jewish identity, as the American synagogue could neither embrace the widening civil spaces and religious factions of American-Jewish life nor give them a particularly Jewish meaning. Thus a "civil" platform for Jewish identity emerged and enabled the modern Jews to appear as Jews and as citizens.

Imitating the popular model of American Odd Fellowship, the Independent Order of B'nai B'rith was independent from congregational and rabbinical authority; it placed Enlightenment thinking at its center and was to serve as a key vehicle to re-introduce and develop a Jewish, yet modern, secular, and respectable religious and bourgeois lifestyle which would reflect both the spirit of Judaism and a strong commitment and close link to American civil society. American freedoms clearly challenged immigrant Jews. Pluralism, individualism and religious, political as well as social opportunities hitherto unexperienced by the immigrants were something with which they had to be familiarized. This was particularly true if they wanted to live their new lives as "modern Jews," taking on a particular religious mission to humankind: they had to define a timely pattern to merge Jewish and civil identities. This included the civic duties Jews had to match after having been given civil rights and an equal status as citizens. The relationship between *individual, community*, and *society* challenged the modern immigrant, who had lost his traditional culture, language, kinship, and religion.

While Jews had sympathized with masonry earlier in Europe,[15] but had usually been excluded from fraternal and Masonic orders there, America, where free associationalism was flourishing, permitted Jews to join such voluntary associations. Masonry of the Scottish Rite and Odd Fellowship had become a favored way for Jews to experience sociability, a port of entry to civil society and modern religiosity together with mainly Protestant Masonic "ébrothers." Indeed, by the year 1840, Masonic or fraternal affiliation was proof that American Jews had overcome social and religious exclusion. It is therefore no surprise that American Jews felt such an organization could ideally serve as a means for general uplift and access to American society, while contributing toward re-defining a modern Jewish identity.

The Lodge, as a small social entity, was replacing traditional forms of family and kinship and was instrumental in maintaining and reshaping cohesion and solidarity among modern Jews. The Lodge and Lodge life as the center of a new Jewish identity helped the individual to redefine his own role as a "Jew" among his religious brethren and within society at large. The grassroots-organization was based on the local need and spirit of its members and was to preserve a sense of communal and ethical belonging, to shape a new role model for modern Jews and to include those who did not belong to any congregation. Rather than living as isolated individuals without any moral standards, its members sought to represent a distinct moral community based on the idea of "mission" as defined by modern Judaism, reaching into society as a whole.[16]

Inside the order, secrecy added to the latter's special significance and attraction as an exclusive group, but was also based on principles of traditional Jewish *chevrot* and protected the circle of men from the curious eyes of outside society during the process of identity formation and learning. The fraternal system supplied instruments to reach far beyond the limits of tradition and particularism. It created a protected space and taught strong dedication to self-improvement, moral and intellectual refinement, and personal morality as vehicles for the development of a civil Jewish identity within society. The degree system and jurisdictional apparatus of the order were crucial mechanisms for self-improvement, moral control, and the raising of a new self-awareness.[17]

After all, upon admittance to the first degree, each member of the order was sworn to self-improvement and active community building under the premises of *brotherly love*. Rooted in Enlightenment thinking, the idea of human brotherhood was elevated to become the guiding principle for the relationship of Jews both among themselves and within the non-Jewish world. This principle was drawn from the covenant-motive and expressed the "fatherhood of God and the brotherhood of men," a concept that was central to the Reform movement. It defined all adherents to monotheistic faiths as "children of God" and as members of one family. This placed Judaism, as the "first-born child," firmly into the human family, but left room for the Jews' distinctiveness and particular mission. Placing an ethical value rather than a religious dogma at the core of the order's identity opened venues for union and consensus among *brothers* of different ethnic and religious backgrounds.[18] Building on this commitment, the candidates were taught to focus on self-improvement and character formation (*Bildung*), and *to act* in accordance with the divine; the aim was to reach full inner harmony and to convert the relationship between men, Jews and non-Jews, into one of a *brotherly nature*. Thus the degree-system not only bound the members of the order to a common mission, but also required them to transcend the boundaries of the group, engage in society at large and present a modern image of Judaism to the outside world, all of which helped the individual members become active participants in American civic life.[19]

To perform their duties as true role models and mediators between group and society, lodge members also learned the details of civil participation such as how to organize voluntary organizations, how to administer business, organize elections, run an organization's finances, hold public speeches or defend one's own or the group's issues publicly. This introduced them into the democratic process and taught American Jews (in particular B'nai B'rith) how to see themselves as integral to the American public sphere and to serve as mediators between individual, community, and society. Such integration allowed them to maintain their Jewish identity and even led to the formation of an American Jewish ethnic group in this process of "becoming American."[20]

Suddenly the performance of a "civil Judaism," civic, public, and political involvement in the public sphere took on a new dynamic within the Jewish world. Civil and civic involvement, active participation, and the development of republican role models in public life almost turned into an act of religious observance. Labeled first "Practical Judaism," then "B'nai B'rithism,"[21] such activity was a vehicle putting the theory of modern Jewish universalism into practice and permitted the members of the order to advance and concentrate their religious energies through the vast network of lodges. This process of identity formation, channeled and coordinated by the lodges, was not only an expression of devotion to a new religiosity, but was meaningful socially as it served the practical needs of American Jews, who found a common ground for joint projects and previously unknown access to civil society. The order planted particular hubs for outreach and civic education through its lodges and its libraries which appeared after 1851 in larger urban centers, such as New York, San Francisco, Philadelphia, and Chicago.[22] These libraries not only constituted the first Jewish public libraries in the country but more importantly also served as the first Jewish community centers, which reached beyond the B'nai B'rith. As communal centers they educated Jewish men and women beyond the lodge room in such important matters as public speech and rational public discourse as vehicles of public and political participation.[23]

In America, the B'nai B'rith quickly grew into a powerful instrument in the public arena uniting and representing American Jews. For the first time, it did not merely offer a national platform for *American Jews*, thus establishing an American Jewish ethnic group; rather, it also gave Jews unprecedented access to identification with American society and polity at large. It allowed them to maintain and even celebrate their Jewish identity while becoming Americans. This happened on several levels of the B'nai B'rith experience and helped shape an American Jewish community that presented itself with a previously unknown civil identity as Jews and Americans.

The order offered a unique platform on a local level for Jews to unite and express their American-Jewish spirit and citizenship through projects of charity and communal involvement. Here they created a public sphere to reach out to the wider society and build alliances with like-minded groups around civic involvement within the local community. Among other projects it was a particularly remarkable achievement of the order to initiate the founding of modern Jewish hospitals in numerous American cities. All such projects presented themselves as open to all faiths and institutions serving the larger community. The opening and ground stone laying ceremonies were conducted by local Jews in cooperation with civic institutions of the city, who often performed key ceremonies to express their appreciation of the Jewish contribution.[24]

The successful creation of an American-Jewish civil religion was instrumental in incorporating this new element of Jewish identity into American civil religion. This found its expression in numerous public acts where American Jews merged Jewish and American symbolism, identifying a common mission and also successfully encouraging American Jews to enact their Jewish identity in the American public arena. How well Jews connected their own history and destiny with the American nation is best portrayed in public ceremonies such as the dedication of the "Statue of Religious Liberty" on the occasion of the centennial celebration of the American Independence in Philadelphia's Fairmount Park in 1876: the statue needs very little explanation. It has a female figure depicting "Liberty," holding the constitution in one hand and shielding a young child, "The Genius of Devotion," with the other. In front of the group, the artist placed the snake, "intolerance," creeping toward "Liberty," and the American Eagle, "Freedom," battling the snake. Not only did this statue connect the B'nai B'rith actively to the world of American religion, confirming the significance of the First Amendment for the Jewish community, it also signaled to the outside world how deeply American Judaism was connected to American civic ideals.[25]

The unparalleled growth of the order between 1851 and 1885 as well as the formation of seven American districts and its national presence by 1856 made the B'nai B'rith America's key Jewish organization, which by the year 1885 represented 25,000 members. Benjamin Peixotto's[26] diplomatic mission as American Consul to Romania, however, has proved that the order's name had long surpassed its original sphere of influence and that the meaning of the "B'nai B'rith order" had become synonymous for a unique Jewish identity, solidarity, system of self-help and access to the modern civil public sphere in the Diaspora, allowing the American Jew to become a role model among European Jewries.[27]

It was striking that, when in 1883 the first lodge abroad was founded in Berlin, it was called "Reichsloge," indicating a close connection between the order and the German nation. The strong American-Jewish civil self-awareness raised suspicion about unwanted *Jewish* political activity and access. The German organization of the order was only allowed to open up its doors in Germany under statutes[28] which stressed that the order was exclusively to serve a *merely philanthropic* purpose, forcing the order to state that it had no intention of engaging in the *political or civil* sphere. This limited the range of the order tremendously, and although the German B'nai B'rith became an extremely popular social organization among German Jews, the organization served different needs of the community. In Germany the order provided a platform for sociability and solidarity of Jews. They even succeeded in merging Jewish identity with that of the emerging German nation, but the nation increasingly rejected Jews. This was not the failure of the B'nai B'rith as such, but the result of the German nation-making process which had started long before and clearly limited the options of the order.[29]

Unlike in the United States, the German nation-making process was long delayed and its democratic and republican elements failed to succeed. The failure of the revolution of 1848 and the defeat of the liberal movements in Germany increasingly gave way to conservative and reactionary forces, which marked the process of identity formation within the emerging German nation: when the nation state materialized in 1871 and all Jews finally reached full emancipation through a constitution, civil liberties had been brought about "from above," instead of being founded on the desire of all elements of society for a modern democratic bourgeois civil society. They envisioned the nation in an ideological framework which stressed anti-modernist elements as well as a romanticist concept of a uniquely *German* way. "Germanness" was not defined as the result of a set of Enlightenment values which could be adopted and supported by any member of society, but as a value based on the identity of its "people." This meant that "Germanness" was determined by ancestry and the adherence to traditional societal patterns, rather than by concepts of citizenship based on Enlightenment thinking. Such a society did not allow a modern civil society to develop since by definition it prevented the integration of all its citizens and minority groups on the basis of equality. Those who stood outside the definition of German peoplehood by birth and ancestry were automatically excluded from finding an equally respectable place therein. The German B'nai B'rith tried to follow the same pattern as the American B'nai B'rith and attempted to define a place for German Jews at the heart of the German nation; they argued that German Jews had a distinct German ethnic identity, like the regional ethnic groups who constituted the German nation—"the Bavarians," "the Rhinelanders," and "the Westphalians"—claiming that after a 2,000-year presence in the German lands, German Jews would constitute a German "Stamm."[30] This effort, however, was doomed to failure from its very inception: while the German territories were accepted as the individual and historic components of the newly founded nation, the German Jews were not. As German nationalism developed it was increasingly built upon a "Germanic" kinship and the idea of a Protestant religious mission: this form of "integral" nationalism was based on the construction of a past and future that did not attribute all members of society the same status and opportunity of participation, but excluded Jews, Catholics, and Socialists.

Even complete assimilation including conversion did not lead to Jews being accepted as "truly German" and thus to becoming an integral part of the nation. Contemporary political discourse claimed that the "social question" and the "Jewish question" were alike.[31] Increasingly the term "völkisch" (folkish) was used in public language, and in 1909, Meyers Grosses Konversations-Lexikon stated that the definition of the adjective "völkisch" equated to the term "national."[32] Even worse, toward the end of the nineteenth century, growing modern and state supported anti-Semitism based on political and racial theories sought to compensate the deficits of the "delayed nation" by constructing a nationalism, a sense of Protestant German national religious mission that destroyed all hopes that Jews would be allowed to find a place within the German nation. The best example of an organization specifically designed to claim and define German-Jewish belonging to the nation is probably the Centralverein deutscher Staatsbürger jüdischen Glaubens (Central Association of German Citizens of the Jewish Faith) founded in 1893. The Centralverein sought to defend the Jewish claim to "Germanness" with political and legal means and tried to support the development of a German-Jewish self-awareness,[33] but tragically failed, as shown by Avraham Barkai, due to the prevailing German "cultural code."[34]

The fact that being Jewish was a major hurdle for inclusion in the German nation was rooted in the Christian image of Judaism earlier in the nineteenth century when Judaism was not considered to be an equally respectable religion but rather a "nation." This view eventually led to the accusation that Jews represented a "state within the state," a distinct ethnic group that could not be integrated into the German nation.[35] While this perspective served as the basis for the acculturation and confessionalization of Judaism as well as for the discourse on Jewish integration into German society and culture, the Protestant church continued to play a seminal role in defining the relationship between religion and nation.[36] Unlike in the case of American national identity where Protestant dissenters had helped to create a civil religion providing an open platform for all its groups to unite in order to form a nation, German national identity increasingly used the polarization of "Germanness" and "Jewishness" in order to define the boundaries of inclusion and exclusion.[37] Unlike the United States, where diversity and cultural difference stood at the core of the nation, the opposite became the ideal of German nationhood where maintaining a distinct Jewish identity would continue to conflict with societal and political acceptance. In the United States secular Jewish organizations became a pattern for an ongoing communication and negotiation of American Jewry with American society and polity. It clearly became American Jews' trademark to engage in the public sphere as both Jews and Americans.

Notes

1. Jürgen Kocka, "Civil Society in Historical Perspective," in *Civil Society: Berlin Perspectives*, ed. John Keane (New York and Oxford: Berghahn Books, 2007), 37–50, here 40.

2. Michael A. Meyer, *Response to Modernity: A History of the Reform Movement* (Detroit, MI: Wayne State University Press, 1988), 227.

3. Cornelia Wilhelm, *Deutsche Juden in Amerika, Bürgerliches Selbstbewusstsein und Jüdische Identität in den Orden B'nai B'rith und Treue Schwestern, 1843–1914* (Stuttgart: Steiner, 2007), 50.

4. Vgl. Uwe Puschner, *Die völkische Bewegung im wilhelminischen Kaiserreich. Sprache—Rasse—Religion* (Darmstadt: Wissenschaftliche Buchgesellschaft, 2001).

5. Jürgen Kocka, "German History before Hitler: The Debate about the German Sonderweg," *Journal of Contemporary History* 23 (1988): 3–16, here 13. Although criticizing Geoff Eley's and David Blackbourn's argument (in their 1984 book, *The Pecularities of German History: Bourgeois Society and Politics in Nineteenth-Century Germany*), Kocka stresses the weakness of civic virtues in German bourgeois civil society.

6. Avraham Barkai, *Branching Out: German Jewish Immigration to the United States, 1820–1914* (New York: Holmes and Maier, 1994), 9.

7. Ibid., 20. Barkai discusses this first wave of immigrants in detail in his first chapter.

8. See Jacob Toury, *Soziale und Politische Geschichte der Juden in Deutschland 1847–1971: Zwischen Revolution, Reaktion und Emanzipation* (Düsseldorf: Droste, 1977), 211–214. See also Ludwig Lesser, *Die Chronik der Gesellschaft der Freunde in Berlin, zur Feier ihres fünfzigjährigen Jubiläums* (Berlin: printed as a manuscript, 1842), 5, 78, 94.

9. See also Stefan-Ludwig Hoffmann, *Die Politik der Geselligkeit. Freimaurerlogen in der deutschen Bürgergesellschaft, 1840–1918* (Göttingen: Vandenhoeck & Ruprecht, 2000), 44–55. See also Helmut Reinalter, ed., *Freimaurer und Geheimbünde im 18. Jahrhundert in Mitteleuropa* (Frankfurt am Main: Suhrkamp 1983).

10. James Reichley, *Faith in Politics* (Washington, DC: Brookings, 2002), 53–112.

11. See, for instance, Deborah L. Madsen, *American Exceptionalism* (Jackson: University Press of Mississippi, 1998).

12. Seymour-Martin Lipset, *American Exceptionalism: A Double Edged Sword* (New York: W. W. Norton, 1996).

13. Reichley, *Faith in Politics*, 53–112.

14. Wilhelm, *Deutsche Juden*, 170–84.

15. Jacob Katz, *Jews and Freemasons in Europe 1723–1939* (Cambridge, MA: Harvard University Press, 1970); see also Jacob Katz, "Echte und imaginäre Beziehung zwischen Freimaurerei und Judentum," in *Geheime Gesellschaften*, ed. Peter Christian Ludz and Ludwig Hammermeyer (Heidelberg: Lambert Schneider, 1979), 51–61, and Jacob Katz, "Samuel Hirsch: Rabbi, Philosopher and Freemason," in Jacob Katz, *Emancipation and Assimilation: Studies in Modern Jewish History* (Farnborough: Gregg, 1972), 159–72.

16. Wilhelm, *Deutsche Juden*, 46, 51–2,173.

17. Ibid., 15, 64–72.

18. Ibid., 50.

19. Ibid., 67–72. It was particularly large scale charitable projects, such as the founding of hospitals and orphanages, which became a transmission belt for activities in American civil society; ibid., 184–207.

20. Ibid., 172–84.

21. "The Progress of the IOBB," *The Menorah* 21 (February 1896): 67–78.

22. Wilhelm, *Deutsche Juden*, 172–84.

23. Ibid., 178–80.

24. Ibid., 187, 190–91.

25. Ibid., 182–3.

26. Benjamin Peixotto's prominence resulted from his former B'nai B'rith presidency.

27. See Lloyd P. Gartner, "Roumania, America and World Jewry: Consul Peixotto in Bucharest, 1870–1876," *American Jewish Historical Quarterly* 58 (1968): 25–116, and Cornelia Wilhelm, "Community in Modernity—Finding Jewish Solidarity within the Independent Order of B'nai B'rith," *Simon Dubnow Yearbook* 1 (2000): 297–319, here 315.

28. Deborah Dash Moore, *B'nai B'rith and the Challenge of Ethnic Leadership* (Albany, NY: SUNY Press, 1982), 39.

29. Andreas Reinke, "'Eine Sammlung des jüdischen Bürgertums': Der Unabhängige Orden B'nai B'rith in Deutschland," in *Juden, Bürger, Deutsche: Zur Geschichte von Vielfalt und Differenz 1800–1933*, ed. Andreas Gotzmann, Rainer Liedke, and Till van Rahden (Tübingen: Mohr Siebeck 2001), 315–40; and see Andreas Gotzmann, "Zwischen Nation und Religion: Die deutschen Juden auf der Suche nach einer bürgerlichen Konfessionalität," in *Juden, Bürger, Deutsche*, 241–61.

30. Reinke, "Eine Sammlung des jüdischen Bürgertums," passim.

31. Derek Penslar, "Philanthropy, the 'Social Question' and Jewish identity in Imperial Germany," *Leo Baeck Institute Yearbook* 38 (1993): 51–73

32. Puschner, *Die völkische Bewegung*, 27.

33. Avraham Barkai, *"Wehr Dich!" Der Centralverein deutscher Staatsbürger jüdischen Glaubens (C.V.) 1893–1938* (Munich: C. H. Beck, 2002), 214.

34. Ibid., 16.

35. Gotzmann, "Zwischen Nation und Religion," 244–5.

36. See Christian Wiese, *Challenging Colonial Discourse: Jewish Studies and Protestant Theology in Wilhelmine Germany* (Leiden and Boston: Brill, 2005).

37. Gotzmann, "Zwischen Nation und Religion," 247.

CHAPTER 8

THE PHILADELPHIA CONFERENCE (1869) AND GERMAN REFORM: A HISTORICAL MOMENT IN A TRANSNATIONAL STORY OF PROXIMITY AND ALIENATION

Christian Wiese

---

1 Prologue: American-Jewish responses to the Abraham Geiger centenary in 1910

On May 28, 1910, on the occasion of the centenary of Abraham Geiger's birth in Frankfurt am Main, the renowned American Reform rabbi and influential theologian Kaufmann Kohler delivered a memorial address entitled "Abraham Geiger: The Master Builder of Modern Judaism." Born in Fürth, Kohler had grown up within the context of Bavarian Orthodoxy and studied with Jacob Ettlinger in Altona as well as with Samson R. Hirsch in Frankfurt, but his intellectual and spiritual path had been strongly influenced by the ideas of the German Jewish reform theologian. It had also been Geiger who had supported Kohler's emigration to America in 1869, suggesting he should leave "for the promised land of progressive Judaism," and recommending him to American rabbinical colleagues.[1] Subsequently Kohler served as a rabbi at the Beth-El Synagogue in Detroit, the Sinai Congregation in Chicago, and Temple Beth-El in New York, before being elected president of the Hebrew Union College in Cincinnati in 1903.[2] His exuberant praise of Geiger shows very clearly to what extent the historian and prominent representative of German Reform Judaism had, since the wave of German Jewish immigrants in the 1850 and 1860s, become a hero and symbolic model of American progressive Judaism. At the same time, Kohler's remarks convey the impression of a cautious critical distance that hinted at a self-confident awareness on his part of the new and independent intellectual achievements of the American rabbinate since Geiger's death in 1874. With Geiger, the "genius of rejuvenation" and "spiritual regenerator of Judaism," with the "prophet to whom God revealed the secret of the age for modern Israel," Judaism, Kohler emphasized, had indeed reached a new stage of its existence. "He broke the spell of centuries and spoke the liberating word which imbued it with new life and vigor," i.e., he gave the Reform movement its scholarly and historical foundation: "Before the torch light of his keen research and the brightness of his vision, the dark recesses of Jewish history were lit up, and order and harmony entered the chaos of Jewish thought."[3]

Moses Mendelssohn's philosophical thought in the eighteenth century and the historical approach of the leading co-founder of *Wissenschaft des Judentums*, Leopold

Zunz, according to Kohler, had not managed to efficiently transform the reality of European Jewry. Instead of bringing about a vital reform of Judaism, their ideas had remained theoretical and caught in rationalism or philological analysis.[4] In contrast to them, Kaufmann Kohler argued, Geiger had achieved much more than the mere negation and destruction of the old traditions. His contribution consisted of a creative blend of historical interpretation of Jewish tradition, a critical diagnosis of traditional Judaism's severe crisis, and a constructive vision of a cautious modernization of Judaism that was at the same time consistent and aware of tradition. Geiger's accomplishments, he claimed, went far beyond the reformist war cry against the persistence of a culturally obsolete stage of Judaism and even transcended the reforms he himself had introduced or proposed, reforms, "which, after all, remained but half-measures compared with what his fellow-champions and particularly the American Reform pioneers did."[5] Geiger's true significance lay particularly in his "ingenious powers as a historian and theologian," which had enabled him to achieve his path-breaking modernizing reinterpretation of Judaism.[6] However, it had needed others to put his ideas into practice in a much more uncompromising fashion. Apparently, Kohler considered the fact that Geiger had embraced the principle of historical continuity and followed an evolutionary rather than a revolutionary strategy one of his most important strengths, but he also indicated that, in the meantime, history had surpassed his activities as a practical reformer. More important than Geiger's contribution to the inner-Jewish reorientation, Kohler suggested, was the impact of his historical research on Judaism's cultural acknowledgment within the non-Jewish society. Far from his being a Christianizer, as opponents of Reform Judaism used to claim, Geiger had proven to be "the most persistent, the most outspoken and the most dreaded antagonist of official Christianity."[7] His research on Jewish antiquity as well as on Judaism's historical relevance for Christianity and Islam had procured the Jewish minority a respected place within European culture, unmasked the traditional contempt for Pharisaic and Rabbinic Judaism as a biased historical error, and unmistakably brought forward the religious superiority of Jewish tradition within the broader horizon of world history.

An abundance of similar voices can be discerned in America during this period, be it Emanuel Schreiber's hagiographic book, *Abraham Geiger: The Greatest Reform Rabbi of the Nineteenth Century*,[8] numerous further sermons and speeches on the occasion of the Geiger centenary in 1910,[9] or contemporary representations of the history of the Reform movement such as the one published by David Philipson in 1907.[10] Philipson, the son of German Jewish immigrants, a graduate of the first generation of rabbinical students at the liberal Hebrew Union College in Cincinnati and later rabbi of the local Congregation Bne Israel, delivered a commemorative speech on July 1, 1910 at the meeting of the Central Conference of American Rabbis, in which he emphasized Geiger's achievements as an advocate of the freedom of critical scholarship, who had paved the way for a prudent reform that avoided schismatic inclinations. He had neither been "a blind worshipper of the past" nor a "ruthless iconoclast," neither a "romanticist" nor an "ultra-modernist," but "in the best sense of the word a reformer, who felt that the present can continue all that is fine and worthy in the past by presenting the everlasting truth of

Judaism in a form which attracts the contemporary generation."[11] As a critical thinker and thoughtful practical reformer he had modernized all aspects of Jewish religious reality, from liturgy through the position of women within Judaism, and, at the same time, taken the role of a "prophet of universalistic Judaism," who had redefined Judaism's role in modern society and overcome Jewish religious and cultural self-ghettoization.[12]

Emil G. Hirsch, who had come to America in 1869 with his father, the philosopher Samuel Hirsch, from Luxembourg, but had returned to Europe in 1872 in order to study with Geiger at the newly established Hochschule für die Wissenschaft des Judentums in Berlin, characterized his teacher's ambivalence between radical freedom regarding his scholarly judgment and his sense of responsibility for the more conservative members of the Jewish community by quoting Geiger's own ironic self-description: To his American students, Hirsch told his readers, the historian had described his attitude "as that of the famous Schulklopfer of the proverb, whose business it was to arouse the pious early in the morning for the hour of worship and who having knocked at the doors went back to his own bed." Geiger's true sympathy, however, had been with the radicals, particularly his intellectual followers in America:

> America was for him the land of promise. That his old companions in arms [David] Einhorn, [Samuel] Adler and [Samuel] Hirsch in the young republic had carried to fruition the work begun in the old fatherland filled him with joy, and that the sons of his yokemates, and other Americans, pilgrimed to the school where he taught in quest of scholarly equipment for continuing the work of the fathers made him young again.[13]

The representatives of the Reform movement in America at the beginning of the twentieth century thus unanimously praised Abraham Geiger as a towering figure of *Wissenschaft des Judentums*, as an exceptionally gifted polemicist against Christianity, and as a prudent and tolerant reformer characterized by a clear sense for historical continuity—in sum: as a scholar-reformer, whose work provided orientation to both European and American Reform Judaism.[14] The same is true for the many rabbis and scholars affiliated with the German Jewish Reform Movement who had found inspiration from his ideas.[15] As we will see, however, a careful reading of the American sources, particularly those published during Geiger's lifetime or immediately after his death in 1874, leads to a more differentiated image and helps discovering other, more ambivalent elements, including traces of serious conflicts between Geiger and some of his friends and disciples who had left Germany behind in the mid-nineteenth century. The impression created by the commemorative speeches and articles in 1910 is that of an attempt to do justice to Geiger's heritage without concealing that American Jews had pushed on with the modernization of Judaism to a degree that went beyond what had been conceivable in Germany. The scholar and reformer Geiger had become a historical figure whose limits, arising from prevailing circumstances in the "Old World," could be ascertained without particular polemics and without being compelled to question his paramount significance for German and American Judaism in the nineteenth century or even the relevance of crucial elements of his work for the present. As we will see, there had been a time in which the need to dissociate American Reform from its German origins engendered a much more ambivalent, emotional and polemical assessment.

This dimension of the American reformers' response to Abraham Geiger's thinking deserves a closer analysis, since it sheds light on the complex relationship between the German Jewish and American Jewish Reform movement since the 1860s. This essay is devoted to the ambivalence characterizing American Jewish perceptions of the German Jewish tradition of Reform in general and of Geiger's Reform agenda in particular— views that, as I would like to argue, oscillated between proximity, even profound admiration on the part of American Jewish intellectuals, and gradual skepticism and alienation. By briefly addressing a skirmish between Geiger and one of his most important friends and ideological allies, the radical Reform rabbi David Einhorn, in the wake of the famous Philadelphia Conference (1869), and by interpreting it in the broader context of the complex and shifting story of the transnational link between German Reform and the classical American Reform movement, I would like to draw attention to the conspicuous tension between German Jewish claims of cultural hegemony on the one hand and the peculiar blend of admiration and emancipatory rhetoric within American Jewish circles on the other hand that seems to have defined the relationship between the two movements during the late nineteenth and the early twentieth century. Even though their devotion to the spiritual heritage of German Jewish scholarship and the gratitude for the inspiration they had received from the reform ideas developed in Germany remained undiminished, the rabbis who had emigrated to America since the 1850s were increasingly disturbed by what they perceived as conservative elements within the development of German Reform Judaism.[16] By the 1870s, they seriously questioned whether Ludwig Philippson, Abraham Geiger, and other reformers could still serve as role models for the Jewish religion in America. The second generation of radical reformers, men like Kaufmann Kohler or Emil G. Hirsch, both sons-in-law of David Einhorn, gradually became aware not only that the younger American Jews preferred to speak English and had begun to reject the German Jewish hegemony, but also that German Reform Judaism had settled into stagnation. At the same time, the German reformers observed with a certain degree of indignation what they perceived as an illegitimate claim to superiority in important circles of the American radical Reform movement.

2 A controversy between German and American Reform: David Einhorn, Abraham Geiger, and the Philadelphia Conference

A telling expression of the mutual alienation and disillusionment during those years can be found in a conflict between David Einhorn and Abraham Geiger triggered by the latter's critical comparison of German and American Reform Judaism published in 1870 in the wake of the Philadelphia Conference (1869), which had been organized under Einhorn's leadership and which aimed at defining the future theological and practical guidelines of American Reform Judaism.[17] At first glance, it might seem as a rather unlikely controversy, since both reformers had been close intellectual allies since the religious-cultural controversies of the 1840s in Germany. During those years, in which Einhorn served as a rabbi, first in Schwerin and later in Budapest, and in which he developed the central elements of his reform philosophy that was to become the basis for the uncompromising attitude he developed since his emigration to America in 1855,[18] his relationship with Geiger had been a respectful, even amicable one. Apparently they agreed on most aspects pertaining to the contemporary debates regarding the legitimacy of Judaism's modernization, as is demonstrated by Einhorn's intervention during the so-called "Geiger-Tiktin affair," which raged in Breslau from 1842 to 1849.[19] One of the core points in this heated controversy lay in the question as to whether a reform-oriented scholar such as Geiger, who in his writings had questioned whether the rabbinical tradition and its hermeneutics of the Bible possessed the quality of divine revelation, and who had applied the criteria of historical science to the sources of Judaism, could legitimately serve a Jewish congregation as rabbi. Geiger himself made a distinction between the strictly scientific approach and the duty of the rabbi to keep to the ordinances as well as to approach customs that were suffused with religious feeling with respect, even if from a scientific point of view they seemed to him to be obsolete.[20] As regards the authority of tradition, Geiger asserted that the Talmud, in contrast to the Bible, could make no claim to canonical significance, and legitimized the renewal of religious life with the aid of the principle—based on the idea of the oral Torah—of a continual adjustment of tradition to the needs of the present.[21]

Einhorn was one of the seventeen reformers who were called upon by the committee of senior chairmen of the Israelite congregation in Breslau to address the question of whether the principle of progress advocated by Geiger was legitimate from a Jewish perspective, whether researchers who questioned the authority of rabbinical literature could really still call themselves Jews, and whether Jewish theology could justify the integration of free scientific research as a new religious and cultural system of interpretation.[22] In his learned expert opinion Einhorn defended above all Geiger's right to research the Talmudic sources historically and, in his reforms of outdated practices, to invoke the principle of development. Far more sharply and trenchantly than many other experts, with all due acknowledgment of the truthfulness of the rabbinical tradition, Einhorn condemned the Orthodox "apotheosis" of the Talmud, its "authority which transforms Judaism into a static swamp and condemns it to eternal stagnation."[23] However, if it were not to be a "frivolous game with what is holy," deviation from the ceremonial laws must be based on "the spirit of Judaism" and on mature, scientific insight.[24] Geiger, he argued, did not mock the Talmud; rather, he displayed the earnest desire of a "mind and soul struggling toward light and truth," to research the sources of Judaism in order to discover "what elements are part of its essential nature—and what elements are accretions, how much of its divine, eternal and developing spirit, under the cloak, is prepared for breakthrough and longs for it, while the various periods of its existence have already gone out into the world, or are yet to come."[25]

Einhorn's defense of Geiger during the controversy marked the beginning of a relationship that was, despite occasional disagreements, characterized by a fundamental consensus. Even though his intellectual alliance with the much more radical reformer Samuel Holdheim became apparent in the 1840s, he seems to have felt, at least until his emigration, a strong sympathy for Geiger's endeavor to provide a cautious rationale for the practical reforms he suggested, without fighting the tradition in which God's will manifested itself, and without undermining the authority of the Bible. After Einhorn's departure for Baltimore, where he was offered the rabbinate of the Reform congregation Har Sinai, the relationship between him and Geiger had remained a cordial and mutually respectful one, despite a few critical comments on Einhorn's part that can be found in the 1850s in reviews published in his journal *Sinai* which anticipated later conflicts. Thus, Einhorn stated in 1857 in a review on Geiger's work on Leone da Modena, that he was actually unsatisfied with everything his friend had written in recent years—the lion who had once roared had now succumbed to sleep and preferred to indulge in historical studies rather than promoting serious reforms.[26] It took, however, many years before others witnessed that the Atlantic Ocean that was separating them had, to some degree, also become an ideological divide that unavoidably had to lead to a public controversy.[27]

When the news of Geiger's sudden death arrived in America in 1874, Einhorn belonged to those who immediately paid tribute to the famous scholar. In an obituary in the *Jewish Times* he gave voice to the profound grief prevailing on both sides of the Atlantic and praised Geiger's ingenious insight, his path-breaking achievements as a historian, his uncompromising religious and moral critique of traditional Judaism, his "magisterial and illuminating reflections on the position of women in Judaism," and the pioneering literary and historical works that had made him a guiding figure of theological scholarship.[28] In his memorial address in honor of Geiger on November 21, 1874 in Temple Beth-El in New York, Einhorn characterized him as a "great luminary in Israel," as one of the "greatest sons of Abraham who bore the name of the Patriarch,"[29] and expressed his regret about the fact that this towering figure of nineteenth-century Jewish Reform had unjustly fallen into oblivion among younger American Jews. A comparison between Einhorn's speech and memorial addresses delivered by other companions of Geiger who had emigrated to America,[30] reveals two elements that were conspicuously absent in Einhorn's depiction: an explicit appreciation of Geiger's prudent and constructive reform on the one hand, and any trace of a critique of the conservative traits of his reform concept on the other. In this moment of mourning David Einhorn refrained from criticizing Geiger or from emphasizing the superiority of the more radical and uncompromising American Reform movement, limiting himself to allusions to a severe clash that had occurred between him and Geiger a few years earlier. This conflict, he indicated, had led to a "long-lasting alienation" that had only been overcome shortly before Geiger's death thanks to the latter's "kind and conciliatory attitude"—a reconciliation that, as Einhorn added, was very important to him because, despite a range of deviating convictions, he had always admired him as the "luminary of exile."[31] Attentive readers of the *Jewish Times* certainly still remembered the rather bitter attack Einhorn had launched against Geiger in 1870 as a response to the latter's critique of the ideological path of the American Reform agenda. As will be shown, the public conflict between the two friends was not just one among the many polemical skirmishes Einhorn had engaged in, among others with Samuel Holdheim and Samuel Hirsch. Rather, at least from Einhorn's point of view, this was a much more fundamental ideological debate in which apparently the legitimacy of his entire philosophy as well as his role as the representative of an increasingly self-confident American Jewish religious movement was at stake.

The controversy had started with an article Geiger had published in 1870 in his widely read journal *Jüdische Zeitschrift für Wissenschaft und Leben* under the title "Die Versammlung zu Leipzig und die zu Philadelphia."[32] This essay had provided a critical comparison between the intellectual and cultural circumstances of the Reform movement in Germany and America and included a few polemical elements that prompted Einhorn to a sharply worded response.[33] In his article, Geiger had responded to or anticipated criticism on the part of his American colleagues regarding the moderate character of the decisions made by the Leipzig Reform Synod in 1869,[34] pointing out that in Germany—because of the principle of unified Jewish congregations—the implementation of uncompromising reforms was much more difficult than in American congregations, which consisted mainly of like-minded members and were thus much better able to agree upon radical reforms and to put them into practice. Since the reformers in Germany had to take the traditionalist attitude of parts of the synagogue members into consideration, he claimed, it would be unfair to compare the relatively unsatisfactory results of the Leipzig Synod to those of the Philadelphia Conference.[35] Einhorn rejected this view outright, arguing that "life in America wasn't a bed of roses either," because rabbis there had to deal with the diversity of congregations consisting of members with immigrants from very different cultural backgrounds.[36]

In his assessment of the Philadelphia Conference, Geiger started with a *captatio benevolentiae*, praising the "capable" American rabbis, whom he characterized as "kind and brave old friends," and emphasized that all of them—the "dignified and considerate" Samuel Adler, who had left behind his propensity for "apologetic conservatism ... on board of the steamship"; David Einhorn, who had "always been glowing with youthful and noble fervour" and was now inspired by the "fresh air of freedom" in America; and the "straightforward and open" reformer Samuel Hirsch, who was now "adapting his philosophical approach and his desire for symbolization to America's practical spirit"—stood in closest relationship to the German Reform movement:

> What we are encountering here is flesh from our flesh, spirit from our spirit: they are Germans, who have crossed the sea, carrying with them their knowledge and theological approach taken from their original fatherland; still feasting on the latter's spiritual sources, they are, however, empowered and inspired by the more liberal circumstances in America to a more forceful and consistent procedure.[37]

Geiger then proceeded to discuss the seven principles proposed by the Philadelphia Conference as binding elements of American Reform Judaism. These principles can be seen as a precise summary of the theological reform theory specific to Einhorn, which he had developed in Germany and then consistently translated into the American cultural and political context. At the center stood the attempt to raise as the standard of Jewish identity, in clear antithetical sentences, the universal "mission" of modern Judaism, divested of all historically determined particularistic elements, in order to distance Judaism programmatically from traditional Orthodoxy and to confront anti-Jewish prejudices. As the American reformers stated, Israel's messianic aim was not the restoration of the Jewish state, the "repeated separation from the peoples," but "the unification of all people as God's children" in recognition of the uniqueness of God as well as of "the unity of all rational beings and their calling to moral observance"; the destruction of the Second Temple and Israel's Exile, the *galut*, were not to be understood as a "punishment for the sinfulness of Israel," but as the expression of the divine intention "to send the members of the Jewish line to all the corners of the Earth, to fulfill their high priestly task of leading the nations to the true acknowledgement and honoring of God"; "Israel's status as the people chosen for the religion" and as the bearer of the highest idea of humanity was to be emphasized, but only in the same breath as the universal mission of Judaism and the idea of the "equal love that God has for all his children."[38] The principles of the Philadelphia Conference had thus voiced central themes of the European and American Reform movement of the nineteenth century which had developed since the Enlightenment as a response to the image of Judaism held by non-Jewish theologies and in the context of politico-social debates about Judaism's social and cultural integration—an option that was allegedly prevented by an indissoluble alien Jewish "special identity." At the same time, these principles aspired to provide a universalistic re-interpretation of fundamental themes of Jewish tradition: Israel's status as the chosen people, exile and suffering in the *galut*, Jewish existence in the Diaspora, the vision of the messianic future, the relationship between Judaism and humanity and other religions, the relevance of ceremonial law for the modern era as well as the relationship between universalism and particularism—a theme that played a crucial role in contemporary debates on Judaism's capability for modernization.[39]

All these key elements of Einhorn's reform philosophy seemed at stake when Geiger undertook his harsh critique of the seven principles and the practical consequences drawn from them. Even though he conceded a "close affinity" between the results of the Leipzig Synod and those of the Philadelphia Conference, he clearly insisted on the superiority of his own ideas[40] and apparently looked at Einhorn's convictions and those of his American colleagues with a certain suspicion, as he quite rightly perceived them as a kind of implicit intellectual and theological declaration of independence on the part of the American Reform movement that embarked on surpassing its German model in terms of theoretical as well as practical radicalism. Einhorn, who did not suffer from an inferiority complex either, accused Geiger of lacking "scholarly and religious earnestness" and of being motivated mainly by huffiness given the American rabbis' "presumption," since they were not in the slightest inclined "to confirm or even take into consideration Geiger's lame theses," rejecting instead the "sanctification of the hesitating, unprincipled and stillborn." Einhorn had never stopped admiring Geiger's acumen, even though the latter had "always been anxious to interfere with and retard determined reforms," but now he had seen him for the first time "theorizing in favor of the lack of principles" und taking sides with "the worst enemies of religious progress."[41] In private letters to his American comrades-in-arms Einhorn was even harsher, for instance when writing to Bernhard Felsenthal that Geiger was slapping the true reformers in the face and that the German reform conferences were full of "characterlessness, hypocrisy and superficiality."[42]

Geiger's detailed critical discussion of the principles of Philadelphia as well as Einhorn's response are multifaceted, referring to fundamental theological and historical convictions, to specific liturgical and halakhic questions as well as to topics (such as the meaning of the Sabbath or the legitimacy of mixed marriages) which had prompted controversies also within the American Reform movement. Some of the issues raised during the debate point to a gradually deepening divide between Geiger's concept of reform and the American radical ideas embodied by Einhorn's philosophy.

A fundamental objection voiced by Geiger referred to the "theorizing" and "dogmatizing" language of the principles which, in his eyes, imposed a full-fledged confession on the part of the Jewish communities to rather doubtable assertions and, on this insufficient basis, drew unjustified conclusions with regard to important practical issues, for instance the receding role Hebrew was to play in the ritual.[43] Einhorn denied that the intention was to impose anything on the communities, but emphasized the need to formulate clear principles which offered orientation, and suggested that what stood behind Geiger's "clamor about the dogma," was the inclination to deprive Judaism of its character as a religion and "to reduce it, with Mendelssohn, to a conglomerate of laws." If this was true, however, he was concerned that it would be quite difficult to make it plausible "in which way it could claim a world mission, or, if—in contrast to Mendelssohn, these laws were only seen as eternally binding with regard to their purely human aspects, it could be ascribed a potential of resistance against Christianity any longer."[44]

Even more important was Geiger's suggestion that the principles of Philadelphia were profoundly contradictory. The first principle, according to which Israel's messianic aim was not the restoration of the old Jewish state and its renewed separation from the other nations, but the "union of all the children of God in the confession of the unity of God, so as to realize the unity of all rational creatures and their call to moral sanctification," Geiger argued, was clearly opposed to the fifth principle which demanded that, in the same breath with the emphasis on God's equal love toward all His children, also the "selection of Israel as the people of religion, as the bearer of the highest idea of humanity" should be underscored.[45] As a much less ambiguous alternative he pointed to his own Leipzig principles which argued that Judaism was "the religion of truth and light," that Israel was aware of its mission to be the "bearer and herold of these teachings," and that the Jews hoped that "these teachings would more and more become the common good of the entire educated world, thus allowing Israel to universalize itself"; however, for this to happen, "Israel's national element had to take a backseat."[46] Einhorn characterized this argument as a completely nebulous definition of the content of messianic hope: "Wouldn't it be possible also for Christianity, atheism or pantheism to confess themselves to this hypothesis-Messiah, this thoroughly mysterious person?" The Jewish character of messianic awareness, he claimed, had been totally lost in Geiger's theology; however, especially with regard to this aspect a "strong emphasis of the fundamental ideas," with which the Jewish religion was at stake, was indispensable. Geiger's failure to clearly define what was essential for Judaism, Einhorn argued, had to do with the fact that he was "on bad terms with Israel's chosenness," because he feared that non-Jews would "sniff at" an overly strong emphasis on this notion. However, the conviction regarding Israel's universal mission, which Geiger shared, as Einhorn conceded, would be untenable without the "proud awareness of our tribe that it had been sent by the Allfather to be a blessing for all families of the earth," and the abandonment of the messianic task to make the universal Jewish teaching of pure humanity the common good of all human beings would deprive Judaism of its religious-historical relevance.[47]

Geiger also strongly criticized the second principle of Philadelphia, according to which the loss of Israel's statehood and the fate of Jewish exile should not be understood as a consequence of Israel's sinfulness, but as the result of the divine purpose revealed to Abraham, which consisted "in the dispersion of the Jews to all parts of the earth, for the realization of their high-priestly mission, to lead the nations to the true knowledge and worship of God"—a dispensable and highly problematic "historico-philosophical construction," as far as Geiger was concerned.[48] The background of this criticism was apparently the historian's skepticism toward Einhorn's philosophical approach which was centered around a reinterpretation of the classical idea of "Israel's mission" and chosenness that could maybe be interpreted with the paradoxical notion of a "particularistic universalism." Einhorn's theology of history, whose main ideas can only be indicated here, aimed at providing a theoretical basis for his interpretation of Judaism as the pure embodiment of religious universalism. Starting from Friedrich W. J. Schelling's idea of an original, pre-biblical monotheism and a divine original revelation that develops into a growing "awareness of God" among humanity,[49] Einhorn postulated the distinction between an "original revelation" to Adam through the breath of creation and the revelation at Sinai—an interpretation that, firstly, permitted a consistent universalistic interpretation of the earliest origins of Judaism. If Judaism—and its revelation—begins not with Abraham or with the special revelation at Sinai, but at the beginning of biblical prehistory, then it becomes the "essence of Man"—"its truths and obligations are by their nature implanted by God, axioms of the human spirit and thus innate in the actual sense of the word."[50] Secondly, in this way the reason that is given by God, part of man's likeness to God, becomes the actual "organ" of revelation, which is imparted in the person's growing awareness.[51] The immutable moral law is part of this rational divine spirit in the person. The revelation of Sinai, which was limited to the people of Israel, and which in spite of the story of the epiphany is not an external but an internal process, brings the people of the covenant and the ceremonial law into play as an educational tool that is limited in time and space; the latter is at the same time divine and subject to change on account of advances in human reason. According to Einhorn, the "actual Shibboleth of Reform Judaism" is as follows:

> In its essence, Judaism is even older than the Israelite line; as pure essence of Man, as the expression of the divine spirit that is innate in us, it is as old—as the human

race. The origin and its course of development—it is rooted in Adam and reaches its pinnacle in messianically perfected humanity. It was not a religion, but a religious people that was newly created on Sinai, a priestly people that was first of all to show the ancient doctrine of God more deeply in itself, and then bring it to general rule.[52]

The "biblical particularism" that came into play at Sinai is thus "nothing other than a lever of unrestricted universalism"[53] and constitutes Israel's specific providential role in history. Reform Judaism, according to Einhorn, rests "on the unshakable cornerstone of a revelation that encompasses all times and all races, and created on Sinai only a central point in the people of the covenant, in which all its rays should be focused, in order to provide light and love for the one great organism of humanity."[54] Based on this notion of a polarity of universalism and particularism, Einhorn strongly accentuated the distinctive character of the Jewish people within history, in order to prevent its absorption by general culture. His concept of Israel as an *am ha-cohanim* (a "priestly people") summoned from history and of a Messiah "wandering" in exile[55] refers to a further crucial aspect of his philosophy: his understanding of the "mission of Israel" which he taught and preached with an intensity unmatched by any other reformer, as well as to his understanding of the relationship between Israel and the nations. He developed these ideas, which had already dominated his early theological comments at the rabbinical conferences in Germany, most impressively in his sermons, for example in 1859 at Tischa Be'Aw in his congregation in Baltimore, in an analysis of Isaiah 9:6: Certainly one should also remember the tears and blood of exile, but contrary to any Orthodox theology of sin and *galut*, this day of remembrance was much more a day of rejoicing, the day on which, from the ruins of the Jewish state with its institutions, "the foundation stone and cornerstone was laid for the enormous edifice of the messianic kingdom": "We celebrate today nothing less than the birthday of the Messiah, in other words Israel at the beginning of its messianic, world-redeeming vocation!"[56] One will hardly be mistaken if one understands this identification of Judaism as the Messiah of the nations as an attempt at a Jewish reclaiming of the idea of the suffering servant of God and as a polemical attack against Christianity's universal messianic claim.

In his sermon, Einhorn explicitly ascribed to the destruction of the Second Temple and the events at Sinai a revelatory quality of equal value, and thus justified that dialectic, characteristic for this thinking, of particularism and universalism which was to justify the autonomous continued existence of Judaism as a minority in Christian America: "From the flames of Sinai, God revealed himself to Israel through Moses, from the flames of the temple mount through Israel—to the whole of humanity!"[57] This is the same radical reinterpretation of exile and Messianism that recurs also in the principles of Philadelphia: the notion of Israel, punished for its sins and hoping for the coming of the Messiah, the return to Zion, and the restoration of the Temple, is replaced by that of a religious community that comes to embody the suffering Servant of the Lord and ths possesses messianic qualities itself. Judaism, according to Einhorn, was the epitome of Divine truth and human morality, and thus, exactly because of this, needed to preserve its uniqueness and distinctiveness in comparison to the other nations.

This interpretation of a Jewish universal mission rendered it possible, on the one hand, to make the case for a complete integration of the Jews into American society; on the other hand, it was meant to counter assimilation and to legitimize the preservation of a distinctive Jewish identity within the American context. A certain separation from the non-Jewish environment belonged, according to Einhorn, to what he used to call Israel's "priestly robes,"[58] which could only be cast off in the messianic era. The Jewish people with its Divine mission, he argued, would have disappeared long time ago, had it eradicated all particularistic boundaries during its history in the Diaspora. With the fulfillment of its messianic role, however, this mission will have been complete and Israel will merge with the nations under which it exists.

We are thus faced with the paradox that Einhorn's radical historico-theological universalism, together with his theory of an Adamitic pre-existence of Judaism before Israel became a people, and of a future messianic self-dissolution of the chosen "priestly people," evidently required as a counterweight a strong particularistic element in the present. Einhorn seems to have seen himself as forced to limit the apparent practical implications of his extreme theoretical universalism. The means for this were provided by the trenchant recourse to the aspect of chosenness, which was associated with a particularly marked consciousness of Judaism's special nature—an emphasis that Geiger considered to be much too strong. A considerable role was evidently played here by the American context, which inspired Einhorn's enthusiastic belief in humanity and progress,[59] but also triggered a strong concern that certain developments posed a threat to the preservation of Jewish identity in America. These developments included not only an increasing tendency toward indifference to and neglect of religious life within the Jewish community, but also the materialistic inclinations which Einhorn felt to be a serious threat to spiritual progress.[60] As long as this danger was not banished, Israel's messianic mission seemed to be not only unfinished, but more necessary than ever.

A comparison between the thinking of both reformers with regard to the relationship between universalism and particularism allows for a twofold explanation of their controversy. One aspect is the differing political and cultural context, particularly the fact that American Jewry's cultural integration was less precarious; in contrast to Geiger, who, in the German context, endeavored to emphasize Judaism's universalism and ability to integrate, Einhorn saw himself forced to underscore its remaining distinctive religious and ethnic element. At the same time, their differing views were also based on opposing theoretical assumptions: in his historico-theological reflections, the philosopher Einhorn advocated a much more radical universalism than the historian Geiger, who criticized that the speculative idea that the Jewish people had been a universal religion of humanity already before the revelation at Sinai and that Judaism, since then, had the task to spread the Divine truth until its ultimate victory, implied a problematic compulsion to emphasize a rhetoric of chosenness which threatened Judaism's universalism rather than making it theologically plausible.

It was not merely the theoretical basis of the seven principles of Philadelphia that triggered Geiger's criticism, but he also harshly attacked his American colleagues with regard to their practical reform proposals. The strongest dissensus between Geiger and

Einhorn concerned the wedding ceremony and its implications for the role of women in Jewish ritual. At first glance, this may be surprising: Since 1837, when he published an article devoted to the position of women in contemporary Judaism,[61] Geiger had consistently criticized rituals which humiliated and excluded women, denigrating them to an object and property of men, and there seems to have been a strong degree of agreement between him and Einhorn. The latter had been the spokesman for the committee dealing with the position of women within Judaism at the German Reform conference in Breslau in 1846 and had provided a masterly analysis of how the rabbis had additionally exacerbated the view of the social, legal and religious inferiority of women that was rooted in Mosaic law; as a consequence, he had demanded the acknowledgment of the complete religious equality of women with men.[62] Inspired by Geiger's article of 1837, and in obvious agreement with Samuel Holdheim's position, who was among the most firm critics of the treatment of women in the Jewish tradition,[63] Einhorn had asked "whether a proportion of our co-religionists which is eminently receptive to religious impressions shall continue—as heretofore—to experience an insulting exclusion from sharing in several duties and rights, to the detriment of themselves and the whole religious community," and called for the antiquated rabbinical views to be overcome:

> From their point of view, the rabbis were however fully entitled to systematically exclude the female sex from a significant portion of the religious obligations and rights, and the poor woman was not permitted to complain about the withholding of high, spiritual favors, since it was believed that God himself had uttered the condemnation of her; with so many insulting setbacks in civil life, she could not even complain that the house of God too was as good as locked against her, that she had to beg the rabbis for permission to make the daily expression of the Israelite creed like alms, she was not permitted to take part in religious instruction nor in certain holy parental duties, the performance of religious acts being sometimes waived, sometimes forbidden, and finally insulted most bitterly in the house of God by the daily benediction for the good fortune of not having been born a woman. . . . But for our religious awareness that all people are accorded an equal degree of natural holiness, and for which the distinctions in the Holy Scripture in this case have only a relative and momentary validity, it is a sacred duty to express the complete religious equality of the female sex most emphatically. In this respect life, which is stronger than any theory, has certainly achieved something; but for complete equality there is much that is still lacking, and even the little that has already been done still lacks legal force. It is thus part of our vocation to express the equal religious obligation and entitlement of woman, as far as possible, as lawful . . .[64]

Only later, in America, was Einhorn to turn his ideas into practice in the congregation. Thus in 1858, in a sermon in Baltimore, he condemned the "gallery cage" of the women's galleries, and granted the women of his congregation the same religious rights and duties.[65] Under his leadership, the Philadelphia Conference advocated a reform of the divorce law and a revision of the liturgy of the wedding ceremony to express the equal rights of the partners.[66] As a liturgical consequence, Einhorn had followed through with the decision that women should take an equal role in speaking the marriage vow during the ceremony and that bride and groom should mutually give each other the wedding ring. Geiger emphatically rejected this—from his point of view unnecessary—practice, emphasizing that what was essential was just a dignified and solemn moment marking the "beginning of the moral life partnership." He was, however, not convinced of the suggested reformulation of a mutual wedding vow that was meant to express the equality between women and men; on the contrary, from his point of view it was an abuse of the idea of gender equality. His own interpretation was based on a bourgeois concept of the appropriate passivity of women:

> Women are undoubtedly equal to men, but they still have a different position within society and within the marital community, and this will remain the same eternally. It is true that, given the current circumstances, much can be said in order to advocate a change in favor of women, but still the man will always remain the master of the house and make the decisions; his task is, first of all, to nourish his wife and the children as well as to maintain the house; his wife carries his name, as will do the children, and, as far as the beginning of marriage is concerned, it is always the man who will court the future wife and not the other way round.[67]

This is why, according to Geiger, men should continue to play the active role in the wedding ceremony, even though this should not be misinterpreted as expressing antiquated notions of female submissiveness. Women should be protected from male domination, but the traditional wedding ceremony should not be seen as disregarding women's rights. Geiger thus concluded that

> it seems much more appropriate to me that the active man should represent both and to set the seal on the mutual bond in word and deed, whereas the virtuous wife, who has whispered her "yes" more than she has spoken it loudly, should not speak and act in the public but should rather listen with soulful eyes to the man's words and eagerly put out her finger in order to receive the ring. In the future too, the man will be the giving part, his wife the receiving part; is it inappropriate that this relationship should also find its expression at the start of the marriage?[68]

Einhorn characterized this as a "monstrous assertion" and a completely astonishing attitude given the fact that it had been Geiger himself who had once "complained about the Jewish woman's bitter fate," whereas now he opposed "with hollow phrases" the effort to overcome a situation that was a disgrace for modern Judaism. Geiger's strategy to gloss over this with a sentimental atmosphere seemed reprehensible to him, since the abandonment of women to the curse of servitude would thus simply be continued under the cover of sentimentality and romanticism.[69] As much as this dissensus may just have emerged from differing individual attitudes toward the question of gender relations, it seems important to point to Karla Goldman's convincing interpretation, according to which it was much easier for Einhorn, due to the differing American circumstances and role ascriptions, to liberate himself from the cultural patterns acquired in Europe than Geiger, who remained under the spell of the German bourgeois concepts of manliness. The generation of immigrant rabbis, as Goldman suggests, were forced to a much greater degree to adapt themselves to the given conditions of American religious life, where the interest in female religiosity and in women's contributions to the religious community was much more distinct than in Europe.[70]

During the controversy about the Philadelphia Conference a series of further disagreements were voiced, among others with regard to the problem of how to deal with mixed marriages. Geiger advocated a full acknowledgment of such marriages "regarding their moral value," even though he was uncertain about whether or not the participation in a religious ceremony should be involved.[71] He also questioned Einhorn's view that circumcision should be obligatory for converts to Judaism.[72] With his attitude toward marriages with non-Jewish partners, Geiger was clearly in conflict with Einhorn. However, this was a controversial topic also among American reformers. In the wake of the Philadelphia Conference Einhorn had also attacked Samuel Hirsch when the latter published a series of articles in which he deplored the rigorous rabbinical rejection of mixed marriages and suggested, very much along the lines of Geiger's views, that Reform Judaism should respect the state law regarding marriage and allow non-Jews the marriage with a Jewish partner without urging the former to convert to Judaism and—in the case of men—to undergo circumcision.[73] Einhorn strictly rejected the consecration of mixed marriages, and indeed not—as he never tired of emphasizing—for the reason of Talmudic "belief in the higher sanctity of the blood of the Jewish line," but because it was his firm conviction that this meant "hammering a nail into the coffin of the tiny Jewish race with its high calling."[74] The polemical sharpness with which Einhorn rejected a more liberal practice had quite evidently to do with his concern about a potential dissolution of Jewish identity; mixed marriages, in his eyes, were not a sign of the overcoming of particularism, but a threat to Israel's universal mission of Israel to spread and deepen the eternal truths and moral laws. In Einhorn's estimation that if the barriers of separation in its history of exile had been lifted, "the tiny Jewish line, a grain of sand among the peoples,"[75] would long since have perished, one can certainly perceive an echo of the anti-Jewish calls—customary at that time above all in Germany—for a gradual dissolution of the "special Jewish character" through assimilation and mixed marriages. Einhorn countered that with the duty of Israel to hold fast to its special character, and asked: "May [Judaism], through mixed marriages, lead its nationality, the actual lever of its missionary activity, gradually toward destruction or even just allow it to be weakened?"[76] Therefore, from his point of view a precondition for marriage between Jews and non-Jews was the formal conversion, including ritual bath or circumcision.[77] With regard to the issue of mixed marriages it was Einhorn who embraced a more conservative view, apparently due to his strong accent on Israel's chosenness and mission, whereas Geiger agreed with Samuel Holdheim's attitude.[78]

3 Conclusion: the beginnings of the emancipation of the American Reform movement

The theological controversy between Geiger and Einhorn in 1870 concerned central questions such as the interpretation of the relationship between the universal "mission of the Jews" and remaining elements of Jewish distinctiveness within modern society, the appropriate understanding of exile and messianic redemption as well as the practical consequences of religious progress for the equality of women in Judaism, for the discussion on the legitimacy of intermarriage and the circumcision of non-Jewish partners in such marriages. While it can be shown that the polemical nature of the controversy had to do both with diverging philosophies of history and the differing social and cultural contexts in Germany and America which entailed different challenges to their Jewish minorities when it came to maintaining Jewish identity in the course of integration into the respective societies,[79] what needs to be emphasized here is the rivalry expressed in the argument of both protagonists. Apparently what mainly caused the American rabbis' chagrin was the tone of Geiger's judgement on American Reform Judaism, oscillating as it was between benevolent acknowledgment and paternalism. Geiger concluded his critical reading of the proceedings of the Philadelphia Conference by calling its results "promising," adding, however, the recommendation that his American colleagues should devote themselves more seriously to scholarship in order to be in a better position "to conquer space for Judaism's world-historical mission" based on a more appropriate scholarly and practical approach. The American rabbis, he suggested, should "give up any jealousy toward the old homeland and rather acknowledge the spiritual profundity granted in Germany"; they should also contribute to this profundity by using the practical flexibility facilitated by the more liberal circumstances without "self-complacency."[80] Provided the American Reform rabbis would display such an attitude (that would be tantamount to acknowledging the *primacy of Wissenschaft des Judentums* in Germany), Geiger was ready to stress the high expectations he harbored with regard to America: "May a fresh stream of air flow to us and revitalize us!"[81] Einhorn responded by characterizing Geiger's comments on the Philadelphia Conference as a deplorable attempt "to galvanize dead bodies on the one hand and to maim vital ideas on the other hand," and accused him of having completely distorted his American colleagues' aspirations.[82]

The condescending tone of Geiger's critique and Einhorn's forceful polemic can thus be interpreted as the expression of an ideological or theological conflict unfolding against the backdrop of the strong tension between the enduring influence of Geiger's thought in America and a certain mutual alienation. The temporary discord between Geiger and some of the American Reform rabbis seems to signify an early exemplary episode of the more general cultural ambivalence characterizing the relationship between the reformers who stayed in Germany and the generation of German rabbis who had emigrated to the *goldene medine*. The former tended to assume that they embodied the origin and ongoing source of a scholarly and cultural superiority over their American counterparts who lived in a country that lacked culture and tradition; the latter, on their part, were torn between an admiring attachment to German Jewish culture, including the achievements of *Wissenschaft des Judentums*,[83] and the increasing feeling that they were about to leave the German model behind and thus entitled to insist on the acknowledgment of their intellectual independence or even their more distinct progressiveness.

Kaufmann Kohler, who was to become one of the leading figures of the second generation of the radical Reform movement in America, which expressed its views in the Pittsburgh Platform of 1885, had already given voice to this emerging sense of superiority over the German Reform movement in his obituary devoted to Abraham Geiger in 1874. Despite his respect for his teacher, he was even more outspoken than Einhorn in identifying the tension between Geiger's critical historical approach and his hesitant attitude when it came to drawing the practical consequences: it was this hesitation that made him "fall back behind the full requirements of the time." Emphasizing the gradual loss of relevance of Geiger's ideas, Kohler came to the harsh conclusion that the latter's thinking was already part of history:

> He reformed and reformed bit by bit and with mounting moderation and fear rather than, as he once wrote to me, "to eradicate the underbrush at once in order to allow the tree of life to unfold in freedom." With a patronizing air he objected to the more uncompromising and noble, fully valid and principled reforms of his American allies and friends of his youth, thus alienating to a certain degree in recent years from his closest spiritual brothers and children. After all, it is the fate of all Jewish intellectual heroes that they are not allowed to access the Promised Land of their inner divine vocation. With sublime majesty, Judaism goes constantly beyond the achievements of their most important men and gratefully accepts only their creative works and achievements, leaving them behind as important milestones during the great progress of history.[84]

The ambivalence inherent in Kohler's obituary, with its admiration for the potential in Geiger's work for a determined reform of Judaism, based on progressive scholarship, and its simultaneous emphasis on the fact that his significance for the theoretical and practical outlook of the contemporary American Jewish Reform communities might be over, can be understood as one among several elements of a comprehensive process of emancipation that characterized the self-understanding particularly of the radical Reform Movement in America at the end of the nineteenth and the beginning of the twentieth century. As we have seen at the beginning of this essay, the retrospective views on Abraham Geiger expressed by representatives of the American Reform movement in 1910, on the occasion of the latter's 100th anniversary, were based on the self-confident awareness that they had created something that transcended the German origins of their religious identity, and that they had long superseded the European model of Judaism's modernization. This awareness was so strong that the ideological controversies that had taken place in the 1870s did no longer play a decisive role and that a more serene appreciation of both the scholar and reformer Geiger was possible. He had eventually become a historical figure, whose achievements and time-bound limits could be stated as a matter of fact, without polemics and without the need to deny the continuing relevance of a part of his ideas for the European as well as the American Reform movement.

Notes

1. Kaufmann Kohler, *Personal Reminiscences of My Early Life* (Cincinnati, OH: Eggers, 1918), 11.

2. For Kohler, see Robert F. Southard, "The Theologian of the 1885 Pittsburgh Platform: Kaufmann Kohler's Vision of Progressive Judaism," in *Platforms and Prayer Books: Theological and Liturgical Perspectives on Reform Judaism*, ed. Dana E. Kaplan (Lanham, MD: Rowman & Littlefield, 2002), 61–79; Yaakov S. Ariel, "'Wissenschaft des Judentums comes to America': Kaufmann Kohler's Scholarly Projects and Jewish-Christian Relations," in *Die Entdeckung des Christentums in der Wissenschaft des Judentums*, ed. Görge K. Hasselhoff (Berlin and New York: de Gruyter, 2010), 165–82.

3. Kaufmann Kohler, "Abraham Geiger: The Master Builder of Modern Judaism," in Kohler, *Hebrew Union College and Other Addresses* (Cincinnati, OH: Ark Publishing Co, 1916), 83–97, here 84–5.

4. Ibid., 86–8.

5. Ibid., 85.

6. Ibid., 90.

7. Ibid., 94.

8. Emanuel Schreiber, *Abraham Geiger: The Greatest Reform Rabbi of the Nineteenth Century* (Spokane, WA: Spokane Printing Co, 1892).

9. See the contributions in the *Yearbook of the Central Conference of American Rabbis* 20 (1910): 96; 197–8; 246–83.

10. David Philipson, *The Reform Movement in Judaism* (London: Macmillan & Co, 1907).

11. David Philipson, "Abraham Geiger," in Philipson, *Centenary Papers and Others* (Cincinnati, OH: Ark Publishing Co, 1919), 99–147, here 102.

12. Ibid., 130–1.

13. Emil G. Hirsch, "One of Modern Judaism's Greatest: A Centenary Address Preached in Anticipation of Abraham Geiger's One Hundredth Birthday," *The Reform Advocate* 40 (1910): 627–31, here 631. Hirsch served as a rabbi in Baltimore in 1877/78, in Louisville from 1878 to 1880 and later at the Congregation Sinai in Chicago; for the important role he played in this congregation and for his significance for the American Reform Movement, see Tobias Brinkmann, *Sundays at Sinai: A Jewish Congregation in Chicago* (Chicago: University of Chicago Press, 2012). As another example, see the speech by Felix Adler, "Abraham Geiger: Address at the Free Synagogue, Sunday May 16, 1910" (typescript), Felix Adler Papers, Columbia University, Box 77, File 17—a very loyal yet still critical assessment of the achievements of his teacher Geiger, with whom he had studied in Berlin. For Felix Adler, see Benny Kraut, *From Reform Judaism to Ethical Culture: The Religious Evolution of Felix Adler* (Cincinnati, OH: Hebrew Union College Press, 1979). Adler, son of the German Reform rabbi Samuel Adler, had studied at Columbia University in New York, before returning to Germany and writing his PhD in Heidelberg, where he came under the influence of Ludwig Feuerbach's thought. During the early 1870s, he studied with Geiger at the Berlin Lehranstalt für die Wissenschaft des Judentums. In 1874 he became professor of Hebrew and Oriental Languages at Cornell University—a position he lost because of the charge of atheism. In 1877 he

founded the Society of Ethical Culture, and in 1903 he was given a chair in Social Ethics at Columbia University. In his New York eulogy in 1910 Adler emphasized that, as a young American student in Berlin, he had very much admired Geiger, especially for his intuitive relationship to the truth of the Jewish religion, for the balance between reason and emotion that characterized his interpretation of Judaism, for his outstanding scholarship as historian and exegete, but mainly, however, for his firm conviction that thinking was the basis for human liberty and that a revitalization of life and the mind could be achieved by knowledge of the past. However, his admiration did not prevent him from criticizing—from the point of view of the generation of German Jewish immigrants to America—Geiger for his role in the fact that the German Reform movement had, after the failed revolution of 1848 and in view of the growing influence of the natural sciences and of materialism, seen a sharp decline, since it failed to achieve a creative reinterpretation of Judaism beyond the pure critique of tradition. Geiger's fault had been, Adler emphasized, that, with his veneration for the past and his neglect of the ethical challenges of the present, he had not grasped the opportunity of becoming a true religious leader and offering the younger generation an ethical-spiritual perspective. This was why Adler had not become a disciple of Geiger, even though he had been profoundly influenced by his intellectual activities as a theologian, philologist, and lover of poetry as well as by his human character.

14. For Geiger's actual influence on American Judaism, see Walter Jacob, "Abraham Geiger and America: His Influence on Jewish Life and Thought," in *Jüdische Existenz in der Moderne: Abraham Geiger und die Wissenschaft des Judentums*, ed. Christian Wiese, Walter Homolka, and Thomas Brechenmacher (Berlin: de Gruyter, 2012), 193–203.

15. See, e.g., Ismar Elbogen, "Abraham Geiger. 1810–1910," *Jahrbuch für jüdische Geschichte und Literatur* 14 (1911): 71–83 and the praising articles devoted to different facets of Geiger's work in *Abraham Geiger. Leben und Lebenswerk*, ed. Ludwig Geiger (Berlin: Georg Reimer, 1910).

16. See Michael A. Meyer, "German-Jewish Identity in Nineteenth-Century America," in *Toward Modernity: The European Jewish Model*, ed. Jacob Katz (New Brunswick, NJ and Oxford: Transaction Books, 1987), 247–67.

17. For the Philadelphia Conference, see Meyer, *Response to Modernity: A History of the Reform Movement in Judaism* (New York and Oxford: Oxford University Press, 1988), 255–8.

18. As a description of Einhorn's biographical and intellectual path, see Christian Wiese, "Samuel Holdheim's 'Most Powerful Comrade in Conviction': David Einhorn and the Discussion about Jewish Universalism in the Radical Reform Movement," in *Redefining Judaism in an Age of Emancipation: Comparative Perspectives on Samuel Holdheim (1806–1860)*, ed. Christian Wiese (Leiden and Boston: Brill, 2007), 303–73.

19. See Michael A. Meyer, *Response to Modernity*, 109–14; Andreas Gotzmann, *Eigenheit und Einheit. Modernisierungsdiskurse des deutschen Judentums der Emanzipationszeit* (Leiden: Brill Publishers, 2002), 193–211.

20. Abraham Geiger, "Die zwei verschiedenen Betrachtungsweisen. Der Schriftsteller und der Rabbiner," *Wissenschaftliche Zeitschrift für jüdische Theologie* 4 (1839): 321–33.

21. Abraham Geiger, *Nachgelassene Schriften*, ed. Ludwig Geiger, Vol. 1 (Hildesheim: Olms, 1999; reprint of the edition of Berlin 1875), 1–112, esp. 14–18, 92–112.

22. *Rabbinische Gutachten über die Verträglichkeit der freien Forschung mit dem Rabbineramte*, 2 vols. (Breslau: L. Freund, 1842/43).

23. "Gutachten des Herrn Rabbiners Dr. David Einhorn im Fürstenthume Birkenfeld," in *Rabbinische Gutachten*, Vol. 1, 125–39, here 127.

24. Ibid., 131.

25. Ibid., 135–6.

26. David Einhorn, Review of Abraham Geiger's *Leon da Modena* (1856), *Sinai* 2 (1857): 435.

27. For the indirect effects of the ideological divide between radical and more moderate approaches within German Reform on the American Reform Movement, see Jakob J. Petuchowski, "Abraham Geiger and Samuel Holdheim: Their Differences in Germany and Repercussions in America," *Leo Baeck Institute Yearbook* 22 (1977): 139–59.

28. David Einhorn, "Abraham Geiger," *The Jewish Times* 6 (1874/75): 621–2.

29. David Einhorn, "Gedächtnisrede, gehalten am 21. November 1874 zu Ehren Abraham Geigers im Tempel der Beth-El-Gemeinde zu New York," in *David Einhorn Memorial Volume: Selected Sermons*, ed. Kaufmann Kohler (New York: Bloch Publishing Company, 1911), 190–3, here 190.

30. See, for instance the obituaries by Bernhard Felsenthal, New York rabbi Samuel Adler, and Chicago rabbi Liebman Adler in *The Jewish Times* 6 (1874/75): 622, 668–71.

31. Einhorn, "Abraham Geiger," 621.

32. Abraham Geiger, "Die Versammlung zu Leipzig und die zu Philadelphia," *Jüdische Zeitschrift für Wissenschaft und Leben* 8 (1870): 1–27.

33. David Einhorn, "Dr. Geiger und die Philadelphier Rabbiner-Conferenz," *The Jewish Times* 2 (1870/71): 107, 123–4, 139, 171, 187–8.

34. See Meyer, *Response to Modernity*, 188–90.

35. Geiger, "Die Versammlung in Leipzig und die zu Philadelphia," 3–5.

36. Einhorn, "Dr. Geiger und die Philadelphier Rabbiner-Conferenz," 123.

37. Geiger, "Die Versammlung in Leipzig und die zu Philadelphia," 6.

38. *Protokolle der Rabbiner-Conferenz abgehalten zu Philadelphia, vom 3. bis zum 6. November 1869* (New York: S. Hecht, 1870), 86; on the practical resolutions in Philadelphia, see Meyer, *Response to Modernity*, 255–8.

39. See Michael A. Meyer, "Should and Can an 'Antiquated' Religion Become Modern? The Jewish Reform Movement in Germany as Seen by Jews and Christians," in Meyer, *Judaism within Modernity: Essays on Jewish History and Religion* (Detroit, MI: Wayne State University Press, 2001), 209–22.

40. See Geiger, "Die Versammlung in Leipzig und die zu Philadelphia," 8–9.

41. Einhorn, "Dr. Geiger und die Philadelphier Rabbiner-Conferenz," 107.

42. Letter from David Einhorn to Bernhard Felsenthal on November 29, 1872, David Einhorn Papers, American Jewish Archives (AJA), Cincinnati, MSS Col. 155.

43. Geiger, "Die Versammlung in Leipzig und die zu Philadelphia," 9.

44. Einhorn, "Dr. Geiger und die Philadelphier Rabbiner-Conferenz," 123. This argument is based on Einhorn's critique of Moses Mendelssohn's rejection of dogma and his definition of Judaism as a "revealed law." Einhorn, in contrast to this, argued that Judaism's true core consisted of—particularly moral—theological teachings which found their expression in symbolical, time-bound ceremonial forms and commandments; see David Einhorn, *Das Princip des Mosaismus und dessen Verhältnis zum Heidenthum und rabbinischen Judenthum* (Leipzig: C. L. Fritzsche, 1854), esp. 4–13.

45. Geiger, "Die Versammlung in Leipzig und die zu Philadelphia," 10.

46. Abraham Geiger, "Thesen für die am 29. d. [M.] in Leipzig zusammentretende Versammlung," *Jüdische Zeitschrift für Wissenschaft und Leben* 7 (1869): 161–7, here 163. For Geiger's understanding of Jewish universalism, see Michael A. Meyer, "Universalism and Jewish Unity

in the Thought of Abraham Geiger," in *The Role of Religion in Modern Jewish History*, ed. Jacob Katz (Cambridge, MA: Association for Jewish Studies, 1975), 91–107.

47. Einhorn, "Dr. Geiger und die Philadelphier Rabbiner-Conferenz," 124.

48. Geiger, "Die Versammlung in Leipzig und die zu Philadelphia," 10.

49. Friedrich W. J. Schelling, *Philosophie der Offenbarung* (1841/42) (Frankfurt am Main: Suhrkamp, 1977); also Friedrich W. J. Schelling, *Philosophie der Mythologie. Nachschrift der letzten Münchner Vorlesungen 1841*, ed. Andreas Roser and Holger Schulten (Stuttgart-Bad Cannstatt: Fromman-Holzboog, 1996).

50. David Einhorn, "Prinzipielle Differenzpunkte zwischen altem und neuem Judentum," *Sinai* 1 (1856/57), no. 6: 162–4; no. 7: 193–7; no. 10: 290–4; no. 11: 333–5; no. 12: 365–71; 2 (1857/58), no. 1: 399–404; no. 5: 540–4; no. 6: 572–6; 7 (1862/63), no. 12: 320–7; here 293.

51. Ibid., 401.

52. Ibid., 539.

53. Ibid., 293.

54. Ibid., 544.

55. Ibid., 327.

56. David Einhorn, "Predigt gehalten am Erinnerungstag der Zerstörung Jerusalems 5619 (1859) im Tempel der Har-Sinai-Gemeinde zu Baltimore," in *Dr. David Einhorn's ausgewählte Predigten und Reden*, ed. Kaufmann Kohler (New York: Steiger, 1881), 324–31, here 325.

57. Ibid., 329.

58. David Einhorn, "Gutachtliche Äußerung eines jüdischen Theologen über den Reformverein an einen sich dafür interessierenden Christen," *Allgemeine Zeitung des Judenthums* 8 / 7 (1844): 87–9, here 88.

59. In this regard, it is worth reading his New York sermon given in 1866 on the occasion of the laying of the Atlantic telegraph line, with the title "Gott redet durch Feuerfunken" [God speaks through sparks of fire]—an enthusiastic paean to the continuing work of the spirit of God, which drives forward enlightenment and brotherhood among humanity; see David Einhorn, "Predigt gehalten am 20. October 1866, aus Anlaß der Legung des atlantischen Telegraphen, im Tempel der Adath-Jeschurun-Gemeinde zu New York," in *Dr. David Einhorn's ausgewählte Predigten und Reden*, 176–82. Einhorn saw in this event a sign that the world was on its way to "reaching our proudest goal," "general enlightenment and unification, brotherhood among all humankind in God, their father" (181).

60. See for example the striking contrasting of the conflict between the achievements of civilization in America and the "hideous" materialism and indifferentism in David Einhorn, "Predigt gehalten am Neujahrstage 5639 (1878) im Tempel der Beth-El-Gemeinde zu New York," in *Dr. David Einhorn's ausgewählte Predigten und Reden*, 197–204, here 203; see also David Einhorn, *Predigt im Tempel Beth-El dahier, am Sabbath Chanukkah* (New York: M. Thalmessinger & Co, 1874), particularly 7: "Our teaching still stands in bitterest enmity against on the one hand the dark superstition that presages the most unreasoning dogmas, and on the other hand a spreading scientific approach that takes pride in denying God, in raw materialism, teaches the similarity of humans to apes instead of their likeness to God, and has blind natural forces rather than the spirit of God hold sway over the surging waves, sets a law without a legislator to rule the world. Light still has to struggle violently with darkness . . ."

61. Abraham Geiger, "Die Stellung des weiblichen Geschlechtes in dem Judenthume unserer Zeit," *Wissenschaftliche Zeitschrift für jüdische Theologie* 3 / 1 (1837): 1–14. For the attitude of the Reform movement toward the question of gender within the context of the German

bourgeoisie, see Benjamin M. Baader, *Gender, Judaism, and Bourgeois Culture in Germany, 1800-1870* (Bloomington and Indianapolis, IN: Indiana University Press, 2006); for Geiger's attitude, see Ken Koltun Fromm, *Abraham Geiger's Liberal Judaism: Personal Meaning and Religious Authority* (Bloomington and Indianapolis, IN: Indiana University Press, 2006), 64–84.

62. *Protokolle der dritten Versammlung deutscher Rabbiner, abgehalten zu Breslau, vom 13. bis 24. Juli 1846* (Breslau: Leuckart, 1847), 253–65.

63. See Samuel Holdheim, *Die religiöse Stellung des weiblichen Geschlechts im talmudischen Judenthum* (Schwerin: C. Kürschner, 1846).

64. *Protokolle der dritten Versammlung deutscher Rabbiner*, 264. The concrete demands of the committee were nevertheless formulated in relatively general terms (see ibid., 265).

65. David Einhorn, "Predigt, vom Herausgeber dieser Blätter gehalten im Tempel der Har Sinai Gemeinde," *Sinai* 3 / 1 (1858/59): 824; David Einhorn, "Über Familiensitze in den Synagogen," *Sinai* 6 / 7 (1861/62): 205–07.

66. See Meyer, *Response to Modernity*, 256–7; and see *Protokolle der Rabbiner-Conferenz abgehalten zu Philadelphia*, 19–39. On the reform of the position of women in American congregations in the nineteenth century, see Karla Goldman, *Beyond the Synagogue Gallery. Finding a Place for Women in American Judaism* (Cambridge, MA: Harvard University Press, 2000).

67. Geiger, "Die Versammlung in Leipzig und die zu Philadelphia," 11.

68. Ibid., 12.

69. Einhorn, "Dr. Geiger und die Philadelphier Rabbiner-Conferenz," 171.

70. Karla Goldman, *Beyond the Synagogue Gallery*, esp. 153–72.

71. Geiger, "Die Versammlung in Leipzig und die zu Philadelphia," 17.

72. Ibid., 24–5.

73. Samuel Hirsch, "Darf ein Reformrabbiner Ehen zwischen Juden und Nichtjuden einsegnen?," *The Jewish Times* 1 (1969/70), no. 27: 9–10; no. 28: 10–11; no. 30: 9–10; no. 31: 10; no. 32: 10; no. 33: 10; no. 34: 10; no. 35: 11; no. 36: 13.

74. David Einhorn, "Noch ein Wort über gemischte Ehen," *The Jewish Times* 1 (1869/70), no. 48: 10–13, here 11.

75. Ibid.

76. Ibid.

77. Ibid. Hirsch thereupon accused Einhorn of thinking in the racist categories of Ernest Renan and of proselytizing. "The hope [of Reform Judaism] is surely not," he objected, "that one day all people shall become Jews, but that without being Jews, they shall live in truth, morality and holiness"; see Samuel Hirsch, "Der Nagel zum Sarge der winzigen jüdischen Race," *The Jewish Times* 1 (1869/70), no. 47, 10–11, here 11.

78. See Samuel Holdheim, *Gemischte Ehen zwischen Juden und Christen. Die Gutachten der Berliner Rabbinatsverwaltung und des Königsberger Konsistoriums beleuchtet* (Berlin: L. Lassar, 1850).

79. See Christian Wiese, "Heros, Ikone, Gegenbild: Abraham Geiger aus der Perspektive der Reformbewegung in Amerika," in Wiese, Brechenmacher, and Homolka, eds., *Jüdische Existenz in der Moderne*, 205–47, esp. 242–7.

80. Geiger, "Die Versammlung in Leipzig und die zu Philadelphia," 21–2.

81. Ibid., 27.

82. Einhorn, "Dr. Geiger und die Philadelphier Rabbiner-Conferenz," 188.

83. For the relationship between German Jewish and American Jewish scholarship during the second half of the nineteenth century, see my chapter on "Translating *Wissenschaft*: The Emergence and Self-Emancipation of American Jewish Scholarship, 1860–1920" in this volume.

84. Kaufmann Kohler, "Dr. Abraham Geiger. Gedächtnisrede," *The Jewish Times* 6 (1874/75): 637–9, here 639.

CHAPTER 9
BEYOND THE SYNAGOGUE GALLERY? WOMEN'S CHANGING ROLES IN NINETEENTH-CENTURY AMERICAN AND GERMAN JUDAISM

Karla Goldman

Tensions between traditional roles assigned to women and expectations for women within modernizing societies have arisen within every Western religion. In Judaism, as in many traditions, responses to changing roles and identities for women have offered powerful indicators of a group's embrace or rejection of the values of the surrounding society. In fact, efforts to accommodate Judaism to changing societal roles for women have been a key element of Jewish modernization wherever it has taken place. At the same time, the extent and nature of these accommodations have always reflected the particular concerns of the specific society in which they developed.

Examination of the changing role of women in Reform Judaism in American and German settings highlights both the shared and distinctive dynamics shaping these movements. At the same time it illustrates the common need to find culturally appropriate gender roles in defining these different versions of a modernized Judaism. The place and roles offered to women within American and German Judaism provide a sensitive barometer of the ways in which Jewish culture responded both to the expectations of the surrounding society and to their own particular needs within those societies.

Historians have long sought to trace the reciprocal influences that shaped the related but often distinctive Reform Judaisms emerging among acculturating Jews in the developing German and American urban cultures of the mid-nineteenth century. German Reform Jewish thought and practice is often portrayed as the primary source and model for American Reform Judaism. Indeed, German Reform synagogue regulations were adopted almost verbatim by many early American synagogues looking to create more decorous modes of synagogue behavior than those associated with traditional Jewish worship.[1]

The large majority of members of many mid-nineteenth-century American synagogues were born in German-speaking regions of Europe.[2] Beyond this, the Judaism practiced within many of these same synagogues was largely shaped by the first generation of American rabbis, most of whom came from German-speaking lands and many of whom had had some contact with the Reform movement there. These spiritual leaders came to the United States prepared to assist Americanizing Jews in identifying a way of being Jewish that could harmonize with their sensibilities as acculturated citizens of a modern society. German-trained rabbis thus became key players in disparate local American efforts to adapt Jewish worship and behavior to the new environment and in bringing such efforts together to create a more formal and organized Reform movement.[3]

Even with these strong connections, however, the German and American versions of Reform Judaism reflected and conformed to the very different political and social environments in which they arose. One of the clearest manifestations of these differences can be seen in the very different ways that American and German reformers sought to accommodate changing roles for women. In both the American and German contexts, modernizers had to take on the problem of adapting traditional roles for Jewish women to the expectations of the bourgeois culture in which they hoped to find a comfortable home. The key defining dynamics for each movement, the achievement of *Bildung* (an educated refined culture) among German Jews and respectability among American Jews, could not be realized without the cultivation of cultural roles for Jewish women that were congruent with the expectations and ideals for women presented by the surrounding societies.

The differences in the ways that German and American Reform responded to the challenge of redefining women's roles reflect both the basic structural differences that shaped the two movements and the different cultural contexts in which they developed. In general, the voluntary and pluralistic character of American religious community made room for the introduction of far more radical innovations than were possible in German synagogues which had to serve the whole range of Jewish community members. We can see the effect of this difference most clearly in American innovations like the removal of head coverings for men, the elimination of the observance of the second day of holidays, and most relevantly here, the introduction of mixed seating for men and women.

In the German context, although it was possible to propose radical ideas such as the celebration of Sunday Sabbath or the elimination of the rite of circumcision, it was impossible to introduce largely symbolic changes like the removal of head coverings— when those practices were understood as the essential markers that defined Jewish presence, practice, and space as Jewish. In the United States, when innovations such as these were initially proposed, many communities completely rejected them. Within a few years, however, as authoritative members or leaders of the community argued that such change could be consistent with Jewish practice and was being practiced elsewhere, and practices—like worship with uncovered heads or the elimination of the second day of a holiday—became more familiar, the very same communities were able to accept these changes with few apparent qualms.[4] Once these innovations became familiar in the 1870s, they spread rapidly, becoming, in many ways, characteristic of acculturated American Jewish practice before the era of mass Eastern European Jewish migration to the USA.[5]

Well before the Reform innovations that began emerging in the 1850s, adjustments in the worship space assigned to women were among the first indications of the tendency of American synagogues to diverge from European models. The rapid appearance of these innovations during the colonial era reflected an American concern for female religiosity and a general emphasis on public expressions of worship that would shape the emergence of a distinctive American Judaism. Given the centrality of churches and public worship in the development of colonial American society, it was hardly surprising that the religious expressions of early American Jews focused on synagogues. The earliest American synagogues, although modest, in keeping with the scale and economic resources of their communities, all demonstrated a clear intent to establish a strong physical and esthetic presence in their new world homes. Their success in this project was exemplified in the admiring observation of the future Yale president Rev. Ezra Stiles in his diary that the new synagogue dedicated in Newport in 1763 was indeed an "edifice the most perfect of the Temple kind perhaps in America."[6] The power of Protestant models for the early American Jewish communities was reflected in exterior synagogue design, internal synagogue behavior, and in the dominant weight given to public worship in the construction of colonial Jewish religious identities.

American Jewish women also very quickly adapted their religious expressions to the colonial and early national religious environment. The relevant dynamic here was not necessarily one of gender equity. Although a small number of early American women found strong public voices and identities as religious leaders, American churches, over all, clearly remained male-led bastions. Yet the dominant presence of women which has consistently defined the American church experience was present from the inception of European settlement in North America.[7] American synagogue-goers thus found themselves in an environment where the strong presence of women in public religious settings framed an unsavory assessment of the space assigned to women in colonial American synagogues. This negative impression found expression in the observations of non-Jewish synagogue visitors, like one at New York's Shearith Israel in 1744, who noted that the women, "of whom some are very pretty, stood up in the gallery like a hen coop."[8]

Jewish communal adjustments to these American emphases on both the centrality of public worship and of women's place within it manifested themselves in the ways that women's presence in early American synagogues quickly diverged from familiar women's spaces and roles in contemporaneous European synagogues. Structural adjustments can be seen early on in the 1763 Newport synagogue so admired by Ezra Stiles. This building was the second synagogue built in what later became the United States and is now the oldest existing synagogue building in the country. In the Newport synagogue, women sat behind a low balustrade, free of the opaque barriers of the European sanctuaries which would have served as the models for the Newport congregation's design. Despite being modeled upon the traditional plan of Sephardic synagogues of Amsterdam and London, the Newport gallery suggests that these colonial Jews were prepared to adjust their observance even in the context of an otherwise traditional synagogue. This innovation was replicated in subsequent American synagogues, including Charleston's Beth Elohim (1794), New York's second Shearith Israel building (1818), and Philadelphia's second Mikveh Israel building (1824). Notably, German and other European synagogues which also adopted the influential Amsterdam model retained the strict separation shown in Amsterdam and London.[9]

The modified structure of Newport's women's gallery reflected many factors starting with the growing synagogue presence of Jewish women who were aware of the church-going predilections of their female neighbors. The synagogue leaders would also have been aware of the disapproving assessments by non-Jews of segregated gallery space for women, who saw in women's relegation to the gallery implication not only of separation (still practiced within many American Protestant churches), but of a lesser religious status. For a society which constructed women as paragons of religious virtue, and which saw balcony seating as suitable for children, servants, and slaves, the sequestering of women within synagogues confirmed unsympathetic understandings of Judaism as an exotic oriental sect, primitively ignorant of the religious virtue which should have graced its female adherents.

American Jews thus realized quickly that their acceptance among the cultured classes of American society depended upon their ability to demonstrate that Jewish women belonged among their virtuous and religiously inclined American Protestant counterparts. In keeping with this societal expectation, the evolution of nineteenth-century American synagogues moved steadily toward increased inclusion for women. Beginning with Newport, most American synagogues displayed a reorientation of the women's presence in the synagogue by removing the grill or lattice work that surmounted the railing of women's galleries in most European synagogues. By mid-century, the processes of Reform and Americanization brought the innovation of replacing women's galleries with family pews. By the 1870s, sanctuaries with family pews had become almost the hallmark of Americanized synagogues. By the end of the century, even the Sephardic traditional stalwarts of Shearith Israel in New York and Mikveh Israel in Philadelphia had to beat back congregational calls for sanctuaries in which husbands and wives could sit side by side.[10]

This pressure to accommodate and redefine women's presence, which actually required rebuilding synagogues in order to include women properly, never came to define German or European Reform efforts. When the Hamburg Temple, the most radical Reform effort to date, was dedicated in 1818, its open synagogue gallery offered the same women's gallery design as the most traditional contemporaneous American synagogue. The more elaborate and ornate synagogues of acculturating Western European Jews of the second half of the nineteenth century came around to offering well-appointed open balconies, but they remained women's galleries, with the congregation's men seated in the sanctuary below.[11] By the First World War, mixed synagogue seating in European settings remained virtually nonexistent. This is not to suggest that reformers in Germany and elsewhere did not find it necessary to critique and address what they saw as women's unequal status in Judaism. As we shall see, acculturating German Jews also found it necessary to reconfigure Jewish female religious identities in conformity with the bourgeois cultural expectations of the surrounding society. It was only in the United States, however, that structural changes in women's place in the synagogue became a central aspect of a broad synagogue–centered Reform program.

There were certainly Jewish leaders in German lands who believed that what they saw as women's marginalized and subservient role within Judaism was emblematic of the backward and "oriental" character of rabbinic Judaism and needed to be transformed. In 1837, Rabbi Abraham Geiger, a pioneering German reformer, described how Judaism's treatment of women illustrated his more general characterization of the way that rabbinic edicts had corrupted the original purity of Biblical Judaism. He pointed to the fundamental respect accorded to women within the Bible, but deplored the exclusions and alienation from public worship enshrined within Talmudic law. Geiger advocated a reconfigured Judaism in which women would feel welcomed and valued as participants and contributors.[12]

In practice, however, German reformers like Geiger and his even more radical colleagues were largely constrained in the degree of reform that they could bring to their communities. Despite a general decline of communal authority, German Jewish communities comprising all resident Jews were invested with economic and juridical authority by the state. To shift communal resources away from traditionalists, Reform leaders had to win the support of the majority of local Jewish residents. Thus, even when they gained communal authority, they still had to meet the needs of the whole community, including residents who had no sympathy for a Reform program. Geiger himself lamented being forced, in response to this situation, to teach "a program of religious instruction in which [he did] not believe."[13] Thus, although German reformers often professed an extreme radicalism including the prohibition of ritual circumcision and the celebration of a Sunday Sabbath, in practice, organized Jewish life continued much as it had been. Even far less radical, more symbolic reforms, like the removal of head coverings or the abolition of women's sections, never came to the fore.[14] In the United States, by contrast, competing congregations could arise, free to alter their practice in order to appeal to those seeking less traditional worship, without having to worry about whether they were meeting the needs of every Jewish resident of their community.

This contrast between the theoretical radicalism possible for German thinkers and the practical reform possible in the United States as it related to women's roles can be seen in the German and American careers of Rabbi David Einhorn. Einhorn articulated the most prominent German call for reform related to Jewish women's roles in his address to the Third Assembly of German Rabbis meeting in Breslau in 1846. Einhorn, then a rabbi in Birkenfeld, equated Judaism's treatment of women with the withholding of political emancipation from Jews. In both cases, he suggested, rhetorical affirmations of equality were useless: "A mere theoretical recognition of women's disenfranchisement" gave "them as little satisfaction as the Israelites are given in civic matters." Like German Jews, Einhorn pointed out, women had "received assurances of their capabilities without however being permitted to become emancipated." In response to this perceived hypocrisy, Einhorn called upon the assembly to declare "the complete religious equality of the female sex." Asking for not just words but action, he demanded that the declaration be borne out in practical reforms that would include counting women in a *minyan* (the quorum required for public prayer defined by the presence of a minimum of ten men), omitting traditional prayers that seemed to disparage women, and a commitment to offering women the same instruction and expecting them to take on the same rights and obligations as men.[15] Einhorn's demands were scheduled to be taken up at the 1847 rabbis' meeting which never took place. It would be another twelve years before Einhorn, as a rabbi in Baltimore, would again become a public advocate for equal rights and duties for women, as he condemned the gallery cage of the traditional synagogue. In the United States, where practical, structural change in women's position could be a central element of a broad reform movement, Einhorn was able to translate his words into action, as his congregation soon brought women down from the women's gallery.[16]

Although nineteenth-century German Reform synagogues never saw the kind of structural shift in women's place and status that marked acculturated American synagogues, they were not untouched by the need to adjust to changing societal understandings of women's roles. As historian Benjamin Baader points out, German synagogues also became sites for a reconfigured public religious identity for women. German Reformers "required" women's presence in the synagogue and incorporated stylistic and programmatic changes which were meant to attract or include women in ways which were substantively different from practices in traditional synagogues. He points especially to the introduction of mixed-gender choirs and of confirmation services for boys and girls as elements of a Jewish culture seeking to change synagogue dynamics from ones in which the members of a *minyan* acted as protagonists to ones in which both men and women served as passive but equal members of a congregational audience.

As Baader and historians Marian A. Kaplan and Paula E. Hyman have pointed out, expectations that German Jews and Jewish communities needed to demonstrate that they were worthy not just of social acceptance, but also of political and civil rights, increased the pressure upon Jewish women to show that they were worthy carriers and transmitters of public and domestic culture. Attention to whether they embodied appropriate models of domestic piety for women proved more important than their roles within public worship. In fact, as the synagogue declined in importance in the lives of many acculturating Jews, the domestic sphere became imperative as a site for adjustment to the expectations of non-Jewish society and culture. Just as American middle-class women were seen as keepers of religious devotion and the mainstays of religious community, German bourgeois society demanded that women serve as moral exemplars and the prime transmitters of religious values. Even though traditional Judaism assigned the responsibilities of religious education for one's children to the father, the ability of mothers to take on this role allowed German Jewish women to connect their families to the emerging values of *Bildung* (the acquisition of culture through education) and bourgeois domesticity. As German Jewish men increasingly absented themselves from the traditional spheres of worship, Jewish women took on more and more responsibility for embodying the religious identity of German Jews through their domestic duties and in raising their children.[17]

Creating more open access to public observance and expression of Judaism was important to the process of overcoming the impression created by traditional gender roles that Judaism represented a backward and "oriental" religious culture. The essential site for the construction of bourgeois Jewish female religiosity, however, turned out to be not the synagogue, but the home. It was in their homes that Jewish women could demonstrate how Jewish practice, ritual, and identity could be turned into solid emblems of bourgeois respectability. Baader, Kaplan, and Hyman all present recollections of nineteenth-century German Jews attesting to their warm memories of tranquil homes where their mothers served as the central virtuous purveyors of Jewish observance and practice. In these recollections, these practices were seen as more important for the way that they elevated and beautified the home, and filled it with clear bourgeois values of refinement, *Gemütlichkeit* (homeyness), and serenity, than for their role in fulfilling the halakhic particularities of Jewish law.[18]

The question as to why the central pressure in the need to re-define female religiosity focused on domestic Judaism in German lands and on public synagogue Judaism in the United States challenges us to understand the distinctive framing contexts that shaped American and German Judaism. Truly satisfying answers may remain elusive, but the question does point us in some suggestive directions.

Nineteenth-century German churches, like their American counterparts, became homes to increasing numbers of female congregants. Like American society, German culture also developed a cultural ideal for women in which religious piety was fundamental. So, we might expect that women's presence in German synagogues would have approached or exceeded the number of men present as they did in the United States. But despite the efforts of synagogue leaders, described by Baader, to reconfigure the practice and ethos of the synagogue to make it more welcoming and comfortable for women, we do not see the same shift in numbers that we see in the United States. Nor do we see any fundamental structural reorientation of the German synagogue to incorporate women's presence.[19]

Although German synagogues became more accessible to and accommodating of women's presence, they did not become major sites for female religiosity. Given that many German churches maintained separate seating of men and women, it is not surprising that German Jews were less likely to challenge the convention of separate seating. Still, if the synagogue had been seen as more important to the validation of Jewish women's religious identities, there might have been some challenge to the continued sequestering of women in synagogue balconies which diverged from German church practice where men and women tended to occupy the main floor and balconies together.[20]

The lack of structural changes related to women's place in German synagogues may mainly, as has been pointed out, have reflected the fact that, in serving broader communities, German synagogues were more resistant to basic reconfigurations than were American synagogues. The introduction of family pews as seen in the United States would have been too radical a departure from the traditions of a public setting intended to serve the whole community. Ultimately, however, it is likely that the main distinction between American and German constructions of Jewish women's roles and identities resulted from the basic salience and importance of public worship in the two societies. As nineteenth-century German society moved in an increasingly secular direction, the church became less central relative to other societal institutions and may have been less important than in the United States as a site to mark the attainment of bourgeois respectability. Despite all its attempts to adjust to modern environment, the German synagogue, in general, receded in importance in the life of individuals and communities. For Jewish men, this was reflected in a withdrawal of men from traditional and public male spheres of Jewish life centered in the synagogue and study hall.[21]

The United States, of course, defined itself from the outset by the separation of church and state. Thus, the emergence of secular institutions did not necessarily challenge the pervasive religious presence that shaped much of American society during the Colonial Era; nor did it imply a decline of religious institutions as it may have in Germany. While Americans did develop influential models of religious domesticity, the most dominant expression of female religiosity remained in the church and in church-based institutions like temperance groups and missionary societies.[22] Structures of public worship remained the essential site for the formulation and expression of appropriate female religious identities.

An abundance of evidence indicates that women came to dominate American synagogue attendance in a fashion that found no parallel (at least none that we know about) in European settings. It is true that the integration of women into the American sanctuary was made possible by the same congregational passivity that Baader describes in his account of German synagogue development. In the United States, however, women's passive presence still resulted in the physical reconfiguration of the synagogue, and in the redefinition of both Jewish female religious identity and the customary numeric dominance of men among regular synagogue worshippers.[23]

Comparison of the ways in which Jewish communities sought to adjust the presence of women in order to meet societal expectations for appropriate female religiosity illuminates both the primacy of negotiating appropriate roles for women in this process and the distinctive paths of American and German Reform Judaism. Such a comparison helps us see that while German models were important to the ways that German Jews in America defined their Jewish identities, they were ultimately more attuned to the expectations of the society in which they lived than to any shared universal plan for the Reform of Judaism.

Notes

1. See for example synagogue regulations proposed in Bene Israel Trustee minutes, February 12, 1848, Cincinnati, Ohio—Bene Israel Collection, Collection #24, American Jewish Archives, Cincinnati, OH (AJA); B'nai Yeshurun minutes, February 10, 1848; February 27, 1848, Cincinnati, Ohio–Bene Yeshurun Collection, Collection #62, AJA. Much of the content and language of the plans considered by these congregations echoes the *Synagogenordnungen* or plans for synagogue regulation collected by Jakob J. Petuchowski in *Prayerbook Reform in Europe: The Liturgy of European Liberal and Reform Judaism* (New York: The World Union for Progressive Judaism, 1968), 105–27.

2. See Alan Silverstein, *Alternatives to Assimilation: The Response of Reform Judaism to American Culture, 1840–1930* (Hanover, NH and London: Brandeis University Press by University Press of New England, 1994), 12–13. Using census data, Silverstein is able to trace the German origins of the membership of the congregations that he studies with great precision (see pp. 12–13, 76). Hasia R. Diner, *The Jews of the United States, 1654–2000* (Berkeley, CA: University of California Press, 2004) and Avraham Barkai, *Branching Out: German-Jewish Immigrants to the United States* (New York: Holmes & Meier, 1994) trace the geographic origins of "German Jews" in the United States with great precision.

3. Leon Jick, *The Americanization of the Synagogue, 1820–1870* (Hanover, NH and London: Brandeis University Press, by the University Press of New England, 1976). I make this argument in Karla Goldman, "The Path to Reform Judaism: An Examination of Religious Leadership in Cincinnati, 1841–1855," *American Jewish History* 90 / 1 (2002): 35–50, as does

Zev Eleff in his recent dissertation, "Power, Pulpits and Pews: Religious Authority and the Formation of American Judaism, 1816–1885" (PhD dissertation, Brandeis University, 2015).

4. See for example evolving discussion of banning head coverings at Cincinnati's Bene Israel Congregation, Bene Israel Trustee Minutes, September 4, 1869; October 11, 1874; February 28, 1875; September 26, 1875; October 31, 1875.

5. Karla Goldman, *Beyond the Synagogue Gallery: Finding a Place for Women in American Judaism* (Cambridge, MA: Harvard University Press, 2000), 132–3; 172–3.

6. Quoted in Morris A. Gutstein, *The Story of the Jews of Newport: Two and a Half Centuries of Judaism, 1658–1908* (New York: Bloch Publishing, 1936), 100–1.

7. Ann Braude, "Women's History *Is* American Religious History," in *Retelling U.S. Religious History*, ed. Thomas A. Tweed (Berkeley, CA: University of California Press, 1997), 87–107. For more recent assessments of women's historical centrality in American religion see the essays in Catherine Brekus, ed., *The Religious History of American Women: Reimagining the Past* (Chapel Hill: University of North Carolina Press, 2007).

8. Quoted in David de Sola Pool and Tamar de Sola Pool, *An Old Faith in a New World; Portrait of Shearith Israel, 1654–1954* (New York: Columbia University Press, 1955), 453.

9. See Goldman, *Beyond the Synagogue Gallery*, 40–6.

10. Ibid.; and see Jonathan D. Sarna, "The Debate Over Mixed Seating in the American Synagogue," in *The American Synagogue: A Sanctuary Transformed*, ed. Jack Wertheimer (New York and London: Cambridge University Press, 1987), 363–93.

11. Benjamin M. Baader, *Gender, Judaism and Bourgeois Culture in Germany, 1800–1870* (Bloomington and Indianapolis, IN: Indiana University Press, 2006), 152–3; Carol Herselle Krinsky, *Synagogues of Europe: Architecture, History, Meaning* (Mineola, NY: Dover Publications, Inc., 1985), 63, 279, 284, 299, 416.

12. Abraham Geiger, "Die Stellung des weiblichen Gesclechtes in dem Judenthume unserer Zeit," *Wissenschaftliche Zeitschrift für jüdische Theologie* 3 (1837): 1–14, here 8.

13. Abraham Geiger, quoted in Max Wiener, *Abraham Geiger and Liberal Judaism: The Challenge of the Nineteenth Century* (Cincinnati, OH: Hebrew Union College Press, 1981), 89.

14. Robert Liberles, *Religious Conflict in Social Context: The Resurgence of Orthodox Judaism in Frankfurt Am Main, 1838–1877* (Westport, CT: Greenwood Press, 1985), 165–72.

15. David Einhorn, quoted in W. Gunther Plaut, *The Rise of Reform Judaism: A Sourcebook of its European Origins* (New York: World Union for Progressive Judaism, 1963), 253–5.

16. David Einhorn, "Predigt,vom Herausgeber dieser Blätter gehalten im Tempel der Har-Sinai-Gemeinde," *Sinai* 3 / 1 (February 1858): 824; David Einhorn, "Über Familiensitze in den Synagogen," *Sinai* 6 / 7 (August 1861): 205–7.

17. See Marion A. Kaplan, *The Making of the Jewish Middle Class: Women, Family and Identity in Imperial Germany* (New York and Oxford: Oxford University Press, 1991); Paula E. Hyman, *Gender and Assimilation in Modern Jewish History: The Roles and Representation of Women* (Seattle: University of Washington Press, 1995).

18. See especially Baader, *Gender, Judaism, and Bourgeois Culture*, 212–16.

19. Ibid., 152–3.

20. Ibid.

21. Ibid., 212, 216–19.

22. See, for example, Patricia R. Hill, *The World Their Household: The American Woman's Foreign Mission Movement and Cultural Transformation, 1870–1920* (Ann Arbor, MI: University of

Michigan Press, 1985); Peggy Pascoe, *Relations of Rescue: The Search for Female Moral Authority in the American West, 1874–1939* (New York and Oxford: Oxford University Press, 1990); Anne Firor Scott, *Natural Allies: Women's Associations in American History* (Urbana: University of Illinois Press, 1992); and Ruth Bordin, *Women and Temperance: The Quest for Power and Liberty, 1873–1900* (Philadelphia: Temple University Press, 1984). On American religious domesticity, see Colleen McDannell, *The Christian Home in Victorian America, 1840–1900* (Bloomington and Indianapolis, IN: Indiana University Press, 1986); Barbara Reeves-Ellington, Kathryn Kish Sklar, and Connie A. Shemo, eds., *Competing Kingdoms: Women, Mission, Nation, and the American Protestant Empire, 1812–1960* (Durham, N.C.: Duke University Press, 2010).

23. See Goldman, *Beyond the Synagogue Gallery*, passim.

CHAPTER 10
SOMETHING OLD, SOMETHING NEW . . . SOMETHING BLUE: NEGOTIATING FOR A NEW RELATIONSHIP BETWEEN JUDAISM AND CHRISTIANITY IN AMERICA, 1865–1917

Yaakov Ariel

The decades following the Civil War in America witnessed the beginning of a shift in the relationship between Judaism and Christianity, and the emergence of new attitudes on the part of both liberal and conservative American Christians toward Judaism and Jews. It was during that era that interfaith dialogue began in America, and American religious leaders convened the first World Parliament of Religions (1893). It was also during that period that a number of Christian leaders in America organized to combat harassment of Jews around the globe, and, at times, lent their support to the fledgling Zionist movement. During that period, Jewish leaders had worked hard to make a case for Judaism, attempting to convince their Christian counterparts of the legitimacy and validity of the Jewish faith. While full recognition and acceptance was not achieved during those years, the efforts were more fully rewarded a generation later, as it took long decades for new attitudes to prevail.

1 An era of renegotiations

It was no coincidence that in America of the period, Jews and Christians began renegotiating the relationship between their faiths. Day to day Jewish-Christian interaction in America had been better than in Europe even before the outbreak of the Civil War. While prejudices and discrimination against Jews were rampant, Jews in America were spared the more brutal elements of Christian negative attitudes toward Jews, and no pogroms or blood libels took place in America.[1] America held a different ethos than European or Asian nations, viewing itself as a democratic country, open to people of all creeds and ethnicities. Moreover, in America Jews encountered a different attitude on the part of the prevailing Christian Churches than in Europe, Africa, or Asia. Influenced by the English Reform tradition, European Pietism, and British and American evangelicalism, Protestant Americans had been strongly influenced by the Old Testament. They understood their commonwealth in biblical terms as a covenant between God and his people.[2] Replacement Theology, the traditional Christian claim to have inherited Israel, was weaker among American Protestant Christians than among their European counterparts. While the period between the Civil War and the First World War saw continuation of old theological claims and accusations on both sides, the time was ripe for change.

The years after the Civil War in America were favorable for a renegotiation of the relationship between the religious communities. Considered formative for the development of religious life in modern America, the period saw major changes in the ethnic and religious composition of American cities.[3] Millions of immigrants settled in America, many of them affiliated with communities whose loyalties were different from those of the Protestant American majority. Rapid industrialization, the growth of multi-ethnic cities, and the rise of a secular culture of leisure, including the early beginnings of the movie industry, challenged the old American cultural and religious establishments.[4] Protestant reactions to the new social and cultural developments ranged from attempts to accommodate Protestant Christianity to the prevailing intellectual and cultural modes of the day to rejection of the premises of modernity.

Protestantism in America began splitting into two camps: liberal modernists and reactionary conservatives, known at that time as fundamentalists. Liberal Christian theology of the period promoted universalistic ideals of progressive millennialism. Looking forward to the building of the kingdom of God on Earth through means of social and political reform, better technology, evangelism, and education, the liberals insisted that humanity could work toward its own redemption.[5]

Liberal Protestants showed interest in a new discipline, History of Religions or Comparative Religion, which emerged in Britain and Germany of the period. The new discipline inspired interest in other religions at the same time that it asserted that the Protestant tradition was standing at the top of the religious, spiritual and moral ladder.[6] A Protestant school of inquiry at its first decades, History of Religions was influenced by theories of evolution, viewing human faiths as developing from primitive "magic" to a more sophisticated "religion."[7] Like their theological ancestors, the Protestant scholars viewed Christianity as a purified, refined version of Judaism, which they considered a progress in relation to heathen religions. The new times offered new means of making claims for superiority on the part of Western Christianity. Aiming at making Christianity relevant for the new epoch, liberal Christians were relying on major premises of the Enlightenment, making their ideals compatible with nineteenth-century notions of progress. Their tradition, they were certain, represented the ideals of the era and went hand in hand with scientific truths.

The period saw willingness on the part of the Protestant elite to give more space to members of other religious groups and allow greater representation in American public life to non-Protestants. Likewise, the Protestant theological elites were reviewing their tradition utilizing historical and comparative tools. In principle, they became committed to adjusting their theological perceptions in accordance with the scientific theories of the time. In the decades following the Civil War, American Protestant theological schools incorporated new techniques of biblical research, namely the Higher Criticism of the Bible, which had emerged in nineteenth-century Germany. According to this school of inquiry, the Hebrew and Greek Bibles were to be examined in the same manner that all other ancient texts were studied, utilizing philological, literary, historical and archeological evidence.[8] The Jewish religious leaders of the period took notice of both developments: the scientific guise that the Protestant elite used in order to assert its primacy and supremacy as well as the window of opportunity that a triumphalist but liberal Christian elite opened before them. Their mission, they believed, was to prove to their Christian colleagues that Judaism stood at the same position or even on a higher level than Christianity.

The renegotiations of a new relationship were carried, for the most part, from above, by the theological elite. While the daily interaction between Christians and Jews in America took place mostly between laypersons on both sides, the negotiation of a new basis for the relationship between the groups was the initiative of the religious leadership of both communities. By the turn of the twentieth century, the majority of American Jews were newly arrived immigrants from Eastern Europe, but the representatives of American Jewry were leaders of the German Jewish elite and, at times, even of the Sephardic community. In fact, on the Jewish side it was only a handful of rabbis who took part in interfaith dialogue. When denominational lines were drawn during the period, one could notice that they were affiliated with the Reform movement, and the fledgling Conservative movement. Conducted by the elite, it would take time for their ideals and attitudes to influence the rest of society.

Renegotiations of relationships between religious communities can be compared to attempts by spouses, usually wives, to reset the relationship with their husbands on more egalitarian grounds. Such wives would refuse to accept their husbands' claims to superior status. In fact they would insist that their merits and accomplishments were just as good as, if not superior to, those of their spouses. The Jewish intellectual rabbinical elite of the period did exactly that.

Jewish apologists argued for the authenticity of Judaism, defending it from the Christian claim that Christianity inherited Israel, long before the 1860s. Exchanges and arguments between Jews and Christians to that effect had taken place in the early centuries of Christianity, as well as in "disputations" in Western Europe in the High Middle Ages. Jews had never accepted the Christian claims for replacing or superseding the Jews as the true heirs to God's promises to Israel and rejected the Christian view that there was no more role or purpose for the separate existence of the Jewish people outside of the Church.[9] Similarly, Jews had consistently refused to adopt the Christian manner of reading the Hebrew Bible as a prelude to the New Testament and had related to the latter as a non-Jewish text. Ironically, such theological debates resurfaced in the nineteenth century as a result of an emancipated, more tolerant era. Jews were making their way into the general society and wished to do so as equal citizens. For that, they had to insist that their heritage deserved the same respect as that of their neighbors. However, Jewish theologians and apologists were facing a new challenge: the means to claim pride in one's heritage were by relying on scholarly theories produced by academicians.

One may again compare the attitudes of the Jewish rabbinical elite to that of leaders of the Women's Movement, a hundred years later, who—in the wake of other movements of liberation—recognized an opportunity to renegotiate their status. And like an assertive wife, their attitude was "everything you can do I can do better." To contend with Christian liberal or conservative triumphalist theologies, Jews built a progressive millennial theology of their own. American Reform rabbis during the period constructed a theology that both retained the Jewish ethos of a chosen nation, with a unique role and mission in history, and adapted it to a progressive philosophy of history intended to counter Christian claims of supremacy. The Jewish thinkers, in the words of Susannah Heschel, "reversed the gaze," adopting the same ideals and claims.[10]

2 Scholarship as a weapon

Jewish leaders such as Isaac M. Wise, Emil G. Hirsch, and Kaufmann Kohler concluded that in order to create a new basis for the relationship between the two faiths, Christians needed to change their attitude toward Judaism in a fundamental manner and come to respect the Jewish religion, its texts, and history. To accomplish that task they utilized the most potent weapon in the relationship between the faiths during the period: academic scholarship.[11]

The decades following the Civil War witnessed an increase in the prestige of academic scholarship. The progressive interpretation of history had viewed scientific research and academic scholarship in linear terms.[12] Scientists, according to the prevailing understanding, were discovering eternal and universal laws that governed nature as well as human society and culture in all times and all places. Liberals in particular trusted and appreciated academic disciplines and asserted that human civilization should build its foundation and choose its direction based on "science," the scientific theories provided by the academy. Academic theories consequently provided political as well as religious groups' arguments in their struggle to legitimize their ideologies or theologies. However, it was already at this stage, a century before the appearance of postmodern theories and Deconstructionism, that Jewish leaders and scholars, such as Isaac M. Wise and Kaufmann Kohler, had noted that "science" was not always about eternal and universal truth and was far from being "blind."[13]

Jewish leaders were concerned over what they considered a serious disparity. Christian academicians and theologians were unwilling to apply the same rigid scholarly standards that they utilized to study the origins of Judaism, when they examined the origins of their own religious tradition. Few, if any, New Testament scholars or those searching for the historical Jesus, for example, were as daring as the Christian scholars of the Old Testament who had no problems smashing the Jewish ethos.[14] Concerned over what they considered to be unfair usage of scholarship, elite American rabbis felt that they had to defend their tradition and assert its legitimacy, this time utilizing scholarship to their advantage. They mustered in particular academic fields of scholarship that related to the relationship between the faiths. Mastering new disciplines along the same line that their Protestant counterparts employed, the American Jewish theological elite practiced what Ahad Ha'am's labeled "chikuy mitoch tacharut," an adaptation of methods created by the majority culture in an attempt to preserve and promote the minority group's self-esteem.[15] Like their Christian counterparts, they, in the last analysis, were scholars in defense of their faith.

Scholarship as a means of Jewish religious and cultural affirmation began in the early nineteenth century in Germany with the establishment of the *Wissenschaft des Judentums*.[16] Scholars affiliated with this academic discipline took interest in various aspects of Jewish history and thought. They established scholarly journals, and provided academic positions for scholars in Judaic Studies, as well as forums for such scholars to meet. Likewise, they created what in our days would be called a graduate program. No Jewish school of such caliber had formed in America of the nineteenth century. In America, rabbi-scholars were studying the history of Judaism and the historical relationship between Judaism and Christianity on their own. While the Hebrew Union College in Cincinnati and the Jewish Theological Seminary in New York were established in the latter decades of the nineteenth century, they were not yet the scholarly centers they would become in the twentieth century. Only at the beginning of the twentieth century Kaufmann Kohler, in Cincinnati, and Solomon Schechter, in New York, turned the Hebrew Union College and the Jewish Theological Seminary into solid academic institutions.

The American Jewish rabbi-scholars of the late nineteenth century did not build historical theories out of thin air. They borrowed from German Jewish scholarship. In fact, in the specific realm of research on early Christianity, they were disciples of Abraham Geiger (1810–74), an architect of the Reform movement and the patriarch of Jewish scholarship on the origins of Christianity. Geiger and his disciples had set out to reclaim Jesus as a teacher in Judea instead of the God of the Gentiles.[17] They insisted that Jesus was a Jew, not unlike many of his contemporaries. Geiger concluded that Jesus was a Pharisee, that his teaching should be read in light of first-century Jewish rabbinical teachings, and that in fact much of it could be found in the *Mishnah*. Geiger's pioneering work served as a model for Jewish scholars in the field, who basically accepted his conclusions. American disciples of Geiger, such as Wise, Hirsch, and Kohler, followed in his footsteps in their understanding of Jesus and his followers as part of the messianic fervor of Second Temple Judaism. They were careful to note that for Jews of that period, Jesus' group was just one of many messianic groups of its kind; and even during the immediate generations that followed Jesus, Christians were but one of a number of Jewish semi-heretical groups.[18]

The Jewish American scholars followed Geiger in his understanding that Christianity augmented out of Judaism, but some of them contributed their own insights. Kohler, for example, saw Jesus as walking in the footsteps of the Hasidim, an avant-garde reformist Pharisee group. The rabbi-scholars concluded that Christianity was a child of Judaism. The merits of Christianity were actually the achievements of Judaism: monotheism, demand for moral values and social justice, and even Jesus, a sympathetic moral and spiritual leader, were all Jewish. In fact, Christianity was a form of Judaism. They saw Judaism as more rational, more purely monotheistic, and holding more integrity than Christianity. In contrast to this, the Jewish rabbi-scholars demonstrated anger at Paul of Tarsos, who, in their opinion, had constructed Christology, the faith in Jesus that theologically separated Christians from Jews.

Who of the two was the more typical Jew? Jesus, the mild, silver-tongued preacher of Galilee, who probably never stepped beyond the boundaries of Judea, nor spoke in other language but that of his countrymen, nor preached to any but Jewish hearers, whose every word is an echo of rabbinical sayings, and who emphatically declared that he had not come to destroy but to fulfil the old covenant? Or Paul, the irritable, ghost-seeing fanatic from the Greek isle of Tarsos, who acted like an infuriated zealot when in Judea, and poured forth all the wrath of his hot temper against the Jews when a preacher of Christ among the Gentiles, whose writings are a quaint mixture of Hellenistic philosophy, of semi-pagan mysticism (or gnosticism) and oriental superstition, and who took a special pride in being a Roman among Romans, a Greek with Greeks, and a Hebrew with Hebrews? There is nothing genuinely Jewish about Paul except the name of Saul, which he in time dropped, whereas every feature of Jesus betrays the influence of rabbinical lore, and particularly the school of Hillel, the meek, the original exponent of the Golden Rule.[19]

In addition to Paul, whom they considered to have led Christianity astray, Jewish American scholars have openly stated their less than appreciative judgment of the Trinity. The concept of the Trinity, they argued, did not make sense. Utilizing modern arguments to make their point, they pointed out that Christian dissatisfaction with Trinitarian theology made Christian thinkers hostile toward Judaism, which did not have to contend with the Trinity.

3 A scholar and theologian of an age of interfaith discussion

Kaufmann Kohler (1843–1923) was the most original and imaginative of all of Geiger's students. Born in Fürth, Bavaria, Kohler moved from Neo-Orthodoxy to Reform. After completing a PhD degree at the University of Erlangen, Kohler immigrated to the United States, where he served as a rabbi in Congregation Sinai in Chicago, Congregation Beth El in New York, and later as president of the Hebrew Union College in Cincinnati. A leader of Reform Judaism in America during the 1870s to 1920s, Kohler's real passion was to bring Christians to respect Judaism. Kohler studied the literature of the new discipline of History of Religions and became fully acquainted with the scholarly arguments of historians of early Christianity.[20] He both followed Geiger and deviated from him in his understanding of some key elements. Kohler speculated that John the Baptist and Jesus were inspired by and were close to the Essenes, the ascetic sect whose stronghold was near the Dead Sea.[21] Jesus, according to Kohler, might have been an Essene himself for some time and drew a number of his followers from people who could neither adhere to the rigid standards of the Essenes nor to the high demands in learning of the Pharisees. Jesus' more democratic sect was inspired by the Hasidim, whom Kohler defined as a virtuous and ascetic group that served as the avant-garde of the Pharisees. He credited the Hasidim for bringing about many of the positive developments in Judaism in the generations before and during Jesus' era. Among other things, he claimed that the Hasidim were the ones who invented the synagogue and turned it into the preferred gathering place in Jewish life.[22] When Kohler writes on the Hasidim one can sense that he sees himself—and the Reform movement in general—as following in the footsteps of what he considers to have been the avant-garde of a self-reforming Judaism, a movement that pioneered in adjusting Judaism to the changing times.

In concluding that the early beginnings of Christianity grew out of and resembled virtuous avant-garde Jewish movements of the time, the Reform leader gave Jesus and his immediate disciples a clean bill of health. The pedigree of Christianity was good since it started as a righteous Jewish sect. It was not an accident that Kohler named one of his books *The Origins of the Synagogue and the Church*, indicating that the origins of the one were connected to those of the other.[23] But further developments, he claimed, led Christianity away from its cradle and compromised its original Jewish character. As much as Kohler was appreciative in his treatment of the origins of Christianity, he was not as generous in his understanding of the development of Christianity after its first generation. Like other Jewish thinkers, Kohler put much of the blame for what he considered the corruption of the early doctrines and character of Christianity on Paul, whose theological system shifted the focus from Jesus' faith to a Christological faith in Jesus. Paul's theology, Kohler complained, was more pagan than Jewish, and he made an effort to distance Paul, even before his conversion, from Judaism.[24]

Kohler is particularly scornful when relating to the Trinity. "The Christian Trinity led mankind in many ways to the lowering of the supreme standard of truth, to an infringement on Justice, and to inhumanity to other creeds, and therefore Judaism could regard it only as a compromise with heathenism."[25] The greatest harm of all, Kohler remarks, was done to Judaism: "Paul made a caricature of the Law … the Paulinian Church … impregnated the Christian World with hostility to Judaism and the Jew." Relating to Paul's concept of grace, Kohler writes:

> The Jewish conception of grace is far deeper and worthier of God than that of Paulinian Christianity … For grace in Paul's sense is arbitrary in action and dependent upon the acceptance of a creed … In Judaism, divine grace is not offered as a bait to make men believe, but as an incentive to moral improvement.[26]

Kohler's major complaint, like that of other Jews before him, relates to the non-appearance of an age of righteousness. "Nor did the church bring to mankind the salvation she promised … She preached and promoted the gospel of love, but failed to recognize the fundamental principle of justice … She had no freedom nor tolerance for those who would not accept her creed. She denied to the Jew the very right of existence."[27] The last remark explains Kohler's critical attitude toward the Christian church as it developed after its parting of the ways with Judaism. He was bitter over what he considered the historical injustice expressed in the offensive measures taken by Christianity against Jews throughout the centuries.

Kohler quoted from the sixteenth-century Karaite polemicist Isaac Troki, whose book *Hizzuk Emunah* ("Strengthening of the Faith") came to defend Judaism against Christian claims.[28] "None of the Messianic promises of a time of perfect peace and unity among men, of love and truth of universal knowledge and undisturbed happiness, of the cessation of all wrong doing, superstition, idolatry, falsehood, and hatred have been fulfilled by the church," Troki asserted, to which Kohler agreed.

Kohler continues Troki's line of thinking: "The medieval church divided men into believers and unbelievers, who are to inherit heaven and hell respectively. With the love which she poured forth ... she also sent forth streams of hatred."[29] "She [the church]," Kohler claims, "did not foster that spirit of true holiness which sanctifies the whole of life—marriage and home, industry and commerce—but in Jewish eyes seemed to cultivate only the feminine virtues of love and humility, not liberty and justice, manhood and independence of thought."[30]

In describing Christian characteristics as "feminine" and Jewish ones as "manly," Kohler reflected the influence of the cultural climate of his day, which differentiated between "manly" and "feminine," placing manly characteristics above the feminine ones. In declaring Judaism to be the "manly" religion and Christianity the "feminine" one, the Jewish polemicist was again "reversing the gaze," and offering the majority culture a taste of its own medicine. In European culture of the time, Jews were often portrayed as effeminate.[31] Their minority status and their "bookish" occupations made the majority group look upon them as cowards. Significantly, Kohler was not satisfied with what he considered to be the manly character of Judaism or wholly unappreciative of what he thought to be the feminine nature of Christianity. Kohler recognizes many merits in the Christian church, including its success in carrying its messages, many of them derived from Judaism, to all corners of the earth. Judaism with its high standards and demanding norms, he contends, could not have done that and remained a smaller community. Kohler also considered Christianity's achievements in art, music, and architecture superior to those of Judaism and derived from Christianity's "feminine character." He sees the role of Jewish women as helping to reform Judaism by feminizing it.[32]

Kohler proposes an alternative to what he considers an exclusivist and triumphalist Christian attitude:[33]

Christianity presents itself as an orb of light, but ... room is left for other spiritual forces ... for all religious and philosophical systems that may yet be evolved in the process of the ages. In fact, whatever constitutes humanity and bears the image of God, whatever man does to unfold the divine life.[34]

While Kohler believed in Israel's unique mission and its covenant with God, he promoted a universal and harmonious future that included reconciliation and cooperation between Judaism and Christianity.[35] He believed that Judaism and Christianity could work together toward the building of the kingdom of God on Earth. Mutual recognition and reconciliation are a requirement for such a development to take place.

So let the flags and emblems, the watchwords of former hostility between the various religious denominations henceforth bespeak peace and friendly recognition for each other and the marks and remnants of prejudice be buried from sight ... Let Christianity and Judaism, let mother and daughter, walk arm in arm while climbing up the heights of Zion, that the day may be near when God will be one and humanity one.[36]

Kohler offers here much of his messianic progressive vision, according to which all human beings would come to recognize the God of Israel and his moral commandments, creating a universal community and bringing about the kingdom of God on Earth through human cooperation. He also offered a vision of Christian-Jewish reconciliation. Kohler was not the only religious leader during the period to advocate the idea of Christian-Jewish dialogue and cooperation. A number of Christian and Jewish leaders had also suggested such ideas.

4 The rise of the interfaith dialogue movement

Interfaith dialogue between Christians and Jews began in America in the latter decades of the nineteenth century, primarily between liberal Protestants and Jews. Dialogue is more than polite conversations, and entails a conscious attempt to overcome long-standing prejudices and injuries and work toward improvement in the relationship between participating groups. The very engagement in dialogue signifies some amount of good will and mutual respect, if not preliminary recognition. During the post-Civil War era, a number of Jewish and Protestant clergymen invited each other to give talks in their respective congregations, cooperated over civic agenda and, at times, organized interfaith meetings. Such interactions took place on a sporadic basis and often entailed personal friendships between Jewish and Christian religious leaders.[37]

A special occasion in the history of interfaith dialogue in America took place in 1893. The World Parliament of Religions convened in Chicago in conjunction with the World Columbian Exposition, bringing together Protestants, Catholics and Greek Orthodox Christians, as well as Jews, Buddhists, Hindus, Bahai, Muslims, Native Americans, and representatives of other faiths as well. Jews were not the initiators of the event, but they took full advantage of the unprecedented opportunities it offered.[38] Committed to changing the relationship between Judaism and other faiths, Jewish religious leaders such as Alexander Kohut, Isaac M. Wise, Kaufmann Kohler, Emil G. Hirsch, and Marcus Jastrow, took the opportunity to present their views to a non-Jewish audience and make a case for Judaism. Emil G. Hirsch, the American born rabbi of Temple Sinai, the largest and richest congregation in Chicago at the time, spoke about the need to overcome parochial differences and create one world religion.[39] Other Jewish representatives used the occasion to defend Judaism against what they considered to be erroneous and degrading Christian views on the Jewish faith.

Protestants were the major initiators of and partners in dialogue between the faiths. But at times, representatives of other faiths also took part in such meetings. Roman Catholic bishops and priests were sporadically also involved in dialogue or cooperation between communities of faith. Cardinal Gibbons, the Archbishop of Baltimore, for example, participated in the World Parliament of Religion, and later lent his support to Zionist initiatives.[40] As a rule, however, the Roman Catholic hierarchy in America played a secondary role in initiatives for interfaith reconciliation during the period.

Interfaith dialogue at that era was at its infancy, but certain characteristics of the dialogue were laid out at this early stage. An important feature of this dialogue, from the early beginnings, was that the actual willingness to meet with Jewish representatives and converse with Jews in the forum of the dialogue was already in itself a litmus test for the attitude of Christian groups in America toward Judaism and Jews. Dialogue entailed an a priori respect, even if limited, toward each other's faith and a willingness to hear, if not always to listen to, religious leaders of other groups discuss their concerns. Christian and Jewish participants in the dialogue would continue to be representatives of liberal wings of their faith. Most Jewish participants at this stage of the dialogue were Reform rabbis or rabbis of the fledgling Conservative movement. However, contrary to a prevailing myth, Orthodox rabbis and communities were also engaged in dialogue with Christians.[41] While many of the issues discussed were not spiritual or theological, the dialogue between Jews and non-Jews was entrusted to clergymen. Representing Judaism and the Jewish community in dialogue with members of other faiths would become an important component of rabbis' work in America. It would greatly add to the prestige of the American rabbinate, as well as make the rabbis' work less parochial and more interesting. Rabbis would become representatives of Judaism and Jewish causes vis-à-vis other faiths in America as well as American society at large.

5 Conservatives and Jews: a new relationship

Conservative Protestants did not take part in Interfaith Dialogue, or in meetings intended to promote good will and cooperation between religious communities. In fact, they objected to such gestures, which meant legitimizing other faiths. The conservatives disapproved of the modernist trends that gained ground among liberal Protestants and cared little for the liberals' enchantment with new academic theories. They insisted that only true Christians, persons who had undergone experiences of conversion and accepted Jesus of Nazareth as their personal Savior, would be saved and rewarded with eternal lives. In their opinion, all others were doomed. They considered it therefore negligence and irresponsibility on the part of the good Christians to allow non-Christians to assume that their faith could provide them with the spiritual assurance that Christianity could. Conservative Christians have therefore viewed the mission as the most appropriate manner to relate to members of other faiths and they took special interest in the Jews.

In the decades following the Civil War, many conservative American Protestants accepted the eschatological faith in the imminent second coming of Jesus to establish the kingdom of God on Earth. In reaction to the liberal endorsement of the Higher Criticism of the Bible, conservatives adopted a more literal manner of reading the sacred Christian texts. Departing from an ancient Christian approach, conservative biblical literalists had come to recognize the Jews as continuers of the historical children of Israel and heirs to the covenant between God and Israel.

Motivated by their messianic faith, those conservative Christians demonstrated a renewed interest in the Jewish people, the prospect of their conversion to Christianity and of their return to Palestine.[42] While the conservatives' view was that their faith, namely Christianity in its conservative evangelical interpretations, was the only legitimate faith, they had come to regard Judaism as an exception, at least in some ways. Judaism could not provide its adherents with the spiritual comfort and moral guidance that Christianity did and Jews could not obtain salvation without accepting Jesus. But Judaism prepared the Jews, at least partially, for their historical mission—helping to re-establish the Davidic kingdom in the Land of Israel. According to the conservatives' eschatological hope, the Jews were to go back to their ancestral land in "unbelief," without having accepted Jesus as their savior.[43] Beginning in the 1880s conservative Protestants became involved in pro-Zionist activities intended to restore Palestine to the Jews. They also established a large missionary network, intended to educate the Jews as to their real role and mission in history and prepare them for the events of the Endtimes.[44]

The new manner, in which conservative Protestant leaders had viewed the Jewish people, had proved throughout the decades to be a lasting revolution that had affected the attitudes toward Jews and Zionism of many conservative Americans for years to come.[45] It was already during that period that eschatologically oriented conservative Americans established contacts with Zionist Jewish leaders. The messianic visions of the groups were not fully identical, but they both shared the wish to build a Jewish commonwealth in Palestine and they cooperated toward that goal. In 1891, William Blackstone, an American evangelist, organized a public petition to the President of the United States calling upon him to act in the international arena toward the restoration of Palestine to the Jews.[46] Blackstone established a friendly relationship with activists of the pre-Herzilian Zionist groups and, later on, the Zionist federation in America. At the request of the Zionist leadership, he organized a second petition in 1916. While the Zionist leaders appreciated the Protestant willingness to advance their cause, they and other Jews reacted very differently toward attempts at evangelizing Jews.

6 Will you please shut down the missions?

One thorny issue in the relationship between Judaism and Christianity during the period was the mission. Influenced by a more literal reading of the Bible, American Protestants saw special merit in evangelizing the Jews. In their own understanding they meant well for the Jews, dedicating themselves to improving their spiritual and moral condition, as well as educating them as to their real role in history.[47] Members of the Jewish elite did not encounter the missionaries very often. Missionaries carried out their work among poor Jewish immigrants from Eastern Europe, offering them a variety of welfare and educational services. The Jewish elite reacted with resentment and alarm toward missionary activity among working class Jews. In their eyes, the missions were more than an attempt to capture Jewish souls, and represented at its core an attempt to eliminate Judaism as a community of faith existing outside the body of Christ. Viewing the missionary endeavor as a demonstration of contempt toward Judaism and Jews, Jewish religious leaders wished to defend Judaism against what they considered to be the unwillingness of Christians to relate to Judaism as a legitimate faith.

Missions were, therefore, a constant item on the agenda of dialogue groups, with the Jewish representatives demanding that Christians give up on evangelizing Jews. Since the Roman period, Jews had not missionized and expected Christians to also refrain from propagating the Christian faith among Jews.[48] But Christianity was not Judaism and thrived on missionizing, calling upon people of different ethnicities and cultures to join its ranks. As the dialogue between Jews and Christians advanced throughout the first half of the twentieth century, Christian groups associated with the dialogue gave up on missionizing Jews. But the evangelizing of Jews would continue vigorously by the more messianically oriented conservatives.

7 Conclusion

The time and place, America of the post-Civil War era, allowed Jews to begin to renegotiate their status as individuals and as a minority community. Jewish leaders took full notice of the new atmosphere and the new forums, which had opened doors to them to state their demands and make a case for Judaism. They concluded that they needed to fundamentally change the Christian attitude toward the Jewish religious tradition and stir the respect of members of a sister religious community that had historically made a claim for supremacy and exclusivity. The ruling Protestant majority was rewriting the rules of engagement between the faiths, putting a high premium on scholarly theories and newly created academic disciplines. Jewish religious leaders rose to the occasion, and the Jewish theological elite of the post-Civil War era mastered the new academic tools and used them to counter the Christian claims to supremacy.

This leads us to a number of conclusions. One relates to the nature of American Christianity and its impact on the position of Jews and Judaism in America. In America, Jews had more space and opportunity than in European societies to befriend the Christian theological elite, present their arguments and demand a theological revision. Jews made a similar effort in Germany, where Jewish scholarship was more advanced than in America, to renegotiate the status of their faith. But no movement of Interfaith Dialogue developed there, and Jewish intellectuals found it difficult to find open Christian ears.

Second, the renegotiation of a relationship between Judaism and Christianity has been central to the creation of American Judaism and American Jewish self-awareness. This community has been more comfortable in America than in the Old Country, enjoyed more opportunities it did not possess before, and being more self-assured, built a better image of itself. The relatively more open and amicable relationship between Christians and Jews contributed to a greater feeling of security and acceptance on the part of Jews in America. While many of them have been unaware of the negotiations that have taken place between Christian and Jewish theologians, such dialogue, and attempts at changing the Christian mind, affected their lives. The renegotiations of a new attitude were made possible by the uniqueness of the American scene, which was more tolerant and inclusive.

Thirdly, one should pay attention to the role of leadership in the negotiations between the faiths. Jewish historiography of the twentieth century did not relate kindly to the German Jewish contribution to the building of American Jewry. Traditionalist, Zionist and Socialist historians looked upon Reform Jews as lapsed Jews, who compromised on authentic Judaism for the sake of middle class respectability. Examination of the Jewish attempt to negotiate the basis for the relationship between the faiths, however, reveals a very different story. A proud and proactive leadership took upon itself the task of challenging the Christian religious elite and arguing with it on its own terms. Those rabbis deserve our respect for the historical breakthrough they helped bring about.

Notes

1. See Leonard Dinnerstein, *Antisemitism in America* (New York and Oxford: Oxford University Press, 1994). And see Benny Kraut's excellent article, "Jewish Survival in Protestant America," in *Minority Faiths and the American Protestant Mainstream*, ed. Jonathan D. Sarna (Urbana, IL: University of Illinois Press, 1998), 15–60.

2. See the classical works: Perry Miller, *Errand Into the Wilderness* (Cambridge, MA: The Belknap Press of Harvard University Press, 1956), and H. Richard Niebuhr, *The Kingdom of God in America* (New York: Harper and Row, 1937).

3. See Samuel Eliot Morrison, Henry Steele Commager and William E. Leuchtenberg, *A Concise History of the American Republic* (New York and Oxford: Oxford University Press, 1977), Chapters 20–27.

4. George M. Marsden, *Fundamentalism and American Culture* (New York and Oxford: Oxford University Press, 1980).

5. See William Hutchison, *The Modernist Impulse in American Protestantism* (Durham, NC: Duke University Press, 1992).

6. See, for example, C. Samuel Preus, *Explaining Religion* (New Haven, CT: Yale University Press, 1987), 131–56; Eric J. Sharpe, *Comparative Religion: A History* (Chicago: University of Chicago Press, 1986), 47–71.

7. See Randall Styers, *Making Magic: Religion, Magic and Science in the Modern World* (New York and Oxford: Oxford University Press, 2002).

8. Martin E. Marty, *Modern American Religion*, Vol. 1: *The Irony of It All* (Chicago: Chicago University Press, 1994).

9. See Frank E. Talmage, ed., *Disputation and Dialogue: Readings in the Jewish-Christian Encounter* (New York: Ktav, 1975).

10. Susannah Heschel, *Abraham Geiger and the Jewish Jesus* (Chicago: University of Chicago Press, 1998).

11. The first Jewish scholarly publication during the period on the origins of Christianity was Isaac M. Wise, *The Origins of Christianity* (Cincinnati, OH: Bloch, 1868). See also George L. Berlin, *Defending the Faith: Nineteenth-Century American Jewish Writings on Christianity and Jesus* (Albany, NY: State University of New York Press, 1989).

12. See Arthur Link and Richard L. McCormick, *Progressivism* (Arlington Heights, Ill.: Harlan Davidson, 1983), Chapter 1; Claude Welch, *Protestant Thoughts*, Vol. 2, 1870–1914 (New Haven, CT: Yale University Press, 1985).

13. See Heschel, *Abraham Geiger and the Jewish Jesus*, passim.

14. See also Arthur Hertzberg, *The French Enlightenment and the Jews* (New York: Columbia University Press, 1968).

15. Yehiel Alfred Gottschalk, *Ahad Ha-Am and the Jewish National Spirit* [hebr.] (Jerusalem: Hassifria Haziyonit, 1992).

16. On the Wissenschaft des Judentums and its influence on Reform thinking, see Michael A. Meyer, *Response to Modernity: A History of the Reform Movement in Judaism* (New York and Oxford: Oxford University Press, 1988), 75–99; Paul Mendes-Flohr, *Hohmat Israel* (Jerusalem: Magness, 1980). On the contribution of the *Wissenschaft des Judentums* in Germany to the intellectual debates with Protestant theology, see Christian Wiese, *Challenging Colonial Discourse: Jewish Studies and Protestant Theology in Wilhelmine Germany* (Leiden and Boston: Brill, 2005).

17. Donald A. Hagner, *The Jewish Reclamation of Jesus* (Grand Rapids, MI: Zondervan, 1984).

18. See the entries "Christians," in *The Jewish Encyclopedia*, Vol. 4, 48, and "Jesus of Nazareth," in *The Jewish Encyclopedia*, Vol. 17, 160–1.

19. Kaufmann Kohler, *Christianity vs. Judaism: A Rejoinder to the Rev. Dr. R. Heber Newton* (New York: Stettiner, Lambert & Co., 1890), 3.

20. On Kaufmann Kohler's scholarship on Christianity, see Yaakov Ariel, "Christianity through Reform Eyes: Kaufmann Kohler's Scholarship on Christianity," *American Jewish History* 89 (2001): 181–91.

21. Kaufmann Kohler, *Studies, Addresses and Personal Papers* (New York: Alumni Association of the Hebrew Union College, 1929), 238–40.

22. Kohler, *Studies, Addresses and Personal Papers*, 29–116. Identification of Jesus with the Essenes can also be found in Heinrich Graetz's understanding of Jesus. Graetz saw such strong similarities between Jesus and the Essenes that he concluded that Jesus was an Essene; see Heinrich Graetz, *History of the Jews* (London: David Nutt, 1891/92), Vol. 11, 150.

23. Kaufmann Kohler, *The Origins of the Synagogue and the Church* (New York: Mcmillan, 1929).

24. Kohler, *Christianity vs. Judaism*, 3–4.

25. Kaufmann Kohler, *Jewish Theology, Systematically and Historically Considered* (New York: Macmillan, 1918), 56.

26. Kohler, *Jewish Theology*, 116–7.

27. Samuel S. Cohon, ed., *A Living Faith: Selected Sermons and Addresses from the Literary Remains of Dr. Kaufmann Kohler* (Cincinnati, OH: Hebrew Union College Press, 1949), 113.

28. See the entry "Troki," in *The Jewish Encyclopedia*, Vol. 12, 265–7.

29. Kohler, "Christianity," in *The Jewish Encyclopedia*, Vol. 4, 58.

30. Ibid.

31. See Daniel Boyarin, Daniel Itzkovitz and Ann Pellegrini, eds., *Queer Theory and the Jewish Question* (New York: Columbia University Press, 2003).

32. On Kohler's view on women's role in Jewish life, see Karla Goldman, *Beyond the Synagogue Gallery: Finding a Place for Women in American Judaism* (Cambridge, MA, and London: Harvard University Press, 2000), 151–71.

33. Heschel, *Abraham Geiger*, 58.

34. Kohler, "Christianity," in *The Jewish Encyclopedia*, Vol. 4, 58.

35. A good example of Kohler's walking a fine line between universalism and the Jewish mission can be found in Kaufmann Kohler, *Guide for the Instruction in Judaism: A Manual for Schools and Homes* (New York: Philip Cowen, 1898).

36. Kohler, *Christianity vs. Judaism*, 8.

37. Lawrence G. Charap, "Accept the Truth from Whomsoever Gives It: Jewish Protestant Dialogue, Interfaith Alliance and Pluralism, 1880–1910," *American Jewish History* 89 (2001): 161–78.

38. On the World Parliament of Religions and its effect on interfaith dialogue, see Marcus Braybrooke, *Pilgrimage of Hope: One Hundred Years of Interfaith Dialogue* (New York: Crossroad, 1992).

39. On Hirsch and his ideas, see David E. Hirsch, *Rabbi Emil G. Hirsch: the Reform Advocate* (Northbrook, IL: Whitehall, 1968); Meyer, *Response to Modernity*, 270–6; Tobias Brinkmann, *Von der Gemeinde zur Community: Jüdische Einwanderer in Chicago, 1840–1900* (Osnabrück: Universitätsverlag Rasch, 2002), 406–22; idem, *Sundays at Sinai: A Jewish Congregation in Chicago* (Chicago: University of Chicago Press, 2012). In the wake of the World Parliament of Religions, some liberal Jewish and Protestant religious leaders further engaged in organized dialogue. Emil G. Hirsch established a particularly friendly relationship with Jenkins Lloyd Jones, a Unitarian minister and an initiator of the Parliament. Both educated and cultured, the two clergymen shared a box at the Chicago Lyric Opera and extended their friendship to each other's family. When Jenkins' ambitious young nephew, Frank, showed up in Chicago, the stern but kind Hirsch helped secure a position for the aspiring young architect at the office of a friend, a son of a fellow rabbi from Chicago, Liebmann Adler. Adler and Louis Sullivan came to regret their offering a job to the protégé of the prestigious rabbi and eventually came to see Frank Lloyd Wright as an eccentric and self-serving employee. But the latter went on to build a brilliant career in architecture, in which he promoted, through the medium of buildings, openness to religious diversity including to Judaism. See Benny Kraut, "The Ambivalent Relations of American Reform Judaism with Unitarianism in the Last Third of the Nineteenth Century," *Journal of Ecumenical Studies* 23 (1986): 58–68.

40. See Yaakov Ariel, "An American Initiative for the Establishment of a Jewish State: William Blackstone and the Petition of 1891," *Studies in Zionism* 10 (1990): 125–38.

41. See Charap, "Accept the Truth from Whomsoever Gives It."

42. See Yaakov Ariel, *On Behalf of Israel: American Fundamentalists Attitudes towards the Jewish People and Zionism, 1865–1945* (New York: Carlson, 1991).

43. For the details of the conservatives' messianic faith, see the premillennialist bestseller of the period: William E Blackstone, *Jesus is Coming* (Chicago: Fleming H. Revell, 1878, 2nd edition 1886, 3rd edition 1908).

44. See Yaakov Ariel, *Evangelizing the Chosen People: Mission to the Jews in America, 1880–2000* (Chapel Hill, NC: University of North Carolina Press, 2000).

45. Peter Grose, *Israel in the Mind of America* (New York: Knopf, 1983).

46. See Yaakov Ariel, "An American Initiative for the Establishment of a Jewish State," passim.

47. See Ariel, *Evangelizing the Chosen People*, passim.

48. See Isaac M. Wise, *A Defense of Judaism versus Proselytizing Christianity* (Cincinnati: American Israelite, 1889).

CHAPTER 11

TRANSLATING *WISSENSCHAFT*: THE EMERGENCE AND SELF-EMANCIPATION OF AMERICAN JEWISH SCHOLARSHIP, 1860–1920[1]

Christian Wiese

Wissenschaft des Judentums originated in Germany in the first quarter of the nineteenth century as the result of the desire on the part of a small number of university-trained Jewish intellectuals to modernize the study of Judaism in accordance with the model of contemporary Western European critical historical and literary scholarship.[2] Its founders also aspired to facilitate a proper understanding of Jewish religion, culture, and history in German society and thus to help overcoming anti-Jewish prejudice that had proven to be a major stumbling block to emancipation despite the Enlightenment. Leopold Zunz, in particular, was convinced that Jews as individuals would never attain full emancipation unless Judaism as a religion and culture was fully acknowledged and Jewish scholarship was raised to its rightful place among academic disciplines.[3] Others, such as Abraham Geiger, Zacharias Frankel, and Heinrich Graetz, emphasized the crucial role *Wissenschaft des Judentums* promised to play in inspiring a rekindling of Jewish self-respect and in promoting Jewish pride and self-respect.[4] *Wissenschaft des Judentums* in Europe, especially in Germany, was excluded from the universities, but founded its institutions of higher learning, for instance in Berlin, Breslau, Budapest, Vienna and elsewhere, which attracted students from all over Europe,[5] and established several well-known scholarly periodicals.[6] Throughout the nineteenth century and before the emergence of new centers of Jewish scholarship in America and later in Palestine (foremost the founding of the Hebrew University in Jerusalem in 1925), German was *the* acknowledged *lingua franca* of Jewish scholarship. The German-speaking tradition of *Wissenschaft des Judentums*, having formulated an ethical and philosophical reinterpretation of the Jewish tradition that highlighted Judaism's contribution to the contemporary social, intellectual and moral challenges, and having transformed Judaism into a "modern universal religion,"[7] was widely respected among Jewish scholars in other parts of the Diaspora as an inspiration for Jewish *Bildung* and scholarship.

The analysis of German Jewish history throughout the nineteenth and the early twentieth century demonstrates that the profound love German Jews harbored for the German language and culture eventually turned out to be an unrequited love, since it was never matched by a sincere and respectful response on the part of non-Jewish German intellectuals. Historical retrospect clearly reveals that the development of the rich history of *Wissenschaft des Judentums* in Germany, rooted as it was in the German intellectual discourse, was at the same time a history of unrealized hopes, of exclusion from universities, of contempt for Jewish scholars and their achievements, and ultimately, a history of discrimination and destruction.[8] During the nineteenth century, however, the strong bond between *Wissenschaft des Judentums*, the German language, and the so-called "German spirit" created enormous energies and hopes, which, as I would like to show in the following passages, did not only exert a strong influence on the creation of American Jewish culture during the formative period of American Reform Judaism, but—in a complex development—led to a profound admiration for German Jewry among American Jews and allowed only a gradual emancipation from its dominant cultural role. At least up to the final decades of the nineteenth century, American Jews seem to have gratefully accepted German Jewry's hegemony with respect to Jewish culture and scholarship.

This does, of course, not mean that the transnational relationship between German Jewish culture and American Reform Judaism unfolded undisputed and without conflicts—on the contrary. Particularly the question regarding the appropriate language of Jewish learning and scholarship was one of the increasingly contested issues that accompanied the history of American Judaism throughout the nineteenth century. From the very beginnings of Jewish emigration from Germany to America in the 1820s and 1830s until the demographic revolution in American Jewry caused by Eastern European immigration at the end of the century,[9] a tension can be discerned between forces favoring the preservation of the domination of German Jewish culture, language, and scholarship, and those arguing for a greater intellectual and spiritual distinctiveness.[10] In a complicated and fluctuating process, acculturation at first slowly and then in greater acceleration worked toward a gradual assertion of independence from the German matrix.

1 Language of the golden age: the period of the hegemony of German Jewish culture

In the early period of the migration of German-speaking Jews from Central Europe to America during the first half of the nineteenth century the later predominance of the German language within American-Jewish culture was not as self-evident and undisputed as it might seem. This is demonstrated particularly by the attitude of Isaac Leeser, one of the most influential early protagonists of a determined Americanization of the first German Jewish immigrants and their religious life. Leeser had emigrated from Westfalia in 1825 and become the *chazan* of the Congregation Mikveh Israel in Philadelphia.[11] A Jewish traditionalist who became a fierce opponent of the Reform movement, Leeser published numerous English textbooks and an English prayerbook, founded the first significant American Jewish newspaper,[12] pioneered the English sermon,[13] translated Mendelssohn's *Jerusalem* into English,[14] and above all translated the Bible into English in 1853/54 since he wanted his fellow Jews to learn English by studying the Bible.[15] One of the constant *leitmotifs* of his editorials in *The Occident* was the demand to replace the German-speaking *chazanim* by rabbis, who, as he wrote on the occasion of the consecration of Baltimore Synagogue in 1845, should be required to be able to speak concerning the ways of God and his law in the language of the country to the rising generation; for we deem it an undeniable truth, that the German language, no matter how eloquent the preacher, must soon become useless as a pulpit language, since the children of the present immigrants will soon know no other than the English; hence persons merely acquainted with the German will not be as useful preachers as those who are familiar with the vernacular.[16]

The practical reason given by Leeser was linked to a call for a deliberate process of acculturation. The country, as he insisted, was "essentially English in its tastes, habits and predilections," and it appeared to him "absolutely requisite that Jews should conform as nearly as possible, consistent with their religion, to the manners of the people among whom they live."[17] Jews, he maintained, should use English exclusively as the language of public and private instruction, while German might be acquired as a useful additional language.

The reason for Leeser's polemical rejection of German as the language of the American synagogue and scholarship was the changing character of American Judaism that can be observed in the course of the second wave of Jewish immigration after 1848. Between 1825 and 1870, the Jewish population in America grew from about 15,000 to 250,000.[18] In the first half of the nineteenth century it had been mostly rural Jews from southern Germany who had immigrated, motivated by social restrictions in their home country and the hope for economic self-improvement. For these immigrants, who had been only superficially Germanized und who had not studied at German universities, Germany and the German language represented primarily the experience of social discrimination and cultural exclusion they had left behind. They felt compelled to learn English quickly and to assimilate in order to make a living and improve their economic situation: Americanization was the key to their economic success and their first experience with integration into the modern world. Already with the immigrants who came after 1848, particularly during the 1860s, this constellation was completely transformed. The culture cherished by most of these new immigrants was German culture of which they were intensely proud. These immigrants also found a large non-Jewish community of German speakers in the United States that offered a good example of how to preserve German language and identity while integrating into the new homeland.[19] By the end of the Civil War, the American Jewish community consisted of more than 200,000, many of them recent immigrants from Central Europe.

During the 1850s, 1860s, and even into the 1870s German remained the language of most Jewish schools, the synagogue liturgy and the sermons. Even as late as 1874, it was estimated that German predominated in the majority of the Jewish congregations in the United States,[20] and only a small number of the representatives of the American rabbinate delivered their sermons in English. By 1870, at least twenty German rabbis had assumed positions in American synagogues and temples, and cultured German-Jewish laymen could be found in every major American city.[21] The later immigrants widely regarded the tradition of Reform Judaism that had been molded in Germany during the first half of the nineteenth century as an integral part of their German heritage. Accustomed to their

German reformed liturgy and to the Reform ideas expounded from liberal German pulpits, and to some extent familiar with the works of German *Wissenschaft des Judentums*, the immigrants learned to use English in business and on the streets, but chose to speak German in their homes and to read German books and newspapers. They insisted that their children study German in school and considered German— no less than Hebrew—as an almost religiously revered sacred language of the synagogue. Congregational records were kept in German, and religious leaders established German-language Jewish newspapers as well as German sections in those published in English. The intellectuals among the German Jews were especially convinced that the future of American Jewry in terms of religion and culture depended on the ability to transmit the heritage of German Jewry's religious values and the achievements of its Jewish scholarship.

Isaac Leeser did not leave this tendency undisputed and started a fierce argument against the predominance of the German-speaking rabbinate. On the occasion of the establishment of the Maimonides College in Philadelphia in 1867, the first American rabbinical seminary, he emphasized the necessity of such an institution which had been created in order to give young American Jews the opportunity to learn "the science of Judaism through the vehicle of the vernacular, which will enable them . . . as ripe scholars, to expound our religion" to the native English-speaking population.[22]

> We are the last to deny the immense influence Germany has exercised over the development of mind for the last century . . . But after all, . . . do our Germanists expect to maintain the Teutonic language for more than two generations in the large cities, unless it be done by excluding Israelites from a general intercourse with society and make a distinct German element here, which will effectually divide the country into two hostile classes? . . . In brief, let the German element be ever so beneficial, German orators ever so great, German scholars ever so learned, they must remain confined to their own class—for Americans they are utterly useless.[23]

The establishment of Maimonides College can be seen as the first attempt to create an independent American Jewish scholarship and to overcome the predominance of German-speaking *Wissenschaft* in America.[24] However, the opponents of this endeavor, embodied by the majority of American Reform rabbis during the period after the Civil War, who continued to advocate German as the language of scholarship and liturgy, turned out to be a delaying factor. The outstanding "Germanizer" among those rabbis was the radical reformer David Einhorn, a friend of Abraham Geiger as well as of Samuel Holdheim, who had left Europe after his failure to implement his radical philosophical views and practical concepts at the rabbinical conferences and in the Reform congregations of Schwerin and Pest. Einhorn had arrived in America in 1855 to serve as rabbi of Congregation Har Sinai in Baltimore and later occupied pulpits in Philadelphia and New York.[25] The influence of his German Reform prayerbook, *Olat Tamid*, which appeared in 1856 and was published in English only in 1896,[26] his intellectual journal

Sinai, published in German,[27] and his German philosophical works were ultimately greater during this period of Reform Judaism in America than the less radical ideas of Isaac Mayer Wise.[28] Until his death Einhorn was probably the most prominent advocate of the conviction held by many intellectuals among the immigrants, according to which the future of American Jewish culture depended on its ability to transplant the values and achievements of German Judaism to the "New World." Until the very end he refused to write and preach in English because the German language appeared to him as the "language of our spirit and our heart, which brought the reform idea into being and continues to bear it, as the caretaker carries the infant, and which still has to make sure not to transfer its high duty to the English tongue and to deprive the child from its mother's protecting arms."[29]

Einhorn's feelings toward America were, as Gershon Greenberg has so lucidly explained, highly ambivalent.[30] On the one hand, there is evidence that America represented to him the environment of freedom that Judaism required in order to flourish, the land of Judaism's future. It was the land in which the Messiah would arrive, because here, after a thousand years of oppression, Israel could finally raise the banner of holiness. From his point of view, religious history culminated in post-Civil War America, the land that promised to be a land of freedom of conscience and of the absence of orthodox authority. Already upon his arrival in Baltimore, Einhorn called America his "promised land," "new Canaan," and "land of Zion," the place for the universal kingdom of God on Earth.[31] Later he praised George Washington and Abraham Lincoln as messianic figures and even thought of Washington, DC as the New Jerusalem and the Capitol building as the new Temple sanctuary.[32] It seems as if Einhorn, disillusioned by the political situation in Europe, had envisioned a "messianic" America that, unfortunately, still lacked what had once inspired his hopes regarding Germany: a spirit of scholarship and religious depth. Despite his religious enthusiasm for the "New World" he felt a strong contempt for what he perceived as a superficial and materialistic American culture, his favorite word for it being "Humbug." He looked to German Reform Judaism for inspiration, and was convinced that the future and success of the Reform movement in America depended on its German intellectual origins, the German cultural heritage and the German language. In an article published in Sinai in 1859, he wrote:

> It takes little familiarity with the condition of American Jewish religious life to recognize that the English element … is an impediment to Reform strivings. German research and science constitute the source of the Jewish Reform idea, and *German* Jewry has the mission to bring life and recognition to this idea upon American soil.[33]

Only German Jews, nurtured on German Jewish religious thought, Einhorn was convinced, could rely on a profound concept of Judaism's historical development or its universal messianic character. At least for the present, he believed, the Reform idea was still too young in America to divest itself of its original German shell. Only after having fully absorbed the German Jewish heritage could American Jewry seek to be more independent, to substitute the English language for the German, and to embark on its own course. How strongly Einhorn continued to be dominated by the language and cultural world of his home country, is demonstrated by his farewell sermon at Congregation Beth El in New York in 1879, in which he expressed his self-understanding as follows:

> Germany is my home. I am an *ivri*, a wanderer, and I journeyed with thousands of my brethren from there to this God-blessed republic! As proud as I am of my adopted citizenship and as much as my heart is glowing for the well-being of this site of freedom, whose star spangled banner grants protection to all those who are downtrodden—I will never forget that the old home is the land of thinkers, presently the foremost land of culture, and above all the land of Mendelssohn, the birthplace of Reform Judaism, which, having been nurtured and raised by the profoundly scholarly spirit and proudly unfolding in an ever richer Jewish literature, gradually advanced into other countries and was eventually carried over the sea. Should you sever from Reform the German spirit or—that amounts to the same thing—the German language, you will have torn it from its native soil and the lovely flower must wilt. In sum: where the German language is banned, the reform of Judaism will be no more than a bright varnish, a beautiful doll without a heart and without a soul, which neither the proudest temples nor the most magnificent chorals will be able to animate![34]

Einhorn was aware, however, that his resistance to the use of the English language would exert little influence in the long run and that the pressure for its introduction was ever present. In the same farewell sermon he concluded with an announcement of surrender, as it were: "Henceforth you will hear the word of God expounded alternately one week in English and one week in German."[35] One could, of course, maintain that, on a personal level, Einhorn's attitude was the expression of the personality of a man who never came to feel fully at home in America. Beyond this, however, it seems that he was simply an extreme example for a more general tendency among most of the German-born rabbis of the Reform movement. Because of their characteristic conviction of the cultural superiority of the German language and their sometimes nostalgic sentiments toward their German past, many of them continued the religious modernization process begun in Germany within an imported German context, thereby paradoxically slowing down their assimilation to the new American cultural context. With the passing of time, however, the need to replace the German language in the synagogue and to introduce the English language in religious services and education became more and more urgent and finally gained general support. In 1872, a German newspaper in Pittsburgh pointed out that the "Israelites of German descent show a tendency to emancipate from remembering the German language, customs, and education … Even in religious service German is progressively displaced and the ritual performed in English." The paper regretted this development but admitted that "one cannot ignore the fact that the German Israelites break away from the language and national customs of a people among whom they have to these days experienced all kinds of oppression and discrimination."[36]

As for Jewish scholarship, a similar process of a rather reluctant and delayed Americanization can be observed. During most of the nineteenth century American rabbis deeply admired the German representatives of *Wissenschaft des Judentums* as modern scholars of Judaism and bearers of Jewish religion and culture. Abraham Geiger's *Jüdische Zeitschrift für Wissenschaft und Leben* as well as Ludwig Philippson's *Allgemeine Zeitung des Judenthums* and Samson Raphael Hirsch's *Jeschurun* found numerous American readers and contributors. American rabbis praised the work of Leopold Zunz and his fellow workers in the vineyard of Jewish scholarship. By comparison, American-Jewish culture seemed to them rather weak and immature. By 1866, Bernhard Felsenthal, who had left Germany in 1854 and served as a rabbi at the Chicago Congregation Sinai since 1861, expressed his attitude in enthusiastic words:

> With regard to the assertion that we should emancipate ourselves from German Jewry and proclaim our independence, we say: Alas, for us if we were now to free ourselves from German Judaism and its influences! As in the Middle Ages, the sun of Jewish scholarship shone loftily and marvellously in Spain ... that sun now stands in the German heavens and from there sends its beneficent light to all Jews and Jewish communities among the modern cultured nations. Germany has replaced Sefarad.

Felsenthal's enthusiasm in the face of the golden age of Jewish scholarship in Germany culminated in the admonition not to turn away from the intellectual and spiritual influences of German Judaism as this would inevitably lead to a disastrous cultural isolation. As a consequence, American Judaism would either "descend into Orthodox ossification" or "find its expression in nihilistic, boisterous and crude wisdom of the taproom." Both phenomena would, however, result in a "genuine native American attitude," open to the influences of Methodism or Puritanism, whereas the Reform movement would sacrifice its religious and moral seriousness to a "young-American presumptuousness." In order to prevent such a development, Felsenthal recommended that they continue sending American candidates for the rabbinate to Germany for training, because American Jewish scholarship could not yet be expected to produce independent scholarly works;[37] and in fact, from the 1870s onward, the Lehranstalt für die Wissenschaft des Judentums in Berlin attracted many students from America. Most leading American rabbis of the last three decades of the nineteenth century studied either in Berlin or at the conservative Breslau Jewish Theological Seminary before moving to the New World. Some of them sent their sons back to Germany for advanced studies at those institutions. Many of the immigrant rabbis maintained correspondence with their European mentors and contemporaries, and those who wanted to remain in the mainstream of scholarship, including Marcus Jastrow, Kaufmann Kohler, and Bernhard Felsenthal, published numerous articles in German Jewish scholarly journals.

2 Language of the future: the emergence of an Americanized *Wissenschaft des Judentums*

The rivalry inherent in the encounter between German Jewish and American Jewish intellectuals, which had already become visible in polemical debates between leaders of the Reform movements in Germany and America,[38] became much more explicit during the 1880s. A telling example is Ludwig Philippson's response in 1880 to a remark in the American Jewish journal *Der Zeitgeist*, according to which German Jewry, due to its lack of freedom, tended to accumulate treasures of knowledge, rummaging in "the rich repositories of scholarship," however, despite all this, Judaism was "not making any progress." Philippson, who frequently referred to developments within American Jewry in the *Allgemeine Zeitung des Judenthums*, struck back by requesting proof of a single product of American Judaism that did not originate in Germany: "The majority of American rabbis are Germans, and quite a few of them have only recently visited German schools. Having arrived in America, they rejoice in comparing themselves to their German colleagues and American to German Judaism—a comparison from which the latter loses out!" The American rabbis, however, he claimed, were unable to point to a single achievement, "including errors, for which no model can be found in Germany." "You are following us," he proclaimed, "you are using the paths we created and extended."[39] Conversely, we find an increasing number of voices, according to which the future of progressive Judaism and Jewish scholarship lay in America,[40] or, as expressed by Kaufmann Kohler in 1886: "American Judaism has learnt from Germany, now it is ready to teach."[41] In contrast to his father-in-law, David Einhorn, Kohler became increasingly determined to promote a politics of Americanization of the *Wissenschaft des Judentums*, and from the 1890s at the latest the message that German Judaism, once a "pioneer of Reform and progress," was in serious decline and that the task to revitalize the Jewish spirit was now the prerogative of the "American Israelite," became a *leitmotif* of his speeches and essays.[42]

Much of the new self-confidence indicated in Kohler's narrative, according to which America, as the "promised land," would now carry on the torch of European Judaism and German Jewish scholarship,[43] resulted from developments fueled by an increasing insistence on promoting American Jewry's linguistic and cultural emancipation from German domination. In this regard it is important to mention one of the most prominent representatives of an alternative to the "Germanizing" element within American Jewry. It was Isaac Mayer Wise who embodied a very different current within the American Reform movement, not only in terms of his more moderate attitude toward practical reforms, but above all in terms of his assessment of the issue of the language of American Jewry and his aspirations regarding American Jewish scholarship. Continuing the efforts of Isaac Leeser, Wise was the most enthusiastically American among the American Jewish reformers. Unlike many of his German rabbinical colleagues, Wise did not identify himself actively as a German Jew or encourage others to do so. Instead he consistently urged his coreligionists to acculturate rapidly in America, leaving behind foreign loyalties while clinging all the more fervently to their inherited identity as Jews.

The modernization and fulfilment of Jewish identity, according to Wise, was to be realized in America, not in Germany, and it was here that the future of Reform Judaism lay. A new stage in Jewish history had begun on this side of the ocean. "American Judaism," he wrote, "that means Judaism reformed and reconstructed by the beneficent influence of political liberty and progressive enlightenment, is the youngest offspring of the ancient and venerable faith of Israel ... It is the American phase of Judaism."[44] As synagogues became more German in the early 1860s, he struggled against this trend, though at that time, even he himself was forced to preach in German in his Cincinnati congregation at least every other week. Sarcastically he wrote in 1855: "The Alexandrine Hebrews had a Greek ritual, the Babylonians adopted the Chaldean, and the American Israelites, in the midst of an English speaking community, should be German. They call that Reform, we call it retrogression."[45]

Wise was thus a staunch "Americanizer" who saw it as his task to establish a distinctly American Judaism unrestrained by its roots in Europe, and he seriously endeavored to transcend his own personal and the collective European-Jewish experience. One of the reasons why he opposed German cultural influence so strongly may be biographical. Born in Bohemia, he had studied in a *yeshivah* near Prague, and although he may have attended some university courses there and in Vienna, he never felt so deeply impressed by German *Wissenschaft*, much in contrast to the university-trained German rabbis. To him, Germany and the Austrian Empire represented above all social and cultural oppression, and he had left Europe because America seemed the only country that promised the liberty of Jewish self-expression. While most of the German rabbis identified with the spirit of German culture and felt a close relationship to it, Wise claimed a deep affinity between the Jewish religion and American democracy which now was to come to its historical fulfilment. It was mainly this vision of America as a promised land of an American Jewish symbiosis that led him to anxiously strive for the thorough Americanization of all Jews as a warrant for the equal participation in political liberty.

English was absolutely necessary, according to Wise, not only for surviving in every-day life and succeeding in business or for bringing Jews into contact with Americans and the American ideals of liberalism, progress and enlightenment, but also to restore their cultural and religious self-respect. It was urgent, he argued, that Jews divorce themselves from the German tongue with its rich vocabulary of anti-Jewish sentiments: "The Jew must be Americanized ... for every German book, every German word reminds him of the old disgrace ... The Jew must become an American in order to gain the self-consciousness of the free-born-man."[46] This conviction explains Wise's impatience with the German-American rabbis of the 1860s who Germanized instead of Americanizing and, as he said, "made Israel a stranger forever in this country": "They may preach and write German one century longer among us, without giving us a position in society, without gaining public acknowledgment for the spirit of Judaism."[47] Furthermore, Germanizing the American Jews appeared to him like surrender to a German and anti-Semitically inspired claim of cultural superiority, and he vehemently reproached those devoted to German language and culture for permitting this German spirit of oppression and intolerance to influence the young American-Jewish generation. In 1879, in the face of the wave of anti-Semitic sentiments accompanying the surge of German nationalism that made itself felt even in America, he wrote in his journal *The American Israelite*:

> Germany has become immensely patriotic, and Cincinnati is full of patriotism, music and hilarity, and the world is going to be Germanic, we expect. The German reformation, philosophy, art and beer have conquered the world. Why should not the rest of things give way before the Germanic muse. There is a proposition set on foot to canonize the German language by placing it on the Curriculum of the Hebrew Union College ... and make it the holy language of the synagogues and temples ...—so faithfully patriotic are we to the old Fatherland. The world is going to be Germanic; the Romanic and Semitic elements will have to submit—to Teuton's braves, to German art and Gemütlichkeit, song and poetry. The countries of the European continent are suburbs of Germany, their languages are corruptions of the German; their arts and sciences culminate in Berlin; their philosophies are Germanic; the world is rapidly Germanizing, no doubt. As long as we sing, poetize and philosophize in the German style there is no harm in the progress of the Berlin civilization, and we can go along conveniently; beyond that however we propose to remain Franco-American democratic and Semitically monotheistic.[48]

Germanization versus Americanization was thus one of the major issues that separated David Einhorn's and Wise's visions regarding the future of Jewish scholarship in America. A comparison of these two positions demonstrates that both thinkers, influenced by different biographical experiences in Europe, treated the issue of the right language for the self-expression of American Judaism in a highly symbolic or metaphorical way. Einhorn revered German as the true language of Jewish scholarship, as the language of the religion of reason in the tradition of Kant and Mendelssohn, and viewed the English language as less valuable, even as the expression of a superficial culture. Wise, in contrast to this, saw in the German tongue a language of oppression and contempt for Judaism and hoped for a renaissance of Jewish religion, culture, and scholarship through the use of English, which he felt was the language of freedom, the language in which Jews for the first time in the history of the *galut* could openly express their self-understanding and their religious mission to the modern world. Consequently, Wise developed a program of rapid and complete Americanization of Jewish religious life and devoted all his energies to creating conditions for the establishment of an independent, self-confident American Jewish culture, convinced that "ignorance swayed the scepter and darkness ruled"[49] as a result of the Germanizing tendencies among American Jews. In order to improve this situation, he wrote a prayer book—*Minhag America*[50]—started the American Jewish newspaper *The American Israelite*, translated numerous excerpts of German Jewish scholarship in the *Asmonean* (Leopold Zunz, Abraham Geiger, Zacharias Frankel, Samuel Holdheim, Isaak Markus Jost, and Heinrich Graetz), composed a *History of the Israelitian Nation* and a *History of the Hebrew's Second Commonwealth*[51]—both in English—struggled for the establishment of a *Union of American Jewish Congregations*, and was especially instrumental in founding the first successful rabbinical seminary—

the Hebrew Union College—in 1875 for which he had fought for years with all his polemical energy. "The question simply is," he addressed the leaders of American Jewry in 1873:

> [D]o you intend to remain Jews, and do you wish that your children should? If you do not, we have no more to say. This is a free country. If you do, please let us have men to teach and expound Judaism in a manner as we in this country understand and appreciate it. If you want to go back to Poland, keep up your Minhag Polin . . . If you want to go back to Germany, well then, keep up your Minhag Ashkenaz and call the introduction of German prayers, hymns and sermons a Reform. But if you want to remain in this country and cling to Judaism here, you must have the Minhag America with so much English in your synagogues and temples as you can adopt; then you must educate Americans for the ministry, to whom the spirit of the country is no foreign element. You must have the college.[52]

The founding of the Hebrew Union College[53] was thus a signal for the thorny but gradual emergence of an independent American Jewish scholarship. As late as the 1870s, however, there were no successful Jewish publishers, no scholarly journals, and significant scholarly achievements were rare. Wise concluded during those years that American Jews were "no literary people as yet,"[54] a reality which was no doubt due in part to their continued reliance on the rich intellectual and spiritual tradition of the larger, wealthier, more established Western European communities, especially in Germany. With its faculty, exclusively educated in Germany—Max Lilienthal, Moses Mielziner, who coined a new terminology for rendering rabbinic writings in English, Gotthard Deutsch, Max Margolis, Moses Buttenwieser and others—the Hebrew Union College soon developed into a centre where American-born young Jews encountered the achievements of *Wissenschaft des Judentums* presented to them in English. We also know, of course, that the students were requested to learn German and that in some cases German textbooks had to be used, for example Samuel Bäck's work on Jewish history.[55] Despite the fact, however, that the Hebrew Union College started from a strongly Germanic scholarly tradition, it represented a major step forward toward the Americanization of Reform Judaism, and engendered the formation of a young generation of scholars and rabbis committed to the American Jewish culture. A strong indication for this is that, by the end of the 1870s, American congregations gradually stopped seeking German rabbis and cantors and advertising for them in Jewish newspapers and journals in Germany. Even Ludwig Philippson praised the Hebrew Union College in 1881, emphasizing that since its establishment "American Jewry has emancipated from the Old World, has become independent and thoroughly American. It would be egoistic from us in the Old World if we were not willing to acknowledge that this is a most desirable event." His vision of the increasing degree of American Jewish independence, however, was still obviously a rather condescending one in that it continued to imply a hegemonic role of German Jewish culture also for the future: "Even if there are still plenty of immature elements to be seen, American Jewry will become mature, and the spiritual connection with Judaism in the Old World and particularly with Germany will not vanish!"[56] These were, of course, remarks that were rather unlikely to overcome the strong sense of asymmetry that had shaped the relationship over decades—an asymmetry characterized by the fact that scholars such as Philippson kept emphasizing the German Jewish influence without ever looking themselves for orientation in American Jewish publications and platforms or admitting the relevance of their American colleagues' voices.

The further development of Hebrew Union College and other institutions emerging since the 1880s indicate, however, that Philippson and other German Jewish observers may have underestimated the many circumstances that promoted American Jewry's increasingly strong striving for cultural and intellectual independence. In part, these developments were linked to the diversification of Jewish scholarship in America during this period. Although Wise had tried hard to make Hebrew Union College a rabbinical seminary for all American Jewry, hoping to overcome the profound differences between the conservative and liberal religious leaderships, he did not succeed. Jewish immigration to the United States from Eastern Europe since the Russian pogroms in 1881/82 made this attempt even more difficult, as the many newcomers did not share the heritage of German Reform but were, with the exception of the politically radical secular Jews, much more traditional. When the 1885 rabbinical conference in Pittsburgh adopted a radical platform—a kind of declaration of independence from traditional concepts and practices[57]—the conservative forces began to withdraw their support and, under the leadership of Sabato Morais and Alexander Kohut, founded the Jewish Theological Seminary Association in New York in 1887.[58] Hebrew Union College thus became an institution confined to the Reform Movement.

This tendency was fostered when Kaufmann Kohler, the foremost representative of the second generation of American Reform Judaism and one of its most influential scholars, became Wise's successor as president of the Hebrew Union College in 1903. Interestingly enough, he published his best-known work, *Jewish Theology Systematically and Historically Considered,* in German in 1910; it was translated into English only a few years later.[59] In contrast to his father-in-law David Einhorn, however, he was determined to push ahead the politics of Americanization within the Reform movement. The most obvious change during his presidency of the College was the total elimination of any instruction in Modern Hebrew. In his first speech to the students he expressed his attitude in the most forceful terms:

> The College should have a thoroughly American character. The students should endeavor to be imbued with the American spirit, and this includes the mastery of English diction. Neo-Hebraic literature may be a necessity for Russian Jews who have no genuine national literature from which to derive culture and idealism. For us the English literature is a source of culture and enlightenment; wherefore Neo-Hebraic Literature will be abolished here.[60]

This approach was not only the result of an anti-Zionist attitude, but also the expression of his conviction that American Jewish scholarship at the turn of the twentieth century especially had to accomplish the task of educating the new Jewish immigrants from Eastern Europe, a quite common attitude among the increasingly acculturated American Jewish establishment. The growing sense that the future of Judaism lay in America rather than Europe as well as the sincere wish to adapt to American culture were precipitated by deteriorating conditions in Europe, especially the resurgence of anti-Semitism in Western Europe, which gradually made American Jews recognize their destiny as the leading force of a free Judaism. In 1893 Moravian-born rabbi Gotthard Deutsch, who had studied in Breslau and Vienna and accepted a professorship in Jewish history and philosophy at Hebrew Union College in Cincinnati in 1891, stressed the necessity of Americanization, particularly because, from his point of view, the predominance of German would prevent integration and social acceptance:

> The German Christian who keeps his mother-tongue is called a German, while the Jew who does the same remains a Jew, or at best politely a Hebrew . . . If therefore the Jew wants to be considered a genuine American he has to speak English. A second reason is anti-Semitism in Germany. This movement has caused many Jews not to want to be reminded of the old fatherland.[61]

One of the main reasons, however, for the acceleration of Americanization and American Jewry's gradual dissociation from its German roots was demographic in nature. The rising tide of Jewish immigration from Eastern Europe greatly increased the population of American Jewry, and led to a radical change of its character. The Jews of German origin, who had dominated the American scene both in numbers and influence for most of the nineteenth century, became a minority. The Yiddish-speaking Eastern European-Jewish population, concentrated in New York's Lower East Side, organized itself in *landsmanshaften* according to their place of origin and remained both economically and culturally separated from the German Jewish group of immigrants, who—at least in the second generation—had largely ascended to the middle class and lived an acculturated life. Many of the new immigrants clung to the religious orthodoxy in which they had grown up, while others broke radically with tradition. The effect was highly ambivalent. On the one hand, this influx of Eastern European Jews was responsible for sustaining the remnants of a separate German Jewish identity in America for a further generation, with many Jews stressing their German ancestry in order not to be identified with the new immigrants; on the other hand, the Jewish establishment tried to Americanize the Eastern European Jews and at the same time to foster their loyalty to Judaism. The Yiddish language, they felt, had to be suppressed and replaced by English, and to this end the teaching of English had to be intensified; at the same time secularism had to be fought by spreading Jewish knowledge. Promoting Jewish scholarship, therefore, was one element of an education strategy aimed at creating an "American Jewish culture" and providing an Americanized, albeit conservative rabbinical leadership.

This was in particular the intention of philanthropists such as Louis Marshall, Jacob H. Schiff and Felix Warburg, who supported the Jewish Theological Seminary (JTS) in New York at the turn of the century. Within a short period of time the group of scholars and laymen who founded the JTS created a whole set of institutions that together resulted in a tremendous growth and spread of Jewish culture in America: The Jewish Publication Society (1888), The American Jewish Historical Society (1892), Gratz College (1893), the Rabbi Isaac Elchanan Theological Seminary (1897), forerunner of the Yeshiva University,[62] the JTS, and the Dropsie College for Hebrew and Cognate Learning (1907), the first post-graduate Jewish institution in the world whose sole purpose was the promotion of academic research.[63] All of these institutions sought to promote religious renewal, improved education, cultural revitalization, the professionalization of Jewish scholarship, and the elevation of American Jewry to a position of greater prominence, if not pre-eminence among the Jews of the world. The American scholar of Semitic Studies, Cyrus Adler, who was a leading figure in most of the above-mentioned institutions (he served as the President of Dropsie College from 1908 to 1940 and as the President of JTS from 1915 to 1940), deliberately aimed for an American Jewish "renaissance" and a "revival of Jewish learning" in the English-speaking world. Jonathan D. Sarna aptly interprets this as the expression of what he calls the "Late Nineteenth-Century American Jewish Awakening" during the years between 1881 and 1914. Jews at that time, he argues, experienced a period of religious and cultural reorientation that included the growth of Conservative Judaism as well as American Zionism and was apparently a response to a sense of crisis that had shaped particularly the younger generation of scholars.[64]

Several of the newly created institutions played a crucial role in the shift of the language of scholarship and the establishment of a self-confident tradition of American Jewish Studies. Of major importance was the Jewish Publication Society of America (JPS) that was founded in 1888 in Philadelphia after two previous attempts had failed. Dedicated to spreading the knowledge of Jewish history and religion, the Society aimed at providing authoritative works in English to a community sorely in need of such books. It continued the tendency of the previous decades that had witnessed intense efforts to enrich Jewish intellectual life in America by translating important works of German *Wissenschaft des Judentums* into English, for example Abraham Geiger's seminal work, *Das Judentum und seine Geschichte*.[65] One of the first undertakings of the Society was the publication of James Gutheim's English translation of Heinrich Graetz's multi-volume *History of the Jews* that had been most influential in Europe.[66] However, the JPS was not merely dependent upon German Jewish literary activity; numerous learned works on Jewish history and religious tradition were soon also written for the Society, including biographies, works in Yiddish Studies and in Bible scholarship. As early as 1892, the Society envisioned a new translation of the Bible with original contributions by American and English Bible scholars, an undertaking that eventually started in 1907 and was completed in 1917.[67]

Inspiration for the shift toward the emergence of an independent English-speaking *Wissenschaft des Judentums* at the end of the century came also from England. Heinrich Graetz himself had helped stimulate the renaissance of Jewish scholarship in England when he visited the country on the occasion of the Anglo-Jewish Exhibition of England and America in 1887 and predicted that the future of Judaism would lie with the English-speaking Jews of England and America.[68] When the German *Monatsschrift für Geschichte und Wissenschaft des Judentums*, of which he was then editor, ceased publication in 1887—being resumed only in 1892—Graetz suggested that a new English journal—the *Jewish Quarterly Review*—take its place.[69] The periodical, founded by Claude G. Montefiore[70] and Israel Abrahams, concentrated in its early volumes on theology, biblical studies and the publication of original sources; Genizah scholarship and the historical and critical study of Rabbinic Judaism were of particular significance, as a result of Jewish scholars being challenged by the distortion of Rabbinic literature by contemporary Christian theologians.[71] Despite the existence of Jew's College in London since 1856, Anglo Jewry had until then produced scarcely any books of serious Jewish historical or rabbinic scholarship and there had not been any substantial interest in the kind of critical scholarship created by nineteenth-century *Wissenschaft des Judentums* in Germany. Between 1888 and 1908, however, the *Jewish Quarterly Review*, as the first English language forum for Jewish scholarship, served as the primary vehicle for establishing and furthering the scientific study of Judaism in England and subsequently promoted the transplantation of *Wissenschaft des Judentums* onto American soil. In 1908, after twenty years in England, the *Jewish Quarterly Review* ceased publication, but two years later, under the auspices of the new Dropsie College for Hebrew and Cognate Learning, it resumed publication in Philadelphia where it became the first and most important periodical of Jewish scholarship in America. In his editorial of the first volume Cyrus Adler wrote:

> It was then resolved not to allow the only organ for Jewish learning in the English language to disappear ... The editors feel it all the more their duty to supply the need, as America is fast becoming the center of Jewry, and in all likelihood will become also the center of Jewish learning in the English world. It would be anomalous if, in the face of this great present growth, the past with its glory and its sacrifices, its ideals and its achievements, its lessons and its inspirations, were not offered the opportunity of that articulate utterance which can be given to it only through the mouth of science and scholarship.[72]

Not only the journal itself was transferred to America, but also its most celebrated contributor, the preeminent Jewish scholar of his generation, Solomon Schechter. Schechter had already given up his chair in Rabbinics at Cambridge University and had come to America to serve as president of the JTS.[73] Schechter's interest in America was based on his conviction that the future of Judaism lay in this country rather than in Europe. Already in 1893 he had written to his friend Alexander Kohut:

> What is your College doing? America must be a place of Torah, because the future of Judaism is across the seas. You must make something great out of your institution if the Torah and wisdom are to remain among us. Everything is at a standstill in Germany, England has too few Jews to exercise any real influence. What will happen to Jewish learning if America remains indifferent?[74]

Schechter's arrival in America and the faculty he established there—including the Lithuanian born scholar Louis Ginzberg, Alexander Marx from Berlin, and the eminent Semitist Israel Friedländer—marks the transformation of the Seminary from a small rabbinical school to a world-class center of Jewish scholarship. As to the language issue, the beginnings were difficult, since—apart from Schechter himself—none of the scholars had a strong command of English, and both Marx and Friedländer had at first to teach in German. During the first years Friedländer, Marx and Ginzberg spent a great deal of time learning the new language from Henrietta Szold, the chief editor of JPS; Szold also translated the first volumes of Ginzberg's famous *Legends of the Jews*, which he had written in German.[75]

The attempts to create a strong and independent American Jewish scholarship and to make America the leading center of Jewish learning culminated in the project of a Jewish Encyclopedia which was realized during the years 1901–6. This remarkable work, the first comprehensive scholarly collection of material pertaining to Jewish history, literature, ritual, sociology, and biography and written by the most outstanding scholars in Europe and in America, is particularly interesting: although marking the highest expression of European Jewish scholarship it was published in English. Earlier attempts in Germany to create an encyclopedia of Judaica in the nineteenth century had proven premature. It was mainly the resurgence of anti-Semitism at the end of the century that provided the external motivation for Western European Jews to undertake such a work and to summarize the studies of nearly a century of European *Wissenschaft des Judentums*. Yet interestingly the project was realized not in Western Europe but in America, where Jewish intellectual life seemed much less developed. Originally its initiator, the Moravian-born scholar Isidore Singer, a student of Adolph Jellinek in Vienna, had conceived it as a German encyclopedia entitled *Allgemeine Encyklopädie für Geschichte und Wissenschaft des Judentums*, designed mainly to fighting anti-Semitism. When this project eventually failed due to the lack of financial support, Singer tried to create a French encyclopedia, but with the outbreak of the Dreyfus Affair in 1894 became strongly disillusioned about the prospects of this project and eventually moved to New York in 1895. There he initially attempted to find support for his original German-language encyclopedia. "I was told by my friends in Paris," he explained, "that American Judaism is a crown colony of Germany-Austria."[76] Only after becoming familiar with the new development of American Jewish scholarship did he decide to pursue an English language work and find an American publisher, while himself beginning to learn English.

Did the shift from the German to the English language imply any change in the concept of the aims of *Wissenschaft*? And what impact did the Jewish Encyclopedia have on the further development of Jewish scholarship in America and German Jewish perceptions of it? With regard to the first question, the assumption that the more liberal, pluralistic and less anti-Semitic context in America may have facilitated a discernible departure from the apologetic motifs so characteristic of German Jewish scholarship during the nineteenth century[77] is actually not corroborated by historical analysis. Substantially, the characteristic threefold intention of *Wissenschaft des Judentums*—fighting prejudice and anti-Semitism, guarding Jewish identity against the influence of indifference and secularism as well as providing an intellectual framework for the scholarly exploration of Jewish history and modern Jewish self-understanding—seems to have basically remained unchanged in the American context. Joseph Silvermann, Rabbi of Temple Emanu-El of New York, for example, praising the "renaissance of Science of Judaism" that expressed itself in the *Jewish Encyclopedia*, described its intentions to be a powerful weapon against anti-Semitism as well as a helpful instrument to awaken new interest in the study of Jewish history and literature and to foster Jewish self-pride.[78] Similar statements could have been written in Germany.

One reason for the continuation of the apologetic motivation of *Wissenschaft des Judentums* in the American context may be, first of all, that many of the participating European scholars had deeply internalized this self-understanding of Jewish scholarship and could not easily depart from it. A further reason was apparently that the representatives of Jewish scholarship in America, though not having to struggle for its acknowledgment as a legitimate discipline, were well aware that American society was not free of anti-Jewish sentiments, prejudices and contempt which had to be fought should the process of Jewish Americanization succeed.[79] As in Germany, the impact of the *Jewish Encyclopedia* in terms of overcoming prejudice by knowledge was rather limited. It may have contributed to increasing Christian understanding of Jews and Judaism, as many reactions indicated, but it hardly prevented anti-Semitism. On the contrary, racial anti-Semitic theories continued to gain popularity also in America, fueling restrictionist sentiments regarding immigration in the first quarter of the twentieth century.[80] The Encyclopedia did, however, albeit only to a certain degree, achieve the goal of increasing Jewish knowledge and became an important resource for many individuals in diverse Jewish communities.

In the final analysis, however, it is in the area of scholarship that the Jewish Encyclopedia made its deepest impact, fulfilling and perhaps even surpassing the expectations of the editors. First of all, it provided a forum for respected scholars to summarize their research for a broader audience. Furthermore, it gave young scholars, especially Louis Ginzberg and Jacob Z. Lauterbach, the opportunity to establish the reputation upon which they built their careers in America. Lauterbach published works in English on the Pharisees and the literary history of the Talmud,[81] while Ginzberg expanded research in the fields of Aggadah, liturgy, and Talmud. Both scholars played major roles in shifting the center of research in Rabbinics to American Jewish scholarship and to the English language. Even more importantly, the Encyclopedia broadened the scope of Jewish scholarship in America, legitimizing new fields such as the history of Zionism and Yiddish literature and establishing an independent American Jewish biblical scholarship.[82] Most dramatically perhaps, by providing the first comprehensive depiction of Jewish life in America, the Encyclopedia served as a catalyst for the emerging discipline of American Jewish history, which was instrumental in strengthening the position and prestige of American Jewry as a whole.[83]

The discernible change in the European Jewish attitude in the first decade of the twentieth century toward America as a home for serious Jewish scholarship was largely a result of the prestige gained by the project of the Encyclopedia. The initial skepticism on the part of European Jewish scholars gradually gave way to a growing recognition of the value of this undertaking and to the willingness to participate. If the Jewish Encyclopedia was to symbolize the future of Jewish scholarship, they wanted to be part of it. The historian and philosopher Joseph Jacobs, for example, who had studied in Berlin with Moritz Steinschneider and Moritz Lazarus before moving to England, went to America and joined the board of the Encyclopedia Committee in 1900, because colleagues persuaded him, as he wrote in his farewell letter, that "there were great hopes that the intellectual center of Judaism may fix its quarters across the Atlantic."[84] Once in America, Jacobs became involved in the JPS and the American Jewish Historical Society, edited the *American Jewish Yearbook* and taught English literature and rhetoric at the JTS.

The significance of the Encyclopedia was, of course, due in large measure to its publication in English. As Shuly Rubin Schwartz has pointed out, the Jewish Encyclopedia, in surpassing the limited attempts throughout the twentieth century "to translate Jewish scholarship," proved to be a "giant leap forward from such tentative beginnings" and turned out to be a catalyst for the furtherance of English language Jewish scholarship.[85] Wilhelm Bacher, the great scholar of Midrash at the Landesrabbinerschule in Budapest, noted in 1906 in the *Allgemeine Zeitung des Judentums*: "The significance that the English language has acquired for the life and future of Judaism can be illustrated through nothing more powerfully than through the Jewish Encyclopedia."[86] By summarizing and preserving Jewish scholarship in English and in America, he admitted, the Encyclopedia signified the transference of both the *center* and the *language* of Jewish scholarship. "America," Bacher had written already in 1901, in the face of Isidore Singer's bold announcement of the creation of a "University of Jewish theology, history, and literature,"

> you are happier and far better than our old continent … What we longed for in Europe during the past century now, at the dawn of a new century, becomes a fact in America … New York City, which of all of the cities of the world contains today the greatest numbers of Jews, has unexpectedly become the center of Jewish scholarship.[87]

Perhaps most important was the Encyclopedia's profound impact on American Jewish intellectual life. Having completed a work that won almost universal acclaim, something that their European mentors had been unable to accomplish, American Jewish scholars were convinced that they had now established their own identity and were finally ready to assume the "mantle of scholarly hegemony" from Germany. The Encyclopedia became "the symbol par excellence of the emerging cultural and intellectual independence of American Jewry."[88] In 1913, Solomon Schechter, assessing his first ten years of activity in America, concluded that

> as to Jewish learning, it has become a fact: American Jewish scholarship is now a recognized factor all over the world … If there is a spot in the world where Jewish learning, which has so often migrated from land to land, should at last find a

resting-place and develop freely in accordance with its own laws, it will be America.[89]

3 Conclusion: a new center of Jewish scholarship

The development of American Jewish scholarship from the turn of the century to the 1920s and 1930s was marked by rapid success. Important new institutions were established, such as the Academy for Jewish Research in 1920 and Stephen S. Wise's Jewish Institute for Religion in New York (1922); Harry A. Woolfson occupied the Nathan Littauer Chair of Hebrew Literature and Philosophy at Harvard University (1925) and Salo W. Baron's appointment as the Nathan L. Miller Professor of Jewish History, Literature and Institutions at Columbia University in 1929 is considered to signify the beginning of the scholarly study of Jewish History in an American University.[90] New scholarly journals were published, such as the *Hebrew Union College Annual* (1924), and the creation of great Jewish libraries, the availability of positions in Jewish Studies as well as the emigration of important Jewish scholars from Europe to America, particularly in the 1930s and early 1940s,[91] underlined America's emergence as *the* center of Jewish scholarship in the Diaspora even before the destruction of European institutions of Jewish scholarship during the Second World War. This profound shift, accompanied by the growing self-esteem of American Jewish scholarship, was intensified by the catastrophe of European Jewry under the Nazi regime.

After the long history of the intense and sometimes controversial transnational relationship between *Wissenschaft des Judentums* in Europe and American Jewish scholarship which reflected the inclination of American Jewry to both cherish and transcend the European experience, particularly the dominating influence of German Jewish culture, and after the long and thorny path toward establishing a viable, independent and productive Jewish scholarship in the "New World," which extended over more than a century, the fate of European Jewry during the early twentieth century completely changed the landscape of Jewish Studies. During this period, American Jewish scholarship as well as American Reform had finally found their new language and assumed a much more independent role, albeit without dissociating themselves completely from the German language and scholarly tradition. This process was eventually accelerated dramatically by the developments that led to the end of the tradition of *Wissenschaft des Judentums* in Germany during the Nazi Period and the Holocaust and made Germany a country in which Jewish scholarship was almost absent for several decades.

This was all the more tragic in view of the hopes during the Weimar Republic for a prosperous development and even for the establishment of the discipline at German universities—one of the central objectives of *Wissenschaft des Judentums* since its inception.[92] A series of lectureships and honorary professorships had been created, giving Jewish scholars the opportunity to teach in the field of Jewish history and literature, even though most of these scholars were marginal figures and obtained only inferior positions.[93] The real achievements of Jewish Studies in Germany during that time, especially the development of Jewish History, took place outside the universities, in independent associations, for instance in the Akademie für die Wissenschaft des Judentums, founded in 1919.[94] Temporarily conditions had generally improved in several respects: the Institute for Jewish Studies in Berlin, for example, was for the first time entitled to describe itself as a "Hochschule," albeit for only a brief period. Jewish scholars were also invited to collaborate on prestigious projects such as the theological encyclopedia *Religion in Geschichte und Gegenwart* [Religion in History and the Present]—an indication of at least a slight change in the perception of Jewish scholarship in Germany.[95] And yet there was never a real breakthrough with regard to the academic integration of Jewish Studies, and the few rudimentary steps taken toward a dialogue on the basis of equality fell victim to the destructive will of National Socialism that was unopposed by any genuinely viable tradition of academic discourse, dialogue and solidarity with the Jews.

On the contrary: there was almost no resistance among non-Jewish scholars in Germany when the Jewish community was deprived of its rights, when Jewish scholars were expelled and Jewish academic institutions banned. It is tragically symbolic of the brutal failure of former hopes for Jewish Studies that at the same time as the *Hochschule* in Berlin was radically reduced in its activities after the November pogrom of 1938 and finally closed down on July 19, 1942,[96] eminent Protestant theologians in Jena created an institute which claimed to be establishing a new, German-Christian form of Jewish Studies: the Institut zur Erforschung und Beseitigung des jüdischen Einflusses auf das deutsche kirchliche Leben (Institute for the Investigation and Eradication of Jewish Influence on German Christian Life), which set itself the objective of cleansing Christianity of every trace of "the Jewish spirit."[97] While Jewish scholars had to bury their dreams of establishing an independent, recognized discipline and were forced to leave Germany, German non-Jewish scholars exploited their knowledge of Jewish sources and history and devoted themselves to a research, motivated by anti-Semitism, on the so-called "Jewish Question." This startling contrast between the rise of anti-Jewish studies and the end of Jewish Studies in Germany makes it possible to gauge the extent of the loss brought about by the expulsion and destruction of the German-Jewish tradition of Jewish Studies during the "Third Reich."

Historian Ismar Elbogen, who had escaped from Nazi-Germany in 1938 and—like Eugen Täubler, Julius Lewy, Alexander Guttmann, Abraham Joshua Heschel and others— had found refuge in America, compiled a survey on "American Jewish scholarship" in honor of the centenary of Kaufmann Kohler for the 1944 issue of the *American Jewish Yearbook* which began with the following words:

Heinrich Heine aptly said that the Jew had a portable fatherland. Wherever the Jew migrated he carried with him his spiritual heritage. Different countries at different periods of Jewish history have held the hegemony in Jewish Studies. During the past fifty years the mantle of Elijah has fallen on the United States. America was fast becoming a center of Jewish scholarship, and within the past decade it has become the sole center—with the exception of Palestine.[98]

Elbogen's article outlined the development of Jewish Studies in America, emphasizing particularly the events in Europe since the First World War that led to the awareness spreading among American Jews that "they were destined to become the center of Jewish life,"[99] and concluded with the following passage:

We are at the end. Our survey shows from what small beginnings Jewish scholarship in America has developed. The growth has been rapid, even great. But it was not an organic growth, it did not spring in the main from America's own soil. For until recently American Jewry has had a constant influx of intellectual forces from Europe. This reservoir is now destroyed. American Jewry will henceforth have to produce native scholars of its own. We shall not prophesy what America's distinctive contribution will be. But let us hope that the next hundred years will be no less creative than were the last.[100]

Notes

1. Part of the following reflections is based on my article, "Inventing a New Language of Jewish Scholarship: The Transition from German Wissenschaft des Judentums to American-Jewish Scholarship in the Nineteenth and Twentieth Centuries," in *Speaking Jewish—Jewish Speak: Multilingualism in Western Ashkenazic Culture*, ed. Shlomo Berger, Aubrey Pomerance, Andrea Schatz, and Emile Schrijvers (Berlin: Metropol, 2004), 273–306; and see Christian Wiese, "Auf Deutsch nach Amerika: Über den Transfer der Wissenschaft des Judentums nach Amerika," in *Sprache, Erkenntnis und Bedeutung—Deutsch in der jüdischen Wissenskultur*, ed. Arndt Engelhardt and Susanne Zepp (Leipzig: Leipziger Universitätsverlag, 2015), 57–86.

2. See Max Wiener, *Jüdische Religion im Zeitalter der Emanzipation* (Berlin: Philo Verlag, 1933); Julius Carlebach, ed., *Chochmat Jisrael—Wissenschaft des Judentums: Anfänge der Judaistik in Europa* (Darmstadt: Wissenschaftliche Buchgesellschaft, 1992).

3. See Leopold Zunz, *Zur Geschichte und Literatur* (Berlin: Veit, 1845); Céline Trautmann-Waller, *Philologie allemande et tradition juive: Le parcours intellectuel de Leopold Zunz* (Paris : Cerf, 1998).

4. See Susannah Heschel, *Abraham Geiger and the Jewish Jesus* (Chicago: University of Chicago Press, 2001); Andreas Brämer, *Rabbiner Zacharias Frankel: Wissenschaft des Judentums und konservative Reform im 19. Jahrhundert* (Hildesheim: Olms, 2000).

5. For Berlin and Breslau, see Marianne Awerbuch, "Die Hochschule für die Wissenschaft des Judentums," in *Geschichtswissenschaft in Berlin im 19. und 20. Jahrhundert: Persönlichkeiten und Institutionen*, ed. Reimer Hansen and Wolfgang Ribbe (Berlin and New York: de Gruyter, 1992), 517–52; Guido Kisch, ed., *Das Breslauer Seminar. Jüdisch-Theologisches Seminar (Fraenckel'scher Stiftung) in Breslau 1854–1938: Gedächtnisschrift* (Tübingen: Mohr-Siebeck, 1963).

6. See Kerstin von der Krone, *Wissenschaft in Öffentlichkeit: Die Wissenschaft des Judentums und ihre Zeitschriften* (Berlin and New York: de Gruyter, 2011).

7. See Shulamith Volkov, "Die Erfindung einer Tradition. Zur Entstehung des modernen Judentums in Deutschland," *Historische Zeitschrift* 253 (1991): 603–28.

8. See Christian Wiese, *Challenging Colonial Discourse: Jewish Studies and Protestant Theology in Wilhelmine Germany* (Boston and Leiden: Brill, 2005).

9. For a characterization of both periods of American Jewish history, see Hasia Diner, *A Time for Gathering: The Second Migration, 1820–1880* (Baltimore, MD and London: Johns Hopkins University Press, 1992); Gerald Sorin, *A Time for Building: The Third Migration, 1880–1920* (Baltimore, MD and London: Johns Hopkins University Press, 1992); Jacob R. Marcus, *United States Jewry 1776–1985*, Vol. II and III: *The Germanic Period*, and Vol. IV: *The East European Period* (Detroit, MI: Wayne State University Press, 1993).

10. See Avraham Barkai, *Branching Out: German-Jewish Immigration to the United States 1820–1914* (New York and London, Holmes & Meier, 1994), 152–90.

11. See Lance Sussman, *Isaac Leeser and the Making of American Judaism* (Detroit, MI: Wayne State University Press, 1995).

12. *The Occident and American Jewish Advocate: A Monthly Periodical Devoted to the Diffusion of Knowledge on Jewish Literature and Religion* (Philadelphia, PA: 1843–1869).

13. See Isaac Leeser, *Discourses on the Jewish Religion*, 10 vols. (Philadelphia, PA: Sherman & Co, 1867).

14. Moses Mendelssohn, *Jerusalem: A Treatise on Religious Power and Judaism*, trans. Isaac Leeser [Supplement to Occident 9 (1852)].

15. Isaac Leeser, *The Twenty-four Books of the Holy Scriptures* (Philadelphia: L. Johnson & Co, 1853/54); see Lance Sussman, "Another Look at Isaac Leeser and the First Jewish Translation of the Bible in the United States," *Modern Judaism* 5 (1985): 159–90.

16. Isaac Leeser, "Consecration of the Synagogue at Baltimore," *The Occident* 3 (1845): 367.

17. Isaac Leeser, "The Demands of the Times," *The Occident* 2 (1844): 412.

18. Barkai, *Branching Out*, 65.

19. See Rudolf Glanz, "Jews in Relation to the Cultural Milieu of the Germans in America Up to the Eighteen Eighties," in Glanz, *Studies in Judaica Americana* (New York: Ktav Publishing House, 1970), 203–55; Kathleen Neils Conzen, "German-Americans and the Invention of Ethnicity," in *America and the Germans: An Assessment of a Three-hundred Year History*, Vol. 1: *Immigrating, Language and Ethnicity*, ed. Frank Trommler (Philadelphia: University of Pennsylvania Press, 1985), 131–47.

20. Michael A. Meyer, *Response to Modernity: A History of the Reform Movement in Judaism* (Detroit, MI: Wayne State University Press, 1988), 252.

21. Jonathan Sarna, *JPS: The Americanization of Jewish Culture 1888–1988* (Philadelphia: Jewish Publication Society, 1989), 5.

22. Isaac Leeser, "A Hebrew College," *The Occident* 25 (1867): 325–6.

23. Leeser, "A Hebrew College," 325–6.

24. See Bertram W. Korn, "The First American Jewish Theological Seminary: Maimonides College, 1867–1873," in Korn, *Eventful Years and Experiences: Studies in Nineteenth Century American Jewish History* (Cincinnati. OH: American Jewish Archives, 1954), 151–213. Unfortunately, the seminar had to close a few years later, shortly after Leeser's death in 1868.

25. For Einhorn's biographical and intellectual profile, see Christian Wiese, "Samuel Holdheim's 'most Powerful Comrade in Conviction': David Einhorn and the Discussion about Jewish Universalism in the Radical Reform Movement," in *Re-Defining Judaism in an Age of Emancipation: Comparative Perspectives on Samuel Holdheim*, ed. Christian Wiese (Leiden and Boston: Brill Publishers, 2007), 306–73.

26. *Dr. David Einhorn's "Olath Tamid": Book of Prayers for Jewish Congregations* (Chicago: s.n., 1896).

27. *Sinai: Ein Organ für Erkenntnis und Veredlung des Judenthums* (Baltimore, 1855–1861).

28. For a comparison of Einhorn's and Wise's concepts, see Meyer, *Response to Modernity*, 235–60.

29. David Einhorn, "Antrittspredigt gehalten am 31. August 1866 in der Adath-Jeschurun-Gemeinde zu New York bei deren gleichzeitiger Tempelweihe," in *Dr. David Einhorns ausgewählte Predigten und Reden*, ed. Kaufmann Kohler (New York: Steiger, 1881), 60–72, here 65.

30. Gershon Greenberg, "The Messianic Foundations of American Jewish Thought: David Einhorn and Samuel Hirsch," in *World Congress of Jewish Studies 1975* (Jerusalem: World Union of Jewish Studies, 1976), 215–26.

31. David Einhorn, "Antrittspredigt gehalten am 27. September 1855 im Tempel des Har-Sinai-Vereins zu Baltimore," in *Dr. David Einhorns ausgewählte Predigten und Reden*, 21–44.

32. David Einhorn, "Abraham Lincoln. Trauerrede am 19. April 1865, Philadelphia," in ibid., 135–9.

33. David Einhorn, cited in Nathan Glazer, *American Judaism*, 2nd edition (Chicago: University of Chicago Press, 1989), 39.

34. David Einhorn, "Abschiedspredigt, gehalten am 12. Juli 1879 im Tempel der Beth-El-Gemeinde zu New York," in *Ausgewählte Predigten und Reden*, 85–92, here 90.

35. Ibid., 92.

36. Cited in Barkai, *Branching Out*, 167–8.

37. For all quotes, see Felsenthal's lecture on "Jüdisches Schulwesen in Amerika," cited in *Allgemeine Zeitung des Judentums* 30 (1866): 202–3, here 202. Felsenthal hoped for an "independent flourishing of Judaism" in America, but he emphasized that to expect it already in the present would "be foolish" and that to claim that it was already happening "would be a crime" (203); for Felsenthal, see Alex J. Goldman, "Bernard Felsenthal; Teacher in Israel," in Goldman, *Giants of Faith: Great American Rabbis* (New York: Citadel Press, 1965), 85–98; for Felsenthal as Germanizer, see Tobias Brinkmann, *Sundays at Sinai: A Jewish Congregation in Chicago* (Chicago: The University of Chicago Press, 2012), 46–8.

38. See my chapter "The Philadelphia Conference (1869) and German Reform: A Historical Moment in a Transnational Story of Proximity and Alienation" in this volume.

39. Ludwig Philippson, "Über das Judenthum in den Vereinigten Staaten von Nordamerika," *Allgemeine Zeitung des Judenthums* 44 (1880): 433–6, here 435 (the anonymous passage from *Der Zeitgeist* is cited in ibid., 435).

40. Adolf Moses, for instance, commented in 1882: "From America salvation will go forth, in this land (and not in Germany) will the religion of Israel celebrate its greatest triumphs"; see *Der Zeitgeist* 3 (1882): 249.

41. Kaufmann Kohler in *The Jewish Reformer*, January 29, 1886, 12; and see Kaufmann Kohler, "The Discovery of America: Its Influence upon the World's Progress, and Its Especial Significance for the Jews," *The Menorah* 13 (1892): 232–42. For Kohler, see Robert F. Southard, "The Theologian of the 1885 Pittsburgh Platform: Kaufmann Kohler's Vision of Progressive Judaism," in *Platforms and Prayer Books: Theological and Liturgical Perspectives on Reform Judaism*, ed. Dana E. Kaplan (Lanham, MD: Rowman & Littlefield, 2002), 61–79.

42. Kaufmann Kohler, "A Well of Living Waters" (1893), in Kohler, *Hebrew Union College and Other Addresses* (Cincinnati, OH: Ark Publishing Co, 1916), 1–10, here 8.

43. See esp. Kaufmann Kohler, "American Judaism. As Represented by the Union of American Hebrew Congregations and the Hebrew Union College," in Kohler, *Hebrew Union College*, 195–213.

44. Cited in Meyer, *Response to Modernity*, 241; for Wise see Sefton D. Temkin, *Creating American Reform Judaism: The Life and Times of Isaac Mayer Wise* (London and Oxford: Littman Library of Civilization, 1998).

45. Isaac M. Wise, in *American Israelite* 2 (1855): 137.

46. Isaac M. Wise, *Reminiscences*, translated from the German and edited with an introduction by David Philippson (Cincinnati, OH: L. Wise and Company, 1901), 331.

47. Isaac M. Wise, "A Retrospect," *American Israelite*, May 6, 1870: 8.

48. Isaac M. Wise, "German Culture," *American Israelite* 27 (1879), No. 24: 4.

49. Wise, *Reminiscences*, 24.

50. Isaac M. Wise, *Minhag America: The Daily Prayers for American Israelites* (Cincinnati, OH: Bloch, 1857).

51. Isaac M. Wise, *History of the Israelite Nation, from Abraham to the Present* (Albany: J. Munsell, 1854); Isaac M. Wise, *History of the Hebrew's Commonwealth, with Special Reference to its Literature, Culture and the Origins of Rabbinism and Christianity* (Cincinnati, OH: Bloch, 1880).

52. Isaac M. Wise, *American Israelite*, June 20, 1873: 4. One cannot, however, explore the crucial role of the Hebrew Union College and other American Jewish institutions evolving at that time for the Americanization of Jewish culture and Jewish scholarship without pointing out that even Wise remained at least ambivalent about the German language and culture: he wrote literary texts in his mother tongue, as well as his *Reminiscences*, which had to be translated into English, and confided more in the female readers of the German-language journal *Die Deborah* than in the larger circle which received his English weekly, the *American Israelite*. Wise mainly used *Die Deborah* to fight—in German—for the dissemination of the English language among Jewish children and adolescents. Despite his wish to uproot the immigrants from their German identity, he was aware that he was dealing with a heritage that nonetheless was of overwhelming importance to those whose American identity he wished to strengthen.

53. For the history of the institution, see Samuel E. Karff, *Hebrew Union College—Jewish Institute of Religion at One Hundred Years* (Cincinnati, OH: Hebrew Union College Press, 1976).

54. Isaac M. Wise, in *American Israelite*, September 15, 1876: 4.

55. Samuel Bäck, *Geschichte des jüdischen Volkes und seiner Literatur vom babylonischen Exile bis auf die Gegenwart*, 2nd edition (Frankfurt a. M.: Kauffmann, 1894).

56. Ludwig Philippson, "Das Hebrew Union College in Cincinnati," *Allgemeine Zeitung des Judenthums* 45 (1881): 351–5, here 352.

57. See Meyer, *Response to Modernity*, 265–70.

58. For this forerunner of the later Jewish Theological Seminary, see Hasia Diner, "Like the Antelope and the Badger. The Founding and Early Years of the Jewish Theological Seminary, 1886–1902," in *Tradition Renewed. A History of the Jewish Theological Seminary of America*, ed. Jack Wertheimer, 2 vols. (New York: Jewish Theological Seminary of America, 1997), esp. vol. 1: *The Making of an Institution of Jewish Higher Learning*, 3–42.

59. Kaufmann Kohler, *Grundriss einer systematischen Theologie des Judentums auf geschichtlicher Grundlage* (Leipzig: Fock, 1910); Kaufmann Kohler, *Jewish Theology: Systematically and Historically Considered* (New York: Macmillan, 1918).

60. Kaufmann Kohler, cited in Karff, ed., *Hebrew Union College*, 59.

61. Gotthard Deutsch, "Briefe aus Amerika," *Allgemeine Zeitung des Judenthums* 57 (1893): 16–18, here 17.

62. See Gilbert Klaperman, *The Story of Yeshiva University: The First Jewish University in America* (London: Collier-Macmillan, 1969).

63. Abraham A. Neumann, "The Dropsie College for Hebrew and Cognate Learning: Basic Principles and Objectives," in *Seventy-Fifth Anniversary of the JQR*, ed. Abraham A. Neumann and Solomon Zeitlin (Philadelphia: Jewish Quarterly Review, 1967), 19–46.

64. Jonathan D. Sarna, "The Late Nineteenth-Century American Jewish Awakening," in *Religious Diversity and American Religious History*, ed. Walter H. Conser Jr. and Sumner B. Twiss (Athens, GA: University of Georgia Press, 1997), 1–25.

65. Abraham Geiger, *Judaism and Its History* (New York: Thalmessinger & Cahn, 1866).

66. Heinrich Graetz, *History of the Jews* (New York: American Jewish Publication Society, 1873); and see Solomon Graytzel, "Graetz's *History* in America," *Historia Judaica* 3 (1941): 53–66.

67. See Jonathan Sarna and Nahum M. Sarna, "Jewish Bible Scholarship and Translations in the United States," in *The Bible and Bibles in America*, ed. Ernest S. Frerichs (Atlanta, GA: Fortress Press, 1988), 83–116.

68. See Shuly Rubin Schwartz, *The Emergence of Jewish Scholarship in America: The Publication of the Jewish Encyclopedia* (Cincinnati: Hebrew Union College Press, 1991), 4.

69. See Solomon Zeitlin, "Seventy-Five Years of the *Jewish Quarterly Review*," in Neumann and Zeitlin, eds., *Seventy-Fifth Anniversary of the JQR*, 60–5.

70. See Daniel R. Langton, *Claude Montefiore: His Life and Thought* (London: Vallentine Mitchell, 2002).

71. See Israel Abrahams, "Professor Schürer on Life under the Jewish Law," *Jewish Quarterly Review* 11 (1898): 626–42; Solomon Schechter, "The Law and Recent Criticism," in Schechter, *Studies in Judaism. First Series* (New York: Macmillan, 1896), 233–51; Solomon Schechter, "Higher Criticism—Higher Anti-Semitism," in Schechter, *Seminary Addresses and Other Papers* (Cincinnati: Ark Publishing Co, 1915), 35–9; for the discussion in Germany, see Wiese, *Challenging Colonial Discourse*, 159–215.

72. Cyrus Adler, "Editorial announcement," *Jewish Quarterly Review* (1910), cited in Zeitlin, "Seventy-Five Years of the *Jewish Quarterly Review*," 63.

73. For Schechter and his activities, see Norman Bentwich, *Solomon Schechter: A Biography* (New York: Jewish Publication Society, 1938); Abraham J. Karp, "American Rabbis for America: Solomon Schechter Comes to the Seminary," in *Karp, Jewish Continuity in America: Creative Survival in a Free Society* (Tuscaloosa, AL and London: University of Alabama Press, 1998), 132–44.

74. Cited in Bentwich, *Solomon Schechter*, 167.

75. Louis Ginzberg, *The Legends of the Jews* (Philadelphia: Jewish Publication Society, 1909–1938); for Szold's translation, see Sarna, *JPS*, 130–5; Baila Round Shargel, *Lost Lover: The Untold Story of Henrietta Szold: Unpublished Diary and Letters* (Philadelphia: Jewish Publication Society, 1997); for Friedländer, see Baila Round Shargel, *Practical Dreamer: Israel Friedlaender and the Shaping of American Judaism* (New York: Jewish Theological Seminary of America, 1985).

76. Cited in Rubin Schwartz, *The Emergence of Jewish Scholarship in America*, 27.

77. See Christian Wiese, "Struggling for Normality: The Apologetics of *Wissenschaft des Judentums* in Wilhelmine Germany as an Anti-Colonial Intellectual Revolt against the Protestant Construction of Judaism," in *Towards Normality: Patterns of Assimilation and Acculturation in German Speaking Jewry*, ed. Rainer Liedke and David Rechter (Tübingen: Mohr-Siebeck, 2003), 77–101.

78. Joseph Silverman, *The Renaissance of the Science of Judaism in America* (New York: Bloch, 1901), 4.

79. See George L. Berlin, *Defending the Faith: Nineteenth-Century American Jewish Writings on Christianity and Jesus* (Albany, NY: State University of New York Press, 1989).

80. See, for instance, Leonard Dinnerstein, *Antisemitism in the United States* (New York and Oxford: Oxford University Press, 1994); Frederic Cople Jaher, *A Scapegoat in the New*

Wilderness: The Origins and Rise of Anti-Semitism in America (Cambridge, MA: Harvard University Press, 1994); Jeffrey S. Gurock, ed., *American Jewish History*, Vol. 6: *Anti-Semitism in America*, in two parts (London and New York: Routledge, 1998).

81. See, for instance, Jacob Z. Lauterbach, *The Ancient Jewish Allegorists in Talmud and Midrasch* (Philadelphia: Jewish Publication Society, 1911).

82. Rubin Schwartz, *The Emergence of Jewish Scholarship in America*, 128–45.

83. Ibid., 112–19.

84. Joseph Jacobs, *Jewish Chronicle*, February 23, 1900: 18–9.

85. Rubin Schwartz, *The Emergence of Jewish Scholarship in America*, 169.

86. Wilhelm Bacher, "Die jüdische Enzyklopädie," *Allgemeine Zeitung des Judentums* 70 (1906): 114–16, here 114–15.

87. Wilhelm Bacher, "Eine Hochschule für die Wissenschaft des Judentums in Amerika," *Allgemeine Zeitung des Judenthums* 65 (1901): 380–2, here 380; and see Gustav Karpeles, "Das Judentum in Amerika," *Allgemeine Zeitung des Judenthums* (1904): 385–6, here 385: "American Judaism will have to receive the scholarly tools for their fight and work from Old Europe for years to come; but while only a few years ago young Jewish theologians from America had to seek support in order to win capable forces for their synagogues, it may well be the case in a few decades that modern theologians from Europe will travel to the young continent in order to extend their knowledge."

88. Rubin Schwartz, *The Emergence of Jewish Scholarship in America*, 16.

89. Solomon Schechter, "The Assistance of the Public," in Schechter, *Seminary Addresses and Other Papers*, 229–37, here 232–3. It sounds like a response to Schechter's assessment when Markus Brann, the editor of the *Monatsschrift für Geschichte und Wissenschaft des Judentums*, gave his Viennese colleague, Victor Aptowitzer, the advice in 1914 to accept an offer from JTS in New York. The "ineradicable anti-Semitism," the persecution of the Russian Jews and the "increasing decomposition of European Judaism," he argued, was a signal "that our future lies in America." As a young man it was Aptowitzer's task to contribute to help the new generation in America to retain its Jewish identity. Schechter's seminary would be a blessing for Judaism—"I can, therefore, only hope that you will decide in favour of America. We old people here in Europe will have to struggle with the task to rescue what can be rescued"; see the letter of Markus Brann to Victor Aptowitzer from January 27, 1914. Aptowitzer responded that Brann was right, but that, from his point of view "European Judaism, as the larger part, should not be given up for the sake of American Judaism," and that he had, therefore, decided to stay in Vienna; see postcard from Victor Aptowitzer to Markus Brann from January 22, 1914 (both documents in the Markus Brann papers, Jewish National Library, Jerusalem, manuscript collection, ARC Ms. Var 308/23).

90. See Paul Ritterband and Harold S. Wechsler, eds., *Learning in American Universities: The First Century* (Bloomington and Indianapolis, IN: Indiana University Press, 1994), 98–123.

91. For the role of Hebrew Union College in rescuing Jewish scholars from Europe between 1935 and 1942, see Michael A. Meyer, "The Refugee Scholars Project of the Hebrew Union College," in Meyer, *Judaism within Modernity: Essays on Jewish History and Religion* (Detroit, MI: Wayne State University Press, 2001), 345–61.

92. See, for instance, Felix Perles, "Eine Ehrenpflicht des gebildeten Judentums," *Ost und West* 14 (1914): 553–60; for the struggle for the emancipation of Jewish Studies in Germany, see Wiese, *Challenging Colonial Discourse*, 351–425.

93. See Henry Wassermann, *False Start: Jewish Studies at German Universities during the Weimar Republic* (Amherst, NY: Humanity Books, 2003).

94. See David N. Myers, "The Fall and Rise of Jewish Historicism: The Evolution of the Akademie für die Wissenschaft des Judentums (1919–1934)," *Hebrew Union College Annual* 63 (1992): 107–44; for the development of Jewish historiography, see Christhard Hoffmann, "Jüdische Geschichtswissenschaft in Deutschland: 1918–1938: Konzepte, Schwerpunkte, Ergebnisse," in Carlebach, ed., *Chochmat Jisrael*, 132–52; Michael Brenner, *The Renaissance of Jewish Culture in Weimar Germany* (New Haven, CT and London: Yale University Press, 1996), 69–126; Michael Brenner, "Jüdische Geschichte an deutschen Universitäten—Bilanz und Perspektiven," *Historische Zeitschrift* 266 (1998): 1–21; Michael Brenner, *Prophets of the Past: Interpreters of Jewish History*, trans. Steven Randall (Princeton, NJ: Princeton University Press, 2010).

95. For the ambivalence of this form of participation, see Leonore Siegele-Wenschkewitz, "Das Verhältnis von protestantischer Theologie und Wissenschaft des Judentums während der Weimarer Republik," in *Juden in der Weimarer Republik*, ed. Walter Grab and Julius H. Schoeps (Stuttgart and Bonn: Burg-Verlag, 1986), 153–78.

96. See Herbert A. Strauss, "Die letzten Jahre der Hochschule (Lehranstalt) für die Wissenschaft des Judentums, Berlin: 1936–1942," in Carlebach, ed., *Chochmat Jisrael*, 36–58.

97. See Susannah Heschel, "Theologen für Hitler: Walter Grundmann und das 'Institut zur Erforschung und Beseitigung des jüdischen Einflusses auf das deutsche kirchliche Leben'," in *Christlicher Antijudaismus und Antisemitismus. Theologische und kirchliche Programme Deutscher Christen*, ed. Leonore Siegele-Wenschkewitz (Frankfurt a. Main: Haag + Herchen, 1994), 125–70; Susannah Heschel, *The Aryan Jesus: Christian Theologians and the Bible in Nazi Germany* (Princeton, NJ: Princeton University Press, 2008). The same happened in the field of history when several anti-Semitic institutes were established: the Institut zur Erforschung der Judenfrage in Berlin (1934), the Forschungsabteilung "Judenfrage" am Reichsinstitut für Geschichte des neuen Deutschland in Munich (1936), and the Institut zur Erforschung der Judenfrage in Frankfurt (1941). For this kind of anti-Semitic research on the "Jewish question," see Dirk Rupnow, *Judenforschung im Dritten Reich. Wissenschaft zwischen Politik, Propaganda und Ideologie* (Baden-Baden: Nomos-Verlag, 2011); Werner Schochow, *Deutsch-Jüdische Geschichtswissenschaft: Eine Geschichte ihrer Organisationsformen unter besonderer Berücksichtigung der Fachbibliographie* (Berlin: Colloquium, 1969), 131–95; Patricia von Papen-Bodek, "Anti-Jewish Research of the *Institut zur Erforschung der Judenfrage* or *Außenstelle* of the High School of the NSDAP in Frankfurt am Main," in *Lessons and Legacies*, Vol 6: *New Currents in Holocaust Research*, ed. Jeffry M. Diefendorf (Evanston, IL: Northwestern University Press 2004) 155–89.

98. Ismar Elbogen, "American Jewish Scholarship: A Survey. In Honor of the Centenary of Kaufmann Kohler," *The American Jewish Year Book* 45 (1943/44): 47–65, here 47.

99. Ibid., 61.

100. Ibid., 65.

PART III
NEW ROLES AND IDENTITIES IN AN AGE OF MASS MIGRATION

CHAPTER 12
"SHUL WITH A POOL" RECONSIDERED
David E. Kaufman

At this moment of transnational comparative study, the notion of American Jewish "exceptionalism" has come under reexamination. What was called by an earlier generation of scholars "Americanization" is now more likely expressed in the more ecumenical terms of modernization, westernization, and feminization. Yet the question remains: Is the historical experience of American Jews unique? How is it distinct from that of other Americans and different from that of other Jews? In my 1999 book, *Shul with a Pool: The "Synagogue-Center" in American Jewish History,*[1] I took such distinctiveness for granted. Now, with some distance from the work, the time has come for some self-criticism, a *mea culpa* in fact—for as in much of the historiography of our field, the book treats its subject as a phenomenon unique to the American Jewish experience and thereby assumes exceptionalism as a given. By eschewing comparative Jewish history and relegating ourselves to the American scene alone, we accept the idea too readily and uncritically. Though I will not reject it out of hand today, I would like to offer a more nuanced view and take the opportunity to review the history of the synagogue-center experiment through a new lens—by raising anew the question of how and why the synagogue-center was a uniquely American case, as claimed all too blithely in *Shul with a Pool*.

A widely noted phenomenon of Jewish America in the post-First World War period, the "synagogue-center" can be defined simply as a combination of synagogue and community center, a "shul with a pool" in the colloquial phrase of the day. As sociologist Marshall Sklare famously noted, the expanded institution became the prototype for the typical American synagogue of today;[2] less often noted is that the synagogue-center of the early decades of the century also served as the genesis of the "JCC," or Jewish Community Center—an ubiquitous institution in today's American Jewish community, and, we might note, an original creation of American Jewry (note the claim to exceptionalism once again). Today, the synagogue and JCC often co-exist in tension, competing over constituencies, funding, programming, and most importantly, the claim to centrality, to being *the* essential institution of American Jewish life.

Not surprisingly, a similar tension characterized the synagogue-center's emergence—it was the modern conflict between competing visions of "Jewishness," one vision rooted in a religious definition of Jewish life, the other defining it in purely social terms, a secular expression of Jewish peoplehood and ethnic community—one concerned primarily with *Judaism*, the other with *Jews*. I chose to study the synagogue-center movement of the early twentieth century in order to better understand this dynamic—what I've called the "social-religious dialectic" of American Jewish life. Of course, as noted by Jewish historians from Heinrich Graetz to Salo Baron to Kaufman, such a dynamic tension between religion and peoplehood has animated Jewish life throughout history—an observation, important to note, deriving from Jewish history rather than American history.[3] As Henry Feingold and others have written, contemporary social science often has trouble categorizing the Jews, tending to limit them within rubrics of ethnicity, religion, race, etc., rather than adopting a more idiosyncratic view of Jewish complexity and multiplicity.[4] For example, the relationship between Jewish ethnicity and religiosity in America is not merely a matter of one being repackaged as the other, but rather is a complex negotiation between two alternate constructions of modern Jewish identity. As we shall see, the interplay of the social and religious spheres of American Jewish life is revealed in the historical dialectic between the American synagogue, Jewish center, and their hybrid, the synagogue-center.

Where did the synagogue-center come from? How, when, and why did it emerge? In the Introduction to *Shul with a Pool*, I outlined the four conventional explanations:

1. Those taking the longer view of Jewish history often point to the ancient and medieval precedents of a multi-functional synagogue which often included social functions and was instrumental in forming Jewish community—any modern version of this must simply be a revival of an earlier tradition in Jewish life. Though this begs the question of why in America and why in the early twentieth century, the historical impulse ought not to be dismissed so easily. Many familiar modes of Jewish life reappear in disparate times and cultures—so why not the synagogue-center? And note how this view contradicts the notion of American exceptionalism—by pointing to the social function of the synagogue in the past, one implies that there is nothing exceptional—in Jewish history—about the American experience.

2. A second view suggests nothing particularly exceptional about the Jewish experience within American history. This perspective focuses on the American environment rather than on Jewish precedent. Turn of the century American Christianity was at the height of its Social Gospel phase, one of whose principal manifestations was the "institutional church," a multi-purpose institution offering social and recreational services as well as religious, a combination church and community center. Certainly, the institutional church and its related movements of Social Christianity were key influences in the creation of a series of Jewish analogs. Yet if the synagogue-center is nothing but an adaptation of a broader trend, then there can be no claim of uniqueness, nothing of particular import about the Jews and their communal life. In the end, the emphasis on outside influence alone is insufficient as it misses the relevant developments within the Jewish community itself.

3. One of those internal Jewish developments, and the third conventional explanation, was the rise of a new leadership and ideological trend that historian Deborah Dash Moore has described as "A New American Judaism."[5] The phrase refers to the early twentieth-century worldview of progressive rabbinic figures such as Stephen S. Wise, Judah L. Magnes, Israel Friedlaender, and most centrally, Mordecai M.

Kaplan—all of whom were profoundly influenced both by Jewish nationalism *and* American Progressivism, guided as much by Ahad Ha'am as by John Dewey. In their common conception, the synagogue would become a center of Jewish peoplehood; and hence the synagogue-center phenomenon can be understood as the institutional expression of their own hybrid ideologies of social Judaism and religious Zionism—in Kaplan's formulation especially, the synagogue-center would be the means toward achieving "Jewish civilization" in America.

4. The problem with this "elite" point of view is that it ignores the great inchoate "folk" urge toward the synagogue-center solution, as demonstrated by the lay builders of synagogue-centers around the country who never had heard of either John Dewey or Mordecai M. Kaplan. This fourth perspective focuses on the second generation Jewish neighborhood as the essential sociological context for the emergence of the synagogue-center. Hence Marshall Sklare explained the development of the synagogue-center as a combination of two factors: first as a means of engaging acculturated American Jews by yielding to their more secular interests—and, Sklare suggested, this compromise with secularism was simultaneously a strategy to "reculturate" its constituency to Judaism.[6] So the synagogue-center's synthesis of social and religious services satisfied both American tastes and Jewish needs. Yet once again, such an illuminating description does not in itself shed light on our starting question—what is exclusively "American-Jewish" about the synagogue-center? Did not German, French, and English Jews of the equivalent generation have the same dual need for acculturation and reculturation? Why, after all, did this phenomenon appear in America and not elsewhere?

Shul with a Pool attempts to answer such questions by describing the discrete origins of the synagogue-center movement. In the first five chapters, I locate the sources of the synagogue-center phenomenon in five separate and precedent institutional movements of American Jewry. Two were explicitly religious "synagogue" movements that developed into something more self-consciously social through the turn of the century; two were secular "community center" movements that began to incorporate more religious activity during the same period; and one was both religious and social from the start, but evolved from a peripheral activity into a central institution of the community. All five yielded the synagogue-center solution, and thus, I argue, exemplify the social-religious synthesis characteristic of American Jewish life.

In retrospect, I should confess that the question of exceptionalism is somewhat cloudy in its original formulation. On the one hand, as implied earlier, all five movements were deeply embedded in an American context, reflecting more general trends in American society. And, at the same time, all five had their analogs in the greater Jewish experience, and were closely related to one another as integral elements of an organic Jewish community. So once again, the argument could be made that these movements are exceptional neither in American nor in Jewish history. And yet I cannot help but continue to assert their uniqueness. Perhaps it is just that they are quintessentially American *and* quintessentially Jewish at the same time—and it is that synthesis that makes American Jewry different (the German-Jewish symbiosis notwithstanding). Or, as asserted in *Shul with a Pool*, they are exceptional in light of their shared social and religious dynamic; this notion will become clearer as I outline the five movements. But in rethinking the subject for this essay, yet another theme jumped out, another possible rationale for the specificity of the American Jewish experience. I will leave that for the end, however, and proceed first to summarize the five source movements:

1. *The Temple Center movement of Classical Reform Judaism.* As employed by Michael Meyer in his authoritative history of Reform Judaism, the term "Classical Reform" refers to the efflorescence of German Reform ideology in the environment of post-Civil War American Judaism.[7] Meyer further describes Classical Reform as the union of the religious radicalism of David Einhorn and Kaufmann Kohler with the social pragmatism of Isaac Mayer Wise and Emil G. Hirsch. The trend peaked at the Pittsburgh Conference of 1885, which crystallized the classical position through its platform of ideological principles, and also marked Reform as a separate denomination in American Judaism.

   But there is a second act of the classical period left out of the narrative—and that was the creation of a new generation of American-born and American-trained Reform rabbis, newly minted by the Hebrew Union College from its first graduation in 1883. Following their careers we discover a new phase in Classical Reform Judaism—one centered on the practical improvement of congregational life. Examples would be the all-encompassing synagogue experiment of Henry Berkowitz's Kansas City congregation in 1888; Joseph Krauskopf's young people's societies in 1890s Philadelphia; and the "institutional temple" launched by Moses Gries in Cleveland at the turn of the century; and so on. What they all share in common is first, the very Jewish concern of the rabbi for the parochial needs of the community; and second, a very American devotion to practical solutions rather than to intellectual deliberation. Paradoxically, this pragmatic trend gave birth to a new legitimating ideology—as expressed in the rabbinic discourse of the CCAR, the new ideology re-conceptualized the temple as a social center, and redefined the synagogue as the communal center of Jewish life. Hence the synagogue-center movement had its first source in the "socialization" of the classical Reform temple.

2. The second source was in the parallel "religionizing" trend of the YMHA, the *Young Men's Hebrew Association.* Obviously inspired by the example of the Young Men's Christian Association (YMCA), a Jewish "Y" movement was made possible by the ethnic diversity of American life—sectarian Y's were founded in other minority communities as well, such as those for Asian and African Americans, and all can be considered constituents of the social trend in contemporary Christianity. Yet the YMHA departed from the Christian precedent in one significant way: whereas the YMCA had begun as a missionary church for young people and grew more social and recreational in nature over time, the YMHA was established as a

secular social center from its earliest beginnings in the 1850s, remained so through its growth as a national movement in the 1870s and only began to adopt synagogue-style programming around the turn of the century—then adding conventionally religious functions such as holiday observances, Jewish education, and even synagogue services. Two particular constituencies played key roles in this transformation. First, the rabbis of the established German Jewish community took a vested interest in the youth activities of the Y. Prior to developing youth programs within the synagogue, rabbis turned to YMHAs to reach Jewish youth, offering lectures and organizing activities. More important than the rabbis, however, were the women.

Uptown Jewish women, infused with the social activism of first phase feminism, took the YMHA model and created their own Young Women's Hebrew Association movement in 1902. From the start, the YWHA departed from its male counterpart in its emphasis on Jewish religious revival. Bella Unterberg, the founding president, dedicated its first building in 1903 and stated in no uncertain terms: "I wish right here to lay stress upon what I deem to be the cornerstone of success of such work, and that is the religious nature of it." A 1912 newspaper article quoted Miss Sophia Berger, superintendent of the YWHA, as saying: "Back of all that we do, is the thought of preserving the essential Jewishness of our people. As Jews we want to save our Judaism. As Jews we bring these girls in here that they may find shelter and help and find, too, the God of their fathers." And thus not surprisingly, in 1918, the newly constructed Young Women's Hebrew Association of New York would include both a synagogue and a swimming pool on its premises—it was a "shul with a pool" just as surely as was the Jewish Center founded by Mordecai M. Kaplan in that same year.[8]

3. *The Jewish Settlement house and Educational Alliance movement.* After the YMHA, the second precedent for the Jewish community center was the Jewish settlement. Like the Y, the idea was originally imported from England, but in the American Jewish context turned into something else again, what I've described as "a department store of Jewish life." Indeed, we might say that while settlement houses blossomed in England, and Jewish department stores flourished in Germany, it was in America that the two come together in a single communal institution. Their synthesis was epitomized by New York's Educational Alliance of 1893—whose founders, not incidentally, included department store magnates Isidor Straus and Joseph Bloomingdale. As a full-service, departmentalized Jewish institution offering social, recreational, educational and religious programs, the Educational Alliance unified the community, bringing together uptown and downtown Jews in common purpose (hence, "alliance"), and ultimately inspired a nationwide movement of similar communal centers. As in the YM/WHA movement, the Jewish settlement also transformed from a paternalistic agency of Americanization into an agency of Judaization. How did this happen? Simply put, following the turn of the century, the "inmates took over the asylum"—that is, the East European immigrant community, for whom the settlement was originally conceived, took

over the reins of the institution and turned it into a "Jewish center" serving the community's needs as they perceived them. First they introduced Yiddish into the program, then Zionism, Jewish education, and ultimately, synagogue services—making the Educational Alliance (and its analogous institutions around the country) a principal source of the synagogue-center phenomenon.

4. *The modern Talmud Torah and Jewish School Center movement.* Both religious and social in function, the field of Jewish education also produced a synagogue-center experiment. American-trained Jewish educators under the tutelage of John Dewey, Mordecai M. Kaplan, and Samson Benderly promoted a new conception of the Jewish school as a community center. At the same time, the Jewish immigrant community also began to modernize and Americanize the Talmud Torah type of Jewish school. Both the former and the latter movements were united by a common ideology—the cultural Zionism of Ahad Ha'am. In 1910, Ahad Ha'am wrote to Judah L. Magnes that "the Synagogue must be the center to which those who want to learn about Judaism resort every day."[9] In the following years, American Jewish educators would incorporate the synagogue and center into one institution—exemplified by the Central Jewish Institute founded in 1916, the "Jewish school center" became yet another essential precedent for the synagogue-center movement of the 1920s.

5. *The modern Orthodox Shul and young people's synagogue movement.* As in the case of the Jewish school, the traditional synagogue was also modernized during this period, and again, both by the elite and the folk of the community. From the turn of the century, forward-thinking rabbis joined with the youth of the immigrant community to establish "young people's synagogues." For example, Jeffrey Gurock has written about the Jewish Endeavor Society, one of the earliest of these groups in 1901.[10] A decade later, Judah L. Magnes would help establish the Young Israel movement on the Lower East Side. And in 1918, two influential Orthodox synagogue-centers were established further uptown: Herbert Goldstein's Institutional Synagogue in Harlem and Mordecai M. Kaplan's Jewish Center on the Upper West Side. All of these experiments combined religious congregation with social recreation. And once again, the synagogue-center concept had grown out of a particular movement in American Jewish life.

Thus, every one of the institutional movements I've delineated exemplifies the social-religious dialectic and the tendency toward synthesis. They all reached this conclusion in order to attract a broader constituency and find success as a communal institution—and in the process, they each asserted a more holistic construction of Jewishness, one incorporating both religious and ethnic identification. All of which still begs the question of "why in America?" Here I take my lead from the work of sociologist Charles Liebman, who described American Judaism as a dichotomy between "elite" and "folk" expressions—"elite" referring to the normative version of religion propounded by the leadership and the learned, and "folk" indicating the popular practice and understanding of religion as found among the people, the *amcha* of the Jewish community.[11] According to

Liebman, American Judaism has often been an elite formulation of folk religion, as epitomized by Mordecai M. Kaplan's Reconstructionism. In his pragmatic religious philosophy, Kaplan elevated the folk concerns with social life, culture, and peoplehood to the elite level of core Jewish values. In this regard, the synagogue-center can be understood as the leadership's recapitulation of the laity's needs and desires. Though this concept should not be confused with the notion of the "ethnic church," a religious container of ethnic content—it represents instead a meeting and merger of both elite and folk concerns.

Let me suggest, in closing, that a distinctive characteristic of the American Jewish experience is a closer, less hierarchal, and more integral relationship between the elite and folk. This idea is borne out by each one of the synagogue-center movements I've described—the Reform temple center was the product of rabbis catering to their constituents; the YMHA was a case of rabbis reaching out to Jewish youth and of Jewish women aspiring to create a center for Judaism; the Jewish settlement brought together the uptown elite with the downtown masses; the Jewish school center merged the concerns of academic educators with neighborhood Zionists; and the young people's Orthodox synagogue joined progressive rabbis with youth once again. How to explain this feature of American Jewish life? Can it be attributed to the anti-intellectualism and democratic populism of American culture? Or shall we look to the American Jewish community's lack of traditional authority structures such as the Kehillah? Or perhaps to the selection process of Jewish immigration whereby the less educated came in far greater numbers than did members of the establishment? Whatever the specific reason, the flattening of the folk/elite dichotomy in early twentieth-century American Judaism surely helps to explain the puzzling existence of synagogues with swimming pools.

Notes

1. David E. Kaufman, *Shul with a Pool: The "Synagogue-Center" in American Jewish History* (Hanover, NH and London: Brandeis University Press by University Press of New England, 1999).

2. Marshall Sklare, *America's Jews* (New York: Random House, 1971), 127.

3. See, e.g., Salo Baron, *A Social and Religious History of the Jews* (Philadelphia: The Jewish Publication Society of America, 1952), Vol. I, 3–4.

4. Henry Feingold, "Jewish Exceptionalism," in *Lest Memory Cease: Finding Meaning in the American Jewish Past* (Syracuse, NY: Syracuse University Press, 1996), 34–52.

5. Deborah Dash Moore, "A New American Judaism," in *Like All the Nations?: The Life and Legacy of Judah L. Magnes*, ed. William Brinner and Moses Rischin (Albany, NY: State University of New York Press, 1987), 41–55.

6. Marshall Sklare, *Conservative Judaism* (New York: Schocken Books, 1972), 129–45.

7. Michael A. Meyer, *Response to Modernity: A History of the Reform Movement in Judaism* (New York and Oxford: Oxford University Press, 1988), 264–95.

8. Kaufman, *Shul with a Pool*, 76–82; also see David Kaufman, "Young Women's Hebrew Association," in *Jewish Women in America: An Historical Encyclopedia*, ed. Paula Hyman and Deborah Dash Moore (New York: Routledge, 1997), 1536–40.

9. Ahad Ha'am, letter to Judah L. Magnes (September 18, 1910), in *The Zionist Idea*, ed. Arthur Hertzberg (New York: Atheneum, 1979), 261.

10. Jeffrey Gurock, "Consensus Building and Conflict over Creating the Young People's Synagogue of the Lower East Side," in *The Americanization of the Jews*, ed. Robert Seltzer and Norman Cohen (New York: New York University Press, 1995), 230–46.

11. Charles Liebman, *The Ambivalent American Jew: Politics, Religion, and Family in American Jewish Life* (Philadelphia: The Jewish Publication Society of America, 1973), 45–77.

CHAPTER 13
"RESISTERS AND ACCOMMODATORS" REVISITED: REFLECTIONS ON THE STUDY OF ORTHODOXY IN AMERICA

Jeffrey S. Gurock

In 1983, I wrote an article that was praised at the time as a "path breaking analysis" of the diversity of opinion and variety of attitudes among Orthodox rabbis toward the challenges of voluntarism, Jewish denominationalism, and mass disaffection from traditional faith commitments that confronted these leaders in America. In "Resisters and Accommodators," I posited that specific and staunch "categories of difference" characterized that denomination's rabbis' outlooks over the prior one hundred years (1883–1983). Indeed, I contended that with "certain notable exceptions or important variations," the American Orthodox rabbinate was "polarized" into two camps. The resisters, primarily those who hailed from, or were trained at, East European yeshivas, in pursuit of their lofty, if unattainable, goal of recreating the Jewish civilization of the past within hostile American soil, "reject[ed] acculturation and disdained cooperation with other American Jewish elements, fearing that alliances would work to dilute traditional faith and practice."

Meanwhile, the accommodators, mostly those born or raised and certainly, those trained in America, whether at the Jewish Theological Seminary of America, in its earliest phases and at the Rabbi Isaac Elchanan Theological Seminary, until today, operated from the perspective that the Americanization of their potential flocks was "inevitable." Accordingly, they often "joined arms with less traditional elements in the community" to perpetuate at least "the essence of ancestral faith." In their efforts, I argued, to gain, or regain, the allegiances of the Americanizing to their form of Orthodoxy, the "moderns" adopted a tripartite strategy. They included in their communal mix, and reached-out to, as broad a constituency of Jews as possible. Here, for them Orthodox behavior often would be defined as what a Jew did in public religious precincts, not in private lives or homes. Also, toward maximizing their reach, accommodators would integrate or simulate, within their synagogues, attractive features of general culture and of more liberal Jewish practice. Essentially, they would modify the social forms of congregational life without violating halakhic norms. And they would find common cause—cooperate—with non-Orthodox Jews and their leaders on matters of non-religious Jewish communal concern.[1]

When this article appeared, that same friendly critic who called my contribution "path breaking" complimented me for realizing that I was "really describing a spectrum of Orthodoxy, with full accommodation on the left, utter resistance on the right, and Orthodox rabbis of various shades ranged along different points of the intervening continuum."[2] But Jonathan D. Sarna was far too generous in his evaluation. For in the piece, I really was, in fact, too absolute in my categories. Indeed, some time later, I started revisiting my thesis in an attempt to show greater texture and tension *within* my categories. And, over the years, I have continued to rethink my assumptions and conceptualizations. In this effort, I am revising "Resisters and Accommodators" once more with an even more critical eye toward offering a more nuanced understanding of both camps' outlooks. I am now prepared to argue that while for many resisters, the recreating of East European ways on these shores was an ideal worth praying and striving for, they, nonetheless, frequently made pragmatic adjustments to American realities.

I also now recognize, far more than I did in 1983, that accommodators have varied significantly in their degrees of simulation of, and cooperation with, other Jewish religious groups and their values. And, when elements within the "modern" camp moved very close to liberal denominations in practices and procedures, some other Americanized Orthodox rabbis could be harshly critical of them. An ultra-accommodator could be judged as no longer a loyal member of the group for having crossed over unbridgeable lines of theological demarcation. Moreover, subsequent research has sensitized me to the reality that the atmospherics that engendered accommodating behavior changed much over time. Sometimes, emulation of what Conservatives did reflect the weakness of their traditional movement. Other times, especially in recent decades, the tacit alliances that have been struck, not only with Conservatives, but also with Reformers and Reconstructionists, evidenced the growing strength of Orthodoxy in America.

My first second thoughts about the initial conceptualization revolved around Rabbi Jacob Joseph, the Chief Rabbi of New York City from 1887 to 1902, whom I originally projected as the paradigmatic resister of his era. My re-thinking began when I investigated the early Orthodox phases in the life of Rabbi Mordecai M. Kaplan, the founder of Reconstructionism. The Joseph-Kaplan connection involved Mordecai's father, Rabbi Israel Kaplan, who upon arrival in America in 1888 linked up with Rabbi Joseph, his erstwhile yeshiva-mate from Volozhin, and served as a religious judge within the downtown religious establishment. Predictably, Israel and Anna Kaplan sent their young boy to the Etz Chaim Yeshiva, the jewel institution of the Association of Orthodox Hebrew Congregations (AOHC), the organization that controlled the Chief Rabbinate initiative. But Mordecai M. Kaplan did not stay long at this school that offered students only the most haphazard of training in American ways and skills. His parents preferred to have their child attend the public schools—just like 99.9 percent of other American Jewish youths of that time. Moreover, when young Kaplan reached his teenage years, his family sent him off to the Jewish Theological Seminary to train as an American Orthodox rabbi, to be an accommodator. So, it appeared to me that in this educational realm, the Kaplans seemingly stood apart from the community of resisters that they were supposed to be a part of. And yet, Israel Kaplan, this transplanted East European rabbi and his wife were not renegades. If anything, a lieutenant to Rabbi Joseph, Israel Kaplan was *within and not without* the epicenter of the chief rabbi's court. Such a position only sustained my questions about how "frum"—to use the parlance of our day—Rabbi Joseph's court really was.[3]

Indeed, additional research suggested that many others who were part of the Chief Rabbi's group—not just Kaplan—were far from unqualifiedly committed to resistance. Its court "historian," Judah David Eisenstein, whom the currents of the Haskalah also touched, saw real value in youngsters receiving quality instruction in the language and ways of this country "for necessity impels us so that we may mingle with the people among whom we live." Moreover, Eisenstein had no problem whatsoever with Orthodox accommodators in America receiving their training at a seminary—even possibly the Jewish Theological Seminary—and not at a yeshiva to lead the next generation back toward observance of the Torah. All told, for the Association, resistance may have been their ideal stance, even as they made tacit accommodations to American realities.[4]

Could the same ambivalence have characterized the early Agudath ha-Rabbanim (Union of Orthodox Rabbis of the United States and Canada, UOR), the successor organization to the Association? Early on in my re-evaluation of my conceptualization, I sustained the argument that a "new era of more strident resistance to Americanization and entrenched opposition to religious opponents began" with the founding of that organization in the years that immediately followed the death of the Chief Rabbi in 1902. My most striking evidence continued to be that, in its first years, the de-legitimization of the Jewish Theological Seminary in the eyes of the immigrant Jewish community ranked high on its list of concerns. In 1904, the UOR castigated professors like Orientalist Solomon Schechter and Talmudist Louis Ginzberg, leaders of the so-called "New Seminary," men who would slowly move that school toward becoming Conservative Judaism's flagship institution, as "expounders of the Higher Criticism which is anything but Orthodox ... [and who] have no place in the world to come."[5] But as I considered other fronts and different occasions, I came to determine that the Orthodox rabbinical group could be far more accepting or tolerant of other Jewish opinions and movements. Consider the circumstances that surrounded the planning meeting in Boston in April 1902 that led to the UOR's founding some three months later.

The leaders who championed, as a national group, the challenges that had undone the Chief Rabbi—the problems of Sabbath desecration, poor Jewish education, kashruth non-regulation and denominational competition—were all in town as delegates to the decidedly non-Orthodox convention of the Federation of American Zionists. There they sat with such seemingly unlikely colleagues as Reform rabbis Richard Gottheil, Stephen S. Wise and Abraham Radin, Conservative spokespeople like Marcus Jastrow and Henrietta Szold and a slew of secular Zionists. There were, understandably, some difficult moments when very different types of Jews met, particularly when "recommendations" and "resolutions" were made that "emphatically opposed and condemned the proposal to abolish the sacred and traditional Sabbath." Some delegates—presumably with the Agudath ha-Rabbanim members in the forefront—believed that it was entirely appropriate for the conclave to speak out against the Reform Jewish "Sunday Sabbath" movement. Others in attendance considered that discussion out of order since "the Zionist movement does not recognize religious questions." Still, the Orthodox rabbis' very presence at this conclave that dealt with a welter of pressing contemporary Jewish issues bespoke a level of recognition of, and willingness to work with, their theological and ideological opponents.[6]

This degree of tolerance, I would then argue, ironically grew out of their own East European background where over *there*, the UOR men of the future were among the most accommodating rabbis of their time and place. Most of the Agudath ha-Rabbanim's founders were Orthodox supporters of Hibbat Zion, disciples of Rabbis Isaac Elchanan Spektor and Isaac Jacob Reines. And they were soon to be members of the American branch of the Mizrachi movement, a faction and a vision within the Zionist camp that was organized the same crucial year of 1902. As such, they subscribed to that proposition that Orthodox Jews must play a major role within the Jewish national revival—and certainly interact with non-Orthodox Jews—to assure that Zionism progressed with regard to the teachings of the Torah. In occupying that position, these "moderns" effectively rejected the millennium-old notion that Jews should play no role in, and work with no one, toward hastening their redemption. In Russia, Poland, and Hungary, this Religious Zionist position was a minority stance within the Orthodox rabbinate. However, in America, it long endured as the majority opinion. Accordingly, it was possible for a good UOR member to resist Americanization and, thus, to stay clear of inter-denominational cooperation while, at the same time, being a modernist, and working with others when it came to steering the Zionist revival in the appropriate direction.[7]

But how "utterly resistant" and fully non-cooperative was the Agudath ha-Rabbanim on its anti-acculturation front? A reexamination of the UOR's mission statement—its Constitution of 1902—suggests that these rabbis harbored a level of realism about conditions in this country, a degree of pragmatism that I had not originally emphasized.

Predictably, when it came to the daunting issue of non-observance of the Sabbath among immigrant Jews, the UOR took a hardline stance. It called upon its members to deny "any certification of Kashrut to Sabbath desecrators," and the rabbis were told, similarly, to "warn the people not to buy bread from bakeries which bake on the Sabbath," declaring that "not only is purchasing such products considered aiding a sinner, but it is practically certain that there is also non-kosher oil and shortening in the baked products." However, the group also spoke, simultaneously, of tactics reminiscent of those that accommodationist Orthodox rabbis used. The UOR rabbis were instructed to reach out, just like an Americanized Sabbath Observers Association might do, "to locate employment for workers desirous of observing the Sabbath" and to "try to influence the owners of factories to employ Sabbath observers." Even more remarkably, the Agudath ha-Rabbanim countenanced concerted cooperation, the creation of a united front, with Jewish labor unions that shared little of, if they did not actively oppose, its religious values. The tacit deal that the UOR *proposed*—the rabbis were the initiators of the plan—to secular elements downtown was that

when there is a strike, the rabbis should influence the workers to include the right for Sabbath observance among their demands. In return for this, the organization will agree to support all the just demands of the workers. The rabbis will pressure the owners and employees to comply with the requests of the union.

The resisters also made concessions to the power of that most powerful of Americanizing agencies, the public schools. For the Agudath ha-Rabbanim, the ideal educational institution was always the old-world style yeshiva. There, its Constitution read that teachers who "must be Godfearing and their deeds in accordance with the Torah" would instruct their youthful charges in "Yiddish, the language of the children's parents." Of course, before entering his heder room, every teacher had to have "a certificate of approbation from one member of the Agudath ha-Rabbanim and two pedagogues . . . testify[ing] to his religious devotion and teaching abilities." Moreover, a "supervising committee" of the UOR was empanelled to be on hand to assure that Torah "study is properly organized so that the yeshiva students will truly succeed in their dedicated endeavors."

Yet, at the same time, in a partial bow to how the public schools ran their operations, the Constitution also spoke of the need "to draw up a proper curriculum for the various levels of study" making clear that "important topics must no longer be left in the hands of individuals on an ad hoc basis." The rabbis' organization also recognized the need for "a graded system of study so that teachers will no longer have various levels of students in one class." Through these moves the East European transplant was reformed with American pedagogic values and models in mind. Most importantly, they assented that when "necessary for the clarification of the topic, the teachers may also utilize English [and] in areas where only English is spoken, it may be the basic tongue." The *rebbes*, presumably rabbis and teachers with East European pedigrees, had to know the language of the new land. This skill would be of particular importance to UOR members who lived in communities like Omaha, Nebraska; Louisville, Kentucky; Denver, Colorado; Bangor, Maine; and Hazleton, Pennsylvania: locales far removed from the metropolis. (Only fourteen of the original fifty-nine members of the UOR hailed from the New York City area.) Moreover, back in New York, home to but two fledgling yeshivas, provision had to be made to teach "necessary . . . secular subjects" in their schools, albeit "by qualified instructors."

What sort of American training these general studies faculty had to have, became clear a year after the Agudath ha-Rabbanim's founding. Then it ruled that "graduates from the normal schools in the employ of the City Boards of Education" should be engaged to moonlight in the all-day yeshivas, a concession to United States law, if not customs.

Finally, while never gainsaying the yeshiva as the ideal educational institution, as early as 1903, the organization was also on record in support of "evening schools for those youths who work or attend secular schools by day," a systematic curriculum and financial support "for all talmud torahs and hedarim," as well as the need to establish Hebrew schools for girls.[8]

My evolving understanding that before the First World War, the UOR could consciously, and in good conscience, strive for certain ideals but did make pragmatic adjustments to American realities also may help explain one of the still unanswered questions that I originally raised in "Resisters and Accommodators." How were Rabbis Moses Sebulun Margolies and Philip Hillel Klein able to remain powerful in the Agudath ha-Rabbanim after they backed the founding of the New York Kehillah, a community-wide organization whose agenda and leadership the rabbinical association disdained?[9]

The story-line here dates to 1908 when this unique, inclusive American Jewish initiative reached out to the Orthodox community—as it did to all other Jewish groups in town—to join its coalition dedicated to solving the New York community's multifarious problems. As an inducement to allay Orthodox Jewish fears of the power and "assimilationist" influence of the German Jewish Reform lay leaders and rabbis who headed up this combine, the Kehillah promised to help its most traditional brethren solve two of their most pressing problems. Money, time and effort would be allocated to upgrade the quality of Jewish education and kashruth supervisions, two of the concerns that had undone poor Rabbi Joseph. Not surprisingly, local accommodationist rabbis agreed to cooperate with the endeavor. Just as predictably, the UOR stood apart from this cooperative venture. However, early on, two of its most distinguished officials, rabbis Margolies and Klein, long-term members of the UOR's own *Presidium* did sign up with the Kehillah. And, as influential rabbis they, arguably, had much to do with some twenty-three of the UOR's forty-six members joining the *Vaad ha-Rabbanim*, a Kehillah "committee of recognized and authoritative rabbis for the control of the whole matter of kashruth, *schechita*, and other religious matters."[10]

In 1983, I explained Margolies' and Klein's willingness to associate themselves with the Kehillah as emblematic of their own affinity for accommodationist values. After all, I reasoned these two rabbis did share pulpits with Orthodox Seminary men—Bernard Drachman and Mordecai Kaplan—in Americanized Orthodox synagogues. Moreover, in Margolies' case, several years before the Kehillah was started, this East European-trained rabbi was already a backer of modern Jewish educational initiatives. And both of these leaders stayed active in the New York Jewish Community's educational endeavors years after the *Vaad ha-Rabbanim* declined—with Margolies' and Klein's active assent—as a presence in the umbrella organization. I explained that these rabbis' willingness to stay as forces within the UOR as indicative of their "aspirations" as "astute communal politicians ... to maintain influence in all religious power bases, even going so far as to stand at the head of avowed anti-Americanization institutions."[11] By the way, I should have noted then, as I am doing now, that Margolies' and Klein's accommodationist views—like the ambivalence shown, decades earlier within the Chief Rabbi's court—offer evidence of multiple degrees of resistance within the transplanted East European rabbinic community. Still, my question remains—as it did in the original article—did not their Americanized perspective raise the hackles of the staunchest rejectionists within that camp and undermine Margolies' and Klein's credibility and power within the UOR's front?

Ultimately, the pragmatism of the Agudath ha-Rabbanim in the pre-First World War period explains Margolies' and Klein's unchallenged leadership. The organization could take a stout public stand against the Kehillah, as an opponent possessed of the wrong types of leaders and with dangerous possibilities. At the same time, it could recognize that umbrella organization as an institution that might be utilized to advance the rabbis' agenda in their all-important pursuit of order in kashruth with New York meat markets and increased enrollment in Orthodox Jewish schools. The UOR might even countenance some tweaking of the way Torah training was delivered in line with the Kehillah's modern techniques, so long as it remained the decisors of what constituted acceptable change.

After all, had not the Agudath ha-Rabbanim spoken, within its own forums some years earlier, about normal school teachers, curricular reform and graded class etc? Thus, Margolies and Klein retained their prestigious positions because most of their fellow East European rabbis understood that, in the end, some concessions to American realities were necessary even if these strategic retreats were never officially acknowledged. These esteemed rabbis may even have been respected for establishing boundaries for dealing with American realities within a resistant community.

Meanwhile, as I have continued to study Orthodox rabbis who accommodated the new world around them, the more I have realized that even as these advocates of flexibility concurred in their analysis of the problems America posed to the maintenance of traditional practice, they often disagreed over how much bending of the halakhah was permissible. Like their resistant brethren, they too were not of one mind-set and were far from a monolithic group. My ongoing investigations have also made clear that the impetuses that led to Orthodox accommodations differed over time reflecting in some eras the weakness and, in other contexts, the strength of that movement in America.

To detail but one example of variance among the "moderns," possessed of a long and suggestive history: while throughout much of the twentieth century, all accommodationists shared the view that the work patterns of most Orthodox synagogue members dictated some adjustments in the time and scope of Sabbath services, they sometimes disagree over the question of how much change was kosher. The long-standing dilemma was that in pursuit of economic mobility and well-being, many if not most, potential worshippers were out working when prayers normally took place. It was an unavoidable American reality.[12]

In meeting that challenge, I have found that there was general agreement that accommodating a working worshipper's desire to pray, with a *minyan*, before going off to labor on a Saturday morning was both permissible and possible. All that was required here, at these incipient "hashkamah minyans," was that those in charge open their doors at an early morning hour and ask no questions or otherwise embarrass miscreants who could not attend the regular eight or nine o'clock service.[13] Similar "don't ask, don't tell" social policies also informed creative Saturday afternoon synagogue programming that Americanized Orthodox rabbis and their students initiated in the first decade of the twentieth century. Here too, I determined that there was no discernible opposition or difference of opinion within American Orthodox ranks.

Where I have found that the accommodators differed with one another was over the question of how to reach out to potential worshippers who stayed on their jobs, or at their stores, until well after sundown on Friday evening. Here the problem was that halakhic guidelines precluded them from postponing Friday evening services. Rabbinic rulings meant a 4–5 p.m. start for *Mincha* (afternoon services) and *Kabbalat Shabbat* (the prayers welcoming the Sabbath) during the winter months, not the more convenient 8 p.m. slot.[14] But if they failed to adjust Orthodoxy's clock and mode of operations, these American Orthodox rabbis risked losing those who might turn out for services after work to rival Conservative and Reform congregations. For beginning as early as the 1920s, that after-dinner hour emerged as a religious prime time for American Jewish synagogue-goers. Among more affluent members of the community, moments of spiritual reflection, prayerful devotion and social interaction with fellow Jews at Friday night services were a fitting close to their mundane week and a bridge to a weekend of rest and recreation. Among these second generation Jews, now making their way toward middle class status, family religious protocol dictated that the Sabbath effectively would begin at home upon the arrival back from work of the major breadwinner—usually the father. Then, after a family meal at home, it was off to the house of worship with the next morning reserved for sleeping-in or possibly set aside for play out of doors.[15]

Of course, during the 1920s, many American Jews did not possess the luxury of weekend time on their hands. Moreover, during the Great Depression, many of those who had achieved much during the prior decade had to face "downward mobility and persistent economic insecurity," even if they did not experience unemployment.[16] Thus, for poorer and working class Jews, the 8 p.m. starting time offered a temporary respite from their continuing workday labors.

Facing up to these American social realities, and anxious to compete for congregants, many accommodationist Orthodox rabbis and congregations, in keeping with a tradition that I had identified back in 1983, relied upon a policy of "simulation" to stem the tide of disaffection. They integrated attractive features of more liberal Jewish practice into synagogue life without violating halakhic norms. Interestingly enough, even the often contrarian UOR, in a partial bow to the proclivities of the irreligious world around it, and the religious competitors that abounded, did not unconditionally condemn late Friday night "lectures." Incidentally, for us, that position is but another sign of tacit accommodation within that resistant organization.[17]

Of even greater significance, however, were those Orthodox ultra-accommodators, who standing as they did in a totally different corner of the Orthodox world, defined simulation in questionable terms. Here on the weighty question of what constituted the appropriate time for services, they demonstrated how variegated that Americanized camp of rabbis and congregations actually was. Indeed, I have found that in their quest for congregants they went so far as to veer away from the regulations of the Code of Jewish Law (*Shulkhan Arukh*). As important, some of their own Americanized colleagues defined those who went too far in their simulations as unworthy miscreants.

For example, in 1942, a harsh critic of these unconventional Orthodox synagogue practices, who was then touring the West Coast, wrote angrily of the "appeasement, compromise and surrender"—words that surely resonated with Second World War readers—within shuls that "add a Service of sorts, late Friday evenings for the so-called younger set." And to make matters worse, since this service was not "in accordance with a 'Din' [Jewish law] or 'Minhag' [Jewish custom] … [it] becomes a caricature, a cross between an entertainment and a religious display." These offenders permit "various innovations … the mixing of the sexes … a mixed choir … a microphone for convenience unconcerned with the problems of Sabbath sanctity." For Rabbi Isadore Goodman, "the path to conservatism [sic] and reform [sic] becomes open, with the specious excuse that we have to meet the popular desire and compete with the attractions of the Temple."[18]

Down South, in Atlanta, Georgia, the late Friday night service came into vogue at Congregation Ahavath Achim to meet not only the economic needs of congregants, but their social desires as well. In 1932, under the leadership of Rabbi Harry Epstein, this synagogue, reportedly, began conducting late Friday night services during winter time—sometimes at 6 p.m., other times at 8 p.m., but not at sundown to permit members "to attend the synagogue after work or before the theatre." And again, to exacerbate the matter from an Orthodox perspective, at these prayers, females were allowed to come down from the balcony and sit across the aisle from males. Together they participated in an innovative service, complete with songs, prayers, English responsive readings and, of course, an English language sermon. Here, not unlike among some Reform or Conservative Jews, there was a palpable desire to attend Sabbath worship while retaining time for other evening activities.[19]

However, for a long time these policies were not widely or officially condemned. For example, neither the Orthodox Union nor for that matter, the Rabbi Isaac Elchanan Theological Seminary castigated those congregations and rabbis that did far more than merely change the sociology of Orthodox synagogue life. Take Rabbi Epstein, for example. No renegade he, the Atlanta rabbi was a member of the national executive committee of the American Orthodox synagogue organization in the 1930s. And note the lack of angst in the very candid remark of Rabbi David de Sola Pool, an Orthodox Union Vice President, who, in 1942, admitted that "no logical or clear line can be drawn today between American Orthodoxy and Conservatism." For him, one of the sure signs of fluidity between groups as "American Orthodoxy . . . is adapting itself to the American environment" was "the late Friday evening service." Such an "innovation," he observed, "would have shocked the worshippers of a generation ago. Today such practices are accepted in numerous congregations." In other words, during the interwar period, even as a strand of accommodationists shared many of the religious values of Conservative Judaism, its actions and policies raised eyebrows in only some Orthodox circles. Arguably, when those with the Americanized Orthodox camp did not staunchly challenge those who had overstepped halakhic bounds, their quietude contributed to—when it did not underscore—the "fluidity" within Jewish denominational life that I have said characterized this period.[20]

By the same token, beginning in the mid-1940s, the issue of late Friday services-forums within Orthodoxy became a point of contention that helped darken the lines of demarcation between Orthodoxy and Conservatism and tighten the definition of acceptable behavior among accommodators. A first step took place in July 1944. Then a Committee on Rabbinical Practice of the Rabbinical Council of America (RCA)—basically the alumni association of rabbis trained at the Rabbi Isaac Elchanan Theological Seminary—was engaged "to study and draw up minimum standards for rabbinic and synagogal practice and conduct." Among the "practices" that necessitated "special clarification" were "mixed choirs," "mixed pews," "the use of a microphone" during Sabbath and Holiday services—elements common to Conservative synagogues—and "the method and program of late Friday evening religious forums." Four months later, the RCA's Executive Committee commissioned the preparation of a "booklet" on proper Forum procedures. A much more significant move toward concretizing standards for what could take place after sundown Friday night in American Orthodox synagogues took place in 1948, when the RCA's Halakhah Committee ruled "that the regular service at the onset of the Sabbath [*Kabbalat Shabbat* and *Maariv*] must be conducted at sunset for it was prohibited by Jewish law to be recited at late Friday night services."[21]

Through this later decision, the Rabbinical Council challenged those rabbis and synagogues that had previously behaved so much like their Conservative counterparts to conform or depart from Orthodoxy. Ultimately, for someone like Harry Epstein, the Council's policy—and maybe its threat—was not of much enduring moment. By the early 1950s this former member of the Rabbinical Council became far more comfortable in the Rabbinical Assembly and defined himself as a proud, committed, Conservative rabbi. So disposed, he influenced his Atlanta congregation to leave the Orthodox Union in 1952 and join the United Synagogue. From then on he would be no longer an Orthodox accommodator.[22]

However, a diversity of outlooks continued to obtain within accommodationist ranks. As it turned out, not all Orthodox synagogues either conformed to this Rabbinical Council of America ruling about late *Kabbalat Shabbat-Maariv* services or switched to Conservatism. Moreover, forums or quasi-services of various sorts continued to be part of the national Orthodox scene. Moreover, in some places they were, in fact, *instituted* in the late 1940s and 1950s as a weapon in that movement's battle against Conservative incursions.[23] For example, in Springfield, Massachusetts during the early 1950s, young rabbi Norman Lamm—destined to be, and identified in my 1983 article, as one of his generation's most thoughtful accommodationist leaders—devised his own version of an attractive Sabbath evening program. His mode of simulation was a way of heading off in his congregation even more substantial breaks with Orthodox tradition.

The story line here was that in the twenty or so years before Lamm's arrival, Kodimoh had been one of America's more idiosyncratic congregations. Its rabbi, Isaac Klein, was arguably one of the Jewish Theological Seminary's most traditional graduates. During Klein's long tenure at Kodimoh (1934–53), the synagogue affiliated neither with the Orthodox Union nor with the Conservative United Synagogue. The congregation evidenced fidelity to Orthodoxy through its *mehitzah* and an affinity for Conservatism through its 8 p.m. *Kabbalat Shabbat-Maariv* service.[24] In the early postwar period, however, Jewish Theological Seminary operatives opened "a Battle of the Seminary on the Springfield Front" at his Kodimoh synagogue.[25]

Faced with bubbling tensions and endemic factionalism, Lamm initially maintained the ritual status quo—including acquiescing to the Conservative Friday night service. But he quickly moved to create his own Orthodox alternative through eliminating *Borchu*, the public call to prayer, and the *Amidah*, the central part of the *Maariv* service. What he gave congregants were some highlights of the best known and loved parts of the Sabbath services as well as the *Shema*, Judaism's most basic creedal prayer; and *Kiddush*, the sanctification over wine. Maybe most significantly and cagily too, with an eye on the battle against Conservative incursions, during his program Lamm permitted men and women to sit together when they sang Sabbath songs or even when they recited the *Shema*. Since this gathering of Jews at Kodimoh was not truly a religious service, he was able to accommodate those who desired some sort of egalitarian seating patterns, though not during regular prayers and never in violation of the Orthodox understanding of Jewish law.[26]

The era of late Friday night services and forums in American Orthodox synagogues waned in the 1960s. The decline in the demand for such religious activities had much to do with a change in the make-up in that movement's rank and file. A "winnowing of American Orthodoxy"—to borrow a phrase from my 1984 article of the same name— was underway as more observant types *replaced* long-standing "nominal Orthodox" constituencies as their men and women in the pews. In some suburban communities, it had been those with "tenuous Orthodox attachments" who built those congregations in the first place during the first decade of postwar Jewish residential relocation. In the late 1960s, other Jews who were more committed to "Orthodox life patterns" arrived in suburbia and effectively took over these shuls. Not incidentally, these newcomers' possession of the economic wherewithal to leave their jobs or businesses to attend *Kabbalat Shabbat* and *Maariv* at sundown contributed substantially to their high religious profile. In this regard too, they were a new breed of American Orthodox Jews, more affluent than their parents and grandparents. Meanwhile, those in their synagogues who would then begin to leave Orthodoxy would find religious meaning and social satisfaction for themselves in other religious venues. They would ensconce themselves comfortably both within Conservative and increasingly traditional Reform congregations where 8 p.m. Friday night continued to be a religious prime time.[27]

Late Friday night religious experiences—this long-standing form of accommodation to non-observant Orthodox Jewish life styles—was destined to return to the synagogue scene in the early 1980s. But reflective of a very different era for American Orthodoxy, the implementers of these activities were not local rabbis and congregations pushing to meet the needs and demands of non-observant members. Nor was this a case of neighborhood Orthodox synagogues under pressure in stark competition with Conservatives and Reformers down their streets battling for the allegiances of local synagogue-goers. Rather, the rabbinic and lay operatives that initiated these activities were emblematic of a far more self-confident, and even aggressive, Orthodoxy on the move. In this venue, they were seeking to influence the many disconnected American Jews who were disinterested in all forms of synagogue life. Moreover, in this contemporary context, instead of fighting against Conservative and Reform leaders, these Orthodox activists, within their continent-wide efforts, often sought to find common cause with— if not to co-opt—their liberal religious counterparts. What has transpired in this context within the last quarter-century—or the more than twenty years since I wrote "Resisters and Accommodators"—has sensitized me to always consider the specific and changing atmospherics that engender accommodationist responses.

The leadership of the Lincoln Square Synagogue on New York City's upper West Side was the driving force behind this new era outreach effort. In 1980, this congregation inaugurated its "Turn Friday Night into Shabbos" program for what it hoped would be a largely youthful, single, and upwardly mobile audience. This intense and attractive religious experience would typically begin not at sundown Friday evening, but at a more convenient hour for young professionals on the make, shades of the old "Forums."[28]

Seven years later, with the help of a Jewish philanthropic foundation, Lincoln Square offered its now tested program to synagogues throughout the United States and Canada. By 1996, it had involved some fifty Orthodox congregations and a "few right-wing Conservative synagogues" in its activities.[29] But ultimately these ambitious Orthodox operatives were out for even larger game. Reconstituted as a not-explicitly Orthodox group in 1997, their National Jewish Outreach Program (NJOP), a "non-denominational organization," sought to "enlist some 300 synagogues and temples" on the same Friday night to its "Shabbat Across America" event. Conservative, Reform and Reconstructionist rabbis did not oppose the NJOP's subtle incursion into their religious space, at least within the 200 or so liberal congregations that signed on.[30]

Still, problems remained in implementing what was ultimately an inter-denominational Jewish endeavor, particularly in a present day climate where Jewish leaders of all expressions are often at loggerheads with each other. Would's the Reform, and even some of the Conservative congregations, accede to the NJOP "respectful request" that "in the spirit of Jewish unity and program uniformity that the meals served be kosher and that shabbat [as Orthodoxy defined it] be observed" even as all parties understood that "it would be impossible to insure that all congregations and organizations will not be *mechalel Shabbos* [desecrate the Sabbath] in some way?" More critically, how would these new era accommodationists' efforts be received within a growing resistant Orthodox community that generally looked askance at religious, and even Jewish political, interaction with Conservative and Reform Jews?[31]

To bolster their position and mission, the NJOP turned to two senior rabbis for high-level approbation. Rabbis Zelig Epstein and Dovid Cohen signed off on this endeavor in the spirit "that many thousands of Jews would benefit from this Shabbos experience, and the publicity value of every Jew in America being invited to a Shabbos meal would be immeasurable."[32] Still, elements within its own contemporary Orthodox community have been outspoken about the NJOP's friendly approach and openness to Conservative, Reform, and Reconstructionist congregations as constituting tacit recognition of the legitimacy of other Jewish religious movement.[33]

In the end, here, as it was for at least the last sixty years, attitudes toward late Friday night synagogue religious activities under modern Orthodox auspices serve as a point of demarcation among the resisters and accommodators who make up that most traditional of Jewish movements in America.

Notes

1. Jeffrey S. Gurock, "Resisters and Accommodators: Varieties of Orthodox Rabbis in America, 1886–1983," *American Jewish Archives* 35 (1983): 109–15, here 108.

2. Jonathan D. Sarna, "Introduction," *American Jewish Archives* 35 (1983): 91–9, here 92.

3. Jeffrey S. Gurock and Jacob J. Schacter, *A Modern Heretic and a Traditional Community, Mordecai M. Kaplan, Orthodoxy and American Judaism* (New York: Columbia University Press, 1997), 10–15, 19.

4. Jeffrey S. Gurock, "How 'Frum' Was Rabbi Jacob Joseph's Court? Americanization Within the Lower East Side's Orthodox Elite, 1886–1902," *Jewish History* (1994): 255–64.

5. Gurock, "How 'Frum,'" 263–4.

6. On *Agudath ha-Rabbanim* presence and activity at the Zionist conference, see *American Jewish Year Book* 5663 (1902–3): 101–2 and "List of Delegates," *The Maccabaean* (June 1902): 337–8.

7. Jeffrey S. Gurock, "American Orthodox Organizations in Support of Zionism, 1880–1930," in *Zionism and Religion*, ed. Shmuel Almog, Jehuda Reinharz, and Anita Shapira (Hanover, NH, Boston, and Jerusalem: Brandeis University Press in association with the Zalman Shazar Institute for Jewish History, 1998), 219–24.

8. All quotations from the "Constitution of the United Orthodox Rabbis of America: Organized 24th of Tamuz 5662 in New York," in Aaron Rakeffet-Rothkoff, *The Silver Era in American Jewish Orthodoxy: Rabbi Eliezer Silver and his Generation* (Jerusalem and New York: Yeshiva University Press and Feldheim Publishers, 1981), 317–20. See that document also for the names and home bases of its fifty-nine founders.

9. Gurock, "Resisters," 122.

10. Arthur A. Goren, *New York Jews and the Quest for Community: The Kehillah Experiment, 1908–1922* (New York: Columbia University Press, 1970), 50–1. See also, Gurock, "Resisters," 119–20.

11. Gurock, "Resisters," 120.

12. On Sabbath work patterns of Orthodox synagogue members, see Jeffrey S. Gurock, "Twentieth-Century American Orthodoxy's Era of Non-Observance, 1900–1960," *The Torah U-Madda Journal* 9 (2000): 87–94.

13. On guilt-ridden Jews praying on the Sabbath before going off to work, see Herbert S. Goldstein, ed., *Forty Years of Struggle for a Principle: The Biography of Harry Fischel* (New York: Bloch, 1928), 17–19 noted in Jonathan D. Sarna, *American Judaism: A History* (New Haven, CT and London: Yale University Press, 2004), 163.

14. On the halakhic issues regarding Kabbalat Shabbat and Maariv services after sun-down Friday night, see Norman Lamm, "The Late Friday Night Service in the Light of the Halacha," *Yeshiva University Rabbinic Alumni Chavrusa* (September 1956): 5–6.

15. On the achievement of middle-class status by the children of immigrants during the 1920s and the connection between residence and place of work in their new neighborhoods, with specific reference to New York, see Deborah Dash Moore, *At Home in America: Second Generation New York Jews* (New York: Columbia University Press, 1981), 30–6.

16. Beth Wenger, *New York Jews and the Great Depression: Uncertain Promises* (New Haven, CT and London: Yale University Press, 1996), 17.

17. Oscar Z. Fasman, "This Friday Night Forum," *The Orthodox Union* (February 1944): 4–7. For a UOR spokesman's opinion of the late service phenomenon, see Samuel Aaron Pardes, "Ha-Hiluf ve ha-temurah," *Ha-Pardes* (December 1930): 5–6.

18. Isadore Goodman, "Trends in Orthodoxy," *The Orthodox Union* (June, 1942): 8–9.

19. Kenneth Stein, *A History of Ahavath Achim* (Atlanta, GA: Standard Press, 1978), 44, discussed in Jeffrey Gurock, *From Fluidity to Rigidity: The Religious Worlds of Conservative and Orthodox Jews in Twentieth Century America* (Ann Arbor, MI: Jean and Samuel Frankel Center for Jewish Studies, University of Michigan, 1998), 26. See also on the time of the services, Mark K. Bauman, *Harry H. Epstein and the Rabbinate as Conduit for Change* (Rutherford, Madison, and Teaneck, NJ: Farleigh Dickinson University Press, 1994), 54.

20. On the Union's toleration of Epstein, see Gurock, *From Fluidity to Rigidity*, 26, 53, note 85 which indicates that as of 1936–37, Epstein was a member of the Union's national executive committee. See also, David De Sola Pool, "Judaism and the Synagogue," in *The American Jew: A Composite Portrait*, ed. Oscar Janowsky (New York and London: Harper and Brothers, 1942), 50–4.

21. Minutes of the Executive Committee of the Rabbinical Council of America, July 11, 1994, November 30, 1944 (records housed at the offices of the RCA, New York City). Phone interview with Rabbi David Hollander, December 9, 2004 (tape of interview deposited in the Yeshiva University Archive). Hollander recalls that he worked on the booklet, but to the best of his knowledge, it was never published. There is no extant record of this booklet having been, in fact, published. See also, Louis Bernstein, *Challenge and Mission: The Emergence of the English Speaking Orthodox Rabbinate* (New York; Shengold Publishers, 1982), 42–3.

22. Bauman, *Harry S. Epstein and the Rabbinate*, 60, 92.

23. For an example of the institutionalization of a late Friday night "Forum," as a weapon against Conservative growth in a small Southern city, see Jeffrey S. Gurock, *Orthodoxy in Charleston: Brith Sholom Beth Israel and American Jewish History* (Charleston, SC: College of Charleston Library, 2004), 32, 41, 46–7.

24. For a biographical sketch of Isaac Klein, see Pamela S. Nadell, *Conservative Judaism in America: A Biographical Dictionary and Sourcebook* (New York, Westport, CT and London: Greenwood Press, 1988), 159–60. There is no record in published lists of United Synagogue members of Kodimoh joining that organization. Indeed, the United Synagogue affiliate in Springfield beginning in the 1910s and continuing into the 1930s was Beth El. See on such membership lists, *Third Annual Report, The United Synagogue of America* (1915), 45 and *Report Seventeenth Annual Convention of the United Synagogue of America, May 19–21* (1929), 14. Kodimoh did not join the Orthodox Union until 1961 but did join the Yeshiva University Synagogue Council in 1956, during Lamm's era. On Klein's sense that he ministered to an ideologically split community, see Klein to Finkelstein, November 14, 1934. (Isaac Klein's Rabbinic Alumni File, Library of the Jewish Theological Seminary.)

25. On the Seminary's campaign to capture Kodimoh, see Max Arzt to Klein, February 2, 1945. (Isaac Klein's Rabbinic Alumni File, Library of the Jewish Theological Seminary.)

26. Interview with Dr. Norman Lamm, December 20, 2004 (tape of interview on deposit at the Yeshiva University Archives). See also *The Kodimoh Guide to Song and Hymn for Sabbath Eves* (Springfield, MA: Congregation Kodimoh, n.d. c. 1954); *A Book of Prayers and Zemiros for Congregational Use of Friday Nights* (Springfield, MA: Congregation Kodimoh, n.d. c. 1954). All of these documents are in Dr. Norman Lamm's personal files. I am indebted to Dr. Lamm for opening his records and for sharing his memories with me.

27. Jeffrey S. Gurock, "The Winnowing of American Orthodoxy," in *Approaches to Modern Judaism II*, ed. Marc Lee Raphael (Chico, CA: Scholars Press, 1984), 41–54. On the relationships between nominal and committed Orthodox Jews in 1980s American Jewish communities, see Samuel C. Heilman and Steven M. Cohen, *Cosmopolitans and Parochials: Modern Orthodox Jews in America* (Chicago and London: University of Chicago Press, 1989), 40–1; Samuel C. Heilman, "Orthodox Jews, the City and the Suburb," *Studies in Contemporary Jewry* 15 (1999): 19–34, here 22–3; and Gurock, *From Fluidity to Rigidity*, 33–8.

28. The texts of these advertising pitches were derived from ephemeral flyers and enrollment blanks from the 1980s all created by Lincoln Square Synagogue. [Files of the National Jewish Outreach Program, hereafter NJOP.] I am indebted to rabbis Yitzhak Rosenbaum and Ephraim Buchwald for making these and other documents relating to their work available to me.

29. "Lincoln Square Synagogue Awarded $65,000 Grant to Promote 'Turn Friday Night into Shabbos' on a National Level" (press release of the Avi Chai Foundation, May 27, 1987 on deposit at NJOP). Phone interview with Yitzhak Rosenbaum, December 9, 2004.

30. On the history of the National Jewish Outreach program, see "Shabbat Across America/ Canada Reaches Out to North American Jews," press release of NJOP, February 21, 2004 (www.njop.org). For the nature of the activities at these gatherings, see Rabbi Ephraim Z. Buchwald and Rabbi Yitzhak Rosenbaum to HaRav Zelig Epstein, 5 Sivan, 5756 (1996), document on file at NJOP. Yitzhak Rosenbaum provided the number of non-Orthodox synagogues that initially participated in the program. On the problems of assimilation and disaffection that motivated synagogues to join the program, see "(Synagogue) Hosts 'Shabbat Across America/ Canada," press release of NJOP, December 9, 2004.

31. On the acknowledged difficulties the NJOP faced in enforcing its protocol on Sabbath observance among non-Orthodox synagogues, see Ephraim Buchwald to Rabbi (Dovid) Cohen, January 15, 1996.

32. See Buchwald to Cohen, January 15, 1996 and Buchwald and Rosenbaum to Epstein, 5 Sivan, 5756 (1996).

33. Reflective of this resistant position was the following editorial, "A Proposed Addition to the Agudah Convention Agenda," *The Jewish Press* (November 6, 2002), online edition.

CHAPTER 14

EXPORTING YIDDISH SOCIALISM: NEW YORK'S ROLE IN THE RUSSIAN JEWISH WORKERS' MOVEMENT[1]

Tony Michels

From the late 1880s to the early 1900s, Jewish socialists in the United States shipped thousands of Yiddish newspapers, journals, and pamphlets to the Russian Empire. The literature was used to spread revolutionary ideas and secular knowledge among a relatively small but growing number of Russian Jews drawn into the nascent Jewish workers' movement. The movement's leaders would surely have preferred to produce their own literature, but they lacked the means, personnel, and political freedom to do so effectively. They therefore looked abroad for assistance. Jewish socialists in England, Germany, and Austria-Hungary played important roles in producing and transporting illegal literature into Russia. Most of the reading materials, however, came from the United States, specifically from New York City. By providing an ample supply of Yiddish publications, New Yorkers successfully exported socialism to Russian Jews.

Previous historians, Jonathan Frankel most notably, have drawn attention to New York's role in the early Russian Jewish workers' movement, but the subject has yet to be examined thoroughly. Which publications were sent? How did they reach Russia and circulate once there? What influence, if any, did they exert? By exploring those questions, this chapter seeks to uncover a formative moment in the history of radical Jewish politics on both sides of the Atlantic. Jewish socialists in New York and, to a lesser extent, London provided crucial materials for the operation of the nascent workers' movement. Indeed, these materials encouraged Russian Jewish revolutionaries to employ Yiddish in the first place. This is not to claim that the Russian Jewish movement came into existence only because of support from New York and London. Rather, it is to argue that Jewish socialists in New York and London played a pivotal role in the movement's early development. That Russian Jewish revolutionaries were willing to risk long prison sentences by trafficking in Yiddish socialist literature from abroad may be taken as recognition of its importance.

The leading role of New York in exporting Yiddish socialist literature to Russia suggests the need to revise the standard view of American Jewry as an outpost of European Jewry. According to that view, the cultural, ideological, and political life of immigrant Jews amounted to little more than a replica—and a pale one at that—of European originals. In fact, a tremendous degree of innovation took place in immigrant Jewish communities, so that what might appear to have been European carryovers were in fact American inventions. A Yiddish commercial newspaper market, certain forms of Yiddish literature (such as protest poetry), and the Jewish labor movement itself arose in the United States well before their emergence in Russia. Moreover, these developments reverberated across the Atlantic. Works of Yiddish fiction, plays, and popular science, in addition to socialist propaganda, were shipped to Russia in large quantities starting in the 1890s.[2] Taken together, this body of literature indicated a significant penetration of American Yiddish culture into Russia. Scholars have just begun to explore how American Yiddish literature, broadly defined, might have influenced its Russian counterpart, but they have firmly established its presence there. Yiddish moved from west to east, not just the other way around.

Thus, instead of a core-periphery model for understanding the relationship between American and Russian Jewry, it would be more helpful to adopt a transnational framework in which individuals, ideas, publications, money, and organizations moved between countries, sometimes in one direction, other times reciprocally.[3] A transnational approach need not negate the significance of the nation as an analytical frame, although some historians have aimed to do just that.[4] On the contrary, New York's role in exporting Yiddish socialist literature demonstrates that both local and national contexts structured how (and why) Jews on both sides of the Atlantic interacted with one another. The rise of a mass Jewish labor movement in New York, Chicago, Philadelphia, and other cities in the mid-1880s, almost ten years before the birth of the Russian Jewish workers' movement and fifteen years before it grew into a significant force, can only be understood in light of the specific combination of forces that obtained in American cities: the extremely rapid, large-scale concentration of Jewish immigrants; their proletarianization in the booming garment industry and other areas of America's robust economy; the practical support offered by preexisting, non-Jewish labor and socialist organizations; the marginal standing of rabbis in immigrant Jewish life; the absence of an entrenched Jewish communal authority that might oppose radicalism; and the freedom, guaranteed by the Constitution, to engage in protest and voice dissent.[5] If these factors draw attention to the salience of local and national contexts, then the growing American involvement in Russian political, economic, and religious (via missionary activity) affairs serve as a reminder that American Jewish ties to Russia, by no means limited to support for the revolutionary movement, paralleled the United States' expanding power overseas.[6] Transnational Jewish politics, in other words, did not transcend place. The local, the national, and the transnational operated as three interrelated planes. By uncovering the flow of Yiddish socialist publications from New York to Russia in the 1890s, this chapter brings to light an important moment in the development of transnational ties between American and Russian Jews.

1

Sometime in or around 1887, the Russian censor in charge of foreign publications issued a ban on a Yiddish newspaper from New York City named *Di nyu-yorker yidishe folkstsaytung* (henceforth, *Di folkstsaytung*). The weekly, founded in June 1886, was the first left-wing Yiddish newspaper of any significance in the United States. The person responsible for shipping it to Russia was Shmuel Rabinovitsh, a Jewish revolutionary from Warsaw living in Paris. Rabinovitsh discovered *Di folkstsaytung* and another Yiddish newspaper, London's *Arbeter fraynd*, in a friend's apartment no more than two months after *Di folkstsaytung's* debut. Both publications made a strong impression on Rabinovitsh, if for no other reason than he had never seen a Yiddish newspaper before, let alone a politically radical one. At that time, only one poorly circulated Yiddish newspaper existed in the Russian Empire.[7] Rabinovitsh's discovery inspired him to order ten copies each of *Di folkstsaytung* and *Arbeter fraynd*, which he shipped to a comrade in Warsaw who, in turn, dispatched them to Bialystok, Brisk, Minsk, and Vilna. It is not known how many individuals saw the newspapers or how they responded, but the government censor in St. Petersburg made his reaction clear. He promptly banned *Di folkstsaytung* (*Arbeter fraynd* seems to have eluded authorities at that point) for its "very harmful" criticism of the tsar and praise for Russian revolutionaries. The Russian government thus recognized that a new, potentially subversive phenomenon—Yiddish-language socialism—had arrived from the West.[8]

Di folkstsaytung and *Arbeter fraynd* were among the first Yiddish socialist publications to reach the Russian Empire, but many more would follow. In 1887, Rabinovitsh translated a Polish-language pamphlet entitled *Kto z czego zyje?* (Who Lives By What?), authored by S. Dikshtein. Printed on *Arbeter fraynd's* press, 500 copies of *Kto z czego zyje?* came out under the Yiddish title *Fun vos eyner lebt?* Rabinovitsh sent several bundles of *Fun vos eyner lebt?* for distribution within the Russia Empire. He himself smuggled a larger quantity across the Russian border as part of a shipment of illegal newspapers and pamphlets in German, Polish, Russian, and Yiddish, including, once again, *Di folkstsaytung* and *Arbeter fraynd*. Rabinovitsh's translation of *Fun vos eyner lebt?* would become a staple of Yiddish socialist propaganda in the Russian Empire, reprinted perhaps as many as eighteen times over the following four decades. The *Bund* (the General Jewish Labor Union in Lithuania, Poland, and Russia) alone printed a total of 15,000 copies in 1900 and 1905. Rabinovitsh's activities, however, were cut short in July 1888, when authorities arrested him in Kovno during his second smuggling mission. He spent the next fifteen months in jail, followed by ten years in Siberia.[9] Importing socialism to the Russian Empire, in Yiddish or any other language, was a dangerous undertaking.

At the time of Rabinovitsh's arrest, the Russian Jewish workers' movement existed only in embryonic form. In Vilna, Jewish revolutionaries had started to conduct propaganda—intensive education in political economy, Marxism, natural science, and the Russian language—for small numbers of Jewish workers, with the expectation that they would eventually become revolutionary propagandists themselves. The Russian-speaking intellectuals who created such study groups, or circles, did not originally intend to build an all-Jewish movement. However, because of the social and cultural gulf separating Jews from gentiles, Vilna's revolutionaries—identifying themselves formally as the Vilna Social Democratic Group—operated entirely among Jewish workers. By 1892, the Vilna Social Democrats consisted of about sixty to seventy intellectuals who belonged to secret groups of ten to fifteen members each. About 150 Jewish workers participated in study circles and, a year later, some 300 Jewish workers were organized into *kassy*, quasi-unions that originated as strike funds. The shoots of a Jewish workers' movement thus began to sprout in the late 1880s, though its leaders did not think of it as such. In their eyes, the Vilna Social Democrats were Russian revolutionaries who happened to conduct propaganda among Jews.[10]

In late 1893, the Vilna Social Democrats embarked on a major change in tactics that would lead directly to the creation of an autonomous, Yiddish-speaking workers' movement. The group's leadership decided to switch from a policy of propaganda to one of agitation, two terms that carried distinct meanings in the lexicon of Russian Marxism. As explained by Gregory Plekhanov, the leading Russian Marxist of the time, "A propagandist gives *many* ideas to one or a few people while an agitator gives only one or only a few ideas but to the masses of people."[11] Agitation required spreading socialism on a broad scale and organizing workers into unions, on the grounds that workers could best develop class consciousness through action as well as study. The Vilna Social Democrats accepted Plekhanov's position. In the preceding years, there had been a sharp increase in the number of strikes among Jewish workers in various cities, lending credence to Plekhanov's argument. Polish socialists had also started to build a workers' movement in Warsaw, and this too had an influence.[12]

The move from propaganda to agitation necessitated a shift in language from Russian to Yiddish, the spoken language of the vast majority of Jewish workers. Jewish revolutionaries had used Yiddish occasionally since the 1880s, facilitated perhaps by publications from abroad such as *Di folkstsaytung* and *Fun vos eyner lebt?* But the new program committed the Vilna Social Democrats to using Yiddish concertedly, for the purpose of creating a popularly based, autonomous Jewish workers' movement—a Jewish branch of the Russian revolutionary movement rather than a "recruiting ground" for it.[13] The Vilna group's new program proved to have far-reaching results. Following Vilna's example, Jewish Social Democrats in Bialystok, Minsk, Odessa, Warsaw, and other cities established local Yiddish-speaking workers' organizations that would, in 1897, unite to create the Bund, the first Jewish political party in Russia and the forerunner to the Russian Social Democratic Workers' Party.[14] According to one calculation, a total of 2,500 Jewish workers were organized in Vilna and Minsk by 1897; six years later, the Bund's membership may have surpassed 30,000.[15]

Yet, as important as the turn to agitation was, the Vilna Social Democrats were ill prepared to embark on their new program. Few of the group's leaders could speak Yiddish well, if at all, and suitable reading material in the language barely existed. Several activists had established a Yiddish library in the fall of 1893, but the collection of roughly fifty volumes contained mostly works of fiction and not a single title on socialism, political economy, or philosophy.[16] The Vilna group did not own a hectograph until July 1894 or a printing press until May 1897.[17] The intellectuals who led workers' study circles often relied on handwritten Yiddish translations of Russian booklets. Yet those texts, produced ten to fifteen copies at a time, were in such short supply that group leaders frequently had to translate them on the spot for participants. In desperate instances, intellectuals tried to memorize a Russian work in advance of a meeting and recount it later in Yiddish. Their translations often left much to be desired, amounting to "gibberish," according to A. Litvak, an important mid-level activist.[18]

The Vilna group made several successful efforts to produce their own literature in the mid-1890s. In 1895, for instance, it established the Zhargonisher Komitet (Jewish Vernacular Committee) "to spread good literature among Jewish workers, found Yiddish workers' libraries in the provinces, and publish popular scientific and belletristic books in Yiddish."[19] During its three years of existence, the Zhargonisher Komitet legally published eight booklets through a sympathetic printer in Warsaw: one each on history, philosophy, and political economy, and five on popular science. With the exception of A. Litvak's *Vinter ovntn* (Winter Evenings), a well-received, two-part series on popular science, all the titles were translations from Polish and Russian.[20] The Zhargonisher Komitet also published a number of illegal pamphlets on socialism through an arrangement with a Jewish socialist group across the border in the Galician city of Lemberg. The pamphlets were written in Vilna, printed in Lemberg, and then smuggled back into Russia.[21] Similarly, the Zhargonisher Komitet established a close relationship with a publishing association in Berlin called Tsayt-gayst. Established in 1898 by the Yiddish writer Dovid Pinsky, Tsayt-gayst published three booklets on physiology, two on Darwinism, and one volume containing two short stories by Pinsky. In addition, the Zhargonisher Komitet used fictional works by Pinsky and Y. L. Perets, both of whom had introduced working-class themes into Yiddish literature during the 1890s.[22] Finally, the Vilna group issued its own news organs, such as the handwritten *Nayes fun rusland*, five issues of which appeared in 1894, and *Der yidisher arbeter*, which was printed abroad in runs of 1,000 copies starting in late 1896.[23]

The Vilna Social Democrats thus made some progress during the mid-1890s, but the organization was far from self-sufficient. They faced constant difficulties caused by a shortage of resources, government censorship, and police repression. On a single night in December 1896, for instance, policemen arrested five members of the Zhargonisher Komitet, one of whom later committed suicide in prison. The committee ceased to exist in 1898.[24]

Unable to achieve self-sufficiency, the Vilna Social Democrats and other Jewish socialist organizations looked to older Jewish socialist movements in New York City and London for assistance. Russian Jewish revolutionaries had, since the late 1880s, gained some sense of the political and cultural ferment happening in the West from personal correspondence, word-of-mouth, and publications in Russian and Yiddish. At a minimum, they knew that popular Jewish workers' movements existed in New York and, on a smaller scale, London and that those movements produced Yiddish publications that could be used in the Russian Empire. New York and London would, soon enough, become the main suppliers of Yiddish socialist literature to Russia.[25]

Of the two cities, New York was the more important. Although London gave rise to the first Jewish socialist group, the Hebrew Socialist Union, in 1876, the first Jewish tailors' union, and the first labor-oriented Yiddish newspaper, *Der poylisher yidl*, socialism and unionism never took hold among London's immigrant Jews on a large scale. The Hebrew Socialist Union disbanded within a year, and subsequent socialist groups were short-lived or debilitated by factionalism. *Der poylisher yidl* was superseded by the outspokenly socialist *Arbeter fraynd* in 1885, but the latter newspaper appeared irregularly by the early 1890s. Meanwhile, trade unions came and went with each round of strikes. As the historian Elyohu Tcherikover writes, "The internal strife, chaotic conditions of work, and consistent failures led to disillusionment and passivity."[26] Frustrated by repeated failures, most of London's leading Jewish radicals relocated, one by one, to New York City, further contributing to London's diminished status in the 1890s. The fact that anarchists predominated over Marxists in London's Jewish labor movement also served to undermine London's influence in Russia. The Marxists who founded and led the Vilna movement had no use for anarchist publications. They naturally wanted ideologically agreeable materials, and those could be found most readily in New York.

New York's Jewish labor movement began in 1885 with the creation of the Jewish Workingmen's Association (JWA). Aided by German immigrants, who provided much in the way of ideological guidance, money, and institutional models, members of the JWA made significant strides in 1886 during a nationwide upsurge in strikes known as "The Great Upheaval." The JWA organized thirteen unions, and two of its members started the aforementioned weekly, *Di folkstsaytung*. Although the JWA, its unions, and *Di folkstsaytung* died out between 1887 and 1889, the newborn Jewish labor movement flourished in the following decade. During the 1890s, tens of thousands of immigrants demonstrated, joined unions, voted for socialist candidates, read left-wing publications, and participated in myriad educational and cultural activities. The movement's core consisted of three interlocking institutions: the United Hebrew Trades (an umbrella organization of Yiddish-speaking unions inspired by the United German Trades), the Arbeter Tsaytung Publishing Association (which published the weekly *Di arbeter tsaytung* and the daily *Dos abend blat*), and the Yiddish-speaking branches of the Socialist Labor Party (which sponsored the monthly *Di tsukunft*). All of those organizations were Marxist in orientation and aligned with the German-dominated Socialist Labor Party, the mainstay of American socialism in the late nineteenth century.[27] Freed from the kinds of constraints imposed on their Russian counterparts, New York's Jewish socialists emerged as powerful leaders of the city's burgeoning Yiddish-speaking population. If one were to identify a capital of Jewish radical politics in the late nineteenth century, it would have to be New York City.

Jewish socialists in New York and London produced three kinds of publications: newspapers, journals, and pamphlets. (Little appeared in book form in the 1880s and 1890s.) One of the earliest and most popular pamphlets to reach Russia was *Yehie or* (Let There Be Light), authored by Morris Vintshevsky, pseudonym of Lipe Ben-Tsien Novakhovitsh (1856–1932). Vintshevsky began his literary career in Hebrew but adopted Yiddish after he moved to London in 1879. He wrote *Yehie or* in that year, though it would not appear in print until late 1884 or 1885. The pamphlet was reissued in Newark, New Jersey, in 1890—four years ahead of Vintshevsky's move to the United States—and both editions were used in Russia.[28]

Yehie or begins with a declaration of socialist principles modeled after Maimonides' "Thirteen Articles of Faith." "I believe with perfect faith," one article reads, "that whoever profits by the labor of his fellow man without doing anything for him in return is a willful plunderer." Another states, "I believe with perfect faith that women will remain the slaves of men, or their playthings, as long as they depend on the will of others instead of enjoying the fruit of their own labor." The remainder of *Yehie or* is a dialogue between the fictional narrator, named Morris Vintshevsky (henceforth the author's permanent nom de plume), and his friend Hyman. During the course of their conversation, "Vintshevsky" poses a number of naïve questions to Hyman, who uses the opportunity to expound on the injustices of capitalist society. Hyman begins on a personal level, decrying the ravages of poverty on children, the elderly, and workers. Somewhat skeptical, "Vintshevsky" asks if poor people themselves are not at least partially responsible for their plight because of their excessive drinking, gambling, and criminality. Hyman corrects him, explaining that poor people are driven to destructive behavior by poverty, not the other way around. Capitalist society is turned around—a *farkerter velt*—where a small number of people own too much wealth and the majority has too little. An individual might succeed in working his or her way out of poverty, Hyman acknowledges (knowing that many Jewish workers strove to do just that), but, even so, an individual's good fortune cannot solve society's problems. With that point, Hyman moves from the personal to the sociological. Capitalism, Hyman tells his friend, causes endemic problems. Machines force human beings out of their jobs, fluctuations in production create unemployment, and large corporations lead to great concentrations of wealth and power. The only solution, Hyman declares, is the abolition of wage labor and private property. "Vintshevsky" walks away from the conversation convinced.[29]

Yehie or secured Vintshevsky's reputation as the "grandfather of Jewish socialism" among radicals on both sides of the Atlantic. Using an accessible, colloquial Yiddish, he formulated an engaging critique of capitalism without straying into the realm of abstraction. It was easily understandable and had an air of common sense. The pamphlet went over well in Russia, as did at least one other by Vintshevsky, *Der alef-beys fun treyd-yunyonizm* (The ABC of Trade-Unionism, 1894). His poetry and essays—notably, the series "Tseshlogene gedanken fun a meshugenem filozof" (The Mixed-up Thoughts of a Crazy Philosopher)—were also widely read within the Jewish workers' movement.[30]

If Vintshevsky was the first Yiddish socialist pamphleteer, Benyomen Faygnboym (1860–1923) can be considered the most prolific. Born into a poor, Hasidic family in Warsaw, Faygnboym joined the Jewish workers' movement in London before immigrating to New York in 1891. The former yeshivah student specialized in withering critiques and parodies of Judaism and its alleged inconsistencies, superstitions, and hypocrisies. His parody of the traditional Passover Haggadah, *Hagode shel peysakh al pi nusakh khadash* (The Passover Haggadah According to the New Version, 1888), offers an excellent example. In response to the Haggadah's customary Four Questions, Faygnboym's version asks:

> Why are we worse than Shmuel the factory owner, Meir the banker, Zorekh the moneylender, and Todros the rabbi? They do nothing but eat and drink, day and night, at least a hundred times, and we toil with all our strength the whole day, and at night we do not eat, not even once.

Why do they have great palaces, decked out and appointed with every comfort, many beautiful rooms that stand empty—and we lie suffocating in a hole, and they still want to throw us out?

Why do they do nothing and yet wear the most expensive clothes—and we toil like oxen and do not even have shirts on our backs?

Why do they eat a good lunch, drink a good glass of wine, and go to sleep in a soft, warm bed—and we are confined to a corner on a straw mattress just so we can get up again for work?[31]

Later in the Haggadah, Faygnboym proposes universal brotherhood as an alternative to religion. "Who knows one?" the traditional Passover Haggadah asks in reference to God, to which Faygnboym responds, "I know one: there is but one humanity in the world."[32] These ideas were nothing if not heretical, but they evidently found appreciative readers. Faygnboym's Haggadah went through four printings in as many cities: London (1888), New York (in modified form, 1896), Geneva (1900), and Kraków (1919).[33] An 1896 report by the Vilna Social Democrats confirms that Faygnboym's Haggadah was read in workers' study circles. Another two of his pamphlets, possibly *Gezets der antviklung* (Law of Evolution, 1890) and *Der sotsyalizmus fun alef biz tes* (Socialism from A to Z, 1894)—a reworking of Karl Kautsky's *Erfurt Program*—were known to have circulated in Russia.[34]

Perhaps Faygnboym's most widely read pamphlet was *Dos gan-eyden hatakhtn: A vunderlekhe emese mayse, vi men iz dergangen dem veg tsum gan-eyden af der velt, un vi mentshn forn ahin* (Paradise on Earth: A Wonderful True Story about How the Road to Paradise Was Found, and How We Can All Get There). With a print run of 3,000 copies, *Dos gan-eyden hatakhtn* was commissioned by a group called the Jewish Socialist Post from America to Poland. The group was created on the initiative of the Polish Socialist Party (PPS), whose leaders, Jozef Pilsudski chief among them, had taken an interest in organizing Jewish workers. Pilsudski hoped to win Jews over to the cause of Polish independence and prevent the spread of Russian cultural influence by promoting the use of Yiddish by Jewish revolutionaries. Toward that end, Pilsudski gave the Vilna Social Democrats their first hectograph and facilitated contact with socialists in Lemberg, the same individuals who eventually printed several of the Zhargonisher Komitet's publications. For its own use, the PPS smuggled 167 Yiddish pamphlets into Russia in 1893 and 788 in 1894.[35] The party failed, however, to sway the Vilna group to its program and consequently decided to establish its own Jewish Section to propagate socialism in Yiddish. At the Jewish Section's urging, the party sent an emissary to New York in 1896 to garner support, which led to the creation of the Jewish Socialist Post from America to Poland. Faygnboym, a PPS sympathizer, was recruited to write *Dos gan-eyden hatakhtn*. The pamphlet's purpose was to convince readers that they should view gentile workers as potential friends and comrades, not as threatening goyim.[36] Through the fictional character of a *folks-mentsh* (ordinary Jew), Faygnboym explains the importance of class solidarity: "To you, poor Jewish artisans, workers from Poland and Russia, your brother, the local Christian worker, is extending his brotherly hand, and asks you to understand that he is rebelling not against you ... but against the rich capitalist thieves, whether Polish, Russian, German, or Jewish."[37] The pamphlet proved successful and, a year after its publication, one of Faygnboym's earlier pamphlets, *Vi kumt a yid tsu sotsyalizmus?* (The Path of a Jew to Socialism, 1891), was reprinted in 3,000 copies for use by the PPS.[38]

In addition to pamphlets by Faygnboym and Vintshevsky, a number of others were known to have reached Russia. Abraham Cahan, the leading figure in New York's Jewish labor movement, contributed no fewer than three titles: *Loyn arbet un kapital* (a loose translation of Marx's *Wage Labor and Capital,* first published in serialized form in 1886); *Vemens got iz beser? A vikuekh tsvishn a rov un a galekh* (Whose God Is Better? An Argument between a Rabbi and a Priest, 1890); and *Der iker fun sotsyalizmus un der kamf far im* (The Fundamental Principle of Socialism and the Struggle to Achieve It, 1892). Philip Krants,[39] editor of the first socialist Yiddish daily in New York, produced at least two pamphlets: *Vos heyst sotsyal-demokratye?* (What Is Social Democracy?, 1892), and *Di lebens bashraybung fun Grinevetski, velkher hot geharget dem dritn kayzer* (The Biography of Grinevetski, Who Assassinated Alexander II, 1892). The titles cited above do not represent a complete bibliography but are a sampling based on available sources.

In addition to pamphlets, New Yorkers supplied educational journals, the aforementioned *Di tsukunft* most importantly. The socialist monthly provided the closest thing to a general secular education available anywhere in Yiddish. Hundreds of articles on political economy, philosophy, all branches of science, and, to a lesser extent, literature and literary criticism appeared in the journal between 1892 and 1897, when it ceased publication until 1902.[40] "The Rise of the Proletariat in America," "On the American Women's Movement," "How Scientific Socialism Has Evolved," "Work and Leisure," "Crime and Criminals," and "The Evolution of Nations" were some of the many *visnshaftlekhe* (scientific) articles that appeared in *Di tsukunft*. Intentionally scholastic, *Di tsukunft* must have been more challenging to read than Vintshevsky's *Yehie or* or Faygnboym's *Dos gan-eyden hatakhtn*. Nonetheless, the magazine, which used a straightforward, albeit often dry, Yiddish, was a staple of socialist propaganda in the Russian Empire, read in workers' study circles and by individuals hungry for secular knowledge.[41] (According to one account, Krants' series "God, Religion, and Morals" was well received by a group of yeshivah students who used to gather in the woods to read the magazine.)[42] Short-lived but similar journals also found their way into Russia. Hundreds of copies of the socialist *Di naye tsayt* and London's *Fraye velt* are said to have circulated in Russia before they became defunct.[43] *Di tsukunft*, however, appeared most consistently and was the most widely read of the three journals.

Yiddish newspapers provide the final examples of socialist literature exported to Russia. Although rarely mentioned in primary accounts, perhaps because of their ephemeral character, newspapers reached Russia in untold numbers, starting with the aforementioned *Di folkstsaytung* and *Arbeter fraynd*. We may surmise that newspaper articles were, on the whole, too topical and specific to America for use in study circles and agitational meetings. Newspapers, however, were important as sources of poetry, which was often recited or sung at workers' gatherings. Most popular were the so-called

Sweatshop Poets, such as Vintshevsky, Dovid Edelshtat, Morris Rosenfeld, and Yoysef Bovshover, who wrote lyrics of an explicitly radical nature, quite unlike traditional folk songs. Whereas folk songs lamented the hardships of daily life, the Sweatshop Poets condemned, albeit not in any uniform way, capitalist exploitation and urged workers to protest against it. Edelshtat's "Wake Up!," published originally in the New York anarchist weekly *Di fraye arbeter shtime* in 1891, provides an example:

How long, oh, how long will you slave and still wait,
Chained in shame and in dread!
How long will you splendid treasures create
For those that rob you of bread?!

How long will you bow, unable to rise,
Debased, with no home and no right!
Day dawns! Wake up! Oh, open your eyes!
Discover your ironclad might!

Proclaiming the freedom of strong barricades,
Let war against foul tyrants be!
Brave comrades, courage and will pervades
And leads you to victory!

The chains and the thrones must all fall away
Under the workers' sword!
With fragrant flowers, in golden array,
Freedom is the earth's reward.

And all will live and love and bloom
In freedom's golden May!
Brothers, don't kneel! See the tyrants' doom!
Swear you'll be free as the day!

Strike everywhere the freedom bell!
Let suffering slaves feel their might!
Inspired in struggle, struggle like hell—
For yourself, for your holiest right![44]

Such poems inspired newly radicalized Jewish workers and activists, who eagerly circulated newspaper clippings and handwritten transcriptions. "Singing agitation," A. Litvak recounts, "spoke more to the heart of the primitive worker" than pamphlets, journals, or lectures.[45] He may have exaggerated his point, but it stands to reason that most workers derived greater enjoyment and inspiration from a rousing poem than, say, a historical survey on the development of social classes. In short, New Yorkers and

Londoners provided the lyrics—if not the melodies, which were usually adopted from Russian songs—of Jewish workers' protest in Russia.[46]

Large quantities of socialist Yiddish literature were smuggled into Russia, but how did it get there? It is worth noting that Jewish members of revolutionary populist organizations, such as Bread and Freedom, had been involved in smuggling as far back as the 1870s. "It was the Jews," the historian Leonard Schapiro writes, "with their long experience of exploiting conditions on Russia's western frontier, which adjoined the Pale, for smuggling and the like, who organized the illegal transport of literature, planned escapes and illegal crossings, and generally kept the wheels of the whole organization running."[47] Thus, activists in the 1890s may have benefited from accumulated experience, learning directly or indirectly from older Jewish revolutionaries involved in other organizations.

The smuggling process often began with Russian Jewish émigrés, typically university students, residing in Austria-Hungary, Germany, and Switzerland. School holidays and Jewish holidays, such as Passover, provided opportune times to transport materials back home. Smugglers would often strap contraband to their bodies or hide it under false bottoms inside their suitcases. In that way, an individual might carry as much as twenty pounds of literature inside a single bag.[48] Larger quantities of literature were smuggled across the border by horse and wagon, driven by Jews who lived in towns near the Russian border.[49] In case of detection, false covers with innocuous titles and incorrect publication information were often attached. For instance, the actual title of Faygnboym's *Dos gan-eyden hatakhtn*, translated here into English, was *The Socialist Movement in Russia and the Local Jewish Population: A Propaganda Brochure Published for Distribution among the Jewish Workers in Russia in General, and in Russian Poland in Particular*. Likewise, instead of using the real publication date, the decoy cover gave a publication year of 1875—that is, almost two decades before the rise of the Russian Jewish workers' movement.[50]

Within Russia, couriers brought literature to various locations. Libraries, for instance, offered effective mechanisms of distribution. With the growth of the labor movement in the second half of the 1890s, workers' libraries appeared in a growing number of cities and towns. In 1897, Vilna boasted several workers' libraries, in addition to two general libraries containing 500 books. Minsk was home to two workers' libraries, which, notably, contained works by Edelshtat and Rosenfeld.[51] In addition to libraries, bookstores were used to disseminate illegal literature. The Zhargonisher Komitet, for instance, stashed some of its publications in the back of a small store in Vilna that sold religious articles and prayer books. The owner's daughter had ties to the local Social Democratic organization and, unbeknownst to her father, used his store as a meeting place for visiting activists who would exchange information and retrieve packages. Between 1898 and 1901, another bookstore in Vilna, which sold "everything more or less interesting that was published in Russia and America," served as a "center of illegal activity" until the police closed it down.[52] Old-fashioned *pakn-tregers*, or book-peddlers, also played a part in the dissemination of illegal literature. Pakn-tregers mostly sold religious books and popular fiction, but, by the late 1890s, some of them began to carry socialist literature, not necessarily because they sympathized with the contents but because they perceived a growing demand for works on popular science, political thought, social problems, and worker-oriented fiction. One member of the Zhargonisher Komitet himself took to peddling the committee's wares in and around Vilna.[53] Finally, couriers sometimes left copies of illegal literature around town in specific locations, such as yeshivahs and synagogue study halls, where rabbinical students would gather to socialize or relax.[54] Borukh Tsukerman, for example, remembers studying in one such *beysmedresh* in Vilna when a stranger arrived with a bundle of proclamations and a pamphlet by Faygnboym on "religion and class contradictions." Intrigued by the pamphlet ("I knew what the word 'religion' meant, but 'class contradictions'—this word I met for the first time"), Tsukerman undertook to read it surreptitiously.[55] In short, a mixture of traditional means (book-peddling) and new outlets (workers' libraries) were used to distribute literature produced by or associated with the Jewish workers' movement. All methods were risky. Authorities did not necessarily distinguish between legal and illegal publications if they suspected one was linked to the other. "At every opportunity," Anna Rozental, a member of the Zhargonisher Komitet, recalls, policemen "confiscated booklets and arrested their distributors."[56]

Did Yiddish socialist literature from abroad exert any influence? Tcherikover, who in 1939 published a groundbreaking article on illegal Yiddish literature, maintained that American publications had "a comparatively small influence on the Jewish workers in Russia."[57] Tcherikover offered several reasons. First, socialists across the ocean could not maintain the kind of sustained, direct contacts needed to exercise a substantial influence. Second, writers in New York used a Germanized Yiddish (*daytshmerish*) that was unintelligible to Russian Jews. Finally, New York socialists promoted a "vulgar" assimilationist perspective, which could only alienate Russian Jewish workers who, on the whole, were traditional in orientation and retained strong Jewish group attachments. Tcherikover, in other words, considered New York's Yiddish socialist literature poorly written and ideologically objectionable.[58]

Tcherikover's conclusions can be questioned in several respects. Although numerous socialists employed *daytshmerish* in their writings, not all did so.[59] Tcherikover cited only one example: a translation of Ferdinand Lassalle by Krants. Other, more widely read authors, such as Vintshevsky, Faygnboym, and Cahan, wrote excellent colloquial and literary Yiddish. Indeed, in a different context, Tcherikover praised Faygnboym's Yiddish as "very good for that time."[60] *Daytshmerish*, furthermore, did not necessarily deter readers. Immigrant Jews in the United States initially found *daytshmerish* extremely difficult but soon learned to read it, as reflected in the steep rise in Yiddish newspaper circulation during the 1880s and 1890s. Their desire to read trumped the difficulties of reading. If that held true in the United States then one can infer that Russian Jewish workers, particularly those motivated enough to join an underground movement, also acquired the skills needed to read the peculiar language of the American Yiddish press. In any case, the use of *daytshmerish* diminished during the 1890s as writers increasingly employed a more natural Yiddish. Cahan, Faygnboym, and Vintshevsky were among those who led the way.[61]

Finally, Tcherikover overstated the prevalence of assimilationist perspectives in the literature produced in New York. True, many socialist intellectuals believed on principle in the complete assimilation of Jews into the larger working class. Yet few preached that goal consistently or in a crude manner. Faygnboym attacked Judaism, but he was an exception among his peers, who commonly avoided Jewish subjects altogether. *Di tsukunft*, for instance, which was edited mostly by Cahan, preferred publishing "scientific" articles, which socialists understood as a more effective way of spreading secular knowledge than direct assaults on religion. Furthermore, certain writers, Vintshevsky most notably, even evinced sympathy for Jewish nationalism.[62] We must also consider the possibility that the ideal of proletarian internationalism, if only as a vague concept, appealed to at least some individuals from traditional backgrounds, like Faygnboym himself. The fact that his Haggadah went through multiple printings suggests that atheism and universalism found interested, even appreciative, readers. Whatever the case, Tcherikover offered almost no evidence for his contentions. He presumed that Russian Jewish readers found little of value in New York's socialist Yiddish literature because he disapproved of its style and content.

Without doubt, literature from New York suffered from deficiencies in the eyes of Russian Jewish readers. The bundist leader Frants Kursky used to poke fun at American Yiddish pamphlets, not because of their difficulty or objectionable ideas but because of their flimsy content. Kursky and his associates spoke of "American *vaserizatsye*" (watered-down socialism), a play on the term *popularizatsye*, or popularized socialism. In addition, there can be no doubt that Russians would have preferred literature specifically adapted to their social and cultural context. That Russian Jewish revolutionaries sometimes modified literature they received from abroad—Faygnboym's Haggadah is a case in point—indicates a certain degree of dissatisfaction. Even so, attitudes seem to have been generally positive. Kursky himself acknowledged that fellow party members generally "loved" *Di tsukunft*.[63] The bundist writer Shakhne Epshteyn (later a communist leader in the Soviet Union and the United States) admitted that pamphlets from New York contained some flaws, which he left unspecified, but that *Di tsukunft* was a very effective tool nonetheless. "The first pioneers of the Jewish workers' movement in Russia," Epshteyn wrote in 1912, "not having their own literature or a very significant one, had to depend on the American Yiddish revolutionary literature for help in their educational work. For beginners, raw elements, this literature was tailor made."[64] In Epshteyn's opinion, New York's socialist Yiddish literature had merit (even if suitable only for beginners, as he implied) and played an indispensable role in spreading socialism in Russia. Sholem Levin, a revolutionary in Minsk, recalls that he and his comrades regarded each new issue of *Di tsukunft* as a "true holiday."[65] The Jewish Social Democratic group in Warsaw reported in 1896 that it distributed "the entire American socialist Yiddish literature, especially *Di tsukunft*."[66] And, as noted above, American Yiddish poetry, a type of literature Tcherikover barely considered, met with perhaps the greatest enthusiasm. Thus, according to contemporaries, New York's publications, whatever their flaws, found an appreciative audience in Russia. Without them, the Jewish workers' movement could not have functioned as well as it did.

How individual readers responded to Yiddish socialist literature is difficult, probably impossible, to assess conclusively. Nonetheless, one can reasonably conclude that it more or less achieved the intended purpose of radicalizing and secularizing workers. Regarding this point, it should be kept in mind that socialist literature was not meant for a mass audience but rather for a relatively small number of recruits to an illegal movement. Those recruits were, by definition, members of a self-selected group prepared to accept new ideas and values associated with socialism: secular education, class solidarity, and egalitarianism. This is not to suggest that workers passively received ideas presented to them. Individuals most certainly brought personal perspectives to a given text (or a lecture based on certain texts), interpreting it differently from the intended meaning.[67] Even so, eclecticism and ideological deviation from officially sanctioned interpretations seem to have diminished the longer one remained in the movement, where members received sustained tutelage in party ideology. Alexander Bittelman, best known as a leader of the American Communist Party, provides an example. Bittelman joined the Bund in Berdichev in 1902 at the age of 13, shortly after he became a bar mitzvah. He continued to practice Judaism even after he joined the Bund, not perceiving any contradiction between piety and socialism; nor did he face any pressure from local party leaders to abandon religion. Yet during his first year in the party, questions arose in Bittelman's mind. "It didn't look quite right to me," he recollects, "to continue paying tribute to the Almighty—reading prayers with the Tefillin on me, going to synagogue on Saturdays and holidays, and observing various religious rules—and at the same time participating in a socialist organization that was non-religious and atheist."[68] Eventually, Bittelman "took leave of [his] religious ideas and beliefs."[69] Bittelman did not necessarily represent all those party members and sympathizers who moved within the Bund's orbit, but it is fair to conclude that the overall socialist message, as absorbed through reading, discussions, lectures, and social and cultural rituals, gained acceptance from year to year. To put it simply: it is clear from the growth of the Jewish workers' movement, and the Bund specifically, that an increasing number of Jews came to identify with Marxism in some sense, although the ways in which Jewish workers understood the specifics of Marxism as part of a new worldview requires further research.[70]

Yiddish socialist literature in New York may be considered important in another respect: its sheer availability encouraged Russian Jewish revolutionaries to adopt Yiddish in the first place. As Julius Martov, one of the leading Vilna Social Democrats, indicates in his memoir, the group's 1893 turn to agitation was undertaken on the presumption that it could "make use of the socialist Yiddish literature coming out in London and New York."[71] Jonathan Frankel has elaborated Martov's point: "The ability of [immigrant Jews] in London—and much more spectacularly in New York—to create a self-supporting Yiddish press and Yiddish-speaking trade-union movement inspired growing respect. Nothing succeeds like success, and in the years 1891–95 socialists throughout eastern Europe sought to repeat what had been achieved in the East End and the Lower East Side."[72] Frankel's insight is important for understanding the eastward influence from New York and London. Jewish socialists in those cities not only helped Russian Jews to disseminate socialism, but they also helped to legitimate the idea of using Yiddish as an instrument of socialist agitation. "The decision to create a Yiddish-speaking labor movement in Lithuania," Frankel concludes, "can largely be explained in terms of the overseas example."[73]

2

New York's influence seems to have been strongest during the Jewish workers' movement's infancy in the 1890s. With the establishment of the Bund in October 1897, its rapid growth in the early 1900s, and the easing of censorship after the 1905 revolution, Russian Jewish revolutionaries—not only bundists but also members of all the new, post-1905, left-wing Jewish parties—produced their own ramified party literatures.[74] To be sure, literature from New York continued to flow into Russia, perhaps in even larger quantities than before. To take just one example, all of the Bund's major branches as well as imprisoned party members in Siberia regularly received copies of *Di tsukunft* between 1907 and 1914.[75] Nonetheless, after 1905, the role of New York publications seems to have been supplemental, filling in gaps in the overall body of Yiddish literature produced in Russia, rather than indispensable. Dependency on New York had come to an end.[76]

Nonetheless, Russian Jewish revolutionaries continued to rely on Jews in the United States in other respects. Escalating violence against Jews, mounting class conflict, and political protest brought tens of thousands of Jews into revolutionary political parties in and around the 1905 revolution. The Bund grew dramatically in size in the years between 1903 and 1907, reaching some 33,000 members, and its expenses increased accordingly. The party needed funds for self-defense groups, propaganda, aid to pogrom victims, strike funds, and other day-to-day operations.[77] The Bund conducted extensive fundraising campaigns in the United States, amid even wider efforts among American Jews to raise funds for pogrom victims that had started in response to the 1903 Kishinev pogrom. Within the context of a highly mobilized, outraged Jewish population, groups such as Friends of the Bund, Central Union of Bundist Organizations, the daily *Forverts*, and Arbeter Ring (a mutual aid society) raised tens of thousands of dollars. Between the fall of 1905 and the spring of 1906, party representatives collected at least $35,000, some of which went toward the purchase of weapons from a Cleveland manufacturer. The Central Union of Bundist Organizations raised another $11,500 by 1907. A report to the Bund's annual convention in 1906 estimated that up to half the money used by local party organizations came from American donors.[78]

Apart from the Bund, other revolutionary parties conducted extensive fund-raising campaigns in the United States. Even non-Jewish parties, such as the Russian Social Democratic Workers' Party and the Party of Socialist Revolutionaries, relied heavily on Jewish support. In 1904, for instance, the Socialist Revolutionaries sent Katerina Breshkovskaia (widely acclaimed as the grandmother of the Russian Revolution) and Chaim Zhitlovsky to the United States as emissaries and, tellingly, based their operations on the Lower East Side, where support was expected to be strongest. Indeed, Zhitlovsky, the foremost socialist theoretician of Yiddish cultural nationalism, was chosen to accompany Breshkovskaia precisely because of his Jewish ties (although she also generated much interest beyond the immigrant Jewish scene). The two raised about $10,000 over five months, a substantial portion of which was used to purchase weapons. In 1906, the Socialist Revolutionary leader Nikolai Tshaikovsky embarked on another fund-raising tour for the party, which, again, met with greatest success among Jews. The failure of gentiles to offer the desired level of support prompted Mark Twain to remark to Tshaikovsky that Christians "have lost our ancient sympathy with oppressed peoples struggling for life and liberty."[79] Maxim Gorky, who came to the United States as a representative of the Bolshevik wing of the Russian Social Democratic Workers' Party, praised Jews as "the most influential bearers and representatives of the new religion, socialism."[80] After the tsar's overthrow and the ensuing civil war, American Jewry lent tremendous financial and technical assistance to Soviet reconstruction efforts. Sidney Hillman, president of the Amalgamated Clothing Workers of America and a former member of the Bund, established the Russian-American Industrial Corporation in 1922 to rebuild Russia's garment industry. During its first two years, the corporation invested two million dollars in the modernization of thirty-four factories employing 17,500 workers.[81] American Jews, socialist and not, gave millions of dollars to the Joint Distribution Committee and other bodies for various aid projects, including the creation of agricultural communes for Russian Jews.[82]

Looking back, then, the export of Yiddish socialist literature from New York to Russia may be seen as the beginning of more extensive efforts to aid the Russian revolutionary movement and, after 1917, Soviet reconstruction efforts. The interplay between Jewish socialists on both sides of the Atlantic expanded into ties with the larger Russian revolutionary movement and, after the Bolshevik seizure of power, Soviet Russia itself.

Notes

1. This chapter originally appeared as an article in *Jewish Social Studies* 16 / 1 (2009): 1–26, and I would like to thank the publisher for the permission to reprint it in this volume. I would also like to thank Hasia Diner, Francine Hirsch, Neil Kodesh, Cecile Kuznitz, Kenneth Moss, David Sorkin, Sarah Stein, and Scott Ury for commenting on drafts of this chapter. Unless otherwise indicated, all translations from Yiddish sources are mine.

2. Hagit Cohen, "The USA-Eastern Europe Book Trade and the Formation of an American Yiddish Cultural Center," *Jews in Russia and Eastern Europe* 2 / 57 (2006): 52–84; Eric J. Goldstein, "'Shmates for Sale': American Imprints in Imperial Russia" (paper presented to the Association for Jewish Studies' annual conference, Dec. 2004); Nina Warnke, "Going East: The Impact of American Yiddish Plays and Players on the Yiddish Stage in Czarist Russia, 1890–1914," *American Jewish History* 92 (2005): 1–30.

3. For recent transnational approaches to American Jewish history, see Rebecca Kobrin, *Jewish Bialystok and Its Diaspora* (Bloomington and Indianapolis, IN: Indiana University Press, 2010), 1–18; Adam Mendelsohn, "Tongue Ties: The Emergence of the Anglophone Jewish Diaspora in the Mid-Nineteenth Century," *American Jewish History* 93 (2007): 177–209; and Daniel Soyer, "Transnationalism and Mutual Influence: American and East European Jewries in the 1920s and 1930s," in *Rethinking European Jewish History*, ed. Jeremy Cohen and Moshe

Rosman (Oxford and Portland, OR: Littman Library of European Jewish Civilization, 2009), 201–20. On the role of Jews in trans-Atlantic business networks, see Sarah Abrevaya Stein, *Plumes: Ostrich Feathers, Jews, and a Lost World of Global Commerce* (New Haven, CT and London: Yale University Press, 2008), 1–27.

4. See, e.g., David Thelen, "The Nation and Beyond: Transnational Perspectives on United States History," *Journal of American History* 86 (1999): 965–75, here 967. On the debate over immigrants and transnationalism, see David G. Gutierrez and Pierette Hondagneu-Sotelo, "Nations and Migration," *American Quarterly* 60 (2008): 503–21.

5. Eli Lederhendler, *Jewish Immigrants and American Capitalism, 1880–1920: From Caste to Class* (Cambridge and New York: Cambridge University Press, 2009), 38–84; Tony Michels, *A Fire in Their Hearts: Yiddish Socialists in New York* (Cambridge, MA: Harvard University Press, 2005), 7–16.

6. David C. Engerman, *Modernization from the Other Shore: American Intellectuals and the Romance of Russian Development* (Cambridge, MA: Harvard University Press, 2003), 17–102; David S. Foglesong, *The American Mission and the Evil Empire* (Cambridge and New York: Cambridge University Press, 2007), 7–45.

7. *Dos yidishes folksblat*, 1881–90. In 1881, members of Narodnaia Volia (People's Will) published the first revolutionary newspaper in Yiddish, *Di arbeter tsaytung*, but it is likely that only one issue appeared and was seen by very few individuals. A. Kirzhnits, "Der onheyb fun der sotsyalistisher prese in Yidish in Rusland," *Biblyografisher zamlbukh* 1 (1930): 61–4; Elias Tcherikover, "Di onheybn fun der umlegaler literatur in Yidish," *Historishe shriftn* 3 (1939): 578.

8. Shmuel Rabinovitsh, "Mit 50 yor tsurik: Fragmentn fun zikhroynes," *Historishe shriftn* 3 (1939): 229–30. The government decree appears, undated, in the original Russian with Yiddish translation, and with an introduction by E. Tcherikover, in *Historishe shriftn* 3 (1939): 801–3.

9. Rabinovitsh, "Mit 50 yor tsurik," 336–40.

10. Ezra Mendelsohn, *Class Struggle in the Pale: The Formative Years of the Jewish Workers' Movement in Tsarist Russia* (Cambridge and London: Cambridge University Press, 1970), 32; Joshua D. Zimmerman, *Poles, Jews, and the Politics of Nationality* (Madison, WI: University of Wisconsin Press, 2004), 45.

11. Quoted in Jonathan Frankel, "The Polarization of Russian Marxism (1883–1903): Plekhanov, Lenin and Akimov," in *Vladimir Akimov on the Dilemmas of Russian Marxism, 1895–1903: Two Texts in Translation*, ed. and trans. Jonathan Frankel (Cambridge and London: Cambridge University Press, 1969), 3–73, here 17.

12. Jonathan Frankel, *Prophecy and Politics: Socialism, Nationalism, and the Russian Jews, 1862–1917* (Cambridge and London: Cambridge University Press, 1981), 185–98; Mendelsohn, *Class Struggle in the Pale*, 47–8; Henry J. Tobias, *The Jewish Bund in Russia: From Its Origins to 1905* (Stanford, CA: Stanford University Press, 1972), 22–5; Zimmerman, *Poles, Jews, and the Politics of Nationality*, 47–53.

13. Frankel, *Prophecy and Politics*, 187.

14. Between 1893 and 1897, the new Vilna program "gradually won almost universal approval from the leading revolutionary Marxists in Russia." Frankel, "Polarization of Russian Marxism," 20.

15. Tobias, *Jewish Bund in Russia*, 37, 239.

16. The library contained only one book on history (a translation of Heinrich Graetz's *Volkstümliche Geschichte der Juden*), one on science (astronomy), and two books on "social questions" (producers' cooperatives). The library survived about six months. A. Litvak, "Di 'Zhargonishe komitetn,'" *Royter pinkes* 1 (1921): 9.

17. L. Yevzerov, "Di yidishe arbeter bavegung in datn (1876–1922)," in *25 yor (1897–1922): zamlbukh* (Warsaw: farlag Di velt, 1922), 112; Zimmerman, *Poles, Jews, and the Politics of Nationality*, 31. See Sholem Levin, "Finf yor in umlegale drukerayen," *Royte bleter* 1 (1929): 1–7, for a first-person account of the Bund's early underground presses. (Note: each article in *Royte bleter* is numbered separately.)

18. A. Litvak, "Di krayzlekh," in *Geklibene shriftn* (New York: Arbeter Ring, 1945), 209. A. Litvak was the party name of Khayim Yankl Helfand (1874–1932).

19. A. Litvak, "Di 'Zhargonishe komitetn,'" 19.

20. Ibid., 22–4; Anna Rozental, "Bletlekh fun a lebns-geshikhte," *Historishe shriftn* 3 (1939): 433–4. See also L. Berman, *In loyf fun yorn* (Warsaw: Dvinsker "Bund" Branch 75, Arbeter Ring in America, 1936), 172.

21. Tcherikover, "Di onheybn fun der umlegaler literatur," 592, 589. On Jewish socialists in Galicia, see Frankel, *Prophecy and Politics*, 169–70, 176–7, and Yoysef Kisman, "Di yidishe sotsyal-demokratishe bavegung in Galitsye un Bukovine," in *Di geshikhte fun Bund*, 5 vols., ed. G. Aronson et al. (New York: Unzer Tsayt, 1966), Vol. 3: 337–480.

22. A. Litvak, "Di 'Zhargonishe komitetn,'" 9–13; Tcherikover, "Di onheybn fun der umlegaler literatur," 580–1; Dovid Pinski, "A 'zhargon' farzamlung," *Dos naye lebn* (Dec. 1912): 37–9.

23. Tcherikover, "Di onheybn fun der umlegaler literatur," 584–6; Tobias, *Jewish Bund in Russia*, 46–7.

24. A. Litvak, "Di 'Zhargonishe komitetn,'" 25.

25. Frankel, *Prophecy and Politics*, 194.

26. Elias Tcherikover, *The Early Jewish Labor Movement in the United States*, trans. and ed. Aaron Antonovsky (New York: YIVO, 1961), 199.

27. Anarchists had a small movement of their own, consisting of political clubs, educational societies, and the weekly *Di fraye arbeter shtime*. Unlike the Marxists, however, they lacked a strong base of support in trade unions and attracted far fewer followers. Michels, *A Fire in Their Hearts*, 68–124.

28. "Materyaln far der kharakteristik fun der arbeter-bavegung ba undz in shtot (Vilna) far di letste 4–5 yor," reprinted in *Di sotsyalistishe literatur af Yidish in 1875–1897*, ed. Shmuel Agurski (Minsk, 1935), Vol. 2: 64, Tcherikover, "Di onheybn fun der umlegaler literatur," 336, 600. Although an anarchist group republished *Yehie or* in New Jersey, Vintshevsky himself was a social democrat.

29. Morris Vintshevsky, *Yehie or* (Newark, NJ: 1890). Located in collection M-2, folder 46A, Bund Archives, YIVO Institute for Jewish Research.

30. Frants Kurski, "Di 'Tsukunft' in untererdishe Rusland," in *Gezamlte shriftn* (New York: Veker, 1952), 258–9.

31. *Hulyot* 2 (Summer 1994): 234.

32. Haya Bar-Yitschak, "Hearot le-hagadat ha-pesakh shel ha-Bund," *Hulyot* 2 (Summer 1994): 255–71, here 257. The quotations are from the fourth edition of the Haggadah, published by the Bund in 1900 with minor changes and reprinted in *Hulyot* 2 (Summer 1994): 239, 243.

33. Bar-Yitschak, "Hearot le-hagadat ha-pesakh shel ha-Bund," 255–7.

34. "Materyaln far der kharakteristik fun der arbeter-bavegung," 64. Mention of the use of *Hagode shel Peysakh* in Minsk can be found in Khanke Kopelyovitsh (Khane Levin), "Der onheyb fun kamf," *Royte bleter* 1 (1929): 3. Two of Faygnboym's other pamphlets known to have reached Russia were *Vi kumt a yid tsu sotsyalizmus?* and *Di yidishe hilf*.

35. Zimmerman, *Poles, Jews, and the Politics of Nationality*, 30–1.

36. Faygnboym's introduction is reprinted as "B. Faygnboym un di 'Yidish-sotsyalistishe post fun Amerike,'" in *Historishe shriftn* 3 (1939): n.p.

37. Quoted in Zimmerman, *Poles, Jews, and the Politics of Nationality*, 130.

38. Tcherikover, "Di onheybn fun der umlegaler literatur," 600; Zimmerman, *Poles, Jews, and the Politics of Nationality*, 127–8, 146–7. Tcherikover refers to the group as the Jewish Socialist Post from America to Russia, but Zimmerman's is the better-researched account. Tcherikover, "Di onheybn fun der umlegaler literatur," 600, n. 74. Faygnboym's biography of George Washington, published in book form, was also available in Russia legally; see Cohen, "USA-Eastern Europe Book Trade," 61.

39. Yakov Rombro (1857–1922).

40. On the relative dearth of "scientific" literature in Russia compared to the United States, see Sh[muel] Niger, "Sotsyalistishe oyfklerungs-literatur," *Di tsukunft* (Oct. 1941): 43.

41. A. Litvak, "Di krayzlekh," 209. Additional examples of Russian Jewish readers of *Di tsukunft* are L. Bernshteyn, *Ershte shprotsungen* (Buenos Aires: Yidbukh, 1956), 80; I. S. Pomerance, "Autobiographical Notes" (1942), p. 20 (RG 102, YIVO Institute for Jewish Research); and Dr. Samuel Siegel, autobiography (1942), p. 98 (RG 102, YIVO Institute for Jewish Research).

42. Shakhne Epshteyn, "Di 'Tsukunft,' Der 'Bund' un di yidishe literatur," *Di tsukunft* (Jan. 1912): 69.

43. Tcherikover, "Di onheybn fun di umlegaler literatur," 600. *Di naye velt* is a rare example of an anarchist journal used in the Russian Jewish workers' movement.

44. In *Sing, Stranger: A Century of American Yiddish Poetry*, ed. Benjamin Harshav, trans. Barbara Harshav and Benjamin Harshav (Stanford, CA: Stanford University Press, 2006), 66–7. On Yiddish folk songs, see Ruth Rubin, *Voices of a People: The Story of Yiddish Folksong* (Philadelphia: Jewish Publication Society of America, 1979), 278–309.

45. Bernshteyn, *Ershte shprotsungen*, 81; A. Litvak, "Di rol fun der revolutsyoner lid in der arbeter bavegung," in *Yidishe literatur*, ed. N. Oyslander et al. (Kiev: Kultur Lige, 1928), 324. A. Litvak recalls being taken aback by a group of matchmakers on strike in Pinsk who were so eager to see poetry by Edelshtat and Vintshevsky that they "simply tore" the texts from his hands. He cites the following as among the most popular songs: by Edelshtat, "Vi kum ikh, brider, freylekhn zingen," "Oh guter fraynt, az ikh vel shtarbn," "In shturem un drang," "O muze, ruf mikh nit," "Mir vern gehast un getribn," "Tsum Sofia Perovskaia," and "Arbeter-froyen"; by Vintshevsky, "Tsum Arbeter-fraynd," "Oh, du geduld," "Di marsellaise," "Az di velt vet vern yunger," and "A bezim un a ker"; and by Rosenfeld, "Der opereyter" and "Ikh hob a kleyne yingele."

46. Although New Yorkers predominated, the Russian Jewish labor movement eventually began to produce its own poets, most notably the Minsk-based activist and writer Avrom Lesin, who debuted in 1896. Lesin, however, moved to the United States in 1897.

47. Leonard Schapiro, "The Role of the Jews in the Russian Revolutionary Movement," *The Slavonic and East European Review* 40 (1961): 148–67, 153. See also Erich Haberer, *Jews and Revolution in Nineteenth-Century Russia* (Cambridge and New York: Cambridge University Press, 1995), 124–5.

48. P. An-Man, "Der bialystoker peryod in lebn fun tsentral-komitet fun 'Bund' (1900–1902)," *Royter pinkes* 1 (1921): 64–5.

49. Sholem Levin, *Untererdishe kemfer* (New York: Sh. Levin Bukh-komite, 1946), 108. See also Arnold, "A nesie mit tshemodanes: An epizod fun dem amolikn umlegaln literatur-transport," *Arbeter-luekh* 3 (1922): 129–42.

50. The falsified title page is reproduced in Tcherikover, "Di onheybn fun der umlegaler literatur," 599.

51. Leybetshke Berman, *In loyf fun yorn* (New York: Dvinsker "Bund" Branch 75, Arbeter Ring in America, 1945), 145–9; Mendelsohn, *Class Struggle in the Pale*, 121; Kh. L. Poznanski, *Memuarn fun a Bundist* (Warsaw: Zetzerei H. Glantz, 1938), Vol. 1: 17–19. Libraries in Dvinsk contained American editions of Yiddish translations of Jules Verne and Tolstoy. On Jewish libraries in Russia and Poland, see Zeev Gries, *The Book in the Jewish World, 1700–1900* (Oxford and Portland, OR: Littman Library of Jewish Civilization, 2007), 57–68, and Jeffrey Veidlinger, *Jewish Public Culture in the Late Russian Empire* (Bloomington and Indianapolis, IN: Indiana University Press, 2009), 24–66.

52. A. Litvak, "Di 'Zhargonishe komitetn,'" 25–7.

53. Ibid., 24–5.

54. An alter bakanter, "Der onheyb fun der yidisher arbeter bavegung in Lodsh," *Royter pinkes* 2 (1924): 59–60.

55. Borukh Tsukerman, *Zikhroynes*, 3 vols. (New York: Yidisher kemfer, 1962), Vol 1: 109–10.

56. Anna Rozental, "Bletlekh fun a lebns-geshikhte," *Historishe shriftn* 3 (1939): 434. See also Levin, *Untererdishe kemfer*, 108–9. It should be added that the successful delivery of literature to a particular city did not guarantee its circulation. In at least one instance, books intended for workers in Berdichev never left the hands of a small group of activists. Poznanski, *Memuarn fun a Bundist*, 28–9.

57. Tcherikover, "Di onheybn fun der umlegaler literatur," 601.

58. Ibid.

59. See, e.g., A. Litvak, "Di krayzlekh," 210. On *daytshmerish*, see Michels, *A Fire in Their Hearts*, 110–11, and Marc Miller, "The Artificiality of German in Modern Yiddish Poetry: A New Perspective on *Daytshmerish*," *Journal of Modern Jewish Studies* 4 (July 2005): 123–35.

60. E. Tcherikover's introduction to Faygnboym's pamphlet, *Der sotsyalizmus fun alef biz tes*, reprinted in *Historishe shriftn* 3 (1939): 758. See also Michels, *A Fire in Their Hearts*, 79–85, and Zimmerman, *Poles, Jews, and the Politics of Nationality*, 146.

61. Michels, *A Fire in Their Hearts*, 91–121.

62. Itshe Goldberg, "Dos natsyonale ponim fun der ershter arbeter-poetn in Amerike," in *Eseyen* (New York: YKUF Farlag, 1981), 163–88. The essay was originally published in *Yidishe kultur* (January 1976).

63. Kursky, "Di 'Tsukunft' in untererdishe Rusland," 257–8.

64. Epshteyn, "Di 'Tsukunft,' Der 'Bund' un di yidishe literatur," 70.

65. Sholem Levin, *Untererdishe kemfer*, 106.

66. Frankel, *Prophecy and Politics*, 194.

67. Roger Chartier, *The Order of Books: Readers, Authors, and Libraries between the Fourteenth and Eighteenth Centuries*, trans. Lydia G. Cochrane (Stanford, CA: Stanford University Press, 1994), 1–24; Carlo Ginzburg, *The Cheese and the Worms: The Cosmos of a Sixteenth-century Miller* (Baltimore: Johns Hopkins University Press, 1992), xii–xiv; Jonathan Rose, *The Intellectual Life of the British Working Classes* (New Haven and London: Yale University Press, 2001), 39–47.

68. Alexander Bittelman, "Things I Have Learned," unpublished ms., n.d., p. 52 (Alexander Bittelman Collection, Tamiment Library, New York University, box 1, folder 6).

69. Ibid., 58.

70. Mendelsohn, *Class Struggle in the Pale*, 116–25, 153–5.

71. Iuli Martov, *Zapiski sotsial-demokrata* (Berlin: zdatel'stvo Z.I. Gržebina, 1922), 227. I thank David McDonald for this translation from the Russian. For a Yiddish translation of Martov's account, see L. Martov, "Di yidishe arbeter-bavegung in Rusland farn Bund," *Der veker*, May 12, 1922: 16. See also B. Mikhalevitsh, "Erev Bund," *Royter pinkes* 1 (1921): 39.

72. Frankel, *Prophecy and Politics*, 176.

73. Ibid., 194.

74. Dmitrii Elyashevich, "A Note on the Jewish Press and Censorship during the First Russian Revolution," in *The Revolution of 1905 and Russia's Jews*, ed. Stefani Hoffman and Ezra Mendelsohn (Philadelphia: University of Pennsylvania Press, 2008), 49–54; Kh. Sh. Kazdan, "Der Bund biz dem finftn tsuzamenfor," in Aronson et al., *Di geshikhte fun Bund*, Vol. 1: 276–86; Barry Trachtenberg, *The Revolutionary Roots of Modern Yiddish, 1903–1917* (Syracuse, NY: Syracuse University Press, 2008), 60–5.

75. Kurski, "Di 'Tsukunft' in untererdishe Rusland," 258.

76. The exceptions were specialized works such as books about political economy and political theory. Michels, *A Fire in Their Hearts*, 149, 196. See also Cohen, "USA-Eastern Europe Book Trade," 62–84.

77. Tobias, *Jewish Bund in Russia*, 295–332.

78. Herts Burgin, *Di geshikhte fun der yiddisher arbeter bavegung in Amerike, Rusland, un England* (New York: United Hebrew Trades, 1915), 667–77; Y. Sh. Herts, "Di ershte ruslender revolutsye," in Aronson et al., *Di geshikhte fun Bund*, Vol. 2: 421; Michels, *A Fire in Their Hearts*, 125–6, 156; Arthur W. Thompson, "The Reception of Russian Revolutionary Leaders in America, 1904–1906," *American Quarterly* 18 (1966): 452–76, here 464; Tobias, Jewish Bund in Russia, 241, 244. A list of donations from Arbeter Ring branches can be found in A. S. Zaks, *Geshikhte fun Arbeter Ring* (New York: Natyonale Ekzekutiv Komite fun Arbeter Ring, 1925), Vol. 2: i–xlv.

79. Quoted in Thompson, "Reception of Russian Revolutionary Leaders in America," 464.

80. Quoted in ibid., 472. Gorky received an enthusiastic reception from immigrant Jews, in contrast to the wide censure of him by the English-speaking public for alleged sexual impropriety in his personal life. Ernest Poole, "Maxim Gorki in New York," *Slavonic and East European Review* 3 (1944): 77–83; Thompson, "The Reception of Russian Revolutionary Leaders in America," 465–72; Nina Warnke, "Of Plays and Politics: Sholem Aleichem's First Visit to America," *YIVO Annual* 20 (1991): 239–76, here 248–9.

81. Steven Fraser, "The 'New Unionism' and the 'New Economic Policy,'" in *Work, Community, and Power: The Experience of Labor in Europe and America, 1900–1925*, ed. James E. Cronin and Carmen Sirianni (Philadelphia: Temple University Press, 1983), 173–96.

82. John L. Dekel-Chen, *Farming the Red Land: Jewish Agricultural Colonization and Local Soviet Power, 1924–1941* (New Haven and London: Yale University Press, 2005), 34–95; Henry Srebnik, "Diaspora, Ethnicity and Dreams of Nationhood: American Jewish Communists and the Birobidzhan Project," in *Yiddish and the Left*, ed. Gennady Estraikh and Mikhail Krutikov (Oxford: Legenda, 2001), 80–108.

CHAPTER 15
ZIONISM IN THE PROMISED LAND[1]
Arthur A. Goren

We believe that if an end is to be made to Jewish misery and to the exceptional position which the Jews occupy—which is the primary cause of Jewish misery—the Jewish nation must be placed once again in a home of its own . . . We believe that such a home can only naturally, and without violence to their past, be found in the land of their fathers—in Palestine

Richard Gottheil, The Aims of Zionism, 1898.

May we never forget . . . and may our descendants never forget the debt of gratitude that we owe to the first Jewish settlers [in the United States], nor the gratitude that we owe to the God of our fathers who has led us out of Egypt to this land of freedom

Louis Marshall, Address, November 30, 1905.

The Gottheil and Marshall quotations frame the issue this essay addresses: the ambiguity American Zionists and American Jews faced when they spoke of the Promised Land. Was it the historic homeland, "the land of our fathers" that Gottheil referred to, or "this land of freedom," the United States, whose citizens they were or would soon become? Both the Gottheil and Marshall texts resonate with the biblical doctrine of the Promised Land, God's summons to Abraham to go "to the land I will show you" where the patriarch's descendants would become "a great nation."[2] This foundation myth of Jewish nationhood became an article of faith for a dispersed people awaiting redemption. In the late nineteenth century, political Zionism bypassed messianic yearnings and called for the restoration of Jewish sovereignty to the ancestral homeland as the answer to the "Jewish problem"— poverty, pogroms and expulsions in Eastern Europe and the social and political discrimination practiced in Central and Western Europe. Richard Gottheil, professor of Semitics at Columbia University and president of the newly established Federation of American Zionists (FAZ), published *The Aims of Zionism* the year following the calling of the first Zionist Congress by Theodor Herzl and the founding of the World Zionist Organization (WZO). The pamphlet, as the historian Arthur Hertzberg noted, was "the first official statement of the philosophy of American Zionism." It opened with a catalogue of the countries closing their doors to Jewish immigrants. Then Gottheil asked, "Shall they all come to America, to the greater New York? . . . It is more than an open secret that we cannot cope with the 400,000 Jews in our city; Boston, Baltimore, Philadelphia, and Chicago will give you the same answer." Reclaiming the ancestral homeland for the "Jewish nation," Gottheil argued, would divert the migration of impoverished East European Jews to Palestine. He also assured American Jews that support of Zionism did not conflict with their allegiance to the United States. "With a home of his own [the Jew] will no longer feel himself a pariah among the nations; he will feel that he belongs somewhere and not everywhere." A Jewish homeland in Palestine would provide not only a refuge for those in need, but serve as a surrogate motherland for America's Jews, placing them on a par with other immigrant nationalities. Gottheil mentioned the example of the great masses of German Americans, Irish Americans, and Scandinavian Americans who proudly maintained their cultural identity and their collective affection for the motherland without compromising their loyalty to the land of their adoption.[3]

Seven years after Gottheil's manifesto when Louis Marshall, one of American Jewry's foremost leaders, delivered his address on the occasion of the nationwide celebration of the 250th anniversary of the founding of the first Jewish settlement in North America, over a million Jews resided in New York City. The celebrations were held in the shadow of the latest wave of pogroms that had taken place in Russia in the spring and fall of 1905. There hardly could have been a greater contrast between the two events, and Marshall linked the Czarist outrages to his hymn to the American republic, "to the God of our fathers who has led us out of Egypt to this land of freedom."[4]

America as the Promised Land was woven into the fabric of the nation's identity. In George Washington's words, the new nation would be "an asylum for the oppressed and persecuted of all Nations and Religions; whom we shall welcome to a participation in all our rights and privileges" (a pledge in fact limited to white Europeans).[5] In the mid-nineteenth century, Herman Melville reaffirmed another tenet of the American creed which harked back to the Puritan/Old Testament inheritance of the New England settlers. In his novel, *White Jacket* (1850), he wrote: "We Americans are the peculiar, chosen people—the Israel of our time; we bear the ark of the liberties of the world. . . . The political Messiah has come. He has come in *us*."[6] Eighteen years later, Max Lilienthal, a Munich-born and educated rabbi who had immigrated to the United States in 1845, transposed those ideals into the idiom of an evolving American Reform Judaism. At the cornerstone laying ceremony of Cincinnati's Temple Bene Israel, he proclaimed:

America is our Palestine; here is our Zion and Jerusalem; Washington and the signers of the glorious Declaration of Independence are our deliverers, and the time when their doctrines will be recognized and carried into effect is the time so hopefully foretold by our great prophets.[7]

This was neither the first nor the last time that the America-as-Zion mantra would be deployed.

Two historical moments define American Zionism's quest for self-definition. The first considers the years 1914–20 when the movement found its American voice and became a major presence on the American Jewish scene. These years coincided with Louis D. Brandeis' leadership of the movement. They were also the years when the European war intensified the on-going debate over the meaning and requirements of American nationhood. Nativist, old-stock Americans charged immigrant and ethnic groups with divided loyalties for lobbying on behalf of the national rights of their European brethren. For Zionists the prospect of achieving such rights culminated in the San Remo Conference (April 1920), where the Supreme Council of European Powers confirmed the award of the Palestine mandate to Great Britain and included the Balfour Declaration as a binding part of the mandate. (Britain's wartime statement, issued on November 2, 1917, by foreign secretary Sir Arthur Balfour, declared the government's "sympathy" for the establishment of a "national home for the Jewish people in Palestine.") Zionists throughout the world hailed the occasion. A Warsaw Zionist daily headline read: "The Trumpet of Salvation Is Blowing." In New York, 100,000 celebrants marched from lower Manhattan to Central Park behind an enormous banner, "Geulah— Redemption."[8] For Brandeis and his followers, Zionism had achieved its political goals. To reap the fruit of victory required new strategies and a new focus: a de-politicized, efficiency-driven agenda, private investments for building the infrastructure in preparation for the mass immigration. To begin with, it was necessary to transcend the political partisanship endemic of the WZO.

The second defining episode the American movement faced occurred during the twenty-third World Zionist Congress which convened in Jerusalem in August 1951. The Congress met under the aura of the establishment of the Jewish State three years earlier. The American Zionist leadership had performed brilliantly in the final push for statehood, mobilizing the political and financial resources of American Jewry and winning the endorsement of a reluctant American government for a Jewish state. However, when the Zionist Congress met, instead of exultation and rededication, the deliberations disclosed a wrenching breach between two sorts of Zionism. The Israeli delegates insisted that the establishment of the state demanded a redefinition of the meaning and goals of Zionism. For the Israelis, the heart of the matter, indeed the raison d'être of the Jewish state, was the "ingathering of the exiles," the consummation of the millennial dream of "the return." *Aliyah*—settling in the ancestral land and participating in building and defending it— transcended all else. To *choose* to remain in "exile" (*galut*)—in the eyes of the Israelis America was "exile"—was a self-deceiving decision. For American Zionists, America was home, not "exile." Zionism was an indelible part of their American Jewish being, assured the continuity of Jewish life, and embodied unconditional support for Israel without compromising one's loyalty to America. Some observers concluded that American Zionism's very success was its downfall: the job was done; a Jewish state existed and the vast majority of American Jews were its supporters and admirers.[9]

1 Early Zionism

Before considering these self-defining turning points, aspects of the formative years of the Zionist movement, 1898 to 1914, require consideration. An uncommon duality characterized the movement. On the one hand, it was small in number; a loose association of organizations that included Yiddish-speaking recent arrivals bearing the full gamut of Zionist ideologies—socialist, Orthodox, and cultural in all their variants. On the other hand, Zionism was a highly visible and contentious presence. The movement was in the eye of an ideological storm, the *bête noire* of both the Reform Jewish establishment and the anti-Zionist radical left. For the former, Jewish nationalism and socialism was anathema, creeds that threatened the civic standing of the Jew as American. Zionism was also the nemesis of the majority of the socialist intelligentsia who faulted Zionism as reactionary and chauvinistic, distracting the Jewish proletariat from the cosmopolitan ideal of working class solidarity. Small in numbers as the Zionists may have been, they occupied a prominent place on the Jewish public agenda.[10]

The FAZ sought to reach out beyond immigrant factionalism to an English-speaking public, and it succeeded in attracting a circle of young activists and intellectuals. Most were offspring of established families of German-speaking Central European origin. Two popular young Reform rabbis who rejected the regnant anti-Zionist stance of Reform Judaism stand out. Stephen S. Wise, son of a rabbi whose family emigrated from Budapest when he was an infant, studied with Richard J. H. Gottheil at Columbia University for his PhD and with Gottheil's father, Gustav Gottheil, senior rabbi of New York's Temple Emanu-el. (The elder Gottheil was born in the Pozen district of Prussia, educated in German universities and ordained by Samuel Holdheim, a leading theologian of German Liberal Judaism.) Wise served briefly as the FAZ's first "honorary" (unsalaried) secretary. After holding a pulpit in Portland, Oregon, he returned to New York and founded the Free Synagogue. In the four decades that followed, he won recognition as an outstanding leader of American Jewry, a major figure in the social reform movements of his time, founder of the World Jewish Congress, and one of American Zionism's most powerful and persuasive voices. Judah L. Magnes was San Francisco-born. His mother and her brothers immigrated from Filehne in the western part of Prussian Poznan and his father from near Lodz. Magnes graduated from Hebrew Union College, continued his studies in Berlin and received his PhD from Heidelberg. He was elected honorary secretary of the FAZ in 1906 when he began his tenure as associate rabbi of Temple Emanu-el. (His sermons on Jewish nationalism and his call for a "counter-reformation," the introduction of more traditional practices in the temple's services, led to his resignation.) Like Wise he was immersed in a score of communal enterprises. He established cordial ties with the Yiddish-speaking radicals and Zionists of "downtown" and became the prime mover of a bold experiment to establish a democratic communal polity, a "kehillah" that would coordinate and improve the community's educational, religious, and philanthropic services. Other members of this socially and intellectually cohesive circle also served for short terms as executive officers of the FAZ. Israel Friedlaender, Polish-born and German-educated (he held a PhD in Semitics from the University of Strasbourg), joined the faculty of the Jewish Theological Seminary (JTS) in 1903 as professor of the Bible. Henrietta Szold, daughter of a Hungarian-born Baltimore rabbi of the Conservative "Historical School," was secretary and editor of the Jewish Publication Society before being accepted as a special student at the JTS. Szold turned a women's study group into the most successful of all Zionist organizations, Hadassah, which fostered health services in Palestine. Finally, in 1911, Louis Lipsky, the founding editor of the FAZ's journal, the *Maccabaean*, was elected chairman of the organization's executive and administrative committees, the most prominent of a growing number of American-born activists of East European families. However, the absence of a firm hand to provide continuity and direction for the Federation proved debilitating for the organization. When Gottheil withdrew from active leadership in 1904, Dr. Harry Friedenwald, a well-known Baltimore ophthalmologist—American-born and identified with traditional Judaism and the cultural strand in Zionism—succeeded him as president. Despite his public stature, Friedenwald's professional commitments and bland leadership style affected the organization adversely. Dependency on part-time volunteers and a woefully underfinanced infrastructure further impaired the organization. The Federation numbered a mere 12,000 dues-paying members in 1914.[11]

Yet the decade prior to the outbreak of the war in August 1914 did bring hopes of a new era in the building of the homeland. Approximately 35,000 Jews migrated to Palestine, mostly from Eastern Europe. (Some 1.2 million Jews migrated to the United States during the same period.) Reports of new settlements including the first agricultural cooperatives and communes, the growth of urban centers, most famously the founding in 1909 of the all-Jewish city of Tel Aviv, were encouraging, as were the accounts of the spread of Hebrew as the vernacular tongue and the establishment of modern educational institutions, a Hebrew press and a budding literary life. On the lecture circuit, American Zionist leaders who visited Palestine, and European and Palestinian officials touring the United States seeking financial help offered eye witness accounts of Zionist progress. Judah Magnes' address to a "mass meeting" at New York's Cooper Union following his visit to Palestine in 1912 is of special interest. He compared his impressions with his first trip in 1907. He described a people who were now "possessed by a new spirit no longer living in fear and trembling" of their Arab neighbors. The *shomrim*, the organization of volunteer armed watchmen, made the difference. They were the nucleus of a "Jewish militia, the beginning of a new type of Jew ... defending their country." Moreover, alongside of self-defense went self-reliance. Magnes described the self-governing agricultural villages. He gave special attention to the first communal and cooperative workers' settlements, which were barely two years old, Um Juni (Deganya) and Fuleh (Merhavia). Magnes also recounted a meeting with an American immigrant, Eliezer Jaffe, who was probably known to many in the audience. "I have written to my friends [in America]," Jaffe told Magnes, "that here I am stronger and happier than I was there [in New York]. I tell them that here I am learning to be a man, I am a full and thorough and harmonious Jew." Magnes concluded his address with a rhetorical flourish that harked back to Jaffe's message: "If you have a love of your people in your hearts and a yearning for the land of your fathers, I say to you, go up into the land!"[12]

For American audiences, Aaron Aaronsohn personified that "new type of Jew." An agronomist, founder of the Jewish Agricultural Experiment Station in Palestine and son of a founding family of Zikhron Yaacov, one of the first of the Zionist settlements, Aaronsohn visited the United States in 1909 and again in 1912–13 for extended speaking tours. He delivered scientific papers, raised funds for his experimental station, and discoursed on the pioneer settlements. The historian, Allon Gal, exploring Louis Brandeis' conversion to Zionism, has portrayed the impact Aaronsohn made upon him.

In one of Brandeis' first Zionist addresses (May 1913), he described a gathering of Boston notables which he hosted in Aaronsohn's honor, "one of the most interesting, brilliant and remarkable men that I have ever met."[13] Besides Aaronsohn's account of his agricultural experiments, he talked about "the little communities which have grown up in the last thirty-two years and now number 150,000 Jewish souls." Responding to a remark Brandeis made concerning Jewish involvement in a New York City crime wave, Aaronsohn noted "that not a single crime was committed by any of our people in the Jewish settlements in Palestine [since their establishment]." Brandeis ascribed the probity of the settlers to the noblesse oblige, moral sensibilities, and traditional values inculcated in the young, and the dedication inspired by the pioneering act of the Zionist return to the homeland.[14]

2 Brandeisian Zionism

The transformation of American Zionism from an organizationally modest undertaking into an efficient popular movement numbering 180,000 in 1919 was in large measure a response to the First World War, which raged in the heartland of the great Jewish population mass in Eastern Europe.[15] The war prompted an enormous outpouring of communal activity. New and old organizations and agencies funneled their energies into overseas relief: mass-action fund-raising campaigns, coordinating the relief efforts of the various sectors of the community, and obtaining government help in transferring and distributing the funds in the war zone. The war also raised hopes that a peace settlement would address the grievances of East European Jewry as it would those of other minorities. The American Jewish Joint Distribution Committee, founded by the American Jewish Committee (AJC), the leading Jewish defense agency, took on the first task; the second task was to be handled by a democratically elected American Jewish Congress, which would speak in the name of a unified American Jewry at a future peace conference. The Zionists took part in both these endeavors. First of all, the movement focused upon the threatened Jewish settlements in Ottoman-controlled Palestine, and then upon attaining international recognition for a Jewish national home in Palestine.[16]

The role of Brandeis is central to these developments. The period is often described as "the Brandeis Era" and his brand of Zionism as "Brandeisian Zionism." Brandeis is quite correctly credited with being instrumental in reconfiguring American Zionism. He made it palatable to a broad American Jewish public; in a word, he presented Zionism and Americanism as sharing the same values of freedom and social justice which he argued were rooted in a common Biblical heritage. In one of his early Zionist addresses (September 1914), he declared: "My approach to Zionism was through Americanism. In time practical experience and observation convinced me that Jews were by reason of their tradition and their character peculiarly fitted in the attainment of American ideals. It became clear to me that *to be good Americans, we must be better Jews, and to be better Jews, we must become Zionists*" (author's emphasis).[17] Of the memorable aphorisms he coined this was the most celebrated. Jerold Auerbach, the historian, commented that "no other prominent American Jew so unerringly identified, and immediately resolved, the implicit conflict between Jewish and American loyalties that defined the nagging dilemma of American Jewish life."[18]

Other elements in the Brandeis legend made him the paradigmatic Zionist American hero. One was his unexpected appearance on the Jewish scene in the role of national leader. Brandeis scholars—Allon Gal, Ben Halpern, Melvin Urofsky, Evyatar Friesel, Jonathan Sarna, and Jerold S. Auerbach—have meticulously traced his tentative and casual interest in Jewish affairs and then his gradual espousal of Zionism. He may have shown some interest in Zionism as early as 1910, although he formally joined a Zionist organization only in 1913 and then politely declined all overtures to take an active part in the movement. However, for the broad Jewish public, the prominent American reformer, the "people's attorney"—Harvard Law School alumnus, architect of "the New Freedom," and advisor to President Woodrow Wilson—was at best only marginally interested in Jewish matters. Then at a critical moment, the outbreak of the war in Europe, Brandeis' legendary return to his people took place, literally overnight, cloaked in the Zionist mantel of Jewish nationhood.

The occasion was the emergency Zionist conference convened in New York on August 30, 1914 by Shmarya Levin, a leading member of the WZO's Actions Comite' (the governing executive body) who was completing a tour of the American movement, and Louis Lipsky in the name of the FAZ. With the WZO headquarters in Berlin incapacitated due to the outbreak of hostilities and members of the Actions Comite' scattered among the belligerent countries and unable to meet, representatives of the American Zionist organizations responded to the call to establish an ad hoc body to fill the void. High on the agenda was the dire state of the Jewish settlements in Palestinian cut off from their European sources of financial support. The emergency conference established the Provisional Executive Committee for General Zionist Affairs (PEC) which included representatives of the FAZ, Zionist factions and fraternal orders unaffiliated to the FAZ, and Hadassah, the women's Zionist organization. The crowning event of the conference was Brandeis' acceptance of the chairmanship of the Provisional Committee. In fact, this was the first Zionist conference he ever attended. Brandeis now stood at the head of a Zionist coalition authorized to act in lieu of the WZO in international affairs.[19] In the national Jewish limelight for the first time, the apologetic note Brandeis struck in his acceptance speech is especially notable and understandable. "I feel my disqualification for this task," he remarked:

Throughout long years which represent my own life, I have been to a great extent separated from Jews. I am very ignorant of things Jewish. But recent experiences, public and professional, have taught me this: I find Jews possessed of those very qualities which we of the twentieth century seek to develop in our struggle for justice and democracy.

A month later, he began his first formal address as chairman of the PZC, delivered in Symphony Hall in Boston, in the same vein. When the address appeared in revised form as a pamphlet, "Zionism and Patriotism," Brandeis opened in the same contrite manner: "During most of my life my contact with Jews and Judaism was slight, and I gave little thought to their problems save in asking myself from time to time whether we were showing by our lives due appreciation of the opportunities which this hospitable country affords." Brandeis began the scores of speeches he delivered in the early months of his chairmanship with some variation of his confession. Obviously the image he wished to project was of the assimilated American Jew who was born again a Zionist.[20]

Brandeis, the social reformer and secularist with a humanistic stance on religion—his brother-in-law, Felix Adler, founder of the Ethical Culture Society, officiated at Brandeis's marriage—appealed to the ideologically fractious immigrant community no less than to the growing number of acculturated Jews. His penchant for casting the causes he represented as moral crusades, and an ethical life style his admirers publicized endowed him with a leadership persona heretofore unknown in the Jewish public realm. Jonathan Sarna has captured this Brandeis "mystique" and his impact on the Jewish scene in an essay entitled, "'The Greatest Jew in the World since Jesus Christ': the Jewish Legacy of Louis D. Brandeis."[21] Brandeis' official "ministry" was also formally brief: from August 1914, when he was elected chairman of the Provisional Council, to July 1916, when he exercised "judicial restraint" and resigned all public offices upon his appointment to the Supreme Court of the United States. Nevertheless, Brandeis continued to direct the movement's affairs in all of their particulars as the discrete behind-the-scenes leader. For his informal circle of aids and advisors, Brandeis remained "the chief." Some were FAZ veterans whom he reactivated while chairman of the Provisional Council like Stephen Wise and Jacob de Haas, an early aide of Herzl who as a Boston journalist played a singular role as Brandeis' Zionist informant. Some were professionals, academics, and businessmen whom he recruited: Judge Julian W. Mack, Felix Frankfurter and Horace Kallen had Harvard connections; Bernard Flexner, Robert Szold, and Benjamin V. Cohen were established lawyers and family friends, and Eugene Meyer Jr., Louis Kirstein, and Nathan Straus were wealthy businessmen. Brandeis maintained close ties with the Wilson administration and served as a conduit for Zionist interests. In 1918 when the FAZ was reorganized as the Zionist Organization of America (ZOA), Brandeis was elected "honorary" president, a post bearing no executive responsibilities; Mack was elected president, Wise vice president, and de Haas executive secretary.[22]

On two occasions, in the summers of 1919, following a visit to Palestine, and again in 1920, when he headed an American delegation to a conference of the WZO in London, Brandeis momentarily played an auspicious public role in international Zionist affairs. These ended in confrontations with the Europeans led by Chaim Weizmann. Brandeis insisted on the need for a reorganization of the world movement, the co-option of non-Zionist notables to the movement's leadership, replacement of Zionist party functionaries with professional administrators, delaying mass migration until such basic problems of sanitation as malaria were alleviated, and the adoption of what was tantamount to an economic-social development policy of a mixed economy of private investments and national (philanthropic) capital was in place. No less upsetting were the jarring political cultures—Brandeis' pragmatic, American progressivism with its emphasis on efficiency colliding with the doctrinal, populistic European Zionism. By 1921, the gulf widened, and disaffected American Zionists and Weizmann followers won control of the ZOA.[23]

However, the Brandeis mystique left an indelible mark on the movement. In addition to his iconic personification of American Zionism and his rhetorical skill in linking Zionism with Americanism—his frequent references to "our Jewish Pilgrim Fathers" in relating to the early "self-governing" Zionist colonies in Palestine, and his axiom, "Let no American imagine that Zionism is inconsistent with Patriotism, multiple loyalties are objectionable only if they are inconsistent"—Brandeis redefined American national identity in the process. Embracing Zionism—acknowledging the Jews as a national entity—required a redefinition of Americanism to reconcile the two. Most famously, in an address on July 4, 1915, in Boston's Faneuil Hall—the cradle of liberty—Brandeis spoke on the theme of "True Americanism." Democratic America, he proclaimed, by its very definition, held that "each race or people, like each individual, have the right and duty to develop, and that only through such differentiated development will high civilization be attained."[24]

Brandeis, most historians agree, was beholden in this regard to the philosopher, Zionist, and fellow Harvard alumnus, Horace Kallen, who is credited with being a prime mentor of the fledgling Zionist. What is notable is not merely Brandeis' theme, "America as a nation of nationalities" reverberating Kallen's notion of America as a federation of nationalities, but how far Brandeis had come in his thinking. Ten years earlier, he warned a Jewish audience that there was no place in the United States for hyphenated Americans. He proceeded to enumerate "the hyphenates"—Irish, Germans, Poles, Slovaks. "This country," he summed up,

> demands that its sons and daughters whatever their race—however intense or diverse their religious connections—be politically merely American citizens ... Habits of living or thought which tend to keep alive difference of origin or to classify men according to their religious belief are inconsistent with the American ideal of brotherhood, and are disloyal.[25]

Wilson himself cautioned an audience of newly naturalized citizens in May 1915: "You cannot become thorough citizens if you think of yourselves in groups. A man who thinks of himself as belonging to a particular national group in America has not yet become an American." However, the war increasingly fixed Wilson's attention on European questions and most prominently on nationalist rivalries. As early as November 1915 he declared America's belief in "the right of every people to choose their own allegiance and be free of masters altogether." By 1918, that belief became Wilson's clarion call of self-determination.[26]

Brandeis moved in a similar direction. In a major address before a conference of Reform rabbis in April 1915, he dwelled upon the European nationalities issue and applied the lessons to the American setting. He quoted Robert W. Seton-Watson, the famous Scottish historian and authority on East Central European nationalism:

America is full of nationalities which, while accepting with enthusiasm their new American citizenship, nevertheless look to some center in the old world as the source and inspiration of their national culture and traditions. The most typical instance is the feeling of the American Jew for Palestine which may well become a locus for his déclassé kinsmen in other parts of the world.

Notable is Seton-Watson's view that for American Jews the "source of inspiration" for their "national culture" was not "the old world" they had come from, but the Palestine of their imagination. Interestingly, Seton-Watson's essay was published prior to the outbreak of the war when American Zionism had not as yet established itself as a popular movement.[27] Nevertheless, for Seton-Watson, American Zionism epitomized the legitimacy and beneficence of maintaining dual identities.

For Brandeis, the war underscored the struggle for political independence of the national minorities controlled by the Habsburg, Russian, and German empires. In January 1916, Brandeis told a rally demanding the holding of an American Jewish Congress,

The position of the Jew is not entirely unique. The history of the Bohemians, the Poles and several other Slavic races, provides remarkable parallels, and among all these nationalities hopes are now high that in the peace that will follow the war their elemental wrongs will be righted. We [the Jews] have not made less, but more sacrifices than they have, and are justified in expecting that our elemental wrongs, too, will be righted.[28]

Noteworthy is Brandeis' full-hearted identification with his European kin: "*We* have made ... more sacrifices. ... *Our* ... wrongs will be righted" (emphasis added).

As the war ignited the homeland anxieties of America's immigrant groups, political realists came to terms with an increasingly assertive ethnic pluralism. Zionist speakers frequently referred to Irish-American support for home rule as an exemplary expression of American patriotism. In his 1915 address to the Reform Rabbis, Brandeis stated:

Every Irish-American who contributed towards advancing home rule was a better man and a better American for the sacrifice he made. Every American Jew who aids in advancing the Jewish settlement in Palestine, though he feels that neither he nor his descendants will ever live there, will likewise be a better man and a better American for doing so.[29]

A sub-theme is discernible in Brandeis' rhetoric. On the one hand, Zion's call to return to the homeland and rebuild it was accompanied by the motif that American Jews who supported those builders were "better Americans for doing so." Brandeis also argued that Zionism was a movement "to enable Jews to exercise the same right now exercised by practically every other people in the world, to live at their option either in the land of their fathers or in some other country; a right which members of small nations as well of large ... may now exercise."[30] Thus Brandeis countered accusations that in embracing Zionism American Jews treaded the dangerous waters of dual loyalty with his universal reading of the free choice inherent in democratic society implying, I suggest, that American Jews were free to join the builders in Zion.

In January 1916, when Wilson nominated Brandeis to the Supreme Court, he knew well enough of Brandeis' Zionist affiliation. If the President still had reservations about ethnic group solidarity within America, in Brandeis' case his American progressive credentials outweighed the other. A caustic cartoon in the Yiddish satirical periodical, *Der Groyse kundes*, sums up the debate. On the right, Jacob Schiff, the German Jewish investment banker and philanthropist, the 100 percent American, declares with passion that a Jew cannot be a Zionist and a good American at the same time. Uncle Sam motions to Brandeis, wearing a judge's robe, to take his seat on the Supreme Court and tells him, "Mr. Brandeis, you are one of my finest Americans." The caption reads: "As is well known, Mr. Brandeis is an ardent nationalist and president of the American Zionists." By simplifying the controversies over the meaning of Americanism, the *Groyse kundes* cartoon touched the heart of the matter, the pride and self-confidence the appointment evoked.[31] However fluctuating the course of American Zionism would be during the years ahead the fact that its most revered figure was also a member of the nation's most august body assured Zionism's civic legitimacy.

3 The Jerusalem Congress

The 1951 Jerusalem Congress, as I suggested, was a wrenching experience for the American delegates. The critic Judd L. Teller, subtitling his review of the Congress, "To be or Not to Be 'Ingathered'" (a pun on the Zionist dogma of "the ingathering of the exiles"), wrote:

> American Zionism had been the big brother of the Jewish independence movement in Palestine. Now the Jews of Palestine are the sovereign people and sovereign government of Israel, and their erstwhile big brother, though proud and happy, could not help but wonder where he stood—especially since there came to his ears brazen murmurings from Israeli sources that he had no place to stand at all.[32]

Emblematic of this turn of events was Abba Hillel Silver's fall from his commanding position on the Jewish political scene following the establishment of the state.[33] During the three climactic years from the surrender of Nazi Germany on May 8, 1945, to David Ben Gurion's proclamation of Israel's independence on May 14, 1948, Silver directed the extraordinary campaign to win the support of American public opinion for a Jewish state. American Jews confronting the enormity of the destruction of European Jewry and the urgent need to resettle and rehabilitate the one-third that had survived responded enthusiastically to Silver's aggressive leadership. Non-Zionists such as Henry Morgenthau, Jr., Bernard Baruch, and Joseph Proskauer put aside their ideological qualms and supported pro-statehood politics. Leading Protestant liberals—Reinhold Niebuhr, Paul Tillich, and John Haynes Holmes—formed the American Christian Palestine Committee and collaborated with the Zionists. Silver, aided by a brilliant group of strategists, political lobbyists, and fund-raisers, transformed the American Zionist Emergency Council (AZEC) into a militant think-tank and task force with a network of regional offices that staged mass meetings, filled the press with political advertisements, solicited statements of support from trade unions, church and synagogue associations, and flooded the White House and Congress with torrents of pro-Zionist letters and petitions. Silver and his advisors established close ties with key presidential aides and congressional leaders and coordinated the unrelenting behind-the-scenes lobbying that secured the UN General Assembly's passage of the partition resolution.[34]

In the Zionist political realm, Silver was Ben-Gurion's American counterpart. The 1946 Zionist Congress, facing Britain's uncompromising implementation of the White Paper severely restricting immigration, deposed the moderate and cautious Weizmann from the presidency of the WZO in favor of a militant coalition leadership. It appointed Silver to the Jerusalem executive of the Jewish Agency, the quasi-state governing body of the *yishuv*, the Palestinian Jewish settlement, which Ben-Gurion chaired. (The Jewish Agency was recognized by the Mandatory government as representing world Jewish interests in matters pertaining to the development of the Jewish national home. It originally included non-Zionist representatives who soon became inactive. The Jewish Agency functioned as the executive arm of the WZO in Palestine.) The Zionist Congress also created an American section of the Jewish Agency executive and placed Silver in charge, responsible for political activities in the United States. Silver now held a double mandate: elected by the American Zionist movement to head the AZEC, and elected by the WZO to chair the American section of the Jewish Agency. Silver and Ben-Gurion, hawkish in their tactics and goals, each dominated one of the two chief centers of the Jewish people, the American Jewish community and the embattled *yishuv* in Palestine. However, deep mistrust existed between the two. Ben-Gurion, rooted in the socialist-Zionist pioneering ethos, headed the social democratic MAPAI party, the largest of the Israeli parties, and single-mindedly argued the "negation of *galut*" dogma, the denial that a creative and secure Jewish life was possible in the Diaspora. Silver dominated the largest of the American Zionist organizations, the mainstream ZOA. He was identified with its right wing. Under Silver's influence, the ZOA increasingly allied itself with its Israeli counterpart, the General Zionist Party, a member of the opposition to Ben-Gurion's MAPAI-led government coalition.[35]

Silver reached the pinnacle of his political career as chief spokesman of the Jewish Agency delegation to the UN. On May 7, 1947, he presented the case for a Jewish state before the General Assembly during the debate over the partition proposal. A year later, on May 14—at midnight Tel Aviv time, May 15, the British mandate ended—in the midst of last-minute efforts by the United States to adopt the proposal for a UN temporary trusteeship for Palestine which would have stalled the impending declaration of a Jewish state, Silver announced that he had received word that a Jewish state was proclaimed in Palestine. Minutes later the chief American delegate was informed of Truman's de facto recognition of the state. (The following year the ZOA published a collection of Silver's addresses. The editor's note introducing his May 14 statement concluded with these words: "History singled out Dr. Abba Hillel Silver as the servant of his people who should stand before the United Nations on the never-to-be-forgotten day to announce the proclamation of Israel's independence.")[36]

From that point on, Israel's diplomatic representatives and not the well-connected American Zionists or Jewish Agency officials negotiated with the State Department, the President of the USA, and the UN. Sovereignty sundered the intimate partnership and stripped the American Zionist leaders of much of their influence and prestige. As Ben-Gurion expressed it, American Zionists were citizens of a foreign state. They were at best "friends of Israel," no different than the growing legion of Israel sympathizers. Once full partners, they were now stigmatized as lapsed Zionists. Abba Eban, who replaced Silver as Israeli representative to the UN, recalled in his autobiography:

The proclamation of our independence was having some curious personal effects. Zionist leaders and representatives now had to make a choice from which the lack of statehood had long shielded them. Would they take Israeli's citizenship and cut themselves loose from all other allegiances? Or would they maintain their Diaspora nationalities and thus be ineligible to represent a "foreign" state? Abba Hillel Silver and Emanuel Neumann made the latter choice. With bewildering rapidity they left the central arena, leaving me and a few other colleagues in solitary vigilance at Sixty-Six Street [the temporary offices of the Israeli delegation] and the United Nations headquarters.[37]

During the months that followed the establishment of the state, in a series of acrimonious confrontations and political maneuvers, Silver and Emanuel Neumann, Silver's close associate in the Zionist establishment (essentially the ZOA leadership), were displaced by those amenable to the Israel government's pressure for preeminence in the triangular relationship of the American Jewish community (now largely pro-Israel), the American Zionists, and Israel. In the intricate Jewish organizational map, this meant, in the first place, controlling the fund-raising apparatus so essential for the fledgling state. (The United Palestine Appeal, in particular, soon renamed the United Israel Appeal, operated within the framework of the United Jewish Appeal with its broad communal base of contributors.)[38]

For the ZOA, in particular, the period leading up to the 1951 Jerusalem Congress was marked by a sharp decline in membership. Ben-Gurion, faced with the enormous task of social and economic absorption of the first great wave of immigrants and insisting on maintaining the state's open door immigration policy, increasingly by-passed the American Zionist organizations which some of the prime minister's Israeli and American advisors considered moribund and stagnant. He cultivated instead Jewish financial figures, key communal functionaries and national organizations who hitherto had been outside the Zionist mainstream. One auspicious example of this strategy was the launching of Israel Bonds, the first direct approach of Israel to American Jewry for assistance through a large-scale loan. Buying Israel Bonds immediately became a popular demonstration of pro-Israel support. Ben-Gurion made his first visit to the United States as prime minister in May 1951 to launch the Bond drive. Following a whirlwind two week tour of the country, at a farewell dinner, Zionist leaders who were present bitterly complained that the prime minister had failed to mention the Zionist movement in any of his addresses. Ben-Gurion replied that he had come to the United States "to [address] all of American Jewry ... because all Jews now had the duty and the opportunity to cooperate in strengthening the State of Israel."[39]

Probably the most sensitive of all issues which accompanied Israel's out-reach policy was what the historian Zvi Ganin called "the specter of dual loyalty."[40] This anxiety was not new. When the Balfour Declaration was issued Brandeis wrote privately to Jacob Schiff, the banker, philanthropist, and key member of the AJC, that he neither advised nor desired an independent state. He considered statehood "a most serious menace." The period immediately prior to and following the establishment of Israel coincided with the early years of the Cold War. Loyalty oaths, security clearances, Senator Joseph McCarthy's rise to notoriety, fear of communist infiltration, and espionage (the arrest in 1950 of Julius and Ethel Rosenberg for handing atomic secrets to the Soviet Union) were high among the public's concerns. Jewish organizations and in particular the conservative AJC were obsessed with the issue. The AJC created a special committee to combat the "Jewish/communist stereotype." "Dual loyalty" carried sinister connotations.[41]

Especially disconcerting were Ben-Gurion's pronouncements calling on American Jews to settle in Israel. Israel needed their professional skills and "know-how." Needed as well were American *halutzim*, young pioneers who in classic Zionist parlance were the vanguard of the Jewish people, volunteering for the challenging tasks of nation building. Israel had doubled its population in its first three years of independence, bringing waves of impoverished, mostly unskilled "displaced-persons," uprooted émigrés from the Soviet satellite states, and indigent refugees from Middle East countries. Soon, some predicted within two years, the reservoir of immigrants from the distressed lands would run dry. To survive the country needed to tap new population sources. In the mind of the AJC, Ben-Gurion's calls for American Jews to settle in Israel constituted "intervention by a foreign state in the internal affairs of the Jewish community." Some Jewish leaders were also distraught by Israeli emissaries sent on educational missions to the United States who were allegedly weaning Jewish youth away from their loyalty to America by recruiting them for a pioneering life in Israel.[42]

From 1949 through 1952, Jacob Blaustein, the AJC president, and his staff were immersed in interminable negotiations with Ben-Gurion, Israeli diplomats in the United States and Foreign Minister Moshe Sharett over these issues. Finally, on August 30, 1950, Blaustein and Ben-Gurion and their advisors met in Jerusalem and agreed upon the text of "An Exchange of Views between American Jews and the State of Israel." At what resembled a treaty-signing ceremony between sovereign nations, Ben-Gurion declared that the Jews of the United States had only one political attachment and that was to the United States. Israel, he continued, "speaks only on behalf of its own citizens and in no way presumes to represent or speak in the name of the Jews who are citizens of any other country." Nor did Israel have any "intention of interfering in any way in the internal affairs of Jewish communities abroad." Thus Ben-Gurion accepted one of the AJC's demands: non-interference in the affairs of Diaspora Jewry. On the issue of calling on American Jews to settle in Israel, Ben-Gurion tempered his usual rhetoric but conceded little more. He hoped that there would be "those [American Jews] who believe that their aspirations as human beings and as Jews can best be fulfilled by life and work in Israel." Blaustein's reply was a fervent disavowal that American Jews were in any sense in "exile":

> American Jews—young and old alike, Zionists and non-Zionists alike—are profoundly attached to America. America welcomed their immigrant parents in their need. Under America's free institutions they and their children have achieved that freedom and sense of security unknown for long centuries of travail. American Jews have truly become Americans; just as have all other oppressed groups that have ever come to America's shores.[43]

Setting the boundaries between Diaspora and the sovereign Jewish state was neither settled by the Ben-Gurion-Blaustein accord, nor would it be resolved by the upcoming Zionist Congress on whose agenda these matters loomed large. In the first instance, the dispute with Blaustein and the AJC was with a circle of new-found friends of Israel who had moved from indifference or opposition to a Zionist homeland to support for the state. In the second instance, the dispute was intramural; the delegates to the Zionist Congress had shared a common vision and had been comrades-in-arms for a half century in building the groundwork for the state.[44]

The twenty-third World Zionist Congress deliberations lasted two weeks, from August 14 to August 30, 1951. The Congress opened with all the accouterments of state sovereignty. A memorial service on Mt. Herzl at the tomb of Theodore Herzl began when a military honor guard snapped to attention and a bugle sounded a fanfare as the Prime Minister, members of the cabinet, the Jewish Agency executive, Knesset and World Zionist leaders took their places. Similarly, the first plenary session began with members of the Israel Cabinet, headed by the Prime Minister, taking their places on the dais, "alongside their *former* [emphasis added] colleagues of the Zionist Executive and Jewish Agency," one press report noted. Three keynoters spoke: Prime Minister Ben-Gurion, Berl Locker, chairman of the Jewish Agency Executive in Jerusalem, and Nahum Goldmann, an old hand in Zionist diplomacy who had replaced Silver as the chairman of the American section of the Jewish Agency. The congress they addressed—445 delegates from thirty-five nations—was dominated by the two main protagonists: the American delegates, products of America's own history of "ingathering," now citizens of the United States, the leader of the free world; and the Israelis, liberators of the historic Promised Land, the cradle and millennial hope of the Jewish people.[45]

The first of two broad issues which preoccupied the Congress revolved around the relationship of Diaspora Zionism and the State. Many of the American delegates, followers of Silver and Neumann, pressed for a Congress resolution calling on the State of Israel, through an appropriate legislative act, "to grant status to the World Zionist

Organization as the representative of the Jewish people in all matters that relate to the organized participation of Jews the world over in the development and building of the land and rapid absorption of newcomers." In the pre-state era, the WZO-Jewish Agency raised the funds, directed the social and economic absorption of immigrants and managed settlement and land development. As we have seen, American Zionist leaders played an increasingly crucial role in the WZO-Jewish Agency governance. "Suddenly and at one stroke," Emanuel Neumann commented, "the Zionist Organization was shorn of its political prerogatives." Ministries and public institutions ultimately responsible to the Knesset assumed most of these functions leaving little more for the Diaspora Zionists to do than raise funds. In essence, the "special status," the quasi-governmental standing the WZO sought, was intended to restore to Diaspora Zionists, dominated by the Americans, their former policy making role. Special status advocates insisted that those who raised the funds should have a voice in the spending of those funds. (The Silver group's slogan was, "No taxation without representation.") Furthermore, only if the Zionist movement possessed a semi-governmental status could it regain its prestige and influence.[46]

In his keynote address Ben-Gurion called for a "loyal partnership" between the State of Israel and World Jewry. The mission of the Zionist Movement was to "encourage and create such a loyal partnership." Only then and with "a great pioneering upsurge" would the Jewish State and the Jewish people be able to contend with the central and vital tasks Israel faced: security, immigrant absorption, and the speedy up building of the land. Ben-Gurion vigorously opposed the notion of the State designating the WZO as representative of Diaspora Jewry in matters pertaining to Israel. "If American Jews wanted a voice in Israeli affairs, they would have to become Israeli citizens." More than a year was required until a watered-down version of the special status proposal passed the Knesset. On the one hand, the Zionist Congress text aroused the protests of American non-Zionists led by the AJC who objected to the phrase stating that the WZO was "the representative of the Jewish people." On the other hand, the Knesset's political factions were divided, either charging that the proposal impinged on Israel's sovereignty or else that it circumscribed the activities of the WZO.[47]

The prolonged verbal scuffle ran deeper than a jurisdictional dispute. In an essay on the eve of the Jerusalem congress, Neumann recalled that at the first meeting of the Jewish Agency's Actions Committee following the establishment of the State in August 1948 he suggested "in private" that "all organized efforts by the Jews of the world on behalf of Israel should be carried on through or under the supervision of the WZO." This meant "a self-imposed limitation on the part of the Government of Israel to refrain from making its own direct approaches to the Jews of the Diaspora." The time had also come for the World Zionist movement to expand its program and "proceed on the basis of an affirmative attitude toward Jewish life in the Diaspora." For example, "in undertaking a more vigorous effort to spread the Hebrew language and literature among our youth, the goal should be not only to prepare them for Israel, but to deepen and to enrich their lives as Jews" in their Diaspora home. The Zionist movement should also be active in other spheres of Jewish concern, like "the defense of Jewish rights the world over." This would lead to the consolidation of existing organizations under the aegis of the WZO. Neumann, as well as Silver and Goldmann, conceived of a WZO which would embrace an organized Diaspora Jewry dedicated to supporting the Jewish state and benefiting in turn from the flourishing cultural and spiritual center in Israel. Two distinctive realms, State and Diaspora—Israel and the WZO—would assure the unity and continuity of the Jewish people.[48]

Ideological issues, goals and definitions, were subsumed under the rubric of the proposed "Jerusalem Program." Its proponents argued that the aim of the Zionist movement as adopted by the first Congress (Basle, 1897), "to create for the Jewish people a home in Palestine secured by public law," had been achieved, hence the need to define a new "aim" appropriate to the post-state reality. The "Jerusalem Program" would define "the final aim of Zionism."[49] In deference to the American delegates' hostility to redefining Zionism at all—which they perceived as challenging their Zionist credentials and triggering a painful and pointless ideological debate—a compromise was reached. One observer called it an "armistice." The operative term "task" replaced "aim" or "ultimate aim" as originally proposed, a semantic sleight of hand. The American delegate, Ezra Shapiro, on presenting the "Report of the Committee on Fundamental Problems" to the plenum explained that "if the Congress and the Zionist Movement wished to remain united, there was no alternative but to formulate the *Task* of Zionism and not its *Aim*." (Apparently, "task" was less binding than "aim.") The original draft formulated by the Agency's executive read: "Zionism aims at the redemption of the people of Israel through the ingathering of its exiles in the Land of Israel and the consolidations of the State of Israel."[50]

"Aim" or "task," "redemption" (*geulah*) and "ingathering of the exiles" (*kibbutz galuyot*) evoked a passionate debate. If American Jews were also in "exile" (*galut*), as the Israelis insisted, then surely the Zionists among them were obliged to join the "ingathering," "to make *aliyah*." In a "post-mortem" of the Congress, Marie Syrkin, a Labor Zionist delegate and an editor of the *Jewish Frontier*, sardonically remarked that "in the committee rooms where the resolutions were being drafted the tug-of-war" between the American Zionists and the Israelis "could be sensed in every cautious comma and prudent phrase. No American Jew was going to find himself spiritually, if not physically, *en route* to Israel because of an oversight in punctuation."[51] Syrkin's bitter witticism was especially appropriate to the controversy over the proposed new doctrine which preoccupied the "Fundamental Problems Committee." American delegates led by Rose Halprin, Hadassah's president and member of the Jewish Agency's American executive, declared that American Jews did not want to be or need to be "redeemed" or "ingathered." Jews are in exile when they live in fear or torture, or cannot immigrate freely. "All of us," Halprin granted,

> recognize and accept the historic and Messianic concept of Ge'ulat Ha'am [the redemption of the people] and kibbutz galuyot. Why then do we differ? The differences arise in the projection of that Messianic historic concept upon the organizational scene today. The differences are sharpened when this concept, with

which we all agree, is translated into a program of implementation of Zionism today.[52]

No less distressing for the American delegates were the Israeli taunts that America's Jews were not exempt from the fate that befell other exiled communities. Hayim Greenberg, the leading Labor Zionist ideologue, captured the essence of the American Zionist view. "If there will be a time when American Jews will go to live in Israel, they will do so not because America will have ejected them, but out of Israel's attraction and inspiration. Not in fear, but in love." Finally, a subcommittee eliminated "redemption," added the phrase, "the fostering of the unity of the Jewish people," and replaced "aim" with "task." The Americans voted with the majority having made their rejection of the America-is-exile argument abundantly clear. Moreover, the fact that Congress rules required the approval of two successive Congresses for a proposed change in the movement's fundamental principles to become binding enabled the Americans to demonstrate their recognition of the need for Zionist unity.[53]

For American Zionists, the Jerusalem Congress turned into an inquest. For two weeks, the American delegates defended the authenticity and legitimacy of their Zionism *and* their Americanism. In his discourse on "Jewish Culture and Education in the Diaspora," Greenberg discussed the exceptionalism of America's national identity. The American Revolution was the most successful revolution in world history, and it produced a "rational patriotism" with none of the "nationalistic mythology" that led Germany astray, "making it drunk and toxic with political idolatry." Jews in America lived in a cultural context at one and the same time American and Jewish, unfettered by the monism of the nation-state. The chief danger was indifference to the whole matter of being a Jew. Neither "platonic Zionism" nor "sentimental Zionism" was enough to overcome indifference. From the standpoint of Jewish survival in the West, education in "Jewishness" was more vital than what some called "Zionist education."[54] Halprin lectured the Congress on the same theme: "Within the wide latitude given by American Democracy to multiple cultures there is room for the concept of Jewish peoplehood. The idea of Jewish peoplehood does not violate the concept of nationhood as we know it in the United States." In this context, the references to the spiritual and religious motifs inherent in Zionism are striking given the engrossment with organizational politics and ideology which dominated the discussions. Summing up the general debate, Nahum Goldmann, an unabashed secularist, expounded on the exiled Jews' "mystical ties to Eretz Israel" during the millennia of their dispersion. "Three times every day they prayed, 'Restore us to Zion.' This was the basis of Zionism." Greenberg placed the question of religion and the religious tradition in Judaism at the heart of what he called "Hebraism," the national-religious civilization. With the indifference and ignorance to religious tradition of the native-born Israeli generation in mind, a rebuke directed to the pioneering generation of the parents and teachers, Greenberg wryly remarked that knowing the Hebrew names of the plants in Israel, or the parts of a tractor in their new Hebrew coinages was not enough if one did not know "to their deepest sounding, and in their context of spiritual tensions such Hebrew expressions as *mitsvah, averah, tikkun, Kiddush ha-shem, devekut, teshuvah.*"[55]

For the American delegates, the first Zionist Congress to be held in the Jewish state underscored the new complexities Zionism faced in America. On the one hand, fragile, new-born Israel required enormous support, more than the American Zionists had provided at the birth of the state. At the same time, an unfolding Jewish communal order at home demanded their involvement. American Jewry was undergoing rapid social and cultural integration into American life. (The 500, 000 Jews who had served in the armed forces during the war was one component in this development.) A new affluence, the move from city to suburb, and the central roles the synagogue centers and community federation of philanthropies played replaced the once ascendant secular ideologies and particularistic interests. Concern for Jewish group survival in America equaled if it did not surpass the angst for the welfare of Israel. The two were often linked. Jewish leaders and communal activist wore several hats—builders of American communal institutions and workers for the many-sided needs of Israel. At the Jerusalem congress, the American Zionist leadership responded to the Israeli challenge of the authenticity of its Zionism by affirming without reservation or apology its dual identity as Americans and Zionists, and its commitment to the cultural and spiritual enrichment of American Jewish life. The American Zionists' faith in the compatibility of believing in two promised lands confronted Israel's exclusive claim to the birthright, dogmas that continued to be debated with changing nuances at Zionist conventions and ideological conferences. The 1951 Jerusalem congress set the agenda for the post-state era with its search for collective self-understanding and the fulfillment of the promises of a promised land or lands.

Notes

1. My deepest thanks to Professor Ezra Mendelsohn of the Hebrew University Jerusalem for reading a number of versions of this essay and for his insightful comments and suggestions.

2. Genesis 12:1–3.

3. Arthur Hertzberg, *The Zionist Idea: A Historical Analysis and Reader* (New York: Atheneum, 1973), 495–500.

4. *The Two Hundred and Fiftieth Anniversary of the Settlement of the Jews in the United States* (New York: n.p., 1906), 105.

5. George Washington to Members of Voluntary Association, New York, Dec. 2, 1783 in *Immigration and the American Tradition*, ed. Moses Rischin (Indianapolis, IN: Bobbs Merrill, 1976), 43.

6. Quoted in Arthur Schlesinger Jr., "The American Experience or Destiny?" *American Historical Review* 82 (1977): 502–22, here 516.

7. David Philipson, *Max Lilienthal, American Rabbi: Life and Writings* (New York: Bloch Publishing Co., 1915), 457.

8. Ben Halpern, *A Clash of Heroes: Brandeis, Weizmann, and American Zionism* (New York and Oxford: Oxford University Press, 1987), 208, 215; Ezra Mendelsohn, *On Modern Jewish Politics* (New York and Oxford: Oxford University Press, 1993), 66; *Maccabaean* 33 (1918): 193; *Der Tog*, May 12, 1920: 1. For a useful overview of American Zionism see Naomi W. Cohen, *American Jews and the Zionist Idea* (New York: KTAV, 1975).

9. Melvin I. Urofsky, *We Are One! American Jewry and Israel* (Garden City, NY: Anchor Press and Doubleday, 1978), 258–97; *Reconstructionist* 17 (June 29, 1951): 3–5.

10. Jonathan Frankel, *Prophecy and Politics: Socialism, Nationalism, and the Russian Jews, 1862–1917* (Cambridge and New York: Cambridge University Press, 1981), 472–547; Naomi W. Cohen, *The Americanization of Zionism* (Hanover, NH and London: Brandeis University Press by University Press of New England, 2003), 39–63.

11. Evyatar Friesel, *The Zionist Movement in the United States, 1897–1914* (Hebrew) (Tel Aviv: Hakibbutz Hmeuchad, 1970), 15–39, 125–59; Melvin I. Urofsky, *American Zionism from Herzl to Holocaust* (Garden City, NY: Anchor Press and Doubleday, 1975), 81–117; Cohen, *Americanization of Zionism*, 15–38.

12. Judah L. Magnes, "A Message from Palestine: Address delivered at Cooper Union, on Saturday evening, May 18, 1912," Magnes Papers, Central Archives for the History of the Jewish People, Jerusalem, P3/1065, 3–13.

13. Allon Gal, *Brandeis of Boston* (Cambridge, MA: Harvard University Press, 1980), 179–81.

14. Barbara Ann Harris, "Zionist Speeches of Louis Dembitz Brandeis: A Critical Edition" (UCLA dissertation, 1967): 85–9.

15. Urofsky, *American Zionism*, 145.

16. Gerald Sorin, *A Time for Building: The Third Migration 1880–1920* (Baltimore, MD: Johns Hopkins University Press, 1992), 109–38; Zosa Szajkowski, "Private and Organized American Jewish Overseas Relief (1914–1938)," *American Jewish Historical Quarterly* 57 (Sept. 1967): 52–98; Zosa Szajkowski, "Concord and Discord in American Jewish Overseas Relief, 1914–1924," *YIVO Annual* 14 (1969): 99–158, here 105; Halpern, *Clash of Heroes*, 114–16, 118–21.

17. Harris, "Zionist Speeches of Louis Dembitz Brandeis," 100.

18. Jerold Auerbach, *Rabbis and Lawyers: The Journey from Torah to Constitution* (Bloomington and Indianapolis, IN: Indiana University Press, 1990), 128.

19. Jacob D. Haas, *Louis D. Brandeis: A Biographical Sketch* (New York: Block Publishing Co., 1929), 56–61; Halpern, *A Clash of Heroes*, 109–12; Urofsky, *American Zionism*, 120–1, 161–3. Evyatar Friesel cites a letter from Jacob de Haas to Brandeis dated August 26, 1914 urging Brandeis to head the Provisional Committee to be established at the Emergency conference ("Brandeis' Role in American Zionism," *American Jewish History* 69 (September, 1979): 34–59, here 42). Sarah Schmidt cites an interview with Horace Kallen in which Kallen described convincing Brandeis, en route to New York, to accept the chairmanship of the Provincial Committee; see *Horace M. Kallen: Prophet of American Zionism* (Brooklyn, NY: Carlson Publishing, 1995), 58–9.

20. Quotations in Harris, "Zionist Speeches of Louis Dembitz Brandeis," 96–7; *Brandeis on Zionism: A Collection of Addresses and Statements by Louis D. Brandeis* (Washington, DC: Zionist Organization of America, 1942), 49.

21. Jonathan D. Sarna, "'The Greatest Jew in the World Since Jesus Christ': The Jewish Legacy of Louis D. Brandeis," *American Jewish History* 81 (1984): 346–64.

22. Urofsky, *American Zionism*, 252–7; Schmidt, *Horace M. Kallen*, 116–19.

23. Halpern, *Clash of Heroes*, 94–100, 113–26, 196–232.

24. *Brandeis on Zionism*, 10; see Melvin I. Urofsky, "Zionism, An American Experiment," *American Jewish Historical Quarterly* 63 (1979): 215–30; Auerbach, *Rabbis and Lawyers*, 133–46.

25. Quoted in Gal, *Brandeis of Boston*, 92–3; see Schmidt, *Horace M. Kallen*, 35–66.

26. Hans Vought, "Division and Reunion: Woodrow Wilson, Immigration and the Myth of American Unity," *Journal of American Ethnic History* 13 (Spring 1994): 24–50, here 33; Michla Pomerance, "The United States and Self-Determination: Perspectives on the Wilsonian Conception," *The American Journal of International Law* 70 / 1 (January 1976): 1–27, here 1–3.

27. Robert W. Seton-Watson, "The Issues of the War," in *The War and Democracy*, ed. Roger W. Seton-Watson et al. (London: Macmillan, 1914), 290, quoted in *Brandeis on Zionism*, 28–9. For background, see Ezra Mendelsohn, "The Paradox of Nationalism: A Comparative Study of Ethnic Nationalism in the U.S.," *Historia* 2 (1998): 87–101 (Hebrew). Joseph P. O'Grady, ed., *The Immigrants' Influence on Wilson's Peace Policies* (Lexington: University of Kentucky Press, 1967), contains essays on ten ethnic groups' pro-homeland activities during the First World War.

28. *Brandeis on Zionism*, 102–3.

29. Quotations in *Brandeis on Zionism*, 28–9.

30. Harris, "Zionist Speeches of Louis Dembitz Brandeis," 100–1.

31. *Der Groyse kundes* 8 (June 9, 1916): 1.

32. Chester Teller, "American Zionists Move Toward Clarity," *Commentary*, 12 (November 1951): 444–50.

33. See Zohar Segev, "American Zionists' Place in Israel after Statehood: From Involved Partners to Outside Supporters," *American Jewish History* 93 (2005): 277–302.

34. Zvi Ganin, *Truman, American Jewry and Israel, 1945–1948* (New York: Holmes & Meier Publishers, 1979), 34–48; Marc Lee Raphael, *Abba Hillel Silver: A Profile in American Judaism* (New York: Holmes & Meier Publishers, 1989), 168–74.

35. Zvi Ganin, *An Uneasy Relationship: American Jewish Leadership and Israel, 1948–1957* (Syracuse, NY: Syracuse University Press, 2005), 18–25, 53–9; Ernest Stock, *Partners and Pursestrings: A History of the United Israel Appeal* (Lanham, MD: University Press of America, 1967), 132–41; Arthur A. Goren, "Between Ideal and Reality: Abba Hillel Silver's Zionist Vision," *The Journal of Israeli History* 17 (Spring 1996): 71–86, here 81–4; Segev, "American Zionists' Place in Israel after Statehood," 283–8; Mark A. Raider, "Where American Zionism Differed: Abba Hillel Silver Reconsidered," *American Jewish History* 93 (2005): 87–121, here 119–20; Rafael Medoff, "Recent Trends in the Historiography of American Zionism," *American Jewish History* 86 (March, 1998): 117–34, here 117–20; Urofsky, *We Are One!*, 115–20.

36. *Vision and Victory: A Collection of Addresses by Dr. Abba Hillel Silver, 1942–1948* (New York: Zionist Organization of America, 1949), 192–3; see Elihu Elath, *The Struggle for Statehood*, vol. 3 (Tel Aviv: Am Oved, 1982), 777 (Hebrew); Ganin, *Truman*, 120–89. My thanks to Dr. Zvi Ganin for bringing this source to my attention.

37. Abba Eban, *An Autobiography* (New York: Random House, 1977) 117–18.

38. Raphael, *Abba Hillel Silver*, 175–82; Urofsky, *We Are One!*, 278–89; Ganin, *An Uneasy Relationship*, 18–25; Ofer Shiff, "Abba Hillel Silver and David Ben-Gurion: A Diaspora Leader Challenges the Revered Status of the 'Founding Father,'" *Studies in Ethnicity and Nationalism* 3 / 3 (2010): 391–412, here 397–8.

39. Urofsky, *We Are One!*, 202; Emanuel Neumann, *In the Arena* (New York: Herzl Press, 1976), 31–4; Ganin, *An Uneasy Relationship*, 115.

40. Ibid., 3–5.

41. Yonathan Shapiro, *Leadership of the American Zionist Organization, 1897–1930* (Urbana, IL.: University of Illinois Press, 1971), 115; Stuart Svonkin, *Jews Against Prejudice: American Jews and the Fight for Civil Liberties* (New York: Columbia University Press, 1997), 161–77.

42. Urofsky, *We Are One!*, 265–70; Ganin, *An Uneasy Relationship*, 36–40, 82–4; *Furrows* 8 (October 1950): 3–4; Arthur A. Goren, *The Political Culture of American Jews* (Bloomington and Indianapolis, IN: Indiana University Press, 1999), 165–6, 182–5.

43. "An Exchange of Views," *American Jewish Yearbook* 53 (1952): 564–8.

44. See Ganin, *An Uneasy Relationship*, 81–130; Auerbach, *Rabbis and Lawyers*, 141; Urofsky, *We Are One!*, 193–5.

45. *Jerusalem Post*, August 15, 1951; *Ha-Aretz*, August 15, 1951; *New York Times*, August 15, 1951. For a penetrating analysis of the complexity of Jewish politics see Ezra Mendelsohn, *On Modern Jewish Politics*, passim.

46. "Dispute Over Zionism," *New York Times*, August 19, 1951; "Split of Zionists," *New York Times*, August 18, 1951; *American Jewish Year Book* 54 (1953): 154–7; "Excerpts from Speeches," in *Fundamental Issues of Zionism at the 23rd Zionist Congress*, ed. S. U. Nahon (Jerusalem: Organization Department of the Zionist Executive, 1952) (Nahum Goldmann, 13–18; Abba Hillel Silver, 80–3); Ganin, *Uneasy Relationship*, 121–3, 141–8.

47. "Excerpts from Speeches" (David Ben Gurion, 10–3); "Ben-Gurion Urges Zionist Harmony," *New York Times*, August 15, 1951; "Dispute Over Zionism," *New York Times*, August 19, 1951; *Ha-Aretz*, August 27, 1951: 1–2; Ganin, *An Uneasy Relationship*, 141–8.

48. Emanuel Neumann, "Towards the World Zionist Congress," *The Zionist Quarterly* 1:1 (Summer 1951) 6–8, 12–13, 15; Segev, "American Zionists' Place in Israel after Statehood," 297–9; Gideon Shimoni, "Reformulations of Zionist Ideology since the Establishment of the State of Israel," *Studies in Contemporary Jewry* 11 (1995): 11–18.

49. Quoted in Nahon, ed., *Fundamental Issues of Zionism*, 119–20.

50. *Jerusalem Post*, August 27, 1951.

51. Nahon, ed., *Fundamental Issues of Zionism*, 80–3, 85–135; Stenographic Report: 23rd Zionist Congress (Hebrew) (Jerusalem: Zionist Executive, 1951), 151–78; Marie Syrkin, "The Zionist Congress—a Post-Mortem," *Jewish Frontier* 18 (October 1951): 21–3, here 21.

52. *Jerusalem Post*, August 27, 1951; *Ha-Aretz*, August 27, 1951; Nahon, ed., *Fundamental Issues of Zionism*, 30.

53. Nahon, ed., *Fundamental Issues of Zionism*, 36.

54. Ibid., 37.

55. Ibid., 30, 106.

CHAPTER 16

"YOU CAN'T RECOGNIZE AMERICA": AMERICAN JEWISH PERCEPTIONS OF ANTI-SEMITISM AS A TRANSNATIONAL PHENOMENON AFTER THE FIRST WORLD WAR

Gil Ribak

In May 1924, just after Congress passed the Johnson-Reed Act, which severely curtailed the number of immigrants from Eastern and Southern Europe, Polish-born Yiddish journalist Gedaliah Bublik declared that "the end of the golden epoch" for American Jews had arrived. Bublik, who would become a key figure in orthodox Zionism, claimed that "the Jewish experience in other countries repeats itself in America": when Jews first came to Spain, Poland, and Russia, they received "liberal treatment." But since "America has become nationalistic in the European sense . . . the hatred toward Jews intensified." Four years beforehand, socialist Hillel Rogoff, who hardly shared Bublik's political convictions, recounted pessimistically how he heard from all sides "you can't recognize America." Rogoff lamented that anyone living in America "for more than five years" could not know the country anymore: "Nowhere has chauvinistic patriotism assumed such a wild character as in America."[1]

The Great War and its aftermath witnessed a succession of events at home and abroad that flung American Jews into a whirlwind of challenges. The unprecedented postwar mass murder of Jews in Eastern Europe and the campaign for minority rights at the Paris Peace Conference had strained Jewish relations with Eastern European immigrants, especially the Poles. At the same time, American-bred anti-Semitism was also on the rise: the strain of xenophobia that underlay the Red Scare, university quotas, immigration restriction, the singling out of minorities, deportation of aliens, and Henry Ford's fulminations had all signaled an ominous path.

The specter of American anti-Semitism clashed with an earlier fundamental axiom in American Jewish life: the belief that "Yankees" or "real" Americans (the common term for old-stock, Anglo-Saxon Protestants in many Jewish sources) were inherently different from Gentiles elsewhere by virtue of their tolerance and openness. Nineteenth-century American Jews, whether native-born or immigrants, Central or Eastern Europeans, tended to agree that Americans could not be anti-Semitic. Henry (Zvi) Gersoni from Vilna, who came to America in 1869 and became active as a rabbi and journalist, sang the praise of the American people, determining "the Americans who live in villages and small towns are lovers of man and their heart is far from any prejudice," and that "an American would never think to defame" immigrants. A pioneer of the Yiddish press in America, Zvi Hirsh Bernstein, arrived in New York in 1870 and shortly thereafter reported to his readers in moderate-orthodox Hebrew periodical *Ha-magid* (The Herald, which came out in Prussia) that "Not a single person among the local Christians" complained against the new immigrants because "In America there is no hatred and no resentment." Even a blunt critic of America, like Russian-born socialist George M. Price, wrote in 1891, after living for nearly a decade in New York, that "[T]he very make-up of an American" might "seem strange to a Russian anti-Semite" because "For the American racial, national or religious differences do not exist." Leading Reform rabbi, Kaufmann Kohler, argued in 1898 that "[T]here is no anti-Semitism in this free land of ours" since it was "antagonistic to the spirit of ... the American people." A year later, during a mass meeting of the American Hebrew League of Brooklyn, a Hungarian-born rabbi, Leopold Wintner, cried that "there is no antisemitism in America," and furthermore "it cannot exist"; the American people are honorable and do not tolerate anti-Semitism. Wintner emphasized that "The Yankees love justice too much to allow [anyone] to persecute Jews."[2]

When anti-Jewish animosity appeared in America, Jewish observers were quick to ascribe it to European immigrants. The idea that European immigrants like the Irish or Germans imported their anti-Jewish hatred to the USA was a common way to reconcile the image of the tolerant American with the existing instances of bigotry. In 1865 the American correspondent of a leading German-Jewish periodical, *Allgemeine Zeitung des Judenthums*, complained about the hostility of German immigrants, including the radical ones, toward Jews in America: "we owe all *rishes* [anti-Semitism] in America to those freedom heroes [a sarcastic reference to German radicals]—originally the American knows nothing about rishes." In 1890 the popular Yiddish poet and wedding bard, Elikum Tsunzer, wrote that in America anti-Jewish venom was on the rise due to demographic changes: "here the whole regime is passing into the hands of the Irish and the Germans, who brought their antisemitism from Europe." In the same year, Polish-born rabbi Marcus Jastrow echoed that attitude, when he said that anti-Jewish "poison ... has been imported" to the country. In 1898 longtime lobbyist Simon Wolf wrote, "Most of it [anti-Semitism] in this country is of foreign origin."[3] After workers attacked the funeral procession of Rabbi Jacob Joseph on the Lower East Side in 1902, Jewish responses referred to hooligans who "come here from abroad" and mistook themselves for Americans, and that anti-Semitism was "impossible" in America. Such attitudes led even the moderate, not to say bland, *Yidishe velt* (Jewish World) to complain that among American Jews you were not allowed to call Americans "anti-Semites"; they were always "loafers," "bums," or "hoodlums."[4]

In cases when blue-blooded Americans like Judge Henry Hilton or Austin Corbin blatantly banned Jews from their resorts, Jewish correspondents interpreted them as the doings of prejudiced individuals, who were atypical of the American character. Moreover, their reports emphasized how the American press and public chided and ridiculed the bigots.[5] By the time of the First World War, however, that idealization of Americans had become all but impossible. The horrendous situation in Eastern Europe further complicated the situation: the simultaneous rise of anti-Semitism on both sides of the Atlantic, though hardly on the same scale or with the same ramifications, had sometimes cast Americans as part of an unspecified, hostile Gentile world.

Jewish attitudes toward the warring sides in the Great War changed dramatically before America entered the war. When word of the Tsar's abdication and arrest was received in New York by mid-March 1917, the initial disbelief soon turned to ecstasy. The demise of a hateful regime, that was seen as the Jews' bitterest tormentor, was welcomed with parades, merriment, and cries of "Long Live the Russian Revolution!" On the streets of the East Side people embraced one another, happily crying and laughing. Radical and conservative papers alike celebrated the revolution, including the orthodox *Morgen zhurnal* (Morning Journal) which only a month earlier asserted, "The simple Slav knows nothing of the dreams of the cultured revolutionist." Some 20,000 blissful celebrants gathered in Madison Square Garden, yelled, and danced in the aisles as socialist leaders like Abraham Cahan, Morris Hillquit, Jacob Panken, and Borekh Charney Vladeck praised the revolution. Yet the enthusiasm did not translate into massive re-emigration to Russia: in 1917 only 864 Jews and 7,557 Russian nationals (many of whom were probably also Jews) left the United States.[6]

The euphoria brought about an instant reversal in attitudes toward the belligerents on the Jewish street: negative references to Russia had all but vanished, while pro-German utterances (considerably encumbered by America's involvement in the war) had drastically decreased. Jews were influenced by the anti-German environment, where scholars dissected the inbred depravity of the German, shocked audiences watched motion pictures about the barbarities of the "Hun," and the Committee on Public Information (CPI) dispatched 75,000 "Four-Minute Men" across the country to whip up enthusiasm for the war through oratorical bombardment before any available spectators.[7]

The surrounding atmosphere against the "Huns" just added to other developments that harmed the image of Germans in Jewish eyes: after the Tsar was toppled, Russian Jews had no reason to support the authoritarian Germany against their former home country, which emancipated its Jewish population. In addition, reports from Eastern Europe pointed to the deteriorating economic conditions under German occupation, which led to hunger and smuggling, and subsequent German punitive measures against local Jewish communities. Already before America entered the war, the nonpartisan, liberal daily *Der tog* (The Day) critically scrutinized the German character, noting that Germans "are too much in love with themselves." Yiddish writer Tashrak (pseudonym of Yisroel Zevin) penned a humoristic sketch in March 1917 that relayed how all things German fell from grace for American Jews: lodge members refused to speak Germanized Yiddish anymore at their meetings, everyone hoped America would beat the Germans, and German Jews pretended to be Litvaks.[8]

Pro-Ally veteran politician Oscar S. Straus did not pretend to be an Eastern European Jew, and he claimed that "in one of the largest Jewish clubs, whose membership consisted almost entirely of Jews of German origin, the pro-Ally sentiment was so strong as to be practically unanimous." Whereas several American Jews of German origin like Straus, Otto Kahn, Louis Marshall, and Rabbi David Philipson held pro-Allied position before 1917, the US entry into the war was decisive in turning many German Jews in America against the fatherland. Financier Jacob H. Schiff, who earlier expressed confidence in the victory of "German manhood," stopped speaking German in public and wholeheartedly took part in pro-war rallies, cooperating with arch-patriotic organizations in propaganda work aimed at the foreign-born. Immediately after the armistice German-born Simon Wolf warned that the "Teutons" were "hungry ... to get even" with the Allies and urged that the strictest measures should be imposed against Germany. In a Memorial Day sermon delivered in 1919 before congregants of mostly German origin, Rabbi Joseph Silverman of Temple Emanu-El (New York) thundered, "the nations responsible for this war should be punished. They are murderers from the Kaiser down."[9]

After the March Revolution in Russia, antipathy to Germany permeated also the circles of previously pro-German Jewish socialists who opposed America's entry into the war. The satirical weekly, *Der groyser kundes* (The Big Stick), depicted Germans as "savages" with a superiority complex. A friend of the influential socialist activist and journalist Tsivyen (Bentsiyen Hofman) described him as "in love with German culture." By August 1917, nonetheless, that very Tsivyen wrote about the "barbaric, bloodthirsty Germans that have to be wiped from the face of the earth so humanity may live in peace." When a German-American New Yorker was called to jury duty, he expressed his loyalty to Germany and hostility to the Allies and the Jews. The *Forverts* (Jewish Daily Forward) wondered why he had to drag the Jews into it: "Apparently he found it impossible to express truly his German patriotism without it [anti-Semitism]."[10]

When the Soviets signed (March 1918) a humiliating separate peace treaty with Germany at Brest-Litovsk, where they ceded vast territories to the Central Powers, many Americans saw it as a Bolshevik betrayal of the Allies. Jewish radicals, in contrast, saw it as German belligerence that emphasized the vulnerability of the young Soviet regime. For the bulk of socialists, those circumstances led to a reversal in their position toward the war: preservation of the revolutionary Russia became the main priority, and Wilson's "capitalistic" war was suddenly an imperative. Even the most pro-German Jewish radical of yesteryear no longer saw the Germans as a bulwark of civilization against the Slavs, but rather as those culpable for the outbursts of anti-Jewish violence and dire food shortage in Eastern Europe. In 1919 a Jewish organizer for the Structural Iron workers, Sol Broad, described "a friction between the Jews and the German-Austrian element because the Jews favored the war after the Brest-Litovsk Treaty. The German-Austrian element has been somewhat antisemitic." By February 1918 Yiddish journalist William Edlin privately claimed that "everybody" on the East Side was becoming anti-German, and that transformation was especially noticeable among Jewish socialists. A week later the German-American secretary of the Socialist Party, Adolph Germer, wrote that "95% of their [Jewish] membership have changed front" and support the war against Germany.[11]

News about the reemergence of political anti-Semitism in postwar Germany fortified Jewish suspicions toward the nation of poets and thinkers. In 1919 critic Re'uven Brainin, who edited a New York Hebrew weekly, *Ha-toren* (The Mast), described how German Jewish soldiers sacrificed themselves for their country yet German anti-Semitism was strengthening. Brainin criticized Jewish thinkers who tried to demonstrate a German-Jewish symbiosis: "The Hebrew spirit and the German spirit ... are opposed to each other like two antagonistic natural elements." Brainin called Germans "the creators of antisemitism" that "Slavic nations had put into practice"; with the outbreak of anti-Jewish violence in Germany, "Germans had become the students of the Slavs." Zionist journalist and children's books author Leon Elbe (nom de plume of Leyb Baseyn) argued that "German hands" wrote the anti-Semitic articles in Henry Ford's newspaper: "the two essays in Ford's weekly are a German product." Voicing a similar view, German-born rabbi Isaac L. Bril argued in 1921, "Scratch a German and you will find an anti-Semite. This hatred of Jews is inherited in all classes in Germany."[12]

During the war and especially its bloody aftershocks American Jews were primarily worried about the events in the areas east of Germany. The news about the horrors that befell Eastern European Jewry and the need to work for an immediate relief for one's family members engulfed nearly every immigrant Jewish family and led to the formation of several relief agencies, most notably the Joint Distribution Committee (JDC), to aid the devastated communities.[13] In the first week of November 1917 two major events abroad occurred almost simultaneously, capturing Jewish attention and exhilaration, and seeming to many as the birth pangs of a new world: the Balfour Declaration and the Bolshevik Revolution. On November 2, 1917, Britain's Foreign Minister, Arthur J. Balfour, wrote to Lord James Rothschild that the British government supports "the establishment in Palestine of a national home for the Jewish people." The Declaration, coupled with General Allenby's dramatic conquest of Jerusalem a few weeks later led to an outpouring of euphoric sentiments in various quarters of American Jewry. As Zionist societies and orders celebrated the eventful developments, the orthodox Agudas ha-Rabonim (Union of Orthodox Rabbis of the United States and Canada) rejoiced, as did the socialist Independent Arbeter Ring (Workmen's Circle) order, which decided to espouse Zionism. The socialist monthly *Di tsukunft* (The Future), which under Avrom Lesin's editorship had become more approving of Jewish nationalism, published a short article by renowned Yiddish writer Sholem Ash titled "The Triumph": Ash interpreted the declaration as a "great repentance by the Christian world for eighteen hundred years of Christian sin and injustice." As Zionist membership swelled, the messianic prospect of fulfilling an almost 2,000-year promise touched even the unlikeliest corners of American Jewish life.[14]

While the Balfour Declaration immensely increased Jewish support for the Allies' cause, the ramifications of the Bolshevik Revolution complicated the situation of American Jews: Jewish leaders became quickly aware how rife was the association of Jews with Bolshevism in American society. Such linkage was made in late 1917 and by 1918 the *New York Exporters Review* claimed that "the majority of East Side (New York) Jews are 'bolshevists.'" Though these voices were weaker than in the postwar panic, the word Bolshevik had become quickly identical with treason. Thus Jewish leaders hastened to deny those charges: as early as November 1917 journalist and communal activist Herman Bernstein deplored the reports that Jews were the main backers of the new regime in Russia, calling them "antisemitic propaganda." Bernstein added that Bolsheviks like Leon Trotsky "are not Jews in the real sense of the word." The president of the Educational Alliance, Judge Samuel Greenbaum, warned in March 1918 that "Our race has been sullied" by the few Jews who wanted to imitate the government of "darkened

Russia." But those accusations and rebuffs were merely precursors to the nativist torrent after 1918 that tied Jews to communism, anarchism, syndicalism, and anything that had to do with wild-eyed, shaggy Russians seeking to bring down the American way of life.[15]

Unlike the March Revolution, numerous Russian-born Jews responded to the Bolshevik takeover of Petrograd with hesitation and distrust. Some even gloated about the turmoil in Russia. Four days after the revolution, writing in his diary at his Bronx apartment, Re'uven Brainin recalled that only a few months beforehand the Bolshevik leader had lived close by in the neighborhood. Brainin's thoughts about the revolution led him to bitter musings that unwittingly and ironically anticipated the rantings of anti-Semites like Henry Ford, who viewed Bolshevism as a Jewish plot. Brainin wrote,

> And if Leon Trotsky and his Jewish friends who now head the Russian government shall destroy Russia—it would be the revenge of the Jewish people on their tormentors, persecutors, haters and also slaughterers of yesterday. The dog—deserves his stick. Until yesterday the Russians ravaged our people, tormented our daughters, tore our children to pieces … Today, maybe the Trotskys and the Goldbergs will destroy their country.[16]

Journalist Yankev Magidov believed that his editor, the conservative Peter (Perets) Wiernik, with "his antipathy to all things Russian," was actually pro-Bolshevik, since "Russia does not deserve a better government."[17]

The reservations of Jewish immigrants included at first the radicals, too. As many Jewish socialists and Bundists identified with the Mensheviks (the socialist rivals of the Bolsheviks), their responses to the revolution were initially skeptical, if not negative: M. Gurevich, M. Baranov, and Moyshe Olgin (the latter subsequently became an adamant Stalinist) attacked the Bolsheviks' dictatorial rule and their attempt to install socialism in a peasant society that was ill-prepared for it. But as the years 1918 and 1919 progressed Jewish Socialists became more and more pro-Soviet: the revolution generated messianic fervor among Jewish radicals (and some of their non-Jewish comrades), promising a brave new world and the rise of a classless humanity. By 1919, Abraham Cahan forbade criticism of the Soviet Union in the *Forverts*.[18]

By 1918, the most compelling reason for many American Jews (not only radical ones) to wish for a Bolshevik victory was quite simple: though Red Army units occasionally assaulted Jewish communities as well, the Communists were often the only force that stood between Jews and violent death. In the civil war that wreaked havoc from late 1917 on in the former Pale of Settlement (especially in Ukraine), Reds (Bolsheviks) fought Whites (counterrevolutionary), Poles fought Ukrainians, Poles fought Bolsheviks, and Ukrainians fought among themselves, there was a vicious circle in motion: Jews were accused of being pro-Bolshevik, and were attacked and murdered in the tens of thousands. That persecution had the effect of turning them pro-Bolshevik for the sake of survival, and that allegiance served to justify further mass murder of Jews. White armies, Polish forces, Ukrainian nationalists under Semyon Petlyura, and marauding bands of peasants and Cossacks, attacked hundreds of Jewish communities, massacring unarmed, non-combatant Jewish families. Famed Russian-Jewish writer Isaac Babel, who traveled with a Red Army cavalry unit as a war correspondent, saw "naked seventy-year-old men with their skulls bashed in and tiny children with their fingers hacked off."[19]

But as the overall mood in America dreaded Bolshevism, and President Wilson sent some 15,000 American troops to Russia to help the Whites, American Jews found themselves in a bind: on the one hand, the overwhelming majority among them was not Bolshevik and wholeheartedly backed the war and loathed the "Teutons." Non-radical Jews (and also some of the radicals) hailed Wilson and the American intervention: anti-Bolsheviks like Rabbi Stephen S. Wise, poet Morris Rosenfeld, and anarchist Shoel Yanovsky constantly attacked the Communists and warned fellow Jews that as unpopular foreigners it was practically dangerous, morally wrong, and ungrateful toward America to back the Soviet regime.[20]

But on the other hand, in spite of the exhortations, quite a few, especially immigrant Jews, continued to view the Red Army as the Jews' savior. Author Upton Sinclair surely exaggerated when he wrote in early 1919, "According to the point of view of the Russian Jews of Hester Street ... American soldiers are shooting down their fathers, their sons, their brothers in Northern Russia and Siberia." Though hyperbolic, a situation where American troops were fighting on the same side with the anti-Semitic and reactionary forces of Alexander Kolchak's White regime did leave a bad taste in the mouths of many an immigrant. As the drive for American military intervention in Russia began in the spring of 1918, numerous individuals and committees poured into the offices of the *Forverts* and other radical newspapers on the East Side, demanding concrete effort against such plans. Jewish immigrants also participated in anti-intervention rallies and signed petitions to that effect. Non-radicals like Harvard law professor and former assistant to the Secretary of War, Felix Frankfurter, and philosopher Horace M. Kallen also opposed American intervention, as did most Yiddish newspapers.[21] Against that backdrop, a few Arbeter Ring's branches and half a dozen *landsmanshaftn* collected money to cover the expenses of the defense for six anarchist Jewish immigrants who were arrested (August 1918) for the distribution of leaflets against the American intervention in Russia. One of them, Jacob Schwartz, was beaten by the police and died in prison. Four of the defendants—Jacob Abrams, Hyman Lachovsky, Samuel Lipman, and Mollie Steimer—were sentenced to long prison terms, but were eventually deported to Russia in 1921.[22]

The radicals' defense of the young Soviet Union did not mean that older, enduring images of the Russian people vanished: Bundist writer Vladimir Kosovsky (penname of Nokhem-Mendel Levinson) described in the *Tsukunft* how Red Army units also initiated pogroms. Yet the editor (Avrom Lesin) hastened to defend the Soviets, as he revealed his perception of the Russian masses: Lesin commented below Kosovsky's article, "Naturally, nobody could believe that under the effect of the Bolshevik regime the Russian people would be transformed from pogromists to angels in a couple of months."[23] By early 1919 the Socialist Party in New York acknowledged the tension between Jews and the Russians and Ukrainians in its midst, and in one branch it became "impossible to create harmony and peace" between those groups. By 1921, Yiddish critic Mordekhai Danzis ridiculed anyone who idealized "the Russian peasant as the liberator of the world," but forgot "the dreadful cruelty of those beasts" who murdered tens of thousands of Jews.[24]

Russians were not seen as the only or chief culprits in shedding Jewish blood. As American Jews celebrated the Armistice, the Yiddish press as well as American papers carried ghastly reports about the horrors that befell Jews in Poland, Romania, and Ukraine: the descriptions of pregnant women ripped open, of eyes gouged out and infants murdered in their sleep, brought Jewish resentment toward the Eastern European nations involved in the atrocities to new heights. The growing anger toward "Slavs" and especially Poles began earlier, and Jewish antagonism intensified as more news arrived: in 1917 the *Tageblat* cautioned, "the antisemitism which is engraved in every Pole remains the same wherever he emigrates to." The events in Poland came quicker to the public's attention in the West than those in Ukraine, and added to the escalation of tensions over the anti-Jewish boycott and violence in Poland during the war. Furthermore, Poles in America were far more conspicuous than Ukrainians or Romanians with their campaign for Polish independence during the war and for Polish territorial demands in the postwar Paris Peace Conference. The American Citizens' Committee of Polish Birth and Descent charged that American Jews were besmirching the people of Poland by spreading "lies" about pogroms. The Polish Citizens' Committee of Cleveland threatened that American Jewish "position" might "force local disturbances."[25]

In November 1918 Jewish leaders like Louis Marshall of the American Jewish Committee (AJC) and Julian W. Mack of the Zionist Organization of America (ZOA) were quick to "deny that the Jews are in any way unfriendly to Polish independence." Yet speakers at a mass meeting organized by Jewish labor unions at Madison Square Garden a few days later, like Sholem Ash, lambasted Poles as anti-Semites. The flood of livid condemnations by Jewish writers only grew stronger with news about pogroms in Vilna and Pinsk in the spring of 1919. The Yiddish poet and essayist, Aren Glanz, wrote a scathing indictment of Polish and Ukrainian "national characteristic": Jews were "intrinsically incapable" of committing "unspeakable massacres like the Poles and Ukrainians." Glanz argued, "The Slavs are the most backward people . . . *The soul of the Slavs . . . is dark, a bleak night*."[26]

Such images became ubiquitous: one Saul Rosen of Forsyth Street, who visited Poland after the war said "with tears in his eyes" how a Pole snatched a Jewish toddler from his mother on a train and threw him out of the window. The *Groyser kundes* published a caricature, "How he looks without the mask," showing a frightening "Polish pogromist" holding a blood-dripping knife between his teeth while holding a mask of a human face bearing the caption "Free Poland." The *Tog* conveyed a similar idea in a caricature that showed a Pole with a blood-soaked knife climbing stairs covered with bodies of babies, women, and old men with a heading, "The Polish road to freedom."[27]

Hundreds of thousands of Jews in New York and Chicago took to the streets to manifest their anger and frustration in two separate days of mass parades and demonstrations against the continued slaughter of Jews in Eastern Europe, which were reminiscent of the mass protest against pogroms fourteen years beforehand. The first day, May 21, 1919, focused on Poland: after noontime nearly all Jewish workers left their shops and Jewish children stepped out of their classrooms to take part in one of the dozens marches and rallies across New York. Wearing black armbands and carrying banners in Yiddish and English, many protestors marched toward Madison Square Garden, where approximately 200,000 people milled outside the hall that hosted a protest meeting. At the meeting Jacob Schiff accused the American press of suppressing news about the wholesale murder of Polish Jewry, and popular Yiddish orator Hirsh Masliansky cried out to a weeping audience, "How many of you should mourn your slaughtered fathers, mothers, sisters and brothers?" Other speakers emphasized the presence of Jewish soldiers in the crowd: they fought for the liberty of Eastern European countries, which were now murdering Jews. In the black-framed *Forverts* on the day of protest, Avrom Lesin blamed "those Poles, those murderers of old men, of women, of children." On November 24, 1919, Jews in New York and Chicago observed a "day of mourning" in protest of the unrelenting murder of Jews in Ukraine: more than half a million Jews in Greater New York left their workplace as a somber procession of 25,000 men, women and children, representing hundreds of Jewish societies and organizations marched from various boroughs to a rally at Carnegie Hall.[28]

At the Madison Square Garden rally (May 1919), Stephen S. Wise said that American Poles themselves and not American Jews should have organized the protest against the pogroms. The *Groyser kundes* acerbically rejected such notion, claiming it was "a classic joke" to expect such a thing: "Rabbi Wise, who is American-born [sic], never had the honor and pleasure of being in close contact" with Poles and Ukrainians. By the spring months of 1919 American-Polish societies and newspapers strengthened their agitation against Jewish "enemies" that "deprecate" all Poles. The Yiddish papers reported that Poles in New England and Newark were following the example of Warsaw, Lodz, and other cities in Poland and boycotting Jewish businesses. Yiddish humorist Aren D. Egoz, who wrote the serialized adventures of a female streetcar conductor called Khashke, portrayed how Poles tried to bully the Jewish passengers on her car, but "since the Bronx is a Jewish country, a second Brownsville," the Poles were a minority and decided instead to boycott her car. As "our fellow Jews, thank God, are not absent from all cars," the Poles had to go on foot.[29]

As contemporary events in Poland like the massacres and boycott buttressed negative stereotypes, Jewish relations to Poles in America also derived from the apprehension that Poles were introducing violent anti-Semitism to a country that was relatively free of it. While a Polish American paper complained in 1919 that Jews assaulted Poles on the East Side, the *American Hebrew* reported in 1919 on a Jewish carpenter in Queens who was beaten up by two Poles. The paper "quoted" what the Poles at the Flushing Court allegedly said to each other: "It's obvious we may do as we like with the Jews ... We needn't fear any punishment." A popular columnist in the Yiddish press, Romanian-born Dovid Hermalin, wrote in 1920, "Recently we have received many letters from shops where Jews and Poles work together. That leads everywhere to quarrels and fights between the two groups." Hermalin published a letter by a mechanic who charged that because of "two Jew-hating Poles" he had to leave his job. Hermalin believed that in addition to the anti-Jewish boycott and incitement, Poles "would have made pogroms against Jews in America, had they felt strong enough, and did not fear Uncle Sam."[30] Jewish anger over the pogroms and persecution was directed at other Eastern European nations as well; yet the focus on Poland was related to the highly visible campaign for independent Poland by Polish Americans and especially Jewish indignation amid what was seen as a Polish attempt to import to America the methods of the Polish boycott and incitement.

Hermalin's aforesaid implication that America would safeguard Jews from anti-Semitism brought over by Polish immigrants belied some of his other assertions. Even as he was writing about the "great and noble heart of the American people," Hermalin believed Jews must be realistic in regard to Americans, too: a few days after writing the above words, Hermalin cautioned American Jews: "You ought to know that even here in America the Gentiles are not strongly enamored with Jews. Naturally, the local Gentiles are simply angels in comparison to the 'noble' Russians and the 'progressive' Poles. But still they do not love us very much."[31]

While American Jews were troubled by the suffering of Eastern European Jews, there were also ominous indications at home that emerged during the war and particularly in its aftermath. Yearning for national conformity, shaken by a wave of labor strife and fearful of Bolshevik subversion, more and more Americans linked Bolshevism or other forms of radicalism with treason and viewed them as synonymous with Jews. Such an attitude was expressed in periodicals like the *Anti-Bolshevist*, which debuted in Brooklyn in September 1918, whose editor stated, "Bolshevism is a Jewish scheme to despoil Christians of their property." The nativist American Defense Society sponsored in 1918 a book by William T. Hornaday that alleged "Russian-Jew [*sic*] anarchists" were the "worst cobras that ever found shelter under the American hearthstone."[32]

These feelings did not remain only in print and intensified after the Armistice on November 11, 1918 as events rapidly unfolded: a series of strikes, totaling more than 500 strikes in New York City alone throughout 1919; the panic following bomb scares and actual bombings against state officials across the country in the spring months of 1919; the creation of the Joint Legislative Committee to Investigate Subversive Activities (also called the Lusk Committee) by the New York State legislature, which conducted a series of raids on the offices of the Soviet government, the Rand School, and the headquarters of the left-wing Socialists; the attacks of soldiers, sailors and members of arch-patriotic organizations on the Russian People's House in Manhattan in March and on May Day 1919, as well as on Socialist parades and meetings; and Attorney General A. Mitchell Palmer's anti-Communist raids (late 1919 and early 1920) in which thousands were arrested and roughed up, and nearly 850 aliens subsequently deported.[33]

It is hard to overestimate the effect, which that nerve-racking succession of events had on American Jewry. If the anxiety about the atrocities in Eastern Europe and the Red Scare at home were not enough, a more malevolent approach toward Jews in different quarters of American society was unmistakably evident. Already during the war Supreme Court Justice Louis Brandeis cautioned his colleagues at a closed meeting of the Zionist leadership in August 1917 "of an anti-Semitic movement. My own mail has an indication of that ... some form of a pogrom would not be at all unlikely." Socialist Congressman

Meyer London, who opposed Brandeis's views on many issues, shared his concern that Jews would be smeared as traitors. In September 1917 London met Jewish socialists in New York and asked them "with tears in his eyes" to stop their dangerous anti-war propaganda, or "expect the most dangerous pogroms."[34]

The habitual practice of employment agencies downtown to specify, "Christians only" or "no Hebrew need apply," and army contractors who rebuffed Jewish applicants prompted Max Pine, Secretary of the United Hebrew Trades, to declare in late 1917 that his organization would fight against such prejudice. In the closing months of 1918 the AJC and the Yiddish papers received dozens of letters from Jewish veterans and workers who complained they suffered discrimination: two shipyard workers from Brooklyn, Jacob Kornbleit and Jacob Goldenberg, wrote to Louis Marshall that they were fired, "although that [sic] Germans and all kinds of nationalities are working without being molested." Three other New York Jews, carpenters by profession, protested that they were turned down for government jobs after saying they were Russian-born. Soon after the Armistice, the *Tog*'s editor, William Edlin, and the president of Manhattan's "Young Israel" synagogue, Harry G. Fromberg, conveyed to the AJC the complaints they received from many Jews, who mentioned how the United States employment offices in New York City discriminated against them.[35]

The amplified clamor for "100 percent Americanism" in those years by a spectrum of ultra-patriotic organizations, city and state officials, and the federal government reinforced the impression that Americans were changing—and not for the best. Various American Jewish agencies and organizations were (often obsessively) engaged in Americanizing the newcomers long beforehand. As the new spirit of "Americanism" increasingly meant also stifling dissent and nativism, however, Leon Elbe bemoaned that until now, "Americanization went on amicably," but now "the air is so stuffed with Americanization that you could suffocate," and it "endangers our existence here as Jews." Writing about the US Senate's Overman subcommittee (which investigated German and Bolshevik subversion in America), socialist essayist Karl Fornberg (pseudonym of Yisha'aya Rosenberg) lamented that America was copying the forced assimilation of "old, dying monarchies." Biblical scholar Israel Friedlaender (who was murdered in Ukraine in 1920 while distributing relief money) warned at a meeting of the Educational Alliance's Board of Trustees in February 1919 that "the immigrant will lose this love [for America] if Americans try to make him do as they say."[36]

Echoing that view, Borekh Vladeck felt in 1919 that "in the past hundred years such open or latent hatred—or suspicion at best—toward immigrants in America was never as dominant as it is today." Vladeck termed the atmosphere in the country as an anti-immigration "stampede," and explained: "It would have been unnatural to expect that the masses in America would be more generous, more tolerant, and more conscious than the masses in England or France." Responding to nativist accusations about the newcomers' purported low mental capacity, Vladeck wrote that in terms of "literature, art, and [cultural] tradition, many immigrants stand higher than the average American masses." By 1919, one found it very difficult to put the character of Americans on a pedestal. But not less important was Vladeck's suggestion that Jews faced the same problems as other immigrants and that the struggle was not against anti-Semitism but a more general form of nativism.[37]

It became indeed harder to view Yankees through rose-tinted glasses, as American public opinion seemed bent on closing America's gates to thousands of Eastern European Jews, who were scrambling to flee starvation or violent death. A rumor that eight million Jews were ready to come to the United States appeared even before the director of the Hebrew Immigrant Aid Society (HIAS), John L. Bernstein, stated in 1921, "if there was in existence a ship that would hold 3,000,000 human beings, the 3,000,000 Jews of Poland would board it to escape to America." Another HIAS official wrote to Louis Marshall, "since the war this country has been flooded with anti-Jewish propaganda and the bogey raised that every Jew wants to come to the United States." The *Groyser kundes* showed a bearded, elderly Jew standing on the brink of an abyss, attacked by three mythological Furies (representing Poland, Romania, and Ukraine), as the bayonets of "immigration laws" prevent him from moving. The Jew clenches his fists and says, "And my sons spilled their blood to make the world safe for democracy!" Reminding his readers in late 1919 that "a large Jewish immigration to America is unavoidable," educator and journalist Yoel Entin considered the "spread of the false accusation that Jews are all Bolsheviks" in addition to the fact that "a bitter hatred against Jews is taking root." Entin claimed that "wherever you go in [various] American circles, even in the truly liberal ones, they foam at the mouth when talking about Jews." Economist and labor tribune Isaac A. Hourwich, who already in 1913 called on American Jews to recognize that anti-Jewish prejudice was "part of a whole social tendency," wrote six years later "that there are many antisemites in America . . . is no news for a long time."[38]

The emergence of a more threatening and oppressive image of the American had an effect on those who were swept up in the wartime Wilsonian idealism. The influential Zionist editor Abe Goldberg, who by the end of 1918 lauded American "free spirit," fairness, and greatness (in comparison to Europe), was much more pessimistic a year later: writing about the "increasing hatred toward Jews," Goldberg sensed "an anxious mood" among American Jews. Goldberg contended that the Poles in America were constantly inciting against Jews, but noted, "The Americans can also commit a bloodbath when dealing with foreigners . . . What the American can do in his anger against a foreign race can be clearly seen in the South" where hot-blooded Americans "raged against their innocent . . . old neighbors, whose only crime was their dark skin." Fellow Zionist Yoel Entin believed that "The American intelligentsia is no less unkind to us than the intelligentsia in other countries." By 1919, Entin warned that "dark clouds" were forming on the American Jewish horizon: immigration restriction, suspicion and hatred of the foreigner "as a Bolshevist and a bomber," while Jews stood "as lonely as before." Equally alarmist, socialist writer A. Voliner (pseudonym of Eliezer Landoy) wrote that Jews in Poland and Russia envy the "prouder, more secure American Jew," but in America, this Jew "is often both a *zhid* [kike] and a Bolshevik . . . and something worse: he is an immigrant, a foreigner."[39]

As Jewish leaders such as Louis Marshall, and labor and communal leader Joseph Barondess were desperately trying to show that the charge of "Judeo-bolshevism" was

Figure 10: "And my sons spilled their blood to make the world safe for democracy!" The cartoonist is Lola (Leon Israel). Courtesy of the Dorot Jewish Division at the New York Public Library.

bogus, Henry Ford's newspaper, *The Dearborn Independent*, instigated its anti-Semitic campaign in 1920. The car magnate's plunge into Judeophobia, and his popularization in America of the Tsarist forgery known as *The Protocols of the Elders of Zion* might have shocked many Jews, to whom Ford was well known:[40] not only as the self-made-man and millionaire, but also as a messenger of peace. When the Hungarian-Jewish pacifist Rosika Schwimmer inspired Ford in 1915 to organize a "Peace Ship" project to end the war in Europe, the Yiddish press lauded the mission: The Zionist *Yidishe folk* predicted that though fools may laugh, "America will not be ashamed of her Ford," and the *Tog* likened Ford's initiative to Tolstoyan pacifism. Stephen S. Wise, who met Ford in Detroit in 1916, privately wrote, "He is a keen, kindly, rugged looking man" and thanked the industrialist for his pacifist efforts. By 1920, however, Wise did not have any illusions about Ford's anti-Jewish obsession.[41]

The attack by one of the most famous icons of Americanism and a Horatio Alger myth by himself was not understood immediately as a grave danger: the *Forverts* called "The International Jew" (the title of the first article in *The Dearborn Independent*'s series) "an antisemitic yet interesting article." After the second essay, the daily asserted it showed "more ignorance and more venom" than the previous one. Dovid Hermalin maintained that Ford fooled everyone when he "played the role of a radical, anti-militarist." Hermalin's counsel was "Every Jew in America, who 'sees' a future for Jews among the Gentiles without Palestine, should learn the lesson" from Ford's attack. Whereas Louis Marshall and Cyrus Adler (AJC) thought at first that silence was the best response, the Yiddish press called for a Jewish boycott of Ford products (which some Jewish communities in the Midwest implemented).[42]

By the early 1920s Jewish voices expressed concern over Ford's insidious impact in Europe, as translations of "The International Jew" into several languages circulated abroad. In 1924, Vladimir Grossman, a Yiddish writer who documented Jewish life in Eastern Europe, described a recent anti-Jewish outburst in Bucharest, where the rioters "carried the picture of Henry Ford." Though Ford in America was "only a nuisance, a worm" according to Grossman, the fact that such "nobodies" managed to reach the masses abroad showed the weakness of American Jews. That year, leading Yiddish theater critic A. Mukdoni (penname of Alexander Kappel), who came to America in 1922, depicted the attackers of Jews in Romania, Poland, and Germany as the "garbage of humanity ... drunk creatures," for whom Henry Ford was the "spiritual leader, thinker, and teacher." The *Tageblat* seconded that view, believing that "Ford had poisoned whole Europe against the Jewish people" and was "directly or indirectly involved" in any anti-Jewish agitation there. As Congress was about to pass the Johnson-Reed Act in 1924, Hebrew and Yiddish writer Y. L. Dalidansky argued that Russian, Hungarian, and German immigrants were leading an anti-Jewish campaign in America: "Antisemitism comes to America with every ship" and "Ford's Millions" funded it.[43] Adolf Hitler, who kept a large portrait of the car magnate on the wall of his private office in Munich and called "Heinrich" Ford "my inspiration," would demonstrate the industrialist's menacing influence in Europe beyond what the said figures could have possibly imagined. In 1922 an Austrian Jewish apostate, Hugo Bettauer, published a dystopian novel, *Die Stadt ohne*

Juden (The City without Jews), where the character of Jonathan Huxtable, a rabidly anti-Semitic American industrialist, was fashioned after Ford.[44]

If the circulation in Europe of American-bred anti-Semitic ideas and literature was not enough, the USA seemed to export a much more direct threat. As thousands of Polish-Americans volunteered for General Józef Haller's army that fought in Poland during 1919–20 against the Bolsheviks, they committed unspeakable violent acts against Jews. Those were Americans who cut off the beards of elderly Jews and reportedly "cut off the ears, lips, and noses" of local Jews. Louis Marshall wrote that General Haller admitted that his soldiers "were violently anti-Semitic" and despite his orders, "were hounding Jews at every opportunity." The Polish Minister of the Interior told Herman Bernstein that "Almost all the excesses" against Jews were committed by soldiers who had "come from America." The "Hallertshikes" had become infamous among Jews on both sides of the Atlantic: in 1920, labor Zionist Zrubavl (Yankev Vitkin), who spent the war years in the USA before returning to Poland, termed Haller's troops the "symbol of Jewish martyrdom."[45]

While Jewish casualties ran in the tens of thousands, and Jewish delegates at the Paris Peace Conference in 1919 struggled to secure the protection of minorities in the new countries of Eastern Europe, Ford's allegations about supposed Jewish world domination seemed especially offensive. An unnamed Jewish satirist "affirmed" those accusations: it was the world Jewish conspiracy that "made the Ukrainians dismember or bury Jews alive," and forced the Hungarians to "tie Jews to tramways" and drag them in the streets. As intolerance and anti-Semitism in America seemed to intensify, some Jewish commentators linked them to the events in Europe and deemed Americans as undistinguishable from the larger Gentile world, which appeared intent on harming Jews. After the bombings of June 2, 1919, orthodox writer Ephraim Caplan prayed that no Jews were involved, because the American public would conclude that all Jews were terrorists: "The non-Jewish world has two norms . . . a Gentile is not responsible for the evil actions of another. And even for the most appalling deeds of millions of Gentiles, one blames neither their faith nor their nationality." When it came to Jews, Caplan explained to his readers, "before and after all, the world wants to see our blood." Writing in the same vein, a newly arrived immigrant in New York, the leading Yiddish critic Shmuel Niger (born Shmuel Charney) also did not see any distinction between Americans and other Gentiles: in a 1920 article titled "The New False Accusation," Niger referred to a united anti-Jewish front, Americans as well as others: the *Protocols* "and all kinds of other documents" reflected "their [the accusers] experience and their psychology: they imagine that we do what they would have done if they were in our place . . . Had they been silent if people had tormented them as they do to us? . . . Hence they cannot imagine that we do not have a thirst for revenge, no thirst for paying death for death."[46]

The impression that Jews faced a hostile Gentile world, which included many, if not most, Americans, led to a short-lived and abortive initiative that anticipated a similar (and successful) attempt in the 1930s: in the fall of 1920 a group of orthodox and Zionist American Jews (mostly immigrants) campaigned for the organization of a World Jewish Congress. The life and soul of that plan was playwright and lawyer Abraham S. Schomer (the son of popular Yiddish writer N. M. Shaykevitsh). Figures who backed his proposal included orthodox Zionists like Rabbi Mayer Berlin, Hirsh Masliansky, Benjamin Koenigsberg, and Joseph I. Bluestone; socialist Zionists such as Yankev Marinoff (editor of the *Groyser kundes*) and Borekh Tsukerman; general Zionists like Reuben Brainin, Shmuel Margoshes, and Leo Wolfson; Yiddish journalists like Ephraim Caplan, Louis Miller, and Getsil Zelikovitsh; social reformer and the former secretary of the National Council of Jewish Women, Sadie American; self-made entrepreneur Harry Fischel; and a few Jewish judges. In the new organization's foundation letter Schomer warned, "At no time in history has the danger to the Jew, everywhere, been so great. THE WHOLE WORLD SEEMS TO BE AGAINST US ... INDIFFERENCE WILL SOONER OR LATER SPELL OUR DESTRUCTION." Eventually the plan failed, not only due to the opposition of the cautious AJC, but also of most American Zionists, who preferred to work on a permanent American Jewish Congress. The detractors of the idea did not dispute there was a grave danger for Jews, but they believed that such congress, in the words of Nathan Straus, "would be considered by the anti-Semites as a proof ... that the Jews are aiming at world dominion."[47]

The identification of Americans as part of the larger, antagonistic Gentile world would grow in the early 1920s. If anyone needed more evidence for the robust anti-immigration mood, the Immigration Act of 1921 and the stricter National Origin Act (1924) served as a stark reminder. While nearly 120,000 Jews were admitted into the USA in 1921, by 1925 the number dropped to 10,292. Besides the sharp curtailment of immigration from Eastern and Southern Europe, the implementation of those acts also stranded thousands of immigrants who were caught in countries of transit due to the changes. Added to the rising power of the Ku Klux Klan and Henry Ford's continued fulminations, it was small wonder that Bublik predicted "the end of the golden epoch" for American Jews.[48]

The gravity of the situation underlined unfavorable depictions of old-stock Americans, many of whom were perceived as adamant, callous restrictionists, and haughty xenophobes. In 1921 Yiddish writer Shmuel Blum analyzed the character of "Our friends the Americans." Blum, who was studying at the University of South Carolina, claimed that despite regional differences, "What all Americans have in common ... They are all stuck-up and think of themselves as humanity's cream of the crop." Blum cautioned that "Americans are very capable of committing violence" and America "might turn out to be the worst of our countries of exile." Dr. Pinchas Churgin, later the president of the orthodox-Zionist Mizrachi movement in America (and founder of Bar Ilan University in Israel) determined in 1924 that "the last sixty years of the previous century were full of persecution of immigrants from Ireland and Germany" and "[t]his primitive hatred has not vanished from the American's heart." That year Yiddish writer Dovid Leyb Mekler described how "American bigots" were convinced that "Slavs, Jews and Italians ... could never mix with the 'chosen' Americans."[49]

Even more than before, the traits ascribed to Americans were indistinguishable from those assigned to Gentiles in general. Perhaps the most extreme case was the book *You Gentiles* (1924) by Romanian-born Zionist intellectual Maurice Samuel. The first in a series of polemical works that repudiated the possibility of Jewish assimilation, the book saw an unbridgeable abyss between Jews and non-Jews: "There will be irritation between us as long as we are in intimate contact." The British-educated Samuel did not expect much of American society, "which tolerates the slaughter of hundreds of negroes," and stressed, "there is no country today" of which Jews could say "In this country anti-Semitism will never become triumphant." In what was perhaps his harshest statement, Samuel wrote, "Compared with each other, you are gentlemen, warriors, democracies: set side by side with us, you are bullies and cowards and mobs." The book's condemning tone was too much for fellow Zionist Louis Lipsky, who privately called it "an impudent, boyish book."[50]

Even if Samuel was "impudent," he was hardly alone. As the debate about the National Origin Bill heated up in 1924, Yiddish journalist and translator Dovid Druk saw the restriction of immigration as a result of America's strengthened relations with Europe. Druk, who emigrated to the USA from Poland in 1920, argued that Americans "import the new European ideologies of hatred." Unwittingly voicing a view that characterized many American isolationists and nativists, Druk bemoaned, "if only America would have remained American forever, if only it would have had no contacts with Europe." Alexander Mukdoni saw Americans as harboring the same anti-Jewish venom as Europeans. Mukdoni was sure that "in the mind of every non-Jew burns, blazes infernal, wild hatred; in the heart of every non-Jew boils and seethes mad rage against us." Providing a more "historical" analysis, writer Shmuel Rosenfeld viewed Jewish-Gentile relations in America as a replica of the "warning signals" that occurred in France and Poland in the past. Rosenfeld, who made a prolific career in Eastern Europe's Jewish press (in Hebrew, Yiddish, and Russian) before arriving in America in 1923, mocked the line of defense of Jewish organizations: "*We* attempt to show *them* that *they* do not understand the spirit of the American revolution, that *they* are unfaithful to these or those principles." But that was the way Jews in Poland reacted, "That is against the principles of Kazimir the Great." Echoing Bublik's gloomy forecast, Rosenfeld believed Americans were following in the Poles and Frenchmen's footsteps.[51]

Writing his memoirs in the 1930s, scholar Cyrus Adler compared contemporary America to that of half a century before: "I feel sure that our America was much broader, much more liberal, much freer from prejudice than it is today." Though sixty years Adler's junior, author Ruth Gay, who grew up in the Bronx in the interwar period, depicted a similar reality, recalling how anti-Semitism "tarnished" the "image of America" and "did the sort of damage that mere taunts and epithets never could."[52] Such impressions were not unique in the interwar period with its crop of bigotry: immigration restriction, universities quotas, anti-Semitic movements, "Christians only" employment advertisements, residential restrictions, and social exclusion had become a fact of life.[53]

Along with the domestic manifestations of anti-Semitism, during the immediate years after the First World War American Jewish commentators from across the spectrum had begun viewing anti-Jewish enmity as an interrelated phenomenon that straddled the Atlantic. On the one hand, they often blamed the growing anti-Semitism in America on immigrant groups like Poles and Germans. On the other, they also saw the simultaneous rise of anti-Jewish hatred in Europe as linked to the circulation of American anti-Jewish literature by Ford and his ilk. Moreover, as anti-Semitism in America coincided with the fact that American troops fought alongside the White forces in Russia and Polish Americans were involved in anti-Jewish atrocities, Jewish observers increasingly cast Americans as part of a larger, antagonistic Gentile world.

To be sure, American Jews remained completely aware of the sea of difference between their situation and that of fellow Jews in Germany or Eastern Europe, and that American anti-Semitism was relatively benign. At the same time, the growing sense of alarm regarding the changing character of American society and its "Europeanization" would prompt American Jews to seek cooperation with other groups as the only viable self-defense approach in a society that seemed to grow ever more hostile.

Notes

1. Bublik wrote in *Yidishes Tageblat* (Jewish Daily News, hereafter *YT*), May 16, 1924: 5. Rogoff wrote in the *Tsukunft*, February 1920: 75. See also what Leon Elbe wrote in *Tog* (The Day), January 21, 1920: 6. Fredrick Lewis Allen expressed a similar opinion in his 1931 classic study *Only Yesterday: An Informal History of the Nineteen-Twenties* (New York: Harper & Row, reprint 1964), 54.

2. All dates are given according to the Gregorian calendar. Gersoni wrote in *Ha-melits* (St. Petersburg), February 12, 1883: 137. Bernstein wrote in *Ha-magid*, June 29, 1870: 196. George M. Price, "The Russian Jews in America," translated by Leo Shpall, *Publications of the American Jewish Historical Society* 48 (1958): 26–62, 78–133, here 124–5. Kohler wrote for the *Reform Advocate*, reprinted in *YT*, April 3, 1898: 8. Leo N. Levi, the future president of B'nai B'rith, and Cyrus Adler expressed a similar view, ibid. Wintner is quoted in *YT*, April 24, 1899: 1; May 1, 1899: 2. One can mention only a fraction of examples for the image of a tolerant American: see the letters of Jewish immigrants in *Yudishes folks-blat* (St. Petersburg), November 23, 1882: 678; Jan. 19, 1882: 11. Isaac M. Wise, *Reminiscences*, transl. and ed. by David Philipson (Cincinnati: Leo Wise, 1901), 34–5; Shomer (Nokhem Meyer Shaykevitsh), *Di farkerte velt*, 5 vols. (New York: Katzenelbogen, 1897), Vol. 1: 14–15; Vol. 2: 11; Vol. 5: 6, 17–18; Sanford Ragins, "The Image of America in Two East European Hebrew Periodicals," *American Jewish Archives Journal* 17 (1965): 143–61, here 146–8; Yehuda David Eisenstein, *Otsar zikhronotay* (New York: By the author, 1929), 203. See also Abraham Cahan's idealized portrayal of "Yankees," in *Abend-blat*, October 1, 1896: 2; October 2, 1896: 2; October 8, 1896: 2.

3. *Allgemeine Zeitung des Judenthums*, March 28, 1865: 202. Tsunzer's comments were reprinted in Elikum Tsunzer, *Ale verk* 2 vols. (New York: Aba Katsenelenboygen, 1920), Vol. 2: 205–6. Incidentally, "an Irishman" assaulted Tsunzer at the Jackson Street Park ten years later—*YT*, September 11, 1900: 4. Jastrow is cited in Naomi W. Cohen, *Encounter with Emancipation: The German Jews in the United States, 1830–1914* (Philadelphia: Jewish Publication Society, 1984), 228. Simon Wolf's words were printed in *YT*, April 3, 1898: 8. See also the letter of a Chicago Jew about German Americans in *Ha-tsefirah*, July 15, 1884: 210.

4. *Yidishe gazetn*, August 22, 1902: 12; *YT*, August 8, 1902: 4; August 5, 1902: 1. "Impossible" was said by an unnamed speaker at a protest rally *New York Times*, August 2, 1902: 2. *Yidishe velt*, August 3, 1902: 4. Leonard Dinnerstein, "The Funeral of Rabbi Jacob Joseph," in *Anti-Semitism in American History*, ed. David A. Gerber (Urbana, IL: University of Illinois Press, 1986), 275–301.

5. Eisenstein, *Otsar zikhronotay*, 43. *Ha-magid*, January 14, 1880: 22. *Ha-tsefirah*, August 1, 1877: 229. See also the *Allgemeine Zeitung des Judenthums*, July 17, 1877: 460; July 24, 1877: 478; September 9, 1879: 577–8. Naomi W. Cohen, "Antisemitism in the Gilded Age: The Jewish View," *Jewish Social Studies* 41 (1979): 187–210.

6. See the front pages in the *Forverts*, *Morgen zhurnal*, and *Yidishes tageblat* between March 16 and March 23, 1917. See also Avrom Lesin's joy in *Tsukunft*, April 1917: 189. The happiness among American Jews is described in the *New York Times* (hereafter *NYT*), March 17, 1917: 1, 8; Zosa Szajkowski, *Jews, Wars, and Communism: The Attitude of American Jews in World War I, the Russian Revolutions of 1917, and Communism (1914–1945)* 4 vols. (New York: Ktav, 1972), Vol. 1: 119–30, 284; and Joseph Rappaport, *Hands Across the Sea: Jewish Immigrants and World War I* (Lanham, MD: Hamilton Books, 2005), 96–8 (*Morgen zhurnal*, hereafter *MZ*, is cited ibid.). See the reservations in *Varhayt*, March 19, 1917: 4; *American Jewish Chronicle*, July 13, 1917: 273.

7. David M. Kennedy, *Over Here: The First World War and American Society* (New York and Oxford: Oxford University Press, 1980), 59–69. John Higham, *Strangers in the Land: Patterns of American Nativism, 1860–1925* (1955, new edition New York: Atheneum, 1978), 204–19, 278–9. Cecilia Elizabeth O'Leary, *To Die For: The Paradox of American Nationalism* (Princeton, NJ: Princeton University Press, 1999), 220–45. On German-Americans in New York see Peter Conolly-Smith, *Translating America: An Immigrant Press Visualizes American Popular Culture, 1895–1918* (Washington DC: Smithsonian, 2004), 245–70.

8. *Tog*, March 31, 1917: 8. Tashrak wrote in *Yidishe gazetn*, March 30, 1917: 11. On the worsening conditions under German occupation in Eastern Europe in 1917 see the recollections in the interview of Pauline Notkoff (Sep. 11, 1985), *Voices from Ellis Island* (Library of Congress), #27: 2; and fellow Bialystoker Gertrude Yellin (February 10, 1986), ibid., #144: 4. See also Vejas Gabriel Liulevicius, *War Land on the Eastern Front: Culture, National Identity, and the German Occupation in World War I* (Cambridge and New York: Cambridge University Press, 2000), 182. Szajkowski, *Jews, Wars, and Communism*, Vol. 1: 211.

9. Oscar S. Straus, *Under Four Administrations: From Cleveland to Taft* (Boston: Houghton Mifflin, 1922), 390. On Schiff see Naomi W. Cohen, *Jacob H. Schiff: A Study in American Jewish Leadership* (Hanover, NH and London: Brandeis University Press by University Press of New England, 1999), 192–3, 200–01. See also Cyrus Adler, ed., *Jacob H. Schiff: His Life and Letters*, 2 vols. (Garden City, NY: Doubleday Doran, 1928), Vol. 2: 210–25, 235–46. Wolf's letter appeared in *Washington Post*, November 15, 1918: 6. Silverman was quoted in *NYT*, June 1, 1919: 27. On Emil G. Hirsch see *Chicago Daily Tribune*, April 12, 1918: 13; *NYT*, April 15, 1918: 10.

10. *Groyser kundes* (hereafter *GK*), July 20, 1917: 6. The friend is Dovid Shub, *Fun di amolike yorn* (New York: Cyco, 1970), 450. Tsivyen wrote in the *Fraynd*, August 1917: 9 (emphasis added). *Forverts* is cited in the *Naye velt*, April 13, 1917: 6.

11. Interview with Sol Broad (March 6, 1919), David J. Saposs Papers (Wisconsin State Historical Society, hereafter WSHS), box #22, folder #2. Edlin wrote to George Creel on February 28, 1918, William Edlin Papers (YIVO), folder #76. Letter from Germer to Morris Hillquit, March 4, 1918, is in the Morris Hillquit papers (WSHS), reel #2.

12. Brainin wrote in *Ha-toren*, November 21, 1919, 1–2. Elbe wrote in *Tog*, June 9, 1920: 4. Bril's article appeared in *YT*, March 10, 1921: 10. Louis Marshall also mentioned German influence in Ford's newspaper—see his letter (July 25, 1921) to President Harding, in Charles Reznikoff, ed., *Louis Marshall: Champion of Liberty* 2 vols. (Philadelphia: Jewish Publication Society, 1957), Vol. 1: 362. See also Nachman Syrkin's letter from Berlin, *Tog*, July 29, 1920: 4.

13. On the relief efforts and destruction in Eastern Europe see Morris Engelman, *Four Years of Relief and War Work by the Jews of America, 1914–1918* (New York: Shoen, 1918). Joseph C. Hyman, "Twenty-Five Years of American Aid to Jews Overseas," *American Jewish Year Book* (hereafter *AJYB*) 41 (1939/40): 141–56; Daniel Soyer, *Jewish Immigrant Associations and American Identity in New York 1880–1939* (1997, reprinted Detroit, MI: Wayne State University Press, 2001), 161–89.

14. On the joy following the declaration see the memoir by Yisroel Iser Katsovitsh, *Zekhtsig yor lebn* (New York: Mayzel, 1919), 371–2; *Yidisher kemfer*, November 23, 1917: 4. Ash's article was published in *Tsukunft*, December 1917, 673–4. The declaration and some of the responses are in Melvin I. Urofsky, *American Zionism from Herzl to the Holocaust* (New York: Anchor, 1975), 202, 212–20. Other responses are quoted in Charles Israel Goldblatt, "The Impact of the Balfour Declaration in America," *American Jewish Historical Quarterly* 57 (1968): 480–92. On the responses to the declaration see also Aaron S. Klieman and Adrian L. Klieman, eds., *American Zionism: A Documentary History*, 15 vols. (New York: Garland, 1990), Vol. 2: 233–6.

15. *New York Exporters Review* is quoted in Michael N. Dobkowski, *The Tarnished Dream: The Basis of American Anti-Semitism* (Westport, CT: Greenwood, 1979), 222 (parenthesis in the original). The speeches of Bernstein and Greenbaum are in the *NYT*, November 19, 1917: 2; March 24, 1918: 22. That was also the argument made in the *Yidishe folk*, November 23, 1917: 2.

16. Brainin, diary entry on November 11, 1917, *Kol kitvey re'uven ben mordecai brainin*, 3 vols. (New York: By a committee, 1940), Vol. 3: 321–2.

17. Yankev Magidov, *Der shpigl fun der ist sayd* (New York: by the author, 1923), 42–4. The anti-Bolshevik stance of Yiddish papers is cited in Rappaport, *Hands Across the Sea*, 122–3. See also Irving Howe, with the assistance of Kenneth Libo, *World of Our Fathers* (1976, reprinted New York: Schocken, 1989), 326.

18. Gurevich wrote in the *Tsukunft*, December 1917: 681. Olgin is cited in an article by Vintshevsky, who defended the Bolsheviks, ibid., March 1918: 134–7. Baranov wrote ibid., June 1918: 364–5. J. S. Herts, *Di yidishe sotsyalistishe bavegung in amerike* (New York: Der veker, 1954), 180–3. Robert K. Murray, *Red Scare: A Study of National Hysteria, 1919–1920* (1955, reprinted New York: McGraw-Hill, 1964), 33–6. Tony Michels, *A Fire in Their Hearts: Yiddish Socialists in New York* (Cambridge, MA: Harvard University Press, 2005), 219.

19. Isaac Babel, "The Killers Must Be Finished Off," *1920 Diary* (edited by Carol J. Evins, translated by H. T. Willetts, New Haven, CT and London: Yale University Press, 1995), 106. See M. Sadikov's account of the pogroms, *In yene teg* (New York: no publisher mentioned, 1926), 32–43. Committee of Jewish Delegates, *The Pogroms in the Ukraine Under the Ukrainian Government, 1917–1920* (London: John Bale, Sons & Danielson, 1927); *AJYB* 5681 (1920/1): 247–83. Norman Davies, *God's Playground: A History of Poland* 2 vols. (New York: Columbia University Press, 1984), Vol. 2: 393–401. Richard Pipes, *Russia Under the Bolshevik Regime* (New York: Alfred A. Knopf, 1993), 99–114.

20. Examples of Jewish anti-Bolshevik warnings are in *MZ*, June 13, 1919: 4; October 27, 1919: 4; *YT*, November 3, 1918: 4; *Yidishe folk*, November 23, 1917: 2. Wise, Rosenfeld, and Yanovsky (among others) are cited in Szajkowski, *Jews, Wars, and Communism*, Vol. 2: 189–94, 204. Zosa Szajkowski, *Kolchack, Jews, and the American Intervention in Northern Russia and Siberia* (New York: by the author, 1977), 27–36. On the American intervention see Thomas J. Knock, *To End All Wars: Woodrow Wilson and the Quest For a New World Order* (New York and Oxford: Oxford University Press, 1992), 155–8; Peter G. Filene, *Americans and the Soviet Experiment, 1917–1933* (Cambridge, MA: Harvard University Press, 1967), 39–63, 164.

21. Sinclair is quoted in Zosa Szajkowski, "Double Jeopardy—The Abrams Case of 1919," *American Jewish Archives Journal* 23 (1971): 8–32, here 22. On the Jewish opposition to American intervention in Russia see Szajkowski, *Kolchack, Jews*, 34–9. See also Lesin's article in *Tsukunft*, September 1918: 503–4.

22. The most comprehensive study of the Abrams case and the Supreme Court decision is by Richard Polenberg, *Fighting Faiths: The Abrams Case, the Supreme Court, and Free Speech* (New York: Viking, 1987), 23–7, 43–81, 88–95, 118–53, 197–242; Szajkowski, "Double Jeopardy," 6–32; Yoysef Kahan, *Di Yidish-anarkhistishe bavegung in amerike* (Philadelphia: Radical Library, Workmen's Circle, 1945), 367–8.

23. *Tsukunft*, September 1919: 530–2 (emphasis added).

24. Isaac Babel described in his diary how Red-Army Cossacks also committed atrocities against Jews—*1920 Diary*, 3–5, 84–5. On pogroms by Red Army units see Elias Tcherikover, *Di ukrayner pogromen in yor 1919* (New York: YIVO, 1965), chapter 12. On the tension in the SP branch see Central Committee minutes, January 11, 1919, *New York Socialist Party Records* (Tamiment), reel #R2638, 5–7. Danzis's article appeared in *YT*, June 9, 1921: 6–7. A similar view was expressed by Dovid Hermalin, *Tog*, November 23, 1920: 8.

25. *YT*, October 22, 1917: 4. See also *Varhayt*, April 19, 1915: 4; *Tog*, March 11, 1919: 4; *Ha-toren*, December 6, 1918: 1; *NYT*, November 15, 1918: 2; November 30, 1918: 3; Harold H. Fisher, *America and the New Poland* (New York: Macmillan, 1928), 155–9. See the essay by Max J. Kohler in *American Hebrew*, November 22, 1918: 50, 68. The Polish Committee's circular, June 9, 1919, is in the Peter Wiernik Papers (Yeshiva University), box #11, folder #20. The Cleveland committee is quoted in Andrzej Kapiszewski, *Conflicts Across the Atlantic: Essays on Polish-Jewish Relation in the United States During World War I and in the Interwar Period* (Krakow: Ksiegarnia Akademicka, 2004), 176.

26. Marshall and Mack are cited in *NYT*, November 30, 1918: 3. Ash is quoted in the *MZ*, December 12, 1918: 1. Glanz (who was among the founders of the *In zikh* literary group and known by his penname Leyles) wrote in *Tog*, May 30, 1919: 6 (emphasis added). A heartrending portrayal of the situation in Pinsk after the pogrom is in a letter by Borekh Tsukerman to his wife (May 1919), cited in his *Zikhroynes* 3 vols. (New York: Yidisher kemfer, 1963), Vol. 2: 160–7. See the reports and memos sent (1919–1920) by Jewish relief workers in Poland (like Boris Bogen), Judah L. Magnes Papers (Central Archives for the History of the Jewish People), folder #1148. Carole Fink, *Defending the Rights of Others: The Great Powers, The Jews, and International Minority Protection, 1878–1938* (Cambridge and New York: Cambridge University Press, 2004), 173–86.

27. Rosen's story appeared in *Tsayt*, November 16, 1920: 3; *GK*, April 25, 1919: 3; *Tog*, April 17, 1919: 4.

28. *NYT*, May 22, 1919: 1, 5; November 25, 1919: 6; *Chicago Daily Tribune*, November 25, 1919: 3. Lesin wrote in the *Forverts*, May 21, 1919: 1; May 22, 1919: 1, 3, 6. See also his comments about Poles in *Tsukunft*, March 1919, 131–2; *Ha-toren*, May 23, 1919: 2; *Yidishe folk*, May 30, 1919: 4–5; *Tog*, November 25, 1919: 1.

29. *GK*, May 30, 1919: 3. Wise was born in Hungary. The Bundist John Mill also wrote about anti-Semitism as a "national phenomenon" in Poland—*Tsukunft*, October 1919: 604; *NYT*, June 5, 1919: 7; June 8, 1919: 20; *Tog*, April 2, 1919: 6; June 1, 1919: 8. June 14, 1919: 1; July 12, 1919: 8; *MZ*, June 3, 1919: 5; June 10, 1919: 2. Egoz's piece appeared in the *MZ*, June 18, 1919: 4.

30. The Polish paper is cited in Kapiszewski, *Conflicts Across the Atlantic*, 176; *American Hebrew*, August 1, 1919: 282. Hermalin's column was published in the *Tog*, May 17, 1920: 8. The *Forverts* also reported on the agitation of a New York Polish priest—May 6, 1919: 1.

31. *Tog*, May 15, 1920: 16; May 26, 1920: 10 (quotes in the original). See also Hermalin's earlier praise of the American people in his *Zhurnalistishe shriftn* (New York: Hebrew Publishing, 1912), 60–3, 147.

32. *Literary Digest*, December 14, 1918: 32. The *Anti-Bolshevist* is cited in Szajkowski, *Jews, Wars, and Communism*, Vol. 2: 159. Hornaday's book, titled *Awake! America! Object Lessons and Warnings*, is quoted in Dobkowski, *The Tarnished Dream*, 223–4.

33. Murray, *Red Scare*, 67–81, 94–104, 190–209, 251; Todd J. Pfannestiel, *Rethinking the Red Scare: The Lusk Committee and New York's Crusade Against Radicalism, 1919-1923* (London and New York: Routledge, 2003), 19–35, 75–96; Higham, *Strangers in the Land*, 229–33, 277–9. William Preston, Jr., *Aliens and Dissenters: The Federal Suppression of Radicals, 1903-1933* (1963, reprinted New York: Harper & Row, 1966), 182–3, 208–37.

34. Brandeis's words were said at a meeting of the Provisional Executive Committee for General Zionist Affairs, cited in an appendix to a letter by Jacob De Haas to Israel Friedlaender, September 11, 1917, *Israel Friedlaender Papers* (Jewish Theological Seminary), box #6, folder "Sep. 1917." The account on London's meeting in New York was given in an ad by a pro-war group, the American Jewish Defense Society, in *Varhayt*, November 4, 1917: 3. The group's depiction seems to be fairly accurate (though it set out to defeat Hillquit's mayoral candidacy): London indeed opposed anti-war agitation and believed it to be dangerous—see Harry Rogoff, *An East Side Epic: The Life and Work of Meyer London* (New York: Vanguard), 104–5.

35. On Pine and discrimination in army camps see in the *New York Call*, November 9, 1917: 1–2. The letter of Kornbleit and Goldenberg (Aug. 27, 1918) and other complaints are in the Louis Marshall Papers (American Jewish Archives, hereafter AJA), box #155, folder "War Department," which also contains many examples of anti-Jewish abuses in the armed forces. See also Marshall's letter to Richard Derby (chair of the Soldiers' Re-Employment Committee), January 5, 1920, ibid., box #1590, folder "Jan. 1920." The letters from Edlin, December 30, 1918 (which cites the *Tog*), and Fromberg, January 5, 1919, are in ibid., box #155, folder "War Department." The situation had worsened a decade later, see Heywood Broun and George Britt, *Christians Only: A Study in Prejudice* (New York: Vanguard Press, 1931), 188–245. See also Lasker's preface in Bruno Lasker, ed., *Jewish Experiences in America: Suggestions for the Study of Jewish Relations with Non-Jews* (New York: The Inquiry, 1930), 3–16.

36. Elbe and Fornberg wrote in the *Tog*, January 16, 1920: 6; June 18, 1919: 6. Friedlaender's words are in the Minutes of a Meeting of the Board of Trustees, February 3, 1919, *Educational Alliance Papers* (YIVO), reel #MK 266.4. For an extreme example of Jewish proponents of Americanization see *Jewish Charities*, February 1919: 207–9. A nationalist who accused those Americanizing agencies of being subservient was Yoel Entin—*Yidisher kemfer*, March 7, 1919: 1–2. On the "Russification" of America see also *Bronzvil un ist nu york progres*, March 23, 1917: 7. See also Tamara K. Hareven, "Un-American America and the *Jewish Daily Forward*," in *East European Jews in Two Worlds: Studies from the YIVO Annual*, ed. Deborah Dash Moore (Evanston, IL: Northwestern University Press, 1990), 314–30.

37. *Tsukunft*, August 1919, 477–8. A similar view is expressed in the recollection of Sam Gordon, *American Jewish Autobiographies Collection* (YIVO) #167: 18.

38. HIAS officials are quoted in Sheldon Morris Neuringer, *American Jewry and United States Immigration Policy, 1881-1953* (1969, reprinted New York: Arno, 1980), 133–4; GK, May 9, 1919: 3. Entin wrote in the *Tog*, November 29, 1919: 9. Hourwich wrote in *Tsukunft*, March 1919, 150. His 1913 article was published in *American Hebrew*, Oct. 17, 1913: 683–4.

39. Goldberg wrote in *MZ*, December 17, 1918: 4; September 24, 1919: 4. The longer quote is in *Yidishe folk*, November 21, 1919: 3. Entin wrote in the *Varhayt*, August 4, 1917: 4–5; August 3,

1917: 4. His 1919 quote appeared in the *Yidisher kemfer*, June 13, 1919: 4. Voliner wrote in *Tog*, January 19, 1920: 4.

40. Neil Baldwin, *Henry Ford and the Jews: The Mass Production of Hate* (New York: Public Affairs, 2001); Albert Lee, *Henry Ford and the Jews* (New York: Stein and Day, 1980); Leo P. Ribufo, "Henry Ford and the *International Jew*," *American Jewish History* 69 (1980): 437–77; David Levering Lewis, "Henry Ford's Anti-Semitism and Its Repercussions," *Michigan Jewish History* 24 (1984): 3–10. On the dissemination of the *Protocols* in America see Robert Singerman, "The American Career of the *Protocols of the Elders of Zion*," *American Jewish History* 71 (1981): 48–78. According to two accounts, two US presidents—Woodrow Wilson and Warren Harding—ordered investigations into whether the *Protocols* contained factual aspects: Cyrus Adler wrote about Wilson in *I Have Considered the Days* (Philadelphia: Jewish Publication Society, 1941), 330. Judge Jonah J. Goldstein mentioned Harding in "Reminiscences of Jonah J. Goldstein" (December 10, 1965), *Columbia University Oral History Research Office Collection*, 1: 44–6.

41. The Yiddish press's reactions are quoted in Rappaport, *Hands Across the Sea*, 63; *MZ*, December 6, 1915: 4. Justin Wise Polier and James Waterman Wise, eds., *The Personal Letters of Stephen Wise* (Boston: Beacon, 1956), 155, 182. Dobkowski, *The Tarnished Dream*, 197–200.

42. *The Dearborn Independent*, May 22, 1920, 1–5; *Forverts*, May 30, 1920: 4; June 5, 1920: 8–9. Hermalin wrote in *Tog*, June 16, 1920 (pagination illegible) ("sees" originally in quotes). Elbe wrote ibid., June 9, 1920: 4. See the letters from Louis Marshall to Julius Rosenwald (June 5, 1920), and to David A. Brown from Detroit (August 13, 1920), warning that Ford was not a local problem that Detroit Jews could handle, Louis Marshall Papers (AJA), box #1590, folders "June 1920" and "August 1920." See also the letter Marshall sent to Ford, June 3, 1920, in Reznikoff, ed., *Louis Marshall*, Vol. 1: 329.

43. Grossman wrote in the *Tog*, April 15, 1924 (pagination illegible). Mukdoni's article appeared in *MZ*, April 13, 1924: 4; *YT*, April 7, 1924: 4. Dalidansky wrote ibid., April 4, 1924: 4. See also the portrayal of Ford as the instigator of anti-Semitism in Europe by Getsil Zelikovitsh, ibid., May 10, 1921: 4. See also the editorial "Fordopia" in *American Hebrew*, January 7, 1921: 228. On the situation of Romanian Jewry in the 1920s see Ezra Mendelsohn, *The Jews of East Central Europe Between the World Wars* (Bloomington and Indianapolis, IN: Indiana University Press, 1983), 183–9.

44. Lee, *Henry Ford*, 45–6, 113–14; Baldwin, *Henry Ford*, 172–91. On Bettauer see Ruth Ellen Gruber, *Virtually Jewish: Reinventing Jewish Culture in Europe* (Berkeley, CA: University of California Press, 2002), 3–4.

45. The report on Haller's soldiers appeared in *Tsayt*, November 24, 1920: 5. Marshall wrote (August 19, 1919) to Abram I. Elkus, in Reznikoff. ed., *Louis Marshall*, Vol. 2: 609. Haller's orders to his soldiers not to attack Jews are in *NYT*, June 21, 1919: 11. Bernstein's report appeared in *The Atlanta Constitution*, September 14, 1919, D18. Zrubavl wrote in *Tog*, November 25, 1920: 3. See also the description of Haller, ibid., August 30, 1920: 1. On Haller's army see James S. Pula, *Polish Americans: An Ethnic Community* (New York: Twayne, 1995), 58–60.

46. The unnamed satirist wrote in the *Tog*, June 15, 1920: 5. Caplan wrote in *MZ*, June 13, 1919: 4; June 20, 1919: 4. Niger wrote in *Tog*, July 24, 1920: 7. See also ibid., October 3, 1919: 8. Iser Ginzburg made a similar point in the socialist *Naye velt*, May 23, 1919: 3. On the Jewish delegates at the peace conference see Oscar I. Janowsky, *The Jews and Minority Rights, 1898–1919* (New York: Columbia University Press, 1933), 264–308, 344–68. On Marshall's role in Paris see Fink, *Defending the Rights of Others*, 197–208.

47. The letter quoted above (November 21, 1920, block letters in the original) is in the Benjamin Koenigsberg Papers (Yeshiva University), box #14, folder #3; and in a slightly different version (November 22, 1920), the William Edlin Papers (YIVO), folder #68. The official Yiddish circular (1920) for the congress is in Abraham S. Schomer Papers (YIVO), folder #23. The letter of Nathan Straus to Schomer, November 3, 1920, is ibid., folder #17. The letter from Benjamin Koenigsberg to Schomer, December 17, 1920, depicted the opposition of American Zionists to the initiative—ibid., folder #11. See Cyrus Adler's letter to Schomer, November 24, 1920, ibid., folder #1.

48. The data is taken from *American Jewish Yearbook* 5690 (1929/30): 325–9. On the suffering of stranded immigrants and torn families see *YT*, March 14, 1921: 2; June 9, 1921: 1; *Tog*, May 29, 1924: 1; *Ha-doar*, July 11, 1924: 2. Bublik wrote in *YT*, May 16, 1924: 5. See also Mae M. Ngai, "The Architecture of Race in American Immigration Law: A Reexamination of the Immigration Act of 1924," *Journal of American History* 86 (1999): 67–92; Henry L. Feingold, *A Time for Searching: Entering the Mainstream 1920–1945* (Baltimore, MD: Johns Hopkins University Press, 1992), 15–20, 29.

49. Blum wrote in the *Tsayt*, April 19, 1921: 5; April 20, 1921: 5. Churgin wrote in *Ha-doar*, July 18, 1924: 3. Churgin also referred to anti-Jewish quotas in elite universities. Mekler wrote in *MZ*, April 21, 1924: 6 (quotes in the original). On Churgin's life and career see Moshe D. Sherman, *Orthodox Judaism in America: A Biographical Dictionary and Sourcebook* (Westport, CT: Greenwood, 1996), 49–50.

50. Maurice Samuel, *You Gentiles* (New York: Harcourt, Brace and Co., 1924), 23, 132, 95, 129. See Louis Lipsky's letter to his wife Charlotte ("Eddie"), August 18, 1924, Louis Lipsky Papers (American Jewish Historical Society), box #20, folder #13. Samuel's other books in that vein are *I, the Jew* (New York: Harcourt, Brace and Co., 1924); and *Jews on Approval* (New York: Liveright, 1932).

51. Druk's feuilleton was published in *MZ*, April 18, 1924: 10. Mukdoni wrote in ibid., March 2, 1924: 4. Rosenfeld wrote in *Tog*, April 24, 1924: 4 (emphasis in the original). On Rosenfeld's wide-ranging career see Zalmen Reyzin, *Leksikon fun der yidisher literature, prese un filologye* (Vilna: Kletzkin, 1929), 4: 169–76.

52. Adler, *I Have Considered*, 54; Ruth Gay, *Unfinished People: Eastern European Jews Encounter America* (New York: W. W. Norton and Co., 1996), 56–7; Beth S. Wenger, *New York Jews and the Great Depression: Uncertain Promise* (1996, reprinted Syracuse, NY: Syracuse University Press, 1999), 197–206.

53. Higham, *Strangers in the Land*, 264–99; Broun and Britt, *Christians Only*, 72–124, 203–45; Leonard Dinnerstein, *Antisemitism in America* (New York and Oxford: Oxford University Press, 1994), 78–127.

PART IV
CHALLENGES FOR AMERICAN JEWRY AFTER THE HOLOCAUST

CHAPTER 17

FROM PERIPHERY TO CENTER: AMERICAN JEWRY, ZION, AND JEWISH HISTORY AFTER THE HOLOCAUST

Jonathan D. Sarna

The *American Jewish Year Book* of 1946, the first to appear following the Shoah, redrew the statistical map of world Jewry. "The major part of the present world Jewish population—about 5,176,000," it disclosed, "lives in the United States and Canada." By contrast, "in Europe only an estimated 3,642,000 remain[ed] of the total Jewish pre-war population of approximately 9,740,000." The two continents had thus "reversed their order of 1939." Where before Europe had been "the greatest center of Jewish population," now, as a consequence of the Shoah, that designation fell to North America.[1] The news was heralded by historians Oscar and Mary Handlin on page one of the fiftieth volume of the *American Jewish Year Book*, published in 1949. "The events of the Second World War," they declared, "left the United States the center of world Judaism. The answers to the most critical questions as to the future of the Jews everywhere will be determined by the attitudes and the position of the five million Jews who are citizens of the American Republic."[2]

America's emergence was not totally unexpected. The Anglo-Jewish novelist, Israel Zangwill, had in a sense predicted its ascent back in his bestselling 1892 novel, *Children of the Ghetto*. Of course, that book was produced for an American audience, and Judge Mayer Sulzberger of the Jewish Publication Society sought a happy American ending for commercial reasons.[3] The German-Jewish historian Heinrich Graetz likewise believed that "salvation would arise for Judaism out of ... America" (and England).[4] Plenty of American Jews, such as the aforementioned Mayer Sulzberger and his nephew, Cyrus Adler, looked forward to a glorious "awakening" of Jewish life in the United States; that, in large part, motivated their untiring efforts to strengthen the cultural and organizational fabric of the American Jewish community. The publication of the *Jewish Encyclopedia*, beginning in 1901; the arrival in America of the preeminent Jewish scholar, Solomon Schechter, in 1902; the central role played by the American Jewish community in responding to the Kishinev pogrom of 1903—all seemed to herald a new twentieth-century Jewish world in which American Jewry would play a far more central part than ever before (just, of course, as America generally was making its presence increasingly felt in world affairs).[5] Mass East European Jewish immigration, which peaked in 1906 when over 153,000 Jews were added to the community's population in a single year, provided demographic confirmation of American Jewry's mounting significance. "We have grown under providence both in numbers and in importance, so that we constitute now the greatest section of Israel living in a single country outside of Russia," the preface to the new 1917 Jewish Publication Society Bible translation proclaimed. It predicted, correctly, that the English language would shortly become "the current speech of the majority of the children of Israel."[6]

The inter-war years, when immigration to America was drastically curtailed and American Jewry, like America generally, stepped back into relative isolationism, forestalled American Jewry's emergence. Nevertheless, the work of the American Jewish Joint Distribution Committee, the Zionist Organization of America, the American Jewish Committee, institutions of higher Jewish learning, and other bodies served notice that American Jewry still carried significant financial, cultural, and even political clout; it could not be ignored. The cataclysm of the Second World War thrust American Jewry into a role that it had not expected to assume as early as 1945, but the community was not wholly unprepared. The Shoah hastened a process that had actually been ongoing for more than half a century.

American Jewry's move from periphery to center in the postwar years transformed the community in myriad ways. Aryeh Goren properly points to "the fashioning of a new communal order and the emergence of a collective self-confidence and sense of well-being."[7] Organization after organization in the Jewish community witnessed significant staff increases, a host of new, highly specialized job titles and divisions, and an influx of young college-trained experts with professional training who gradually supplanted the once dominant lay leaders. During these years, New York cemented its position as the "capital" of world Jewry, and a professional bureaucracy, the so-called Jewish civil service, emerged to staff these Jewish organizations. Indicative of these trends is the transformation, during these years, of the Union of American Hebrew Congregations. In 1951, it left Cincinnati for its new House of Living Judaism "in the thick of things" in New York and thereafter it grew and rapidly professionalized under the leadership of Rabbi Maurice Eisendrath. The American Jewish Committee doubled its staff and tripled its budget just between 1939 and the late 1940s, and continued to grow thereafter. Other Jewish organizations experienced similar developments. It was a good time to work in the field of Jewish communal service.[8]

Of course, the "self-confidence" that Goren pointed to in his discussion of American Jewry's "golden decade" looked different to those with whom American Jews interacted abroad. With some justification, they viewed this "self-confidence" as bristling arrogance. The famous 1950 exchange between Jacob Blaustein, President of the American Jewish Committee, and David Ben Gurion, Prime Minister of the State of Israel, illustrates this. The episode has been interpreted in different ways by Israeli scholars and by those who study the relationship of Israel and the Diaspora, but what is most important for our purposes is the self-perception on the part of Blaustein that he, as President of the American Jewish Committee, represented American Jewry, and that the Committee's will should become the State of Israel's command. Blaustein warned Israeli leaders not to interfere in American Jewish affairs, not to promote *aliyah* from America, and not to attempt to speak for the Jews of the world. What was at stake, he privately made clear, was "not only the continuance of American philanthropic and economic assistance, but also the general good will of American Jewry." Publicly, he lectured Ben Gurion that it was American Jewry that assumed "a major part of the responsibility of securing equality of rights and providing generous material help to Jews in other countries." Insisting that "to American Jews, America is home," Blaustein bluntly warned Ben Gurion against "unwise and unwarranted statements and appeals which ignore the feelings and aspirations of American Jewry."[9]

Blaustein viewed Israel within the context of President Harry Truman's 1949 inaugural address, the fourth point of which called upon Americans to "embark on a bold new program for making the benefits of our scientific advances and industrial progress available for the improvement and growth of underdeveloped areas."[10] He actually referred to Truman's program in his address, where he portrayed Israel as a model for how "under-developed peoples" might "improve their conditions and raise their standards of living."[11] It is fascinating to see this same American context invoked by Louis Finkelstein, Chancellor of the Jewish Theological Seminary. The occasion was the appearance of the first three volumes of the great Talmudist Saul Lieberman's *Tosefta* in 1955. In a letter to America's ambassador to Israel, Edward Lawson, Finkelstein proposed that the ambassador present this seminal work of rabbinic scholarship to the president of the State of Israel in a public relations ceremony as part of what he described as a "Spiritual Point Four program, by which America may contribute to older civilizations new insights into their own cultural products." The event in due course took place, and the headline in the *New York Times* reflected the cultural politics of the day. It read: "U.S. Gives Israel New Study of Jewish Code."[12] Viewed in transnational terms, American Jews, in the immediate postwar decade, viewed themselves and their government as generous "donors" and their Israeli cousins as "underdeveloped beneficiaries." This "self-confidence" (as Goren calls it) or "arrogance" (as we might call it) was a trope that echoed deeply in the history of Jewish philanthropy, as well as in the traditional rhetoric of colonialism, but it surely did not endear America's Jewish leaders to their Israeli counterparts.

American Jewry's swaggering self-confidence during these years masked a substantial degree of insecurity that the community tried hard to keep hidden. It is easy to exaggerate the "golden era" image that Goren has so powerfully drawn.[13] True, anti-Semitism had markedly declined, but it was neither eradicated nor forgotten. Moreover, the "great fear" of the immediate postwar era was Communism, and everybody knew that the majority of Communists, suspected Communists and former Communists, as well as Communist sympathizers and even Communist spies and traitors (such as Julius Rosenberg) were Jewish or had Jewish-sounding names. Just as in our day *all* Muslims in America find themselves suspected of terrorism because *some* Muslims are indeed terrorists, so in the early and mid-1950s *all* Jews labored under the suspicion of Communism, just because some Jews were active Communists.[14]

As a result, anti-Communism, in many forms and guises, shaped the postwar American Jewish communal agenda for at least a decade. The collapse of Jewish secularism; the strident anti-Communism of the American Jewish Committee, many Jewish labor unions leaders and of other Jewish organizations that purged Communists from their ranks; even the unprecedented spike in rates of synagogue affiliation all reflect a conscious effort to distance the American Jewish community from the "taint" of Communism. The collapse of Yiddish secularism is quantifiable: by 1958, fewer than two percent of American Jewish children were studying in Jewish secular ("Yiddishist") schools, a decline of more than 50 percent in just a dozen years.[15]

Unlike those who moved far to the political right in response to Communism (which some Jews did), the bulk of the American Jewish community embraced what we would today call liberal anti-Communism. Even as Jews distanced themselves from the Communist Party, they battled prejudice and discrimination against all groups, believing, as the American Jewish Committee explained, "that there is the closest relation between the protection of the civil rights of all citizens and the protection of the civil rights of the members of particular groups [meaning Jews]." This widely held theory, dubbed by historian John Higham as "the theory of the unitary character of prejudice,"[16] made it self-evident to many Jews that they should "join with other groups in the protection of the civil rights ... irrespective of race, religion, color or national origin."[17] The fact that non-Jewish organizations like the National Council of Churches, the National Conference of Christians and Jews, and the American Civil Liberties Union, had cooperated with Jewish defense organizations during the war, and now sought to continue to work with them on a common social agenda, strengthened this trend.[18] As a result, American Jewish communal organizations concentrated during these years on issues like civil rights, civil liberties, church-state relations, and discrimination in housing, education, and employment. Anti-Communism did not drive most 1950s Jews into the conservative camp.[19]

The tercentenary celebration of American Jewish life, in 1954, which, as Goren notes, highlighted many trends in the era, was, at least in my reading, a public demonstration of these two trends: liberalism and anti-Communism. Its very slogan, "man's opportunities and responsibilities under freedom," coined by David Sarnoff and used as the theme of the celebration, suggests this. The American Jewish Committee cleverly referred both to freedom and to anti-Communism in its fundraising for the celebration.[20] That, of course, helps to explain why the commemoration highlighted the values of America even as leftist scholars like Morris Schappes and Louis Harap were completely excluded from the mainstream celebration. From the point of view of the American Jewish community, these people (Communists and Communist sympathizers) represented "the danger within," and anxious community leaders, therefore, did all that they could to drown them out and suppress them.

Liberal anti-Communism likewise characterized the foreign policies of the American Jewish community during the 1950s. Support for Israel, support (albeit grudging) for America's policy in rebuilding Germany, and growing attention to anti-Semitism behind the iron curtain all reflected the liberal anti-Communist ethos of the postwar American Jewish community. At the same time, the general unwillingness to openly challenge American foreign policy—even at the time of the 1956 Suez war—bespoke the community's continuing anxieties. However self-confident Jews may have felt in confronting Jewish communities abroad (witness Blaustein's confrontation with Israeli leaders), they certainly did not yet feel the same degree of self-confidence in confronting their own government at home.[21]

Beneath the surface in the 1950s, two seismic shifts were taking place that, while scarcely noticed at the time, would ultimately transform American Jewish life in ways that nobody could have predicted in 1945. These seismic shifts set the stage for developments that we may only appreciate sixty years later.

The first seismic shift, which I have written about at greater length elsewhere,[22] was the impact of the 300,000 or so refugees, survivors, and "displaced persons" who migrated to America between 1933 and 1950. These immigrants, some from Germany, some from Eastern Europe, included some of Judaism's most illustrious rabbis and scholars, such as the Lubavitcher rebbe (Rabbi Joseph I. Schneersohn and his son-in-law and successor, Rabbi Menahem Mendel Schneerson), as well as many other Hasidic rebbes; the rabbinic decisor, Rabbi Moshe Feinstein; the founder of advanced Talmudic academies (*kollelim*) in America, Rabbi Aaron Kotler; the German Reform rabbis, Leo Baeck and Joachim Prinz; the theologian, Abraham Joshua Heschel; and a parade of other luminaries.

Besides these towering figures, scores of future leaders and shapers of American Judaism settled in America during these years as children and teens, "embers plucked from the fires of the Holocaust," eager to complete their education and start life anew. These included three of the most influential figures in late twentieth-century American Reform Judaism, Alfred Gottschalk, W. Gunther Plaut, and Alexander Schindler; the future chancellor of the Jewish Theological Seminary, Ismar Schorsch; the charismatic Orthodox Jewish female "evangelist," Esther Jungreis; the influential composer, singer, and spiritual revivalist, Shlomo Carlebach; and the founder of the Jewish renewal movement, Zalman Schachter.

Few American Jews in the 1950s paid much attention to these immigrants, who spoke with thick accents and tended to live apart from the mainstream community. But as it turned out, these men and women, notwithstanding the vast ideological chasms that divided them, became the most influential figures of late twentieth-century American Jewish life: they strengthened and revitalized practically every aspect of American Judaism and American Jewish culture, and they played a tremendous role in reordering American Jewry's communal priorities as well. They were the first to memorialize the Shoah and did more than anybody else to make it central in American culture; they renewed and reshaped American Orthodoxy in particular and also Conservative and Reform Judaism; they took over the leadership of both religious and secular Jewish organizations; they created new forms of Jewish music and spirituality; they broadened and strengthened American Jewish scholarship; and much, much more. In short, this remarkable intellectual migration transformed America into a religious and cultural and intellectual center of world Jewry in the postwar era. Some of the changes the immigrants wrought might have happened anyway, but the impact of these immigrants can, nevertheless, scarcely be overestimated.

The second seismic shift that took place actually happened not in America, but in Israel, and its implications are only now beginning to be appreciated. I refer to the massive postwar global Jewish population transfer that multiplied Israel's Jewish population by 840 percent between 1948 and 2005, from 650,000 to 5,260,000 Jews. This demographic leap, which was accompanied by substantial economic advances, had vast political and cultural implications. Decade by decade, Israel came to feel less like a dependent under-developed colony, and more like a first-world independent state (which in fact it became). As it did so, it challenged American Jewry's claim to centrality in Jewish life.

The later history of the Blaustein-Ben Gurion agreement vividly illustrates this development. As time went on, Israel paid less and less attention to the substance of that agreement, and by 1961, when under AJC pressure it was reaffirmed, the American Jewish Committee was forced to admit that "it is perfectly natural for differences of view to exist on the essence and the meaning of Jewish and Jewishness"—a far cry indeed from the imperious tone employed eleven years earlier. By 1977, political scientist Charles S. Liebman concluded that the agreement had become "of purely symbolic importance, and only to the AJC at that."[23] In practice, Israel no longer needed to march to the beat of the American Jewish community's drummer.

Actually, David Ben Gurion *never* made peace with American Jewry's domination of world Jewish affairs. A remarkable protocol of a high-level meeting called by him back on July 25, 1950 to discuss "Our Attitude Toward American Jewry" shows that even while his hands were tied by Blaustein, he and his colleagues sought to promote *aliyah* from America and to strengthen the Jewish identity and Zionist sympathies of American Jews. The protocol bespeaks a very different view of the Jewish world than that which held sway in America. Indeed, it presumed that the State of Israel, through its own actions and emissaries, would transform American Jewry; not vice versa.[24] Israel's heart was thus squarely located in the postcolonial world (to use contemporary jargon) even if it was still forced to dance to old colonial tunes. Israeli Jewry at that time was perhaps one-fifth the size of American Jewry and in practical terms, it rapidly bent to American Jewish demands. Nevertheless, it imagined itself, even then, as the very center of the Jewish world, responsible for the welfare of all Jews everywhere. It did not expect to kowtow to American Jewry forever.

And slowly but surely Israel *did* move from the periphery to the center. The Israel Bonds Program, launched in 1951, marked an initial step in this quest for self-determination. Without undermining other bodies, like the United Israel Appeal or the Jewish Agency, the Bonds program, centered in Israel, underscored such themes as state sovereignty and patriotism; it was modeled, reputedly, on US Savings Bonds, not on charity programs. American Jews may not always themselves have appreciated Israel Bonds for what they were—an investment vehicle—nevertheless, from Israel's perspective, the difference between charitable giving and investment was both symbolic and profound. The very word "bond" hinted at the kind of relationship that Israel wanted to have with American Jewry: one that bonded American Jews to Israel but did not make Israel a totally dependent partner in that relationship.[25]

This is not the place for a full-scale analysis of how Israel came increasingly to challenge American Jewry's claims to centrality. The Soviet Jewry movement and especially the bitter battle over *"Noshrim"* ("dropouts"), Russian Jews who upon their departure from the Soviet Union elected to settle in the United States, is an important part of that story. So is the Jonathan Pollard affair of 1985 which reflected, among many other things, Israel's unwillingness to play by American Jewish rules. So is the "who is a Jew" controversy and the battle over religious pluralism in Israel.[26] In fact, throughout the Jewish world today it is abundantly clear that the days of American Jewish "centrality" are over. American Jews are being forced to come to terms with a new model of Jewish life, a two-center model in which the role of Israel is substantially larger than it was back when Blaustein and Ben Gurion met together in 1950, while the role of American Jewry is considerably diminished.

Indeed, amidst the commemoration of 350 years of American Jewish life in 2005, a news item of immense historical and symbolic significance passed practically unnoticed though it bears on precisely this point. On May 10, 2005, Israel's Central Bureau of Statistics announced that the country's population of Jews and people closely related to Jews (who are not deemed Jewish by the Ministry of the Interior) had reached a grand total of 5,550,000.[27] The parallel number for Jews and people closely related to Jews in the United States (where the figures are admittedly less precise and more controversial) is 5,290,000 (and that may be a high figure).[28] Israel in 2005 has overtaken the United States as the largest Jewish population center in the world. This is a development of immense portent—one of only a handful of such transformations in all of Jewish history—and it marks the first time since the days of the Bible (though others claim since the days of the crusades) that the largest population center of world Jewry is actually found in the land of Israel. Along the same lines, it is noteworthy that Greater Tel Aviv (in Israel) has overtaken greater New York (in the United States) as the metropolitan area with the world's largest core Jewish population. There are 2,663,000 Jews living in Greater Tel Aviv and 2,051,000 in Greater New York. "The greatest Jewish city in the world," as journalist Harry Golden once dubbed New York, is now only the second greatest.[29]

With this news, an era that began in 1945, when the statistical map of world Jewry was redrawn leaving the United States all alone at the center of world Jewry, has with little fanfare come to a close. A new era, characterized by a different definition of Jewry's center (likely a two-center model) and a different relationship between the Jews of Israel and the Jews of the United States, seems poised to begin.

Notes

1. *American Jewish Year Book (=AJYB)* 48 (1946–47): 599.

2. *AJYB* 50 (1948–49): 1.

3. See Meri-Jane Rochelson's introduction to the reprint edition of *Children of the Ghetto* (Detroit: Wayne State University Press, 1998) and Jonathan D. Sarna, *JPS: The Americanization of Jewish Culture, 1888–1988* (Philadelphia: Jewish Publication Society, 1988), 39–42.

4. Quoted in Sarna, *JPS*, 37.

5. Shuly Rubin Schwartz, *The Emergence of Jewish Scholarship in America: The Publication of the Jewish Encyclopedia* (Cincinnati: Hebrew Union College Press, 1991); Abraham J. Karp, "Solomon Schechter Comes to America," *American Jewish Historical Quarterly* 53 (1963): 44–62; Philip E. Schoenberg, "The American Reaction to the Kishinev Pogrom of 1903," *American Jewish Historical Quarterly* 63 (1974): 262–83.

6. Quoted in Sarna, *JPS,* 112.

7. Arthur A. Goren, *The Politics and Public Culture of American Jews* (Bloomington and Indianapolis, IN: Indiana University Press, 1999), 186.

8. Stuart Svonkin, *Jews Against Prejudice: American Jews and the Fight for Civil Liberties* (New York: Columbia University Press, 1997), 16–7; Michael A. Meyer, "From Cincinnati to New York: A Symbolic Move," in *The Jewish Condition: Essays on Contemporary Judaism Honoring Rabbi Alexander Schindler* (New York: Union of American Hebrew Congregations Press, 1995), 302–13, here 311; Naomi W. Cohen, *Not Free to Desist: The American Jewish Committee, 1906–1966* (Philadelphia: Jewish Publication Society, 1972), 238–9, 334–5.

9. Charles S. Liebman, *Pressure Without Sanctions: The Influence of World Jewry on Israel* (Rutherford, NJ: Fairleigh Dickenson University Press, 1977), 122; *AJYB* 53 (1952): 564–8; Zvi Ganin, *An Uneasy Relationship: American Jewish Leadership and Israel, 1948–1957* (Syracuse, NY: Syracuse University Press, 2005), 81–104.

10. The text of the address is available at http://www.trumanlibrary.org/calendar/viewpapers. php?pid=1030.

11. *AJYB* 53 (1952): 566.

12. Jonathan D. Sarna, "Two Traditions of Seminary Scholarship," in *Tradition Renewed: A History of the Jewish Theological Seminary,* ed. Jack Wertheimer (New York: Jewish Theological Seminary, 1997), vol. II, 53–85, here 69–70; see Ben Gurion's comments on the Point Four Program analogy in the 1950 document ("On The Agenda: Our Attitude Towards American Jewry") reprinted by Zvi Ganin in *Kivunim: The Journal of Zionism and Judaism* 4 (April 1993): 49–89, here 86 [in Hebrew].

13. See his caveats; Goren, *Politics and Public Culture of American Jews,* 200.

14. Arthur Liebman, *Jews and the Left* (New York: John Wiley, 1979), 514–7; David Caute, *The Great Fear: The Anti-Communist Purges under Truman and Eisenhower* (New York: Simon and Schuster, 1978); John Earl Haynes and Harvey Klehr, *Venona: Decoding Soviet Espionage in America* (New Haven, CT and London: Yale University Press, 1999).

15. Stephen J. Whitfield, *The Culture of the Cold War* (Baltimore: Johns Hopkins University Press, 1996), 77–100; Judah Pilch, *A History of Jewish Education in America* (New York: American Association for Jewish Education, 1969), 130; Jonathan D. Sarna, *American Judaism: A History* (New Haven, CT and London: Yale University Press, 2004), 281–2.

16. John Higham, *Send These to Me: Immigrants in Urban America* (Baltimore: Johns Hopkins University Press, 1984), 155.

17. *AJYB* 50 (1948–49): 826.

18. Svonkin, *Jews against Prejudice,* 18, 25.

19. Some of those who did become conservatives in this era are discussed in George H. Nash, "Forgotten Godfathers: Premature Jewish Conservatives and the Rise of *National Review, American Jewish History* 87 (June–September 1999): 123–157; see also Murray Friedman, *The Neoconservative Revolution* (Cambridge and New York: Cambridge University Press, 2005), 28–99.

20. Goren, *Politics and Public Culture of American Jews,* 195.

21. See my discussion of "the issues of the '50s" in Jonathan D. Sarna and Jonathan J. Golden, "The Twentieth Century Through American Jewish Eyes: A History of the *American Jewish Year Book, 1899–1999," American Jewish Year Book* 100 (2000): 59–65.

22. For what follows, see Sarna, *American Judaism,* 293–306.

23. Liebman, *Pressure without Sanctions,* 130.

24. "On The Agenda: Our Attitude towards American Jewry," passim.

25. Allon Gal, ed., *Envisioning Israel: The Changing Ideals and Images of North American Jews* (Detroit, MI: Wayne State University Press, 1996), 207–17, 254–67; Henry Morgenthau III, *Mostly Morgenthaus: A Family History* (New York: Ticknor & Fields, 1991), 418–22.

26. See generally Fred A. Lazin, *The Struggle for Soviet Jewry in American Politics: Israel Versus the American Jewish Establishment* (Lanham, MD: Lexington Books, 2005) and Steven T. Rosenthal, *Irreconcilable Differences? The Waning of the American Jewish Love Affair With Israel* (Hanover, NH and London: Brandeis University Press by University Press of New England, 2001).

27. "Press Release: Eve of 57th Independence Day: 6.9 Million Residents in the State of Israel," Jerusalem: Central Bureau of Statistics 100/2005 (May 10, 2005), available at www.cbs.gov.il/press205-ettm. The development was noticed by Arutz Sheva: "After 1,000 Years, Israel is Largest Jewish Center" (May 1, 2005/22 Nisan 5765), available at www.israelnationalnews.com/news.php3?id=81071.

28. *AJYB* 104 (2004): 501–5.

29. *AJYB* 104 (2004): 520; Harry Golden, *The Greatest Jewish City in the World* (Garden City, NY: Doubleday, 1972).

CHAPTER 18

CAN LESS BE MORE? THE AMERICAN JEWISH EFFORT TO "RESCUE" GERMAN AND SOVIET JEWRY

Henry Feingold

The use of a familiar Bauhaus principle, "less is more," to throw light on a historical event may seem peculiar at first glance. But it is actually a practical way to gain entrée into a quandary of recent American Jewish historiography where less did come to more. By all measures, numbers, communal adherence and coherence, American Jewry should have been in a weaker position to "rescue" Soviet Jewry than it was to "rescue" the German Jews of the 1930s. Yet precisely the reverse turned out to be the case. Its performance in the Soviet Jewry crises was more effective than it was in the 1930s. None of the bugaboos of modern Jewish life, disunity, indifference, and privatism, had disappeared but American Jewish leaders acted with greater confidence to find the levers of power and to pull them. In this discussion the many factors to account for this unexpected phenomenon are probed. We focus particularly on the impact of its imagined failing witness role during the Holocaust which haunted the new rescue effort.

But first a word of warning. We need to be wary of reading too much into seemingly analogous events. There was, of course, a multiplicity of reasons for the growth in effectiveness. Two communities may undergo similar experiences but historical contexts differ. Like fingerprints responses to crisis are never the same. Baked in different historical ovens for centuries there is as much cultural dissonance between German and Russian Jews, as there is between Teutons and Slavs. First overcooked and now undercooked, the cultural differences between Eastern and Western Jews, are nevertheless real.[1] It is primarily their Jewish condition of non-acceptability in the host culture which they hold in common. Though it took different forms, anti-Semitism was a common denominator of pre-war German and Soviet society. We can note simply that both migrations are products of the internal dynamics of twentieth-century totalitarian social orders.

However, that almost exhausts what they held in common. The National Socialists spared no effort to make the Reich *judenrein* and were faced with the refusal of receiving nations to accept their Jewish discards. On the other hand, almost as if it adored them, the Soviets did not want to let its Jews go. We begin then with the reality that these migrations began as involuntary emigrations. Had the Nazi Reich and the Soviet Union assured its Jews a normal measure of human rights and security there would have been no mass emigration, certainly not in the case of Germany. The rejection was not mutual. There was an element of love unrequited for the host society in both migrations, or at least in some initial part of it. These immigration codas are composed of immigrants who in some respects are more German than the Germans, more Russian than the Russians.[2] German and Soviet Jews drank deeply from the well springs of the host culture which they served as carriers and generators and were, up to a point, willing to accommodate their own cultures to fit-in. In both cases they were eminently successful in doing so.[3] That success was at the heart of Nazi anti-Semitic plaint that German culture has been captured by the Jews. Goebbels' cry was that German culture must be retrieved and purified of its Jewish taint. The Soviets were more secure about their culture but had other problems with an imagined Jewish taint. The idea that Communism was somehow a Jewish idea which was a major theme of anti-Soviet propaganda plagued the Soviet leadership who went to great lengths to counteract the idea of *Judeobolshevism*.

Before they were declassed the Soviet refuseniks and the German "Transfer agreement" emigrants both stemmed from the urban/urbane middle class of their respective societies. But they were reluctant immigrants not anxious to give up the lives they had built for themselves. The Zionist refuseniks who mounted a worldwide struggle to emigrate and risked giving up their middle class position, or at least the Soviet version of it, were not representative of Soviet Jewry which was far less willing to expose itself to the Soviet control system. The real Soviet Jewish emigrant did not make his debut in force until 1977. Like his predecessors at the turn of the century he preferred to settle in the USA and used the Israeli visa, the only visa available to leave the Soviet Union, to realize that hope. The Soviet "dropout" to America was in fact a reversion to a normal immigrant with normal motivation similar to the Russian immigrants who arrived in great numbers after 1870. In that sense they were "Tevye's" children.

Only in the anti-Semitic imagination were all Jewish emigrants cut from the same cloth. The German Jewish Transfer agreement emigrants of the 1930s who resettled in Palestine were a far cry from the adolescents who were recruited for *Youth Aliyah*.[4] The German Jewish immigrants who settled in the "Fourth Reich," the unloving nickname given to the new German Jewish enclave in the Washington Heights neighborhood of Manhattan, and the sundry artists, musicians, and filmmakers who ended up in Los Angeles in the purview of Hollywood or the physicists who manned the Manhattan project, often had only a birthplace and language in common.[5] Similarly, the refuseniks that spearheaded the Soviet emigration were a far cry from the "dropouts" who dominated the emigration after 1987. The former were zionized and wanted to be ingathered in a Jewish homeland. The settlers of "little Odessa" in the Brighton Beach section of Brooklyn could barely muster the cultural energy required to build a network of synagogues and self-help agencies that are everywhere the hallmark of Jewish communalism. The Soviet intent to liquidate Jewish life and culture may not have been as bloody as that of the National Socialist but it was a far more sustained campaign and seemingly more effective.

The candidates for rescue were quite different from each other especially in their relationship to matters of faith. With the exception of the Breuer group of Frankfurt Hasidim, the German Jewish refugees were more or less secular. Still in the throes of Jewish communalism the Jews of Washington Heights established the full panoply of philanthropic communal and religious congregations.[6] On the other hand the highly secularized Soviet Jewish emigrants of "little Odessa" in Brooklyn retained little desire to recreate a community of faith. Perhaps they no longer remembered how to do so. Often the only thing immediately recognizably Jewish about this group is their overriding concern about the future of their children who had been systematically excluded from the schools and institutions that served as the instruments of mobility in the closed Soviet system.

Time and circumstance had also created a wide gulf between the candidates for rescue and the host Jewish community mobilized to receive them. The rustic "Landjuden" from Bavaria and Alsace and Posen who composed the nineteenth-century immigration were a far cry from the urbanized, highly professionalized cohort that followed them in the 1930s. These were older and probably more generally and Jewishly learned, and certainly more *großstädtisch* (urbane).[7] The same sharp contrast is discernible when the eastern Jews who arrived after 1870 are compared with the emigrants who arrived in the final three decades of the twentieth century. America modernized and Americanized its immigrants with great zest and success but on its own terms. When the "coda" immigrants arrived they encountered the result of that process, their hosts had become modern Americans who differed markedly from their European counterparts.

The emigrants of the 1930s also arrived under far different circumstances than the later Soviet arrivals. Despite the severe depression of the 1930s, the original German Jews in America had done comparatively well for themselves. Never a very large migration they were clearly on the decline as a distinct community in the 1930s. Their right to communal governance was challenged by the Congress movement which held America's first ethnic election in 1918 to determine the American Jewish delegation to Versailles. Thereafter the flow of power moved steadily "downtown." Jacob Schiff had passed away in 1921 and Louis Marshall, who managed communal affairs under "Marshall Law," passed away in 1929. The Soviet "dropout" emigrants, for whom HIAS had to acquire a *vyzov* (affidavit) from a close relative encountered a community that had fully participated in the embourgouisement process and would soon boast the nation's highest rate of professionalization and per-capita income.[8] Normally emigration processes entail a declassing, at least temporarily. That was essentially true of our codas which were by pre-selection basically either already middle class, or aspiring to be so. That would influence the adjustment of the new arrivals and accelerate their mobility.[9]

That process was probably more challenging for the Soviet than the German Jewish emigrant. The Soviet emigrant was the end product of a society that had undergone cataclysmic changes followed by a brutal war. But as a Jew he was also subjected to a government policy which sought to fit him in by first destroying the Jewish communal structure and then re-tailoring the culture to fit into the new Socialist order. Unlike the National Socialists, the Soviets did not assume a biological base for their Judeophobia. Since the Jewish disease was not in the blood the Soviets had not given up on the possibility of reshaping its Jewish clay. It sought to do so by dismantling its communal institutions and decapitating its leadership. The consequences of that social engineering were startlingly successful so that the Soviet emigrant barely remembered the once rich

Jewish communal culture that had incubated virtually every movement of modern Judaism from Haskalah to Zionism. With the exception of certain self or geographically isolated communities beyond the Urals, the Soviet Jewish identity that survived was based only on a memory of a memory. Between 1968 and 1980, more Soviet Jews exited the Jewish fold by changing their identity designation on their internal passport than by choosing to emigrate from the Soviet Union. The Soviet immigrant who was often seen in Israel and America as barely Jewish was in fact the more strongly identified segment of Soviet Jewry, those that had not yet abandoned their Jewish identity entirely.

The numbers involved in these codas are important because in general the more that come the more problematic the reception.[10] The immigration of a quarter million German Jews in the nineteenth century to a largely rural agricultural economy enveloped in a much larger German immigration wave is barely noticed on the historical monitor compared to the estimated 2.4 million Eastern European Jews who arrived between 1870 and 1924. Perhaps more important than scale was the historical moment the emigration occurred. Though much smaller than the later Soviet emigration, the argument opposed to receiving the German Jewish refugees of the 1930s was, not only that they were the wrong kind, professors and lawyers and sundry white collar types, but that there were too many to be absorbed in a period when according to Roosevelt "one third of the nation was ill housed, ill clothed and ill fed." That was less true of the Soviet emigration. The German Jewish coda of the 1930s came to about 132,000, which is quite negotiable in a community of over four million, which formed about 3.7 percent of the population and was about 17 percent foreign-born in 1930. But they arrived during the Depression into a community whose leadership had but recently been assumed by the descendants of eastern Jews. Such Jews forget nothing including real and imagined trespasses from within the tribe. Some liked to recall the unpleasantness their parents experienced upon first contact with German Jews on their way to America.

Since many American Jews signed the close-relatives *vyzov*, family ties played some role in the resettlement process but in fact the kinship tie with their Soviet relatives had long since lapsed. As in the case of the German Jewish coda, the Soviet dropouts who came to America were basically foreign to their hosts. Generations of life in different cultures had left their mark. It soon became apparent that the difference between Soviet *dropouts* and their American Jewish hosts went beyond their metallic dental work. They were also disaffected from anything that smacked of state control or the liberal sensibility which prevailed among their American Jewish hosts. The greatest contrast seemed to be, as one social worker put it, "the loss of their Jewish edge." They were slow in ridding themselves of their dependency on the help agencies like NYANA and too smart in milking the philanthropic network for anything they could get. It aroused animosity on the grass roots level. "They lie, they cheat, anything to get what they want, [many] lack the basic concepts of humanity, let alone Judaism," observed one Queens rabbi, blaming the Soviet system for having "done its work only too well."[11] But generally the cycle of Jewish immigrant success was repeated by the Soviet Jews who today are distinguishable only by their insistent rejection of the personal article when they speak English.

In both cases the hopes invested in the "American dream" were realized. The German Jews who arrived in the 1930s in the midst of the depression did quite well. I am not speaking only about the Kissingers, Einsteins, and Schoenbergs and the enormous impact they had on American culture in arts, marketing research, and American science or even the cohort of German Jewish professors who found posts in small southern colleges and surfaced during the Civil Rights struggle. That has been well documented.[12] The German immigrant of the 1930s participated fully in the general rise of Jews in the postwar decades. A displaced middle class group was able to recoup its position in their new homes in record breaking time. The role of refugee physicists, many of Jewish origin, in developing the A-bomb at Los Alamos is becoming a subject of increasing interest for researchers.[13]

The Soviet Jewish immigrants experienced a parallel successful adjustment but there are also considerable variations. In scale it is larger than the German-Jewish migration of the 1930s and arrives at a Jewish host community which had grown proportionately smaller.[14]

We need first to note that in terms of scale, time in history and general circumstances comparisons are possible but strained. Historically, however, the cast of characters has remained constant. Center stage there is a beleaguered threatened Jewry. There are the witnessing Diaspora and other Jewish communities, there is a separate Zionist interest represented by the *Yishuv* in the 1930s and by Israel later, and finally there is the role reserved for powerful witnessing nations like the USA and others. In both cases the emigration is perpetrated by a highly threatening totalitarian society but the precise nature of the threat was different. German Jewry ultimately faced physical annihilation while Soviet Jewry had been subject to cultural and communal annihilation but only a passing threat to physical destruction during the "Doctor's plot" year in 1953.

We are above all else interested in communal response to crises. It should come as no surprise that the American Jewish communal effort to extricate Soviet Jewry surpassed in scope and intensity the effort to rescue the Jews of Central Europe, the first group that required rescue during the Holocaust. The primary reason for that may be explained by a simple case of chronological sequence. The Soviet case occurred after the Holocaust. The fact that the Holocaust itself haunted the American Soviet Jewry movement may account for the greater activism mounted by a succeeding generation anxious for redemption. Young American Jewish activists would do for the Soviet Jewish emigrants what they imagined their parents had failed to do for the Jews of Europe.

What we witness is a more energetic, more confident rescue effort mounted by a community that is, after an additional generation of assimilation, proportionately smaller in numbers and organizationally less cohesive. A smaller, seemingly weaker community had in fact become more effective. Less has become more. American Jewry's political influence reached unprecedented heights after the 1967 war. Its strong position in American politics would go on to become legendary in the Islamic world where we can note that exaggerated notion of Jewish power fueling the anti-Semitic imagination.[15] But the fact is that after the June war a change in American Jewish political culture occurred. There began a movement from acting behind the scenes to seeking and holding political office.[16] A disproportionate number of Jews, many serving non-Jewish constituencies, began to seek and win offices on all levels of government and in the judiciary. Jews have always held some offices but their influence was traditionally amplified through the role they played in the professional aspects of politics as pundits, pollsters, journalists, speech writers, campaign managers, and fund raisers.

After the Jackson Vanik amendment which threatened to withhold Most Favorite Nation status and the access to credit that accompanied it unless Moscow allowed its Jews to emigrate and put a halt to its depredations, Jewish political leaders like Senator Jacob K. Javitz and Abraham A. Ribicoff who strongly supported the amendments risked being accused of "hijacking" American foreign policy. At one stroke Senator Henry "Scoop" Jackson was able to hold Henry Kissinger's détente policy hostage over the Soviet Union's immigration policy. It created an opportunity to wield the Soviet emigration problem as a weapon in the hands of those opposed to détente. That was precisely the reverse situation of the 1930s when above all, Roosevelt was anxious to convince a class- and race-driven nation to go to war and rejected the idea that mobilization could be mounted based on the idea of "rescuing" the Jews of Europe.

American Jewry found itself in the middle of a bitter struggle over the tenets of Cold War strategy. It was complicated by the fact that at the same time the amendment was also a factor in the perennial struggle over who should control foreign policy, congress or the president. The conflict between the two branches was intensified by the weakened post-Watergate Nixon presidency. But a half-century after the Holocaust American Jewish discomfort at occupying the center of the historical stage was balanced by its need to this time play its advocacy role fully, something it imagined it had failed to do during the Roosevelt years.

Of course an increased number of Jewish office holders do not automatically translate into Jewish influence. With the exception of the security of Israel issue there is no agreed upon Jewish agenda. There are many Jewish voters who do not think much of Joe Lieberman or Russel Feingold. During the Soviet Jewry crisis those legislators on the Hill most active on behalf of Soviet Jewry, like Senator "Scoop" Jackson, were not Jewish. One needs to be reminded that Richard Nixon, who sat in the Oval Office during the early crucial years of the Soviet Jewry crisis, may have been a staunch supporter of Israel but in domestic politics he also had a disproportionate number of Jews on his "hit" list.

Nor is the period when the Soviet Jewry issue came to the fore in American politics the first time in American history that Jews played an important role in the policy making process. Ted Roosevelt had his Oscar Strauss, Franklin Roosevelt had his "Jew Deal," and even Nixon had his Kissinger. But after the June war in 1967, a new aspect of Jewish political influence made its debut. The customary professional role exercised by Jews in American politics was supplemented by a remarkable increase in the actual exercise of power through office holding and appointments rather than merely advising those who have it. That has taken its place with other means Jews have traditionally used to amplify their influence such as "fat catism"[17] and a fuller engagement in the political process. Jews are more likely to vote, to write letters to their Congressmen, to write letters to the editor of their local newspaper, and often to be the editor of that paper.

Withal, that power is so individuated and amorphous that by itself it is insufficient to explain Jewish effectiveness for Soviet Jewry as compared to its ineffectiveness for European Jewry during the Holocaust.

For a fuller explanation we need to turn to the impact of the Holocaust on American Jewish political culture. The fact is that much of the difference in the American Jewish reaction to crisis of Soviet and German Jewry is rooted in the fact that after the Holocaust the communal perception of threat was far keener. American Jewry's view of the Soviet Jewry problem was conditioned by its recent experience with what they believed was the analogous crisis with German Jewry in the immediate pre-Holocaust years. They naturally imagined that Soviet Jews were victims of an oppressive anti-Semitic regime, much like the Jews of Europe were during the Holocaust years. They thought that history was repeating itself and might end in genocide, as it was rumored Stalin planned before his timely death in 1953.

So pervasive was the analogy that the profound difference between the National Socialist and Communist case were swept aside. The murder of European Jewry during the Second World War, in which Soviet Jewry suffered disproportionate losses, became part of a single continuous process, as if a totalitarian power of similar ilk was continuing the Final Solution. It invested the American activists with an urgency to act. They saw the Soviet Jews as victims of a vicious regime and the discovery that not all Soviet Jews saw themselves as needing to be rescued was ignored. They would not stand idly by, as they imagined their parents had done during the Holocaust.

In retrospect, the ability of the American branch of the Soviet Jewry movement to sustain itself for more than three decades before there were tangible rewards for its efforts finds much of its roots in the Holocaust. It was an important movement for American Jewry because of the opportunity it offered for some kind of redemption from the guilt felt regarding its failing witness role during those terrible years. It is not necessary here to ponder the question of whether that sense of guilt was justified. But we need to be aware of the fact of its existence in many forms, from the impact of the Jewish Defense League's (JDL) "Never Again" slogan to the proliferation of museums, memorials, books, and research projects, to conclude that in the years between 1967 and 1989, concern about the Holocaust and particularly its witness role was a near obsession which the historian ignores at considerable risk.[18] Most activists opposed the violent confrontational tactics favored by the JDL. But despite that, its "Never Again" slogan had high resonance precisely because it linked the "rescue" of Soviet Jewry to the Holocaust. The slogan could be heard in all corners of American Jewry but especially among the young activists of the Student Struggle for Soviet Jewry and the Union of Councils for Soviet Jewry who had learned of the failing witness role from a plethora of books and documentaries including my own.[19]

American Jewry's intense emotion surfaced in April 1985, when Reagan's pending visit to a military cemetery in Bitburg, where forty-seven members of the Waffen SS were buried, was announced.[20] The strength of that Holocaust obsession was also evidenced in the budget priorities within the local community federations where memorialization became an important concern especially among the survivors who had reestablished themselves in the USA.[21] So powerful was the Holocaust consciousness that by the end of the twentieth century, there remained few religious congregations that did not have some physical memorial and some manifestation in the traditional religious prayer ritual.[22]

Small wonder that in a communal atmosphere where the memory of the Holocaust was so pervasive Jewish activists assumed that the threat faced by Soviet Jews was analogous. The advent of a more liberal Gorbachev regime in 1985, which within two years removed most of the remaining signs of physical threat to Jewish dissenters and seemed ready to restore banned cultural institutions, had little impact. Some were wary of the Holocaust analogy. Phil Baum, the executive director of the American Jewish Congress, dared to point out that after Gorbachev, Soviet Jewry did not require rescue any more than any other Soviet ethnic groups.[23] But that opinion ran against the stream. It was as if the Jewish world could not take "yes" for an answer. "Never Again" remained the communal war cry and "rescuing" Soviet Jewry was its objective.

The Bitburg incident cast light on a related factor in the Soviet Jewry story. It again brought the Jewish role as historical victim to the attention of the American public though whether it generated public empathy for the plight of Soviet Jews remains an unknown. With the exception of those involved with the civil and human rights movements, together with certain liberal Protestant churchmen, selected members of Congress and certain government officials, the Soviet Jewish problem remained largely an intra-Jewish community concern. Not all American Jews were happy about the attention Jewish victimization was bringing to the community. Becoming a victim of history was not considered a positive factor in strengthening group identity. Better to be history's master than its victim, counseled the prevailing Zionist ideology.

It would not have mattered much if Holocaust obsession were confined to Jews who, from monotheism to messianism, are after all a people well known in history for having some world shaking obsessions. But it changed not only Jewish perception of the world but that of America as well. By the 1980s there was not an American university that did not have one or two courses on the Holocaust. The churches became involved. It became part of the high school social studies curriculum. Films and books poured from the presses. Finally, almost as if in a kind of government repentance for its indifference during those bitter years, a Holocaust museum was built on the Mall, subsidized partly with federal funds.[24]

The Holocaust obsession effected perception. Soviet Jewry was beleaguered perhaps more than other ethnics in the Soviet "prison house of nations." But we have noted that the analogy with the position of the refugees of the 1930s was a misperception. That is the reason why I have placed the word "rescue" in quotation marks in the title of this discussion.

In the end there were many reasons why "less became more." The expansion of Jewish political influence, the fortuitous linking of the Soviet Jewry issue to the Cold War, the rise of Human Rights as an important lever as a result of the Helsinki accords and the follow up conferences and not least, the enormous courage of the refuseniks in confronting the Soviet control system. But it was American Jewry's effectiveness in its advocacy that compelled the American government to use diplomatic intercession. It was one of those rare times in history that a Jewish community chose the right side and the right time to act.

There was of course the crucial role of Israel and the world Zionist movement. It found the "lost" Jews of the Soviet Union and built the net and connection to the West. Ultimately that enabled Jewish activists to broadcast KGB depredations to a listening world. If a Jewish foot was stepped on in Moscow, the world would know about it within an hour. That was enormously important. But for most of these years the Soviet Union would not enter into diplomatic relations with Israel. It was American Jewry acting through the American government that finally opened the door. The key to that door has the term Holocaust written on it. In historical terms the great contrast between the German and Soviet Jewish refugee crisis was that the former presaged the Holocaust while the latter echoed it.

Notes

1. Hasia Diner finds the differences between "Uptown" and "Downtown" Jews in the American context overstated. See her *A Time for Gathering: The Second Immigration, 1820–1880* (Baltimore, MD: Johns Hopkins Press, 1992), Vol. II of *The Jewish People in America*, ed. Henry L. Feingold.

2. Borrowed from musical composition, the term coda refers to the repetition of a recognizable collective theme in the final movement.

3. Alec Nove and John A. Newth, "The Jewish Population: Demographic Trends and Occupational Patterns," in *The Jews in Soviet Russia Since 1917*, ed. Lionel Kochan (New York and Oxford: Oxford University Press, 1978), 132–67. Jews made up the most highly formally educated group in the Soviet Union. It had four times the number of university graduates as the general population and composed 8.8 percent of its scientists and 14 percent of scientists who held the advanced PhD degree. In 1970, 5.6 percent of Soviet Jews qualified as professionals. Victor Zaslawski and Robert J. Brym, *Soviet Jewish Emigration and Soviet Nationality Policy* (New York: Macmillan, 1983), 14–15. Occupational profile of German Jewry was similarly comparatively high. See Steven M. Lowenstein, *Frankfurt on the Hudson: The German Jewish Community of Washington Heights, 1933–83, its Structure and Culture* (Detroit: Wayne State University Press, 1989), 32–3.

4. A movement organized by the Jewish Agency whose goal it was to bring young European Jews to Palestine.

5. The exodus of technocrats and scientists and other members of the operational elite of Germany deserve a special study, especially the role of refugee physicists in the Manhattan Project which developed the atomic bomb. See Donald Fleming and Bernard Bailyn, eds., *The Intellectual Migration: Europe and America, 1930–1960* (Cambridge, MA: Harvard University Press, 1968).

6. Lowenstein, *Frankfurt on the Hudson*, 140–62. These refugees were probably "frommer" and less affluent than German Jews who settled outside of New York City.

7. The average age of the German Jewish peddler from Bavaria of the nineteenth century was somewhere between fourteen and seventeen.

8. The Soviet Union did not have an emigration law as such. Instead a series of ad-hoc regulations governed the emigration process. Jews who desired to leave required a document

that they were reunifying themselves with family who would be responsible for their support. The Soviet emigration bureau (*Ovir*) would then issue an exit permit based on an Israeli visa. In 1988, a change in the regulations allowed a vouching relative to be an American.

9. We need more research on how many of the new immigrants used an ethnic bridge to "regain" their lost status. Their success in doing so may also account in a peculiar way for the tensions between old and new settlers.

10. About 132,000 refugees settled in the USA between 1933 and 1941, compared to about 850,000 Soviet Jews who settled between 1968 and 1991. Between 1967 and 1994, approximately 1.3 million Jews were able to leave the Soviet Union. The scale of emigration of Soviet Jewry vastly outnumbered the German Jewish coda of the 1930s.

11. Quoted in Howard M. Sachar, *A History of the Jews in America* (New York: Knopf and Vintage, 1992), 927.

12. For a popular account see Anthony Heilbut, *Exiled In Paradise: German Refugee Artists and Intellectuals in America from the 1930s to the Present* (Berkeley, CA: University of California Press, 1997, 3rd edition). The best collection of essays remains Donald Fleming and Bernard Bailyn, eds., *The Intellectual Migration: Europe and America, 1930–1960* (Cambridge: Charles Warren Center, 1968). There are some who go as far as to claim that the scientific and technological boom which placed the USA in the forefront of the world is in some measure based on imported Jewish intellectual capital incubated in Germany and Europe in the prewar period and carried by the refugees and their children.

13. See, e.g., Jennet Conant, *Robert Oppenheimer and the Secret City of Alamos* (New York: Simon & Schuster, 2005). See also Charles Weiner, "A New Site For the Seminar: The Refugees in American Physics in the Thirties," in Fleming and Bailyn, eds., *Intellectual Migration*, 190–234. Laura Fermi, *Illustrious Immigrants: The Intellectual Migration From Europe* (Chicago: University of Chicago Press, 1968). The earliest mention of the role of the refugees was in Henry D. Smyth, *Atomic Energy for Military Purposes* (Washington, DC: US Government Printing Office, 1945).

14. In the 1970s, the Jewish population hovered between 5.1 and 5.3 million, but its proportion of the general population had declined from about 3.5 to perhaps 2.4 percent.

15. That was particularly apparent in the statement by the former prime minister of Malaysia, Mohammed Mahathir in 2004.

16. In 1941, Jews were about 3.7 percent of the electorate. By 2000, that had declined to about 2.3 percent. Nevertheless Jewish representation in Congress and on the local level rose. By 1992, there were ten Jewish Senators a decade late there were twelve.

17. Sixty-eight percent of campaign funds for the Democratic Party can be traced to Jewish donors.

18. Historians have not ignored it. See Peter Novick, *The Holocaust In American Life* (New York: Houghton Mifflin Co., 1999).

19. The publication of Arthur Morse's *While Six Million Died: A Chronicle of American Apathy* (New York: Hart Publishing Co., 1967) followed by my own *The Politics of Rescue, The Roosevelt Administration and the Holocaust, 1938–1945* (New Brunswick, NJ: Ruthers University Press, 1970), had a considerable impact on the younger generation. There are now seven studies and numerous scholarly articles dealing with the American reaction; see, e.g., David S. Wyman, *The Abandonment of the Jews: America and the Holocaust, 1941–1945* (New York: Pantheon Books, 1984); Gulie Ne'eman Arad, *America, its Jews and the Rise of Nazism* (Bloomington and Indianapolis, IN: Indiana University Press, 2001).

20. It was clear days before Eli Wiesel's plea at the White House Medal of Achievement award ceremony that a public relations disaster was in the making. But once scheduled it was

staunchly supported by Pat Buchanan, a right-wing speech writer for Reagan who was also a Holocaust denier. Strangely enough, the Bitburg incident did not there after alter the amicable relationship of the American Jewish electorate with the Reagan administration.

21. The survivors influence could be noted in the fact that virtually every American Jewish community and congregation had either already built or had on the drawing board some kind of Holocaust memorial. The larger urban communities were planning museums focused on the Holocaust. At its apogee was an enormous fund-raising effort to build a huge Holocaust museum on the Mall in the nation's capital. The campaign also included an effort to get the government to assume a financial role in helping to maintain the museum, as if to compensate for government indifference during the Holocaust. Such direct government involvement in an ethnic enterprise was unprecedented.

22. The near obsessional quality of the belated American Jewish reaction and its penchant for memorials is examined in Novick, *The Holocaust in American Life*, 207–63.

23. New York Public Library, Dorot Jewish Division, Wiener Oral History Archive, Interview with Phil Baum, Assistant Director, American Jewish Congress.

24. Edward T. Linenthal, *Preserving Memory: The Struggle to Create America's Holocaust Museum* (New York: Columbia University Press, 1995).

CHAPTER 19
AMERICAN JEWS AND THE MIDDLE EAST CRISIS
Michael E. Staub

1

In the course of the first decade of the twenty-first century, under the quadruple impact of the second Palestinian intifada and the Israeli government's multifaceted responses to it, the terrorist attacks on the World Trade Center in New York and the ensuing "global war on terror," the launching of the second Gulf War in 2003, and then the reconfiguration of the American political and cultural scene with George W. Bush's reelection in 2004, the terms of debate among American Jews over the Middle East were suddenly transformed with breathtaking rapidity. Among the consequences of that peculiar juncture were some remarkable inversions of positions previously considered immovable.

As recently as the late 1990s, for instance, the Israeli government's most vocal supporters in the USA, along with both Labor and Likud leaders in Israel itself, had announced that a Palestinian state would "never happen." But in 2005, prominent right-wing Jewish intellectuals—to say nothing of moderate conservatives and liberals—abruptly and solemnly declared themselves visionary advocates of a Palestinian state. The middle-of-the-roaders, in turn, were able to style themselves as both courageous and evenhanded in their critiques of extremist settlers and even of the "separation wall" that was beginning to be built. In other words, chiding the Israeli government in print in the US press (once considered an outrageous airing of dirty linen and a betrayal of loyalty) became not just acceptable but almost de rigueur as a space-clearing gesture, before right-wing and centrist commentators then moved on, variously, to describe the positive qualities of the Palestinian state they envisioned or to decry the Palestinians as the ones holding out on the peace process. On the other hand, as recently as the 1990s, Israel had consistently been able to count on the American Jewish community for monetary assistance and emotional affirmation. By 2005, however, and although many American Jews still eloquently defended not only Israel as a nation but also Israeli government and military policies, new surveys revealed a steady erosion in strong identification with (and donations to) Israel. This decline, in turn, among other things also prompted some Jewish organizations to seek greater financial and ideological support from evangelical Christian groups.

This essay will consider several aspects of American Jews' recent reactions to developments in Israel as well as Iraq (as the war there, as of 2011, was officially wound down). First, I will examine the ways prominent American Jewish opinion-makers—

among them journalists, academics, activists, and spokespeople for major American Jewish organizations—were framing both the wider educated American public's conversation about the Middle East and the intra-Jewish conflicts about the Middle East during President George W. Bush's second term in office. Second, and more briefly, I will look at the evidence on the American Jewish public's views on Israel and Iraq—including American Jewry's apparent tendency to be more, rather than less, politically progressive than its spokespeople (a definitive reversal of the tendency in the 1960s and 1970s, when the spokespeople tended toward greater liberality than the American Jewish public). Third, I will consider the dramatic rise of cooperation between right-wing evangelical Christians and American Jewish organizations during the first decade of the twenty-first century and the implications of that for American Middle East policy. And finally, I survey the latest reversals in American Jewish opinion (as of early 2012) as a further set of developments—from President Barack Obama's decision to continue (rather than undo) many of President Bush's policies in the "war on terror" and in the Middle East to the global uprisings following in the wake of the "Arab Spring" of 2011 to the political and cultural rise of ultra-Orthodoxy within Israel—have had both predictable and unpredictable effects on US–Israel relations. I will suggest that although the terms of debate about Israeli–Palestinian relations indisputably have been reconfigured in the last decade, this fact has not necessarily resulted in forward movement toward prospects for either justice or peace.

2

To many observers, the early months of 2005 appeared auspicious. There were numerous indications that the seeming deadlock in which the Middle East crisis had been stuck for some time was over. James Bennet, former Jerusalem bureau chief for the New York Times, summarized the prevailing sense of optimism (even as he also demonstrated a new tendency toward a deliberate attitude of balance in discussions of the crisis). "The Israeli–Palestinian conflict—a narcissistic face-off that pays little notice to the world around it—counsels cynicism as the safest guide," wrote Bennet in March: "Yet the seemingly endless, and in fact episodic, violence disguises the fact that over the last 20 years, the two peoples have moved toward recognizing each other's rights to statehood."[1] Or as The Forward noted in May 2005: "Three years after the Passover Eve bombing at Netanya's Park Hotel, arguably the low point in Israel's war against Palestinian terrorism, the Israeli people are in a soaring mood."[2]

Furthermore, in 2005, one increasingly heard reports from those with first-hand knowledge of Israel that developments there might just finally be turning an historic corner for the better. Many attributed this to the death of Yasir Arafat in October 2004 and the subsequent rise to power of Mahmoud Abbas as the chairman of the Palestinian Authority. Also cited were Prime Minister Ariel Sharon's decision to challenge the settler movement and the relatively smooth disengagement from Gaza that ensued in late summer. In the course of 2005, many political observers also effused over what they saw as a wave of democratization sweeping through several countries (including Egypt, Iraq, and Afghanistan) in the Arab world.

In the midst of all these developments, American Jewish commentators writing both in mainstream and in predominantly Jewish venues recurrently sought to shape how the Middle East would be discussed and debated. Those who weighed in on both Israel and the (then still rather young) war in Iraq ranged over the entire ideological spectrum, from Charles Krauthammer, William Kristol, David Brooks, and Norman Podhoretz on the right to Alan Dershowitz and Thomas L. Friedman in the center, to Michael Lerner, Eric Alterman, Paul Krugman, Sara Roy, Judith Butler, Tony Kushner, Alisa Solomon, and Henry Siegman on the liberal left. In their essays and columns, the Jewishness of these writers both did and did not matter. (For instance, someone like David Brooks does not routinely self-identify as a Jewish commentator, though he also has written about Jewish communal issues very much as an insider.) With regard to reception, readers at times did and at other times did not factor in the authors' Jewishness in their evaluations of the authors' merits. Yet there remained no question that readers, both Jewish and gentile, understood that these commentators were not only contributing to the mainstream public's ability to make sense of events in the Middle East, but were also engaged in an intra-Jewish conflict over what the proper response of American Jews should be to these events.

In 2005, *Washington Post* syndicated columnist Charles Krauthammer was as good a representative of the right's position as any. At that time, Krauthammer was a member of the now-defunct Project for the New American Century, a neoconservative think-tank whose chairman was William Kristol, son of Irving Kristol and editor of the *Weekly Standard*, and whose past members included Richard Perle, Paul Wolfowitz, Donald Rumsfeld, and Dick Cheney. Krauthammer was (and remains) a consistently strong booster of "the democracy project" (as he then called US Middle East policy).[3] He was also adamant in his support for the Iraq war, asserting in March 2005 that

> America, using power harnessed to democratic ideals, [has begun] a transformation of the Arab world from endless tyranny and intolerance to decent governance and democratization. Two years ago, shortly before the invasion of Iraq, I argued ... that forcefully deposing Saddam Hussein was, more than anything, about America "coming ashore" to effect a "pan-Arab reformation"—a dangerous, "risky and, yes, arrogant" but necessary attempt to change the very culture of the Middle East, to open its doors to democracy and modernity.[4]

As for the future of the Israeli–Palestinian conflict, Krauthammer expressed admiration for Prime Minister Ariel Sharon's decision to disengage from Gaza, asking rhetorically

> Why did Ariel Sharon do this? Did the father of the settlement movement go soft? Defeatist? No. The Israeli right has grown up and given up the false dream of Greater Israel, encompassing the Palestinian territories. And the Israeli left has grown up too, being mugged by the intifada into understanding that you do not

trust the lives of your children to the word of an enemy bent on your destruction ... Sharon is no dreamer like Yitzhak Rabin and Shimon Peres, who bargained away land for a piece of paper. Sharon, like any good general—and he was a great general—is giving up land for a stable defensive line.[5]

Notably, then, an overtly conservative commentator like Krauthammer also sought at the time to represent the crisis in terms which could be characterized as "balanced."

Yet Krauthammer also decisively insisted that there should be no further dismantling of settlements. In the wake of the Gaza disengagement, Krauthammer wrote:

The Gaza withdrawal is not the beginning but the end. Apart from perhaps some evacuations of outlying settlements on the West Bank, it is the end of the concession road for Israel. And it is the beginning of the new era of self-sufficiency and separation in which Israel ensures its security not by concessions but by fortification, barrier creation, realism and patient waiting.[6]

In the ideological center, the *New York Times'* Thomas L. Friedman recurrently concurred with quite a few of Krauthammer's conclusions. He too, for instance, was a consistent defender of the Iraq war (though a critic of how the Bush administration handled the aftermath), and also placed considerable emphasis on US prospects for democratizing the Middle East.[7] (In the run-up to war, Friedman made plain his position that even if the war against Iraq had nothing to do with weapons of mass destruction, had nothing to do with the war on terror, and was a war for oil—then it was still justified. And he still supported it.)[8] But in contrast to Krauthammer's views on Israel, Friedman explicitly identified the settler movement as an impediment to lasting peace in the Middle East, and did so in blunt terms. Already in late 2002, for instance, Friedman had written: "The settlement policy Israel has been pursuing is going to lead to the demise of the Jewish state. No, settlements are not the reason for the Israeli–Palestinian conflict, but to think they do not exacerbate it, and are not locking Israel into a permanent occupation, is also dishonest."[9] Subsequently, in 2004, Friedman wrote: "Israel must get out of the West Bank and Gaza Strip as soon as possible and evacuate most of the settlements."[10]

Moreover, Friedman pointedly diverged from those on the right on the issue of the separation wall, citing in particular his hostility toward the wall's path into Palestinian territory. As Friedman wrote: "If the wall heads way off the Green Line, deep into the West Bank, as Mr. Sharon hinted it might, we are headed for a disaster." And he has written as well: "Good fences make good neighbors, but only if your fence runs along a logical, fair, consensual boundary—not through the middle of your neighbor's backyard."[11] This remained a significant contrast to the more conservative position advanced, for instance, by James Tisch, chairman of the Conference of Presidents of Major American Jewish Organizations. Tisch held that Israel's defiance of the International Court of Justice (ICJ) by building the wall through Palestinian territory was fully acceptable—arguing in addition that Israel should not be held to a higher standard than countries like France or the United States, for instance, both of whom, Tisch noted, "have defied the ICJ on grounds of national security and sovereignty without any threat of sanctions."[12]

Yet Friedman—in his ongoing defense of US intervention in Iraq—also argued that the eventual outcome of the Iraq war was intimately linked to the Israeli–Palestinian crisis, and he emphasized the parallelisms in the two locales. In a column published in spring of 2005 (aptly titled "Rooting for the Good Guys"), Friedman made pretty much this precise point:

> Politics in places like Iraq and Palestine have been based for decades on "Oriental despotism"—top-down monologues by dictators buttressed by a politics of fear. What Iraqis and Palestinians are trying to do is make a transition from one system to the other. But the fundamentalists and Nasserites within their societies—who for years have been nourished by their Oriental despots as a way of keeping the people backward, divided and focused on the wrong things—are still powerful and virulent. They, too, will not go quietly. The more they are seen to be losing, the crazier they will get.

"The birth of democracy in the Arab world and the sustaining of democracy in Israel are now on the table," Friedman wrote, adding: "I am an optimist about both in the long run—but brace yourself for the short run."[13] Again in December 2005, and despite the evident problems in the Iraqi elections he also enumerated, Friedman reiterated that he remained "guardedly hopeful."[14] And here too he positioned himself as even-handed in his critiques of both left and right, stressing that leftists were too pessimistic about prospects for peace and democracy in Iraq while conservatives were too oblivious to the hard work that building democracy would inevitably take.

Harvard law professor Alan Dershowitz, in defending his book, *The Case for Peace* (2005), made very similar strategic moves.[15] He too aimed for the impression of balance in the sense that he argued that "both sides"—Israelis and Palestinians—had to give up some rights in order to establish a permanent resolution to the conflict. Strikingly, he averred that Israel should get a "C+ or B-" for its record in honoring human rights while combating terrorism, as he also contended that this was a better record than that of any other country, including the USA. At the same time, he emphasized repeatedly that a main problem with left and liberal critics of the Israeli government was their relentless negativity. In Dershowitz's view, left and liberal commentators were too Shakespearean in their desire for perfect symmetry and justice (as Dershowitz pointed out, at the end of a Shakespeare play almost all the characters are dead). Dershowitz instead called for a Chekhovian ending: everyone is cynical, embittered, disillusioned, heartbroken—but alive. Dershowitz called on left commentators "who have supported the Palestinian cause to stop demonizing Israel, to stop de-legitimating Israel, to stop defaming Israel, to stop applying a double standard to Israel, to stop divestiture and boycotts of Israel, and most importantly, to stop being more Palestinian than the Palestinians themselves." In their skepticism about the possibilities for peace, Dershowitz argued, leftists were impeding the prospects for peace. By contrast, Dershowitz declared, "*I* believe peace is possible."[16]

Leftists and liberals were unlikely to recognize themselves in Dershowitz's summaries. On the left and liberal end of the spectrum, there are of course a range of perspectives, but shared tendencies certainly exist. For instance, while conservatives and centrists tended to emphasize the defensive qualities of Israel's militarism, leftists and left-liberals repeatedly pointed to both structural inequities and personalized violence that was not just defensive. Critics of the Israeli government routinely referred to what they saw as the occupation's cruelties, and they stressed the desolation and prison-like conditions in the occupied territories.[17] They called attention to the bulldozing and bombing of Palestinian homes. They noted that the Palestinian death toll at the hands of the Israeli Defense Forces was considerably higher than the death toll for Israelis due to suicide bombers and other Palestinian violence. Left-leaning critics also stressed Israel's bid to control water rights for the region. In 2005, left and liberal commentators underscored how Prime Minister Sharon's withdrawal of all Jewish settlers from Gaza actually coincided with a dramatic expansion of West Bank settlements and actually was a critical piece of a larger plan by the Israeli government to ensure that any future Palestinian state be non-contiguous, bereft of natural resources, and economically unviable.

Throughout this period, a prominent voice on the American Jewish left has been Henry Siegman, a senior fellow of the Council on Foreign Relations. Siegman, an Orthodox rabbi, who has been active in Jewish communal affairs for many decades and is a former head of the American Jewish Congress as well as the Synagogue Council of America, consistently attempted to expose what he saw as Ariel Sharon's lack of credibility and even duplicity. For instance, Siegman wrote in late 2004:

> It is one of the ironies of history that Jews—whether in the US, Europe, or Israel—who were disproportionately involved in struggles for universal human rights and civil liberties should now be supporting policies of a right-wing Israeli government that is threatening to turn Israel into a racist state. For if Sharon leverages his promised withdrawal from Gaza into an Israeli presence in the West Bank that is impossible to dislodge—a point that some observers insist has already been reached—a racist regime is surely what his policies will produce.[18]

And of the separation barrier, Siegman wrote: "The argument that the fence's intrusions into Palestinian territory are necessary to protect the settlements establishes a new standard for chutzpah. In effect, Palestinians are being told that Israel must steal more Palestinian land to protect Israelis living on previously stolen Palestinian land."[19] Also in the wake of Israeli disengagement from Gaza as well as Ariel Sharon's subsequent decision to leave Likud for a new centrist party, Siegman continued to contend that further land concessions by Israel remained a prerequisite for a lasting peace.[20]

In short, the Jewish left in the USA has tended to place special emphasis on how the occupation has undermined the democratic cast of Israeli society as well as brought tremendous suffering to the Palestinians. As *Tikkun* editor Michael Lerner has written:

The Israeli land grab in the West Bank continues under cover of peace moves. The Wall continues to be built. Palestinian homes continue to be bulldozed by machines constructed for that purpose by the Caterpillar corporation in the United States. A recent Knesset decision allows Israel to seize hundreds of properties in East Jerusalem owned by Palestinians.[21]

Lerner routinely combined this sort of basic marshaling of empirical evidence with an insistence on emphasizing how both Palestinians and Israeli Jews have damaged themselves spiritually through their ongoing spiral of violence. In general, Lerner and *Tikkun* consistently criticized *both* Palestinian and Israeli violence—not least as a way to ward off potential accusations that left-leaning critics of Israel were insensitive to Jews' sense of vulnerability and very real suffering and loss.

Yet other progressive commentators, like Judith Butler, emphasized their anguish that points like those of Siegman and Lerner can hardly be made without being immediately attacked. Gentiles who make them are quickly accused of anti-Semitism and liberal-left Jews are accused of self-hatred. One of the most noticeable phenomena, in reaction to this epistemological impasse, was that liberal-left Jews—and this was particularly evident, for instance, in the work of Tony Kushner, Alisa Solomon, Eric Alterman, and Butler herself—was how strenuously they foregrounded their own passionately Jewish identities and emphasized that they were motivated by specifically Jewish ethics.[22]

Meanwhile, in contrast to the self-described "liberal hawks" (such as Paul Berman, Michael Walzer, and Leon Wieseltier), all of whom also happen to be Jewish, the left-liberal critics of Israeli policies were opposed to the Iraq war from the very beginning.[23] They opposed as well the continued occupation of Iraq. In so doing, they not only emphasized the irresponsible adventurism that spawned the war, but also stressed the severe problems for American security that the war has caused. As *New York Times* columnist Paul Krugman wrote in mid-2005:

The people who sold us this war continue to insist that success is just around the corner, and that things would be fine if the media would just stop reporting bad news. But the administration has declared victory in Iraq at least four times. January's election, it seems, was yet another turning point that wasn't.

And Krugman added: "The American military isn't just bogged down in Iraq; it's deteriorating under the strain . . . And every year that the war goes on, our military gets weaker."[24] (Strikingly similar arguments were also made on the left about Israeli policy toward Palestinians, as critics of Israeli policy repeatedly contended that the ongoing occupation made Israel less rather than more secure.)

3

What, then, of the American Jewish public in the first decade of the twenty-first century? Where did those who do not publish books or have a regular op-ed column in a major American newspaper stand in terms of these debates concerning the Middle East conflicts? The results were mixed, although they appeared generally to reflect a far greater liberality among the rank-and-file than among the most influential of the media pundits.

For instance, and according to the American Jewish Committee's 2005 Annual Survey of American Jewish Opinion, opposition to the war in Iraq among Jews in the USA increased sharply after the war began in 2003. Whereas only 54 percent opposed the war in 2003, by late 2005 opposition to the war climbed to 70 percent. The AJC survey also found that 67 percent supported Israel's disengagement from Gaza, while only 26 percent were opposed. Additionally, more than 60 percent of American Jews believed Israel ought to be willing to abandon all or some of the settlements on the West Bank in the context of a peace agreement. And the 2005 AJC poll found that 56 percent of American Jews supported the creation of a Palestinian state. At the same time, however, American Jews showed strong support for the separation wall. More than 70 percent declared themselves in favor, while only 24 percent were opposed.[25]

There was as well among the rank-and-file of the American Jewish community a strong perception of anti-Israel bias in the US media. As Mitchell Baird, author of *Myths and Facts: A Guide to the Arab-Israeli Conflict* put the matter in 2005: "We all know the cliché that for every two Jews there are three opinions. Well, American Jews are unanimous about at least one thing: the conviction that the [US] media is irrevocably biased against Israel."[26] National Public Radio (NPR) was referred to as "National Palestine Radio," due to its perceived anti-Israel bias, and the editorial views of the *New York Times*, the *Washington Post*, and the major television network evening news programs (especially ABC) were also labeled too pro-Palestinian.[27]

Strikingly, however, American Jews were increasingly hesitant to defend Israel in too public a fashion. According to a poll commissioned by The Israel Project, a pro-Israel advocacy group, and conducted by pollster Frank Luntz, there were "disturbing signs that support could shift in the wrong direction." Although American Jews overwhelmingly supported Israel in private, the poll found

> a problem in translating this support to an active pro-Israeli discourse in the American society. When asked if they engage in conversation about Israel or defend Israel while talking to non-Jews, most of the participants replied negatively. Only 29% talk about Israel frequently, while 61% almost never do so.[28]

Confirmation of—and tentative explanation for—this tendency among American Jews not to speak out publicly in support of Israel were found in a 2005 survey conducted by sociologist Steven M. Cohen of the Hebrew University in Jerusalem. Cohen concluded: "The attachment of American Jews to Israel has weakened measurably in the last two years ... Respondents were less likely than in comparable earlier surveys to say they care about Israel, talk about Israel with others or engage in a range of pro-Israel activities." Cohen also found that a sizable proportion expressed at least some negative feelings toward Israel. More than two-thirds said they are at least sometimes "disturbed" by Israel's policies or actions, and nearly as many said they are "confused." Almost half said they were at least sometimes "ashamed," and fully 39% said they were at least sometimes "alienated" by Israel.[29]

4

How did pro-Israel activists and the leaders of major American Jewish organizations respond to this state of affairs? One move was to invite successful advertising executives to help develop Israel as a "brand" that evoked more attractive, warmer, and more positive associations for gentile and Jewish Americans alike.[30] This also meant specifically offering pro-Israeli advocacy groups the advice that if they were to reach disaffected young American Jews, they should—as for instance the online resource booklet *Israel in the Age of Eminem* put it—present pro-Israel messages as above all also being pro-peace, and should at all costs avoid the appearance of overt racism against Arabs.[31]

But although this was only infrequently discussed in op-ed columns or framed as questions asked by pollsters, another major move among mainstream Jewish organizations was to turn to evangelical Christians for support. The influence of Christian evangelicals on US policy toward the Middle East as well as the impact Christian Zionism exerted on professional American Jewish organizations grew steadily in the first years of the twenty-first century. No doubt this was due in no small part to the fact that Christian Zionists in turn took center stage in those years—with an evangelical Christian in the White House—as champions of Israeli policies.

This was a significant new turn of events, not least because the tenets of Christian Zionism were highly problematic when it came to Jews. Christian Zionists were zealous supporters of Israel because they believed that unless Jews lived in the Holy Land and fulfilled the ancient prophecies, the second coming of Christ would be delayed. These views reached wide audiences not least through the wildly successful *Left Behind* apocalyptic novel series by Tim LaHaye and Jerry Jenkins, in which Israel played a central role.[32] But—as religious studies scholar Karen Armstrong succinctly pointed out—the Israeli Jews in the Holy Land were "simply in a 'holding' capacity, because [unless they convert to Christianity] once the last days have begun, the Antichrist will massacre them all."[33]

In other words, Jewish Zionists and Christian Zionists became the oddest of bedfellows—even as most Jewish Zionists hardly respected or especially liked their new-found Christian allies. To the contrary, and as Leon Wieseltier astutely suggested, the alliance between Jewish and Christian Zionists was really "a grim comedy of mutual condescension."[34] Or, as Orthodox Jew and former Bush speechwriter David Frum, for instance, wrote, his "attendance at Bible study [at the Bush White House] was, if not compulsory, not quite uncompulsory, either, [and] was disconcerting to a non-Christian like me."[35]

Nonetheless, and although it remained relatively unpublicized, it was certainly remarkable how intertwined some American Jewish organizations and the evangelical movement had become. Noteworthy was not only the support given to Israel by the Christians' Israel Public Action Campaign (or CIPAC) and the Christian Coalition, and from evangelical leaders like Pat Robertson, Gary Bauer, Jerry Falwell, Ralph Reed, and Tom DeLay—all of whom were hardliners in their support for Israel—as well as the seven million evangelicals at 25,000 churches worldwide who observed (on October 17, 2004) an Annual Day of Prayer and Solidarity with Israel.[36] Perhaps even more important, although it was also not widely discussed, some Bush White House Middle East policy decisions needed to receive clearance from powerful evangelical groups before they were being finalized. In March 2004, for instance, the National Security Council's Near East and North African affairs director Elliott Abrams met with several dozen evangelical ministers to inform them about Bush's plan to back Sharon's disengagement from Gaza. According to a memo of the meeting, Abrams reassured the ministers that "the Gaza Strip had no significant Biblical influence such as Joseph's tomb or Rachel's tomb and therefore is a piece of land that can be sacrificed for the cause of peace."[37]

Additionally, as journalist Esther Kaplan wrote, Christian Zionists "donate millions of dollars to projects in Jewish settlements." Evangelical leaders have called for "a united Jerusalem" at least since 1997, and have also been conducting major fund-raising campaigns for Israel since that time.[38] The American Israel Public Affairs Committee (AIPAC) was also building close relations with the evangelical movement, for instance inviting right-wing evangelical politician Gary Bauer to give the keynote address at its annual convention in March 2003. (In defense of the settler movement, Bauer said: "I oppose ethnic cleansing, and the idea that the West Bank or Gaza should be a Jew-free zone is deeply offensive.")[39] And as the *Christian Century* reported, the Likud Party also actively fostered a financial relationship with American Christian Zionists:

> In the late 1990s donations to Israel and to the Jewish National Fund declined because of the tensions between Orthodox Jews in Israel and Reform and Conservative Jews in the U.S. The loss of funding caused the Likud to turn to Christian Zionists for assistance, an appeal that met with a quick response. Additional support came through a campaign led by the International Fellowship of Christians and Jews, headed by a former Anti-Defamation League employee, the Orthodox rabbi Yechiel Eckstein.[40]

Indeed, the ADL was at the forefront of forging alliances with the Christian right, printing an ad signed by former Christian coalition executive director Ralph Reed, headlined "We People of Faith Stand Firmly with Israel."[41] Abraham Foxman, the ADL's national director, stated directly that "American Jews should not be apologetic or defensive about cultivating Evangelical support for Israel."[42] (Only later would Foxman change course a bit, arguing that "the key domestic challenge" facing Jews was the campaign by the leadership of the Christian right to "Christianize all aspects of American life.")[43]

Where these developments might lead in view of an ever-greater blurring between religion and politics in American culture remained unclear. What did appear clear was that the relationships between ethnic/religious identity and ideology were now completely scrambled. "Identity politics" no longer operated in any kind of predictable way. By 2005, American Jews were sharply at odds with one another over the Israeli government's policies toward the Palestinians, and the majority were at best uncomfortable if not outright appalled that conservative Christians were now directing how the USA responded to the twists and turns in the "roadmap for peace."

5

If 2005 represented a moment of relative optimism (and general liberality) among American Jews with respect to the future of Israel and the crisis in the Middle East, it was not to last. Events in the remainder of this first decade of the twenty-first century resulted principally in heightened feelings among many American Jews of anxiety and frustration when it came to the topic of Israeli policies toward the Palestinians and the Arab world.

Several developments deserve special mention. Early in 2006, and soon after Israeli Prime Minister Ariel Sharon suffered an incapacitating stroke and was replaced by Deputy Prime Minister Ehud Omert, the radical Islamic party Hamas unexpectedly won a majority in the Palestinian parliament. In the summer of that same year, Israel went to war in Lebanon against Hezbollah, while at the same time Hamas gained political control of Gaza. In 2009, right-wing Likud leader Benjamin Netanyahu became prime minister of Israel, and the following year Israeli commandos prevented a flotilla of ships carrying humanitarian aid for Gaza to reach their destination. And early in 2011, Al Jazeera television reported that secret documents showed that Palestinian negotiators had long been far *more* willing to make concessions to and compromises with Israel than had been previously revealed.

Yet there can be little question, however, that it was the year 2011 that marked a major turning point in the history of the Middle East due to the cataclysmic upheavals in a series of nations across the Arab world. Revolutions that began in Tunisia already in December of 2010 quickly spread in the spring of 2011 to Egypt, Libya, Yemen, Syria, Bahrain, as well as elsewhere in the region. By the year's end, pro-democracy uprisings had toppled tyrannical governments in Tunisia, Egypt, and Libya in a movement that had come collectively to be known as the "Arab Spring."

As for the consequences of these revolutionary events on the state of Israel—both at home and abroad—they were nothing if not ambiguous all over again. In April 2011, the *New York Times* ran a lead editorial entitled "President Obama and the Peace Process," addressing the need for the USA to take a more active role in the negotiations toward a Israeli–Palestinian peace settlement. Citing the monumental and historic upheavals across the Arab world in 2011 as additional evidence for why it was critical for a peace deal to be struck as soon as possible, and why the United States needed to make its commitment to such negotiations of preeminent importance, the *New York*

Times favorably cited Defense Secretary Robert Gates who had opined that "there is a need and an opportunity for bold action to move toward a two-state solution." Furthermore, concerning the continued and ongoing settlement construction in the West Bank and East Jerusalem, the *New York Times* observed—in what might only be construed as stating the obvious—that "the more settlers [Israeli government officials] let in, the harder it will be politically for any Israeli leader to cut a deal."

Certainly American Jewish pundits in the ideological center tended in the course of 2011 to echo such sentiments—and with an increasing sense of urgency. There was for some leading American Jews by the fall of 2011 a growing sense of anxiety and anguish that Israel was becoming dangerously isolated in the court of world opinion. *New York Times* columnist (and long-time Israel observer) Thomas L. Friedman wrote in September 2011, for instance, that he had "never been more worried about Israel's future" as he went on to vent frustrations at Prime Minister Benjamin Netanyahu's ruling coalition, characterizing it as "the most diplomatically inept and strategically incompetent in Israel's history."[44] By the year's end, too, and despite the mood among many Jews in the United States that Israel needed to make progress with the Palestinians toward peace, there appeared to be no hope for negotiations in the foreseeable future. As Aaron David Miller, public policy scholar at the Woodrow Wilson International Center for Scholars, tersely summarized the situation at the year's end: "The pursuit of Arab-Israel peace is closed for the season."[45]

Yet at the same moment, public opinion polls revealed that the attitudes of American Jews toward the Middle East crisis had undergone their own new seismic shifts. No longer was a Palestinian state—considered a reasonable position by many across the ideological spectrum only half a dozen years earlier—still acceptable to the majority of American Jews. Most notably, the annual survey of American Jewish opinion conducted by the American Jewish Committee asked respondents: "In the current situation, do you favor or oppose the establishment of a Palestinian state?" In 2010, those who favored Palestinian statehood (48 percent) slightly outnumbered those who opposed it (45 percent). Yet a strange thing happened on the way to Jewish opinion by the middle of the following year; in 2011 those American Jews who favored Palestinian statehood had dropped considerably (to 38 percent), while those who opposed it had risen by an equal percentage (to 55 percent). The tide of public opinion was definitely perceived to be moving in a more conservative direction.

Likewise, the AJC survey reflected American Jewish disenchantment with the Obama administration, with a mere 45 percent approval rating of the president in 2011—quite a drop given that an estimated 78 percent of American Jews had voted for Obama in 2008 (and 57 percent still reported approval of him in 2010). And by contrast, and Thomas Friedman's undisguised frustration notwithstanding, the 2011 AJC poll of American Jewish political attitudes found that 54 percent of American Jews actually approved of Netanyahu's government. In this respect at least, it would appear that American Jewish attitudes had slipped to the right of where Friedman, long considered a classic centrist, now stood.

In the same period of time, and as the Arab world witnessed historic change—although the direction of that change remained highly uncertain—many in Israel expressed their own grim forebodings about the present and possible future of their nation. These events did not always receive widespread coverage in the US press—including the American Jewish press. This sense of foreboding had partly to do with the country's economic problems, a fact dramatically crystallized by the hundreds of thousands of Israelis who demonstrated in 2011 to protest the country's harsh socioeconomic inequalities. Beginning that summer, demands for affordable housing swept through Israel; in August a major demonstration in Tel Aviv held aloft a banner that read: "Egypt is here!"[46] Encampments in Israel to protest high housing costs served as a striking precursor to the global Occupy Wall Street movement that would commence in early fall.

Far more publicity was accrued in 2011 to leaked reports that Netanyahu with the backing of Defense Secretary Ehud Barak as well as members of the security cabinet were deep in the planning stage of a preemptive military strike against Iranian nuclear facilities. Concurrent with these reports were statements that Iran had made considerable progress toward the building of a nuclear bomb in recent years—if not months. A report from the International Atomic Energy Agency (IAEA) released in November 2011 was widely said to support this claim.[47] (Though the New York Times would also conclude that "it is true that the basic allegations in the report are not substantially new, and have been discussed by experts for years," and it was an open question whether in fact Iran had made said progress.)[48] Regardless of the significance of the new IAEA report, however, the perceived threat posed by Iran to Israel soon became a prominent talking point in American—and American Jewish—political life. Notably, for instance, the same AJC 2011 public opinion poll found 68 percent of American Jews showing support for Israel "taking military action against Iran to prevent it from developing nuclear weapons" if "diplomacy and sanctions fail." It would be most indicative, perhaps, that one of the first comments in the new year of 2012 from the Israel Project announced that "Iran threatens to attack U.S. bases in the region," and that Iran "rejected demands they halt their nuclear development program."[49]

Drowned out amidst demands that Israel—or the United States—"bomb Iran" was the moderate stance of American Jews who challenged such calls. Longtime activist M. J. Rosenberg, for instance, acknowledged in the fall of 2011 that Israel had "every right to be concerned about a nuclear-armed Iran," but added that Israel "does not have the right to steamroll Americans into supporting (or waging) a war that would jeopardize all our vital interests in the Middle East."[50]

Finally, and far from incidentally, there was much discussion among Americans—both Jewish and gentile—of the place of women and girls in Israel, as the ultra-Orthodox there were exerting an ever-expanded role in public life. At particular stake were controversies over whether women should sit at the rear of public buses—separated from men—as well as whether they should be expected to cover their legs and arms. The Israeli transportation minister concluded in 2010 that such sex segregation on public buses was perfectly legal, a point that led some American Jewish commentators to draw comparisons between ultra-Orthodox Judaism and Islamic fundamentalism. In late 2011, Ruth Marcus wrote for the *Washington Post*:

> Women are forced to board public buses from the back and stay there. Billboards with images of women are defaced. Public streets are cordoned off during religious holidays so that women cannot enter. Saudi Arabia in the misogynistic grip of sharia law? Sadly, astonishingly, infuriatingly, it is Israel under the growing influence and increasingly assertive demands of the ultra-Orthodox.[51]

Secretary of State Hillary Clinton too, while certainly a staunch supporter of Israel in military matters, nonetheless drew comparisons between the struggle for African American civil rights in the United States and the deteriorating status of women in Israel. As summarized in *Haaretz*, Clinton said that as she read reports of the discrimination faced by Israeli women on public transportation, "she was reminded of Rosa Parks, the African American activist who in 1955 refused to yield her seat on a bus to a white man."[52] By the year's end, tensions between the secular and ultra-Orthodox in Israel would spill into the mainstream when it was reported on Israeli television (and subsequently to the world) that an eight-year-old girl "had become terrified of walking to her elementary school" after ultra-Orthodox men "spit on her, insulted her and called her a prostitute because her modest dress did not adhere exactly to their more rigorous dress code." The *New York Times* reported that the ultra-Orthodox "blamed the news media" for the ensuing uproar because the news media "had come into the ultra-Orthodox neighborhoods to sow hatred and to persecute the residents for their religious beliefs."[53]

Small wonder, then, that the conclusion of 2011 also witnessed the deepening of a mood of despair among more secular Jews both in Israel and in the United States. As *Haaretz* commentator Gideon Levy wrote in a column that was widely circulated and discussed also in the USA, what he felt at year's end was the sobering fact that Israel was sliding precipitously into an existential crisis of its own design. Levy bluntly commented of his own nation: "The pretension of being an enlightened Western democracy is giving way, with terrifying speed, to a different reality—that of a benighted, racist, religious, ultranationalist, fundamentalist Middle Eastern country." And as Levy caustically lamented: "This is not the kind of integration into the region we had hoped for."[54]

Notes

1. James Bennet, "The Interregnum," *New York Times Magazine* (March 13, 2005): 41–2.
2. Ofer Shelah, "Israeli Public is Upbeat, But Leaders Fear the Worst," *The Forward*, May 6, 2005. As the article's title suggests, however, all was not copacetic: "The traditional preholiday interviews with military leaders . . . were filled with foreboding."
3. Charles Krauthammer, "What's Left? Shame," *Washington Post*, March 18, 2005, A23. Krauthammer elaborated: "The democracy project is, of course, just beginning. We do not yet know whether the Middle East today is Europe 1989 or Europe 1848. In 1989 we saw the swift collapse of the Soviet empire; in 1848 there was a flowering of liberal revolutions throughout

Europe that, within a short time, were all suppressed. Nonetheless, 1848 did presage the coming of the liberal idea throughout Europe. (By 1871, it had been restored to France, for example.) It marked a turning point from which there was no going back. The Arab Spring of 2005 will be noted by history as a similar turning point for the Arab world."

4. Charles Krauthammer, "Three Cheers for the Bush Doctrine," *Time*, March 7, 2005.

5. Charles Krauthammer, "Israel Draws the Line," *Washington Post*, February 25, 2005, A21.

6. Charles Krauthammer, "Settling In for a Long Wait," *Washington Post*, August 19, 2005, A21. Also see his "The Stakes After Gaza," *Washington Post*, August 26, 2005, A21.

7. For example, see Thomas L. Friedman, "What Were They Thinking?," *New York Times*, October 7, 2005, A29.

8. See Thomas L. Friedman, "A War for Oil?," *New York Times*, January 5, 2003, section 4, 11.

9. Thomas L. Friedman, "Campus Hypocrisy," *New York Times*, October 16, 2002, A23.

10. See Thomas L. Friedman, "War of Ideas, Part 4," *New York Times*, January 18, 2004, section 4, 11.

11. Thomas L. Friedman, "The Wailing Wall?," *New York Times*, September 7, 2003, section 4, 13.

12. James S. Tisch, "Who's Defying the World Court?," *The Jewish Week*, July 23, 2004.

13. Thomas L. Friedman, "Rooting for the Good Guys," *New York Times*, April 20, 2005, A25. Note as well Friedman's parallelism between Iraqis and Palestinians in a column two weeks earlier: "Until the recent elections in Iraq and among the Palestinians, the modern Arab world was largely immune to the winds of democracy that have blown everywhere else in the world." Thomas L. Friedman, "Arabs Lift Their Voices," *New York Times*, April 7, 2005, A23. Also see historian Juan Cole's rebuttal of Friedman's analysis on his weblog for April 10, 2005 at www.juancole.com.

14. Thomas L. Friedman, "The Measure of Success," *New York Times*, December 21, 2005, A39.

15. Note also that Dershowitz is well known to rationalize the US's right to use torture in a "ticking bomb" scenario. See his contribution to Sanford Levinson, ed., *Torture: A Collection* (New York and Oxford: Oxford University Press, 2004); and *The Nation* special issue (December 26, 2005) on torture.

16. Alan Dershowitz, "Israel and Palestine After Disengagement" (debating Noam Chomsky), Harvard University, Institute of Politics, November 29, 2005.

17. For example, see Sara Roy, *The Gaza Strip: The Political Economy of De-development* (Washington, DC: Institute for Palestine Studies, 2001) and *The Economics of Middle East Peace: A Reassessment* (Stamford, CT: JAI Press, 1999).

18. Henry Siegman, "Sharon and the Future of Palestine," *New York Review of Books*, December 2, 2004. See also the interview with Dov Weissglas, a close friend and colleague of Sharon's, that appeared in *Haaretz*, October 8, 2004.

19. Henry Siegman, "Israel: The Threat from Within," *New York Review of Books* (February 26, 2004): 15.

20. Henry Siegman cited in Karby Leggett, "Latest Answer To Mideast Crisis: Fix the Economy," *Wall Street Journal*, December 28, 2005, A12.

21. Michael Lerner, "Divestment and More: A Strategy Exploration," *Tikkun* (March/April 2005): 33.

22. See especially Tony Kushner and Alisa Solomon, eds., *Wrestling with Zion: Progressive Jewish-American Responses to the Israeli-Palestinian Conflict* (New York: Grove, 2003); Judith Butler, *Precarious Live: The Powers of Mourning and Violence* (New York: Verso, 2004); and "The Liberal Media" columns by Eric Alterman for *The Nation*.

23. See George Packer, "The Liberal Quandary Over Iraq," *New York Times Magazine*, December 8, 2002. Also see Edward Rothstein, "Left Has Hard Time in Era of Terrorism," *New York Times*, December 21, 2002; and Kate Zernike, "Liberals for War: Some of Intellectual Left's Longtime Doves Taking on Role of Hawks," *New York Times*, March 14, 2003. Michael Walzer's is a curious but significant case. Walzer, an expert on "just war" doctrine, is cited in an essay by Garry Wills in *The New York Review of Books* (November 18, 2004) as a thoughtful opponent of the invasion of Iraq. And yet Walzer's position in late 2002 and early 2003 was more complicated and ambivalent. Even right up to the moment of invasion, Walzer urged that a "limited war" be waged against Iraq. He further insisted that the international anti-war movement only served to strengthen and embolden Saddam Hussein. Additionally, already in 2002, Walzer had chided the left as largely knee-jerk anti-American Americans with little perspective on the consequences of their actions. See his "Can There Be a Decent Left?," *Dissent* 49 / 2 (Spring 2002): 19–20, 35–6.

24. Paul Krugman, "Staying What Course?," *New York Times*, May 16, 2005, 25.

25. See the 2005 Annual Survey of American Jewish Opinion, sponsored by the American Jewish Committee. The survey can be found on the AJC website at www.ajc.org.

26. Mitchell G. Baird, "Does the Media's Anti-Israel Bias Matter?," *Jewsweek*, April 22, 2005.

27. For the view that, *The New York Times* gets attacked for its coverage of the Israel-Palestine conflict no matter what it prints, see Daniel Okrent, "The Hottest Button: How the Times Covers Israel and Palestine," *New York Times*, April 24, 2005. For the centrality of the Middle East conflict in the dispute over the future of NPR, also see Stephen Labaton, "NPR Conflict with Overseer is Growing," *New York Times*, May 16, 2005, C1.

28. Nathan Guttman, "U.S. Jews Support Israel, Don't Speak Up," *Jerusalem Post*, December 1, 2005.

29. Steven M. Cohen, "Poll: Attachment of U.S. Jews To Israel Falls in Past 2 Years," *The Forward*, March 4, 2005.

30. For example, see Haim Handwerker, "It isn't enough to defend your position in the U.S., say the marketeers," *Haaretz*, December 22, 2005. One of the advertising specialists consulted found that the average American tends to think of Israel "as a militaristic place and as a very religious, male-controlled society . . . 'There is no "fun" there.'" It was also found that Americans thought of Israel as something that got the U.S. "embroiled in troubles." The goal of a "rebranding" campaign would be to represent more of the "human face" of Israel.

31. Frank Luntz, *Israel in the Age of Eminem: A Creative Brief for Israel Messaging* (Clear Agenda, March 2003), available at www.myisraelsource.com.

32. For two excellent analyses of the *Left Behind* series, see Melani McAllister, "An Empire of Their Own," *The Nation*, September 22, 2003; and Joan Didion, "Mr. Bush and the Divine," *New York Review of Books*, November 6, 2003.

33. Karen Armstrong, "Root out this sinister cultural flaw," *Guardian* (UK), April 6, 2005.

34. Quoted in Maureen Dowd, "Rapture and Power," *New York Times*, October 6, 2002. Wieseltier continued: "The evangelical Christians condescend to the Jews by offering their support before they convert or kill them. And the conservative Jews condescend to Christians by accepting their support while believing that their eschatology is nonsense. This is a fine example of the political exploitation of religion."

35. Quoted in Esther Kaplan, *With God on their Side: How Christian Fundamentalists Trampled Science, Policy, and Democracy in George W. Bush's White House* (New York: New Press, 2004), 5.

36. See Max Blumenthal, "Born-agains for Sharon," *Salon.com*, October 30, 2004. The complete text is available at: www.academicsforjustice.org/pMachine/more.php?id=1718_0_1_0_M3.

Note also that Tom DeLay, "an Evangelical Christian who recently blocked Bush administration plans to provide direct aid to the Palestinian Authority," found strong support from several right-wing Jewish organizations as he faced charges that he violated the House ethics rules. See E. J. Kessler, "Right-wing Jews Rally to Defense of Embattled DeLay," *The Forward*, April 15, 2005.

37. See Rick Perlstein, "The Jesus Landing Pad," *Village Voice*, May 18, 2004. Also see Esther Kaplan's cogent discussion of Christian Zionists' impact on US Middle East policy in her *With God on Their Side*, 23–9.

38. The full-page ad for "Christians Call for a United Jerusalem" appeared in the *New York Times* on April 18, 1997. Included in the ad is the following: "We support Israel's efforts to reach reconciliation with its Arab neighbors, but we believe that Jerusalem or any portion of it shall not be negotiable in the peace process. Jerusalem must remain undivided as the eternal capital of the Jewish people."

39. See Blumenthal, "Born-agains for Sharon."

40. Donald Wagner, "The Evangelical-Jewish Alliance," *The Christian Century*, June 28, 2003.

41. This ADL ad with text by Ralph Reed appeared in the *New York Times*, May 2, 2002, A22. Also see "The Rebirth of Ralph Reed," *Atlanta Jewish Times*, July 23, 1999.

42. Abraham Foxman, "Why Evangelical Support for Israel is a Good Thing," available at http://www.adl.org/Israel/evangelical.asp and dated July 16, 2002.

43. Richard N. Ostling, "Conservative Jews, Evangelical Protestants talk," *Washington Times*, December 10, 2005.

44. Thomas L. Friedman, "Israel: Adrift at Sea Alone," *New York Times*, September 17, 2011.

45. Aaron David Miller quoted in Nathan Guttman, "Officials Speak Sharply but Few See Intentional Snub," *Forward*, December 16, 2011.

46. See Eyal Press, "Rising Up in Israel," *New York Review of Books*, November 24, 2011.

47. David Sanger and William J. Broad, "U.N. Agency Says Iran Data Points to A-Bomb Work," *New York Times*, November 8, 2011.

48. Robert F. Worth, "Report Undercuts Iran's Defense on Nuclear Effort," *New York Times*, November 8, 2011. Also see Seymour Hersh, "Iran and the I.A.E.A.," *New Yorker*, November 18, 2011: http://www.newyorker.com/online/blogs/comment/2011/11/iran-and-the-iaea.html.

49. The Israel Project, "Iran Tests Missiles; Threatens Attacks on Region," January 2, 2012: http://www.theisraelproject.org/site/apps/nlnet/content3.aspx?c=ewJXKcOUJ llaG&b=7712197&ct=11571037&notoc=1#.TwNi1fmnJ8E.

50. M. J. Rosenberg, "Israel's Possible Strike at Iran," *Tikkun*, November 18, 2011.

51. Ruth Marcus, "In Israel, women's rights come under siege," *Washington Post*, December 1, 2011. See also Peter Beinart, "Ultra-Orthodox Attacks on Israel's Women Linked to Arab Inequality, *Daily Beast*, December 29, 2011.

52. Barak Ravid, "Clinton warns of Israel's eroding democratic values," *Haaretz*, December 5, 2011.

53. Isabel Kershner, "Israeli Girl, 8, at Center of Tension Over Religious Extremism," *New York Times*, December 27, 2011. Note as well the saga of Tanya Rosenblit, who refused to give up her seat on a bus in Jerusalem and was immediately dubbed an "Israeli Rosa Parks." See Ophir Bar-Zohar, "'Israeli Rosa Parks' receives death threats after refusing to move to back of ultra-Orthodox bus," *Haaretz*, January 4, 2012.

54. Gideon Levy, "Israel is in the midst of a culture war," *Haaretz*, December 11, 2011.

CHAPTER 20
THE MEANING OF THE JEWISH EXPERIENCE FOR AMERICAN CULTURE
Stephen J. Whitfield

About seven decades ago, the head of production at Metro-Goldwyn-Mayer (MGM), Irving Thalberg, was watching an unreleased film when something he heard on the sound track bothered him. "What is that?" he demanded to know. "What is that in the music? It's awful, I hate it!" An assistant explained: "That's a minor chord, Mr. Thalberg." The following day, the producer sent an inter-office memo to the music department and insisted that the memo be conspicuously posted. It read as follows: "From the above date onward, no music in an MGM film is to contain a 'minor chord.'"[1] Those instructions reflect a sensibility that suggests what may be distinctive about the national culture within which Jewish immigrants and their descendants have operated. Just as American movies were famous for promoting affirmative endings, no matter how implausibly they wrapped their stories up, American culture has defined happiness as the proper end of life itself; and the authority of this jolly imperative represents the greatest challenge to the viability of Judaism itself.

The Declaration of Independence made the pursuit of happiness into an imprescriptible right; and even though Jefferson meant something more political than merely personal, even though he wanted to encourage the public dimension and not only private enjoyment, he did consider happiness to be the measure of civilization. What is remarkable is how easily the *pursuit* of happiness could shade into the right to *attain* it. Another of the Framers, George Mason, inserted that new entitlement into the Virginia bill of rights; and not to be outdone, even the crusty John Adams included it in the Massachusetts bill of rights. A truth that was self-evident had become a guarantee to be self-satisfied. From the American Revolution until the very end of the nineteenth century, the states drafted about 120 constitutions—of which about two-thirds, according to Henry Steele Commager, "provide some kind of guarantee of happiness ... Most of these [state constitutions] guarantee[d] not only the right to seek it but the right to obtain it as well."[2] The United States converted happiness not only into a moral ideal but into a legal provision as well. Unfortunately Commager failed to mention how many lawsuits had been filed against state governments by plaintiffs who somehow failed to overcome their own melancholy.

Such expectations of felicity have nevertheless persisted. In 1953, the literary critic Alfred Alvarez, who was born and based in London, visited the former outpost of the British Empire for the first time. The first American cab-driver whom Alvarez met surprised him by wishing him a nice day. "It had never crossed my British mind," Alvarez recalled, "that a nice day could possibly be an option." Fourteen years later, the daughter of Joseph Stalin defected from the Soviet Union. When she arrived in the United States, Svetlana Alliluyeva announced that she was tired of her "grim" compatriots, that she had had enough of "pessimism."[3] No one has exerted a greater influence in American culture than Walt Disney, whose optimistic pledge to make life more fun is honored at California's Disneyland and at Florida's Disney World, both of which incorporate a section called Tomorrowland. That area is omitted from the European counterpart of these theme parks, Disneyland Paris, as though in recognition of the argument made in *Civilization and Its Discontents.* There Sigmund Freud insisted that "the intention that man should be 'happy' is not included in the plan of 'Creation.'"[4] In contrast to Jefferson, who made happiness the proof of civilization, Freud argued that happiness must be forfeited for the *sake* of civilization.

But a nation that has often imagined itself as exempt from the historic conflicts of the blood-soaked Old World, from the cruelties and miseries and animosities of the past, offered the prospect of becoming a novelty item in Jewish history. In Shakespeare's *The Merchant of Venice,* Shylock shrugs that pain—he uses the archaic term "sufferance"—"is the badge of all our tribe"; and he thus exemplifies the "lachrymose" version of the cultural memory of Exile. A century ago, roughly two-and-a-half million Jews from Eastern and Central Europe flocked to the land where its inhabitants sang (in "America the Beautiful") of "alabaster cities gleam[ing], undimmed by human tears." The overwhelming majority of these newcomers spoke Yiddish, a language for which the compilers of one thesaurus needed nineteen columns to cover all the variations of the word "misfortune" (*tsuris*). Only five columns were needed to record the synonyms for "good fortune."[5] But *glick* is what America seemed to offer. In the last, unfinished novel of Sholem Aleichem, *Motl the Cantor's Son,* a greenhorn realizes that Purim isn't a holiday of liberation that is celebrated only once a year; in the United States "every day is Purim." That sort of jauntiness, interestingly enough, was not entirely outside the imaginative range of the most haunted literary voice of Central European *Kulturpessimismus.* Franz Kafka never saw America. But when he had to envision it, in his own inevitably unfinished, posthumously published *Amerika,* the resulting novel was carnivalesque. It consists of a series of exuberant adventures in the wide open spaces of the empire of the fun, in the so-called Nature Theatre of Oklahoma, where no one is put on trial for an unspecified crime, where no one must wait in the antechambers of authority for a summons that never comes.[6]

Other evidence can be cited for the distinctive appeal of America. Take a lullaby like "Shlof mein kind," published first in Odessa in 1892; the lyrics were by Sholem Aleichem. He evokes how the cradle will rock as a mother tells her sleepy young son of the wonders of America, where the child's father has already found refuge. In the New World, she reassures her child, "they know not of exile, oppression, persecution . . . There, they say, Jews are rich." Indeed they can afford to eat *challah* even on weekdays. Everyone in America "lives contently [and] all are equal." There Jewish history would be put out of its misery. In "Lebn Zol Columbus!" (1915), the lyrics by the Yiddish theatrical impresario Boris Thomashefsky urge his "brothers" to "be happy!" in "the new land" that Columbus had discovered. Here even girls without dowries can get married, and matchmakers are superfluous because "it will be like the Garden of Eden."[7] Paradise (does it need saying?), New York City wasn't. But from the autobiography of one Russian Jew who lived briefly in one New York City borough can be inferred some sort of proof of the comforts that induced others to remain. Leon Trotsky, his wife and two sons came to the Bronx in 1916; and he recalled that even their rented apartment "in a workers' district" came "equipped with all sorts of conveniences that we Europeans were quite unused to: electric lights, gas cooking-range, bath, telephone, automatic service-elevator, and even a chute for the garbage. These things completely won the boys over to New York."[8]

In the following year, Abraham Cahan published his novel of upward mobility, *The Rise of David Levinsky*, and the first words in English that the protagonist learns upon arriving in New York are suitably upbeat: "all right."[9] (That is an analog of the reassuring "OK," which may be the most familiar phrase on the planet.) A decade after the publication of Cahan's canonical novel came the release of the canonical film of upward mobility, *The Jazz Singer*; and the first song that audiences heard Al Jolson sing was a paean to the "Blue Skies" that were shining on him. There would be nothing but blue skies, presumably, from now on. When the star died in Los Angeles in 1950, he was eulogized by the comedian George Jessel, who summed up what the Lithuanian-born son of a cantor had symbolized. Jessel stressed what "a sad lot" the Jewish immigrants had been when they arrived half a century earlier. "And then there came on the scene a young man, vibrantly pulsing with life," the eulogist proclaimed, "who marched on the stage . . . with a gaiety that was militant, uninhibited and unafraid, and told the world that the Jew in America did not have to sing in sorrow but could shout happily about Dixie."[10]

Jolson's persona seemed to confirm the belief among his co-religionists that in America desires could be satisfied, that promises could be fulfilled on earth, that the bitterness of Exile could be assuaged. The "bread of affliction" need not be consumed, when the Happy Meals of McDonald's are also available. If psychological problems nevertheless persisted, one recourse was the couch, despite the objection of the most famous Roman Catholic prelate of the 1950s, Bishop Fulton J. Sheen. He insisted that psychoanalysis was no substitute for the sense of sin and the need for confession and expurgation, that the Freudian outlook was based on "materialism, hedonism, infantilism and eroticism."[11] Such qualities are precisely what the New World often seemed to offer in contrast to the grim struggles of the Old World. Elsewhere in the Diaspora Jews had been unlucky enough to live in countries ruled by the likes of Pedro the Cruel, or Vlad the Impaler, or Ivan the Terrible, or Mad King Ludwig; and even England had been ruled by Bloody Mary. But in the United States, representative government was far more benign. No president ever captured the hearts of Jewish citizens more completely than Franklin D. Roosevelt, who happened to love screening movies in the White House. But they had to satisfy two criteria, his widow later noted: "He hated a picture to be too long, and it must not be sad."[12] Two films in particular flunked that second test, even though they framed the Depression decade so aptly; and Roosevelt could thereby avoid seeing Paul Muni as a fugitive from a chain gang and Henry Fonda as a fugitive from vigilante justice in *The Grapes of Wrath*.

The first of FDR's predecessors had promised "to bigotry no sanction, to persecution no assistance"; and to an astonishing degree, George Washington's pledge to the Jewish minority has not been violated. With the conspicuous and shameful historical exception of blacks, other minorities have been included—and felt themselves to be full participants in the national experiment. The executive director of the Select Commission on Immigration and Refugee Policy, appointed by President Jimmy Carter in 1979, was Lawrence H. Fuchs, an authority on race and ethnicity. In conjunction with his duties to the Commission, Fuchs visited a third-grade class in Denver, noticed a portrait of George Washington, and asked an Anglo kid to identify him. The third-grader did so correctly but then was stumped when Fuchs asked him what Washington did ("He died"). Fuchs then asked a Vietnamese kid wearing a Cub Scout shirt. After naming George Washington correctly, the son of Vietnamese immigrants replied to the question of what Washington did as follows: "Oh, he's the father of our country." Newcomers arrive in the United States, Fuchs concluded, "and feel it's their country right away."[13]

The rapid upward mobility of Jews often made it difficult for them to acknowledge that they were living in Exile, that estrangement and marginality were integral to the experience of the Diaspora. The ascent was so sudden and so dramatic that one generation could not have anticipated how fluid the boundaries were, how limitless the possibilities might be. Before Arthur Goldberg became an Associate Justice of the Supreme Court, before he became the US Ambassador to the United Nations, he served in the Cabinet of John F. Kennedy. Once, while the Secretary of Labor was visiting his mother in Chicago, Kennedy phoned him and announced himself to Goldberg's mother as "the President." Goldberg overheard his mother inquire: "From which *shul*?"[14] The United States has thus generated an irrational number in the equation of Jewish experience. The Polish-born Sir Lewis B. (for Bernstein) Namier had eschewed the opportunity to explore the past of the Jews, who didn't have a history, but "only a martyrology."[15] The history of American Jewry has served as an exception to that rule.

In the precincts of mass culture in the United States, a little night music could be permitted—but only a little; and in a general atmosphere that has been so relentlessly positive, tragedy could seem elusive and incomprehensible. The popular arts have often been impervious to the sadness, anguish and torment that serious artists have tried to convey, and have almost compulsively promoted the need for feel-good resolutions to insoluble conditions. Billy Wilder, born in Galicia, once tried to pitch a story to a prominent Hollywood producer: a biopic of the life of Vaslav Nijinsky, whose spectacular career with the Ballets Russes had ended in a mental asylum. "What kind of picture is this?," Wilder was asked. "A man who thinks he's a horse?" Undoubtedly sensing that so dispiriting a movie would not get made, Wilder offered at least the assurance of a happy ending: "In the final scene we show Nijinsky winning the Kentucky Derby!"[16]

Hollywood was not the first culprit, however. Early in the nineteenth century, the playwright Nahum Tate's revised version of *King Lear* became popular with American audiences because Edgar and Cordelia fall in love and because she and her father remain alive at the end. Scorned for perpetrating so radical a textual deviation, actor Edmund Kean claimed to have tried to be faithful to the original, but "ascertained that a large majority of the public—whom we live to please, and must please to be popular—liked Tate better than Shakespeare." It was left to the novelist William Dean Howells to explain why, after he accompanied Edith Wharton to the New York opening of the dramatization of her novel, *The House of Mirth*. The play failed, and Howells mordantly observed: "What the American public always wants is a tragedy with a happy ending."[17]

Tragedy entails the necessity for choice—for which neither option is satisfactory, and terrible consequences will ensue regardless of which value the protagonist chooses to uphold. How can Jack Robin become a show biz success in *The Jazz Singer*, if he must meet the liturgical needs of the synagogue by chanting *Kol Nidre* in the place of his father, Cantor Rabinowitz, who is dying? The dilemma turns out to be false one—at least in America. Jack Robin gets to obey the Fifth Commandment and thus honor his father, while still opening at the Winter Garden right after the somber observance of Yom Kippur is over. The Yiddish-language counterpart to *The Jazz Singer* serves as its contrast. Released in 1940, *Der Vilner Shtot-Khazn*, or *Overture to Glory*, follows Cantor Yoel Strashunsky (Moishe Oysher) as he leaves his family and his *shul* for a chance to perform in the Warsaw opera. He becomes a star. But, alas, he realizes too late the price exacted upon his loved ones whom he had abandoned in Vilna so that he could embark on his quest for glory. The cantor returns on the eve of Yom Kippur but, after chanting *Kol Nidre*, collapses and dies in the synagogue.[18] In Eastern Europe there was no way to split the difference, no way to reduce the odds against happiness, no way to defy the dictates of tragedy.

Despair is often so foreign to the popular arts in America that even the representation of the Holocaust was expected to conform to the yearning for an upbeat ending. But that is what the public presumably wanted to make of the death of Anne Frank, which could scarcely have been more haunting or terrible. In 1945, the fifteen-year-old inmate of typhus-ridden Bergen-Belsen was last seen shivering in the cold, covered with only a blanket. What was left of her physically had been reduced to bones and tears. Hers was the fate of only one of the nearly six million. Though her diary had proclaimed, on July 15, 1944, that "in spite of everything, I still believe that people are really good at heart," the evidence did not support such a declaration of faith. In the bleakest and most unmistakable terms, the *Shoah* disproved that testament of faith, though during the horror of her ordeal, Anne Frank had surely earned the right to grasp at such a hope. But the American dramatization of her diary, as well as the 1959 film version, makes that gallant statement into the conclusion of the story, and omits entirely the words that follow it, in which she anticipates "the ever-approaching thunder" and senses the doom of "the suffering millions."[19] Though the Holocaust surely does not permit the impertinence of an optimistic note, it was needed to ensure that audiences would somehow be inspired rather than disenchanted.

Of course no historian would claim that the proclivity for happy endings is an American monopoly, nor would any scholar assert that the United States has an exclusive franchise on hedonism—which emerged well after Puritanism had entrenched itself in New England. The pursuit of happiness has not gone uncontested in what is, after all, the "land of the Pilgrims' pride." "Let's party" was not exactly their motto as they engaged in their errand in the wilderness. But Jefferson's startling, third inalienable right does pose a formidable challenge to the exercise of piety, and has certainly threatened the seriousness of Christianity itself. Its own demands were not to be taken lightly. But the calling to try to imitate Christ—to enact an ethos of universal mercy, even at the risk of martyrdom—can gain little traction in a nation where contentment and well-being are often presented as a by-product of faith. Observing Protestant preachers during the Second Great Awakening, Alexis de Tocqueville found it "often difficult to discern from their discourses whether the principal object of religion is to procure eternal felicity in the other world or prosperity in this."[20]

Let a couple of examples suffice. Half a century ago, virtually no clergyman was more influential than Norman Vincent Peale of Marble Collegiate Church in New York City. His version of Christianity was presented as a source of psychic reassurance, as a remedy for personal dissatisfaction, "as a workable instrument" to achieve success: "It is astounding how defeated persons can be changed into victorious individuals when they actually utilize their religious faith." His 1940 volume, *Faith is the Answer*, was co-authored with a psychoanalyst with too perfect a name, Dr. Smiley Blanton. *The Power of Positive Thinking* (1952) ranked for two years as the leading non-fiction best-seller. But its readers were offered not the challenge of sustaining or applying a transformative faith, but rather the prospect of mastery over daily problems through "spirit lifters." The searing austerity of the legacy of St. Paul, for example, was thereby jettisoned; and no wonder that Adlai Stevenson was provoked to claim that he found "Paul appealing and Peale appalling."[21] In a remissive culture, not even the clergyman is willing to be Dr. No.

Religion is supposed to boost confidence and to be cheerful. Television viewers in 1993 got a chance to observe the logic of this orientation when the most consistently admired American of the second half of the twentieth century chatted with four Jewish comedians. The Reverend Billy Graham assured Milton Berle, George Burns, Red Buttons, and Shecky Green that God loves those who make other people laugh. These favorites of Las Vegas were thus God's favorites too. To support Graham's guarantee of salvation, the evangelist cited no Biblical passage (nor did he indicate any other reference). But why risk popularity in a nation of optimists by alluding to the severity of the final judgment? Nine Americans in ten believe in heaven, and regard their own chances of getting there as fair-to-excellent—but only a paltry 6 percent have admitted to pollsters their own expectations of suffering eternal damnation.[22] Their Jewish neighbors are undoubtedly relieved to live among sunny-side-up Christians who are also so virtuous.

Yet the pleasure principle is surely incompatible with any of the main varieties of religious experience. The life of a believer is not supposed to be duty-free but is rather a struggle to be waged. An ideal of sensation which endorses self-satisfaction therefore wreaks special havoc on those who are expected to form "a kingdom of priests and a holy nation" (Exodus 19:6). A lavish and unmodulated commitment to the pursuit of happiness should at least be recognized as a rupture of Judaic tradition. Though Freud described himself as "a godless Jew," he had the authority of tradition behind him in describing happiness as something to be renounced, rather than embraced. At the very base of Mount Sinai, the Hebrews were worshipping the golden calf. But the transmission of the Torah to Moses was supposed to make a difference; and Judaism, insofar as it can be framed in historic and normative terms, has thereafter consisted of a lifelong set of duties—Ten Commandments, 613 *mitzvot*, tractates full of laws, endless inconveniences. To be a Jew in America usually does not bring any trouble; but it can be trouble to practice Judaism, which is a product of both the ancient world and of the Old World. A relentless quest for self-gratification therefore collides with the interdictory claims of historic Judaism.

In engaging a culture that is so often noteworthy for its triviality and superficiality, Judaism is hardly the only vehicle through which to articulate a sensibility of sobriety. But it is a heritage that has been available, braced to offset the compulsive denial of the pervasiveness of human suffering. A Judaism that can be reckoned with has generally generated friction with a dominant ethos that seeks the suppression of the tragic spirit. A Judaism that would clarify the ethical dilemmas associated with success and comfort would not only be consistent with a sinuously long heritage of sensitivity to the perennial abuses of power and wealth; such a critical stance would also be of service to public culture. Judaism, like its adherents, cannot hope to resist entirely the influence of the nation's values—not when the appeal of those values is so often justified. But an unambivalent accommodation to the entitlement to seek happiness would snap the lines of continuity with Judaic tradition, without offering the prospect of enriching the nation's culture either.

Notes

1. André Previn, *No Minor Chords: My Days in Hollywood* (New York: Doubleday, 1991), 86.

2. Henry Steele Commager, *Jefferson, Nationalism, and the Enlightenment* (New York: George Braziller, 1975), 109–10.

3. Alfred Alvarez, *Where Did It All Go Right?: A Memoir* (New York: William Morrow, 1999), 145; Svetlana Alliluyeva, *Only One Year*, tr. Paul Chavchavadze (New York: Harper & Row, 1969), 354.

4. Sigmund Freud, *Civilization and Its Discontents*, tr. and ed. James Strachey (New York: W. W. Norton, 1962), 23.

5. Gerald Sorin, *A Time for Building: The Third Migration, 1880–1920* (Baltimore, MD: Johns Hopkins University Press, 1992), 14.

6. Sidra DeKoven Ezrahi, *Booking Passage: Exile and Homecoming in the Modern Jewish Imagination* (Berkeley, CA: University of California Press, 2000), 116–17, 123.

7. "Two Versions of Sholem Aleichem's Lullaby about America in Music Archives," *YIVO News*, Winter 2002, 22; Victor Greene, *A Singing Ambivalence: American Immigrants Between Old World and New* (Kent, OH: Kent State University Press, 2004), 63–4; "Songs of Immigrants to the 'Golden Land'," *YIVO News*, Winter 2003, 24.

8. Leon Trotsky, *My Life: An Attempt at an Autobiography* (New York: Charles Scribner's Sons, 1930), 271.

9. Abraham Cahan, *The Rise of David Levinsky* (New York: Harper & Row, 1960), 91.

10. Quoted in Herbert G. Goldman, *Jolson: The Legend Comes to Life* (New York and Oxford: Oxford University Press, 1988), 301–2; Jeffrey Melnick, *A Right to Sing the Blues: African*

Americans, Jews, and American Popular Song (Cambridge, MA: Harvard University Press, 1999), 262.

11. Quoted in Andrew R. Heinze, *Jews and the American Soul: Human Nature in the 20th Century* (Princeton, NJ: Princeton University Press, 2004), 243.

12. Quoted in Alan Schroeder, *Celebrity-in-Chief: How Show Business Took Over the White House* (Boulder, CO: Westview, 2004), 179.

13. John Stickney, "To Open the Door or Close It: An Expert Evaluates the Explosive Issues of Immigration," *People*, December 6, 1982, 108.

14. Ruth Bader Ginsburg, "Jews and the Rule of Law," *American Jewish Historical Society Heritage*, May 2005, 2–4, here 4.

15. Quoted in Edmund Wilson, *A Piece of My Mind: Reflections at Sixty* (New York: Farrar, Straus & Cudahy, 1956), 156.

16. Quoted in Maurice Zolotow, *Billy Wilder in Hollywood* (New York: G. P. Putnam's Sons, 1977), 236.

17. Quoted in Edith Wharton, *A Backward Glance* (New York: D. Appleton-Century, 1934), 147.

18. Jim Hoberman, *Bridge of Light: Yiddish Film Between Two Worlds* (New York: Schocken, 1991), 270–2.

19. Anne Frank, *The Diary of a Young Girl*, tr. B. M. Mooyaart (Garden City, NY: Doubleday, 1953), 237.

20. Alexis de Tocqueville, *Democracy in America*, ed. Phillips Bradley (New York: Vintage Books, 1990), Vol. II, 127.

21. Quoted in Richard Hofstadter, *Anti-intellectualism in American Life* (New York: Alfred A. Knopf, 1970), 265; Donald Meyer, *The Positive Thinkers: Religion as Pop Psychology from Mary Baker Eddy to Oral Roberts* (New York: Pantheon, 1980), 260–68; John Bartlow Martin, *Adlai Stevenson and the World* (Garden City, NY: Doubleday, 1977), 543.

22. Neil Postman, *Amusing Ourselves to Death: Public Discourse in the Age of Show Business* (New York: Penguin, 1985), 5; Martin Gottfried, *George Burns and the Hundred-Year Dash* (New York: Simon & Schuster, 1996), 293–4; Russell Shorto, "Belief by the Numbers," *New York Times Magazine*, December 7, 1997, 61.

CHAPTER 21
LOOKING BACK ON AMERICAN JEWISH HISTORY
Hasia R. Diner

We, the historians who specialize in American Jewish history, will long remember the academic year 2004–5, as an *annus mirabilis*, a year of wonder. It has been a banner year for broad interest in our field of study, and I think I am not overstating the case by declaring that never before have so many of us been invited to so many places to give so many talks to so many audiences as we have over the course of that long year of the 350th anniversary of Jewish settlement in North America. Since the summer of 2004 the subject of American Jewish history has been examined in multiple and diverse venues and media, with programs of one kind or another springing forth around the country. Some of these presentations have focused on the "big picture"—that is, attempting to make sense of the full sweep of that history—while others have focused on particular aspects of it, conceptualized around specific time periods, certain themes, and distinctive places. Whether the programs took place in specifically Jewish settings or in more general gatherings, whether they targeted scholars alone or if they brought scholars into conversation with community audiences, whether they involved single speakers, multiple speaker lecture series, symposia, exhibitions, film projects, television documentaries, publications—books, articles, pamphlets, journalistic accounts— sermons, or oral history projects, these texts and events will someday be used by historians to explore how American Jews at the onset of the twenty-first century made sense of their history.

All of these presentations, regardless of intended audience or preferred mode of communication, shared a basic view of the past, and no doubt of the present. We—the scholars who have participated in the endeavor—have all contended that America made possible, and its Jews created there the largest, most elaborately organized, well endowed, least fettered, institutionally plastic and culturally pluralistic Jewish community in the world today and indeed in all of Jewish history.

These performances of American Jewish history, from the most scholarly to the most popular have emphasized that this state of affairs, with its high levels of accomplishment and acceptance, evolved over the course of time. It did not just begin that way. This development, both its internal and external condition, had to be won, or achieved. Jews did not arrive in seventeenth-century North America with anything like the bundle of rights and the communal élan which would develop over time. Our lectures and writings have emphasized several key trajectories that brought the Jews of America to their present state of integration and communal fullness.

We, the scholars of American Jewish history, have demonstrated a process by which the Jews in America moved from being a numerically insignificant band of "23" who interacted with the larger American society devoid of any assumed entitlements to a point in their history now where they could claim utter privilege, chained down by no fetters as they enjoyed access to every "nook and cranny" of American life.

Projects for the 350th anniversary have likewise depicted the movement by which the Jewish women and men of America proceeded from a history where they affirmatively sought anonymity as Jews, occupying in their early history literally unmarked Jewish spaces, to ultimately boldly and assertively putting their particularistic stamp on the American landscape. That is, the trajectory which the programs, be they coolly analytic or boisterously celebratory, have depicted, involved showing an arc by which Jews came over time in America to feel comfortable and empowered to make their case (or better cases) in their own name. At some point in their history they felt able to state that as Jews they had a group-specific stake in the great public issues of the day.

Likewise much of the discourse of the year 2004/5 has sketched out the ways in which Jews, as demonstrated by the words and actions of their organizations, organs of public opinion, networks of communication, and network brokers, moved from quietly asking the vastly larger Christian society to give to Judaism some of the same privileges which the Protestant denominations enjoyed to eventually standing up and demanding not only equal rights for Jews and Judaism, but pushing American society to change itself. From a population that figuratively pleaded that Judaism be considered a legitimate American faith community, Jews ultimately felt able to take on America, and demand that some of the nation's most fundamental institutions change.

Three examples should suffice here. By the late nineteenth century many American Jews began to chide America for its deep commitment to the idea of laissez-faire as the best way to structure relations between the classes. Many American Jews including the leaders of some of the most prestigious bodies came to demand that the state enter into the economic life of the nation not as an advocate for business but as an advocate for workers and for the poor.[1] By the early twentieth century, American Jewish organs of public opinion, in English and Yiddish, joined in an avant-garde assault on American race relations, lambasting the United States for the pervasiveness of racism and calling upon Americans to fully live up to the nation's rhetorical creed of equality.[2] Finally Jews by the middle of the twentieth century willingly stood out and apart from the many times larger Christian population, in their critique of the persistence of cracks in the wall between church and state. They willingly told the overwhelmingly Christian population of the United States that they did not in fact have the right to claim America as a Christian nation.[3] By laying out these profound changes in the ways in which American Jews interfaced with the larger society, historians associated with the 350th anniversary events have shown how the status of the Jews has changed, how America underwent profound change, and how Jews played a crucial role in making that change possible.

Finally, as we historians of the American Jewish past have engaged with our many audiences we have described how the Jewish people in America came to define and redefine Judaism and the nature of Jewish life as a malleable entity, as something which they, often quite ordinary and unlettered women and men, could mold to fit their various beliefs, sensibilities, and tastes. Over such deeply significant issues of language, ritual, governance, and structure, American Jews in their local communities—we have shown—created religious practices and institutions that worked for them.

No issue has been more central to this part of the discussion in the 2004/5 year than that of gender and women's rights. The historians who have spoken and written about the distinctiveness of the American Jewish historical trajectory, have repeatedly outlined the ways in which in America Jewish women moved from behind the curtains of public invisibility to the centre stage of the leadership of American Judaism. "Only in America"— to invoke a hackneyed but still useful phrase—did Jewish women find ways to give themselves voice and make demands upon the male leadership of their community to decouple religious responsibilities and rights from gender. Women, they asserted, should literally count and when it came to participating in the public manifestations of Judaism, biology should not be thought of as destiny.

In short, we the historians have spent the year 2004/5, if we admitted it or not, detailing both the exceptionalism of America and the contributions of the Jews to America. The titles of our talks, the labels affixed to the exhibitions, and the basic assumptions which underlay our presentations have been that Jews brought something distinctive to America and that America had a particular—and particularly positive—impact upon the Jews.

By framing our public discussions around the distinctiveness of the American experience of the Jews, we have reflected a long held view in the field of Jewish history. America, and the history of its Jews, stood in a class by themselves. Notably in the academy only American Jewish history is thought of as a field separate from modern Jewish history. While obviously some historians specialize in German Jewish history, Polish Jewish history, French Jewish history and the like, only we American Jewish historians have a journal, a society, a biennial conference of our own. Courses in "modern Jewish history" do not include America but take Europe, and increasingly the Ottoman Empire and North Africa, as their geographic focus. The rationale behind this organization of knowledge assumes, probably rightly, that not only was America different but that—as the embodiment of the idea of modernity—the history of the Jews in America deserves its own intellectual context.

In large measure the history of American Jewry has been built around the fact of the absence of a process of emancipation. American Jewry never went through this excruciating and excruciatingly long ordeal. Likewise, however, many American Jewish historians have documented instances of anti-Semitism, manifested in both rhetoric and deed, the giant shadows cast by European ghettoes, pogroms, expulsions, and ultimately the Holocaust on modern Jewish history, have made the American experience not only a basically upbeat one, but have forced us to think about it in its own terms and not as part of the larger "modern" narrative. As such, we have, even when we strove for dispassionate analysis, articulated our basically whiggish view of this history.

If the historians, committed as they are to "objectivity," have basically sketched out an upbeat narrative, how much more so the community "celebrations," as they have been generally described? Certainly on the popular level a good deal of the rhetoric has tended to valorize American Jewry, to celebrate its achievements and to assert that certain characteristics of an entity referred to as "Jewish culture" have made all of this possible. Hard work, a traditional commitment to education, strong families, grit, determination, courage, intellect, all somehow have figured in these discussions as explanations for how the Jews "made it" in America. These sterling qualities tend to be posited as particularly Jewish and as particularly prominent in the Jews' unique cultural tool kit.

To the credit of the individuals involved in making these public programs possible, none that I have seen have overtly compared Jews to other Americans. Such distinctions, however, do hover just below the surface. Much of the rhetoric implies that the political, economic, and cultural achievements—the impressive output of the writers, artists, scholars, scientists, entrepreneurs, fighters for social justice who counted themselves as Jews—reflected essential Jewish characteristics and not just those of all immigrants, for example, or all Americans. The "Jewish" component figures prominently here and as such the differences between what the Jews accomplished and what others did, need not be said but could be easily imagined.

From the obverse side of the equation in these "celebrations" of American Jewish history, public programs have emphasized the special attributes of the place, the United States. The phrase "America is different" has been repeatedly invoked and always in the most positive of terms. Because the United States, its government and its people, made room over time for Jews and Judaism to achieve what they did, it has emerged in the 350th anniversary drama as a "best supporting actor," of almost equal billing to the Jews themselves.

Let me here just cite some salient statements from the call to "Celebrate 350: An Invitation" which launched the year's festivities. The document, which appeared on the Celebrate 350 website, stated quite boldly that "we," the coordinators of the year's events "need to reaffirm the reverence for justice, freedom, equality and respect for diversity that has made America the haven it has been for us and all Americans." The invitation to celebrate continued in a similar vein, urging that the participants in this historic moment remember and venerate, "our commitment to sustaining America's role as the champion of freedom and democracy throughout the world." This document, as embodied in these two statements, typical of the text as a whole, captured the ethos of the 350th anniversary moment. American Jews saw themselves as grateful for and celebratory of the United States, both past and present. The historians who helped craft this text and those who lectured under its banner or consulted with the museum and film projects that it spawned participated then in a discourse about American history and its particular impact on the Jews.

From my tone and from the particular words that I chose to highlight here, it must be clear that as an historian I found myself uncomfortable with this kind of rhetoric. I had, and continue to have, problems with the idea of historians operating under the banner of "celebration" as much our professional project involves critical distance from our subject. "Analysis" or "criticism" rather than "celebration" seem to me to be the focus of our activities.[4]

As such, I would like in this short essay to offer an alternative way of making sense of the larger narrative of the 350 years under consideration. I concur with the assertion that in the context of modern Jewish history the experience of the Jews of the United States has stood in a class by itself. I agree with the basic premise that the nature of that experience has in fact produced a "community"—however amorphously defined—that had a history that would best be analyzed quite apart from that of other Jewish communities, and that America—the United States—played a key role in making that possible. What I would like to offer, however, is a set of contexts for exploring and explaining those conclusions.

At least five overarching realities of American life, extending from the seventeenth century outward, provided the basic soil in which American Jewish communal life could take root and then flourish. Let me state them and then return to each one in some detail. Each one of these notably existed in conjunction with the others and in each case we could say that the confluence of these forces functioned as the matrix around which this singular history—that of American Jews—proceeded. The factors that I will be developing involved the nature of immigration to America, America's enduring obsession with color, American materialism and the degree to which the society's basic nature sprang from economic forces, the role of religion in America, and finally, the structure of America's political life. I cannot say with certainty that if any one of these had been different or absent that the history of the Jews would have taken a different course. I do not believe in the practice of counter-history, but suffice it to say here that these factors did all exist and they did all pivot around each other. Therefore we should focus on them to understand how and why, vis-a-vis the Jews, America did differ.[5]

1 Immigration

That America, both before national independence and after, owed its basic character to the fact of constant flows, indeed floods, of voluntary immigration has been well documented by historians. While the size of those population movements into America waxed and waned, with the period after 1924 until the early 1970s representing the nadir due to congressional policy, American social and cultural life took much of its tone and shape to the fact that most Americans—native Americans, the descendants of African slaves, and residents of certain parts of the southwest excluded—stemmed from women and men who had with some degree of volition chosen to leave someplace else and to transplant themselves to America. At the high water period of European immigration, the late nineteenth into the early twentieth century, Jews differed little from most of their neighbors as a result of their overwhelmingly foreign birth, their accented and limited (or nonexistent) English, and the newness of their American experience. Likewise their American-born children resembled the children of other immigrants around them, who also stood between parents of non-American nativity and the larger expanses of American culture.

America was the Western world's largest receiver of immigrants. In the great century of migration, from 1820 through 1924—again a coincidence between the experience of Jews and of all other European immigrants—three-fifths of all Europeans who shifted residence across national borders chose the United States. While Americans, from a number of political perspectives, have generally overstated the degree to which the romance of America propelled the emigration and the uniqueness of America as an immigrant destination and have as such minimized the importance of immigration to the histories of Canada, Brazil, Argentina, Australia, and even Great Britain, the fact remained that immigration to the United States had certain distinctive characteristics which in turn left their mark on the Jews who participated in this historic transfer of population.

Immigration to the United States differed from all of the flows to all the other places by the sheer diversity of its immigrants. To Brazil and Argentina, for example, two places which immigration shaped, the vast majority came from the Italian peninsula, with Spain sending a sizable but decidedly smaller percentage. Of those who chose Canada and Australia, the British Isles sent an overwhelmingly large proportion.

Yet as to the United States, a vast variety of Europeans, with none dominating the flow, contributed to the "national character." While certain decades saw larger and then declining migrations from certain places, over time no one group could be held up as the core population or as embodying the quintessential immigrant experience. Over the course of the century of migration Italians and Germans—both obviously complicated "national" groups to highlight here given the political ambiguities involved in naming those places—arrived in just about equal number and immigrants from Eastern Europe more than doubled the number from the British Isles.

Additionally, the flow into the United States proceeded on a continuous basis. For sure, some years, those characterized by a vigorous economy, saw more immigrants than others, and other years, when the state of the economy went into a temporary decline, witnessed a dip in immigration. But over the course of the great century of migration, the steady and inexorable process of Europeans choosing America continued apace. Again this tended to distinguish immigration to the United States from the other immigrations in that those extended over more limited spans of time.

In this the Jews of America resembled their non-Jewish neighbors for their immigrant status and the immigrant nativity of their parents. Since no one group dominated the population, of the large cities in particular, Jews like all the other immigrants and their children learned to negotiate America from the reality of this on-the-ground diversity. That the official creed, however problematically operationalized, valorized immigration as central to the fulfilling of America's exceptional mission, gave Jews a claim to one key aspect of the nation's central narrative.

Furthermore in the discourse launched by nativists from the 1850s onward about the defects of "the immigrants" and in their crusades to limit the rights of immigrants, Jews did not figure centrally. Unlike the Irish of the pre-Civil War period and Italians of the late nineteenth century, both of whom functioned as the chief European targets of xenophobic fantasies, Jews attracted relatively little negative attention. Without understating the degree to which anti-Jewish rhetoric flourished, the bulk of the discourse about Jews as immigrants tended to see them as hard-working, studious, adept when it came to entrepreneurship, and set on a course, albeit one a bit too rapid, toward economic mobility. In the United States, as such, words like "foreigner" or "alien" did not connote Jew. Jews might be included under those usually negative labels but they did not stand out prominently as embodying them.

Not so in many of the other destination points for central and east European Jews. In those countries, Australia and South Africa, which constituted colonial outposts of larger empires, the Lithuanian or Polish Jews who came to settle, stood out as distinctive for their language, citizenship, and relationship to the imperial project. For those Jews who opted for Argentina, the overwhelming predominance of Italians as the main immigrant group who quickly constituted the majority of the entire population, differences in religion and language made the Jews obtrusive "others." And finally, the Jews who moved westward to Germany, France, and Great Britain in the last half of the nineteenth century found themselves relatively alone as occupying the immigrant category. In England, for example, except for colonials from Ireland, whose right to residence in the metropole could not be changed, barring changing the structure of the empire, Jews made up the largest group of newcomers, and the largest category of non-native, non-English speakers. In the halls of Parliament and in the press the debate over passage of the Aliens Act at the start of the twentieth century discussion about the "aliens" amounted to primarily a debate about the Jews, their merits and mostly demerits. Jews there and in other non-American receiving societies, stood out as quintessential immigrants, foreigners, and problems in the construction of a national "type."[6]

2 Race and color

When contemplating the broad contours of American history and trying to understand the points of intersection between it and the history of its Jews the issue of race and color cannot be ignored. Indeed no aspect of American history can be conceptualized without factoring in the deep, wide, and pervasive American obsession with color. The entire history of America has been a history of color and racial classifications. This has been the dominant motif of the national experience and the very existence of the nation grew out of the encounter of Europeans, native people, and Africans on the shores of North America. The history of its Jews must follow suit.

In this place, since the earliest moments of European colonization, perceived color mattered greatly. In fact, historians can, and have, rightly postulated that no other factor mattered as much, including gender. Color, assumed and constructed as it was as a category, meant the difference between rights and no rights, control over one's body or no control, entitlement to the protection of the state or not. To be on the wrong side of the color equation, which obviously meant the non-white side, not only subjected individuals to the absence of the privileges which accrued from basic definitions of being human or being a citizen, but it exposed them to the full fury of the power of the state and society which served as agents of subjugation and violence.

Despite some recent assertions to the contrary, in every meaningful way, Jews in America always enjoyed the benefits of whiteness. At no time did the formal apparatus of the society, the state and its agents, declare them to be unable to acquire naturalization and citizenship because of their color. At no time did Jews, men in the main, not expect the protection of courts in which to press their claims, equal access to the ballot boxes to voice their opinions, and freedom of movement to go unimpeded wherever they chose. As white men they could enter contracts, hold office, serve on juries, and all the other basic rights that came with being an American.

Certainly rhetoric, particularly by the last quarter of the nineteenth century, could be heard which questioned the whiteness of the Jews. Particularly with the rise of scientific racism and the respectable proliferation of biologized views of difference, some writers, thinkers, and others categorized Jews as something other than white. But these voices remained just that.

Even in the many places where Jews in America suffered limitations and discrimination, in particular in the housing field, in employment, access to higher education, and in entry to places of leisure like clubs and hotels, anti-Jewish practices came from private individuals. The state stood aloof from all these matters. It would take in fact almost the entire course of the 350 years before the state, the federal government, wiped away the distinction between discrimination perpetrated by private sources versus discrimination which came from the state. The 1964 and 1965 civil rights acts (and on a state-by-state basis the civil rights laws passed after 1945) made private acts of discrimination the business of the state.

Jews, unlike African Americans, Americans of Chinese and Japanese ancestry, and Native Americans, never needed to view government—the formal apparatus of the society, its courts, its legislature, its elected leaders, and indeed even its key text, the Constitution—as the source of their sorrows. In all matters relating to the fundamental and extensive formal privileges which flowed from the state, the Jews in America benefited from the fact that phenotypically other Americans saw them as white.

Having this privilege represented in some ways a unique moment in Jewish history. Here, in the United States, for probably the first time, they did not have access to the fewest rights and the sparsest bundle of privileges the society had to offer. Others stood many rungs below them in the scale of entitlement. Here, in the United States, they could distinguish between their enemies—particular colleges, particular hotels, particular companies—and the state, the standard of the nation. The former, they condemned for its hostility to the Jews, while the latter, they lauded for the privileges it gave them. Keenly aware that they benefited from American realities, including those which accrued to them from the right skin color, some American Jews recognized that their entitlements came from the deep and profound stigmatization endured by others. That our subjects—American Jews of the past— recognized that they fell on the other side of the color line means that we historians should also be aware of this history of racial privileging. Being seen as white made all the difference for Jews in the positive fit that took place between them and America.[7]

3 Making a living: Jews and the American economy

So too, in a much less problematic, but no less significant context, we can think about the synergy between Jews and America, in matters economic. The massive transfer of Jewish population to America—about 85 percent of Europe's cross-border migrating Jews chose the United States—brought these millions of Jews from places of low productivity and stagnant development to the most dynamic economy in the world. America from its earliest days until well into the twentieth century experienced a constant and chronic labor shortage, set amidst the vast natural resources waiting to be exploited.

This reality undergirded the entire European immigrant flood to America, that of the Jews as well. Like all other Europeans Jews left settled places where economic opportunities did not exist and opted for America where they did. However much the American Jewish communal narrative has focused on the outbreaks of anti-Jewish violence of life in Europe—the pogroms in particular—as the engines which drove the population transfer, analytically the more mundane story of a group of people, Jews, seeking out places to live better—and ultimately to live well—has greater validity.

The American-Jewish economic fit also reflected the long history of Jews and commerce and the long-observed, and often deprecated, American proclivity toward material acquisition. In nearly every period of American Jewish history we can see a confluence between American material needs, or better wants, and Jewish economic skills. Let me briefly sketch out two eras in American Jewish history as they reveal this symbiotic relationship.

From the middle of the nineteenth century into the earliest years of the twentieth, as the American white population moved westward to the remote and least settled areas, families and communities of "settlers" articulated a desire for cosmopolitan goods. The westward movement of Americans across the continent made it possible for the commercial interests to gain access to vast stretches of "uninhabited" land which could be farmed, mined, and logged. The nation's penetration of the hinterlands, romantically and jingoistically, described as "manifest destiny," required capital, and it required women and men willing to work the land, fell the forests, dig the mines, lay the railroad tracks, and the like. It also needed intermediaries to bring to these people the kinds of "stuff" that made it bearable for them to live in these undeveloped places.

Some central and east European Jews met America on the shifting peddlers' frontier. Tens of thousands of Jewish men, well-acquainted with itinerant merchandising after centuries of life in Europe, turned their long time economic niche into an American opportunity. The Jewish peddlers, many of whom became the owners of Jewish dry goods stores in the small towns which served the hinterlands, the Jewish retailers in the big cities who outfitted the peddlers, and the Jewish tailors who sewed the clothes which then traveled in the peddlers' wagons and ended up on the bodies of rural dwellers, made up a Jewish economy that served the basic needs of the expanding United States. While behind this historic drama lay many complicated economic and political relationships, on the surface what transpired involved a marriage between Americans' desire for consumer goods—buttons, thread, needles, curtains, eye glasses, pictures and picture frames, fabric and readymade clothing—and the willingness of Jews to pick up the familiar peddler's pack and venture out to pretty much anywhere they could find paying customers.

By the 1860s yet another match took place between American economic needs and Jewish history. The expansion of the garment industry which began with the invention of the sewing machine at nearly the same moment in time as the Civil War coincided with a series of linked, but independent developments, which transformed not just America but European Jewry. Late nineteenth-century urbanization, the movement of young women into industrial and white collar jobs in the years before marriage, the rise of the advertising industry, the emergence of "style" as something within the reach of working class women, new sanitary standards, all led to the reality that by the end of the nineteenth century the garment industry took off as one of the most dynamic sectors of the American economy. Factories, heavily although not exclusively housed in New York, sewed the garments which clothed women and men around the world. The ready-to-wear clothing industry spread its dresses and blouses, shirtwaists, hats, and undergarments around the nation and the world fueling American economic development.[8]

In this sector Jews as employers and workers found, and helped create, a niche for themselves. Jews in Europe had long made a living by means of the needle, but in America, they could use that lowly skill to create a vast enterprise which did nothing less than clothe Americans and others, employ in massive numbers successive streams of Jewish immigrants, both women and men, and indeed show Jewish women who worked in factories side by side with their "brothers," that gender inequities mattered greatly and limited their options. In addition this field with its relatively low need for startup capital provided to Jews one of the few means by which immigrant industrial laborers could move into the ranks of the employing class.[9]

These two convergences between Jewish history, the peddling and the garment making, and the needs of the American economy had tremendous implications for Jewish economic mobility. Here we can see writ large an example of being in the right place, at the right time, with the right skill set.

4 American religion and the Jews

The Jewish encounter with America, an encounter that took place in a relatively harmonious manner, reflected the significance of religion as a factor in American history. Here at least three factors shaped that meeting. Those factors made it possible for the Jews to be helped by the fact of their particular religion rather than hindered by it, as they were elsewhere.

First among these reflected the reality that to the primarily Protestant population which dominated America from the colonial period well into the early twentieth century, Jews were not Catholics. Jews could, in America, breathe easily in that for much of American history anti-Catholicism functioned as a powerful force in public life. Catholicism had long been deemed unsuitable for a democratic, egalitarian nation which venerated personal freedom and individual choice. An aggressive strain of anti-"Papism" dominated the public discourse of the Protestant nation and spilled over from the churches to the political realm. One of the country's most successful third parties, the Know Nothings, made anti-Catholicism a core principle and with this it enjoyed a brief, but still notable, hour in the political spotlight.[10]

Judaism, by contrast, while seen as overly legalistic, at times, medieval and retrograde, particularly vis-a-vis the status of its women in public ritual, enjoyed a place of respectability in the American setting. From a negative standpoint, antipathy to it spawned no political movements, nor did its arrival and transplantation into America cause American Christians to redefine public policy in order to lessen Judaism's possible and pernicious impact.

From a positive perspective, from the middle of the nineteenth century onward the appearance of Christian Protestant clergy—at the dedication of synagogues and the pulpit exchanges between rabbis and ministers indicated that Judaism found for itself a legitimate space on the American religious landscape. While a hint of exoticism can be discerned in the Christian discourse on Judaism as well as a note that signaled the desire of evangelicals to convert the Jews, by and large, Protestantism in America did not demonize the planting of Judaism on American shores.

This no doubt reflected the general valorization of religion in America. Americans, observed since the days of Alexis de Tocqueville's now storied visit to the relatively new nation, saw religion—in part because it had been decoupled from state power—as a benign force for promoting civic virtue. While historians of the American Jewish experience may debate the degree to which the veneration of religion in America pushed Jews to repackage themselves as a "faith community" as opposed to a people or a nation, the prevailing positive view of religion in America allowed Jews to argue for extending to their religion the benefits which all other denominations enjoyed. By being bound to each other through a "religion," a concept somewhat extraneous to normative Judaism, American Jews could stand under the protective umbrella of American culture.

Finally, no discussion of the harmonious relationship which evolved between the Jews and the United States would be complete without considering the impact of religious diversity and the concomitant political commitment of the society to the constitutional principle of the separation of church and state. Obviously the complicated history of this twinned phenomenon has been the subject of vast scholarly and legal analysis. To simplify in order to detail this crucial issue within the constraints of time and space here, the fact is that even from before the creation of the Republic, too many denominations had established themselves in British North America and its successor state—and states— to allow any one church to impose an iron grip on civic life. While many gray areas, such as Sunday closings continued to vex groups of religious outsiders, most aspects of public life fell outside the gray zone. Even so simple a fact that the state did not collect statistics on the number of members of particular denominations meant that private beliefs, that is, matters of the spirit, did not require public declarations. No check-off boxes on census forms or on tax statements which demanded, or suggested, that individuals divulge to government officials their religious affiliations, made a world of difference.

In matters of faith and society, the decoupling of religion and government rendered the former powerless to control peoples' lives and slowly forced the latter to validate many religions rather than any one. Religion, without the strong backing of the state, lost its authority and essentially defanged it. Religious institutions either conformed to the demands of their dues paying members or they died out.

For Jews the divorce between state and church not only afforded them the possibility of participating, over time, in the polity as equals to Christians, but it gave them the freedom to mold Judaism to fit their wishes, tastes, and sensibilities. Jews like all others enjoyed the freedom to structure their institutions as they wanted and the state could do little, indeed nothing, to stymie creativity.[11]

5 Politics

A final aspect of American history left an indelible mark on the Jews, facilitated their political integration, and should be included in this survey. This involves an analysis of the political sphere directly. In nearly all paeans to America and its ability to integrate (white, male) immigrants, stump speakers and historians alike have cited the ease of the naturalization process for those of foreign birth and the fact that the political realm did not exclude anyone because of their religion. Vis-à-vis politics and governance, for nearly all of American history, not only did religion not matter in terms of naturalization, acquisition of citizenship, voting, and office-holding, but neither did nativity. With the exception of the constitutional requirement that the president of the United States needed to be native born, no barriers to political participation needed to be overcome for white men (and later women), regardless of how (or if) they prayed and where they had been born. This obvious fact deserves to be stated here because of its tremendous impact.

But it does not represent the totality of the political context for understanding how the Jews "met" America and how America "met" the Jews. Rather in politics, on a more abstract yet equally formative level, the long reality of the two-party system facilitated the American-Jewish symbiosis. The United States, for reasons well beyond the scope of this essay maintained a long tradition of living with two parties relatively evenly matched with each other. Third parties, for sure, developed and nearly all of them failed. While those parties, from the right and the left nudged the two giants in one direction or another, and as such cannot be dismissed analytically as having had no significance, they still died and since the 1850s the political scene has been dominated by the Republicans and the Democrats alone.

Particularly since the end of the Civil War and the resolution of the issue of slavery, the two parties tended to converge ideologically. These two parties, which have functioned without formal membership and only the vaguest of platforms, have often been issueless and as such, have valorized pragmatic majoritarianism. What mattered over the course of much of American history in this kind of politics was simply who got the most votes. Political scientist Daniel Bell offered a powerful image to think about this historic reality. American parties, he wrote, resembled giant bazaars, under whose canopies, multiple hucksters sold their wares. The same hucksters appeared in each of the big tents and peddled their "stuff."

The barkers in the twin bazaars represented the various interest groups: labor, farmers, manufacturers, ethnic groups and the like. While both parties essentially served the interests of business, under the shelter of the two tents, the parties brokered among these constituencies. The parties wanted votes and each group had a particular, and usually practical, agenda.

Compromise and accommodation ruled the parties and in all of this politics, like religion, became tamed. America saw no party of the aristocracy or the clergy, the peasants or the urban proletariat. Rather each party sought to claim as many constituency groups as possible and had little incentive to offend any identifiable block and as such write off any potential voters.

And here, Jews fit in. Neither party defined "the Jews" as a problem, but rather both wanted their votes. Neither party wrote them off as not potential voters, nor did either refuse to provide them with some tangible rewards for voting correctly. Even when Jews had by the late 1920s become comfortably ensconced in the ranks of the Democratic Party, the Republicans did not incorporate antipathy toward the Jews into their political rhetoric. They rather, actually, hoped to woo the Jews over to their camp. By functioning in this bazaar type setting, Jews could literally shop around and make their case to both parties on the local, state, and national levels. They—no differently than midwestern farmers, blue-collar workers, or "members" of nearly every ethnic and religious group— could see who would make them the best deal in exchange for showing up on election day. In this non-ideological political structure which quashed extremism, Jewish men since the middle of the nineteenth century (and then women as well by the end of the first quarter of the twentieth century) found ample space to join in the competition for the attention and rewards that accompanied political participation.

This non-ideological defanged political process may not have helped the Jews secure everything they wanted. Obviously the tragic history of their mighty efforts and limited results in the Hitler era to influence American policy stands as a great failure. But in this they were comparable to other interest groups, particularly those which represented ethnic and immigrant communities. The hurly-burly of the political marketplace made it possible for them to get some of what they wanted, but clearly not everything. They got just enough to allow them to feel part of the civic whole and to believe in the basic goodness of the system.[12]

And as a result of this system as well as the other overarching attributes of American history and the culture which evolved from it and in tandem with it, Jews arrived into an environment which synergistically worked well for them. They arrived in a large enough—but not too large—number to be able to thrive, to build the communities that they wanted, to take advantage of fundamental realities which often worked to the disadvantage of others, and to apply their economic skills sharpened in very different environments to American material realities. In the process they helped make the history which we have spent all the "celebrations" of 2004/5 thinking about.

These five factors may not, in the end, be the stuff of celebration, but hopefully they offer analysts a way to think about what this particular history involved. It may not facilitate celebration, but in the ideal it can help stimulate analysis, the activity which in fact represents the historian's project.

Notes

1. Melech Epstein, *Jewish Labor, U.S.A.: An Industrial, Political and Cultural Hsitory of the Jewish Labor Movement* (New York: Trade Union Sponsoring Committee, 1950–53).

2. Hasia R. Diner, *In the Almost Promised Land: American Jews and Blacks, 1915–1935* (Baltimore: Johns Hopkins University Press, 1992); Cheryl Greenberg, *Troubling the Waters: Black-Jewish Relations in the American Century* (Princeton, NJ: Princeton University Press, 2006).

3. Gregg Ivers, *To Build a Wall: American Jews and the Separation of Church and State* (Charlottesville, VA: University of Virginia Press, 1995).

4. See "The Invitation" on the website of the "Celebrate 350" Commission (http://350th.org).

5. The points of this paper have been vastly amplified in Hasia Diner, *The Jews of the United States, 1654–2000* (Berkeley, CA: University of California Press, 2004).

6. See Walter Nugent, *Crossings: The Great Transatlantic Migration, 1870–1914* (Bloomington and Indianapolis, IN: Indiana University Press, 1992).

7. See Eric Goldstein, *The Price of Whiteness: Jews, Race, and American Identity* (Princeton, NJ: Princeton University Press, 2006).

8. Jewish economic activities in the middle of the nineteenth century can be further accessed in Hasia R. Diner, *A Time for Gathering: The Second Migration, 1820–1880*, Volume 2, *The Jewish People in America* (Baltimore, MD: Johns Hopkins University Press, 1992).

9. On the nature of the garment industry, see Susan Glenn, *Daughters of the Shtetl: Life and Labor in the Immigrant Generation* (Ithaca, NY: Cornell University Press, 1990).

10. Ray Allen Billington, *Protestant Crusade, 1800–1860: A Study of the Origins of American Nativism* (New York: Macmillan, 1938); John Higham, *Strangers in the Land: Patterns of American Nativism, 1860–1925* (Westport, CT: Greenwood Press, 1963).

11. For one example in the vast literature on the role of religion in American life and the expansion of religious diversity, see John Butler, Grant Wacker, and Randall Balmer, *Religion in American Life: A Short History* (New York and Oxford: Oxford University Press, 2003).

12. Everett C. Ladd, *American Political Parties: Social Change and Political Responses* (New York: W.W. Norton, 1970); Roy F. Nichols, *The Invention of the American Political Parties* (New York: Macmillan, 1967). A comprehensive history of Jews and the American party system is yet to be written.

INDEX

Index

Index

Index

Index

Index

Strashunsky, Yoel (Moishe Oysher) 348
Straus, Isidore 219
Straus, Nathan 266, 296
Straus, Oscar S. 283, 321
Strauss, Leo 38
Struve, Gustav 111
St. Thomas (Recife) 52, 54–7
    Hebrew congregation 57
Stuyvesant, Peter 31–2, 38, 48
Sullivan, Louis 183 n.39
Sulzberger, Mayer 307
Suriname 65, 67, 79, 81–4, 86
Switzerland 20, 111, 248
synagogue-center (movement) 18, 215–17, 221, 277
Synagogue Council of America 332
synagogues
    American 161–2, 165–6
    European 161–2
    German 165
    Sephardic 161
Syria 337
Szold, Henrietta 200, 262
Szold, Robert 266

Täubler, Eugen 204
Tate, Nahum 347
Tcherikover, Elyohu 243, 249–50
Tel Aviv 263, 270, 313, 339
Teller, Judd L. 269
Thalberg, Irving 344
Thomashefsky, Boris 345
Tillich, Paul 270
Tisch, James 330–1
Tocqueville, Alexis de 349, 362
tolerance 9, 34, 125
    America as a land of tolerance 34
Toronto 27 n.2
    Beth Tzedek Synagogue 26 n.2
traditionalism 17
transnational (approach), transnationalism 2, 5, 7–9, 11, 13, 23
Trilling, Lionel 38–9
Triumphalism, Christian 176
Trotsky, Leon 285–6, 346
Truman, Harry S. 270, 309
Tshaikovsky, Nikolai 253
Tsukerman, Borukh 249, 296
Tsunzer, Elikum 282
Tunis 100
Tunisia 337
Turner, James 34
Twain, Mark 253

Ukraine 286, 288–9, 291–2
    Ukrainian Jews 289
Union of American Hebrew Congregations 58, 308

Union of Councils for Soviet Jewry 322
United States of America *see* America
    constitution 10, 132, 98–9, 117
universalism, religious 143, 145–7, 150
Unterberg, Bella 219
Urovsky, Melvin 265

Vaad ha-Rabbanim 228
Vanik, Jackson 321
Venezuela 51, 57
Vienna 5, 112, 118 n.1, 185, 193, 197, 200
Vilna 5, 20, 240–3, 245, 248–9, 251, 281, 348
    Vilna (social democratic) group 240–3, 248, 251
Vintshevsky, Morris (Lipe Ben-Tsien Novakhovitsh) 243–4, 246–7, 250
violence, anti-Jewish *see also* pogroms 20–1, 360
Virginia 94, 98, 113, 115
    Virginia Bill of Rights 344
Vitkin, Yankev (Zrubavl) 295
Vladeck, Borekh Charney 283, 291
Voliner, A. (Eliezer Landoy) 292
Volozhin 224
voluntarism 3

Wagenaar, P. 74–6
Wagner, Richard 115
Walzer, Michael 333, 342 n.23
Warburg, Felix 197
Warsaw 5, 240–2, 244, 250, 261, 289
    Jewish Social Democratic group 250
Washington, DC 107, 109–10, 112–14, 189
Washington, George 99, 189, 260, 347
Washington Heights 317
Waskow, Arthur 37
Watson, Karl 79
Weissglass, Dov 341 n.18
Weizmann, Chaim 266–7, 270
Westfalia 186
West India companies 49
Wharton, Edith 348
Whitfield, Stephen J. 25, 101 n.12
Wiernik, Peter (Perets) 286
Wiese, Christian 15–16
Wiesel, Eli 325 n.20
Wieseltier, Leon 333, 335
Wilder, Billy 347
Wilhelm, Cornelia 14
Williams, James Holmer 53
Wilson, Woodrow 265–7, 269, 284, 287, 303 n.40
Wintner, Leopold 282
Wisconsin 120 n.23
Wise, Isaac Mayer 14, 106, 114–15, 117, 123 n.46, 172, 177, 189, 192–6, 208 n.52, 218
Wise, Stephen S. 203, 216, 225, 262, 262, 287, 294, 301 n.29

378